Caroline Lee I

Love After Marriage and Other Stories of the Heart

Caroline Lee Hentz

Love After Marriage and Other Stories of the Heart

1st Edition | ISBN: 978-3-75233-723-5

Place of Publication: Frankfurt am Main, Germany

Year of Publication: 2020

Outlook Verlag GmbH, Germany.

LOVE AFTER MARRIAGE

AND

OTHER STORIES OF THE HEART.

BY

MRS. CAROLINE LEE HENTZ.

1

LOVE AFTER MARRIAGE.

A stranger was ushered into the parlour, where two young ladies were seated, one bonneted and shawled, evidently a morning visiter, the other in a fashionable undress, as evidently a daughter or inmate of the mansion. The latter rose with a slight inclination of the head, and requested the gentleman to take a chair. "Was Mr. Temple at home?" "No! but he was expected in directly." The young ladies exchanged mirthful glances, as the stranger drew nearer, and certainly his extraordinary figure might justify a passing sensation of mirth, if politeness and good feeling had restrained its expression. His extreme spareness and the livid hue of his complexion indicated recent illness, and as he was apparently young, the almost total baldness of his head was probably owing to the same cause. His lofty forehead was above the green shade that covered his eyes in unshadowed majesty, unrelieved by a single lock of hair, and the lower part of his face assumed a still more cadaverous hue, from the reflection of the green colour above. There was something inexpressibly forlorn and piteous in his whole appearance, notwithstanding an air of gentlemanly dignity pervaded his melancholy person. He drew forth his pocket-book, and taking out a folded paper, was about to present it to Miss Temple, who, drawing back with a suppressed laugh, said—"A petition, sir, I suppose?"—then added in a low whisper to her companion—"the poor fellow is perhaps getting up a subscription for a wig." The whisper was very low, but the stranger's shaded though penetrating eyes were fixed upon her face, and the motion of her lips assisted him in a knowledge of their sound; he replaced the paper in his pocket-book—"I am no petitioner for your bounty, madam," said he, in a voice, whose sweetness fell like a reproach on her ear, "nor have I any claims on your compassion, save being a stranger and an invalid. I am the bearer of a letter to your father, from a friend of his youth, who, even on his death-bed, remembered him with gratitude and affection; will you have the goodness to present to him my name and direction?"

Then laying his card upon the table, he made a low bow and retreated, before Miss Temple had time to apologize, if indeed any apology could be offered for her levity and rudeness. She approached the table and took up the card —"Gracious Heavens!" she exclaimed—"it cannot be possible?—Sydney Allison—that bald, yellow, horrid-looking creature—Sydney Allison! they described him as the perfection of manly beauty—I never will believe it—he is an impostor—the wretch!"

The young lady who was with her, beheld with astonishment, the passion that

2

lighted up Miss Temple's face, and her looks besought an explanation. "Have you not heard," said Miss Temple, "since you came to this city, that I was betrothed; that I had been so from a child, to a young gentleman residing in Cuba, whose uncle was the bosom friend of my father? You must have heard it, for my father has always taken pains to circulate the report, so that no one might presume upon my favour. And this is the delectable bridegroom! the one who has been represented as clothed in every grace calculated to fascinate a female heart—and I, fool that I was, I believed it, and looked forward with rapture to the hour of our first meeting." Here she paused, and throwing herself back in her chair, burst into a passion of tears.

Mary Manning, her more rational companion, endeavoured to soothe the excited feelings of her friend, and suggested to her, that whatever disappointment she might feel with regard to his personal appearance, his character might be such as to awaken a very ardent attachment. "Indeed," added Mary, "I thought there was something quite interesting in his address, and his voice was remarkably persuasive in its tones. He has evidently been very ill, and his bad looks are owing to this circumstance. He will become handsomer by and by. Besides, my dear Augusta, what is mere beauty in a man? It is the prerogative of a woman, and you are so highly gifted in that respect yourself, you should be willing that your husband should excel in those qualities which men generally arrogate to themselves."

"Husband!" repeated Augusta; "I would as soon take a death's-head for my husband. I care nothing about mere beauty, provided there is intelligence and spirit. But with such a bald, livid-looking wretch at my side, such a living memento of mortality, I should sink into my grave in a fortnight. I never will marry him, unless I am dragged to the altar." Here Mr Temple entered the room, and interrupted her rash speech. Miss Manning too retired, feeling that her presence might be an intrusion. He looked astonished at the agitation of his daughter, who handed him the card, and turning away leaned against the mantel-piece, the image of woe.

"Sydney Allison arrived!" exclaimed Mr. Temple; "where is he? when was he here? and why is he gone?—why—what is the matter with you, Augusta? The first wish of my heart seems accomplished, and I find you weeping. Tell me the meaning of all this?"

"Oh! father," sobbed Augusta, covering her face with her handkerchief, "he is *so* ugly, and you told me he was so *very* handsome."

Mr. Temple could not forbear laughing at the piteous tone in which Augusta uttered this melancholy truth, though he immediately resumed, in an accent of displeasure, "I am ashamed of your folly—I have always given you credit for being a girl of sense, but you talk like a little fool;—ugly! if a man is not ugly

3

enough to frighten his horse, he is handsome enough. Besides, it is nothing but a whim; I saw him when a child, and he was an uncommonly beautiful boy. I hope you did not behave in this manner before him—why did you suffer him to go away?"

"Why, I did not know him," said Augusta, in considerable trepidation, for she feared her father's anger; "and he looked so thin and woe-begone, I thought he was some foreigner asking charity, and when he took out a paper I thought it a petition, and said something about one—so he was angry, I believe, and went away, saying he had letters for you, from a friend, who was dead."

"And is he dead!—the good old man!—the best, the earliest friend I ever had in the world—dead and gone!" Mr. Temple leaned his face over on his hands, and sat in silence several moments, as if struggling with powerful emotions. After a while, Mr. Temple lifted his hands, and fixed his darkened eyes upon his daughter. He took her hand with affection and solemnity. "Augusta, you are the child of affluence as well as of indulgence; you are my only child, and all the wealth, which now surrounds you with luxury, will be at your disposal after my death."

"Oh! father, do not speak of such a thing."

"Do not interrupt me. Mr. Allison, the uncle of this young man, was my benefactor and friend, when all the world looked dark upon me. He extricated me from difficulties which it is unnecessary to explain—gave me the means of making an ample fortune, and asked no recompense, but a knowledge of my success. It was through his influence I was united to your now angel mother—yes! I owe everything to him—wealth, reputation, and a brief, but rare portion of domestic bliss. This dear, benevolent, romantic old man, had one nephew, the orphan child of his adoption, whom he most tenderly loved. When commercial affairs carried me to Cuba, about ten years ago, Sydney was a charming boy,"—here Augusta groaned—"a charming boy; and when I spoke with a father's pride of my own little girl whom I had left behind, my friend gladdened at the thought, that the union which had bound our hearts together would be perpetuated in our children; we pledged our solemn promise to each other, that this union should take place at a fitting age; you have long been aware of this betrothal, and I have seen with great pleasure, that you seemed to enter into my views, and to look forward with hope and animation to the fulfilment of this contract. The engagement is now doubly binding, since death has set his awful seal upon it. It must be fulfilled. Do not, by your unprecedented folly, make me unhappy at a moment like this."

"Forgive me, my dear father, but indeed when you see him, you will not wonder at the shock I have received. After all you had said of him, after reading his uncle's letters so full of glowing descriptions, after dwelling so long on the graceful image my fancy drew, to find such a dreadful contrast."

"Dreadful contrast! why surely he cannot be transformed into such a monster."

"You have not seen him yet," said she mournfully.

"No! you remind me of my negligence. After the strange reception you have given him, it is doubly urgent that I should hasten to him. Have a care, Augusta, you have always found me a very indulgent father, but in this instance I shall enforce implicit obedience. I have only one fear, that you have already so disgusted him with your levity, that he may refuse, *himself*, the honour of the alliance."

"*He* refuse *me*!" murmured Augusta, in a low voice, as she glanced at herself in a mirror that shone above the mantelpiece. As the nature of her reflections may be well imagined, it may be interesting to follow the young man, whose figure had made so unfortunate an impression on his intended bride, and learn something of the feelings that are passing through his mind.

Sydney Allison returned to his lonely apartment at the hotel with a chilled and aching heart. The bright day-dream, whose beauty had cheered and gilded him, even while mourning over the death-bed of his uncle, while languishing himself on the bed of sickness, and while, a sea-sick mariner, he was tossed upon the boisterous waves—this dream was fled. She, who had always risen upon his imagination as the morning star of his destiny—this being he had met, after years of romantic anticipation—what a meeting! He was well aware of the sad ravages one of the violent fevers of a tropical clime had made upon his beauty, but, never attaching much value to his own personal attractions, he could not believe that the marks of a divine visitation would expose him to ridicule, or unkindness; of an extremely sensitive disposition, he was peculiarly alive to the stings of satire, and the sarcastic whisper of Miss Temple wounded him to the quick.

"What!" said he, to himself, as he folded his arms in melancholy abstraction, in the solitude of his chamber, "what, if the dark luxuriance of waving hair which once shadowed my temples, is now gone, is not thought and intelligence still lingering on my brow? Are there no warm and animated veins of feeling in my heart, because the tide of health no longer colours my wan and faded cheek? These enfeebled eyes, which I must now shelter from the too dazzling light, can they not still emit the rays of tenderness, and the beams of soul? This proud beauty! May she live to know what a heart she has wounded!"

He rose and walked slowly across the floor, pausing before a large looking glass, which fully reflected his person. He could not forbear a smile, in the

5

midst of his melancholy, at the ludicrous contrast to his former self, and acknowledge it was preposterous to expect to charm at first sight, under the present disastrous eclipse. He almost excused the covert ridicule of which he had been the object, and began to pity the beautiful Augusta for the disappointment she must have endured. It was under the influence of these feelings Mr. Temple found him.

"My dear fellow," said the latter, warmly grasping his hand, and gazing earnestly at him—"My poor boy! how ill you must have been!—your uncle, too"—the warm-hearted man was incapable of uttering another syllable, not more moved at that moment, by the recollection of his friend, than affected by the transformation of the blooming boy, whose waving locks were once so singularly beautiful.

His sympathy was so unaffected, his welcome so warm, and his affection expressed in so heartfelt a manner, that Sydney, who had just been arming himself with proud philosophy against the indifference and neglect of the world, melted into woman's softness. He had been so long among strangers, and those of rougher natures—had experienced so cold a disappointment in his warmest hopes—he had felt so blighted, so alone—the reaction was too powerful, it unmanned him. Mr. Temple was a remarkable instance of a man who retained a youthful enthusiasm and frankness of character, after a long and prosperous intercourse with the world of business. The rapid accumulation of wealth, instead of narrowing, as it too often does, enlarged his benevolent heart. When, in a long and confidential conversation with Sydney, he learned that Mr. Allison had left but a small fortune for his support, instead of the immense one he had been led to expect, he was more than ever anxious to promote his union with his daughter. However mysterious it seemed that Mr. Allison's property should be so diminished, or have been so much overrated, he rather rejoiced at the circumstance, as it gave him an opportunity of showing his gratitude and disinterestedness. But Sydney was proud. He felt the circumstance of his altered fortunes, and, though not a poor man, was no longer the heir of that wealth which was his in reversion when Mr. Temple had plighted his daughter to him. In his short interview with her he had gained such an insight into her character, that he recoiled from the idea of appearing before her as her betrothed lover.

"Receive me as a friend," said he to Mr. Temple; "let your daughter learn to look upon me as such, and I ask no more; unless I could win her *affections*, nothing would induce me to accept of her hand—under existing circumstances, I believe that impossible. Much as I feel your kindness, and sacred as I hold the wishes of the dead, I hold your daughter's happiness paramount to every other consideration. This must not be sacrificed for me.

Promise me, sir, that it shall not. I should be more wretched than words can express, if I thought the slightest force were imposed upon her sentiments."

"Be satisfied on that score; say nothing about it; only let her get fully acquainted with you, and there will be no occasion to employ *force*. You must forget the mistake of the morning. This yellow fever makes sad work of a man when it gets hold of him, but you will soon revive from its effects."

––––––––––

Sydney Allison became a daily visiter at Mr. Temple's. Had he assumed the privileges of a lover, Augusta would have probably manifested, in a wounding manner, the aversion she felt for him in that character; but it was impossible to treat with disdain one who never presumed to offer any attentions beyond the civilities of friendship. Though rendered vain from adulation, and selfish from indulgence, and though her thoughtless vivacity often made her forgetful of the feelings of others, Augusta Temple was not destitute of redeeming virtues. Nature had gifted her with very ardent affections, and opened but few channels in which those affections could flow. She had the great misfortune to be the only child of a rich, widowed, and doting parent, and from infancy had been accustomed to see every one around her subservient to her will. She had reached the age of womanhood without knowing one real sorrow, or meeting with a being who had excited in any degree the affections of her heart. Her warm and undisciplined imagination had dwelt for years on one image. She had clothed it in the most splendid hues that fancy ever spread upon her palette; and had poor Sydney appeared before her in his original brightness, the reality would probably have been dim, to the visions of ideal beauty by which she had been so long haunted. In the greatness of her disappointment, she became unjust and unreasonable, violent in her prejudices, and extravagant in the manifestations of them. But after the first ebullition of her grief, she grew more guarded, from the dread of her father's anger; and as Sydney continued the same reserved and dignified deportment, she began to think her father's prediction was fulfilled, and that their aversion was mutual. She did not derive as much comfort from this supposition as might be anticipated. She had dreaded his importunity, but she could not endure his indifference. It was in vain Mr. Temple urged his young friend to a different course of conduct; he always answered, "Let her cease to dread me as a lover, then she may learn to prize me as a friend."

One evening, there was a concert at Mr. Temple's. Sydney, who was passionately fond of music, forgot every cause of inquietude, while abandoned to its heavenly influence. He stood near the fair songstress of the hour, keeping time to the harmony, while in a pier-glass opposite, he had a full view of the groups behind. Augusta was a little in the rear, leaning on the arm of Miss Manning. He could gaze on her image thus reflected, without her being conscious of the act, and he sighed as he paid involuntary homage to her brilliant beauty. Her figure was of superb proportions, her features formed on the model of oriental symmetry, while her eyes glittered through their dark sweeping lashes, like sunbeams through the forest foliage. She stood with her head a little averted, and her profile presented the softened outline of the lineaments ascribed to the beautiful daughters of Judah. He forgot himself entirely, in the contemplation of her loveliness, when he saw her turn, with an arch smile, and hold up her hands in a whimsical attitude in the direction of his head, as if in the act of warming them; for the full blaze of the chandeliers seemed concentrated in that point, and all eyes, lured by Augusta's gesture, were turned upon his illuminated skull. For one moment Sydney lost his self-possession, and the angry spot was seen distinctly burning on his sallow cheek. The next, he smiled superior to such weakness, and retreating a few steps, bowed for her to pass forward. She had relied on the shade that covered his eyes, for security from detection, unconscious of the piercing glances that were darting beneath. Her conscience now upbraided her for her folly, and she felt with bitterness how low she must be in the opinion of the man whose admiration she secretly coveted, notwithstanding the ridicule she dared to throw upon his person. After the company dispersed, she remained alone in the drawing-room, dissatisfied with herself and sickening at the pleasure that surrounded her. The door softly opened. It was Sydney, who had returned for his gloves, which he had left on the mantel-piece. It was the first time she had found herself alone with him, and she felt excessively embarrassed. In that tone, which even *she* acknowledged to be irresistibly sweet, he apologized for his intrusion, and taking his gloves, was retiring, when she, ever impulsive, arrested his motions.

"Stay one moment, Mr. Allison—you have great reason to despise me—I have treated you with unpardonable levity and rudeness. Though I can hardly hope your forgiveness, I cannot withhold this acknowledgment of my errors; your calm forbearance has done more for my reformation, than a thousand reproofs."

Surprised and softened by this unexpected avowal from the cold sarcastic Augusta, whose fluctuating complexion and agitated voice bore witness to her sincerity, Allison was at first incapable of replying.

"Your present candour," at length he said, "would indemnify me for much greater suffering than you have ever inflicted on me. Allow me, Miss Temple, to take advantage of this first moment of confidence, to disarm you of all fear on my account. The relative situation in which we have been placed by others, has given us both much embarrassment; but be assured my only wish is to be looked upon as your friend. Consider yourself as entirely unshackled. In brighter hours I might have aspired to the distinction our parents designed for me; but, worn down by sickness, the shadow of my former self, I feel but too sensibly, that the only sentiment I can now inspire in the female heart, is that of compassion."

Augusta was so much impressed by his delicacy and generosity, she began to hate herself for not having more justly appreciated his worth. She raised her eyes to his face and sighed—"Ah!" said she to herself, "I must respect and esteem, but I can never love him." Mr. Temple, who had been absent the whole evening, returned at this moment, and his countenance expressed his pleasure in finding them thus alone, in apparently confidential conversation with each other.

"Do not go, Allison," said he; "I have been oppressed with business to-night, and I want a little social enjoyment before I sleep. Besides, I do not feel quite well."

They now observed that he looked unusually pale, and pressed his hand upon his head, as if in pain.

"Father," said Augusta, "you do indeed look ill; you have fatigued yourself too much. A glass of wine will revive you."

She brought him the glass, but just as he took it from her hand with a smile, a sudden spasm came over him, and he fell back in his chair, speechless and convulsed. Augusta's piercing shriek alarmed the servants, who, rushing in, beheld their master supported in the arms of Allison, gasping for breath, while Augusta was trying to loosen his cravat with hands nerveless from terror. A physician was directly summoned, who bled him profusely, and after a few hours consciousness was restored. He was removed to his chamber, and Allison remained with him during the remainder of the night. Augusta sat by her father's bedside holding his hand, almost stunned by the suddenness of the calamity. Never, since her recollection, had her father known an hour's sickness; and now to be prostrated at once, in the midst of florid health, it was awful. She dared not ask the physician if there was danger, lest he should confirm her worst fears. She looked at Allison, and, in his pale and anxious countenance, she saw a reflection of her own anxiety and sorrow. Towards morning Mr. Temple opened his eyes, and looked earnestly round him.

"My children," said he, "come near me—both—both."

"Father," cried Augusta, "we *are* near thee—oh! my father, say that you are better—only say that you will *live*."

As she uttered the last word she bowed her head upon the bedcover, and sobbed as if her heart were breaking.

"My child," said Mr. Temple, faintly, "you must call upon God to sustain you, for there is need. I feel that the hand of death is on me. Sudden and awful is the summons—but it must be obeyed. Doctor, I would see my minister. Not to give peace to my parting soul—for all is peace *here*," said he, laying his hand feebly on his heart, "peace with God and man—but there is one thing I would witness before I die."

Sydney, who stood at the bed's head, trembled at the import of these words; Augusta in her agony comprehended them not.

"Sydney, my son, give me your hand; Augusta, is this your hand I hold? My children, if you would bless my last hour, you must let my dying eyes behold your union. It will gladden my friend, when I meet him in another world, to tell him his last wishes are consummated. Do you consent, my children?"

He looked up to Sydney, with that earnest expression which is never seen except in the eye of the dying, and pressed their hands together in his, already cold and dewy with the damps of death. Sydney sunk upon his knees, unutterably affected. All the happiness of his future life was at stake, but it seemed as nothing at that moment.

"Your daughter, sir?" was all he could utter.

"Augusta," repeated Mr. Temple, in a voice fearfully hollow, "will you not speak?"

"Oh! my father," she murmured, "do with me as you will, only take me with you."

The reverend figure of the minister was now added to the group that surrounded that bed of death. Strange and awful was the bridal ceremony, performed at such a moment, and attended by such solemnities. Sydney felt that he was mysteriously and irresistibly impelled on to the fulfilment of his destiny, without any volition of his own; and he supported, with a firm arm, the sinking form of her he was now to call his own. It was with bloodless lips and deadened perceptions Augusta repeated her vows; but low as they were, they fell like music on the ear that was so shortly to close to all earthly sound.

"There is a blessing above, mingling with mine," faintly articulated the dying man. "I bless you, my dear children, and ye will be blessed."

These were the last words he ever uttered. Augusta fell almost lifeless on her father's bosom, but what was a moment before the temple of an immortal spirit, was now but dust and ashes. At the same moment an orphan and a bride, she was incapable of comprehending the startling realities of her situation. The images that flitted through her mind, were like the phantasmagoria of a dream—a vague impression of something awful and indescribable having occurred, a wild fear of something more awful still impending, filled her imagination and paralyzed her frame. But Allison had a full and aching sense of the responsibilities so unexpectedly imposed upon him. He mourned for the venerated and generous friend so suddenly snatched away; but he grieved most of all, that his last act had placed in his keeping that to which he felt he had no legitimate right. No selfish repinings filled his heart—but to find himself *married*, joined irrevocably to a woman who had given him so many proofs of personal aversion; who never, till that evening, had evinced towards him the slightest sensibility—a woman whom he did not love, and whose superior fortune burdened him with a painful sense of obligation—there was something inexpressibly galling and humbling in these circumstances, to the sensitive and high-minded Allison. Tenderness, however, mingled with the bitterness of his reflections; and even then, he could have taken her to his heart, and wept over her tears of sympathy and sorrow, had he not dreaded that she would recoil from his embraces. He did not intrude on the sacredness of her grief, and for days she buried herself in the solitude of her chamber. She admitted no one but her chosen friend, Miss Manning, who represented her as inconsolable, either sunk in a torpor, from which nothing could arouse her, or in a state of nervous excitement still more distressing. He waited, hoping that time would restore her to comparative composure, and that she would be willing to receive from him the consolations of friendship. Finding, at length, that she persevered in her system of solitary grief, and that time, while it must, according to its immutable laws, soften her anguish for her father's death, probably increased her dread of the shackles that bound her, his resolution was taken. In a short time everything was arranged for his departure to a foreign land. The ship, in which he was bound a passenger, was ready to sail, when he requested a parting interview with Augusta. A parting interview!—Augusta was roused at that sound, from the selfishness of her grief. He was going into banishment, and she was the cause. For the first time since the bridal ceremony, the thought forced itself into her mind, that *he* too might have cause for sorrow, and that *his* happiness might be sacrificed as well as her own. Allison was greatly shocked, to see the change wrought in her radiant face. He was so much agitated, he forgot everything he purposed to say, and remembered only the strangeness of their situation. He endeavoured to repress his own emotion, that he might not increase hers; while she, unused to self-control, abandoned herself to a passion of tears. He approached her with tenderness and solemnity, and entreated her to listen to him, as a *friend*, as one willing to promote her happiness by any sacrifice she might require. "I go," said he, "Augusta, to another clime, whose genial influence may restore me again some portion of my former vigour. I go, too, in the hope, that in my absence you will learn submission to a destiny which my presence renders insupportable. If you knew the anguish that fills my heart, when I think of myself as the involuntary cause of your wretchedness, you would pity me, even as much as you abhor. Hear me, Augusta, while I repeat with all the solemnity of the vows that bound us to each other, that I will never claim the name of husband, till your own free affections hallow the sacred title. In the mean time I leave you with one who will be to you as a loving sister, in whose father you will find a faithful and affectionate guardian—will you not part from me, at least in kindness?"

Augusta sat, with her arms thrown around Miss Manning, weeping, yet subdued. All the best impulses of her nature were wakened and active. She would have given worlds to say something expressive of her remorse and regret for her selfishness and waywardness. Clasping her hands together she exclaimed, "Oh! forgive me, Sydney, that I cannot love you;" then, conscious that she was only wounding more deeply when she wished to heal, she only uttered, "what an unfortunate wretch I am!"

"We are both unfortunate," said he, moved beyond his power of control—"but we may not be always miserable. Something whispers me, that we shall meet again with chastened feelings, capable of appreciating all that is excellent in each other, and both earnest in the endeavour to merit the blessing that hallowed our nuptial tie. I leave you that you may be restored to tranquillity— I may never return—I pray to God, that he may find me a grave in that ocean to whose bosom I am about to commit myself, if I am only to live for the misery of others."

"No, no," cried Augusta, "this must not be, you must not become an exile for me."

"Listen to her," said Miss Manning, earnestly, her whole soul wrought up into the most painful excitement, at the sight of their mutual distress—"indeed, sir, you are doing what is rash and uncalled for—oh! why, with so much to bind you together, with qualities capable of inspiring the strongest attachment in each other, will ye close up your hearts in this manner, and resolve to be miserable?"

"I cannot now remain if I would, as I have taken steps which cannot well be recalled—your father, Miss Manning, knows and approves my intention. He is the delegated guardian and protector of Augusta. I will not, I cannot prolong the pain of these moments. Farewell, Augusta! think of me, if possible, with kindness—should I live to return, I will be to you friend, brother, or husband, as your own heart shall dictate."

He pressed her cold and passive hand in his—turned, and was gone. Augusta would have spoken, but she seemed as if under the influence of a nightmare. Her faculties were spell-bound; she would have returned the parting pressure of his hand, but her fingers seemed icicles. She shuddered with superstitious dread. Her father's upbraiding spirit appeared to her imagination, armed with the terrors of the grave, and threatening her with the retribution of heaven. Poor Augusta! her mind required the stern, but salutary discipline of adversity, and that discipline was preparing. How she profited by the teachings of this monitress, whose lessons, however hard, have such high and celestial bearings, the events of after years may show.

Augusta and her friend are once more presented to the view of the reader, but the destiny of the former is changed. They are seated in a parlour side by side, but it is not the same, rich in all the adornments of wealth and fashion, that Augusta once occupied. It is in a neat rural cottage, in the very heart of the country, embosomed in trees and flowers. A few words will explain the past. Mr. Temple's open, generous, uncalculating disposition had exposed him to the designs of the mercenary and treacherous. He never could refuse to endorse a note for a friend, or to loan money when it was asked with a look of distress. He believed his resources as exhaustless as his benevolence; but by the failure of several houses with which he was largely connected, his estate was involved in ruin, and his daughter left destitute of fortune. Mr. Manning suffered so much himself in the general loss, he was obliged to sell all that he still possessed in the city and retire into the country, with limited means of subsistence. But, though limited, he had sufficient for all the comforts of life, and what he deemed its luxuries—books, music, the socialities of friendship, and the exercise of the kindly charities. A cherished member of this charming family, Augusta no longer the spoiled child of fortune, but the chastened disciple of sorrow, learned to estimate the purposes of her being, and to mourn over her former perversity. With such ennobled views of life and its enjoyments, she began to think she might be happy with a husband, with such irreproachable worth and exalted attributes as Sydney Allison, even though he had the misfortune to be bald and sallow. But him she had banished, and when would he return? He had written to her once or twice, in the most affectionate manner, as a brother would write; he had spoken of amended health and reviving spirits, but he spoke of his return as of something indefinite and even remote. She too had written, and her letters were transcripts of the progressive elevation of her character, and expressed with candour and warmth the just appreciation she now had of his own. She was uncertain whether they had ever reached him. It was long since she had received any tidings, and she felt at times that sickness of the heart, which suspense unfed by hope creates.

"I bring you a messenger, who I trust is the bearer of glad tidings," said Mr. Manning, entering, with a benevolent smile, and ushering in a young gentleman, whom he introduced by the name of Clarence. "Augusta, you will greet him with joy, for he comes with letters from Mr. Allison, your husband."

Augusta sprang forward, scarcely waiting to go through the customary form of introduction, and took the letter with a trembling hand. "Tell me, sir, do you know him, and is he well?" The stranger bent his dark and lustrous eyes upon her face, with a look of undisguised admiration.

"I know him intimately, madam; when I last saw him, he was in perfect health, and animated by the prospect of a speedy return."

Augusta waited to hear no more, but retired to her own chamber, to peruse the epistle she had so anxiously anticipated. It was in answer to her last, and breathed the language of hope and confidence. There was a warmth, a fervour of sentiment, far different from his former cold, but kind communications. He rejoiced in the knowledge of her altered fortune, for he could prove his disinterestedness, and show her that he loved her for herself alone, by returning and devoting himself to the task of winning her affections. "Say not, my Augusta," said he in conclusion, "that I cannot win the prize. All the energies of my heart and soul are enlisted for the contest. I could look on your beauty, all dazzling as it is, without much emotion; but the humility, the trust, the gentleness and feeling expressed in your letter has melted me into tenderness. Dare I indulge in the blissful dream, that even now gilds this page with the hues of heaven? Augusta, the sad, reluctant bride, transformed into the fond and faithful wife, cherished in my yearning bosom, and diffusing there the life, the warmth, the fragrance of love!"

Augusta's tears rained over the paper. "Oh! Allison," she cried, "the task shall not be in vain; I *will* love thee for thy virtues, and the blessing my dying father called down, may yet rest upon us." She was about to fold the letter, when a postscript on the envelope met her eye. "Receive Clarence," it said, "as my friend—he knows all my history, and the peculiarity of our situation— he is interested in you, for my sake—as a stranger and my especial friend, may I ask for him the hospitable attentions of Mr. Manning's family?"

When she descended into the room, where Clarence was seated, she could not repress a painful blush, from the consciousness that he was familiar with her singular history. "He must despise me," thought she; but the deference, and respect of his manner forbade such an impression. Gradually recovering from her embarrassment, and finding him directing his conversation principally to Mr. Manning, she had leisure to observe one who possessed strong interest in her eyes, as the friend of Allison. And seldom does the eye of woman rest upon a more graceful or interesting figure, or a more expressive and glowing countenance. There was a lambent brightness in his eyes, a mantling bloom upon his cheek, that indicated indwelling light and conscious youth. His hair clustered in soft waves round his temples, relieving by its darkness the unsunned whiteness of his forehead. Yet the prevailing charm was manner, that indescribable charm, that, like sunshine in the summer landscape, gilded and vivified the whole. The acquisition of such a guest gave life and animation to the domestic circle. Mr. Manning was a man of varied information, and the society of this accomplished traveller recalled the classic enthusiasm of his earlier days. Mary, though usually reserved to strangers, seemed fascinated into a forgetfulness of herself, and found herself a partaker of a conversation to which at first she was only a timid listener. Augusta, while she acknowledged the stranger's uncommon power to please, was preoccupied by the contents of her husband's letter, and longed to be alone with Mary, whose sympathy was always as spontaneous as it was sincere. She was not disappointed in the readiness of Mary's sympathy; but after having listened again and again, and expressed her hope and joy that all would yet be for the happiest and the best, she returned to the subject next in interest, the bearer of this precious document. "Ah! my dear Augusta," said she, "if Allison's noble spirit had been enshrined in such a temple, you had not been parted now." Augusta felt the comparison *odious*. It brought before her the person of Allison in too melancholy a contrast with the engaging stranger. "I thought it was Mary Manning," answered she in a grave tone, "who once reproved me for attaching too much importance to manly beauty—I never thought you foolish or unkind till this moment."

"Forgive me," cried Mary, with irresistible frankness; "foolish I may be, indeed I know I am; but intentionally unkind to you—never—never." It did not require the recollection of all Mary's tried friendship and sincerity, for Augusta to accord her forgiveness. Mary was more guarded afterwards in the expression of her admiration, but Augusta, in her imagination, had drawn the horoscope of Mary's destiny, and Clarence shone there, as the star that was to give it radiance. A constant guest of her father's, she thought it impossible for him to witness Mary's mild, yet energetic virtues, without feeling their influence. She was interesting without being beautiful, and Clarence evidently delighted in her conversation. To her, he was always more reserved, yet there was a deference, an interest, a constant reference to her wishes and opinions, that was as delicate as it was flattering. He was the companion of their walks, and nature, never more lovely than in this delightful season, acquired new charms from the enthusiasm with which he sought out and expatiated on its beauties. Mr. Manning was passionately fond of music, and every evening

Mary and Augusta were called upon for his favourite songs. Now the music was finer than ever, for Clarence accompanied them with his flute, and sometimes with his voice, which was uncommonly sweet and melodious. One evening Augusta was seated at the piano; she was not an excelling performer, but she played with taste and feeling, and she had endeavoured to cultivate her talent, for she remembered that Allison was a lover of music. She had played all Mr. Manning's songs, and turned over the leaves, without thinking of any particular tune, when Clarence arrested her at one, which he said was Allison's favourite air. "Let us play and sing that," said he, repeating the words, "your husband loves it, we were together when he first heard it; it was sung by an Italian songstress, whom you have often struck me as resembling. The manner in which your hair is now parted in front, with those falling curls behind, increases the resemblance; it is very striking at this moment."

Augusta felt a strange pang penetrate her heart, when he asked her for her husband's favourite. There was something, too, in his allusion to her personal appearance that embarrassed her. He had paid her no compliment, yet she blushed as if guilty of receiving one. "I cannot play it," answered she, looking up, "but I will try to learn it for his sake." She could not prevent her voice from faltering; there was an expression in his eyes, when they met hers, that bowed them down, in shame and apprehension. It was so intense and thrilling —she had never met such a glance before, and she feared to interpret it.

"Shall I sing it for you?" asked he; and leaning over the instrument, he sang in a low, mellow voice, one of those impassioned strains, which the fervid genius of Italy alone can produce. The words were eloquent of love and passion, and Augusta, charmed, melted by their influence, could not divest herself of a feeling of guilt as she listened. A new and powerful light was breaking upon her; truth held up its blazing torch, flashing its rays into the darkest corners of her heart; and conscience, discovering passions, of whose very existence she had been previously unconscious. She saw revealed in prophetic vision, the misery of her future existence, the misery she was entailing on herself, on others, and a cold shudder ran through her frame. Mary, alarmed at her excessive paleness, brought her a glass of water, and asked her if she were ill. Grateful for an excuse to retire, she rose and took Mary's arm to leave the room; but as she passed through the door, which Clarence opened and held, she could not avoid encountering again a glance so tender and impassioned, she could not veil to herself the language it conveyed. Augusta had thought herself miserable before, but never had she shed such bitter tears as bathed her pillow that night. Just as she had schooled herself to submission; just as she was cherishing the most tender and grateful feelings towards her husband, resolving to make her future life one long task of expiation, a being crossed her path, who realized all her early visions of romance, and who gently and insidiously had entwined himself into the very chords of her existence; and now, when she felt the fold, and struggled to free herself from the enthralment, she found herself bound as with fetters of iron and clasps of steel. That Clarence loved her, she could not doubt. Enlightened as to the state of her own heart, she now recollected a thousand covert marks of tenderness and regard. He had been admitted to the most unreserved intercourse with her, as the friend of her husband. Like herself, he had been cherishing sentiments of whose strength he was unaware, and which, when revealed in their full force, would make him tremble. She now constantly avoided his society. Her manners were cold and constrained, and her conscious eyes sought the ground. But Clarence, though he saw the change, and could not be ignorant of the cause, was not rebuked or chilled by her coldness. He seemed to call forth, with more animation, the rich resources of his mind, his enthusiasm was more glowing, his voice had more music, and his smile more brightness. It was evident she alone was unhappy; whatever were his feelings, they inspired no remorse. She began to believe her own vanity had misled her, and that he only looked upon her as the wife of his friend. She had mistaken the luminousness of his eyes for the fire of passion. Her credulity abased her in her own estimation.

One afternoon Clarence found her alone. She had declined accompanying Mary and her father in a walk, because she thought Clarence was to be with them. "I did not expect to find you alone," said he, taking a seat by her side —"but since I have gained such a privilege, may I ask, without increasing your displeasure, in what I have offended? You shun my society—your averted looks, your altered mien"—he paused, for her embarrassment was contagious, and the sentence remained unfinished. The appeal was a bold one, but as a *friend* he had a right to make it.

"You have not offended me," at length she answered, "but you know the peculiar circumstances of my life, and cannot wonder if my spirits sometimes droop, when reflecting on the misery of the past, and the uncertainty of the future."

"If," said he, "the uncertainty of the future makes you unhappy as it regards yourself, you may perhaps have cause of uneasiness, but as it respects Allison, as far as I know his sentiments, he has the fullest confidence, and the brightest hopes of felicity. I once looked upon him as the most unfortunate, but I now view him as the most blessed of men. When he told me the circumstances of his exile, how lone and hopeless seemed his lot! Now, when I see all that woos him to return, angels might covet his destiny."

"You forget yourself," cried Augusta, not daring to take in the full meaning of his words—"it is not the office of a friend to flatter—Allison never flattered

—I always revered him for his truth."

"Yes!" exclaimed Clarence, "he has truth and integrity. They call him upright, and honourable, and just; but is he not cold and senseless to remain in banishment so long, leaving his beautiful wife in widowhood and sorrow! and was he not worse than mad to send me here the herald of himself, to expose me to the influence of your loveliness, knowing that to see you, to be near you, must be to love, nay, even to worship."

"You have driven me from you for ever!" cried Augusta, rising in indignant astonishment, at the audacity of this avowal. "Allison shall learn in what a friend he has confided."

"I am prepared for your anger," continued he, with increasing impetuosity, "but I brave it; your husband will soon return, and I shall leave you. Tell him of all my boldness, and all my sincerity; tell him too all the emotions that are struggling in your heart for me, for oh! you cannot deny it, there is a voice pleading for my pardon, in your bosom now, and telling you, that, if it is a crime to love, that one crime is mutual."

"Then I am indeed a wretch!" exclaimed Augusta, sinking down into a chair, and clasping her hands despairingly over her face; "but I deserve this humiliation." Clarence drew nearer to her—she hesitated—he trembled. The triumphant fire that revelled in his eyes was quenched; compassion, tenderness, and self-reproach softened their beams. He was in the very act of kneeling before her, to deprecate her forgiveness, when the door softly opened, and Mary Manning entered. Her step was always gentle, and she had approached unheard. She looked at them first with a smile, but Augusta's countenance was not one that could reflect a smile; and on Mary's face, at that moment, it appeared to her as a smile of derision. Clarence lingered a moment, as if unwilling to depart, yet uncertain whether to remain or go— then asking Mary for her father, he hastily retired, leaving Augusta in a state of such agitation, that Mary, seriously alarmed, entreated her to explain the cause of her distress.

"Explain!" cried Augusta. "You have witnessed my humiliation, and yet ask me the cause. I do not claim your sympathy, the grief I now feel admits of none; I was born to be unhappy, and whichever way I turn, I am wretched."

"Only tell me one thing, dear Augusta, is all your grief owing to the discovery of your love for Clarence, and to the sentiments with which you have inspired him? There is no humiliation in loving Clarence—for who could know him and not love him?"

Augusta looked in Mary's face, assured that she was uttering the language of mockery. Mary, the pure moralist, the mild, but uncompromising advocate for duty and virtue, thus to palliate the indulgence of a forbidden passion! It could only be in derision; yet her eye was so serene, and her smile so kind, it was impossible to believe that contempt was lurking beneath. "Then you *do* love him, Mary, and I am doubly treacherous!"

Mary blushed—"with the affection of a sister, the tenderness of a friend, do I regard him; I admire his talents, I venerate his virtues."

"Virtues! oh! Mary, he is a traitor to his friend; what reliance is there on those virtues, which, having no root in the heart, are swept away by the first storm of passion?"

"Passion may enter the purest heart," answered Mary; "guilt consists in yielding to its influence. I would pledge my life that Clarence would never give himself up to the influence of a guilty passion."

"Talk not of him, let me forget his existence, if I can; I think of one, who will return from his long exile, only to find his hopes deceived, his confidence betrayed, his heart broken."

Here Augusta wept in such anguish, that Mary, finding it in vain to console her, threw her arms around her, and wept in sympathy; yet still she smiled through her tears, and again and again repeated to her, that heaven had long years of happiness yet in store.

Augusta, in the solitude of her own chamber, recovered an appearance of outward composure, but there was a deadly sickness in her soul, that seemed to her like a foretaste of mortality. The slightest sound made her tremble, and when Mary returned to her, softly, but hurriedly, and told her her father wished to see her, she went to him, with a blanched cheek and trembling step, like a criminal who is about to hear her sentence of doom.

"I have something to communicate to you," said he, kindly taking her hand, and leading her to a seat. "But I fear you will be too much agitated."

"Is he come?" cried she, grasping his arm with sudden energy; "only tell me, is he come?"

"Your husband *is* arrived; I have just received tidings that he is in the city, and will shortly be here."

Augusta gasped for breath, she pressed her hands on her bosom, there was such a cold, intolerable weight there; she felt the letter of her husband, which she had constantly worn as a talisman against the evil she most dreaded. That tender, confiding letter, which, when she had first received it, she had hailed as the precursor of the purest felicity.

"It is all over now," sighed she, unconscious of the presence of Mr. Manning.

"Poor unhappy Allison, I will tell him all, and then I will lie down and die."

"I hear a carriage approaching," said Mr. Manning; "the gate opens—support yourself, my dear child, and give him the welcome he merits." Augusta could not move, her limbs were powerless, but perception and sensibility remained; she saw Mr. Manning leave the room, heard steps and voices in the passage, and then the door reopen. The shades of twilight were beginning to fall, and a mist was over her eyes, but she distinctly recognised the figure that entered—what was her astonishment, to behold, instead of the lank form, bald brows, and green shade, marked in such indelible characters on her memory—the graceful lineaments, clustering looks, and lustrous eyes of Clarence? She looked beyond in wild alarm for her husband. "Leave me," she exclaimed, "leave me, or you drive me to desperation!"

But Clarence eagerly approached her, as if defying all consequences, and reckless of her resentment. He clasped her in his arms, he pressed her to his heart, and imprinted on her brow, cheek, and lips, unnumbered kisses. "My bride, my wife, my own beloved Augusta, do you not know me? and can you forgive me for this trial of your love? I did not mean to cause you so much suffering, but I could not resist the temptation of proving whether your love was mine, through duty or inclination. I have been the rival of myself, and I have exulted in finding, that love in all its strength has still been mastered by duty. Augusta, I glory in my wife."

Augusta looked up, in bewildered rapture, hardly knowing in what world she existed. She had never dreamed of such a transformation. Even now it seemed incredible—it could not be true—her present felicity was too great to be real —"Can Allison and Clarence be one?"

"Yes, my Augusta, these arms have a right to enfold thee, or they would not clasp you thus. No miracle has been wrought, but the skeleton is reclothed with flesh, the locks of youth have been renewed, the tide of health has flowed back again into the wasted veins, lending a glow to the wan cheek, and a brightness to the dim eye; and more than all, the worn and feeble spirit, always sympathizing with its frail companion, as replumed its drooping wings, and been soaring in regions of hope, and joy, and love."

Without speaking metaphorically, Augusta's heart actually ached with its excess of happiness.

"I have not room here," she cried, "for such fulness of joy," again laying her hand where that precious letter was deposited, but with such different emotions. "My friends must participate in my happiness, it is selfish to withhold it from them so long."

"They know it already," said Allison, smiling; "they have known my secret from the first, and assisted me in concealing my identity."

Augusta now understood Mary's apparent inconsistency, and vindicated her from all unkindness and wilful palliation of guilt. "I am not quite an impostor," continued her husband, "for my name is Sydney Clarence Allison —and let me still wear the appellation you have learned to love. It was my uncle's, and he left a condition in his will that I should assume it as my own. I find myself, too, the heir of sufficient wealth to be almost a burden; for my uncle, romantic to the last, only caused the report of the failure of his wealth, that I might prove the sincerity of your father's friendship. My wife, my own Augusta, is not his blessing resting on us now?"

Mr. Manning and his daughter sympathized largely in the happiness of their friends. Their only sorrow was the approaching separation. Mary, whose disposition was naturally serious, was exalted on this occasion to an unwonted vein of humour. When she saw Augusta's eyes turning with fond admiration towards her husband, she whispered in her ear—"Is it possible, that bald, yellow, horrid-looking creature is your husband? I would not marry him, unless I were dragged to the altar."

And Allison, passing his hand over his luxuriant hair, reminded her, with a smile, of the *subscription* and the *wig*.

THE VICTIM OF EXCITEMENT.

Intemperance is a vice which is generally considered of the masculine sex. In the pictured scenes of the ravages it has wrought woman is seldom introduced but as the patient victim of brutality, or as the admonishing angel of transgressing man. There are instances on record, however, of a sad reverse. Not alone in the lower classes of life, amid the dregs of society, but in higher walks, where intelligence, wit, beauty, and wealth, virgin worth, wedded love, and Christian grace, are all cast as unvalued offerings at the beastly shrine of intemperance. One of these fatal examples (of which, to the honour of our sex be it said, there are so few) once came under the observation of the writer. Her character and history form the subject of the following sketch.

Mr. Manly first met Anne Weston in a ball-room. It was on the evening of the Fourth of July, and the fairest ladies of the country were assembled to celebrate the national jubilee. He was a lawyer, and had been the orator of the day; an eloquent one, and therefore entitled to distinguished attention. He came from an adjoining town, of which he had recently become an inhabitant, and now found himself in a scene which scarcely presented one familiar countenance. He was a very proud man, and had the air of one who felt himself too superior to the multitude to mingle in the general amusement. He stood with folded arms, as remote as possible from the dancers despising those who were engaged in that exercise on such a sultry night. In vain the obsequious master of ceremonies begged to introduce him to this and that fair lady. He declined the honour with a cold bow, declaring his utter disinclination to dancing. He was told that his disinclination would cease as soon as Miss Weston arrived. She was the belle of the place, the daughter of the richest gentleman in town—had received the most finished education, and refused the most splendid offers. In short, she was irresistible, and it was predicted that he would find her so. It cannot be denied, that the fame of this all-conquering lady had previously reached his ears, but unfortunately he had a detestation of belles, and predetermined to close his eyes, and shut his ears, and steel his heart against her vaunted attractions. He had never yet sacrificed his independence to woman. He had placed his standard of female excellence very high. He had seen no one that reached its altitude. "No," said he to himself, "let me live on in singleness of heart and loneliness of purpose, all the days of my life, rather than unite myself with one of those vain, flimsy, garrulous, and superficial beings who win the smiles, and fix the attention of the many. I despise a weak woman, I hate a masculine one, and a pedantic one I abhor. I turn with fear from the glittering belle, whose home is the crowded hall, whose incense the homage of fools, whose altar the shrine of fashion. Can *she* sit down contented in the privacy of domestic love who has lived on the adulation of the world, or be satisfied with the affection of one true heart, who has claimed as her due, the vows of all? No, better the fool, the pedant, than the belle. Who can find that woman, whose price is above rubies? Ah! 'tis certain I never shall marry." He was aroused from these reflections, by a movement in the hall, and he felt a conviction that the vaunted lady was arrived. In spite of his boasted indifference, he could not repress a slight sensation of curiosity to see one who was represented as so transcendent. But he moved not, he did not even turn his eyes towards the spot where so many were clustering. "The late hour of her arrival," said he, "shows equal vanity and affectation. She evidently wishes to be conspicuous—studies everything for effect." The lady moved towards that part of the hall where he was stationed. She held the arm of one gentleman, and was followed by some half-dozen others. He was compelled to gaze upon her, for they passed so near, the folds of her white muslin dress fluttered against him. He was pleased to see that she was much less beautiful than he had expected. He scarcely thought her handsome. Her complexion was pale, even sallow, and her face wanted that soft, flowing outline, which is necessary to the perfection of beauty. He could not but acknowledge, however, that her figure was very fine, her motions graceful, and her air spirited and intellectual. "I am glad she is not beautiful," said he, "for I might have been tempted to have admired her, against my sober judgment. Oppressed by the heat of the apartment, he left the hall and sauntered for a long time in the piazza, till a certain feeling of curiosity, to know whether a lady whose bearing expressed so much pride of soul, could be foolish enough to dance, led him to return. The first object he beheld, was the figure of Miss Weston, moving in most harmonious time, to an exhilarating air, her countenance lighted up with an animation, a fire, that had as magical an effect upon her features, as the morning sunbeams on the face of nature. The deepest colour was glowing on her cheek,—her very soul was shining forth from her darkening eyes. She danced with infinite spirit, but equal grace. He had never witnessed anything to compare with it, not even on the stage. "She dances entirely too well," thought he; "she cannot have much intellect, yet she carries on a constant conversation with her partner through all the mazes of the dance. It must be admirable nonsense, from the broad smiles it elicits. I am half resolved to be introduced and invite her to dance— from mere *curiosity*, and to prove the correctness of my opinion." He sought the introduction, became her partner in the dance, and certainly forgot, while he listened to her "admirable nonsense," that she was that object of his detestation—a *belle*. Her conversation was sprightly, unstudied, and original. She seemed more eager to listen than to talk, more willing to admire than to be admired. She did not tell him that she admired his oration, but she spoke warmly on the subject of eloquence, and quoted in the happiest manner, a passage of his own speech, *one* which he himself judged superb. It proved her to have listened with deep attention. He had never received so delicate or gratifying a compliment. His vanity was touched, and his pride slumbered. He called forth those powers of pleasing, with which he was eminently endowed, and he began to feel a dawning ambition to make the conquest of a heart which so many had found indomitable. He admired the simplicity of her dress, its fitness and elegance. A lady's dress is always indicative of her character. Then her voice was singularly persuasive in its tones, it breathed of feminine gentleness and sensibility, with just enough spirit and independence for a woman. Mr. Manly came to these wise conclusions before the end of the first dance—at the termination of the second, he admired the *depth*, as well as the brilliancy of her mind, and when he bade her adieu for the night, he was equally convinced of the purity of her feelings and the goodness of her heart. Such is the strength of man's wisdom, the stability of his opinions, the steadiness of his purpose, when placed in competition with the fascinations of a woman who has made the determination to please. In after years Mr. Manly told a friend of a dream which that night haunted his pillow. He was not superstitious, or disposed to attach the slightest importance to dreams. But this was a vivid picture, and succeeding events caused him to recall it, as one having the power of prophecy. He lived over again the events of the evening. The winning accents of Miss Weston mingled in his ear with the gay notes of the violin. Still, ever and anon, discordant sounds marred the sweet harmony. The malicious whisper, the stifled, deriding laugh, and the open scoff came from every corner. Sometimes he saw, through the crowd, the slow finger of scorn pointing at him. As he turned, with a fierce glance of defiance, Miss Weston seemed to meet him still, holding a goblet in her hand, which she pressed him to drain. Her cheeks and lips burned with a scarlet radiance, and her eyes sparkled with unnatural brightness. "Taste it not," whispered a soft voice in his ear, "it is poison." "It is the cup of immortality," exclaimed the syren, and she drained the goblet to its last drop. In a few moments her countenance changed—her face became bloated, her features disfigured, and her eyes heavy and sunken. He turned with disgust from the former enchantress, but she pursued him, she wound her arms around him. In the vain struggle of liberating himself from her embrace, he awoke. It was long before he could overcome the sensation of loathing and horror excited by the unhallowed vision, and even when, overcome by heaviness and exhaustion, he again slept, the same bloated phantom presented her intoxicating draught. The morning found him feverish and unrefreshed. He could not shake off the impression of his dream, and the image of Miss Weston seemed deprived of the witchery that had enthralled his imagination the preceding evening. He was beginning to despise himself, for having yielded up so soon his prejudices and pride, when an invitation to dine at Mr. Weston's, interrupted the severe tenor of his thoughts. Politeness obliged him to accept, and in the society of Miss Weston, graceful, animated, and intellectual, presiding with unaffected dignity and ease at her father's board, he forgot the hideous metamorphose of his dream.

From that day his fate was sealed. It was the first time his heart had ever been seriously interested, and he loved with all the strength and ardour of his proud and ardent character. The triumph, too, of winning one whom so many had sought in vain, threw a kind of glory over his conquest, and exalted his estimation of his own attributes. The wedding-day was appointed. The evening previous to his nuptials, Anne Weston sat in her own chamber, with one of the chosen friends of her girlhood, Emily Spencer. Anne had no sisters, and from childhood, Emily had stood to her almost in that dear relation. She was to accompany her to her new home, for Anne refused to be separated from her, and had playfully told Mr. Manly, "that if he married *her*, he must take Emily too, for she could not and would not be parted from her."

The thought of the future occupied the minds of the two friends. Anne sat in silence. The lamp that partially illumined the apartment, gave additional paleness to her pale and spiritual countenance. Her thoughts appeared to have rolled within herself, and, from the gloom of her eye, did not appear to be such as usually rest in the bosom of one about to be wedded to the object of her affection and her trust.

"I fear," said she at length, as if forgetting the presence of her friend, "that I have been too hasty. The very qualities that won my admiration, and determined me to fix his regard, now cause me to tremble. I have been too much accustomed to self-indulgence, to bear restraint, and should it ever be imposed by a master's hand, my rebellious spirit would break the bonds of duty, and assert its independence. I fear I am not formed to be a happy wife, or to *constitute* the happiness of a husband. I live too much upon excitement, and when the deep monotony of domestic life steals on, what will become of me?"

"How can there be monotony," answered Emily, warmly, "with such a companion as Manly? Oh, trust him, Anne, love him as he merits to be loved, as you yourself are loved, and your lot may be envied among women."

"He has awakened all the capabilities my heart has of loving," cried Anne, "but I wish I could shake off this dull weight from my spirits." She rose as she spoke, approached a side table, and, turning out a glass of rich cordial, drank it, as if conscious, from experience, of its renovating influence. Emily's anxious gaze followed her movements. A deep sigh escaped her lips. When her friend resumed her seat, she drew nearer to her, she took her hand in hers, and, while her colour heightened, and her breath shortened, she said—

"Anne Weston, I should not deserve the name of friend, if in this hour, the last, perhaps, of unrestrained confidence between us, I did not dare—"

"Dare what?" interrupted Anne, shame and resentment kindling in her eye.

"To tell you, that the habit you indulge in, of resorting to artificial means to exhilarate your spirits, though now attended with no obvious danger, may exercise most fatal influence on your future peace. I have long struggled for resolution to utter this startling truth, and I gather boldness as I speak. By all our friendship and sincerity, by the past splendour of your reputation, by the bright hopes of the future, by the trusting vows of a lover, and the gray hairs of a father, I pray you to relinquish a habit, whose growing strength is now only known to me." Emily paused, strong emotions impeded her utterance. "What is it you fear?" asked Anne, in a low, stern voice; "speak, for you see that I am calm." "You know what I dread," continued Emily. "I see a speck on the bright character of my friend. It may spread and dim all its lustre. We all know the fearful strength of habit, we cannot shake off the serpent when once its coils are around us. Oh, Anne, gifted by nature with such brilliancy of intellect and gayety of heart, why have you ever had recourse to the exciting draught, as if art could exalt the original buoyancy of your spirits, or care had laid his blighting hand upon you?"

"Forbear," cried Anne, impetuously, "and hear me, before you blast me with your contempt. It was not till bitter disappointment pressed, crushed me, that I knew art could renovate the languor of nature. Yes, *I, the* courted and admired of all, was doomed to love one whose affections I could not win. You knew him well, but you never knew how my ineffectual efforts to attach him maddened my pride, or how the triumph of my beautiful rival goaded my feelings. The world guessed not my secret, for still I laughed and glittered with mocking splendour, but with such a cold void within! I could not bear it. My unnatural spirits failed me. I *must* still shine on, or the secret of my humiliation be discovered. I began in despair, but I have accomplished my purpose. And now," added she, "I have done. The necessity of shining and deceiving is over. I thank you for the warmth of friendship that suggested your admonition. But, indeed, Emily, your apprehensions are exaggerated. I have a restraining power within me that must always save me from degradation. Habit, alone, makes slaves of the weak; it becomes the slave of the strong in mind. I know what's due to Manly. He never shall blush for his choice in a wife."

She began with vehemence and ended with deliberation. There was something in the cold composure of her manner that forbid a renewal of the subject. Emily felt that she had fulfilled her duty as a friend, and delicacy commanded her to forbear a renewal of her admonitions. Force of feeling had betrayed her into a warmth of expression she now regretted. She loved Anne, but she looked with many misgivings to being the sharer of her wedded home. She had deeply studied the character of Manly, and trembled to think of the reaction that might one day take place in his mind, should he ever discover the dark spot on the disk of his sun—of his destiny. Though she had told Anne that the secret of her growing love for the exciting draught was *known* only to herself, it was whispered among the servants, suspected by a few discreet individuals, and had been several times hinted in a private circle of friends. It had never yet reached the ears of Manly, for there was something in his demeanour that repelled the most distant approach to familiarity. He married with the most romantic and enthusiastic ideas of domestic felicity. Were those bright visions of bliss realized? Time, the great disenchanter, alone could answer.

It was about five years after the scenes we have recorded, that Mr. and Mrs. Manly took up their residence in the town of G——. Usually, when strangers are about to become inhabitants of a new place, there is some annunciation of their arrival; but they came, without any previous intimation being given for the speculation of the curious, or bringing any letters of introduction for the satisfaction of the proud. They hired an elegant house, furnished it rich and fashionably, and evidently prepared for the socialities of life, as enjoyed in the highest circles. The appearance of wealth always commands the respect of the many, and this respect was heightened by their personal claims to admiration. Five years, however, had wrought a change in both, not from the fading touch of time, for they were not of an age when the green leaf begins to grow sere, but other causes were operating with a power as silent and unpausing. The fine, intelligent face of Mrs. Manly had lost much of its delicacy of outline, and her cheek, that formerly was pale or roseate as sensibility or enthusiasm ruled the hour, now wore a stationary glow, deeper than the blush of feminine modesty, less bright than the carnation of health. The unrivalled beauty of her figure had given place to grosser lineaments, over which, however, grace and dignity still lingered, as if unwilling to leave a shrine so worshipped. Mr. Manly's majestic person was invested with an air of deeper haughtiness, and his dark brow was contracted into an expression of prevailing gloom and austerity. Two lovely children, one almost an infant, who were carried abroad every fair day by their nurse, shared the attention their parents excited; and many appealed to *her* for information respecting the strangers. She was unable to satisfy their curiosity, as she had been a member of their household but a short time, her services having been hired while journeying to the place. The other servants were hired after their arrival. Thus, one of the most fruitful sources from which the inquisitive derive their aliment, was denied to the inhabitants of G——. It was not long before the house of Mr. and Mrs. Manly was frequented by those whose society she most wished to cultivate. The suavity of her manners, the vivacity of her conversation, her politeness and disinterestedness, captivated the hearts of all. Mr. Manly too received his guests with a cordiality that surprised, while it gratified. Awed by the external dignity of his deportment, they expected to be repulsed, rather than welcomed, but it was universally acknowledged, that no man could be more delightful than Mr. Manly, when he chose to unbend. As a lawyer, his fame soon rose. His integrity and eloquence became the theme of every tongue. Amidst all the admiration they excited, there were some dark surmises. The malicious, the censorious, the evil-disposed are found in every circle, and in every land. It was noticed that Mr. Manly watched his wife with painful scrutiny, that she seemed uneasy whenever his glance met hers, that her manner was at times hurried and disturbed, as if some secret cause of sorrow preyed upon her mind. It was *settled* in the opinion of many, that Mr. Manly was a domestic tyrant, and that his wife was the meek victim of this despotism. Some suggested that he had been convicted of crime, and had fled from the pursuit of justice, while his devoted wife refused to separate her destiny from his. They gave a large and elegant party. The entertainment was superior to anything witnessed before in the precincts of G——. The graceful hostess, dressed in unwonted splendour, moved through her drawing-rooms, with the step of one accustomed to the homage of crowds, yet her smiles sought out the most undistinguished of her guests, and the most diffident gathered confidence from her condescending regards. Still the eye of Mr. Manly followed her with that anxious, mysterious glance, and her hurried movements often betrayed inexplicable perturbation. In the course of the evening, a gentleman refused wine, on the plea of belonging to the Temperance Society. Many voices were lifted in condemnation against him, for excluding one of the gladdeners of existence, what, the Scriptures themselves recommended, and the Saviour of men had consecrated by a miracle. The subject grew interesting, the circle narrowed round the advocate of Temperance, and many were pressing eagerly forward to listen to the debate. The opinion of Mrs. Manly was demanded. She drew back at first, as if unwilling to take the lead of her guests. At length she seemed warmed by the subject, and painted the evils of intemperance in the strongest and most appalling colours. She painted woman as its victim, till every heart recoiled at the image she drew. So forcible was her language, so impressive her gestures, so unaffected her emotions, every eye was riveted, and every ear bent on the eloquent mourner of her sex's degradation. She paused, oppressed by the notice she attracted, and moved from the circle, that widened for her as she passed, and gazed after her, with as much respect as if she were an Empress. During this spontaneous burst of oratory, Mr. Manly remained aloof, but those who had marked him in their minds as the harsh domestic tyrant, were now confirmed in their belief. Instead of admiring the wonderful talents of his wife, or sympathizing in the applause she excited, a gloom thick as night lowered upon his brow, his face actually grew of a livid paleness, till at last, as if unable to control his temper, he left the drawing-room.

"Poor Mrs. Manly," said one, "how much is her destiny to be lamented! To be united to a man who is incapable of appreciating her genius, and even seems guilty of the meanness of annoying her."

Thus the world judges; and had the tortured heart of Manly known the sentence that was passing upon him, he would have rejoiced that the shaft was directed to *his* bosom, rather than *hers*, which he would fain shield from the proud man's contumely, though it might never more be the resting-place of love and confidence. Is it necessary to go back and relate the history of those years which had elapsed since Anne Weston was presented to the reader as a triumphant belle, and plighted bride! Is it not already seen that the dark speck had enlarged, throwing into gradual, but deepening shade, the soul's original brightness, obscuring the sunshine of domestic joy, converting the home of love into a prison-house of shame, and blighting, chilling, palsying the loftiest energies and noblest purposes? The warning accents of Emily Spencer were breathed in vain. That fatal habit had already become a passion—a passion which, like the rising tide, grows deeper and higher, rolling onward and onward, till the landmarks of reason, and honour, and principle, are swept over by its waves—a tide that ebbs not but with ebbing life. She had looked "upon the wine when it was red, when it gave its colour to the cup," till she found, by fatal experience, that it biteth like a serpent, and stingeth like an adder. It were vain to attempt a description of the feelings of Manly when he first discovered the idol of his imagination under an influence that, in his opinion, brutalized a man. But a woman!—and that woman—his wife! In the agony, the madness of the moment, he could have lifted the hand of suicide, but Emily Spencer hovered near and held him back from the brink to which he was rushing. She pleaded the cause of her unhappy friend, she prayed him not to cast her off. She dwelt on the bright and sparkling mind, the warm, impulsive heart that might yet be saved from utter degradation by his exerted influence. She pledged herself to labour for him, and with him, and faithfully did she redeem her pledge. After the first terrible shock, Manly's passionate emotion settled down into a misanthropic gloom. Sometimes when he witnessed the remorse which followed such self-abandonment, the grace and beauty with which she would emerge from the disfiguring cloud, and the strong efforts she would make to reinstate herself in his estimation, a ray of brightness would shine in on his mind, and he would try to think of the past as a frightful dream. Then his prophetic dream would return to him, and he shuddered at its confirmation—once it seemed as if the demon had withdrawn its unhallowed presence, unable to exist in the holy atmosphere that surrounds a mother's bosom.

For a long time the burning essence was not permitted to mingle with the fountain of maternal tenderness. Even Manly's blasted spirit revived, and Emily hoped all, and believed all. But Anne had once passed the Rubicon, and though she often paused and looked back with yearnings that could not be uttered, upon the fair bounds she had left, the very poignancy of her shame goaded her on, though every step she took, evidenced the shame that was separating her from the affections of a husband whom she loved and respected, and who had once idolized her. It has been said that when woman once becomes a transgressor, her rapid progress in sin mocks the speed of man. As the glacier, that has long shone in dazzling purity, when loosened from its mountain stay, rushes down with a velocity accelerated by its impenetrability and coldness, when any shameful passion has melted the virgin snow of a woman's character, a moral avalanche ensues, destroying "whatsoever is venerable and lovely, and of good report."

Manly occasionally sought to conceal from the world the fatal propensities of his wife. She had occupied too conspicuous a station in society—she had been too highly exalted—to humble herself with impunity. Her father, whose lavish indulgence probably paved the way to her ruin, was unable to bear himself up under the weight of mortification and grief thus unexpectedly brought upon him. His constitution had long been feeble; and now the *bowl was, indeed, broken at the fountain.* The filial hand which he once hoped would have scattered roses on his dying pillow, struck the deathblow. Physicians talked of a chronic disease; of the gradual decay of nature; but Anne's conscience told her she had winged the dart. The agony of her remorse seemed a foretaste of the quenchless fire, and the undying worm. She made the most solemn promises of reformation—vowed never again to taste the poisonous liquor. She threw herself on the forgiveness of her husband, and prayed him to remove her where her name was never breathed; that she might begin life anew, and establish for their children an unblemished reputation. On the faith of these ardent resolutions, Manly broke his connexion with every former friend—sold all his possessions, and sought a new home, in a place far removed from the scene of their present unhappiness. Circumstances in her own family prevented Emily Spencer from accompanying them, but she was to follow them the earliest opportunity, hoping miracles from the change.

Mrs Manly, from the death of her father, came into the possession of a large and independent fortune. She was not sordid enough to deem money an equivalent for a wounded reputation; but it was soothing to her pride, to be able to fill her husband's coffers so richly, and to fit up their new establishment in a style so magnificent. Manly allowed her to exercise her own taste in everything. He knew the effect of external pomp, and thought it was well to dazzle the judgment of the world. He was determined to seek society; to open every source of gratification and rational excitement to his wife, to save her from monotony and solitude. His whole aim seemed to be, "that she might not be led into temptation." If with all these cares for her safety, he could have blended the tenderness that once softened his proud manners, could he have banished from his once beaming eye the look of vigilance and distrust; could she have felt herself once more enthroned in his heart, gratitude might, perhaps, have completed the regeneration begun by remorse. But Anne felt that she was an object of constant suspicion and fear; she felt that he had not faith in her good resolutions. She was no longer the sharer of his counsels—the inspirer of his hopes—or the companion in whom his soul delighted. His ruling passion supported him in society; but in those hours when they were necessarily thrown upon each other's resources, he was accustomed to sit in gloomy abstraction, brooding over his own melancholy thoughts. Anne was only too conscious of the subject of these reveries, and it kept alive a painful sense of her humiliation. She had, hitherto, kept her promise sacred, through struggles known only to herself, and she began to feel impatient and indignant that the reward for which she looked was still withheld. Had she been more deeply skilled in the mysteries of the human heart, she might have addressed the Genius of the household shrine, in the language of the avenging Moor, who first apostrophizes the torch that flares on his deed of darkness:

If I quench thee, thou flaming minister,

I can again thy former light restore,

Should I repent me—but once put out thine,

I know not where is the Promethean heat

That can thy light relume."

Mr. Manly was called away by professional business, which would probably detain him many weeks from home. He regretted this necessity; particularly before the arrival of Emily, whose coming was daily expected. He urged his wife to invite some friends to remain as her guests during his absence, to enliven her solitude. His request, so earnestly repeated, might have been gratifying to her feelings, if she had not known the distrust of her faith and strength of resolution it implied. The last words he said to her, at parting, were, "Remember, Anne, everything depends on yourself." She experienced a sensation of unspeakable relief in his absence. The eagle glance was withdrawn from her soul, and it expanded and exulted in its newly acquired freedom. She had a constant succession of visiters, who, remarking the elasticity of her spirits, failed not to cast additional obloquy on Mr. Manly, for the tyranny he evidently exercised over his wife. Emily did not arrive, and Mrs. Manly could not regret the delay. Her presence reminded her of all she wished to forget; for her days of triumph were returned, and the desire of shining rekindled from the ashes of scorn, that had for a while smothered the flame.

It wanted about a week of Mr. Manly's return. She felt a strong inclination to renew the splendours of her party. She had received so many compliments on the subject:—"Mrs. Manly's delightful party!" "Her conversational powers!" "Such a literary banquet!" &c. Invitations were given and accepted. The morning of the day, which was somewhat warm and oppressive, she was summoned by the kitchen council, where the business of preparation was going on. Suddenly, however, they came to a stand. There was no brandy to give flavour to the cake; and the cook declared it was impossible to make it without, or to use anything as a substitute.

Mrs. Manly's cheeks flushed high with shame. Her husband had retained the key of the closet that contained the forbidden article. He was afraid to trust it in her keeping. The mildest cordials were alone left at her disposal, for the entertainment of her guests. What would her husband think if she purchased, in his absence, what he had himself secreted from her? What would the servants believe if she refused to provide them with what was deemed indispensable? The fear of her secret being detected, combined with resentment at her husband's unyielding distrust, decided her conduct. She bought—she *tasted*. The cook asserted there was something peculiar in its flavour, and asked her to judge for herself. Would it not excite suspicion, if she refused? She broke her solemn vow—she *tasted*—and was *undone*. The burning thirst once kindled, in those who have been victims to this fatal passion, it rages with the strength of madness. In the secrecy of the closet where she hid the poison, she yielded to the tempter, who whispered, that, as she had been *compelled* to taste, her promise had been innocently broken: there could be no harm in a *little more*—the last that should ever pass her lips. In the delirium of the moment, she yielded, till, incapable of self-control, she continued the inebriating draught. Judgment—reason—at length, perception, vanished. The approach of evening found her still prostrate on her bed, a melancholy instance of the futility of the best human resolutions, unsupported by the divine principle of religion. The servants were at first struck with consternation. They thought some sudden disease had overtaken her. But the marks of intemperance, that, like the brand on the brow of Cain, single out its votaries from the rest of mankind, those revolting traces, were but too visible. They knew not what to do. Uncertain what guests were invited, they could not send apologies, nor ask them to defer their visit. The shades of evening were beginning to fall; the children were crying, deprived of the usual cares of their nurse; and in the general bustle, clung to their mother, whose ear was deaf to the appeal of nature. The little one, weary of shedding so many unavailing tears, at last crawled up on the bed, and fell asleep by her side, though there was scarcely room for her to stretch her little limbs, where she had found the means of climbing. As her slumbers deepened, her limbs relaxed from the rigid posture they had assumed: her arms dropped unconsciously over the bed, and she fell. In her fall she was thrown against one of the posts, and a sharp corner cutting her head, inflicted a deep wound. The screams of the little sufferer roused the household, and pierced even the leaden slumbers of intemperance. It was long, however, before Mrs. Manly came to a clear perception of what was passing around her. The sight of the streaming blood, however, acted like a shock of electricity. She sprang up, and endeavoured to stanch the bleeding wound. The effusion was soon stopped; the child sunk into a peaceful sleep, and the alarm subsided.

Children are liable to so many falls, and bruises, and wounds, it is not strange that Mrs. Manly, in the confused state of her mind, should soon forget the accident, and try to prepare herself for the reception of her guests, who were already assembling in the drawing-room. Every time the bell rung, she started, with a thrill of horror, conscious how unfit she was to sustain the enviable reputation she had acquired. Her head ached almost to bursting, her hands trembled, and a deadly sickness oppressed her. The visions of an upbraiding husband, a scoffing world, rose before her—and dim, but awful, in the dark perspective, she seemed to behold the shadow of a sin-avenging Deity. Another ring—the guests were thronging. Unhappy woman! What was to be done? She would have pleaded sudden indisposition—the accident of her child—but the fear that the servants would reveal the truth—the hope of being able to rally her spirits—determined her to descend into the drawing-room. As she cast a last hurried glance into the mirror, and saw the wild, haggard countenance it reflected, she recoiled at her own image. The jewels with which she had profusely adorned herself, served but to mock the ravages the destroying scourge had made upon her beauty. No cosmetic art could restore the purity of her complexion; nor the costliest perfumes conceal the odour of the fiery liquor. She called for a glass of cordial—kindled up a smile of welcome, and descended to perform the honours of her household. She made a thousand apologies for her delay; related, in glowing colours, the accident that happened to her child, and flew from one subject to another, as if she feared to trust herself with a pause. There was something so unnatural in her countenance, so overstrained in her manner, and so extravagant in her conversation, it was impossible for the company not to be aware of her situation. Silent glances were exchanged, low whispers passed round; but they had no inclination to lose the entertainment they anticipated. They remembered the luxuries of her table, and hoped, at least, if not a "feast of reason," a feast of the good things of earth.

It was at this crisis Emily Spencer arrived. Her travelling dress, and the fatigue of a journey, were sufficient excuses for her declining to appear in the drawing-room; but the moment she saw Mrs. Manly, her eye, too well experienced, perceived the backsliding of Anne, and hope died within her bosom. Sick at heart, wounded, and indignant, she sat down in the chamber where the children slept—those innocent beings, doomed to an orphanage more sad than death even makes. Anne's conscious spirit quailed before the deep reproach of Emily's silent glances. She stammered out an explanation of the bloody bandage that was bound around the infant's, head, assured her there was no cause of alarm, and hurried down to the *friends* who had passed the period of her absence in covert sarcasm, and open animadversion on her conduct.

Emily sat down on the side of the bed, and leaned over the sleeping infant. Though Mrs. Manly had assured her there was no cause of alarm, she felt there was no reliance on her judgment; and the excessive paleness and languor of its countenance, excited an anxiety its peaceful slumbers could not entirely relieve. "It is all over," thought she, "a relapse in sin is always a thousand times more dangerous than the first yielding. She is at this moment blazoning her disgrace, and there will be no restraining influence left. Oh! unfortunate Manly! was it for this you sacrificed home, friends, and splendid prospects, and came a stranger to a strange land!" Absorbed in the contemplation of Manly's unhappy destiny, she remained till the company dispersed, and Mrs. Manly dragged her weary footsteps to her chamber. Completely exhausted by her efforts to command her bewildered faculties, she threw herself on the bed, and sunk into a lethargy; the natural consequence of inebriation. The infant, disturbed by the sudden motion, awakened, with a languid cry, expressive of feebleness and pain. Emily raised it in her arms, endeavoured to soothe its complaining; but it continued restless and wailing, till the blood gushed afresh through the bandage. Greatly alarmed, she shook Mrs. Manly's arm, and called upon her to awake. It was in vain; she could not rouse her from her torpor. Instantly ringing the bell, she summoned the nurse, who was revelling, with the other servants, over the relics of the feast, and told her to send immediately for a physician. Fortunately there was one in the neighbourhood, and he came speedily. He shook his head mournfully when he examined the condition of the child, and pronounced its case beyond the reach of human skill. The injury produced by the fall had reached the brain. The very depth of its slumbers was but a fatal symptom of approaching dissolution. The tears of Emily fell fast and thick on the pallid face of the innocent victim. She looked upon its mother—thought upon its father, and pressed the child in agony to her bosom. The kind physician was summoned to another chamber of sickness. He had done all he could to mitigate, where he could not heal. Emily felt that this dispensation was sent in mercy. She could not pray for the child's life, but she prayed that it might die in the arms of its father; and it seemed that her prayer was heard. It was a singular providence that brought him that very night—a week sooner than he anticipated—urged on by a restless presentiment of evil; a dread that all was not well. Imagination, however, had not pictured the scene that awaited him. His wife, clothed in her richest raiments, and glittering with jewels, lying in the deep torpor of inebriation. Emily, seated by the side of the bed, bathed in tears, holding in her lap the dying infant, her dress stained with the blood with which the fair locks of the child were matted. What a spectacle! He stood for a moment on the threshold of the apartment, as if a bolt had transfixed him. Emily was not roused from her grief by the sound of his footsteps, but she saw the shadow that darkened the wall, and at once recognised his lineaments. The startling cry she uttered brought him to her side, where, kneeling down over his expiring infant, he gazed on its altering features and quivering frame with a countenance so pale and stern, Emily's blood ran cold. Silently and fixedly he knelt, while the deepening shades of dissolution gathered over the beautiful waxen features and the dark film grew over the eyes, so lately bright with that heavenly blue, which is alone seen in the eyes of infancy. He inhaled its last, cold, struggling breath; saw it stretched in the awful immobility of death; then slowly rising, he turned towards the gaudy figure that lay as if in mockery of the desolation it had created. Then Manly's imprisoned spirit burst its bonds. He grasped his wife's arm, with a strength that might have been felt, even were her limbs of steel, and calling forth her name in a voice deep and thrilling as the trumpet's blast, he commanded her to rise. With a faint foretaste of the feeling with which the guilty soul shall meet the awakening summons of the archangel, the wretched woman raised herself on her elbow, and gazed around her with a wild and glassy stare. "Woman," cried he, still retaining his desperate grasp, and pointing to the dead child, extended on the lap of the weeping Emily, "woman! is this your work? Is this the welcome you have prepared for my return? Oh! most perjured wife and most abandoned mother! You have filled, to overflowing, the vials of indignation; on your own head shall they be poured, blasting and destroying. You have broken the last tie that bound me— it withers like flax in the flame. Was it not enough to bring down the gray hairs of your father to the grave? to steep your own soul in perjury and shame, but that fair innocent must be a sacrifice to your drunken revels? One other victim remains. Your husband—who lives to curse the hour he ever yielded to a syren, who lured him to the brink of hell!"

He paused suddenly—relaxed his iron hold, and fell back perfectly insensible. It is an awful thing to see man fall down in his strength, struck, too, by the lightning of passion. Anne sprang upon her feet. The benumbing spell was broken. His last words had reached her naked soul. She believed him dead, and that he had indeed died *her* victim. Every other thought and feeling was swallowed up in this belief; she threw herself by his side, uttering the most piercing shrieks, and rending her sable tresses, in the impotence of despair. Poor Emily! it was for her a night of horror; but her fortitude and presence of mind seemed to increase with the strength of the occasion. She turned her cares from the dead to the living. She bathed with restorative waters the pale brow of Manly; she chafed his cold hands, till their icy chill began to melt in the warmth of returning animation. All the while his wretched wife continued her useless and appalling ravings.

The morning dawned upon a scene of desolation. In one darkened room lay the snowy corpse, dressed in the white garments of the grave; in another, the almost unconscious Manly, in the first stages of a burning fever; Anne, crouched in a dark corner, her face buried in her hands; and Emily, pale and wan, but energetic and untiring, still the ministering and healing spirit of this house of grief. Yes! darkness and mourning was in that house; but the visitation of God had not come upon it: Pestilence had not walked in the darkness, nor Destruction, at the noon-day hour. Had Anne resisted the voice of the tempter, her child might have still smiled in his cherub beauty; her husband might have still presided at his board, and she, herself, at his side; if not in the sunshine of love, in the light of increasing confidence. Her frame was worn by the long, silent struggles of contending passions, hopes, and fears. This last blow prostrated her in the dust. Had *Anne resisted the voice of the tempter*, all might yet have been well; but having once again steeped her lips in the pollution, the very consciousness of her degradation plunged her deeper in sin. She fled from the writhing of remorse to the oblivious draught. She gave herself up, body and soul, irredeemably. She was hurrying on, with fearful strides, to that brink from which so many immortal beings have plunged into the fathomless gulf of perdition.

Manly rose from the couch of sickness an altered man: his proud spirit was humbled—chastened—purified. Brought to the confines of the unseen world, he was made to feel the vanity—the nothingness of this—and while his soul seemed floating on the shoreless ocean of eternity, the billows of human passion sunk before the immensity, the awfulness of the scene. The holy resolutions, formed on what he believed his death-bed, did not vanish with returning health. He saw the bitter cup prepared for him to drain, and though he prayed that it might be permitted to pass from him, he could say, in the resignation of his heart, "Not my will, oh, Father! but *thine* be done." He looked upon his degraded wife rather with pity, than indignation. He no longer reproached her, or used the language of denunciation. But sometimes, in her lucid intervals, when she witnessed the subdued expression of his once haughty countenance—his deep paleness—the mildness of his deportment to all around him; the watchful guard he held over his own spirit; and all this accompanied by an energy in action—a devotedness in duty—such as she had never seen before—Anne trembled, and felt that he had been near unto his Maker, while she was holding closer and closer companionship with the powers of darkness. The wall of separation she had been building up between them, was it to become high as the heavens—deep as the regions of irremediable woe?

Emily was no longer their guest. While Manly lingered between life and death, she watched over him with all a sister's tenderness. Insensible to fatigue—forgetful of sleep—and regardless of food, she was sustained by the intensity of her anxiety; but as soon as his renovated glance could answer her attentions with speechless gratitude, and he became conscious of the cares that had done more than the physician's skill in bringing him back to life, she gradually yielded to others the place she had occupied as nurse—that place, which she who should have claimed it as her right, was incapacitated to fill. When Manly was restored to health, Emily felt that she could no longer remain. There was no more fellowship with Anne; and the sympathy that bound her to her husband she could not, with propriety, indulge. Manly, himself, did not oppose her departure; he felt it was best she should go. She took with her the little Anne, with the grateful consent of her father. The opposition of the mother was not allowed to triumph over what Manly knew was for the blessing of his child. "Let her go," said he, mildly, but determinately; "she will not feel the want of a mother's care."

—

It was a dark and tempestuous night. The winds of autumn swept against the windows, with the mournful rustle of the withered leaves, fluttering in the blast: the sky was moonless and starless. Everything abroad presented an aspect of gloom and desolation. Even those who were gathered in the halls of pleasure, felt saddened by the melancholy sighing of the gust; and a cold, whispered mortality breathed into the hearts of the thoughtless and gay. It was on this night that Manly sat by the dying couch of Anne. Every one is familiar with the rapid progress of disease, when it attacks the votary of intemperance. The burning blood soon withers up the veins; the fountain, itself, becomes dry. Fearfully rapid, in this instance, had been the steps of the destroyer. Here she lay, her frame tortured with the agonies of approaching dissolution, and her spirit strong and clear from the mists that had so long and so fatally obscured it. She saw herself in that mirror which the hand of truth holds up to the eye of the dying. Memory, which acquires, at that awful moment, such supernatural power, brought before her all the past—the *wasted past*—the *irretrievable past*. Her innocent childhood—her bright and glowing youth; her blasted womanhood, seemed embodied to her eyes. Her father rose from his grave, and standing by her bedside, waving his mournful locks, warned her of her broken oath. Her little infant, with his fair hair dabbled with blood, came gliding in its shroud, and accused her of being its murderer. Her husband! As her frenzied spirit called up this last image, she turned her dim eye to him, who was hanging over her couch with a countenance of such grief and compassion, the dry agony of her despair softened into a gush of remorseful tenderness: "Oh! no—no!" cried she, in difficult accents, "you do not curse me; you live to pardon the wretch who has undone herself and you. Oh! could I live over the past; could I carry back to our bridal the experience of this awful hour, what long years of happiness might be ours!"

The recollection of what she had been—of what she *might have been*— contrasted with what she then was, and with what she still *might be*, was too terrible. Her agonies became wordless. Manly knelt by her side: he sought to soothe her departing spirit by assurances of his own pardon; and to lead her, by penitence and prayer, to the feet of Him, "in whose sight the heavens are not clean." He poured into her soul the experience of his, when he had travelled to the boundaries of the dark valley: his despair—his penitence, and his hopes. He spoke of the mercy that is boundless—the grace that is infinite —till the phantoms, accusing conscience called up, seemed to change their maledictions into prayers for her behalf. Her ravings gradually died away, and she sunk into a troubled sleep.

As Manly gazed upon her features, on which death was already fixing its dim, mysterious impress,—those features whose original beauty was so fearfully marred by the ravages of intemperance,—the waters of time rolled back, and revealed that green, enchanted spot in life's waste, where he was first gilded by her presence. Was that the form whose graceful movements then fascinated his senses; or those the eyes, whose kindling glances had flashed like a glory over his soul? The love, then so idolatrous and impassioned—so long crushed and buried—rose up from the ruins to hallow the vigils of that solemn night.

The morning dawned, but the slumbers of Anne were never to be broken, till the resurrection morn. In the bloom of life—the midst of affluence—with talents created to exalt society, and graces to adorn it; a heart full of warm and generous impulses; a husband as much the object of her pride as of her affections; children, lovely in their innocence, she fell a sacrifice to one brutalizing passion. Seldom, indeed, is it that woman, in the higher walks of life, presents such a melancholy example; but were there but *one*, and that one Anne Weston, let her name be revealed, as a beacon, whose warning light should be seen by the daughters of the land.

Another year glided by. The approach of another autumn, found Manly girded for enterprise. He had marked out a new path, and was about to become a dweller of a young and powerful city, born on one of the mighty rivers of the West. His child could there grow up, unwithered by the associations of her mother's disgrace. Amidst the hopes and anticipations gathering around a new home, in a new land, his own spirit might shake off the memories that oppressed its energies. He was still young. The future might offer something of brightness, to indemnify for the darkness of the past.

He once more sought the native place of his unhappy wife; for his child was there, under the cherishing care of Emily Spencer. He passed that ball-room, in whose illuminated walls his destiny was sealed. The chamber selected for the traveller's resting-place was the one where the prophetic dream had haunted his pillow. His brow was saddened by the gloom of remembrance, when he entered the dwelling-place of his child; but when he saw the bright, beautiful little creature, who sprang into his arms, with spontaneous rapture, and witnessed the emotion that Emily strove vainly to conquer, he felt he was not alone in the world: and the future triumphed over the past. He unfolded all his views, and described the new scenes in which he was soon to become an actor, with reviving eloquence.

"Are you going to carry me there too, father?" said the little girl, whose earnest blue eyes were riveted on his face.

"Are you not willing to go with me, my child? or must I leave you behind?"

"I should like to go, if you will take Emily, but I cannot leave her behind," cried the affectionate child, clinging to that beloved friend, who had devoted herself to her with all a mother's tenderness.

"We will not leave her," exclaimed Manly, a warm glow spreading over his melancholy features, "if she will go with us, and bless our western home."

Emily turned pale, but she did not speak—she could not, if her existence had depended upon it. She was no sickly sentimentalist, but she had ardent affections, though always under the government of upright principles. Her mind was well balanced, and though passion might enter, it was never suffered to gain the ascendancy. From her earliest acquaintance with Manly, she had admired his talents, and respected his character; but the idea of *loving* the husband of her friend, never entered her pure imagination. It was not till she saw him borne down by domestic sorrow, on the bed of sickness, thrown by the neglect of his wife on her tenderness and care, that she felt the danger and depth of her sympathy. The moment she became aware of her involuntary departure from integrity of feeling she fled, and in the tranquillity of her own home, devoted to his child the love she shuddered to think began to flow in an illegitimate channel. That Manly ever cherished any sentiments towards her, warmer than those of esteem and gratitude, she did not believe, but now he came before her, freed by heaven from the shackles that bound him, and duty no longer opposed its barrier to her affections, her heart told her she could follow him to the ends of the earth, and deem its coldest, darkest region, a Paradise, if warmed and illumed by his love! The simplicity of childhood had unveiled the hearts of each to the other. It was not with the romance of his earlier passion that Manly now wooed Emily Spencer to be his wife. It was love, approved by reason, and sanctified by religion. It was the Christian, seeking a fellow labourer in the work of duty; the father, yearning for a mother to watch over an orphan child—the man awakened to the loftiest, holiest purposes of his being.

In a beautiful mansion, looking down on one of the most magnificent landscapes unfolded in the rich valley of the West, Manly and Emily now reside. All the happiness capable of being enjoyed around the household shrine is theirs—and the only shade that ever dims their brows, is caused by the remembrance of the highly gifted—but ill-fated Anne.

THE BLIND GIRL'S STORY.

All is still and solitary—the lamp burns on the table, with wasting splendour. The writing-desk is open before me, with the last letter unfolded—the letter I have cherished so fondly, though every word seems an arrow to my conscience. I cannot solace myself by the act, yet I must give utterance to the feelings with which my heart is bursting. On these unwritten sheets I will breathe my soul—I will trace its early history, and, perchance, *his* eye may see them when mine are veiled in a darkness deeper than that which once sealed them. Yet what shall I write? How shall I commence? What great events rise up in the records of memory, over which imagination may throw its rich empurpling dyes? Alas! mine is but a record of the heart—but of a *blind* girl's heart—and that Being who bound my eyes with a fillet of darkness, till the hand of science lifted the thick film, and flooded them with the glories of creation, alone knows the mysteries of the spirit he has made. *His* eye is upon me at this moment, and as this awful conviction comes over me, a kind of deathlike calmness settles on the restless sea of passion. Oh! when I was blind, what was my conception of the All-seeing eye! It seemed to me as if it filled the world with its effulgence. I felt as if I, in my blindness, were placed in the hollow of that rock where Moses hid, when the glory of the Lord passed by. Would that no daring hand had drawn me from that protecting shade! The beams that enlighten me have withered up the fountains of joy, and though surrounded by light, as with a garment, my soul is wrapped in the gloom of midnight. I was a blind child—blind from my birth—with one brother, older than myself, and a widowed father—for we were motherless— motherless, sisterless—yet blind. What a world of dependence is expressed in these few words! But, though thus helpless and dependent, I was scarcely conscious of my peculiar claim to sympathy and care.

My father was wealthy, and my childhood was crowned with every indulgence that wealth could purchase, or parental tenderness devise. My brother was devotedly attached to me, giving up all his leisure to my amusement—for I was looked upon as hallowed by the misfortune which excluded me from communion with the visible world—and my wishes became laws, and my happiness the paramount object of the household. Heaven, perhaps, as a kind of indemnification for depriving me of one of the wonted blessings of life, moulded me in a form which pleased the fond eyes of my relatives, and, as it was my father's pride to array me in the most graceful and becoming attire, my sightless eyes being constantly covered by a silken screen, I was a happy child. If it had not been for the epithet, *poor*, so

41

often attached to my name, I should never have dreamed that mine was a forlorn destiny. "My *poor* little blind girl," my father would exclaim, as he took me in his lap, after his return from his business abroad—"My *poor* little sister," was the constant appellation given me by my affectionate brother, yet I was happy. When he led me in the garden, through the odorous flowers, I felt a kind of aching rapture at the sweetness they exhaled—their soft, velvet texture, was ecstasy to the touch, and the wind-harps that played amid the branches of the trees were like the lyres of angels to my ears. Then the songs of birds, with what thrilling sensations would I listen to these harmonists of nature, these winged minstrels of God's own choir, as they lifted their strains of living harmony in the dim corridors of the woods! They painted to me the beauty of the world, and I believed them—but I could conceive of nothing so beautiful as sound. I associated the idea of everything that was lovely with music. It was my passion, and also my peculiar talent. Every facility which art has furnished to supply the deficiencies of nature was given me, and my progress was considered astonishing by those who are not aware of the power and acuteness of touch bestowed upon the sightless. I love to linger on the days of my childhood, when sunshine flowed in upon my heart in one unclouded stream. The serpent slumbered in the bottom of the fountain—had no one gone down into its depths, its venom might have slumbered yet.

My first cause of sorrow was parting with my brother—"my guide, my companion, my familiar friend." He was sent to a distant college, and I felt for a while as if I were alone in the world, for my father was in public life, and it was only at evening he had leisure to indulge in the tenderness of domestic feeling. He had never given up the hope that I might recover my sight. When I was very small there was an operation performed upon my eyes, but it was by an unskilful oculist, and unsuccessful. After this I had an unspeakable dread of any future attempt,—the slightest allusion to the subject threw me into such nervous agitation, my father at last forbore to mention it. "Let me live and die under this shade," I would say, "like the flower that blooms in the cleft of the rock. The sunshine and the dew are not for me." Time glided away. In one year more Henry would complete his collegiate course. I was in the morning of womanhood, but my helpless condition preserved to me all the privileges and indulgences of the child. It was at this era—why did I here dash aside my pen, and press my hands upon my temples to still the throbbings of a thousand pulses, starting simultaneously into motion? Why cannot we always be children? Why was I not suffered to remain blind?—A young physician came into the neighbourhood, who had already acquired some fame as an oculist. He visited in our family—he became almost identified with our household. Philanthropy guided him in his choice of a profession. He knew himself gifted with extraordinary talents, and that he had it in his power to mitigate the woes of mankind. But though the votary of duty, he was a worshipper at the shrine of intellect and taste. He loved poetry, and, next to music, it was my passion. He read to me the melodious strains of the sons of song, in a voice more eloquent, in its low depth of sweetness, than the minstrels whose harmony he breathed. When I touched the keys of the piano, his voice was raised, in unison with mine. If I wandered in the garden, his hand was ever ready to guide, and his arm to sustain me. He brought me the wild-flower of the field, and the exotic of the green-house, and, as he described their hues and outlines, I scarcely regretted the want of vision. Here, in this book, I have pressed each faded gift. I remember the very words he uttered when he gave me this cluster.—"See," said he, "nay, *feel* this upright stem, so lofty, till bending from the weight of the flower it bears. It is a lily—I plucked it from the margin of a stream, in which it seemed gazing on its white, waxen leaves. Touch gently the briars of this wild rose. Thus heaven guards the innocence and beauty that gladdens the eyes of the wayfaring man. Cecilia, would you not like to look upon these flowers?" "Yes, but far rather on the faces of those I love—my father's—my brother's. Man is made in the image of his Maker, and his face must be divine." "Oh!" added I, in the secrecy of my own soul, "how divine must be the features of that friend, who has unfolded to me such unspeakable treasures of genius and feeling, whose companionship seems a foretaste of the felicities of heaven." It was then, for the first time, he dared to suggest to me a hope that my blindness was not incurable. He told me he had been devoting all his leisure to this one subject, and that he was sure he had mastered every difficulty; that though mine was a peculiar case, and had once baffled the efforts of the optician, he dared to assure himself of complete success. "And if I fail," said he, "if through my means no light should visit your darkened orbs, then," continued he, with an expression of feeling that seemed wholly irrepressible, "suffer me to be a light to your eyes and a lamp to your feet. But if it should be my lot to bestow upon you the most glorious of the gifts of God, to meet from you one glance of gratitude and love, were a recompense I would purchase with life itself." Did I dream? or were these words breathed to me?—me, the helpless, blind girl! to receive the unmeasured devotion of one of the most gifted and interesting of created beings. I had thought that he pitied me, that he felt for me the kindness of a brother, that he found in me some congenial tastes—but that he loved me so entirely, it was a confession as unlooked for as overpowering. My heart ached, from the oppression of its joy. Let not the cold-hearted and vain smile, when I repeat the broken accents of gratitude, trust, and love, that fell from my lips. My helplessness sanctified the offer, and I received his pledge of faith as a holy thing, to be kept holy through time and eternity.

Never shall I forget that moment, when the first ray of light penetrated the long midnight that had shrouded my vision. It was in a darkened apartment. My father, one female friend, and Clinton, the beloved physician—these were around me. Faint, dim, and uncertain, as the first gray of the dawn, was that ray, but it was the herald of coming light, and hailed as a day-spring from on high. A bandage was immediately drawn over my brow, but during the weeks in which I was condemned to remain in darkness, the memory of that dim radiance was ever glimmering round me. There was a figure kneeling, with clasped hands and upraised head, pale and venerable—I knew it was my father's—for the same figure folded me to his heart the next moment, and wept like an infant. There was one with soft flowing outline, and loose robes, by my side,—and bending over me, with eyes gazing down into the mysteries of my being, shadowy but glorious, was he, who received the first glance of the being he had awakened to a new creation. Slowly, gradually was I allowed to emerge from my eclipse, but when I was at last led from my darkened chamber, when I looked abroad on the face of nature, clothed as she was in the magnificent garniture of summer, when I saw the heavens unrolled in their majesty, the sun travelling in the greatness of his strength, the flowers glowing in the beams that enamelled them, I closed my eyes, almost fainting from the excessive glory. I will not attempt to describe my sensations when I first distinctly saw the lineaments of my lover. Creation contained nothing so lovely to my sight. To see the soul, the thinking, feeling, immortal soul, flashing with enthusiasm, or darkening with tenderness, looking forth from his eyes, and feel my own mingling with his! No one but those who have once been blind, and now see, can imagine the intensity of my emotions. Next to my Creator, I felt my homage was due to him, and surely it is not impious to apply to him the sublime language of Scripture—"He said, let there be light, and there was light."

Our mansion was transformed. My father gathered all his friends around him to participate in his joy. My brother was summoned home. There seemed one continual jubilee. I turned coldly, however, from all these festivities, occupied almost exclusively with one feeling. I could not feign an interest in others I did not feel. I began even at this early period to experience the first symptoms of that passion, which has since consumed me. Clinton, though still, as ever, the kind, devoted, and watchful guardian, hovering round my steps, as if to shield me from every danger, Clinton, I saw, shared in the pleasures of sociality, and returned the smiles that kindled wherever he moved. He was a universal favourite in society, and knew how to adapt himself to others, not from a vague desire of popularity, but from a benevolence, a sunny glow of feeling, shedding light and warmth all around. Even then there were moments when I regretted my blindness, and wished I had never seen those smiles and glances, which I would fain rivet for ever on myself. Henry, my brother, once whispered to me, as I was turning, in a languid manner, the leaves of a music book, not caring to play because Clinton was not bending over my chair, "My dear Cecilia, do not let Clinton see too glaringly his power over you. There is scarcely a man in the world who can be trusted with unlimited power. We are ungrateful creatures, my sweet sister, and you do not know us half as well as we know each other. You ought to love Clinton, for he merits it, but be mistress of yourself. Do not love him too well for *his* peace and your *own*." Alas! poor Henry—how little have I heeded your brotherly admonitions? But when did passion ever listen to the counsels of reason—when will it? When the cygnet's down proves a barrier to the tempest's breath. We were married. I became the inmate of a home, fashioned after the model of my own taste. Everything was arranged with a view to my happiness. The curtains and decorations of the house were all of the softest green, for the repose of my still feeble eyes. Oh! thou benefactor of my life—friend, lover, husband, would that I could go back to the hour when we plighted our wedded vows, and live over the past, convinced, though too late, how deeply I have wronged thee—confiding implicitly in thy love and truth, we might live together the life of angels! And we were happy for a while. We withdrew as much as possible from the gay world. He saw that I loved retirement, and he consulted my feelings as far as was consistent with the duties of his profession. I might have been convinced by this of the injustice of my suspicions. I might have known that he loved me better than all the world beside. During the day he was but seldom with me, as his practice was extensive, and often called him to a distance from home, but the evening was mine, and it seemed my peculiar province, for I shrunk from the full blaze of sunlight. The brightness was too intense, but when the moon was gliding over the firmament, in her sweet, approachable loveliness, and the soft glitter of the stars was around, I could lift my undazzled eyes, and marvel at the wonderful works of God. Clinton was a devout astronomer—he taught me the name of every planet that burned—of every star known to science. He was rich in the wisdom of ancient days, and his lips distilled instruction as naturally and constantly as the girl in the fairy tale dropped the gems of the Orient. I have made mention of a female friend—she was the daughter of a deceased friend of my father, and, as such, came under his especial guardianship. Since my marriage she had remained with him, to cheer his loneliness, but her health becoming very delicate, he sent her to be my guest, that she might receive medical aid from my husband. She was not a decided invalid, but her mother had died of a consumption, and it was feared she had a hereditary tendency to that disease. Alice was a pale, delicate-looking girl, with sometimes a hectic flush on her cheek, a frail, drooping form, and extremely pensive cast of countenance. The dread of this constitutional malady hung over her like a death-cloud, and aggravated symptoms slight in themselves. Though there was nothing very attractive in the appearance of this poor girl, she was calculated to excite pity and sympathy, and surely she had every claim to mine. I did pity her, and sought, by every attention and kindness, to enliven her despondency, and rouse her to hope and vivacity. But I soon found that my father had encroached sadly on my domestic happiness by giving this charge to my husband. Air, exercise, and gentle recreation, were the remedies prescribed by the physician, and it was his duty to promote these by every means in his power. She often accompanied him on horseback in his rides, a pleasure from which I was completely debarred, for, in my blindness, I was incapacitated, and the timidity which originated from my situation remained after the cause was removed. It was some time before I was willing to acknowledge to myself the pain which this arrangement gave me. I felt as if my dearest privileges were invaded. I had been so accustomed, from infancy, to be the sole object of every attention, these daily offices bestowed upon another, though dictated by kindness and humanity, were intolerable to me. Had I seen the congregated world around her, offering every homage, it would not have given me one envious pang—but Clinton, my husband, he was more precious to me than ten thousand worlds. She leaned too exclusively on his guardian care. I tried to subdue my feelings—I tried to assume an appearance of indifference. My manners gradually became cold and constrained, and instead of greeting my husband with the joyous smile of welcome, on his return, I would avert from his the eyes which had received from him their living rays. Frank and unsuspicious himself, he did not seem to divine the cause of my altered demeanour. When he asked me why I was so silent, or so sad, I pleaded indisposition, lassitude—anything but the truth. I blamed him for his want of penetration, for I felt as if my soul were bare, and that the eye of affection could read the tidings revealed by my changing cheek and troubled brow. In justice to myself, let me say, that Alice, by her manner, justified my emotions.

Enlightened by the sentiment in my own bosom, I could not but mark that the hectic flush always became brighter when Clinton approached, that her glance, kindling as it moved, followed his steps with a kind of idolatry. Then she hung upon his words with an attention so flattering. Was she reading, reclining on the sofa, apparently languid and uninterested, the moment he spoke she would close her book, or lean forward, as if fearful of losing the faintest sound of that voice, which was the music of my life. I could have borne this for a day, a week, a month—but to be doomed to endure it for an indefinite term, perhaps for life, it was unendurable. A hundred times I was on the point of going to my father, and, telling him the secret of my unhappiness, entreat him to recall my too encroaching guest, but shame and pride restrained me. Chilled and wounded by my coldness, my husband gradually learned to copy it, and no longer sought the smiles and caresses my foolish, too exciting heart, deemed he no longer valued. Oh! blissful days of early confidence and love! were ye for ever flown? Was no beam of tenderness permitted to penetrate the cold frost-work of ceremony deepening between us? It is in vain to cherish love with the memory of what has been. It must be fed with daily living offerings, or the vestal fire will wax dim and perish—then fearful is the penalty that ensues. The doom denounced upon the virgins of the temple, when they suffered the holy flame to become extinct, was less terrible. Alice, when the mildness of the weather allowed, almost made her home in the garden. She must have felt that I shrunk from her society, and I knew she could not love the wife of Clinton. She carried her books and pencil there—she watched the opening blossoms, and gathered the sweetest, to make her offering at the shrine she loved. My husband was evidently pleased with these attentions, flowing, as he thought, from a gentle and grateful heart, and his glance and voice grew softer when he turned to address the invalid.

Once during the absence of Alice I went into her chamber for a book I had lent her, which contained a passage I wished to recall. I took up several others, which lay upon the table. There was one which belonged to my husband, and in it was a piece of folded paper, embalmed with flowers, like some holy relic. It was not sealed—it was open—it was a medical prescription, written by Clinton, thus tenderly, romantically preserved. On another half-torn sheet were some broken lines, breathing passion and despair. They were in the handwriting of Alice, and apparently original, without address or signature, but it was easy for my excited imagination to supply them. Poor victim of passion—by the side of this record of all my fears was the composing draught, prepared to check the consumptive cough—the elixir to sustain the failing principles of vitality. How is it that we dare to kindle an unhallowed flame, even on the ashes of decaying mortality? I left the chamber, and retired to my own. I knew not in what manner to act. I endeavoured to reflect on what I ought to do. Alice and myself could not live long under the same roof, yet how could I bid her depart, or betray her to my husband? I could not believe such feelings could be excited in her without sufficient encouragement. I laid myself down on the bed, and wished I might never rise again. I closed my eyes, and prayed that the dark fillet of night might rest on them again and forevermore. My cheeks burned as with consuming fire, but it was in my heart. When Clinton returned, not finding me in the drawing-room, he sought me in my own chamber. He seemed really alarmed at my situation. He forgot all his former constraint, and hung over me with a tenderness and anxiety that might have proved to me how dear I was. He sat by me, holding my burning hand, and uttering every endearing expression affection could suggest. Melted by his caresses, I yearned to unbosom to him my whole heart—my pride, my jealousy was subdued. I endeavoured to speak, but the words died on my tongue. Confused images flitted across my brain—then came a dreary blank. For weeks I lay on that bed of sickness, unconscious of everything around me. My recovery was for a long time doubtful—but when I at last opened my languid eyes, they rested on the face of my husband, who had kept his unwearied vigils by my pillow, and still he held my feeble hand in his, as if he had never unloosed his clasp. He looked pale and wan, but a ray of divine joy flashed from his eye as he met my glance of recognition.

Humbled and chastened by this visitation from heaven, renovated by the warm and gracious influences exerted for my restoration, animated by new-born hope, I rose from my sick-bed. The vulture had unloosened its fangs, and the dove once more returned to its nest. I could even pity the misguided girl who had caused me so much unhappiness. I treated her with a kindness, of late very unwonted—but she evidently shunned my companionship, and in proportion as my spirits rose from the weight that had crushed them to the dust, hers became depressed and fitful. Let me hurry on—I linger too long on feelings. Few events have marked my brief history, yet some have left traces that all the waves of time can never wash out.

It was Sunday—it was the first time I had attended church since my illness. My husband accompanied me, while Alice, as usual, remained at home. The preacher was eloquent—the music sweet and solemn—the aspirations of faith warm and kindling. I had never before felt such a glow of gratitude and trust; and while my mind was in this state of devout abstraction, Clinton whispered to me that he was obliged to withdraw a short time, to visit a patient who was dangerously sick—"but I will return," said he, "to accompany you home." My thoughts were brought back to earth by this interruption, and wandered from the evangelical eloquence of the pulpit. The services were unusually long, and my head began to ache from the effort of listening. I experienced the lingering effects of sickness, and feeling that dimness of sight come over me, which was a never-failing symptom of a malady of the brain, I left the church, and returned home, without waiting for the coming of my husband. When I crossed the threshold, my spirit was free from a shadow of suspicion. I had been in an exalted mood—I felt as if I had been sitting under the outspread wings of the cherubim, and had brought away with me some faint reflection of the celestial glory. I was conscious of being in a high state of nervous excitement. The reaction produced by the unexpected scene that presented itself, was, in consequence, more terrible. There, on a sofa, half supported in the arms of my husband, whose hand she was grasping with a kind of convulsive energy, her hair unbound and wet, and exhaling the odorous essence with which it had been just bathed, sat Alice, and the words that passed her lips, as I entered, at first unperceived by them, were these —"Never, never—she hates me—she must ever hate me." I stood transfixed —the expression of my countenance must have been awful, for they looked as if confronted by an avenging spirit. Alice actually shrieked, and her pale features writhed, as the scroll when the scorching blaze comes near it. My resolution was instantaneous. I waited not for explanations—the scene to my mind admitted none. The sudden withdrawal of my husband from church, upon the pretence of an errand of duty, the singular agitation of Alice—all that I saw and heard, filled me with the most maddening emotions—all the ties of wedded love seemed broken and withered, at once, like the withes that bound the awakening giant. "Clinton," exclaimed I, "you have deceived me— but it is for the last time." Before he could reply, or arrest my motions, I was gone. The carriage was still at the door. "Drive me to my father's, directly," was all I could utter, and it was done.

Swiftly the carriage rolled on—I thought I heard my name borne after me on the wind, but I looked not behind. I felt strong in the conviction of my wrongs. It would have been weakness to have wept. My scorn of such duplicity lifted me above mere sorrow. It was in the gloom of twilight when I reached my father's door. I rushed into the drawing-room, and found myself in the arms of my brother. "Cecilia, my sister! what brings you here?" He was alarmed at my sudden entrance, and through the dusky shade he could discover the wild flashing of my eyes, the disorder of my whole appearance. The presence of human sympathy softened the sternness of my despair. Tears gushed violently forth. I tried to explain to him my wretchedness and its cause, but could only exclaim, "Clinton, Alice, cruel, deliberate deceivers!" Henry bit his lip, and ground his teeth till their ivory was tinged with blood, but he made no comments. He spoke then with his usual calmness, and urged me to retire to my chamber, and compose myself before my father's return. He almost carried me there in his arms, soothing and comforting me. He called for an attendant, again whispered the duty and necessity of self-control, then left me, promising a speedy return. I watched for the footsteps of Henry, but hour after hour passed away, and he returned not. I asked the servants where he had gone? They knew not. I asked myself, and something told me, in an awful voice—"Gone to avenge thee." The moment this idea flashed into my mind, I felt as if I were a murderess. I would convince myself of the truth. I knew my brother's chamber—thither I ran, and drawing back the bed curtains, looked for the silver mounted pistols that always hung over the bed's head. They were gone—and a coat dashed hastily on the counterpane, a pocket-book fallen on the carpet, all denoted a hurried departure on some fatal errand. The agony I had previously suffered was light to what pierced me now. To follow him was my only impulse. I rushed out of the house—it was a late hour in the evening—there was no moon in the sky, and I felt the dampness of the falling dew, as I flew, with uncovered head, like an unblessed spirit, through the darkness. My brain began to be thronged with wild images. It seemed to me, legions of dark forms were impeding my steps. "Oh! let me pass," cried I, "it is my husband and brother I have slain. Let me pass," continued I, shrieking, for an arm of flesh and blood was thrown around me, and held me struggling. "Gracious heavens, it is the voice of my Cecilia!" It was my father that spoke. I remember that I recognised him, and that was all. My cries were changed to cries of madness. I was borne back raving. The malady that had so recently brought me to the door of the grave, had renewed its attack with increased malignancy. My brain had been too much weakened to bear the tension of its agony. For long months I was confined within my chamber walls, sometimes tossing in delirious anguish, at others lying in marble unconsciousness, an image of the death they prayed might soon release me from my sufferings. They prayed that I might die, rather than be doomed to a living death. But I lived—lived to know the ruin I had wrought.

My father was a man of majestic person, and time had scarcely touched his raven locks. His hair was now profusely silvered, and there were lines on his brow which age never furrowed. It was long before I learned all that had transpired during this fearful chasm in my existence, but gradually the truth was revealed. All that I was at first told, was, that my husband and brother lived—then, when it was supposed I had sufficient strength to bear the agitation, this letter from my husband was given me.

"Cecilia, how shall I address you? I will not reproach you, for you have had too bitter a lesson. I would fain have seen you before my departure, but you decline the interview, and perhaps it is well. Should I live to return—Oh! Cecilia, what wretchedness have you brought upon us all! If your alienated heart does not turn from any memento of me, you will read these lines, and I know you will believe them. I have been, as it were, to the very threshold of the presence-chamber of the King of Kings, and am just emerging from the shadows of approaching death. This is the first effort of my feeble hand. Most rash and misjudging woman, what have you done? How madly have I doted on you, how blindly have I worshipped! yet all the devotion of my life, my truth, love and integrity, weighed nothing in the balance with one moment's mystery. I leave my vindication to Alice. She will not deceive you. She will tell you that never did the heart of man throb with a more undivided passion for another than mine for you. She will tell you—but what avails it? You have cast me from you, unvalued and untrusted. Your poor, unhappy brother! his avenging hand sought my life—the life of him who he believed had betrayed his sister's happiness, the wretch almost unworthy of a brave man's resentment. In wresting the weapon from his frenzied grasp, I received an almost deadly wound. His wrath was slaked in my blood. He believes me innocent. He has been to me more than a brother. He will accompany me to another clime, whither I am going, to try the effect of more genial air on my shattered frame. Would to God we could have met before we parted—perhaps for ever. Your father says you have been ill, that you fear the effect of the meeting on both. You have been ill—my ever adored, still tenderly beloved Cecilia, I write not to reproach you. Bitter is the penalty paid for one moment of passion. Had I ever swerved in my affection for you, even in thought, I should deserve all I have suffered. I recall your sadness, your coldness, and averted looks. I now know the cause, and mourn over it. Why did you not confide in me? We might yet have been happy—but the will of God be done. The vessel waits that is to bear us to a transatlantic clime—farewell. Should I return, bearing with me some portion of my former vigour, should your confidence in my love be restored, then, perchance, through the mercy of heaven, two chastened and humble hearts may once more be united on earth. If I am never permitted to revisit my native soil, if I die in a foreign land, know, that, faithful to you to my latest hour, my last thought, prayer, and sigh, will be yours."

And he was gone—gone—sick, wounded, perhaps dying, he was gone to another land, and the blood that was drained from him on my soul. My father forbade him to see me—he was too feeble to bear the shock of beholding me in the condition I then was. My real situation was concealed from him. The only means of making the prohibition effectual, was to word it as proceeding from myself. Thus, he believed me cold and selfish to the last. My father talked to me of better days, of the hope of my husband's speedy restoration, and of our future reunion. I could only listen and weep. I dared not murmur. I felt too deeply the justice of the judgment the Almighty had passed against me. I had one ordeal yet to pass—an interview with Alice. She also was under my father's roof, confined by increasing debility to her own apartment. As soon as my strength allowed, I made it a religious duty to visit the poor invalid. I was shocked to see the ravages of her malady. Her eye of glassy brightness turned on me with such a look of woe and remorse, it cut me to the heart. I took the pale thin hand she extended towards me, and burst into tears. Yes! I saw it but too clearly. Here was another victim. The steps of the destroyer were fearfully accelerated. She had had a profuse hemorrhage from the lungs, and her voice was so weak and husky, it was with difficulty I could understand her. She drew me down near to her pillow, and, placing my hand on her heart, said, in a careful whisper—"Remorse, Cecilia, it is here. It is this which gives the sting to death." She then drew from beneath her pillow a paper that she had written for me, which she begged me to read when I was alone. I did read it. It was the transcript of a warm, romantic heart, erring and misguided, yet even in its aberrations discovering an innate love for virtue and truth. Her whole soul was bared before me—all her love, imprudence, and remorse. She described my husband as an angel of light and purity, soaring high above the clouds of passion that gathered darkly around herself. She spoke of that scene, followed by such irremediable woe. "Even now," continued Alice, "wasting as I am on the bed of death, with the shadows of earthly feeling dimly floating round me, knowing that I shall soon turn to cold, impassive clay, the memory of that hour presses with scorching weight on my brain. I must have been mad. Surely I had not the control of my reason. I had taken the previous night an unusual quantity of opium, which, instead of composing me to sleep, had excited my nerves, and strung them as with fire. Your husband came in only a short time before your sudden entrance, evidently on some errand; and though he kindly paused to speak to me, his looks expressed haste to depart. Just as he was about to leave the room, I was attacked with one of those spasms you have sometimes witnessed. He came to my relief—he administered every restorative. I know not all I uttered, but when I recovered I remember many wild expressions that escaped my lips. It seemed to me that I was going to die, and while his arms thus kindly supported me, I felt as if it would be joy to die. With this conviction, was it so black a crime to breathe forth the love that had so long pervaded my frail and lonely existence? Cecilia, he recoiled from me with horror. He proclaimed his inviolable love and devotion for you—his glance was stern and upbraiding. Then seeing me sinking in despair, the kindness of his nature triumphed, and he sought to calm my overwrought and troubled spirit. He expressed the affection of a brother, the pity of a friend, the admonitions of a Christian. "Above all," said he, "make a friend of Cecilia. She will always cherish you with a sister's love." "Never!" I exclaimed, "she hates me, she must ever hate me." The vision of an injured wife arrested my unhallowed accents. You know the dreadful tragedy that followed. Never since that hour have I had one moment's calm. Conscience, with her thousand scorpions, lashes me— whether sleeping or waking there is no rest. 'There is no peace,' saith my God, 'to the wicked,' Yet mine was not deliberate guilt. Had I only wrecked my own happiness!—but the wide desolation, the irretrievable ruin! I shudder, I weep, I lift my feeble hands to that Power whose laws I have transgressed, and pray for pardon. To you, whose home of love I have laid waste, dare I turn my fading eyes, and hope for forgiveness? To him whom I have driven from his native land, shorn of the brightness of his manhood—Oh! sinful dust and ashes"——here the unhappy writer broke off—the blank was stained with tears. Probably in that broken sentence the embers of passion flashed out their last fires, through the "dust and ashes" of withering mortality. Poor Alice! may'st thou be forgiven by a merciful Creator as freely as thou art by me. Gentle be thy passage through the valley of the shadow of death, to that country where no storms desolate the heart, where passion and penitence are unknown. As for me—why and for what do I live? For hope or despair? I pray for tidings from the beloved exiles, yet dread to receive them. If the night gale sweeps with hasty gust against the window, I tremble lest they be exposed to the stormy deep. When I gaze on the moon and stars, I ask myself if they are lighting the wanderers on their homeward way, and sometimes gather hope from their heavenly brightness.

The manuscript of Cecilia here abruptly closes. It has fallen to the lot of one who afterwards became the devoted friend of Clinton, to relate the sequel of their melancholy history.

"It was in the spring of the year 18——, I was sitting on the deck, watching the rapid motion of the boat, as it glided over the waves, thinking earnestly of the place of my destination, when I first beheld Cecilia, the wife of Clinton. I was a stranger on board, and gazed around me with that indefinite expression, which marks the stranger to the experienced eye. At length my glance was riveted by the appearance of a lady, leaning on the arm of a gray-haired gentleman, slowly promenading the deck. They passed and repassed me, while I continued to lean over the railing, fearing, by a change of position, to disturb the silent strangers. There was something in the figure of the lady inexpressibly interesting. She wore a mourning-dress, and her eyes were covered with a green shade. Notwithstanding her face was thus partially obscured, the most exquisite beauty of outline and colouring was visible I ever saw in any human countenance. She wore no bonnet or veil, for the sun was verging towards the west, and its rays stole soft and mellow over the golden waters. Fair and meek as the virgin mother's was the brow that rose above the silken screen, defined with beauteous distinctness by dark, divided hair, whose luxuriance was confined by a golden band. At length they seated themselves very near me, and began to converse in a low tone. There was a melancholy sweetness in her accents, and I was sure they were speaking of some sorrowful theme. We were now entering the —— bay, and the boat rocked and laboured as she plunged through the increased volume of the waters. Now, just visible on the glowing horizon, was the topmast of a vessel. On she came, with sails full spread, her canvas swelling in the breeze, her majestic outline softened by the sunset hues. The gentleman pointed out the object to his companion, who lifted the shade from her brow, revealing as she did so, eyes of such melting softness, I wondered I had thought her lovely before. She pressed the arm of the gentleman, and gazed eagerly on the vessel which now bore down 'majestically near.' She rose, she bent forward with earnest gestures, her face kindled, and sparkled like the waters themselves. The ship approached so near we could discern figures on the deck. The boat had diverged from her path to give place to the nobler craft. She was sailing with great rapidity, and the noise of the engine and the dashing of the waves drowned the sound of the voices near me. I began to feel a strange interest in the vessel on which the eyes of the strangers were so earnestly riveted. Amid the figures that walked her deck, I distinguished one, which was aloof from the others, of a more lofty bearing—a cloak was gathered round him, and from this circumstance, together with his extremely pallid complexion, I judged him to be an invalid. From the rapid motion of both vessels, it was but a glance I obtained, after we were near enough to trace these lineaments. At this moment the lady sprang upon the bench beneath the railing—she stretched forth her arms, with a startling cry. I saw her for an instant, bending far over the edge of the boat. I rose and rushed towards her to warn her of her danger, but a plunging sound in the water, that closed darkly over her sinking form, froze my veins with horror. 'Oh! my God!' exclaimed the father, 'save her! My daughter! Oh, my daughter!' then fell back, almost paralyzed, on the seat. To throw off my coat and plunge in after the ill-fated lady, in whom I had become so painfully interested, was an instantaneous deed. Alas! all my efforts were unavailing. The current was so powerful, I found it in vain to struggle with its force. I relaxed not, however, till my failing strength warned me that I was seeking a grave for myself, without being able to rescue the victim for whom I had willingly periled my life.

"I will not attempt to describe the grief of the half-distracted father. I never left him till he reached his own home. What a scene of agony awaited him there! The husband and brother, so long absent, were returned, yearning to behold once more that beloved being, whose involuntary sin had been so fearfully expiated. It was Clinton whom I had seen on the vessel's deck. As he afterwards told me, the dazzle of the rays on the water, in that direction, had prevented him from distinguishing the features for ever engraven on his heart. The hoarse sound of the waves swallowed her drowning shriek—onward they bore him, and he saw not the fond arms that would have embraced him, even over that watery chasm. I have witnessed many a scene of sorrow, but never saw I one like this. From the peculiar circumstances that brought us together, I became almost identified with this unhappy family. Clinton was the most interesting man I ever saw. He was a confirmed invalid, never having recovered from the effects of his wound. I never saw a smile upon his face, nor could I ever smile in his presence. He seldom spoke, and never but once did he mention the name of Cecilia. It was one night when he was unusually ill, and I was sitting alone with him in his chamber. He gave me the manuscript for perusal which is here transcribed, an act of confidence he considered due to me, who would have been her saviour. Through the watches of that night he poured into my ear the hoarded agonies of his grief. Never before did I know how deep human sorrow could be, or how holy was that love which clings to the memory of the dead.

"Alice dwelt in 'the dark and narrow house.' She was spared the knowledge of the fatal catastrophe, for she died before her victim. Yes—*her victim*! Had she guarded against the first inroads of a forbidden passion, there might have been 'beauty for ashes, the oil of joy for mourning, and the garment of praise for the spirit of heaviness.' The angel form that lies low, wrapped in the winding-sheet of the waves, might now be moving in the light of loveliness, love, and joy. But who shall dare to arraign the doings of the Almighty?"

THE PARLOUR SERPENT.

Mrs. Wentworth and Miss Hart entered the breakfast-room together, the latter speaking earnestly and in a low confidential tone to the other, whose countenance was slightly discomposed.

"There is nothing that provokes me so much as to hear such remarks," said Miss Hart, "I have no patience to listen to them. Indeed, I think they are made as much to wound my feelings as anything else, for they all know the great affection I have for you."

"But you do not say what the remarks were, that gave you so much pain," answered Mrs. Wentworth. "I would much prefer that you would tell me plainly, than speak in such vague hints. You will not make me angry, for I am entirely indifferent to the opinion of the world."

Now there was not a woman in the world more sensitively alive to censure than Mrs. Wentworth, and in proportion to her sensitiveness, was her anxiety to know the observations of others.

"If you had overheard Miss Bentley and Miss Wheeler talking of you last night as I did," continued Miss Hart, "you would not have believed your own ears. They said they thought it was ridiculous in you to make such a nun of yourself, because Captain Wentworth was absent, and to dress so plain and look so moping. One of them said, you did not dare to visit or receive visiters while he was away, for that you were as much afraid of him as if you were his slave, and that he had made you promise not to stir out of the house, or to invite any company while he was gone."

"Ridiculous!—nonsense!" exclaimed Mrs. Wentworth, "there never was such an absurd idea. Captain Wentworth never imposed such a restraint upon me, though I know he would rather I would live retired, when he cannot attend me himself in the gay world. It is not despotism, but affection, that prompts the wish, and I am sure I feel no pleasure in dressing, shining, and mingling in society, when he is exposed to danger, and perhaps death, on the far deep sea."

"I know all that, my dear Mrs. Wentworth," replied Miss Hart, insinuatingly, "and so I told them; but how little can a heartless and censorious world judge of the feelings of the refined and the sensitive! It seems to be a general impression that you fear your husband more than you love him, and that this fear keeps you in a kind of bondage to his will. If I were you, I would invite a large party and make it as brilliant as possible, and be myself as gay as possible, and then that will be giving the lie at once to their innuendoes."

"It is so mortifying to have such reports in circulation," said Mrs. Wentworth, her colour becoming more and more heightened and her voice more tremulous. "I don't care what they say at all, and yet I am half resolved to follow your advice, if it were only to vex them. I *will* do it, and let them know that I am not afraid to be mistress of my own house while its master is absent."

"That is exactly the right spirit," answered the delighted Miss Hart; "I am glad you take it in that way. I was afraid your feelings would be wounded, and that is the reason I was so unwilling to tell you."

But though Mrs. Wentworth boasted of her spirit and her indifference, her feelings were deeply wounded, and she sat at the breakfast-table, cutting her toast into the most minute pieces, without tasting any, while Miss Hart was regaling herself with an unimpaired appetite, and luxuriating in fancy on the delightful party, she had so skilfully brought into promised existence, at least. She had no idea of spending the time of her visit to Mrs. Wentworth, in dullness and seclusion, sympathizing in the anxieties of a fond and timid wife, and listening to a detail of domestic plans and enjoyments. She knew the weak side of her character, and mingling the gall she extracted from others, with the honey of her own flattery, and building her influence on their ruined reputations, imagined it firm and secure on such a crumbling foundation. It is unnecessary to dwell on the genealogy of Miss Hart. She was well known as Miss Hart, and yet it would be very difficult for anybody to tell precisely who Miss Hart was. She was a general visiter; one of those young ladies who are always ready to fill up any sudden vacuum made in a family—a kind of bird of passage, who, having no abiding place of her own, went fluttering about, generally resting where she could find the softest and most comfortable nest. She was what was called *excellent company*, always had something new and interesting to say about everybody; then she knew so many secrets, and had the art of exciting a person's curiosity so keenly, and making them dissatisfied with everybody but herself, it would be impossible to follow all the windings, or discover all the nooks and corners of her remarkable character. It was astonishing to see the influence she acquired over the minds of those with whom she associated, male as well as female. She was a showy, well-dressing, attractive-looking girl, with a great deal of manner, a large, piercing, dark eye, and an uncommonly sweet and persuasive tone of voice. Mrs. Wentworth became acquainted with her a very short time before Captain Wentworth's departure, and esteemed it a most delightful privilege to have such a pleasing companion to charm away the lingering hours of his absence. Acting upon the suggestions of her friend, and following up the determination she had so much applauded, she opened her doors to visiters, and appeared in society with a gay dress and smiling countenance.

"What a change there is in Mrs. Wentworth!" observed Miss Bentley to Miss Hart, as they met one morning at the house of a mutual friend. "I never saw any one so transformed in my life. She looks and dresses like the most complete flirt I ever saw; I suspect Captain Wentworth has very good reason to watch her as he does."

Miss Hart shrugged her shoulders and smiled significantly, but did not say anything.

"It must be a very pleasant alteration to you," continued Miss Bentley, "the house seems to be frequented by gentlemen from morning till night. I suppose you have the grace to appropriate their visits to yourself."

"I have nothing to say about myself," answered Miss Hart, "and I do not wish to speak of Mrs. Wentworth otherwise than kindly. You know she is excessively kind to me, and it would be ungrateful in me to condemn her conduct. To be sure I must have my own thoughts on the subject. She is certainly very imprudent, and too fond of admiration. But I would not have you repeat what I have said, for the world, for being in the family it would have such weight. Be very careful what you say, and above all, don't mention *my* name."

Miss Bentley was very careful to repeat the remarks to every one she saw, with as many additions of her own as she pleased, and the unutterable language of the smile and the shrug was added too, to give force to the comments. Mrs. Wentworth, in the mean while, unconscious of the serpent she was nursing in her bosom, suffered herself to be borne along on the current on which she had thoughtlessly embarked, without the power to arrest her progress, or turn back into the quiet channel she had quitted. The arrival of her brother, a gay and handsome young man, gave additional animation to her household, and company flowed in still more continuously. Henry More, the brother of Mrs. Wentworth, was the favourite of every circle in which he moved. With an uncommon flow of spirits, a ready and graceful wit, a fluent and flattering tongue, he mingled in society unaffected by its contrasts, unwounded by its asperities, and unruffled by its contentions. He seemed to revel in the happy consciousness of being able to impart pleasure to all, and was equally willing to receive it. He was delighted to find a fine-looking, amiable girl, an inmate of his sister's dwelling, and immediately addressing her in his accustomed strain of sportive gallantry, found that she not only lent a willing ear, but was well skilled in the same language. Though Miss Hart was still young, she had outlived the romance and credulity of youth. She had a precocious experience and wisdom in the ways of this world. She had seen the affections of many a young man, with a disposition open and ingenuous as Henry's, won through the medium of their vanity, by women, too, who could not boast of attractions equal to her own. She believed that juxtaposition could work miracles, and as long as they were the inmates of the same house, participating in the same pleasures, engaged in the same pursuits, and often perusing the same book, she feared no rival. She rejoiced, too, in the close-drawing socialities of the winter fireside, and delighted when a friendly storm compelled them to find all their enjoyment within their own little circle. Mrs. Wentworth, who had once been cheerful and serene in clouds as well as sunshine, was now subject to fits of despondency and silence. It was only when excited by company, that her eyes were lighted up with animation, and her lips with smiles. She dreaded the reproaches of her husband on his return, for acting so contrary to his wishes, and when she heard the night-gust sweep by her windows, and thought of him exposed to the warring elements, perhaps even then clinging to the drifting wreck, or floating in a watery grave, and recollected the scenes of levity and folly in which she was now constantly acting a part, merely to avoid the censures of the very people she detested and despised, she sighed and wept, and wished she had followed her bosom counsellor, rather than the suggestions of the friend in whom she still confided, and on whose affection she relied with unwavering trust. It was strange, she could hear Miss Hart ridicule others, and join in the laugh; she could sit quietly and see her breathe the subtle venom of slander over the fairest characters, till they blackened and became polluted under her touch, and yet she felt herself as secure as if she were placed on the summit of Mont Blanc, in a region of inaccessible purity and splendour. So blinding is the influence of self-love, pampered by flattery, strengthened by indulgence, and unrestrained by religious principle.

One evening, and it chanced to be the evening of the Sabbath day, Henry sat unusually silent, and Miss Hart thought that his eyes were fixed upon her face with a very deep and peculiar expression—"No," he suddenly exclaimed, "I never saw such a countenance in my life."

"What do you see so remarkable in it?" asked she, laughing, delighted at what she supposed a spontaneous burst of admiration.

"I don't know; I can no more describe it, than one of those soft, fleecy clouds that roll melting away from the face of the moon. But it haunts me like a dream."

Miss Hart modestly cast down her eyes, then turned them towards the moon, which at that moment gleamed with pallid lustre through the window.

"Your imagination is so glowing," replied she, "that it invests, like the moonlight, every object with its own mellow and beautiful tints."

"Jane," continued he, without noticing the compliment to his imagination, and turning to his sister, who was reading intently, "Jane, you must have noticed her—you were at the same church."

"Noticed her!" repeated Miss Hart to herself, in utter dismay; "who can he mean?"

"Noticed who?" said Mrs. Wentworth, laying down her book, "I have not heard a syllable you have been saying."

"Why, that young lady dressed in black, with such a sweet, modest, celestial expression of face. She sat at the right hand of the pulpit, with another lady in mourning, who was very tall and pale."

"What coloured hair and eyes had she?" asked his sister.

"I could no more tell the colour of her eyes, than I could paint yon twinkling star, or her hair either. I only know that they shed a kind of glory over her countenance, and mantled her brow with the softest and most exquisite shades."

"I declare, Henry," cried Mrs. Wentworth, "you are the most extravagant being I ever knew. I don't know whether you are in jest or earnest."

"Oh! you may be sure he is in earnest," said Miss Hart. "I know whom he means very well. It is Miss Carroll. Lois Carroll, the grand-daughter of old Mr. Carroll, the former minister of —— church. The old lady with whom she sat is her aunt. They live somewhere in the suburbs of the city—but never go anywhere except to church. They say she is the most complete little methodist in the world."

"What do you mean by a methodist?" asked Henry abruptly—"an enthusiast?"

"One who never goes to the theatre, never attends the ballroom, thinks it a sin to laugh, and goes about among poor people to give them doctor's stuff, and read the Bible."

"Well," answered Henry, "I see nothing very appalling in this description. If ever I marry, I have no very great desire that my wife should frequent the theatre or the ballroom. She might admire artificial graces at the one and exhibit them in the other, but the loveliest traits of her sex must fade and wither in the heated atmosphere of both. And I am sure it is a divine office to go about ministering to the wants of the poor and healing the sick. As to the last item, I may not be a proper judge, but I do think a beautiful woman reading the Bible to the afflicted and dying, must be the most angelic object in the universe."

"Why, brother," said Mrs. Wentworth, "what a strange compound you are! Such a rattle-brain as you, moralizing like a second Johnson!"

"I may be a wild rattle-brain, and sport like a thousand others in the waves of fashion, but there is something here, Jane," answered he, laying his hand half seriously, half sportively on his breast, "that tells me that I was created for immortality; that, spendthrift of time, I am still bound for eternity. I have often pictured the future, in my musing hours, and imagined a woman's gentle hand was guiding me in the path that leads to heaven."

Mrs. Wentworth looked at her brother in astonishment. There was something in the solemnity of his expressions that alarmed her, coming from one so gay and apparently thoughtless. Miss Hart was alarmed too, but from a different cause. She thought it time to aim her shaft, and she knew in what course to direct it.

"This Miss Carroll," said she, "whom you admire so much, has lately lost her lover, to whom she was devotedly attached. He was her cousin, and they had been brought up together from childhood, and betrothed from that period. She nursed him during a long sickness, day and night, and many thought she would follow him to the grave, her grief was so great."

"Her lover!" exclaimed Henry, in a mock tragedy tone. "Then it is all over with me—I never would accept the second place in any maiden's heart, even if I could be enshrined there in heaven's crystal. Give me the rose before the sunbeams have exhaled the dew of the morning, or it wears no charms for me."

Miss Hart and Mrs. Wentworth laughed, rallied Henry upon his heroics, and the beautiful stranger was mentioned no more. Miss Hart congratulated herself upon the master stroke by which she had dispelled his enchantment, if indeed it existed at all. She had often heard Henry declare his resolution never to marry a woman who had acknowledged a previous affection, and she seized upon a vague report of Miss Carroll's being in mourning for a cousin who had recently died, and to whom she thought she might possibly be betrothed, and presented it as a positive truth. Finding that Henry's ideas of female perfection were very different from what she had imagined, she was not sorry when an opportunity offered of displaying those domestic virtues, which he so much extolled. One night, when Mrs. Wentworth was prepared to attend a private ball, she expressed her wish to remain at home, declaring that she was weary of dissipation, and preferred reading and meditation. She expected Henry would steal away from the party, and join her in the course of the evening, but her real motive was a violent toothache, which she concealed that she might have the credit of a voluntary act. After Mrs. Wentworth's departure, she bound a handkerchief round her aching jaw, and having found relief from some powerful anodyne, she reclined back on the sofa and fell at last into a deep sleep. The candles burned dim from their long, unsnuffed wicks, and threw a very dubious light through the spacious apartment. She was awakened by a tall, dark figure, bending over her, with outspread arms, as if about to embrace her, and starting up, her first thought was that it was Henry, who had stolen on her solitude, and was about to declare the love she had no doubt he secretly cherished for her. But the figure drew back, with a sudden recoil, when she rose, and uttered her name in a tone of disappointment.

"Captain Wentworth," exclaimed she, "is it you?"

"I beg your pardon," said he, extending his hand cordially towards her, "I thought for a moment it was my wife, my Jane, Mrs. Wentworth—where is she? Is she well? Why do I not see her here?"

"Oh! Captain Wentworth, she had no expectation of your coming so soon. She is perfectly well. She is gone to a quadrille party, and will probably not be at home for several hours—I will send for her directly."

"No, Miss Hart," said he, in a cold and altered voice, "no, I would not shorten her evening's amusement. A quadrille party—I thought she had no taste for such pleasures."

"She seems to enjoy them very much," replied Miss Hart, "and it is very natural she should. She is young and handsome, and very much admired, and in your absence she found her own home comparatively dull."

The captain rose, and walked the room with a sailor's manly stride. His brows were knit, his lips compressed, and his cheek flushed. She saw the iron of jealousy was entering his soul, and she went on mercilessly deepening the wound she had made.

"You will be delighted when you see Mrs. Wentworth—she looks so blooming and lovely. You have reason to be quite proud of your wife—she is the belle of every party and ball-room. I think it is well that you have returned." This she added, with an arch, innocent smile, though she knew every word she uttered penetrated like a dagger, where he was most vulnerable. "How thoughtless I am!" she exclaimed; "you must be weary and hungry—I will order your supper."

"No, no," said he, "I have no appetite—I will not trouble you. Don't disturb yourself on my account—I will amuse myself with a book till she returns."

He sat down and took up a book, but his eyes were fixed moodily on the carpet, and his hands trembled as he unconsciously turned the leaves. Miss Hart suffered occasional agony from her tooth, the more as she had taken off the disfiguring bandage, but she would not retire, anticipating with a kind of savage delight, the unpleasant scene that would ensue on Mrs. Wentworth's return. The clock struck twelve before the carriage stopped at the door. Mrs. Wentworth came lightly into the room, unaccompanied by her brother, her cloak falling from her shoulders, her head uncovered, most fashionably and elegantly dressed. She did not see her husband when she first entered, and throwing her cloak on a chair, exclaimed, "Oh! Miss Hart, I'm so sorry you were not there, we had such a delightful party—the pleasantest of the whole season." Her eye at this moment fell upon her husband, who had risen upon her entrance, but stood back in the shade, without making one step to meet her. With a scream of surprise, joy, and perhaps terror too, she rushed towards him, and threw her arms around him. He suffered her clinging arms to remain round his neck for a moment while he remained as passive as the rock on the seabeat shore when the white foam wreathes and curls over its surface, then drawing back, he looked her steadfastly in the face, with a glance that made her own to quail, and her lip and cheek blanch. She looked down upon her jewelled neck and airy robes, and wished herself clothed in sackcloth and ashes. She began to stammer forth some excuse for her absence, something about his unexpected return, but the sentence died on her lips. The very blood seemed to congeal in her heart, under the influence of his freezing glance.

"Don't say anything, Jane," said he, sternly. "It is better as it is—I had deluded myself with the idea, that in all my dangers and hardships, to which I have exposed myself chiefly for your sake, I had a fond and faithful wife, who pined at my absence and yearned for my return. I was not aware of the new character you had assumed. No," continued he impetuously, entirely forgetful of the presence of Miss Hart "I was not prepared for a welcome like this. I expected to have met a wife—not a flirt, a belle, a vain, false-hearted, deceitful woman." Thus saying, he suddenly left the room, closing the door with a force that made every article of the furniture tremble. Mrs. Wentworth, bursting into hysterical sobs, was about to rush after him, but Miss Hart held her back—"Don't be a fool," said she; "he'll get over it directly-you've done nothing at which he ought to be angry; I had no idea he was such a tyrant."

"He was always kind to me before," sobbed Mrs. Wentworth. "He thinks my heart is weaned from him. Now, I wish I had disregarded the sneer of the world! It can never repay me for the loss of his love."

"My dear Mrs. Wentworth," said Miss Hart, putting her arms soothingly round her, "I feel for you deeply, but I hope you will not reproach yourself unnecessarily, or suffer your husband to suppose you condemn your own conduct. If you do, he will tyrannize over you, through life—what possible harm could there be in your going to a private party with your own brother, when you did not look for his return? You have taken no more liberty than every married lady in the city would have done, and a husband who really loved his wife, would be pleased and gratified that she should be an object of attention and admiration to others. Come, dry up your tears, and exert the pride and spirit every woman of delicacy and sense should exercise on such occasions."

Mrs. Wentworth listened, and the natural pride and waywardness of the human heart strengthening the counsels of her treacherous companion, her sorrow and contrition became merged in resentment. She resolved to return coldness for coldness and scorn for scorn, to seek no reconciliation, nor even to grant it, until he humbly sued for her forgiveness. The husband and wife met at the breakfast-table without speaking. Henry was unusually taciturn, and the whole burthen of keeping up the conversation rested on Miss Hart, who endeavoured to entertain and enliven the whole. Captain Wentworth, who had all the frankness and politeness of a sailor, unbent his stern brow when he addressed her, and it was in so kind a voice, that the tears started into his wife's eyes at the sound. He had no words, no glance for her, from whom he had been parted so long, and whom he had once loved so tenderly. Henry, who had been absorbed in his own reflections, and who had not been present at their first meeting, now noticed the silence of his sister, and the gloom of her husband, and looking from one to the other, first in astonishment, and then in mirth, he exclaimed, "Well, I believe I shall remain a bachelor, if this is a specimen of a matrimonial meeting. Jane looks as if she were doing penance for the sins of her whole life, and Captain Wentworth as if he were about to give a broadside's thunder. What has happened? Miss Hart resembles a beam of sunshine between two clouds."

Had Henry been aware of the real state of things, he would never have indulged his mirth at the expense of his sister's feelings. He had no suspicion that the clouds to which he alluded, arose from estrangement from each other, and when Mrs. Wentworth burst into tears and left the table, and Captain Wentworth set back his chair so suddenly as to upset the teaboard and produce a terrible crash among the china, the smile forsook his lips, and, turning to the captain in rather an authoritative manner, he demanded an explanation.

"Ask your sister," answered the captain, "and she may give it—as for me, sir, my feelings are not to be made a subject of unfeeling merriment. They have been already too keenly tortured, and should at least be sacred from your jest. But one thing let me tell you, sir, if you had had more regard to your sister's reputation, than to have escorted her to scenes of folly and corruption during her husband's absence, you might perhaps have spared me the misery I now endure."

"Do you threaten me, Captain Wentworth?" said Henry, advancing nearer to him with a flushed brow and raised tone. Miss Hart here interposed, and begged and entreated, and laid her hand on Henry's arm, and looked softly and imploringly at Captain Wentworth, who snatched up his hat and left the room, leaving Henry angry, distressed, and bewildered. Miss Hart explained the whole as the most causeless and ridiculous jealousy, which would soon pass away and was not worth noticing, and urged him to treat the matter as unworthy of indignation. She feared she had carried matters a little too far; she had no wish that they should fight, and Henry, perhaps, fall a victim to excited passions. She was anxious to allay the storm she had raised, and she succeeded in preventing the outbreakings of wrath, but she could not restore the happiness she had destroyed, the domestic peace she had disturbed, the love and confidence she had so wantonly invaded. Nor did she desire it. Incapable herself of feeling happiness from the evil passions that reigned in her bosom, she looked upon the bliss of others as a personal injury to herself; and where the flowers were fairest and the hopes the brightest, she loved to trample and shed her blasting influence. As the serpent goes trailing its dark length through the long grasses and sweet blossoms that veil its path, silent and deadly, she glided amid the sacred shades of domestic life, darting in ambush her venomed sting, and winding her coil in the very bosoms that warmed and caressed her. She now flitted about, describing what she called the best and most ridiculous scene imaginable; and the names of Captain Wentworth and his wife were bandied from lip to lip, one speaking of *him* as a tyrant, a bear, a domestic tiger—another of *her* as a heartless devotee of fashion, or a contemner of the laws of God and man. Most truly has it been said in holy writ, that the tongue of the slanderer is set on fire of hell, nor can the waters of the multitudinous sea quench its baleful flames. One evening Henry was returning at a late hour from the country, and passing a mansion in the outskirts of the city, whose shaded walls and modest situation called up ideas of domestic comfort and retirement; he thought it might be the residence of Miss Carroll, for, notwithstanding Miss Hart's damper, he had not forgotten her. He passed the house very slowly, gazing at one illuminated window, over which a white muslin curtain softly floated, and wishing he could catch another glimpse of a countenance that haunted him, as he said, like a dream. All was still, and he passed on, through a narrow alley that shortened his way. At the end of the alley was a small, low dwelling, where a light still glimmered, and the door being partially open, he heard groans and wailing sounds, indicating distress within. He approached the door, thinking he might render relief or assistance, and stood at the threshold, gazing on the unexpected scene presented to his view. On a low seat, not far from the door, sat a young lady, in a loose white robe, thrown around her in evident haste and disorder, her hair partly knotted up behind and partly falling in golden waves on her shoulders, holding in her lap a child of about three years old, from whose bandaged head the blood slowly oozed and dripped down on her snowy dress—one hand was placed tenderly under the wounded head, the other gently wiped away the stains from its bloody brow. A woman, whose emaciated features and sunken eyes spoke the ravages of consumption, sat leaning against the wall, gazing with a ghastly expression on the little sufferer, whose pains she had no power to relieve, and a little boy about ten years of age stood near her, weeping bitterly. Here was a scene of poverty, and sickness, and distress that baffled description, and in the midst appeared the outlines of that fair figure, like a descended angel of mercy, sent down to console the sorrows of humanity.

"This was a dreadful accident," said the young lady, "dreadful," raising her head as she spoke, and shading back her hair, revealing at the same time the heavenly countenance which had once before beamed on Henry's gaze. It was Lois Carroll, true to the character Miss Hart had sarcastically given her, a ministering spirit of compassion and benevolence.

"She will die," said the poor mother, "she'll never get over such a blow as that. She fell with such force, and struck her head on such a dangerous part too. Well, why should I wish her to live, when I must leave her behind so soon?"

"The doctor said there was some hope," answered the fair Lois, in a sweet, soothing voice, "and if it is God's will that she should recover, you ought to bless Him for it, and trust Him who feedeth the young ravens when they cry to Him for food. Lie down and compose yourself to rest. I will remain here through the night, and nurse the poor little patient. If she is kept very quiet, I think she will be better in the morning."

"How kind, how good you are!" said the mother, wiping the tear from her wasted cheek, "what should I do without you? But I never can think of your sitting up the whole night for us."

"And why not for you?" asked Lois, earnestly. "Can I ever repay your kindness to poor Charles, when he was sick, and you sat up, night after night, and refused to leave him? And now, when you are sick and helpless, would you deprive me of the opportunity of doing for you, what you have done for one so dear to me?"

A pang shot through Henry's heart. This poor *Charles* must have been the lover for whom she mourned, and at the mention of his name, he felt as if wakening from a dream. The love that bound the living to the dead, was a bond his hand would never attempt to loosen, and turning away with a sigh, he thought it would be sacrilege to linger there longer. Still he looked back to catch one more glimpse of a face where all the beatitudes dwelt. He had beheld the daughters of beauty, with all the charms of nature aided by the fascinations of art and fashion, but never had he witnessed anything so lovely as this young girl, in her simplicity, purity, and gentleness, unconscious that any eye was upon her, but the poor widow's and weeping orphan's. He had seen a fair belle in ill-humour for an hour, because a slight accident had soiled a new dress, or defaced a new ornament, but Lois sat in her blood-spotted robes, regardless of the stains, intent only on the object of her tenderness, and that a miserable child.

"Surely," thought he, as he pursued his way homeward, "there must be a divine influence operating on the heart, when a character like this is formed. Even were her affections free and not wedded to the dead, I should no more dare to love such a being, so spiritual, so holy, so little of the earth, earthy, than one of those pure spirits that live in the realms of ether. *I!* what has my life hitherto been? Nothing but a tissue of recklessness, folly, and madness. I have been trying to quench the heaven-born spark within me, but it still burns, and will continue to burn, while the throne of the Everlasting endures."

Henry felt more, reflected more that night, than he had done for five years before. He rose in the morning with a fixed resolve, to make that night an era in his existence. During the day the poor widow's heart was made to "sing for joy," for a supply was received from an unknown hand, so bounteous and unlooked for, she welcomed it as a gift from heaven. And so it was, for heaven inspired and also blessed the act.

Miss Hart began to be uneasy at Henry's deportment, and she had no reason to think she advanced in his good graces, and she had a vague fear of that Lois Carroll, whom she trusted she had robbed of all power to fascinate his imagination.

"By the way," said she to him, one day, as if struck by a sudden thought, "have you seen that pretty Miss Carroll since the evening you were speaking of her?"

"Yes," answered Henry, colouring very high, "I have met her several times—why do you ask?"

"No matter," said she, petrified at this information; "I saw a lady yesterday, who knows her intimately, and her conversation reminded me of ours on the same subject."

"What does the lady say of her character?" asked Henry.

"What every one else does, who knows her—that she is the greatest hypocrite that ever breathed. Perfectly selfish, self-righteous, and uncharitable. She says, notwithstanding her sweet countenance, she has a very bad temper, and that no one is willing to live in the same house with her."

"You told me formerly," said Henry, "that she was *over* charitable and kind, constantly engaged in labours of love."

"Oh, yes!" answered she, with perfect self-possession; "there is no end to the parade she makes about her *good works*, as she calls them, but it is for ostentation, and to obtain the reputation of a saint, that she does them."

"But," said Henry, very warmly, "supposing she exercised this same heavenly charity when she believed no eye beheld her, but the poor whom she relieved, and the sick whom she healed, and the God whom she adores; would you call that ostentation?"

"Oh, my dear Mr. More," cried Miss Hart, with a musical laugh, "you do not know half the arts of the sex. There is a young minister and young physician too, in the neighbourhood, who know all her secret movements, and hear her praises from morning till night—they say they are both in love with her, but as her cousin hasn't been dead long, she thinks it proper to be very demure—I must say frankly and honestly, I have no faith in these female *Tartuffes*."

"Nor I neither," added Henry, with so peculiar a manner, that Miss Hart started and looked inquisitively at him, with her dark, dilated eyes. She feared she had hazarded too much, and immediately observed,

"Perhaps, in my abhorrence of duplicity and hypocrisy, I run into the opposite extreme, and express my sentiments too openly. You think me severe, but I can have no possible motive to depreciate Miss Carroll, but as she herself stretches every one on the bed of Procrustes, I feel at liberty to speak my opinion of her character, not mine only, but that of the whole world."

Henry made some evasive reply, and turned the conversation to another topic, leaving Miss Hart lost in a labyrinth of conjecture, as to the impression she had made on his mind—where and when had he met Lois Carroll, and why was he so reserved upon a theme, upon which he had once been so eloquent?

She sat for half an hour after Henry left her, pondering on these things, and looking at one figure in the carpet, as if her eyes grew upon the spot, when her thoughts were turned into another channel by the entrance of Captain Wentworth.

She believed that she stood very high in his favour, for he was extremely polite to her, and showed her so much deference and attention, that she had no doubt that if Mrs. Wentworth were out of the way, he would be at no loss whom to choose as a successor. Her prospects with Henry grew more and more dubious—she thought, upon the whole, the captain the finer-looking and most agreeable man of the two. There was no knowing but he might separate from his wife, and as they seemed divorced in heart, she thought it would be much better than to remain together so cold and distant to each other. There was nothing she feared so much as a reconciliation; and as long as she could prevent Mrs. Wentworth from manifesting any symptoms of submission and sorrow, she was sure her husband's pride would be unyielding. She had a scheme on hand at present, which would promote her own gratification, and widen the breach between them.

There was a celebrated actor in the city, whom she was very desirous of seeing, and of whom Captain Wentworth had a particular dislike; he disliked the theatre and everything connected with it, and Miss Hart had vainly endeavoured to persuade Mrs. Wentworth to go with her brother, in open defiance of her husband. Henry manifested no disposition himself, and never would understand the oblique hints she gave him; she was determined to make a bold attack upon the captain himself.

"Captain Wentworth," said she, carelessly looking over the morning paper, "don't you mean to take Mrs. Wentworth to see this superb actor? she is dying to see him, and yet does not like to ask you."

"She's at perfect liberty to go as often as she pleases," replied the captain coldly—"I've no wish to control her inclinations."

"But she will not go, of course, unless you accompany her," replied Miss Hart, "not even with her brother."

"Did she commission you to make this request?"

"Not precisely; but knowing her wishes, I could not forbear doing it, even at the risk of your displeasure."

"If her heart is in such scenes, there can be no possible gratification to confine her body within the precincts of home."

The captain walked several times up and down the room, as was his custom when agitated, then abruptly asked Miss Hart if she wished to go herself.

She wished it, she said, merely to avoid singularity, as everybody else went; but had it not been for Mrs. Wentworth, she would never have mentioned it.

The captain declared that if she had the slightest desire, it was a command to him, and the tickets were accordingly purchased.

Late in the afternoon, Captain Wentworth sat in the dining-room, reading. As the sun drew near the horizon, and the light grew fainter, he sat down in a recess by a window, and the curtain falling down, completely concealed him. In this position he remained while the twilight darkened around him, and no longer able to read, he gave himself up to those dark and gloomy reflections which had lately filled his mind. He thought of the hours when, tossed upon the foaming billows, he had turned in heart towards his home,

And she, the dim and melancholy star,

Whose ray of beauty reached him from afar,"

rose upon the clouds of memory, with soft and gilding lustre. Now he was safely anchored in the haven of his hopes and wishes, but his soul was drifted by storms, wilder than any that swept the boisterous seas. The very effort of preserving outward calmness, only made the tempest fiercer within. This new instance of his wife's unconquerable levity and heartlessness, filled him with despair. He believed her too much demoralized by vanity and love of pleasure, ever to return to her duty and allegiance as a wife.

While indulging these bitter feelings, Miss Hart and Mrs. Wentworth entered the dining-room, unaware of his presence. Miss Hart, as usual, was speaking in an earnest, confidential tone, as if she feared some one was listening to her counsels.

"I beg, I entreat," said she, "that you would rally your spirits, and not let the world see that you are cast down by his ill treatment. All the fashionable people will be there tonight, and you must remember that many eyes will be upon you; and pray don't wear that horrid unbecoming dress, it makes a perfect fright of you, muffling you up to the chin."

"It is no matter," replied Mrs. Wentworth, despondingly, "I don't care how I look—the only eyes I ever really wished to charm, now turn from me in disgust; I'm weary of acting the part of a hypocrite, of smiling and chattering, and talking nonsense, when I feel as if my heart were breaking. Oh! that I had not weakly yielded my better reason to that fear of the world's censure, which has been the ruin of my happiness."

"I would never suffer my happiness to be affected one way or the other," cried Miss Hart, "by a man who showed so little tenderness or delicacy towards me. I wonder your affection is not chilled, nay utterly destroyed by his harshness and despotism."

"Oh! you little know the strength or depth of a woman's love, if you deem it so soon uprooted. My heart yearns to be admitted once more into the foldings of his—a hundred times have I been tempted to throw myself into his arms, implore his forgiveness, and entreat him to commence a new life of confidence and love."

Miss Hart began to laugh at this romantic speech, but the laugh froze on her lips when she saw the window-curtains suddenly part, and Captain Wentworth rushing forward, clasp his astonished wife in his arms, exclaiming "Jane, dear Jane, that life is begun!" He could not utter another word.

When, after a few moments of intense emotion, he raised his head, tears which were no stain upon his manhood, were glistening on his dark cheek. Miss Hart looked on with feelings similar to those which we may suppose animate the spirits of darkness, when they witness the restoration of man to the forfeited favour of his Maker. There was wormwood and bitterness in her heart, but her undaunted spirit still saw a way of extrication from all her difficulties.

"Really, Captain Wentworth," exclaimed she, laughing violently, "the next time you hide yourself behind a curtain, you must draw your boots under; I saw the cloven foot peeping out, and spoke of you as I did, just to see what Mrs. Wentworth would say, and I thought very likely it would have a happy result—I am sure this is a finer scene than any we shall see at the theatre."

"That you have deceived me, Miss Hart," answered the captain, "I acknowledge to my shame, but my eyes are now opened. My situation was accidental; no, I should say providential, for I have made discoveries, for which I can never be sufficiently grateful. Jane, I have been harsh and unjustly suspicious, I know, and richly deserve all I have suffered; but from the first hour of my return, this treacherous friend of yours, discovering the weakness of my character, has fanned the flame of jealousy, and fed the fires that were consuming me. I despise myself for being her dupe."

"Oh! Miss Hart," cried Mrs. Wentworth, "how could you be so cruel? you whom I so trusted, and thought my best and truest friend!"

"I have said nothing but the truth to either," cried Miss Hart boldly, seeing all subterfuge was now vain, "and you had better profit by it. Everybody has a weak side, and if they leave it unguarded and open to the attacks of the enemy, they have no one to blame but themselves. I never made you jealous, Captain Wentworth, nor your wife credulous; and, as I leave you wiser than I found you, I think you both ought to be very much obliged to me."

Thus saying, with an unblushing countenance, she left the apartment, and recollecting the next morning that a certain lady had given her a most pressing invitation to visit her, she departed, and no one said "God bless her."

Henry, who had seen full as much as he desired of her, hardly knew which rejoiced him more, her departure or his sister's happiness. Indeed the last seemed the consequence of the first, for never was there such a transformation in a household. There was blue sky for stormy clouds—spring gales for chill east winds—love and joy for distrust and sorrow.

Henry had seen the physician and minister whom Miss Hart had mentioned as the lovers of Lois Carroll. The *young physician* happened to be a bald, broad-faced man, with a long nose, which turned up at the end, as if looking at his forehead, and the *young* minister, a man whose hair was frosted with the snow of sixty winters, and on whose evangelical countenance disease had written deeper lines than those of age. Charles, too, the lover-cousin, proved to be an only brother, whose lingering hours of disease she had soothed with a Christian sister's holy ministration. Henry became a frequent, and, as he had reason to believe, a welcome visiter, at the house. He found Lois skilled in all the graceful accomplishments of her sex—her mind was enriched with oriental and classical literature, her memory stored with the brightest and purest gems of genius and taste; yet, like the wise men of the East, who brought their gold and frankincense and myrrh to the manger of the babe of Bethlehem, she laid these precious offerings in lowliness of spirit, at the feet of her Redeemer. All at once, Henry perceived a cloud come over the confidence in which he was established there. The good aunt was cold and distant; Lois, though still gentle and kind, was silent and reserved, and he thought he caught her melting blue eyes fixed upon him more than once with a sad and pitying expression.

"What has occurred?" asked he with the frankness so peculiar to him—when for a moment he was left alone with her "I am no longer a welcome guest."

"Forgive us," answered Lois, her face mantling with earnest blushes, "if we feel constrained to deny ourselves the pleasure we have derived from your society. As long as we believed you the friend of religion, though not her acknowledged votary, our hearts acknowledged a sympathy with yours, and indulged a hope that you would ere long go goal for goal with us for the same immortal prize. But an infidel, Mr. More! Oh! my soul!" continued she, clasping her hands fervently together, and looking upward, "come not thou into his secret!"

"An infidel!" cried Henry, "and do you believe me such, and condemn me as such, unheard, without granting me an opportunity of vindication?"

"We would not have admitted the belief from an authority less respectable. The intelligence came from one who had been an inmate of your family, and expressed for you the warmest friendship. We were told that you ridicule our faith, make the Bible a scorn and mockery, and expose us as individuals to contempt and derision."

"It must have been that serpent of a Miss Hart!" exclaimed Henry, trembling with passion; "that scorpion, that fiend in woman's form, whose path may be traced by the slime and the poison she leaves behind! The lips which could brand *you*, Lois, as a hypocrite, would not leave my name unblackened. My sister received her into her household, and her domestic happiness came near being the wreck of her malignant arts—I could give you any proof you may ask of her falsehood and turpitude."

73

"I ask none," cried Lois, with an irradiated countenance, "I believe your assurance, and rejoice in it. I cannot describe the pain, the grief I felt that one so kind to others, could be so cruel to himself."

Lois, in the godly simplicity of her heart, knew not of the warmth with which she spoke, or of the vivid expression that lighted up her eyes. Henry thought if ever there was a moment when he could dare to address her as a being born to love, and to be loved with human tenderness, it was the present. He began with faltering lips, but in the intensity of his feelings he soon forgot everything, but the object for which he was pleading, with an ardour and a vehemence that made the unsophisticated Lois tremble. She trembled and wept Her heart melted before his impassioned declaration, but she feared to yield immediately to its dictates.

Their course of life had hitherto been so different, their early associations, their pursuits and habits—she dreaded lest he should mistake the fervour of his attachment for her, for the warmth of religious sentiment, and that the temptations of the world would resume their influence over his heart. "Let us still be friends," said she, smiling through her tears, "till time has more fully unfolded our characters to each other. We are as yet but acquaintances of a day, as it were, and if we hope to pass an eternity together, we should pause a little before we become fellow-travellers in our pilgrimage. The love of a Christian," continued she, a holy enthusiasm illuminating her face, "cannot be limited to the transient union of this world—it soars far, far beyond it, illimitable as space, and everlasting as the soul's existence." Henry felt, while listening to this burst of hallowed feeling, that to possess the love of Lois Carroll here, without a hope of reunion beyond the grave, would be a dark and cheerless destiny, compared to the glorious hopes that now animated his being.

It was about two years after this, Miss Hart took passage in the stage, and started for the habitation of some obscure relative who lived in a distant town. She had gone from family to family, indulging her odious propensity, flattering the present, and slandering the absent, till, her character becoming fully known, all doors were closed against her, and she was compelled to seek a home, among kindred she was ashamed to acknowledge. "Whose beautiful country-seats are those?" asked a fellow-passenger, pointing to two elegant mansions, that stood side by side as if claiming consanguinity with each other. "The first belongs to Captain Wentworth, and the other to Mr. Henry More, his brother-in-law," answered Miss Hart, putting her head from the window, as they passed—"you must have heard of them." "No," said the stranger; "is there anything remarkable connected with them?" "Nothing," replied she, with one of her significant shrugs, "only the captain is one of your dark

Spanish Knights, who lock up their wives, and fight everybody who looks at them; and his lady likes every other gentleman better than her husband—and they could not agree, and the whole city were talking about them, so he took her into the country, and makes her fast and pray, and do penance for her sins. The other gentleman, Mr. More, married a low, ignorant girl, who had never been accustomed to good society; so, being ashamed to introduce her among his friends, he immured himself in the country also. They say he is so wretched in his choice, he has turned a fanatic, and there is some danger of his losing his reason." At this moment one of the horses took fright, and springing from the road, the stage was upset, with a terrible crash. Miss Hart, whose head was projecting from the window, was the only one who was seriously injured. She was dreadfully bruised and mangled, and carried insensible into Captain Wentworth's house. The stranger, whose curiosity was excited by the description he had just heard, and seeing the inhabitants of both dwellings were gathering together in consequence of the accident, assisted in carrying her, and lingered as long as he could find a reasonable excuse for doing so. "I believe that young woman's jaw is broken," said he, when he rejoined his fellow-passengers; "and it is a judgment upon her—I know there is not a word of truth in what she has been saying. If ever domestic happiness, as well as benevolence, dwelt on earth, I verily believe it is in those two families."

It was long before Miss Hart recovered her consciousness, and when she did, and endeavoured to speak, she felt such an excruciating pain in her jaw, as prevented her utterance. It seemed a remarkable instance of the retribution of Providence, that she should be afflicted in the very part which she had made an instrument of so much evil to others. Her jawbone was indeed broken, and there she lay, writhing in agony, incapable of speech, indebted to the beings she hated because she had injured, for the cares that prolonged her miserable existence. She could not speak, but she could see and hear, and her senses seemed sharpened by the bondage of her tongue. Mrs. Wentworth, and Lois too, hovered round her, with gentle steps and pitying looks, and the tenderest alleviations; and for this she might have been prepared. But when, through the shades of evening, she heard the deep voice of the once haughty and ungovernable Captain Wentworth, breathing forth humble and heartfelt prayers, while his wife knelt meek and lowly by his side, when she heard the gay and gallant Henry More, reading with reverence God's holy word, and joining with Lois in hymns to the Redeemer's praise, she rolled her eyes in wild amazement, and her dark spirit was troubled within her. "There seems a reality in this," thought she. "The worldling become the saint, and the lion transformed into the lamb! How happy they look, while I—poor, wretched, mangled creature that I am!" Paroxysms of agony followed these reflections, for which there seemed no mitigation.

She lingered for a long time speechless and in great suffering, but at length recovered with a frightful distortion in the lower part of the face. When she first beheld herself in a mirror, the shock was so great as to produce delirium, and when that subsided, a gloom and despair succeeded, from which they vainly endeavoured to rouse her by the soothings of sympathy and the consolations of religion. She felt that, like Cain, she must carry about an indelible brand upon her face, and cried like him, in bitterness of spirit, "My punishment is greater than I can bear." It was intolerable to her to look upon the fair, serene countenances of Mrs. Wentworth and Lois, and to see too the eyes of their husbands follow them with such love and delight, and then to draw the contrast between them and her own disfigured beauty and desolate lot. She expressed a wish to be sent to her relatives, and the wish was not opposed. She received from them a grudging welcome, for they had felt her sting, and feared that serpent tongue of slander, whose ancestral venom is derived from the arch reptile that lurked in the bowers of Eden.

Woe to the slanderer!—To use the language of the wise man, "her end is bitter as wormwood, and sharp as a two-edged sword—Her feet go down to death, her steps take hold on hell!"

THE SHAKER GIRL.

It was on a Sunday morning, when Roland Gray entered the village of ——. Though his mind was intent on the object of his journey, he could not but admire the singular neatness and uniformity of the houses, the velvet smoothness of the grass on the wayside, and the even surface of the street, from which every pebble seemed to have been removed. An air of perfect tranquillity reigned over the whole—not a being was seen moving abroad, not a human face beaming through the windows; yet far as the eye could reach, it roamed over a vast, cultivated plain, covered with all the animated hues of vegetation, giving evidence that the spirit of life was there, or had been recently active. "Surely," thought Roland, "I have entered one of those cities, described in the Arabian Nights, where some magician has suddenly converted the inhabitants into stone. I will dismount and explore some of these buildings—perchance I shall find some man, who is only half marble, who can explain this enchantment of silence." He had scarcely dismounted, and fastened his horse to a part of the snow-white railing which guarded every avenue to the dwellings, when he saw a most singular figure emerging from one, and approaching the spot where he stood. It was a boy of about twelve years old, clad in the ancient costume of our forefathers—with large breeches, fastened at the knees with square shining buckles—a coat, whose skirts were of surprising breadth, and a low-crowned hat, whose enormous brim shaded his round and ruddy visage. Roland could not forbear smiling at this extraordinary figure, but habitual politeness checked his mirth. He inquired the name of the village, and found to his surprise he was in the midst of one of those Shaker establishments, of whose existence, and of whose singular doctrines, he was well aware, but which, his own home being remote, he had never had an opportunity of witnessing. Delighted with the circumstance, for the love of novelty and excitement was predominant in his character, he determined to avail himself of it to its fullest extent. An old man, dressed in the same obsolete fashion, came up the path and accosted him:

"Are you a traveller," said he, "and seeking refreshments? If so, I am sorry you have chosen this day, but nevertheless we never refuse to perform the rites of hospitality."

Roland confessed he had no claims upon their hospitality, having partaken of a hearty breakfast two hours before in a town not far distant, and he wondered within himself why they had not mentioned the vicinity of this interesting establishment; forgetting that to those who live within the reach of any object of curiosity, it loses its interest. It is said there are some, who live where the echo of Niagara's eternal thunders are ringing in their ears, who have never gazed upon its foam. "If you come to witness our manner of worship, young man," said the elder, "and come in a sober, godly spirit, I give you welcome. The world's people often visit us, some, I am sorry to say, to scoff and to jest; but you have an honest, comely countenance, and I trust are led by better motives."

Roland was no hypocrite, but the good Shaker opened for him so fair a door of excuse for his intrusion, he was unwilling to deny that he was moved by a laudable desire to behold their peculiar form of worship. Pleased by the sunny openness of his countenance, the elder led the way to the house set apart for the service of the Most High, exhorting him at the same time to renounce the pomps and vanities of the world, and unite with them in that *oneness* of spirit, which distinguished their society from the children of mankind. No lofty spire marked out the temple of the Lord, nor did its form differ from that of a common dwelling-place. They entered a spacious hall, the floor of which presented such a dazzling expanse of white, the foot of the traveller hesitated before pressing its polished surface. The walls were of the same shining whiteness, chilling the eye by their cold uniformity—and benches arranged with the most exact precision on each side of the building, marked the boundaries of either sex Roland seated himself at some distance from the prescribed limits, and waited with proper solemnity the entrance of the worshippers. He observed that the men invariably entered at one door, the women at another, and that they had as little intercourse as if they belonged to different worlds. The men were all clothed in the ancient costume we have just described, and the women were dressed in garments as peculiar and unbecoming. A shirt of the purest white, short gown of the same texture, a 'kerchief folded in stiff unbending plaits, a mob cap of linen fastened close around the face, from which every tress of hair was combed carefully back, constituted their chill and ghost-like attire. As one by one these pallid figures glided in, and took their appointed seat, Roland felt as if he were gazing on the phantasmagoria of a dream, so pale and unearthly did they seem. The countenances of the males were generally suffused with a ruddy glow, but cold and colourless as marble were the cheeks of that sex he had been wont to see adorned with the roses of beauty and health. They arose and arranged themselves in a triangular form, while several of the aged stood in the centre, commencing the worship by a hymn of praise. Their voices were harsh and broken, but the devotion of their manner sanctified the strains, and Roland felt not, as he feared he should, a disposition for mirth. But when they gradually formed into a procession, marching two and two in a regular line, all joining in the wild and dissonant notes, then warming as they continued, changing the solemn march into the liveliest dance, clapping their hands simultaneously and shouting till the cold white walls resounded with the strange hosannas; all the while, those hueless, passionless faces gleaming by him, so still and ghastly mid their shroud-like garments, his brain began to reel, and he almost imagined himself attending the orgies of the dead, of resuscitated bodies, with the motions of life, but without the living soul. Still, over the whole group there was a pervading solemnity and devotion, an apparent abandonment of the whole world—an anticipation of the loneliness and lifelessness of the tomb, that redeemed it from ridicule, and inspired emotions kindred to awe. This awe, however, soon melted away in pity at such delusion, and this sensation became at length converted into admiration for an object, at first unnoticed in the general uniformity of the scene, but which grew upon his eye, like the outline of the landscape through the morning mist. There was one young girl moving in this throng of worshippers, whose superior bearing could not long elude the stranger's scrutiny. Her age might be fourteen or fifteen, perhaps younger; it was difficult to decide through the muffling folds of a dress which levelled every distinction of form and comeliness. As she passed and repassed him, in the evolutions of their dance, he caught occasional glimpses of a face, which, though pale, betrayed the flitting colour through the transparent skin; and once or twice the soft, thoughtful gray eyes were turned towards him, with a wistful and earnest expression, as if claiming sympathy and kindness from some congenial being. Fixing his gaze upon the spot where he first beheld her, he watched her returning figure with an intensity that at last became visible to the object of it, for the pale rose of her cheek grew deeper and deeper, and her beautiful gray eyes were bent upon the floor. Roland leaned from the window near which he was seated, to see if it was actually the same world he had inhabited that morning, so strangely were his senses affected by the shrill music, growing louder and louder, the shuffling, gliding motions, increasing in velocity, and this sweet apparition so unexpectedly mingling in such an incongruous scene. The breath of summer redolent with a thousand perfumes stole over his brow—the blue sky was arching over his head; never had creation seemed more lovely or glowing; yet the worshippers within deemed they were offering an acceptable sacrifice on the altar of God, the sacrifice of those social affections, which find such beautiful emblems in the works of nature. Roland became so lost in these reflections, he hardly noticed the closing of the exercise, or heard the monotonous tones of one of the elders, who was exhorting in the peculiar dialect of his sect. When the services were concluded, he left the hall, still watching the motions of the gray-eyed damsel, in the bold resolution of accosting her, and discovering if she were a willing devotee. As she walked along with a light step, in spite of her clumsy high-heeled shoes, by the side of an ancient dame, Roland, unconscious of the extreme audacity of the act, and hardly knowing himself in what manner to address her, crossed her path, and was in the very act of apologizing for the intrusion, when his arm was seized with a sturdy grasp, and he saw the old Shaker who had introduced him into the assembly, standing by his side. "Young man," said he, in a stern voice —"do you come here, a wolf in sheep's clothing, in the very midst of the flock? what is your business with this child, whom our rules forbid you to address?" Roland felt at first very indignant, but a moment's reflection convinced him he had erred, and transgressed their rigid rules. He felt too that he had placed himself in rather a ridiculous situation, and he stood before the rebuking elder with a blush of ingenuous shame, that completely disarmed his wrath. "You are young, very young," said the old man—"and I forgive you— you have been brought up in the midst of the vanities of the world, and I pity you; yet my heart cleaves to you, young man, and when you become weary of those vanities, as you shortly will, come to us, and you will find that peace which the world can neither give nor take away."

He shook hands with Roland after he had spoken, who acknowledged his offence, thanked him for his counsel and kindness, and, mounting his horse, left him with a sentiment of unfeigned respect; so true it is, that sincerity of faith gives dignity to the professor of many a creed revolting to human reason. Roland looked back upon the beautiful village, and wondered at what he had just witnessed. He felt a strong disposition to linger, that he might discover something more of the peculiarities of this singular and isolated people. Had he known their incorruptible honesty, their unwearied industry, their trusting hospitality, their kindness and charity—had he seen the pale sisterhood extending their cherishing cares to the children of orphanage and want, he would have been convinced that warm streams of living tenderness were flowing beneath the cold forms of their austere religion.

Roland Gray was very young, and had seen but little of the world. He had led the secluded life of a student, and, but lately freed from collegiate restraints, he had been trying his wings, preparatory to a bolder flight across the Atlantic. He was now on the way to his sister, who, with himself, was placed under the guardianship of the excellent Mr. Worthington, for they were orphans, left with an independent fortune, but singularly destitute of kindred, being the last of their race. An invalid gentleman, one of his father's early friends, was about to travel in foreign climes to try the benefit of a milder atmosphere, and he urged Roland to be his companion. Such a proposal was accepted with gratitude, and Roland, with buoyant spirits, returned to his sister, to bid her farewell, before launching on the "deep blue sea." Lucy Gray was older than her brother, and from childhood had exercised over him the influence with which a few additional years, joined to a strength of mind far beyond her years, invested her. He was the object no less of her love than her pride. She looked upon him as the last representative of a family, honoured among the most honourable, and destined to transmit to posterity his ancestral name, with unblemished and still more exalted lustre. She resolved he should ennoble himself by marriage, and would have scorned, as degrading, the thought that love might make the youth a rebel to her will. She believed the affections entirely under the control of the reason, and looked upon the passions as vassals to be dragged at its chariot wheels. Lucy was not loved by her friends, but she was respected and esteemed for the firmness of her principles, and the strength of her mind. But Roland loved as much as he revered her. His heart was a fountain of warm and generous affections, and it flowed out towards her, his only sister, in the fulness of a current, that found no other legitimate channel. Accustomed to yield his rash and ardent impulses to the direction of her cooler judgment, he looked up to her as the mentor of his follies, rather than as the companion of his youthful amusements, and now, after an absence of several months, partly from pleasure and partly from business, he looked forward to meeting her with something of the feelings of a son, blended with the affection of a brother. His arrival at Mr. Worthington's was hailed with a burst of joy, for Roland had a face of sunshine and a voice of melody, that shed light and music wherever he went. In relating his adventures, he failed not to give due interest to his interview with the Shakers, and laughed over the Quixotism that exposed him to so stern a rebuke. The pretty little Shakeress did not lose any of her attractions in his romantic description, and he dwelt upon her dovelike eyes, melting beneath the snows of her antiquated cap, her sweet, appealing countenance and spiritual air, till Mr. Worthington's childless heart warmed within him, and Lucy listened with apprehensive pride lest her brother's excited imagination should convert this obscure unknown into a heroine of romance. It was but a transient alarm, for she knew that the waves of the Atlantic would soon roll between them, and Roland, surrounded by all the glorious associations of an elder world, would cast aside every light and ignoble fancy, and fit himself for the high station in society she felt he was born to fill.

After an absence of four years Roland Gray appeared once more in the family circle of Mr. Worthington. His hair had assumed a darker shade, and his cheek a darker glow, but the same sunshiny spirit lighted up his brow and animated his lips; it was Roland Gray still, only the bloom of boyhood was lost in the sunniness of manhood. Lucy's handsome, but severe countenance was so irradiated with joy, it was almost dazzling from the effect of contrast: and as she sat by his side, and gazed in his face, she felt that all her affections and her hopes were so completely centered in him, they could be separated only with the breaking of her heart. Happy as Roland was in being reunited to his sister, his attention was not so engrossed as to forget the kindly greetings due to the other members of Mr. Worthington's household.

"I have an adopted daughter to introduce you to," said Mr. Worthington, drawing forward a young girl who, on the entrance of Roland, had retreated behind a stand of geraniums, and busied herself in picking off the faded leaves. Roland had become too familiar with beauty in foreign climes, to be surprised into admiration of a face however fair, but there was a sweetness, a modesty and simplicity diffused over the young face before him, that interested his feelings and disarmed his judgment. He could scarcely tell the colour of her eyes, for they were downcast, but there was something in the play of her features, that implied she sympathized in the pleasure his coming had excited. "Roland," continued Mr. Worthington, evidently delighted with the reception he had given his favourite, "this is my daughter Grace, whom Providence has kindly given to cheer a widowed and childless heart. You know I look upon you almost as my son, so you will find in her, I trust, another sister to love." Roland held out his hand with great alacrity to seal this new compact, but the pretty Grace drew back with an embarrassment he was unwilling to increase, seeing it was entirely unaffected; and there was something in Lucy's glance that told him she resented the idea of such a partnership in his affections. He could not but marvel where good old Mr. Worthington had found such a fairy gift, but believing the mystery would be explained in due time, he promised himself no slight gratification in studying a character, concealed under such a veil of bashfulness and reserve. The twilight hour found the brother and sister walking together towards their accustomed seat under the sycamore boughs, the scene of many of Lucy's former counsels, and Roland's high resolves. She wanted to be alone with him —to guard him against a thousand dangers and snares, visible only to her proud and jealous eye. "Oh! Roland," said she, taking his hand and looking earnestly in his face—"do you return unchanged?—may I still, as wont, presume to counsel, to direct, and to sustain?" "Unchanged in everything as regards my affection for you, my dear sister," replied he—"be still my mentor and my guide, for I fear, with all the worldly wisdom I have acquired, I am often the same impulsive being you have so long tried in vain to bring under the square and compass of reason and right. Now, I feel at this moment an irresistible impulse to know who is this pretty God-send of Mr. Worthington's; did she drop down from the skies, or did she come on the wings of the wind?"

"I am glad you have opened the subject, Roland, for I brought you here to warn you of that girl's influence. Do not laugh, for, knowing you so well, I feel bound to prevent any imposition on your open, generous nature. I do not know who she is, probably some poor child of shame and desertion, whom Mr. Worthington discovered and educated, for it is but a year since he brought her from school, and introduced her as his adopted daughter. He made a long visit to his relatives, since you left us, and found her, I believe, in the family of his brother, in a dependent and perhaps menial situation. Charmed by her beauty and beguiled by her arts, the good man conceived the romantic design of educating her as his own, and now he is felicitating himself with another project, that of securing for this nameless foundling the heart and the fortune of Roland Gray." Roland had heard too much about gentle blood and honourable parentage, and been too much under the influence of his aristocratic sister, not to shrink from the supposition of such an union, but he protested against the word *arts*, which Lucy had used in reference to Grace, for she looked the most artless of human beings; and he accused her of injustice towards Mr. Worthington, who in his singleness of heart was incapable of making a project of any kind. "You must not think it strange," said Lucy, "that I, a woman should not be blinded by the beauty of one of my own sex, and I know I am superior to the weakness of envy. With an insight into character which has never deceived me, I know that girl to be vain, selfish, and calculating. Mr. Worthington may claim her as *his daughter*, but he shall never impose her on me, by the name of *sister*." Those who have witnessed the empire an elder sister of commanding mind and manners is capable of obtaining over a younger brother's judgment, will not be surprised that Roland learned to look upon Grace with distrustful eyes, though he could not believe in the duplicity Lucy ascribed to her character, and he invariably treated her with that consideration due to the situation she held in Mr. Worthington's family. It was impossible, however, to be domesticated with her, to be seated at the same table, parties in the same amusements, near each other in the evening circle, and the moonlight walks, notwithstanding the unsleeping vigilance of Lucy, not to feel the reality of her loveliness, her simplicity and truth. There was something about her that haunted him like a dream, and whenever she turned her eyes towards him, he experienced a sudden thrill of recollection, as if he had seen that fair face before. In the evening Mr. Worthington often challenged Lucy to a game of chess, for though not a skilful performer, he was extravagantly fond of the game, and Lucy had no rival in the art. She now regretted this accomplishment, as it threw her brother more immediately into companionship with Grace, whose conversation, when unrestrained, was perfectly bewitching, from a mixture of bright intelligence, quick sensibility, and profound ignorance of the vices and customs of the world. It was evident she felt oppressed by Lucy's scrutinizing gaze, for when she was conscious of its withdrawal, her spirits rebounded with an unobtrusive gayety, that harmonized admirably with the life and vivacity of Roland's disposition.

One evening, as Lucy was absorbed in the crisis of the game, Grace was busily plying her needle, making some garments for a poor woman, whose house and wardrobe were completely consumed by fire, the previous night; all the ladies in the neighbourhood were contributing their part towards relieving her wants, and a very pretty little girl, with a basket half-filled with her mother's offerings, was waiting till Grace had put the last stitches into a cap, whose fashion seemed to fix the particular attention of Roland. The child, who was a petted favourite in the family, caught up the cap the moment it was completed, and drawing it over the soft brown locks of Grace, laughingly fastened the linen bands. Roland uttered so sudden an exclamation, it made Lucy start from her seat, upsetting bishop, knight, and royalty itself. The mystery was revealed, the pretty little Shakeress stood before him. The close linen border, under which every lock of hair was concealed, transformed at once the fashionable and elegant young lady into the simple and humble Shaker girl. A scene, which the lapse of years and the crowding events of a transatlantic tour had effaced from his memory, returned vividly to his recollection. He wondered he had not recognised her earlier, but the hue of the soft gray eye was darkened, and its light more warm and shifting, her complexion had a richer colouring, and shadows of bright hair relieved the fairness of a brow where intelligence and sensibility now sat enthroned. Then her figure—now revealed in all the graces of womanhood, was it the same he had seen muffled in the stiff starched shirt and 'kerchief, moving on high-heeled shoes with large shining buckles? Grace blushed deeply beneath his riveted gaze, and hastily snatching the cap from her head, folded it with the other garments she had made into the basket, and bade the little girl hasten to her mother. "What is the meaning of all this bustle?" said Lucy, looking at Grace with so much asperity it made her involuntarily draw closer to Mr. Worthington. "It means," said Roland, delighted and excited by the discovery he had made, and forgetting his sister's daily cautions—"it means that I have found my pretty Shakeress at last. Ah! Mr. Worthington, why did not you tell me that your adopted daughter and my fair unknown were one?" Mr. Worthington laughed, and taking the hand of Grace drew her upon his knee. "Because the world is full of prejudice, and I did not like to expose my girl to its influence. I always wanted to tell *you*, but Grace insisted I should allow you to find it out yourself, for she told me about the bold youth, who almost stared her out of her devotion and her wits. Nay, Grace, I owe him a thousand thanks, for had he not warmed my old heart by a description of your loveliness, I never should have gone so far out of my journey to visit your village, begged you of the good people for my own, nor would I now have such a sweet blossom to shed fragrance over my declining years."

"And how," exclaimed Roland with irresistible curiosity, "how came she amongst them?" Before Mr. Worthington could reply, Grace clasped her hands earnestly together, and cried, "I was a stranger, and they took me in; I was an orphan and they clothed me, sheltered and—" Previously much agitated, Grace here entirely lost her self-command, and leaning her head on the shoulder of Mr. Worthington, she wept audibly. Lucy actually trembled and turned pale. She saw that her empire was tottering from its foundation. Accustomed to interpret every change of her brother's countenance, she read with terror the intense expression with which his eyes were fixed on Grace. She was willing he should marry from ambition, but not for love. She had never for a moment admitted the idea that another should supplant her in his affections—a jealousy far more dark and vindictive than that excited by love, the jealousy of power, took possession of her soul, mingled with a bitter hatred towards the innocent cause of these emotions. Through life she had bowed the will of others to her own, and as long as no opposition roused the strength of her passions, she maintained a character of integrity and virtue, that bid defiance to scandal and reproach. She did not know herself the evil of which she was capable, but now the lion was unchained in her bosom, and chafed and wrestled for its prey. Too politic to attempt checking too suddenly the tide of feeling, yet too angry to hide her own chagrin, she left the room, and meditated in what manner she could best arrest the evil she dreaded. She failed not, however, to breathe a warning whisper into her brother's ear as she passed out. Here Mr. Worthington entreated Grace to tell Roland all she knew of herself, assuring her, in his simplicity, that no one, next to himself, felt so deep an interest in her, as he did. Roland felt no disposition to contradict this assertion, and joined his own entreaties so earnestly to Mr. Worthington's, Grace hesitated not to relate her simple history. It could be comprised in a few words. She told of her sad and almost desolate childhood, of her dwelling in a little cottage deep in the woods, remote from neighbours or friends; of a dark and cruel man she called father—here Grace's voice grew low and husky—of a pale, sick, and dying mother, who was found by a good Shaker, on the bed of death, and who committed her orphan child to the care of the kind Samaritan. The man who had deserted her mother, in the extremity of her wants, never appeared to claim his child. She was cherished in the bosom of that benevolent society, where Roland first beheld her, grateful for their kindness, though yearning after freedom and the fellowship of youth, till Mr. Worthington came, and offered her the love and guardianship of a father, if she would occupy a daughter's place in his heart and home. Her father's name was Goldman, which she had willingly resigned for that of Worthington, for the memory she had of him, was like a dark and terrible dream—fearful to remember. The dread that he might appear some day to claim her, often made her shudder in the midst of her happiness; but as so many years had passed away, it was more natural to suppose he had expiated his cruelty with his life.

Had Mr. Worthington conceived the project that Lucy had suggested, and been aware at the same time of Roland's family pride, it is not probable he would have induced her to reveal to him the sad events of her childhood; and had Grace been the artful being described, she would never have told with such straightforward simplicity and deep sensibility of her father's brutality and vices, nor expressed the startling fear, that he might still assert the forfeited rights of nature, and tear her from the arms of her benefactor. Such thoughts as these filled the breast of Roland, as Grace continued her affecting recital, where truth was attested by her blushes and her tears. She unclasped from her neck a golden chain, from which a miniature was suspended, the sole relic of her mother. The chain was beautifully wrought, and indicated that however abject was the condition to which the owner had been reduced, she had once been accustomed to the decorations of wealth. The miniature was that of a gentleman in the prime of life, with a dark, but interesting countenance, and dignified bearing. Grace knew not whether it was her father's picture, for she had but a faint recollection of his features, and the Shaker who discovered it around her mother's neck, after she was speechless in death, could give her no information.

Here was mystery and romance, innocence, beauty, and youth; and Roland felt as if he would gladly twine them together, and bind them around his heart, as all "he guessed of heaven." But while his imagination was weaving the garland and revelling in its fragrance, the vision of

A sister's jealous care,

A cruel sister she,"

rose before him, and the wreath faded and the blossoms fell. With a stinging sensation of shame, he admitted the conviction, that he *feared* his sister. He had long worn her fetters unconsciously, but now, when for the first time they galled and restrained him, his pride and his heart rebelled against the hand that bound him in thraldom. Grace retired that night, with a thousand bright hopes hovering round her pillow. Roland then was her first benefactor. It was he, who had awakened the interest of Mr. Worthington, and directed him to her retreat. He, the handsome and noble-looking youth, whose dark piercing eyes had kindled in her such yearnings after the world from which she was excluded, and who for four years had been the morning and evening star on the horizon of her memory. She knew something of this before, but she had never realized it so fully as now; for he had himself confirmed it, by words, which, though simple in themselves, were unutterably eloquent, accompanied by such looks—she blushed even in the darkness, as she caught herself involuntarily repeating, "and have I found my pretty Shakeress at last?" For two or three days, Roland avoided being alone with Lucy, but to his surprise, she did not seem to desire an opportunity to renew her warnings. On the contrary, she was more kind and affectionate towards Grace than she had ever been before, who, in the confidingness of innocence, relied on her unwonted testimonies of favour, as the harbingers of her dearest wishes. "Grace," said Lucy—they were alone and secure of interruption, for Mr. Worthington and Roland were both absent on business—"Grace, are you willing to tell me of what you are now thinking?" Grace started—she had fallen into an unconscious revery, and her work lay idly in her lap; her cheeks glowed painfully, but with that habitual reverence for truth which always distinguished her, she answered, "I was thinking of Roland." Unprepared for such perfect ingenuousness, Lucy hesitated a moment, and conscience upbraided her for the part she was about to act, but again fixing her keen eye on a countenance as transparent as crystal, she continued: "Has Roland ever told you that he loved you?" Grace crimsoned still more deeply from wounded modesty and shame, while she answered in a low voice, "Never!" "Then," said the inquisitor, drawing a relieving breath, "Grace, your task is easy, and I rejoice that he has made it so; you must not think of Roland, you must not love him, for he never can be to you anything more than he now is." Grace turned deadly pale, but she did not speak, and Lucy went on—"My brother was my father's only son, and is sole heir of a name long conspicuous for its honours. Our parents died when we were both young; but I, as the elder, became the guardian and guide. To me, on his death-bed, my father committed my young brother, charging me with the solemnity of that awful hour, to guard his honour from stain, and his name from degradation. My father was a proud and haughty man, and he has transmitted to his children a portion of his own spirit. Grace, you have told me all the circumstances of your life; you know there is mystery, but you may not know in your extreme simplicity, that there may be disgrace in your birth. The golden chain that wreathes your neck, shows that your mother was not born to poverty. Why then did she flee from her friends, to bury herself in solitude with the dark and cruel man you called father; and why are you an alien from your kindred? You ought to know these truths, which the mistaken kindness of your friends conceals from you, and I reveal them to you, that you may not encourage hopes that never can be realized; to convince you, you can never be the wife of Roland. For myself, hear me, Grace, to the end—if Roland could forget himself so far as to think of such an union, I would forever disown him as a brother, and load with maledictions the being who had brought such misery on us both." All the strong passions at work in Lucy's bosom, sent their baleful lustre to her eyes, and poor Grace shrunk from their beams as if they were withering her very heart. Brought up in the midst of that gentle and subdued sisterhood, in whose uniform existence the passions seemed cradled into unbroken slumber, she had almost forgotten their existence. The terrible dreams of her childhood were brought back to her. The curses of her father again rung in her ears—the helpless cries of her mother. She clasped her hands despairingly over her eyes—she knew she had been poor and wretched; but benevolence and charity had administered to her wants, and the very remembrance of poverty had faded from her mind; but disgrace—that there was a disgrace attached to her that made it sinful in her to love Roland Gray, that debarred her from an union with the honourable and good—that was the thought that crushed her, that chilled her blood, and turned her cheeks to marble and her lips to ashes. Lucy paused, and attempted to soothe the agony she had excited. Cold herself to the softer emotions, she had no faith in the eternity of love. Grace, like a child robbed of its plaything, now wept and refused to be comforted, but she would soon smile animated by some new-born hope. Thus Lucy tried to reason, while she held her chill grasp on the heart of Grace, and bound her still more closely to her will. "Promise me," said she, "that you will not reveal to any one the conversation of this morning —Mr. Worthington has deceived you, and you would not meanly appeal to the compassion of Roland—promise this, and you shall find in me a friend who will never forsake you in weal or woe. Deny it, and you will create an enemy whose power can make you tremble." Grace, with all her woman's pride rising to her relief, at the idea of appealing to the compassion of Roland, gave the desired promise, and still more—she voluntarily declared she would rather die than think of Roland, after what Lucy had just uttered. Lucy, satisfied with her promise, for she knew her truth, embraced her with commendations which fell heedlessly on poor Grace's paralyzed ears—she withdrew to her chamber, "for her whole head was pained and her whole heart sick;" and when Mr. Worthington and Roland returned, Grace was said to be unable, from indisposition, to join the circle, where she was wont to preside an angel of light and joy. The sympathy and sorrow excited by so common an event, reconciled Lucy more than anything else, to her selfishness and cruelty. But was she happy in the success of her operations! She had planted thorns in the bosom of another—but were there none rankling in her own! Could she, a daughter of this land of republicanism, shelter herself under the cold shadow of family pride, from the reproaches of her own conscience? Ah! no! the heart is its own avenger, and for every drop of sorrow wilfully wrung from the eyes of another, shall be doomed to give only tears of blood.

Roland wondered at the change that had come over Grace, and sought by every means to ascertain the cause, but she seemed wrapped in a cloud of impenetrable reserve. She avoided him, but in so quiet a manner, it appeared to him more the result of sudden indifference or aversion, than unexplained resentment. The sunshine of her smile was gone, and an expression of calm apathy settled on her brow, where the alternations of feeling had lately flitted, like the lights and shadows of a moonlight landscape. Roland sometimes had a painful suspicion of his sister, but she had always been so open in all her actions, so undisguised in her least amiable traits, that notwithstanding all the prejudice she had manifested towards Grace, he believed her incapable of any mean or dark designings. Mr. Worthington was anxious and alarmed. He was sure some incipient and insidious disease was the cause of her pale and dispirited appearance. He was constantly feeling her pulse, and inquiring her symptoms, and insisting upon calling in a physician, till poor Grace, really glad to shelter herself from observation, under the pretext held out, acknowledged herself ill, and passively submitted to a course of medicine, which reduced her soon to a state of real debility and suffering. They applied blisters to her forehead to still its hot throbbings; they drew blood from her veins to reduce her feverish pulse, and Lucy sat by her bedside and administered to her unweariedly, and discussed the nature of her malady, and talked of its different stages; while all the time she knew it was herself who had coldly and deliberately dried up the fountain of hope and joy, and love, which had sent such roses to her cheek and sunbeams to her eye. She sometimes trembled in the darkness of night, at the possibility that Grace might die, under the regimen of this imaginary disease; and then a voice whispered in hollow murmurs, in her ears, "Thou shalt sleep no more, for thou hast murdered sleep." But in day's broad light a witness to Roland's abstraction, anxiety and gloom, she steeled her conscience, in reflecting on the necessity of the act. Let not Grace be condemned, as too weak and yielding, as too blind an instrument in the hands of another. Her education had been peculiar, and her natural disposition was extremely sensitive and timid. The first years of her life had been passed in terror and sorrow—terror for her father's cruelty, and sorrow for her mother's woe. Everything around her was tumultuous and fearful, and she learned to shudder at the awful manifestations of evil passions, before she knew them by name. Transplanted to a scene, where everything breathed of peace and silence, where industry, neatness, and order were heaven's first laws, where the voice of dissension was unheard, and the storms of passion unfelt, her spirit had been so hushed and subdued, her sensibilities so repressed, and her energies held down, she moved along her daily path a piece of beautiful and exquisite mechanism, but whose most powerful springs had never been touched. It is true she loved the kind and gentle Shakers, but it was with a tranquil feeling of gratitude and trust. The visit of Roland Gray acted as an electrical communication between her and the world to which he belonged. It seemed to her it must be inhabited by angels; and when Mr. Worthington came and induced her benefactor to resign her to his care, she welcomed the change as into the garden of Eden. In the seclusion of a school, her timidity still induced her to shrink within herself; in the companionship of Lucy, she felt awe-struck and abashed; but Roland came, and then she realized the paradise of her imagination. Everything around her was music and beauty and love—flowers sprang up in the waste places, water gushed from the rock, and melody filled the air. To be forbidden to think of him, to be commanded to wrench him from her heart, to be made to think of herself as a low and disgraced being—Grace would have shuddered at the idea of impiety, but when she laid her head on her pillow, willing to be thought sick, rather than wretched, she certainly wished to die. But the strength of youth, though prostrated, rebounded from the pressure. She was not doomed to the *curse of a granted prayer*. The Providence that had so long watched over her destiny, still kept its unseen but slumbering vigils. Grace remembered her old friends, the Shakers, and yearned once more for their still and passionless existence. She prayed Mr. Worthington to take her there so earnestly, he did not hesitate to grant her request, believing the journey would invigorate her constitution and change of scene animate her mind. She spoke not of remaining, and the wish was so natural and grateful, it could not excite surprise or censure.

"You see," said Lucy to her brother, the night before Grace's departure, "the influence of early habits. Perhaps all this time Grace has been pining after the Shakers. She has been suffering from a kind of calenture, and when she sees their green plain, and quiet village, she will be happy." "Impossible!" cried Roland, completely thrown off his guard by Lucy's sudden insinuation. "She is strange and unaccountable, but I never will believe anything so preposterous. She, that sweet, lovely, spiritual creature, to be immured again in their cold walls, and to wish it, and pine after it! By heavens! Lucy, if I could believe such a thing, I would go this moment and prevent the immolation. I will not deceive you; I do not care any longer for pride and empty sounding names, and birth and parentage. It is ridiculous to think of such things in this republican country. Grace is equal to the highest; for she claims her birthright from the Almighty himself, and carries on her brow the signet of heaven." "Stop, Roland, for heaven's sake, and hear me." "I will not stop," continued Roland, a spirit of determination flashing from his eyes she had never seen in them before; "shall I sacrifice my happiness to a shadow, a bubble? No! I have hesitated too long; I love Grace; I love her with all my heart and soul, and I will go this moment and tell her so." He laid his hand upon the latch, but Lucy sprang forward like lightning, and seized it in her own. "One moment, Roland, only one moment; I, your only sister, ask it." Roland saw she was very pale, and he felt her hand tremble as it grasped him. She was indeed his only sister, whom he had so much loved, and he felt he had met her prejudices with too much impetuosity; they might yield, perhaps, to softer measures. "What is it you would say, Lucy? You asked for one moment, and I have given you more." "Only promise to wait till her return;

that is all I ask; I spoke in jest; you knew she would not remain; Mr. Worthington will never leave her. Promise me this, dear Roland, and I will not oppose my pride to your happiness." Lucy knew that she was uttering a falsehood, for she herself had confirmed Grace in her resolution to remain; but she had begun to weave the tangled web of deceit, and she wound herself deeper and deeper in its folds. All she wanted now was to gain time, and she then felt she should be safe. Roland promised, for delay was not sacrifice, and he was surprised and grateful for Lucy's concession.

"Grace," whispered Lucy, as she embraced and bid her farewell, "you are acting right; you will find peace and happiness in the path you seek. Be assured of my friendship and also my gratitude." Grace was mute, but she gave Lucy a look that might have melted a heart of stone.

"Grace," said Roland, "come back to us soon." He kept his promise to his sister, but his voice trembled, his hand lingered as it pressed hers in parting, and his eyes spoke a language she must have understood, had not her own been blinded with tears. She met a warm reception from the friends of her early days. The kind Susan, who had taken the first charge of her, and acted toward her a mother's part, opened her arms to receive her, and when she saw her faded colour and drooping eyes, she felt as the patriarch did when he took in his weary dove to the ark, for she knew the wanderer brought back no green olive branch of hope and joy. Susan had once known the gayeties of the world, and tasted its pleasures, but her heart had been blighted and her hopes betrayed, and finding all was vanity, to use her own expressive language she had "taken up her cross and followed her Saviour." The seal of silence was placed on the history of her heart, and Grace dreamed not that one of that tranquil tribe had ever known the tumult of human passions. By some mysterious communion, however, between soul and soul, Grace felt an assurance of Susan's sympathy, and clung to her with increased affection. It was long before Mr. Worthington would consent to leave her behind. "Only a few months," pleaded she, "and then I shall be well and strong again; all I need is quiet." "The child is right," added Susan; "she is weary of the world, and wants rest. She shall dwell in my tabernacle, and share my pillow, and I will nourish and cherish her as my own flesh and blood. She will not be compelled to join our worship, or follow our rites, for we now look upon her as our guest, our daughter in love, but not our sister in the spirit of the Lord." Satisfied with this promise, Mr. Worthington blessed Grace, embraced her, and left her, bidding her be ready to return when the first leaf of autumn fell. She did not sit down and brood over the blighted hopes of her youth. She interested herself in all their neat and regular occupations, assisted them in gathering the leaves of the medicinal plants, in spreading them on pieces of pure white linen to dry; in collecting the garden seeds and shelling them out of their shrunken capsules, with as much readiness and grace as if she had never learned to touch the keys of the piano, or to school her steps by the dancing master's rule. Dressed in the plainest robes the fashions of the world allow, so as not to offend the austerity of their taste, with no other ornament than her shining hair, simply parted on her brow, she looked the incarnation of sweetness and humility; and Susan, seeing her dawning colour, believed she had found peace. "Thus will I live," thought Grace, "till Roland marries, and then if my adopted father claims me, I will try to find happiness in administering to his."

One evening, just as the sun had set, she returned from the garden, her white apron gathered up before her, full of damask rose leaves, while exercise and a bending position had given her cheeks a hue, warm as the twilight's glow, and calling eagerly to Susan, to present her offering for distillation, she crossed the threshold and stood before—Roland Gray. Electrified at the sight, she let go her apron, and the leaves fell in a rosy shower around her. "Grace, dear Grace!" exclaimed Roland, and both hands were clasped in his own. Now she had been called dear Grace, and sweet Grace, and pretty Grace, a thousand times in her life, but never in such a tone, and with such eyes looking down into her heart. It is easy to imagine why Roland came, and how eloquently he proved to Grace that he loved her better than all the world beside, and that he could not, and would not live without her. For a moment a flood of rapture, deep and overwhelming, flowed in upon her heart from the conviction that she was thus beloved; the next, a cold and freezing thought shot through it and turned the current to ice. Lucy—her threatened curse, her withering enmity, her own promise of never thinking of Roland, and of never revealing what had passed between Lucy and herself—all was remembered, and suddenly withdrawing her hand from his, she turned away and wept, without the power of self-control.

Roland was amazed. She had met his avowal with such a radiant blush and smile—such love and joy had just lighted up her modest eye, and now he witnessed every demonstration of the most passionate grief. "Oh, no!" she cried, "it never can be—I had forgotten it all; but I must not listen to you—oh, no!" and she repeated the interjection in such a plaintive accent, Roland was convinced there was no deception in her woe. In vain he entreated her for an explanation. She could not give any consistent with her promise to Lucy; she could only declare her unworthiness, her poor and perhaps disgraceful origin; and this only called forth a more impassioned assurance of his disinterested love, and his disdain of such scruples. He endeavoured to soothe and caress, till Grace felt her resolution and her truth fast yielding before his influence. If she could see Lucy, and be released from her rash promise, all might yet be well. Perhaps Lucy herself, finding her brother's pride had yielded to his love, would sanction the union. This idea once admitted, changed despair into hope. "Wait," said she, "till I return, and then, if the obstacle I fear no longer exists,"—she paused a moment, and her truth-telling lips constrained her to utter—"I shall be the happiest of human beings." Roland, now believing the obstacle to be Lucy, resolved she should not stand any longer in the way of their happiness, pressed for no further explanation. He had departed unknown to her, for he dreaded her violence. When Mr. Worthington returned alone, he dreaded Grace might sacrifice herself, as Lucy insinuated, and determined to bear her away ere it was too late. Grace poured into Susan's calm but sympathizing ear the story of her love and the obstacles that opposed it. Her single heart was too narrow to contain the fulness of her emotions. Susan applauded her integrity, but trembled at her idolatry. She reminded her of the mutability and uncertainty of all earthly things, and strengthened her in the resolution never to accept the vows of Roland, with the threatened vengeance of Lucy hanging over her love. "Oh, she will relent!" cried Grace; "Roland's sister cannot be such a monster." Had the chastened Susan witnessed her parting with Roland, she would have read a still more solemn lesson on the sinfulness of earthly affections; but she only saw the consequent sorrow, which she was too gentle to reprove.

The leaves of autumn soon fell, and then everything was changed in the destiny of Grace. Mr. Worthington claimed his child, and when Susan resigned her, her last words bid her pray for strength to keep her virtuous resolution.

It would be difficult to describe the passions that struggled for mastery in Lucy's breast, when she learned from her brother the part he had acted. Incapable of concealing them at first, and believing she had lost the affection of Roland, she no longer disguised the bitterness of her heart. She hated Grace still more, since she was conscious she had injured her, and when she, appealing in behalf of Roland's happiness as well as her own, entreated her to free her from her promise, she turned a deaf ear to the prayer, and claimed the fulfilment of her word, renewing the same fearful penalty—"Unless," she added, with a scornful smile, "you can prove your family equal to ours, and that your alliance will bring no disgrace."

Strange paradox of the human heart! Had Lucy taken scorpions into her bosom, she could not have suffered keener pangs than the consciousness of Roland's alienated affection caused her; yet she refused to bend her stubborn pride, and wrapped herself up in the sulliness of self-will, feeling a kind of stern joy that she had made others as wretched as herself.

Grace was standing in a lighted saloon, leaning on the arm of Mr.

Worthington, and an unwilling partaker of the gay scene. A tall and majestic-looking man passed the spot where she stood, whose appearance excited her interest and curiosity, for he was evidently a stranger in the throng of fashion and wealth, then gathered together. The suns of warmer climes had darkened his face, and added gloom to features of a fine and noble expression. As Grace lifted her mild gray eyes his somewhat stern countenance relaxed, and turning round he gazed earnestly in her face. Abashed by his scrutiny, she moved into another part of the room; still the tall stranger followed, with his melancholy eyes, pursuing her figure. Roland, never far from the object of his apparently hopeless devotion, now jealous and irritated, drew to her side. "Oh, Roland," said she, suddenly agitated by a new emotion, "there is something in that stranger's face, resembling this!"—and she drew from her bosom the miniature suspended from the golden chain. There was indeed a resemblance, only the face of the picture was younger, and the sable locks unbleached. The stranger observed the motions of Grace, and pressed forward, while the miniature was still open in her hand. "Pardon me, madam," said he, earnestly, "I must be pardoned—but allow me to look at that picture." Grace with trembling fingers unloosed the chain, and gave it into the stranger's hand. "It was once my mother's," said she, in a faltering voice, "and her name was Grace Goldman." "*Was*"—said the stranger—"and yet how could it be otherwise?—she was my sister—my only sister—and you"—he became too much agitated to finish the sentence, and entirely forgetting the throng that surrounded them, he clasped Grace to his bosom, as the living representative of his lost and lamented sister. Yes! in Mr. Maitland, the rich merchant, just returned from the East Indies, Grace had found an uncle, which proved her lineage to be such, that even the proud Lucy must acknowledge to be equal to her own. His sister, the mother of Grace, had eloped, when very young, with a handsome but profligate man, and being cast off by her parents, she was soon doomed to eat the bread of poverty, in consequence of her husband's excesses. Her brother, as soon as he learned her situation, offered to support her through life, declaring his intention never to marry, if she would leave her unprincipled husband. But she, in the strength of that passion which hopes all, believes all, and endures all, refused to leave the man she still loved, and whom she still trusted she might reclaim. Her brother, finding her wedded to her fate, left her with a purse of gold and his own miniature as a parting pledge of love, and departed for a foreign land. Forced to fly from the clamours of his creditors, Goldman removed his wife from place to place, till she was far out of the reach of former friends, when, plunging deeper and deeper in the gulf of inebriation, he left her to die, as we have described, of a broken heart. For himself, he died a drunkard's death by the wayside, and was buried by the same humane society that protected his orphan child. This circumstance had been concealed from Grace, nor did she learn it, till her subsequent visit to the Shaker village. Mr. Maitland, who had dwelt long in other lands, accumulating wealth, which his generous heart longed to share with the friends of his early youth, returned to mourn over the graves of his parents, and to seek in vain intelligence of his lost sister, till he saw in the crowd the lovely form of Grace, such as her ill-fated mother was in the days of her beauty and youth. Lucy could with sincerity offer her congratulations and welcome as a sister the niece of Mr. Maitland, though she had scorned the alliance of the humble Shaker girl. But she felt she was degraded in her eyes, and this was a punishment to her proud spirit, keener than the task-master's lash. Mr. Maitland's gratitude to Mr. Worthington was boundless as it was warm; but he longed to see the kind Samaritans, who had soothed his sister's dying hours and guarded her orphan child.

It was a happy day for Grace, when, as the bride of Roland, she accompanied her husband and her uncle to the home of her early youth. She introduced with pride the noble-looking stranger to all her true and single-hearted friends. "But here," said she, throwing her arms round Susan, "here is my mother and my mother's friend." Mr. Maitland would gladly have lavished wealth upon them, in remuneration for their cares, but they steadfastly refused his gifts, asserting they had only done their duty, and merited no reward. "Do unto others, as we have done towards yours," replied these followers of our Saviour's golden rule. "When you hear us reviled by the world, and our worship scorned, and our rites ridiculed, defend us if you can; and if one of the disciples of our creed should be in need of succour, be unto him as a brother, and we ask no more." "Dear Susan," said Grace, when the parting hour arrived, as she lingered behind to bid her farewell, "am I not the happiest of human beings?" "I bless God that you *are* happy, my child," answered Susan, laying her hand solemnly on her head—"and long, long may you remain so; but forget not, days of darkness may come, that the bridal garments may be changed for sackcloth, and ashes be scattered over the garlands of love. Remember then, O Grace, there is a refuge from the woes and vanities of the world, where the spirit may wait in peace for its everlasting home." Grace wept, but she smiled through her tears, and, seated once more at Roland's side, she felt as if darkness and sorrow could never be *her* portion.

A RAINY EVENING.
A SKETCH.

A pleasant little group was gathered round Uncle Ned's domestic hearth. He sat on one side of the fire-place, opposite Aunt Mary, who, with her book in her hand, watched the children seated at the table, some reading, others sewing, all occupied, but one, a child "of larger growth," a young lady, who, being a guest of the family, was suffered to indulge in the pleasure of idleness without reproof.

"Oh! I *love* a rainy evening," said little Ann, looking up from her book, and meeting her mother's smiling glance, "it is so nice to sit by a good fire and hear the rain pattering against the windows. Only I pity the poor people who have no house to cover them, to keep off the rain and the cold."

"And I love a rainy evening, too," cried George, a boy of about twelve. "I can study so much better. My thoughts stay at home, and don't keep rambling out after the bright moon and stars. My heart feels warmer, and I really believe I love everybody better than I do when the weather is fair."

Uncle Ned smiled, and gave the boy an approving pat on the shoulder. Every one smiled but the young lady, who with a languid, discontented air, now played with a pair of scissors, now turned over the leaves of a book, then, with an ill-suppressed yawn, leaned idly on her elbow, and looked into the fire.

"And what do you think of a rainy evening, Elizabeth?" asked Uncle Ned. "I should like to hear your opinion also."

"I think it over dull and uninteresting, indeed," answered she. "I always feel so stupid, I can hardly keep myself awake—one cannot go abroad, or hope to see company at home; and one gets so tired of seeing the same faces all the time. I cannot imagine what George and Ann see to admire so much in a disagreeable rainy evening like this."

"Supposing I tell you a story, to enliven you?" said Uncle Ned.

"Oh! yes, father, please tell us a story," exclaimed the children, simultaneously.

Little Ann was perched upon his knee as if by magic, and even Elizabeth moved her chair, as if excited to some degree of interest. George still held his book in his hand, but his bright eyes, sparkling with unusual animation, were riveted upon his uncle's face.

"I am going to tell you a story about a *rainy evening*," said Uncle Ned.

"Oh! that will be *so* pretty!" cried Ann, clapping her hands; but Elizabeth's countenance fell below zero. It was an ominous annunciation.

"Yes," continued Uncle Ned, "a rainy evening. But though clouds darker than those which now mantle the sky were lowering abroad, and the rain fell heavier and faster, the rainbow of my life was drawn most beautifully on those dark clouds, and its fair colours still shine most lovely on the sight. It is no longer, however, the bow of promise, but the realization of my fondest dreams."

George saw his uncle cast an expressive glance towards the handsome matron in the opposite corner, whose colour perceptibly heightened, and he could not forbear exclaiming—

"Ah! Aunt Mary is blushing. I understand uncle's metaphor. *She* is his rainbow, and he thinks life one long rainy day."

"Not exactly so. I mean your last conclusion. But don't interrupt me, my boy, and you shall hear a lesson, which, young as you are, I trust you will never forget. When I was a young man I was thought quite handsome—"

"Pa is as pretty as he can be, now," interrupted little Ann, passing her hand fondly over his manly cheek.

Uncle Ned was not displeased with the compliment, for he pressed her closer to him, while he continued—

"Well, when I was young I was of a gay spirit, and a great favourite in society. The young ladies liked me for a partner in the dance, at the chess-board, or the evening walk, and I had reason to think several of them would have made no objection to take me as a partner for life. Among all my young acquaintances, there was no one whose companionship was so pleasing as that of a maiden whose name was Mary. Now, there are a great many Marys in the world, so you must not take it for granted I mean your mother or aunt. At any rate, you must not look so significant till I have finished my story. Mary was a sweet and lovely girl—with a current of cheerfulness running through her disposition that made music as it flowed. It was an under current, however, always gentle, and kept within its legitimate channel; never overflowing into boisterous mirth or unmeaning levity. She was the only daughter of her mother, *and she a widow*. Mrs. Carlton, such was her mother's name, was in lowly circumstances, and Mary had none of the appliances of wealth and fashion to decorate her person, or gild her home. A very modest competency was all her portion, and she wished for nothing more. I have seen her, in a simple white dress, without a single ornament, unless it was a natural rose, transcend all the gaudy belles, who sought by the attractions of dress to win the admiration of the multitude. But, alas! for poor human nature. One of these dashing belles so fascinated my attention, that the gentle Mary was for a while forgotten. Theresa Vane was, indeed, a rare piece of mortal mechanism. Her figure was the perfection of beauty, and she moved as if strung upon wires, so elastic and springing were her gestures. I never saw such lustrous hair—it was perfectly black, and shone like burnished steel; and then such ringlets! How they waved and rippled down her beautiful neck! She dressed with the most exquisite taste, delicacy, and neatness, and whatever she wore assumed a peculiar grace and fitness, as if art loved to adorn what nature made so fair. But what charmed me most was, the sunshiny smile that was always waiting to light up her countenance. To be sure, she sometimes laughed a little too loud, but then her laugh was so musical, and her teeth so white, it was impossible to believe her guilty of rudeness, or want of grace. Often, when I saw her in the social circle, so brilliant and smiling, the life and charm of everything around her, I thought how happy the constant companionship of such a being would make me—what brightness she would impart to the fireside of home—what light, what joy, to the darkest scenes of existence!"

"Oh! uncle," interrupted George, laughing, "if I were Aunt Mary, I would not let you praise any other lady so warmly. You are so taken up with her beauty, you have forgotten all about the rainy evening."

Aunt Mary smiled, but it is more than probable that George really touched one of the hidden springs of her woman's heart, for she looked down, and said nothing.

"Don't be impatient," said Uncle Ned, "and you shall not be cheated out of your story. I began it for Elizabeth's sake, rather than yours, and I see she is wide awake. She thinks I was by this time more than half in love with Theresa Vane, and she thinks more than half right. There had been a great many parties of pleasure, riding parties, sailing parties, and talking parties; and summer slipped by, almost unconsciously. At length the autumnal equinox approached, and gathering clouds, north-eastern gales, and drizzling rains, succeeded to the soft breezes, mellow skies, and glowing sunsets, peculiar to that beautiful season. For two or three days I was confined within doors by the continuous rains, and I am sorry to confess it, but the blue devils actually got complete possession of me—one strided upon my nose, another danced on the top of my head, one pinched my ear, and another turned somersets on my chin. You laugh, little Nanny; but they are terrible creatures, these blue gentlemen, and I could not endure them any longer. So the third rainy evening, I put on my overcoat, buttoned it up to my chin, and taking my umbrella in my hand, set out in the direction of Mrs. Vane's. 'Here,' thought I, as my fingers pressed the latch, 'I shall find the moonlight smile, that will illumine the darkness of my night—the dull vapours will disperse before her radiant glance, and this interminable equinoctial storm be transformed into a mere vernal shower, melting away in sunbeams in her presence.' My gentle knock not being apparently heard, I stepped into the ante-room, set down my umbrella, took off my drenched overcoat, arranged my hair in the most graceful manner, and, claiming a privilege to which, perhaps, I had no legitimate right, opened the door of the family sitting-room, and found myself in the presence of the beautiful Theresa—"

Here Uncle Ned made a provoking pause.

"Pray, go on." "How was she dressed?" "And was she glad to see you?" assailed him on every side.

"How was she dressed?" repeated he. "I am not very well skilled in the technicalities of a lady's wardrobe, but I can give you the general impression of her personal appearance. In the first place, there was a jumping up and an off-hand sliding step towards an opposite door, as I entered; but a disobliging chair was in the way, and I was making my lowest bow, before she found an opportunity of disappearing. Confused and mortified, she scarcely returned my salutation, while Mrs. Vane offered me a chair, and expressed, in somewhat dubious terms, their gratification at such an unexpected pleasure. I have no doubt Theresa wished me at the bottom of the Frozen Ocean, if I might judge by the freezing glances she shot at me through her long lashes. She sat uneasily in her chair, trying to conceal her slipshod shoes, and furtively arranging her dress about the shoulders and waist. It was a most rebellious subject, for the body and skirt were at open warfare, refusing to have any communion with each other. Where was the graceful shape I had so much admired? In vain I sought its exquisite outlines in the folds of that loose, slovenly robe. Where were those glistening ringlets and burnished locks that had so lately rivalled the tresses of Medusa? Her hair was put in tangled bunches behind her ears, and tucked up behind in a kind of Gordian knot, which would have required the sword of an Alexander to untie. Her frock was a soiled and dingy silk, with trimmings of sallow blonde, and a faded fancy handkerchief was thrown over one shoulder.

"'You have caught me completely *en déshabille*,' said she, recovering partially from her embarrassment; 'but the evening was so rainy, and no one but mother and myself, I never dreamed of such an exhibition of gallantry as this.'

"She could not disguise her vexation, with all her efforts to conceal it, and Mrs. Vane evidently shared her daughter's chagrin. I was wicked enough to enjoy their confusion, and never appeared more at my ease, or played the agreeable with more signal success. I was disenchanted at once, and my mind revelled in its recovered freedom. My goddess had fallen from the pedestal on which my imagination had enthroned her, despoiled of the beautiful drapery which had imparted to her such ideal loveliness. I knew that I was a favourite in the family, for I was wealthy and independent, and perhaps of all Theresa's admirers what the world would call the best match. I maliciously asked her to play on the piano, but she made a thousand excuses, studiously keeping back the true reason, her disordered attire. I asked her to play a game of chess, but 'she had a headache; she was too stupid; she never *could* do anything on a *rainy evening.*'

"At length I took my leave, inwardly blessing the moving spirit which had led me abroad that night, that the spell which had so long enthralled my senses might be broken. Theresa called up one of her lambent smiles as I bade her adieu.

"'Never call again on a rainy evening,' said she, sportively; 'I am always so wretchedly dull. I believe I was born to live among the sunbeams, the moonlight, and the stars. Clouds will never do for me.'

"'Amen,' I silently responded, as I closed the door. While I was putting on my coat, I overheard, without the smallest intention of listening, a passionate exclamation from Theresa.

"'Good heavens, mother! was there ever anything so unlucky? I never thought of seeing my neighbour's *dog* to-night. If I have not been completely caught!'

"'I hope you will mind my advice next time,' replied her mother, in a grieved tone. 'I told you not to sit down in that slovenly dress. I have no doubt you have lost him for ever.'

"Here I made good my retreat, not wishing to enter the *penetralia* of family secrets.

"The rain still continued unabated, but my social feelings were very far from being damped. I had the curiosity to make another experiment. The evening was not very far advanced, and as I turned from Mrs. Vane's fashionable mansion, I saw a modest light glimmering in the distance, and I hailed it as the shipwrecked mariner hails the star that guides him o'er ocean's foam to the home he has left behind. Though I was gay and young, and a passionate admirer of beauty, I had very exalted ideas of domestic felicity. I knew that there was many a rainy day in life, and I thought the companion who was born alone for sunbeams and moonlight, would not aid me to dissipate their gloom. I had, moreover, a shrewd suspicion that the daughter who thought it a sufficient excuse for shameful personal neglect, that there was no one present but her *mother*, would, as a wife, be equally regardless of a *husband's* presence. While I pursued these reflections, my feet involuntarily drew nearer and more near to the light, which had been the lodestone of my opening manhood. I had continued to meet Mary in the gay circles I frequented, but I had lately become almost a stranger to her home. 'Shall I be a welcome guest?' said I to myself, as I crossed the threshold. 'Shall I find her *en déshabille*, likewise, and discover that feminine beauty and grace are incompatible with a rainy evening?' I heard a sweet voice reading aloud as I opened the door, and I knew it was the voice which was once music to my ears. Mary rose at my entrance, laying her book quietly on the table, and greeted me with a modest grace and self-possession peculiar to herself. She looked surprised, a little embarrassed, but very far from being displeased. She made no allusion to my estrangement or neglect; expressed no astonishment at my untimely visit, nor once hinted that, being alone with her mother, and not anticipating visiters, she thought it unnecessary to wear the habiliments of a *lady*. Never, in my life, had I seen her look so lovely. Her dress was perfectly plain, but every fold was arranged by the hand of the Graces. Her dark-brown hair, which had a natural wave in it, now uncurled by the dampness, was put back in smooth ringlets from her brow, revealing a face which did not consider its beauty wasted because a mother's eye alone rested on its bloom. A beautiful cluster of autumnal roses, placed in a glass vase on the table, perfumed the apartment, and a bright blaze on the hearth diffused a spirit of cheerfulness around, while it relieved the atmosphere of its excessive moisture. Mrs. Carlton was an invalid, and suffered also from an inflammation of the eyes. Mary had been reading aloud to her from her favourite book. What do you think it was? It was a very old-fashioned one, indeed. No other than the Bible. And Mary was not ashamed to have such a fashionable young gentleman as I then was to see what her occupation had been. What a contrast to the scene I had just quitted! How I loathed myself for the infatuation which had led me to prefer the artificial graces of a belle to this pure child of nature! I drew my chair to the table, and entreated that they would not look upon me as a stranger, but as a friend, anxious to be restored to the forfeited privileges of an old acquaintance. I was understood in a moment, and, without a single reproach, was admitted again to confidence and familiarity. The hours I had wasted with Theresa seemed a kind of mesmeric slumber, a blank in my existence, or, at least, a feverish dream. 'What do you think of a rainy evening, Mary?' asked I, before I left her.

"'I love it of all things,' replied she, with animation. 'There is something so home-drawing, so heart-knitting, in its influence. The dependencies which bind us to the world seem withdrawn; and, retiring within ourselves, we learn more of the deep mysteries of our own being.'

"Mary's soul beamed from her eye as it turned, with a transient obliquity, towards heaven. She paused, as if fearful of unsealing the fountains of her heart. I said that Mrs. Carlton was an invalid, and consequently retired early to her chamber; but I lingered till a late hour, nor did I go till I had made a full confession of my folly, repentance, and awakened love; and, as Mary did not shut the door in my face, you may imagine she was not sorely displeased."

"Ah! I know who Mary was. I knew all the time," exclaimed George, looking archly at Aunt Mary. A bright tear, which at that moment fell into her lap, showed that though a silent, she was no uninterested auditor.

"You haven't done, father?" said little Ann, in a disappointed tone; "I thought you were going to tell a story. You have been talking about yourself all the time."

"I have been something of an egotist, to be sure, my little girl, but I wanted to show my dear young friend here how much might depend upon a rainy evening. Life is not made all of sunshine. The happiest and most prosperous must have their seasons of gloom and darkness, and woe be to those from whose souls no rays of brightness emanate to gild those darkened hours. I bless the God of the rain as well as the sunshine. I can read His mercy and His love as well in the tempest, whose wings obscure the visible glories of His creation, as in the splendour of the rising sun, or the soft dews that descend after his setting radiance. I began with a metaphor. I said a rainbow was drawn on the clouds that lowered on that eventful day, and that it still continued to shine with undiminished beauty. Woman, my children, was sent by God to be the rainbow of man's darker destiny. From the glowing red, emblematic of that love which warms and gladdens his existence, to the violet melting into the blue of heaven, symbolical of the faith which links him to a purer world, her blending virtues, mingling with each other in beautiful harmony, are a token of God's mercy here, and an earnest of future blessings in those regions where no *rainy evenings* ever come to obscure the brightness of eternal day."

THREE SCENES IN THE LIFE OF A BELLE.

There was a rushing to and fro in the chamber of Ellen Loring, a tread of hurrying feet, a mingled hum of voices, an opening and shutting of doors, as if some event of overwhelming importance agitated the feelings, and moved the frames of every individual in the house. A stranger, in the apartment below, might have imagined an individual was dying, and that all were gathering round to offer the appliances of love and sympathy. But Ellen Loring, the object of all this commotion, was in all the bloom and beauty of health. She sat in a low chair and in front of a large mirror, half-arrayed in the habiliments of the ball-room, her head glowing with flowers, and streaming with ringlets, her feet encased in silk cobweb and white satin, her face flushed with excitement, her waist compressed into the smallest possible compass, while the strongest fingers the household could supply, were drawing together the last reluctant hook and eye, which fastened the rich and airy mixture of satin blonde, that fell in redundant folds round her slender person. "I am afraid, Ellen, your dress is *rather* too tight," said Mrs. Loring, who was superintending the process with a keen and experienced eye; "you had better not wear it, it may give you a consumption." "Ridiculous!" exclaimed Ellen, "it feels perfectly loose and comfortable; I am sure it fits delightfully. Look, Agnes," addressing a weary-looking girl who had been standing more than half an hour over her, arranging her hair in the most fashionable style. "Look, Agnes, is it not beautiful?"

"Very beautiful," answered Agnes; "but I think it would look much better if it were not so very low, and the night is so cold, I am sure you will suffer without something thrown over your shoulders. These pearl beads are very ornamental, but they will not give warmth," lifting them up as she spoke, from a neck that "rivalled their whiteness." Ellen burst into a scornful laugh, and declared she would rather catch her death-cold, than look so old-fashioned and old-womanish. Mrs. Loring here interposed, and insisted that Ellen should wear a shawl into the ball-room, and to be sure to put it around her when she was not dancing, "for you must remember," added she, "the dreadful cough you had last winter; when you caught cold, I was really apprehensive of a consumption."

"I do think, mother, you must be haunted by the ghost of consumption. Everything you say begins and ends with *consumption—I* am not afraid of the ghost, or the reality, while such roses as these bloom on my cheeks, and such elastic limbs as these bear me through the dance."

Mrs. Loring looked with admiring fondness on her daughter, as she danced gayly before the looking-glass, called her a "wild, thoughtless thing," and thought it would be indeed a pity to muffle such a beautiful neck in a clumsy 'kerchief. The carriage was announced, and Agnes was despatched in a hundred directions for the embroidered handkerchief, the scented gloves, and all the *et ceteras*, which crowd on the memory at the last moment. Agnes followed the retreating form of Ellen with a long and wistful gaze, then turned with a sigh to collect the scattered articles of finery that strewed the room. "Happy Ellen!" said she to herself, "happy, beautiful Ellen! favoured by nature and fortune. Every desire of her heart is gratified. She moves but to be admired, flattered, and caressed. While I, a poor, dependent relative, am compelled to administer to her vanity and wait upon her caprices—oh! if I were only rich and beautiful like Ellen! I would willingly walk over burning ploughshares to obtain the happiness that is in store for her to-night."

While the repining Agnes followed Ellen, in imagination, to scenes which appeared to her fancy like the dazzling pictures described in the Arabian Nights, let us enter the ball-room and follow the footsteps of her, whose favoured lot led her through the enchanted land. The hall was brilliantly lighted, the music was of the most animating kind, airy forms floated on the gaze, most elaborately and elegantly adorned, and in the midst of these Ellen shone transcendent. For a while, her enjoyment realized even the dreams of Agnes. Conscious of being admired, she glided through the dance, gracefully holding her flowing drapery, smiling, blushing, coquetting and flirting. Compliments were breathed continually into her ears. She was compared to the sylphs, the graces, the muses, the houris, and even to the angels that inhabit the celestial city. Yes; this daughter of fashion, this devotee of pleasure, this vain and thoughtless being, who lived without God in the world, was told by flattering lips, that she resembled those pure and glorified spirits which surround the throne of the Most High, and sing the everlasting song of Moses and the Lamb—and she believed it. Perhaps some may assert that the daughters of fashion are not always forgetful of their God, for they are often heard to call upon his great and holy name, in a moment of sudden astonishment or passion, and were a saint to witness their uplifted eyes and clasped hands, he might deem them wrapt in an ecstasy of devotion.

Ellen, in the midst of almost universal homage, began to feel dissatisfied and weary. There was one who had been in the train of her admirers, himself the star of fashion, who was evidently offering incense at a new shrine. A fair young stranger, who seemed a novice in the splendid scene, drew him from her side, and from that moment the adulation of others ceased to charm. She danced more gayly, she laughed more loudly, to conceal the mortification and envy that was spreading through her heart; but the triumph, the joy was over.

She began to feel a thousand inconveniences, of whose existence she seemed previously unconscious. Her feet ached from the lightness of her slippers, her respiration was difficult from the tightness of her dress; she was glad when the hour of her departure arrived. Warm from the exercise of the dance, and panting from fatigue, she stood a few moments on the pavement, waiting for some obstructions to be removed in the way of the carriage. The ground was covered with a sheet of snow, which had fallen during the evening, and made a chill bed for her feet, so ill defended from the inclement season. The night air blew damp and cold on her neck and shoulders, for her cloak was thrown loosely around her, that her beauty might not be entirely veiled, till the gaze of admiration was withdrawn.

Agnes sat by the lonely fireside, waiting for the return of Ellen. For a while she kept up a cheerful blaze, and as she heard the gust sweep by the windows, it reminded her that Ellen would probably come in shivering with cold and reproach her, if she did not find a glowing hearth to welcome her. She applied fresh fuel, till, lulled by the monotonous sound of the wind, she fell asleep in her chair, nor waked till the voice of Ellen roused her from her slumbers. A few dull embers were all that was left of the fire, the candle gleamed faintly beneath a long, gloomy wick—everything looked cold and comfortless. It was long before poor Agnes could recall the cheering warmth. In the mean time, Ellen poured upon her a torrent of reproaches, and tossing her cloak on a chair, declared she would never go to another ball as long as she lived—she had been tired *to death*, chilled *to death*, and now to be vexed *to death*, by such a stupid, selfish creature as Agnes. It was too much for human nature to endure. Agnes bore it all in silence, for she ate the bread of dependence, and dared not express the bitter feelings that rose to her lips. But she no longer said in her heart "happy, beautiful Ellen;" she wished her admirers could see her as she then did, and be disenchanted.

"Take off this horrid dress," cried Ellen, pulling the roses from her hair, now uncurled by the damp, and hanging in long straight tresses over her face. What a contrast did she now present to the brilliant figure which had left the chamber a few hours before! Her cheeks were pale, her eyes heavy, her limbs relaxed, her buoyant spirits gone. The terrible misfortune of not having reigned an unrivalled *belle*, completely overwhelmed her! He, whose admiration she most prized, had devoted himself to another, and she hated the fair, unconscious stranger, who had attracted him from his allegiance. The costly dress which the mantuamaker had sat up all night to complete, was thrown aside as a worthless rag; her flowers were scattered on the floor; every article of her dress bore witness to her ill-humour.

"I cannot get warm," said she; "I believe I *have* caught my death-cold;" and throwing her still shivering limbs on the bed, she told Agnes to bury her in blankets, and then let her sleep. Can we suppose that guardian angels hovered over the couch, and watched the slumbers of this youthful beauty? There was no hallowed spot in her chamber, where she was accustomed to kneel in penitence, gratitude, and adoration, before the King of Kings and Lord of Lords. Perhaps, when a mere child, she had been taught to repeat the Lord's Prayer at her nurse's knee, but never had her heart ascended unto Him, who created her for his glory, and breathed into her frame a portion of his own immortal Spirit. She had been educated solely for the circles of fashion, to glitter and be admired—to dance, to sing, to dress, to talk, and that was all. She knew that she must one day die, and when the bell tolled, and the long funeral darkened the way, she was reluctantly reminded of her own mortality. But she banished the dreadful and mysterious thought, as one with which youth, beauty, and health had nothing to do, and as suited only to the infirmities of age, and the agonies of disease. As for the judgment beyond the grave, that scene of indescribable grandeur, when every created being must stand before the presence of uncreated glory, "to give an account of the deeds done in the body," she deemed it shocking and sacrilegious to think of a subject so awful; and, to do her justice, she never heard it mentioned except from the pulpit (for there are fashionable churches, and Ellen was the belle of the church as well as of the ball-room). Thus living in practical atheism, labouring to bring every thought and feeling in subjection to the bondage of fashion, endeavouring to annihilate the great principle of immortality struggling within her, Ellen Loring was as much the slave of vice as the votary of pleasure. Like the king of Babylon, who took the golden vessels from the temple of the Lord, and desecrated them at his unhallowed banquet, she had robbed her *soul*, that temple of the living God, of its sacred treasures, and appropriated them to the revelries of life. But the hour was approaching, when the invisible angel of conscience was to write on the walls of memory those mystic characters which a greater than Daniel alone can interpret.

It was the afternoon of a mild summer's day, a lovely, smiling, joyous summer day, when two female figures were seen slowly walking along a shaded path, that led from a neat white cottage towards a neighbouring grove. One was beautiful, and both were young, but the beautiful one was so pale and languid, so fragile and fading, it was impossible to behold her without the deepest commiseration. She moved listlessly on, leaning on the arm of her less fair, but healthier companion, apparently insensible of the sweet and glowing scenery around her. The birds sung in melodious concert, from every green bough, but their music could not gladden her ear; the air played softly through her heavy locks, but awaked no elastic spring in her once bounding

106

spirits. It was the late blooming Ellen Loring, who, according to the advice of her physician, was inhaling the country air, to see if it could not impart an invigorating influence. She had never recovered from the deadly chill occasioned by her exposure, the night of the ball, when she stood with her thin slippers and uncovered neck in the snow and the blast, in all the "madness of superfluous health." It was said she had caught a "dreadful cold," which the warm season would undoubtedly relieve, and when the summer came, and her cough continued with unabated violence, and her flesh and her strength wasted, she was sent into the country, assured that a change of air and daily exercise would infallibly restore her. The fearful word *consumption*, which in the days of Ellen's health was so often on the mother's lips, was never mentioned now; and whenever friends inquired after Ellen, she always told them, "she had caught a bad cold, which hung on a long time, but that she was so young, and had so fine a constitution, she did not apprehend any danger." Ellen was very unwilling to follow the prescriptions of her medical friend. She left the city with great reluctance, dreading the loneliness of a country life. Agnes accompanied her, on whom was imposed the difficult task of amusing and cheering the invalid, and of beguiling her of every sense of her danger. "Be sure," said Mrs. Loring, when she gave her parting injunctions to Agnes, "that you do not suffer her to be alone: there is nothing so disadvantageous to a sick person as to brood over their own thoughts. It always occasions low spirits. I have put up a large supply of novels, and when she is tired of reading herself, you must read to her, or sing to her, or amuse her in every possible manner. If she should be very ill, you must send for me immediately, but I have no doubt that in a few weeks she will be as well as ever."

Poor Agnes sometimes was tempted to sink under the weary burden of her cares. She wondered she had ever thought it a task to array her for the ball-room, or to wait her return at the midnight-hour. But she no longer envied her, for Ellen pale and faded, and dejected, was a very different object from Ellen triumphant in beauty and bloom. The kind lady with whom they boarded, had had a rustic seat constructed under the trees, in the above-mentioned grove, for the accommodation of the invalid. As they now approached it, they found it already occupied by a gentleman, who was so intently reading he did not seem aware of their vicinity. They were about to retire, when lifting his eyes, he rose, and with a benignant countenance, requested them to be seated. Ellen was exhausted from the exercise of her walk; and, as the stranger was past the meridian of life, she did not hesitate to accept his offer, at the same time thanking him for his courtesy. His mild, yet serious eyes, rested on her face, with a look of extreme commiseration, as with a deep sigh of fatigue she leaned on the shoulder of Agnes, while the hectic flush flitting over her cheek, betrayed the feverish current that was flowing in her veins.

"You seem an invalid, my dear young lady," said he, so kindly and respectfully, it was impossible to be offended with the freedom of the address; "I trust you find there is a balm in Gilead, a heavenly Physician near."

Ellen gave him a glance of unspeakable astonishment, and coldly answered, "I have a severe cold, sir—nothing more."

The dry, continuous cough that succeeded, was a fearful commentary upon her words. The stranger seemed one not easily repulsed, and one, too, who had conceived a sudden and irrepressible interest in his young companions. Agnes, in arranging Ellen's scarf, dropped a book from her hand, which he stooped to raise, and as his eye glanced on the title, the gravity of his countenance deepened. It was one of ——'s last works, in which that master of glowing language and impassioned images, has thrown his most powerful spell around the senses of the reader, and dazzled and bewildered his perceptions of right and wrong.

"Suffer me to ask you, young lady," said he, laying down the book, with a sigh, "if you find in these pages instruction, consolation, or support? anything that as a rational being you ought to seek, as a moral one to approve, as an immortal one to desire?"

Ellen was roused to a portion of her former animation, by this attack upon her favourite author; and, in language warm as his from whom she drew her inspiration, she defended his sentiments and exalted his genius—she spoke of his godlike mind, when the stranger entreated her to forbear, in words of supplication, but in accents of command.

"Draw not a similitude," said he, "between a holy God, and a being who has perverted the noblest powers that God has given. Bear with me a little while, and I will show you what is truly godlike, a book as far transcending the productions of him you so much admire, as the rays of the sun excel in glory the wan light of a taper."

Then, taking from his bosom the volume which had excited the curiosity of Ellen, on account of its apparent fascination, and seating himself by her side, he unfolded its sacred pages. She caught a glimpse of the golden letters on the binding, and drew back with a feeling of superstitious dread. It seemed to her, that he was about to read her death-warrant, and she involuntarily put out her hand, with a repulsive motion. Without appearing to regard it, he looked upon her with sweet and solemn countenance, while he repeated this passage, from a bard who had drank of the waters of a holier fountain than Grecian poets ever knew:

This book, this holy book, on every line

Marked with the seal of high divinity,

On every leaf bedewed with drops of love

Divine, and with the eternal heraldry

And signature of God Almighty stamped

From first to last; this ray of sacred light,

This lamp, from off the everlasting throne,

Mercy took down, and in the night of time,

Stood, casting on the dark her gracious bow;

And evermore, beseeching men, with tears

And earnest sighs, to read, believe, and live."

Ellen listened with indescribable awe. There was a power and sensibility in his accent, a depth of expression in his occasional upturned glance, that impressed and affected her as she had never been before.

"Forgive me," said he, "if, as a stranger, I seem intrusive; but I look upon every son and daughter of Adam, with the tenderness of a brother, and upon whom the Almighty has laid his chastening hand, with feelings of peculiar interest. If I were wandering through a barren wilderness, and found a fountain of living water, and suffered my fellow-pilgrim to slake his thirst at the noisome pool by the wayside, without calling him to drink of the pure stream, would he not have reason to upbraid me for my selfishness? Oh! doubly selfish then should I be, if, after tasting the waters of everlasting life, for ever flowing from this blessed Book, I should not seek to draw you from the polluted sources in which you vainly endeavour to quench the thirst of an immortal spirit. Dear young fellow-traveller to eternity, suffer me to lend you a guiding hand."

Ellen Loring, who had been famed in the circles of fashion for her ready wit and brilliant repartee, found no words in which to reply to this affectionate and solemn appeal. She turned aside her head, to hide the tears which she could no longer repress from flowing down her cheeks. As the polished, but darkened Athenians, when Paul, standing on Mars Hill, explained to them "that unknown God, whom they ignorantly worshipped," trembled before an eloquence they could not comprehend, she was oppressed by a power she could not define. Agnes, who began to be alarmed at the consequences of this agitation, and who saw in perspective Mrs. Loring's displeasure and reproaches, here whispered Ellen it was time to return, and Ellen, glad to be released from an influence to which she was constrained to bow, obeyed the signal. Their new friend rose also; "I cannot but believe," said he, "that this meeting is providential. It seems to me that heaven directed my steps hither, that I might lead you to those green pastures and still waters where the Shepherd of Israel gathers his flock. You are both young, but there is one of you whose cheek is pale, and whose saddened glance tells a touching history of the vanity of all earthly things. Take this blessed volume, and substitute it for the one you now hold, and believe me you will find in it an inexhaustible supply of entertainment and delight, a perennial spring of light, and love, and joy. You will find it an unerring guide in life, and a torch to illumine the dark valley of the shadow of death. Farewell—the blessing of Israel's God be yours!"

He placed the book in the hand of Agnes, and turned in a different path. They walked home in silence. Neither expressed to the other the thoughts that filled the bosom of each. Had an angel from heaven come down and met them in the grove, the interview could hardly have had a more solemnizing influence. It was the first time they had ever been individually addressed as immortal beings, the first time they had been personally reminded that they were pilgrims of earth, and doomed to be dwellers of the tomb. The voice of the stranger still rung in their ears, deep and mellow as the sound of the church-going bell. Those warning accents, they could not forget them, for there was an echo in their own hearts, and an answer too, affirming the truth of what he uttered. That night, when Ellen, unusually exhausted, reclined on her restless couch, she suddenly asked Agnes to read her something from *that book*, so mysteriously given. It was the first time she had addressed her, since their return, and there was something startling in the sound of her voice, it was so altered. There was humility in the tone, that usually breathed pride or discontent. Agnes sat down, and turned the leaves with a trembling hand.

"What shall I read? where shall I commence?" asked she, fearful and irresolute, in utter ignorance of its hallowed contents.

"Alas! I know not," replied Ellen, then raising herself on her elbow, with a wild and earnest look, "see if you can find where it speaks of that dark valley, of which he told—the dark valley of death."

By one of those unexpected coincidences which sometimes occur, Agnes at that moment opened at the twenty-third Psalm, and the verse containing this sublime allusion met her eye. She read aloud—"Though I walk through the valley of the shadow of death, I will fear no evil, for thou art with me—thy rod and thy staff, they comfort me."

"Strange," repeated Ellen, and making a motion for her to continue, Agnes read the remainder of that beautiful Psalm, and the two succeeding ones, before she paused. Dark as was their understanding with regard to spiritual things, and deep as was their ignorance, they were yet capable of taking in some faint glimpses of the glory of the Lord, pervading these strains of inspiration. Agnes was a pleasing reader, and her voice, now modulated by new emotions, was peculiarly impressive. Ellen repeated again and again to herself, after Agnes had ceased, "Who is this King of glory? The Lord strong and mighty?" She had never thought of God, but as of a Being dreadful in power, avenging in his judgments, and awful in his mystery. She had remembered him only in the whirlwind and the storm, the lightning and the thunder, never in the still small voice. She had thought of death, but it was of the winding sheet and the dark coffin lid, and the lonely grave—her fears had rested there, on the shuddering brink of decaying mortality. Oh! as she lay awake during the long watches of that night, and conscience, aroused from its deadly lethargy, entered the silent chambers of memory and waked the slumbering shadows of the past—how cheerless, how dark was the retrospect! Far as the eye of memory could revert, she could read nothing but *vanity, vanity*! A wide, wide blank, on which a spectral hand was writing *vanity*, and something told her, too, that that same hand would ere long write this great moral of life on her mouldering ashes. She cast her fearful gaze upon the future, but recoiled in shivering dread, from the vast illimitable abyss that darkened before her. No ray of hope illumined the dread immense. The Star of Bethlehem had never yet shed its holy beams on the horoscope of her destiny; not that its beams had ever ceased to shine, since that memorable night when, following its silvery pathway in the heavens, the wise men of the East were guided to the cradle of the infant Redeemer, to offer their adoration at his feet; but her eyes had never looked beyond the clouds of time, and in its high and pure resplendence it had shone in vain for her.

"I will seek him to-morrow, this holy man," said she, as hour after hour she lay gazing, through her curtains, on the starry depths of night, "and ask him to enlighten and direct me."

The morrow came, but Ellen was not able to take her accustomed walk. For several days she was confined from debility to her own room, and had ample leisure to continue the great work of self-examination. As soon as she was permitted to go into the open air, she sought her wonted retreat, and it was with feelings of mingled joy and dread, she recognised the stranger, apparently waiting their approach. This truly good man, though a stranger to them, was well known in the neighbourhood for his deeds of charity and labours of love. His name was M——, and as there was no mystery in his character or life, he may be here introduced to the reader, that the appellation of stranger may no longer be necessary. He greeted them both with even more than his former kindness, and noticed with pain the increased debility of

Ellen. He saw, too, from her restless glance, that her soul was disquieted within her.

"Oh, sir," said Ellen, mournfully, "you promised me joy, and you have given me wretchedness."

"My daughter," replied Mr. M——, "before the sick found healing virtue in the waters at Bethesda, an angel came down and troubled the stillness of the pool."

Then, at her own request, he sat down by her side, and endeavoured to explain to her the grand yet simple truths of Christianity. And beginning with the law and the prophets, he carried her with him to the mount that burned with fire and thick smoke, where the Almighty, descending in shrouded majesty, proclaimed his will to a trembling world, in thunder and lightning and flame; he led her on with him, through the wilderness, pointing out the smitten rock, the descending manna, the brazen serpent, and all the miraculous manifestations of God's love to his chosen people; then, taking up the lofty strains of prophecy, from the melodious harp of David to the sublimer lyre of Isaiah, he shadowed forth the promised Messiah. In more persuasive accents he dwelt on the fulfilment of those wondrous prophecies. Gently, solemnly he guided her on, from the manger to the cross, unfolding as he went the glorious mysteries of redemption, the depth, the grandeur, the extent, and the exaltation of a Saviour's love. Ellen listened and wept. She felt as if she could have listened for ever. At one moment she was oppressed by the greatness of the theme, at another melted by its tenderness. Those who from infancy have been accustomed to hear these divine truths explained, who from their earliest years have surrounded the household altar, and daily read God's holy word, can have no conception of the overpowering emotions of Ellen and Agnes; neither can they, whose infant glances have taken in the visible glories of creation, comprehend the rapture and amazement of those who, being born blind, are made in after years to see.

From this hour Ellen and Agnes became the willing pupils of Mr. M——, in the most interesting study in the universe; but it is with Ellen the reader is supposed most strongly to sympathize; the feelings of Agnes may be inferred from her going hand in hand with her invalid friend. Ellen lingered in the country till the golden leaves of autumn began to strew the ground, and its chill gales to sigh through the grove. What progress she made during this time in the lore of heaven, under the teachings and prayers of her beloved instructor, may be gathered from *another, and the last scene*, through which this once glittering belle was destined to pass.

***

The chamber in which Ellen Loring was first presented to the reader, surrounded by the paraphernalia of the ball-room, was once more lighted— but what a change now met the eye! She, who then sat before the mirror to be arrayed in the adornments of fashion, whose vain eye gazed with unrepressed admiration on her own loveliness, and who laughed to scorn the apprehensions of her fatally indulgent mother, now lay pale and emaciated on her couch. No roses now bloomed in her damp, unbraided locks, no decorating pearl surrounded her wan neck, no sparkling ray of anticipated triumph flashed from her sunken eye. Pride, vanity, vainglory, strength, beauty—all were fled.

Come hither, ye daughters of pleasure, ye who live alone for the fleeting joys of sense, who give to the world the homage that God requires, and waste in the pursuits of time the energies given for eternity, and look upon a scene through which you must one day pass! There is more eloquence in one dying bed, than Grecian or Roman orator ever uttered.

The dim eyes of Ellen turned towards the door, with a wistful glance. "I fear it will be too late," said she; "mother, if he should not come before I die—"

"Die!" almost shrieked Mrs. Loring; "you are not going to die, Ellen. Do not talk so frightfully. You will be better soon—Agnes, bathe her temples. She is only faint."

"No, mother," answered Ellen, and her voice was surprisingly clear in its tones, "I feel the truth of what I utter, here," laying her wasted hand on her breast, as she spoke. "I did hope that I might live to hear once more the voice of him who taught me the way of salvation, and revealed to my benighted mind the God who created, the Saviour who redeemed me, that I might breathe out to him my parting blessing, and hear his hallowed prayer rise over my dying bed. But oh, my dear mother, it is for your sake, more than mine, I yearn for his presence—I looked to him to comfort you, when I am gone." Mrs. Loring here burst into a violent paroxysm of tears, and wrung her hands in uncontrollable agony.

"Oh! I cannot give thee up," she again and again repeated, "my beautiful Ellen, my good, my beautiful child!"

Mournfully, painfully did these exclamations fall on the chastened ears of the dying Ellen.

"Recall not the image of departed beauty, oh my mother! I made it my idol, and my heavenly Father, in infinite mercy, consumed it with the breath of his mouth. Speak not of goodness—my life has been one long act of sin and ingratitude. I can look back upon nothing but wasted mercies, neglected opportunities, and perverted talents. But blessed be God, since I have been led in penitence and faith to the feet of a crucified Saviour, I dare to believe that my sins are forgiven, and that my trembling spirit will soon find rest in the bosom of Him, who lived to instruct and died to redeem me."

Ellen paused, for difficult breathing had often impeded her utterance; but her prayerful eyes, raised to heaven, told the intercourse her soul was holding with One "whom not having seen she loved, but in whom believing, she rejoiced with joy unspeakable and full of glory." At this moment, the door softly opened, and the gentle footsteps of him, whom on earth she most longed to behold, entered the chamber. As she caught a glimpse of that benign, that venerated countenance, she felt a glow of happiness pervading her being, of which she thought her waning life almost incapable. She clasped her feeble hands together, and exclaimed, "Oh! Mr. M——." It was all she could utter, for tears, whose fountains she had thought dried for ever, gushed into her eyes and rolled down her pallid cheeks. Mr. M—— took one of her cold hands in his, and looked upon her, for a time, without speaking.

"My daughter," at length he said, and he did not speak without much emotion, "do you find the hand of God laid heavy upon your soul, or is it gentle, even as a father's hand?"

"Gentle, most gentle," she answered. "Oh! blessed, for ever blessed be the hour that sent you, heaven-directed, to guide the wanderer in the paths of peace! Had it not been for you, I should now be trembling on the verge of a dark eternity, without one ray to illumine the unfathomable abyss. Pray for me once more, my beloved friend, and pray too for my dear mother, that she may be enabled to seek Him in faith, who can make a dying bed 'feel soft as downy pillows are.'"

Ellen clasped her feeble hands together, while Mr. M——, kneeling by her bed-side, in that low, sweet solemn tone, for which he was so remarkable, breathed forth one of those deep and fervent prayers, which are, as it were, wings to the soul, and bear it up to heaven. Mrs. Loring knelt too, by the weeping Agnes, but her spirit, unused to devotion, lingered below, and her eyes wandered from the heavenly countenance of that man of God, to the death-like face of that child, whose beauty had once been her pride. She remembered how short a time since, she had seen that form float in airy grace before the mirror clothed in fair and flowing robes, and how soon she should see it extended in the awful immobility of death, wrapped in the still winding-sheet, that garment whose folds are never more waved by the breath of life. Then, conscience whispered in her shuddering ear, that, had she acted a mother's part, and disciplined her daughter to prudence and obedience, the blasts of death had not thus blighted her in her early bloom. And it whispered also, that *she* had no comfort to offer her dying child, in this last conflict of

dissolving nature. It was for this world she had lived herself, it was for this world she had taught *her* to live, but for that untravelled world beyond, she had no guiding hand to extend. It was to a stranger's face the fading eyes of Ellen were directed. It was a stranger's prayers that hallowed her passage to the tomb. The realities of eternity for the first time pressed home, on that vain mother's heart. She felt, too, that *she* must one day die, and that earth with all its riches and pleasures could yield her no support in that awful moment. That there was something which earth could not impart, which had power to soothe and animate the departing spirit, she knew by the angelic expression of Ellen's upturned eyes, and by the look of unutterable serenity that was diffused over her whole countenance. The voice of Mr. M—— died away on her ear, and an unbroken silence reigned through the apartment. Her stormy grief had been stilled into calmness, during that holy prayer. The eyes of Ellen were now gently closed, and as they rose from their knees they sat down by her side, fearing, even by a deep-drawn breath, to disturb her slumbers. A faint hope began to dawn in the mother's heart, from the placidity and duration of her slumbers.

"I have never known her sleep so calm before," said she, in a low voice, to Mr. M——. Mr. M—— bent forward and laid his hand softly on her marble brow.

"Calm indeed are her slumbers," said he, looking solemnly upward; "she sleeps now, I trust, in the bosom of her Saviour and her God."

Thus died Ellen Loring—just one year from that night when Agnes followed her retreating figure, with such a wistful gaze, as she left her for the ball-room, exclaiming to herself, "Happy, beautiful Ellen!" and Agnes now said within herself, even while she wept over her clay-cold form, "Happy Ellen!" but with far different emotions; for she now followed, with the eye of faith, her ascending spirit to the regions of the blest, and saw her, in imagination, enter those golden gates, which never will be closed against the humble and penitent believer.

A few evenings after, a brilliant party was assembled in one of those halls, where pleasure welcomes its votaries.—"Did you know that Ellen Loring was dead?" observed some one to a beautiful girl, the very counterpart of what Ellen once was. "Dead!" exclaimed the startled beauty, for one moment alarmed into reflection; "I did not think she would have died so soon. I am sorry you told me—it will throw a damp over my spirits the whole evening— poor Ellen!" It was but a moment, and the music breathed forth its joyous strains. She was led in haste to the dance, and Ellen Loring was forgotten.

THE FATAL COSMETIC.

Charles Brown sat with Mr. Hall in a corner of the room, apart from the rest of the company. Mr. Hall was a stranger, Charles the familiar acquaintance of all present. The former evidently retained his seat out of politeness to the latter for his eyes wandered continually to the other side of the room, where a group of young ladies was gathered round a piano, so closely as to conceal the musician to whom they were apparently listening. The voice that accompanied the instrument was weak and irregular, and the high tones excessively shrill and disagreeable, yet the performer continued her songs with unwearied patience, thinking the young gentlemen were turned into the very stones that Orpheus changed into breathing things, to remain insensible to her minstrelsy. There was one fair, blue-eyed girl, with a very sweet countenance, who stood behind her chair and cast many a mirthful glance towards Charles, while she urged the songstress to continue at every pause, as if she were spell-bound by the melody. Charles laughed, and kept time with his foot, but Mr. Hall bit his lips, and a frown passed over his handsome and serious countenance. "What a wretched state of society!" exclaimed he, "that admits, nay, even demands such insincerity. Look at the ingenuous countenance of that young girl—would you not expect from her sincerity and truth? Yet, with what practical falsehood she encourages her companion in her odious screeching!"

"Take care," answered Charles, "you must not be too severe. That young lady is a very particular friend of mine, and a very charming girl. She has remarkably popular manners, and if she *is* guilty of a few little innocent deceptions, such, for instance, as the present, I see no possible harm in them to herself, and they certainly give great pleasure to others. She makes Miss Lewis very happy, by her apparent admiration, and I do not see that she injures any one else."

Mr. Hall sighed.

"I fear," said he, "I am becoming a misanthropist. I find I have very peculiar views, such as set me apart and isolate me from my fellow beings. I cannot enjoy an artificial state of society. I consider *truth* as the corner stone of the great social fabric, and where this is wanting, I am constantly looking for ruin and desolation. The person deficient in this virtue, however fair and fascinating, is no more to me than the whited sepulchre and painted wall."

"You have, indeed, peculiar views," answered Charles, colouring with a vexation he was too polite to express in any other way; "and if you look upon

116

the necessary dissimulations practised in society as falsehoods, and brand them as such, I can only say, that you have created a standard of morality more exalted and pure than human nature can ever reach."

"I cannot claim the merit of *creating* a standard, which the divine Moralist gave to man, when he marked out his duties from the sacred mount, in characters so clear and deep, that the very blind might see and the cold ear of deafness hear."

Mr. Hall spoke with warmth. The eyes of the company were directed towards him. He was disconcerted and remained silent. Miss Lewis rose from the piano, and drew towards the fire.

"I am getting terribly tired of the piano," said she. "I don't think it suits my voice at all. I am going to take lessons on the guitar and the harp—one has so much more scope with them; and then they are much more graceful instruments."

"You are perfectly right," replied Miss Ellis, the young lady with the ingenuous countenance, "I have no doubt you would excel on either, and your singing would be much better appreciated. Don't you think so, Margaret?" added she, turning to a young lady, who had hitherto been silent, and apparently unobserved.

"You know I do not," answered she, who was so abruptly addressed, in a perfectly quiet manner, and fixing her eyes serenely on her face; "I should be sorry to induce Miss Lewis to do anything disadvantageous to herself, and consequently painful to her friends."

"Really, Miss Howard," cried Miss Lewis, bridling, and tossing her head with a disdainful air, "you need not be so afraid of my giving you so much pain—I will not intrude my singing upon your delicate and refined ears."

Mr. Hall made a movement forward, attracted by the uncommon sincerity of Miss Howard's remark.

"There," whispered Charles, "is a girl after your own heart—Margaret Howard *will* speak the truth, however unpalatable it may be, and see what wry faces poor Miss Lewis makes in trying *not* to swallow it—I am sure Mary Ellis's flattery is a thousand times kinder and more amiable."

Mr. Hall did not answer. His eyes were perusing the face of her, whose lips had just given such honourable testimony to a virtue so rarely respected by the world of fashion. A decent boldness lighted up the clear hazel eyes that did not seem to be unconscious of the dark and penetrating glances at that moment resting upon them. She was dressed with remarkable simplicity. No decoration in colour relieved the spotless whiteness of her attire. Her hair of pale, yet shining brown, was plainly parted over a brow somewhat too lofty for mere feminine beauty, but white and smooth as Parian marble. Her features, altogether, bore more resemblance to a Pallas than a Venus. They were calm and pure, but somewhat cold and passionless—and under that pale, transparent skin, there seemed no under current, ebbing and flowing with the crimson tide of the heart. Her figure, veiled to the throat, was of fine, though not very slender proportions. There was evidently no artificial compression about the waist, no binding ligatures to prevent the elastic motions of the limbs, the pliable and graceful movements of nature.

"She has a fine face—a very handsome face," repeated Charles, responding to what Mr. Hall *looked*, for as yet he had uttered nothing; "but to me, it is an uninteresting one. She is not generally liked—respected, it is true, but feared—and fear is a feeling which few young ladies would wish to inspire. It is a dangerous thing to live above the world—at least, for a woman."

Charles availed himself of the earliest opportunity of introducing his friend to Miss Howard, glad to be liberated for a while from the close companionship of a man who made him feel strangely uncomfortable with regard to himself, and well pleased with the opportunity of conversing with his favourite, Mary Ellis.

"I feel quite vexed with Margaret," said this thoughtless girl, "for spoiling my compliment to Miss Lewis. I would give one of my little fingers to catch her for once in a white lie."

"Ask her if she does not think herself handsome," said Charles; "no woman ever acknowledged that truth, though none be more firmly believed."

He little expected she would act upon his suggestion, but Mary was too much delighted at the thought of seeing the uncompromising Margaret guilty of a prevarication, to suffer it to pass unheeded.

"Margaret," cried she, approaching her, unawed by the proximity of the majestic stranger—"Mr. Brown says you will deny that you think yourself handsome. Tell me the truth—don't you believe yourself *very* handsome?"

"I will tell you the truth, Mary," replied Margaret, blushing so brightly, as to give an actual radiance to her face, "that is, if I speak at all. But I would rather decline giving any opinion of myself."

"Ah! Margaret," persisted Miss Ellis, "I have heard you say that to *conceal* the truth, when it was required of us, unless some moral duty were involved, was equivalent to a falsehood. Bear witness, Charles, here is one subject on which even Margaret Howard dares not speak the truth."

"You are mistaken," replied Miss Howard; "since you force me to speak, by attacking my principles, I am very willing to say, I *do* think myself handsome; but not so conspicuously as to allow me to claim a superiority over my sex, or to justify so singular and unnecessary a question."

All laughed—even the grave Mr. Hall smiled at the frankness of the avowal—all but Miss Lewis, who, turning up her eyes and raising her hands, exclaimed, "Really, Miss Howard's modesty is equal to her politeness. I thought she despised beauty."

"The gifts of God are never to be despised," answered Miss Howard, mildly. "If he has graced the outer temple, we should only be more careful to keep the indwelling spirit pure."

She drew back, as if pained by the observation she had excited; and the deep and modest colour gradually faded from her cheek. Mr. Hall had not been an uninterested listener. He was a sad and disappointed man. He had been the victim of a woman's perfidy and falsehood—and was consequently distrustful of the whole sex; and his health had suffered from the corrosion of his feelings, and he had been compelled to seek, in a milder clime, a balm which time alone could yield. He had been absent several years, and was just returned to his native country, but not to the scene of his former residence. The wound was healed, but the hardness of the scar remained.

One greater and purer than the Genius of the Arabian Tale, had placed in his breast a mirror, whose lustre would be instantaneously dimmed by the breath of falsehood or dissimulation. It was in this mirror he saw reflected the actions of his fellow beings, and it pained him to see its bright surface so constantly sullied. Never, since the hour he was so fatally deceived, had he been in the presence of woman, without a melancholy conviction that she was incapable of standing the test of this bosom talisman. Here, however, was one, whose lips cast no cloud upon its lustre. He witnessed the marvellous spectacle of a young, beautiful, and accomplished woman, surrounded by the artifices and embellishments of fashionable life, speaking the truth, in all simplicity and godly sincerity, as commanded by the holy men of old. There was something in the sight that renovated and refreshed his blighted feelings. The dew falling on the parched herbage, prepares it for the influence of a kinder ray. Even so the voice of Margaret Howard, gentle in itself and persuasive, advocating the cause he most venerated, operated this night on the heart of Mr. Hall.

For many weeks the same party frequently met at the dwelling of Mrs. Astor. This lady was a professed patroness and admirer of genius and the fine arts. To be a fine painter, a fine singer, a fine writer, a traveller, or a foreigner, was a direct passport to her favour. To be distinguished in any manner in society was sufficient, provided it was not "bad eminence" which was attained by the individual. She admired Mr. Hall for the stately gloom of his mien, his dark and foreign air, his peculiar and high-wrought sentiments. She sought an intimacy with Margaret Howard, for it was a *distinction* to be her friend, and, moreover, she had an exquisite taste and skill in drawing and painting. Mary Ellis was a particular favourite of hers, because her own favourite cousin Charles Brown thought her the most fascinating young lady of his acquaintance. Mrs. Astor's house was elegantly furnished, and her rooms were adorned with rare and beautiful specimens of painting and statuary. She had one apartment which she called her Gallery of Fine Arts, and every new guest was duly ushered into this sanctuary, and called upon to look and admire the glowing canvas and the breathing marble. A magnificent pier-glass was placed on one side of the hall, so as to reflect and multiply these classic beauties. It had been purchased in Europe, and was remarkable for its thickness, brilliancy, and fidelity of reflection. It was a favourite piece of furniture of Mrs. Astor's, and all her servants were warned to be particularly careful, whenever they dusted its surface. As this glass is of some importance in the story, it deserves a minute description. Mrs. Astor thought the only thing necessary to complete the furnishing of the gallery, were transparencies for the windows. Miss Howard, upon hearing the remark, immediately offered to supply the deficiency, an offer at once eagerly accepted, and Mrs. Astor insisted that her painting apparatus should be placed in the very room, that she might receive all the inspiration to be derived from the mute yet eloquent relics of genius, that there solicited the gaze. Nothing could be more delightful than the progress of the work. Margaret was an enthusiast in the art, and her kindling cheek always attested the triumph of her creating hand. Mrs. Astor was in a constant state of excitement, till the whole was completed, and it was no light task, as four were required, and the windows were of an extra size. Almost every day saw the fair artist seated at her easel, with the same group gathered round her. Mary Ellis admired everything so indiscriminately, it was impossible to attach much value to her praise; but Mr. Hall criticised as well as admired, and as he had the painter's eye, and the poet's tongue, Margaret felt the value of his suggestions, and the interest they added to her employment. Above all things, she felt their *truth*. She saw that he never flattered, that he dared to blame, and when he did commend, she was conscious the tribute was deserved. Margaret was not one of those beings, who cannot do but one thing at a time. She could talk and listen, while her hands were applying the brush or arranging the colours, and look up too from the canvas, with a glance that showed how entirely she participated in what was passing around her.

"I wonder you are not tired to death of that everlasting easel," said Mary Ellis to Margaret, who grew every day more interested in her task. "I could not endure such confinement."

"*Death* and *everlasting* are solemn words to be so lightly used, my dear Mary," answered Margaret, whose religious ear was always pained by levity on sacred themes.

"I would not be as serious as you are, for a thousand worlds," replied Mary, laughing; "I really believe you think it a sin to smile. Give me the roses of life, let who will take the thorns. I am going now to gather some, if I can, and leave you and Mr. Hall to enjoy all the briers you can find."

She left the room gayly singing, sure to be immediately followed by Charles, and Mr. Hall was left sole companion of the artist. Mary had associated their names together, for the purpose of disturbing the self-possession of Margaret, and she certainly succeeded in her object. Had Mr. Hall perceived her heightened colour, his vanity might have drawn a flattering inference; but he was standing behind her easel, and his eyes were fixed on the beautiful personification of Faith, Hope, and Charity—those three immortal graces— she was delineating, as kneeling and embracing, with upturned eyes and celestial wings. It was a lovely group—the last of the transparencies, and Margaret lavished on it some of the finest touches of her genius. Mary had repeated a hundred times that it was finished, that another stroke of the pencil would ruin it, and Mrs. Astor declared it perfect, and more than perfect, but still Margaret lingered at the frame, believing every tint should be the last. Every lover of the arts knows the fascination attending the successful exercise and development of their genius—of seeing bright and warm imaginings assume a colouring and form, and giving to others a transcript of the mind's glorious creations; but every artist does not know what deeper charm may be added by the conversation and companionship of such a being as Mr. Hall. He was what might be called a fascinating man, notwithstanding the occasional gloom and general seriousness of his manners. For, when flashes of sensibility lighted up that gloom, and intellect, excited and brought fully into action, illumined that seriousness—it was like moonlight shining on some ruined castle, beauty and grandeur meeting together and exalting each other, from the effect of contrast. Then there was a deep vein of piety pervading all his sentiments and expressions. The comparison of the ruined castle is imperfect. The moonbeams falling on some lofty cathedral, with its pillared dome and "long-drawn aisles," is a better similitude, for devotion hallowed and elevated every faculty of his soul. Margaret, who had lived in a world of her own, surrounded by a purer atmosphere, lonely and somewhat unapproachable, felt as if she were no longer solitary, for here was one who thought and sympathized with her; one, too, who seemed sanctified and set apart from others, by a kind of mysterious sorrow, which the instinct of woman told her had its source in the heart.

"I believe I am too serious, as Mary says," cried Margaret, first breaking the silence; "but it seems to me the thoughtless alone can be gay. I am young in years, but I began to reflect early, and from the moment I took in the mystery of life and all its awful dependencies, I ceased to be mirthful. I am doomed to pay a constant penalty for the singularity of my feelings: like the priestess of the ancient temples, I am accused of uttering dark sayings of old, and casting the shadows of the future over the joys of the present."

Margaret seldom alluded to herself, but Mary's accusation about the thorns and briers had touched her, where perhaps alone she was vulnerable; and in the frankness of her nature, she uttered what was paramount in her thoughts.

"Happy they who are taught by reflection, not experience, to look seriously, though not sadly on the world," said Mr. Hall, earnestly; "who mourn from philanthropy over its folly and falsehood, not because that falsehood and folly have blighted their dearest hopes, nay, cut them off, root and branch, for ever."

Margaret was agitated, and for a moment the pencil wavered in her hand. She knew Mr. Hall must have been unhappy—that he was still suffering from corroding remembrances—and often had she wished to pierce through the mystery that hung over his past life; but now, when he himself alluded to it, she shrunk from an explanation. He seemed himself to regret the warmth of his expressions, and to wish to efface the impression they had made, for his attention became riveted on the picture, which he declared wanted only one thing to make it perfect—"And what was that?"—"Truth encircling the trio with her golden band."

"It may yet be done," cried Margaret; and, with great animation and skill, she sketched the outline suggested.

It is delightful to have one's own favourite sentiments and feelings embodied by another, and that too with a graceful readiness and apparent pleasure, that shows a congeniality of thought and taste. Mr. Hall was not insensible to this charm in Margaret Howard. He esteemed, revered, admired, he wished that he dared to love her. But all charming and true as she seemed, she was still a woman, and he might be again deceived. It would be a terrible thing to embark his happiness once more on the waves which had once overwhelmed it; and find himself again a shipwrecked mariner, cast upon the cruel desert of existence. The feelings which Margaret inspired were so different from the stormy passions which had reigned over him, it is no wonder he was unconscious of their strength and believed himself still his own master.

"Bless me," said Mary, who, entering soon after, *banished*, as she said, Mr. Hall from her presence, for he retired; "if you have not added another figure to the group. I have a great mind to blot Faith, Hope, and Charity, as well as Truth from existence," and playfully catching hold of the frame, she pretended to sweep her arm over their faces.

"Oh! Mary, beware!" exclaimed Margaret; but the warning came too late. The easel tottered and fell instantaneously against the magnificent glass, upon which Mrs. Astor set such an immense value, and broke it into a thousand pieces. Mary looked aghast, and Margaret turned pale as she lifted her picture from amid the ruins.

"It is not spoiled," said she; "but the glass!"

"Oh! the glass!" cried Mary, looking the image of despair; "what shall I do? What will Mrs. Astor say? She will never forgive me!"

"She cannot be so vindictive!" replied Margaret; "but it is indeed an unfortunate accident, and one for which I feel particularly responsible."

"Do not tell her how it happened," cried Mary, shrinking with moral cowardice from the revealing of the truth. "I cannot brave her displeasure!— Charles, too, will be angry with me, and I cannot bear that. Oh! pray, dearest Margaret, pray do not tell her that it was I who did it—you know it would be so natural for the easel to fall without any rash hand to push it. Promise me, Margaret."

Margaret turned her clear, rebuking eye upon the speaker with a mingled feeling of indignation and pity.

"I will not expose you, Mary," said she, calmly; and, withdrawing herself from the rapturous embrace, in which Mary expressed her gratitude, she began to pick up the fragments of the mirror, while Mary, unwilling to look on the wreck she had made, flew out to regain her composure. It happened that Mr. Hall passed the window while Margaret was thus occupied; and he paused a moment to watch her, for in spite of himself, he felt a deep and increasing interest in every action of Margaret's. Margaret saw his shadow as it lingered, but she continued her employment. He did not doubt that she had caused the accident, for he had left her alone, a few moments before, and he was not conscious that any one had entered since his departure. Though he regretted any circumstance which might give pain to her, he anticipated a pleasure in seeing the openness and readiness with which she would avow herself the aggressor, and blame herself for her carelessness.

Margaret found herself in a very unpleasant situation. She had promised not to betray the cowardly Mary, and she knew that whatever blame would be attached to the act, would rest upon herself. But were Mrs. Astor to question her upon the subject, she could not deviate from the truth, by acknowledging a fault she had never committed. She felt an unspeakable contempt for Mary's weakness, for, had *she* been in *her* place, she would have acknowledged the part she had acted, unhesitatingly, secure of the indulgence of friendship and benevolence. "Better to leave the circumstance to speak for itself," said Margaret to herself, "and of course the burden will rest upon me." She sighed as she thought of the happy hours she had passed, by the side of that mirror, and how often she had seen it reflect the speaking countenance of Mr. Hall, that tablet of "unutterable thoughts," and then thinking how *his* hopes seemed shattered like that frail glass, and his memories of sorrow multiplied, she came to the conclusion that all earthly hopes were vain and all earthly memories fraught with sadness. Never had Margaret moralized so deeply as in the long solitary walk she stole that evening, to escape the evil of being drawn into the tacit sanction of a falsehood. Like many others, with equally pure intentions, in trying to avoid one misfortune she incurred a greater.

Mrs. Astor was very much grieved and astonished when she discovered her loss. With all her efforts to veil her feelings, Mary saw she was displeased with Margaret, and would probably never value as they deserved, the beautiful transparencies on which she had so faithfully laboured.

"I would not have cared if any other article had been broken," said Mrs. Astor, whose weak point Mary well knew; "but this can never be replaced. I do not so much value the cost, great as it was, but it was perfectly unique. I never saw another like it."

Mary's conscience smote her, for suffering another to bear the imputation she herself deserved. A sudden plan occurred to her. She had concealed the truth, she was now determined to save her friend, even at the cost of a lie.

"I do not believe Margaret broke it," said she. "I saw Dinah, your little black girl in the room, just before Margaret left it, and you know how often you have punished her for putting her hands on forbidden articles. You know if Margaret had done it, she would have acknowledged it, at once."

"True," exclaimed Mrs. Astor; "how stupid I have been!" and glad to find a channel in which her anger could flow, unchecked by the restraints of politeness, she rung the bell and summoned the unconscious Dinah.

In vain she protested her innocence. She was black, and it was considered a matter of course that she would lie. Mrs. Astor took her arm in silence, and led her from the room, in spite of her prayers and protestations. We should be sorry to reveal the secrets of the prison-house, but from the cries that issued through the shut door, and from a certain whizzing sound in the air, one might judge of the nature of the punishment inflicted on the innocent victim of unmerited wrath. Mary closed her ears. Every sound pierced her heart. Something told her those shrieks would rise up in judgment against her at the last day. "Oh! how," thought she, "if I fear the rebuke of my fellow-creature for an unintentional offence, how can I ever appear before my Creator, with the blackness of falsehood and the hardness of cruelty on my soul?" She wished she had had the courage to have acted right in the first place, but now it was too late. Charles would despise her, and that very day he had told her that he loved her better than all the world beside. She tried, too, to soothe her conscience, by reflecting that Dinah would have been whipped for something else, and that as it was a common event to her, it was, after all, a matter of no great consequence. Mrs. Astor, having found a legitimate vent for her displeasure, chased the cloud from her brow, and greeted Margaret with a smile, on her return, slightly alluding to the accident, evidently trying to rise superior to the event. Margaret was surprised and pleased. She expressed her own regret, but as she imputed to herself no blame, Mrs. Astor was confirmed in the justice of her verdict. Margaret knew not what had passed in her absence, for Mrs. Astor was too refined to bring her domestic troubles before her guests. Mary, who was the only one necessarily initiated, was too deeply implicated to repeat it, and the subject was dismissed. But the impression remained on one mind, painful and ineffaceable.

Mr. Hall marked Margaret's conscious blush on her entrance, he had heard the cries and sobs of poor Dinah, and was not ignorant of the cause. He believed Margaret was aware of the fact—she, the true offender. A pang, keen as cold steel can create, shot through his heart at this conviction. He had thought her so pure, so true, so holy, the very incarnation of his worshipped virtue—and now, to sacrifice her principles for such a bauble—a bit of frail glass. He could not remain in her presence, but, complaining of a headache, suddenly retired, but not before he had cast a glance on Margaret, so cold and freezing, it seemed to congeal her very soul.

"He believes me cowardly and false," thought she, for she divined what was passing in his mind; and if ever she was tempted to be so, it was in the hope of reinstating herself in his esteem. She had given her promise to Mary, however, and it was not to be broken. Mary, whose feelings were as evanescent as her principles were weak, soon forgot the whole affair in the preparations of her approaching marriage with Charles, an event which absorbed all her thoughts, as it involved all her hopes of happiness.

Margaret finished her task, but the charm which had gilded the occupation was fled. Mr. Hall seldom called, and when he did, he wore all his original reserve. Margaret felt she had not deserved this alienation, and tried to cheer herself with the conviction of her own integrity; but her spirits were occasionally dejected, and the figure of Truth, which had such a beaming outline, assumed the aspect of utter despondency. Dissatisfied with her work, she at last swept her brush over the design, and mingling Truth with the dark shades of the back ground, gave up her office as an artist, declaring her sketches completed. Mrs. Astor was enraptured with the whole, and said she intended to reserve them for the night of Mary's wedding, when they would burst upon the sight, in one grand *coup d'œil*, in the full blaze of chandeliers, bridal lamps, and nuptial ornaments. Margaret was to officiate as one of the bridemaids, but she gave a reluctant consent. She could not esteem Mary, and she shrunk from her flattery and caresses with an instinctive loathing. She had once set her foot on a flowery bank, that edged a beautiful stream. The turf trembled and gave way, for it was hollow below, and Margaret narrowly escaped death. She often shuddered at the recollection. With similar emotions she turned from Mary Ellis's smiles and graces. There was beauty and bloom on the surface, but hollowness and perhaps ruin beneath.

A short time before the important day, a slight efflorescence appeared on the fair cheek and neck of Mary. She was in despair, lest her loveliness should be marred, when she most of all wished to shine. It increased instead of diminishing, and she resolved to have recourse to any remedy, that would remove the disfiguring eruption. She recollected having seen a violent erysipelas cured immediately by a solution of corrosive sublimate; and without consulting any one, she sent Dinah to the apothecary to purchase some, charging her to tell no one whose errand she was bearing, for she was not willing to confess her occasion for such a cosmetic. Dinah told the apothecary her mistress sent her, and it was given without questioning or hesitation. Her only confidant was Margaret, who shared her chamber and toilet, and who warned her to be exceedingly cautious in the use of an article so poisonous; and Mary promised with her usual heedlessness, without dreaming of any evil consequences. The eruption disappeared—Mary looked fairer than ever, and, clad in her bridal paraphernalia of white satin, white roses, and blonde lace, was pronounced the most beautiful bride of the season. Mr. Hall was present, though he had refused to take any part in the ceremony. He could not, without singularity, decline the invitation and, notwithstanding the blow his confidence in Margaret's character had received, he still found the spot where *she* was, enchanted ground, and he lingered near, unwilling to break at once the only charm that still bound him to society. After the short but solemn rite, that made the young and thoughtless, *one* by indissoluble ties, and the rush of congratulation took place, Margaret was forced by the pressure close to Mr. Hall's side. He involuntarily offered his arm as a protection, and a thrill of irrepressible happiness pervaded his heart, at this unexpected and unsought proximity. He forgot his coldness—the broken glass, everything but the feeling of the present moment. Margaret was determined to avail herself of the tide of returning confidence. Her just womanly modesty and pride prevented her *seeking* an explanation and reconciliation, but she knew without breaking her promise to Mary, she could not justify herself in Mr. Hall's opinion, if even the opportunity offered. She was to depart in the morning, with the new-married pair, who were going to take an excursion of pleasure, so fashionable after the wedding ceremony. She might never see him again. He had looked pale, his face was now flushed high with excited feeling.

"You have wronged me, Mr. Hall," said she, blushing, but without hesitation; "if you think I have been capable of wilful deception or concealment. The mirror was not broken by me, though I know you thought me guilty, and afraid or ashamed to avow the truth. I would not say so much to justify myself, if I did not think you would believe me, and if I did not value the esteem of one who sacrifices even friendship at the shrine of truth."

She smiled, for she saw she was believed, and there was such a glow of pleasure irradiating Mr. Hall's countenance, it was like the breaking and gushing forth of sunbeams. There are few faces, on which a smile has such a magic effect as on Margaret's. Her smile was never forced. It was the inspiration of truth, and all the light of her soul shone through it. Perhaps neither ever experienced an hour of deeper happiness than that which followed this simple explanation. Margaret felt a springtide of hope and joy swelling in her heart, for there was a deference, a tenderness in Mr. Hall's manner she had never seen before. He seemed entirely to have forgotten the presence of others, when a name uttered by one near, arrested his attention.

"That is Mrs. St. Henry," observed a lady, stretching eagerly forward. "She arrived in town this morning, and had letters of introduction to Mrs. Astor. She was the beauty of ——, before her marriage, and is still the leader of fashion and taste."

Margaret felt her companion start, as if a ball had penetrated him, and looking up, she saw his altered glance, fixed on the lady, who had just entered, with a dashing escort, and was advancing towards the centre of the room. She was dressed in the extremity of the reigning mode—her arms and neck entirely uncovered, and their dazzling whiteness, thus lavishly displayed, might have mocked the polish and purity of alabaster. Her brilliant black eyes flashed on either side, with the freedom of conscious beauty, and disdain of the homage it inspired. She moved with the air of a queen, attended by her vassals, directly forward, when suddenly her proud step faltered, her cheek and lips became wan, and uttering a sudden ejaculation, she stood for a moment perfectly still. She was opposite Mr. Hall, whose eye, fixed upon hers, seemed to have the effect of fascination. Though darkened by the burning sun of a tropical clime, and faded from the untimely blighting of the heart, that face could never be forgotten. It told her of perjury, remorse, sorrow—yes, of sorrow, for in spite of the splendour that surrounded her, this glittering beauty was wretched. She had sacrificed herself at the shrine of Mammon, and had learned too late the horror of such ties, unsanctified by affection. Appreciating but too well the value of the love she had forsaken, goaded by remorse for her conduct to him, whom she believed wasting away in a foreign land—she flew from one scene of dissipation to another, seeking in the admiration of the world an equivalent for her lost happiness. The unexpected apparition of her lover was as startling and appalling as if she had met an inhabitant of another world. She tried to rally herself and to pass on, but the effort was in vain—sight, strength, and recollection forsook her.

"Mrs. St. Henry has fainted! Mrs. St. Henry has fainted!"—was now echoed from mouth to mouth. A lady's fainting, whether in church, ball-room, or assembly, always creates a great sensation; but when that lady happens to be the centre of attraction and admiration, when every eye that has a loop-hole to peep through is gazing on her brilliant features, to behold her suddenly fall, as if smitten by the angel of death, pallid and moveless—the effect is inconceivably heightened. When, too, as in the present instance, a sad, romantic-looking stranger rushes forward to support her, the interest of the scene admits of no increase. At least Margaret felt so, as she saw the beautiful Mrs. St. Henry borne in the arms of Mr. Hall through the crowd, that fell back as he passed, into an adjoining apartment, speedily followed by Mrs. Astor, all wonder and excitement, and many others all curiosity and expectation, to witness the termination of the scene. Mr. Hall drew back, while the usual appliances were administered for her resuscitation. He heeded not the

scrutinizing glances bent upon him. His thoughts were rolled within himself,
and

The soul of other days came rushing in."

The lava that had hardened over the ruin it created, melted anew, and the
greenness and fragrance of new-born hopes were lost under the burning tide.
When Mrs. St. Henry opened her eyes, she looked round her in wild alarm;
then shading her brow with her hand, her glance rested where Mr. Hall stood,
pale and abstracted, with folded arms, leaning against the wall—"I thought
so," said she, in a low voice, "I thought so;"—then covered her eyes and
remained silent. Mr. Hall, the moment he heard the sound of her voice and
was assured of her recovery, precipitately retired, leaving behind him matter
of deep speculation. Margaret was sitting in a window of the drawing-room,
through which he passed. She was alone, for even the bride was forgotten in
the excitement of the past scene. He paused—he felt an explanation was due
to her, but that it was impossible to make it. He was softened by the sad and
sympathizing expression of her countenance, and seated himself a moment by
her side.

"I have been painfully awakened from a dream of bliss," said he, "which I
was foolish enough to imagine might yet be realized. But the heart rudely
shattered as mine has been, must never hope to be healed. I cannot command
myself sufficiently to say more, only let me make one assurance, that
whatever misery has been and may yet be my doom, guilt has no share in my
wretchedness—I cannot refuse myself the consolation of your esteem."

Margaret made no reply—she could not. Had her existence depended on the
utterance of one word, she could not have commanded it. She extended her
hand, however, in token of that friendship she believed was hereafter to be the
only bond that was to unite them. Long after Mr. Hall was gone, she sat in the
same attitude, pale and immovable as a statue; but who can tell the changes
and conflicts of her spirit, in that brief period?

Mrs. St. Henry was too ill to be removed, and Mrs. Astor was unbounded in
her attentions. She could hardly regret a circumstance which forced so
interesting and distinguished a personage upon the acceptance of her
hospitality. Margaret remained with her during the greater part of the night,
apprehensive of a renewal of the fainting fits, to which she acknowledged she
was constitutionally subject. Margaret watched her as she lay, her face
scarcely to be distinguished from the sheet, it was so exquisitely fair, were it
not for the shading of the dark locks, that fell unbound over the pillow, still
heavy with the moisture with which they had been saturated; and, as she
contemplated her marvellous loveliness, she wondered not at the influence
she exercised over the destiny of another. Mr. Hall had once spoken of

himself as being the victim of falsehood. Could she have been false—and loving him, how could she have married another? If she had voluntarily broken her troth, why such an agitation at his sight? and if she were worthy of his love, why such a glaring display of her person, such manifest courting of the free gaze of admiration? These, and a thousand similar interrogations, did Margaret make to herself during the vigils of the night, but they found no answer. Towards morning, the lady slept; but Margaret was incapable of sleep, and her wakeful eyes caught the first gray tint of the dawn, and marked it deepening and kindling, till the east was robed with flame, the morning livery of the skies. All was bustle till the bridal party was on their way. Mrs. St. Henry still slept, under the influence of an opiate, and Margaret saw her no more. Farewells were exchanged, kind wishes breathed, and the travellers commenced their journey. Margaret's thoughts wandered from Mrs. St. Henry to Mr. Hall, and back again, till they were weary of wandering and would gladly have found rest; but the waters had not subsided, there was no green spot where the dove of peace could fold her drooping wings. Charles and Mary were too much occupied by each other to notice her silence; and it was not till they paused in their journey, she was recalled to existing realities. Mary regretted something she had left behind—a sudden recollection came over Margaret.

"Oh! Mary," said she, "I hope you have been cautious, and not left any of that dangerous medicine, where mischief could result from it. I intended to remind you of it before our departure."

"Certainly—to be sure I took especial care of it, I have it with me in my trunk," replied Mary, but her conscience gave her a remorseful twinge as she uttered the *white lie*, for she had forgotten it, and where she had left it, she could not remember. As Margaret had given her several warnings, she was ashamed to acknowledge her negligence, and took refuge in the shelter she had too often successfully sought. Had she anticipated the fatal consequences of her oblivion, her bridal felicity would have been converted into agony and despair. She had left the paper containing the powder, yet undissolved, on the mantelpiece of her chamber. The chambermaid who arranged the room after her departure, seeing it and supposing it to be medicine, put it in the box which Mrs. Astor devoted to that department, in the midst of calomel, salts, antimony, &c. It was folded in brown paper, like the rest, and there was no label to indicate its deadly qualities. Mrs. St. Henry continued the guest of Mrs. Astor, for her indisposition assumed a more serious aspect, and it was impossible to remove her. She appeared feverish and restless, and a physician was called in to prescribe for her, greatly in opposition to her wishes. She could not bear to acknowledge herself ill. It was the heat of the room that had oppressed her—a transient cold, which would soon pass away—she would not long trespass on Mrs. Astor's hospitality. The doctor was not much skilled in diseases of the heart, though he ranked high in his profession. His grand panacea for almost all diseases was calomel, which he recommended to his patient, as the most efficient and speediest remedy. She received the prescription with a very ill grace, declaring she had never tasted of any in her life, and had a horror of all medicines. Mrs. Astor said she had an apothecary's shop at command in her closet, and that she kept doses constantly prepared for her own use. After the doctor's departure, Mrs. St. Henry seemed much dejected, and her eyes had an anxious, inquiring expression as they turned on Mrs. Astor.

"You say," said she to her, in a low tone, "that friends have been kind in their inquiries for me? Most of them are strangers, and yet I thank them."

"Mr. Hall has called more than once," replied Mrs. Astor, "he, I believe, is well known to you."

"He is indeed," said Mrs. St. Henry—"I wish I could see him—but it cannot be; no, it would not answer."

Mrs. Astor longed to ask the nature of their former acquaintance, but a conviction that the question would be painful, restrained the expression of her curiosity.

"Would you not like to send for some of your friends?" inquired Mrs. Astor —"your husband? My servants shall be at your disposal."

"You are very kind," answered Mrs. St. Henry, quickly—"but it is not necessary—my husband is too infirm to travel, and believing me well, he will suffer no anxiety on my account—I think I shall be quite well, after taking your sovereign medicine. Give it me now, if you please, while I am in a vein of compliance."

She turned, with so lovely a smile, and extended her hand with so much grace, Mrs. Astor stood a moment, thinking what a beautiful picture she would make; then taking the lamp in her hand, she opened her closet, and took down the medicine casket. It happened that the first paper she touched was that which Mary had left, and which the servant had mingled with the others.

"Here is one already prepared," cried she—"I always keep them ready, the exact number of grains usually given, as we often want it suddenly and at night."

She mixed the fatal powder with some delicious jelly, and holding it to the lips of her patient, said with a cheering smile—"Come, it has no disagreeable taste at all."

Mrs. St. Henry gave a nervous shudder, but took it, unconscious of its deadly properties; and Mrs. Astor, praising her resolution, seated herself in an easy chair by the bedside, and began to read. She became deeply interested in her book, though she occasionally glanced towards her patient to see if she slept. She had placed the lamp so that its light would not shine on the bed, and the most perfect quietness reigned in the apartment. How long this tranquillity lasted it is impossible to tell, for she was so absorbed in her book, time passed unheeded. At length Mrs. St. Henry began to moan, and toss her arms over the covering, as if in sudden pain. Mrs. Astor leaned over her, and took her hand. It was hot and burning, her cheek had a scarlet flush on it, and when she opened her eyes they had a wild and alarming expression.

"Water," she exclaimed, leaning on her elbow, and shading back her hair hurriedly from her brow—"Give me water, for I die of thirst."

"I dare not," said Mrs. Astor, terrified by her manner—"anything but that to quench your thirst."

She continued still more frantically to call for water, till Mrs. Astor, excessively alarmed, sent for the doctor, and called in other attendants. As he was in the neighbourhood, he came immediately. He looked aghast at the situation of his patient, for she was in a paroxysm of agony at his entrance, and his experienced eye took in the danger of the case. "What have you given her, madam?" said he, turning to Mrs Astor, with a countenance that made her tremble.

"What have you given me?" exclaimed Mrs. St. Henry, grasping her wrist with frenzied strength—"You have killed me—it was poison—I feel it in my heart and in my brain!"

Mrs. Astor uttered a scream, and snatched up the paper which had fallen on the carpet.

"Look at it, doctor—it was calomel, just as you prescribed—what else could it be!"

The doctor examined the paper—there was a little powder still sticking to it.

"Good heavens, doctor," cried Mrs. Astor, "what makes you look so?—what is it?—what was it?"

"Where did you get this?" said he, sternly.

"At the apothecary's—I took it from that chest—examine it, pray."

The doctor turned away with a groan, and approached his beautiful patient, now gasping and convulsed. He applied the most powerful antidotes, but without effect.

"I am dying," she cried, "I am dying—I am poisoned—but oh, doctor, save me—save me—let me see him, if I must die—let me see him again;" and she held out her hands imploringly to Mrs. Astor, who was in a state little short of distraction.

"Only tell me, if you mean Mr. Hall."

"Who should I mean but Augustus?" she cried. "Perhaps in death he may forgive me."

The doctor made a motion that her request should be complied with, and a messenger was despatched.

What an awful scene was presented, when he entered that chamber of death! Was that the idol of his young heart, the morning star of his manhood; she, who lay livid, writhing and raving there? Her long, dark hair hung in dishevelled masses over her neck and arms, her large black eyes were fearfully dilated, and full of that unutterable agony which makes the spirit quail before the might of human suffering. Cold sweat-drops gleamed on her marble brow, and her hands were damp with that dew which no morning sunbeam can ever exhale.

"Almighty Father!" exclaimed Mr. Hall, "what a sight is this!"

The sound of that voice had the power to check the ravings of delirium. She shrieked, and stretched out her arms towards him, who sunk kneeling by the bedside, covering his face with his hands, to shut out the appalling spectacle.

"Forgive me," she cried, in hollow and altered accents—"Augustus, you are terribly avenged—I loved you, even when I left you for another. Oh! pray for me to that great and dreadful God, who is consuming me, to have mercy on me hereafter."

He did pray, but it was in spirit, his lips could not articulate; but his uplifted hands and streaming eyes called down pardon and peace on the dying penitent. The reason, that had flashed out for a moment, rekindled by memory and passion, was now gone for ever. All the rest was but the striving of mortal pain, the rending asunder of body and soul. In a short time all was over, and the living were left to read one of the most tremendous lessons on the vanity of beauty, and the frailty of life, mortality could offer in all its gloomy annals.

"This is no place for you, now," said the doctor, taking Mr. Hall's arm, and drawing him into another apartment, where, secure from intrusion, he could be alone with God and his own heart. There was another duty to perform—to investigate the mystery that involved this horrible tragedy. The apothecary was summoned, who, after recovering from his first consternation, recollected that a short time before, he had sold a quantity of corrosive sublimate to a little black girl, according to her mistress's orders. The servants were called for examination, and Dinah was pointed out as the culprit—Dinah, the imputed destroyer of the mirror, whose terror was now deemed the result of conscious guilt. Mrs. Astor vehemently protested she had never sent her, that it was the blackest falsehood; and Dinah, though she told the whole truth, how Mary had forbid her telling it was for her, and she merely used her mistress's name on that account, gained no belief. The chambermaid, who had found the paper and put it in the chest, withheld her testimony, fearing she might be implicated in the guilt. Everything tended to deepen the evidence against Dinah. The affair of the broken looking-glass was revived. She had been heard to say, after her memorable flagellation, that she wished her mistress was dead, that she would kill her if she could; and many other expressions, the result of a smarting back and a wounded spirit, were brought up against her. It was a piteous thing to see the fright, and hear the pleadings of the wretched girl: "Oh! don't send me to jail—don't hang me—send for Miss Mary," she repeated, wringing her hands, and rolling her eyes like a poor animal whom the hunters have at bay. But to jail she was sent—for who could doubt her crime, or pity her after witnessing its terrific consequences?—a damp, dreary prison-house, where, seated on a pallet of straw, she was left to brood day after day over her accumulated wrongs, hopeless of sympathy or redress. Let those who consider a *white lie* a venial offence, who look upon deception as necessary to the happiness and harmony of society, reflect on the consequences of Mary Ellis's moral delinquency, and tremble at the view. She had not done more than a thousand others have done, and are daily doing; and yet what was the result? The soul of the lovely, the erring, and the unprepared had been sent shuddering into eternity, a household made wretched, the innocent condemned, a neighbourhood thrown into consternation and gloom. Had Mary confessed her negligence to Margaret, instead of telling an unnecessary and untempted falsehood, a warning message could have then been easily sent back, and the wide-spread ruin prevented. There is no such thing as a *white lie*; they are all black as the blackest shades of midnight; and no fuller on earth can whiten them.

When Mrs. Astor had recovered from the shock of these events in a sufficient degree, she wrote to Mary a detailed account, begging her and Margaret to return immediately, and cheer the home which now seemed so desolate. The letter was long in reaching her, for the travellers were taking a devious course, and could leave behind them no precise directions. Mary was in one of her gayest, brightest humours, when she received the epistle. She was putting on some new ornaments, which Charles had presented to her, and he was looking over her shoulder at the fair image reflected in the glass, whose brow was lighted up with the triumph of conscious beauty.

"I look shockingly ugly to-day," said she, with a smile that belied her words.

"You tell stories with such a grace," replied her flattering husband, "I am afraid we shall be in love with falsehood."

"A letter from our dear Mrs. Astor; open it, Charles, while I clasp this bracelet; and read it aloud, then Margaret and I both can hear it."

Before Charles had read one page, Mary sunk down at his feet, rending the air with hysterical screams. Her husband, who was totally unaware of the terrible agency she had had in the affair, raised her in indescribable alarm. Her own wild expressions, however, revealed the truth, which Margaret's shivering lips confirmed.

"Oh! had you told me but the *truth*," cried Margaret, raising her prayerful eyes and joined hands to heaven—"how simple, how easy it had been— Charles, Charles," added she, with startling energy, "praise not this rash, misguided girl, for the grace with which she *lies*—I will not recall the word. By the worth of your own soul and hers, teach her, that as there is a God above, he requires truth in the inward heart."

Charles trembled at the solemnity of the adjuration; and conscience told him, that all the agonies his wife suffered, and all the remorse which was yet to be her portion, were just. Margaret sought the solitude of her chamber, and there, on her knees, she endeavoured to find calmness. The image of Mr. Hall, mourning over the death-bed of her once so madly loved, the witness of her expiring throes, the receiver of her last repentant sigh rose, between her and her Creator. Then, that radiant face, that matchless form, which had so lately excited a pang of envy, even in *her* pure heart, now blasted by consuming poison, and mouldering in the cold grave; how awful was the thought, and how fearful the retribution! She, whose vain heart had by falsehood endangered the very existence of another, was the victim of the very vice that had blackened her own spirit. Yes! there is retribution even in this world.

Mary returned, but how changed from the gay and blooming bride! Her cheek was pale, and her eye heavy. She hastened to repair the only wrong now capable of any remedy. The prison doors of poor Dinah were thrown open, and her innocence declared: but could the long and lonely days and nights spent in that weary, gloomy abode be blotted out? Could the pangs of cold, shuddering fear, the dream of the gallows, the rope, the hangman's grasp round the gurgling throat, the dark coffin seat, the scoffing multitude, be forgotten? No!—Dinah's spirit was broken, for though her skin was black, there was sensibility and delicacy too beneath her ebon colouring. Could Mary bring back the gladness that once pervaded the dwelling of Mrs. Astor? Everything there was changed. The room in which Mrs. St. Henry died was closed, for it was haunted by too terrible remembrances. Bitterly did Mary mourn over the grave of her victim; but she could not recall her by her tears. No remorse could open the gates of the tomb, or reclothe with beauty and bloom the ruins of life.

Margaret, the true, the pure-hearted and upright Margaret, was not destined, like Mary, to gather the thorns and briers of existence. Long did the fragrance of *her* roses last, for she had not plucked them with too rash a hand. She and Mr. Hall again met. The moral sympathy that had drawn them together, was not weakened by the tragic event that had intervened; it had rather strengthened through suffering and sorrow. Mr. Hall could never forget the death scene of Laura St. Henry. The love expressed for him at a moment when all earthly dissimulation was over had inexpressibly affected him. Her unparalleled sufferings seemed an expiation for her broken faith. It was at her grave that he and Margaret first met after their sad separation, when the falling shades of evening deepened the solemnity of the scene. Sorrow, sympathy, devotion, and truth, form a holy groundwork for love; and when once the temple is raised on such a foundation, the winds and waves may beat against it in vain. Mr. Hall found by his own experience, that the bruised heart can be healed, for Margaret's hand poured oil and balm on its wounds. He could repose on her faith as firmly as on the rock which ages have planted. He knew that she loved him, and felt it due to her happiness as well as his own, to ask her to be the companion of his pilgrimage. If they looked back upon the clouds that had darkened their morning, it was without self-reproach, and remembrance gradually lost its sting. Who will say she was not happier than Mary, who carried in her bosom, through life, that which "biteth like a serpent, and stingeth like an adder?"

THE ABYSSINIAN NEOPHYTE.

Adellan, an Abyssinian youth, approached one of those consecrated buildings, which crown almost every hill of his native country. Before entering, he drew off his shoes, and gave them in charge to a servant, that he might not soil the temple of the Lord, with the dust of the valley; then bending down, slowly and reverentially, he pressed his lips to the threshold, performed the same act of homage to each post of the door, then passed into the second division of the church, within view of the curtained square, answering to the mysterious *holy of holies* in the Jewish temple. He gazed upon the pictured saints that adorned the walls, long and earnestly, when, kneeling before them, he repeated, with deep solemnity, his customary prayers. He rose, looked towards the mystic veil, which no hand but that of the priest was permitted to raise, and anticipated with inexplicable emotions the time when, invested with the sacred dignity of that office, he might devote himself exclusively to Heaven. From early childhood, Adellan had been destined to the priesthood. His first years were passed mid the stormy scenes of war, for his father was a soldier, fighting those bloody battles, with which the province of Tigre had been more than once laid waste. Then followed the dreadful discipline of famine, for the destroying locusts, the scourge of the country, had followed up the desolation of war, and year succeeding year, gleaned the last hope of man. The parents of Adellan fled from these scenes of devastation, crossed the once beautiful and fertile banks of the Tacazze, and sought refuge in the ample monastery of Walduba, where a brother of his father then resided. Here, he was placed entirely under the protection of his uncle, for his father, sickened with the horrors he had witnessed, and loathing the ties which were once so dear to him, recrossed his native stream, became a gloomy monk in another convent, where, with several hundred of his brethren, he soon after perished a victim to those barbarities, which had robbed him of all that gave value to life. Adellan had never known the joys of childhood. The greenness and bloom of spring had been blotted from his existence. Famine had hollowed his boyish cheek, and fear and distrust chilled and depressed his young heart. After entering the convent of Walduba, where all his physical wants were supplied, the roundness and elasticity of health were restored to his limbs, but his cheek was kept pale by midnight vigils, and long and painful fastings. The teacher, whom his uncle placed over him, was severe and exacting. He gave him no relaxation by day, and the stars of night witnessed his laborious tasks. He was compelled to commit lessons to memory, in a language which he did not then understand, a drudgery from which every ardent mind must recoil. Yet, such was his thirst for knowledge, that he found a pleasure, even in this, that sweetened his toils. All the strains of the devout Psalmist were familiar to his lips, but they were in an *unknown tongue*, for in this manner are the youth of those benighted regions taught. Often, when gazing on the magnificent jewelry of a tropical sky, shining down on the darkness and solitude of night, had he unconsciously repeated the words of the royal penitent—"The heavens declare the glory of God. The firmament showeth his handy work." He understood not their meaning, but the principle of immortality was striving within him, and every star that gemmed the violet canopy, seemed to him eye-beams of that all-seeing Divinity he then darkly adored.

Adellan left the enclosure of the church, and lingered beneath the shade of the cedars, whose trunks supported the roof, and thus formed a pleasant colonnade sheltered from the sun and the rain. Beautiful was the prospect that here stretched itself around him. All the luxuriance of a mountainous country, constantly bathed with the dews of heaven, and warmed by the beams of a vertical sun, was richly unfolded. Odoriferous perfumes, wafted from the forest trees, and exhaled from the roses, jessamines, and wild blossoms, with which the fields were covered, scented the gale. Borne from afar, the fragrance of Judea's balm mingled with the incense of the flowers and the richer breath of the myrrh. A cool stream murmured near, where those who came up to worship, were accustomed to perform their ablutions and purifying rites, in conformance with the ancient Levitical law. Wherever Adellan turned his eyes, he beheld some object associated with the ceremonies of his austere religion. In that consecrated stream he had bathed, he had made an altar beneath every spreading tree, and every rock had witnessed his prostrations. He thought of the unwearied nature of his devotions, and pride began to swell his heart. He knew nothing of that meek and lowly spirit, that humiliation of soul, which marks the followers of a crucified Redeemer. He had been taught to believe that salvation was to be found in the observance of outward forms, but never had been led to purify the inner temple so as to make it a meet residence for a holy God.

Near the close of the day, he again walked forth, meditating on his contemplated journey to Jerusalem, the holy city, where he was not only to receive the remission of his own sins, but even for seven generations yet unborn, according to the superstitious belief of his ancestors. He was passing a low, thatched dwelling, so lost in his own meditations, as scarcely to be aware of its vicinity, when a strain of low, sweet music, rose like a stream of "rich distilled perfumes." Woman's softer accents mingled with a voice of manly melody and strength; and as the blending strains stole by his ear, he paused, convinced that the music he heard was an act of adoration to God, though he understood not the language in which it was uttered. The door of the cabin was open, and he had a full view of the group near the entrance. A man, dressed in a foreign costume, whose prevailing colour was black, sat just within the shade of the cedars that sheltered the roof. Adellan immediately recognised the pale face of the European, and an instinctive feeling of dislike and suspicion urged him to turn away. There was something, however, in the countenance of the stranger that solicited and obtained more than a passing glance. There was beauty in the calm, thoughtful features, the high marble brow, the mild devotional dark eye, and the soft masses of sable heir that fell somewhat neglected over his lofty temples. There was a tranquillity, a peace, an elevation diffused over that pallid face, which was reflected back upon the heart of the beholder: a kind of moonlight brightness, communicating its own peculiar sweetness and quietude to every object it shone upon. Seated near him, and leaning over the arm of his chair, was a female, whose slight delicate figure, and dazzlingly fair complexion, gave her a supernatural appearance to the unaccustomed eye of the dark Abyssinian. Her drooping attitude and fragile frame appealed at once to sympathy and protection, while her placid eyes, alternately lifted to heaven and turned towards him on whose arm she leaned, were expressive not only of meekness and submission, but even of holy rapture. A third figure belonged to this interesting group: that of an infant girl, about eighteen months old, who, seated on a straw matting, at the feet of her parents, raised her cherub head as if in the act of listening, and tossed back her flaxen ringlets with the playful grace of infancy.

Adellan had heard that a Christian missionary was in the neighbourhood of Adorva, and he doubted not that he now beheld one whom he had been taught to believe his most dangerous enemy. Unwilling to remain longer in his vicinity, he was about to pass on, when the stranger arose and addressed him in the language of his country. Surprised at the salutation, and charmed, in spite of himself, with the mild courtesy of his accents, Adellan was constrained to linger. The fair-haired lady greeted him with a benign smile, and the little child clapped its hands as if pleased with the novelty and grace of his appearance; for though the hue of the olive dyed his cheek, his features presented the classic lineaments of manly beauty, and though the long folds of his white robe veiled the outlines of his figure, he was formed in the finest model of European symmetry. The missionary spoke to him of his country, of the blandness of the climate, the magnificence of the trees, the fragrance of the air, till Adellan forgot his distrust, and answered him with frankness and interest. Following the dictates of his own ardent curiosity, he questioned the missionary with regard to his name, his native country, and his object in coming to his own far land. He learned that his name was M——, that he came from the banks of the Rhine to the borders of the Nile, and, following its branches, had found a resting-place near the waters of the beautiful Tacazze.

"And why do you come to this land of strangers?" asked the abrupt

Abyssinian.

"I came as an humble servant of my divine Master," replied the missionary, meekly; "as a messenger of 'glad tidings of great joy,' to all who will receive me, and as a friend and brother, even to those who may persecute and revile me."

"What tidings can you bring us," said Adellan, haughtily, "that our priests and teachers can not impart to us?"

"I bring my credentials with me," answered Mr. M——, and taking a Testament, translated into the Amharic language, he offered it to Adellan; but he shrunk back with horror, and refused to open it.

"I do not wish for your books," said he; "keep them. We are satisfied with our own. Look at our churches. They stand on every hill, far as your eye can reach. See that stream that winds near your dwelling. There we wash away the pollution of our souls. I fast by day, I watch by night. The saints hear my prayers, and the stars bear witness to my penances. I am going to the holy city, where I shall obtain remission for all my sins, and those of generations yet unborn. I shall return holy and happy."

Mr. M—— sighed, while the youth rapidly repeated his claims to holiness and heaven.

"You believe that God is a spirit," said he; "and the worship that is acceptable in his eyes must be spiritual also. In vain is the nightly vigil and the daily fast, unless the soul is humbled in his eyes. We may kneel till the rock is worn by our prostrations, and torture the flesh till every nerve is wakened to agony, but we can no more work out our own salvation by such means, than our feeble hands can create a new heaven and a new earth, or our mortal breath animate the dust beneath our feet, with the spirit of the living God."

The missionary spoke with warmth. His wife laid her gentle hand on his arm. There was something in the glance of the young Abyssinian that alarmed her. But the spirit of the martyr was kindled within him, and would not be quenched.

"See," said he, directing the eye of the youth towards the neighbouring hills, now clothed in the purple drapery of sunset; "as sure as those hills now stand, the banner of the cross shall float from their summits, and tell to the winds of heaven the triumphs of the Redeemer's kingdom. Ethiopia shall stretch out her sable hands unto God, and the farthest isles of the ocean behold the glory of his salvation."

Adellan looked into the glowing face of the missionary, remembered the cold and gloomy countenance of his religious teacher, and wondered at the contrast. But his prejudices were unshaken, and his pride rose up in rebellion against the man who esteemed him an idolater.

"Come to us again," said the missionary, in a subdued tone, as Adellan turned to depart; "let us compare our different creeds, by the light of reason and revelation, and see what will be the result."

"Come to us again," said the lady, in Adellan's native tongue; and her soft, low voice sounded sweet in his ears, as the fancied accents of the virgin mother. That night, as he sat in his lonely chamber, at the convent, conning his task in the stillness of the midnight hour, the solemn words of the missionary, his inspired countenance, the ethereal form of his wife, and the cherub face of that fair child, kept floating in his memory. He was angry with himself at the influence they exercised. He resolved to avoid his path, and to hasten his departure to Jerusalem, where he could be not only secure from his arts, but from the legions of the powers of darkness.

———————

Months passed away. The humble cabin of the missionary was gradually thronged with those who came from curiosity, or better motives, to hear the words of one who came from such a far country. His pious heart rejoiced in the hope, that the shadows of idolatry which darkened their religion would melt away before the healing beams of the Sun of Righteousness. But he looked in vain for the stately figure of the young Adellan. His spirit yearned after the youth, and whenever he bent his knees at the altar of his God, he prayed for his conversion, with a kind of holy confidence that his prayer would be answered. At length he once more presented himself before them, but so changed they could scarcely recognise his former lineaments. His face was haggard and emaciated, his hair had lost its raven brightness, and his garments were worn and soiled with dust. He scarcely answered the anxious inquiries of Mr. M——, but sinking into a seat, and covering his face with his hands, large tears, gathering faster and faster, glided through his fingers, and rained upon his knees. Mary, the sympathizing wife of the missionary, wept in unison; but she did not limit her sympathy to tears, she gave him water to wash, and food to eat, and it was not until he rested his weary limbs, that they sought to learn the history of his sufferings. It would be tedious to detail them at length, though he had indeed experienced "a sad variety of woe." He had commenced his journey under the guidance and protection of a man in whose honour he placed unlimited confidence, had been deceived and betrayed, sold as a slave, and, though he had escaped this degradation, he had been exposed to famine and nakedness, and the sword.

"I have been deserted by man," said Adellan; "the saints have turned a deaf ear to my prayers; I have come to you to learn if there is a power in *your*

Christianity to heal a wounded spirit, and to bind up a broken heart."

The missionary raised his eyes in gratitude to Heaven.

"The Spirit of the Lord God is upon me," cried he, repeating the language of the sublimest of the prophets: "because the Lord hath anointed me to preach good tidings unto the meek; he hath sent me to bind up the broken-hearted, to proclaim liberty to the captive, and the opening of the prison to them that are bound."

"Blessed are they that mourn, for they shall be comforted," repeated Mary, softly; and never were promises of mercy pronounced in a sweeter voice. Afflictions had humbled the proud spirit of Adellan. But his was not the humility of the Christian. It was rather a gloomy misanthropy, that made him turn in loathing from all he had once valued, and to doubt the efficacy of those forms and penances, in which he had wasted the bloom of his youth, and the morning strength of his manhood. But he no longer rejected the proffered kindness of his new friends. He made his home beneath their roof. The Testament he had formerly refused, he now gratefully received, and studied it with all the characteristic ardour of his mind. Persevering as he was zealous, as patient in investigation as he was quick of apprehension, he compared text with text, and evidence with evidence, till the prejudices of education yielded to the irresistible force of conviction. When once his understanding had received a doctrine, he cherished it as a sacred and eternal truth, immutable as the word of God, and immortal as his own soul.

He now went down into the hitherto untravelled chambers of his own heart, and, throwing into their darkest recesses the full blaze of revelation, he shuddered to find them infested by inmates more deadly than the serpent of the Nile. Passions, of whose existence he had been unconscious, rose up from their hiding places, and endeavoured to wrap him in their giant folds. Long and fearful was the struggle, but Adellan opposed to their power the shield of Faith and the sword of the Spirit, and at last came off conqueror, and laid down his spoils at the foot of the cross. The missionary wept over him, "tears such as angels shed." "Now," exclaimed he, "I am rewarded for all my privations, and my hitherto unavailing toils. Oh! Adellan, now the friend and brother of my soul, I feel something like the power of prophecy come over me, when I look forward to your future destiny. The time will shortly come, when you will stand in the high places of the land, and shake down the strong holds of ancient idolatry and sin. The temples, so long desecrated by adoration of senseless images, shall be dedicated to the worship of the living God. Sinners, who so long have sought salvation in the purifying waters of the stream, shall turn to the precious fountain of the Redeemer's blood. Oh! glorious, life-giving prospect! They who refuse to listen to the pale-faced stranger, will hearken to the accents of their native hills. Rejoice, my beloved Mary! though I may be forced to bear back that fading frame of yours to a more congenial clime, our Saviour will not be left without a witness, to attest his glory, and confirm his power."

To fulfil this prophecy became the ruling desire of Adellan's life. He longed to liberate his deluded countrymen from the thraldom of that superstition to which he himself had served such a long and gloomy apprenticeship. He longed, too, for some opportunity of showing his gratitude to his new friends. But there is no need of signal occasions to show what is passing in the heart. His was of a transparent texture, and its emotions were visible as the pebbles that gleam through the clear waters of the Tacazze. The beautiful child of the missionary was the object of his tenderest love. He would carry it in his arms for hours, through the wild groves that surrounded their dwelling, and, gathering for it the choicest productions of nature, delight in its smiles and infantine caresses. Sometimes, as he gazed on the soft azure of its eyes, and felt its golden ringlets playing on his cheek, he would clasp it to his bosom and exclaim, "Of such is the kingdom of heaven."

Mary idolized her child, and Adellan's great tenderness for it, inexpressibly endeared him to her heart. She loved to see the fair face of her infant leaning against the dark cheek of Adellan, and its flaxen locks mingling with his jetty hair. One evening, as it fell asleep in his arms, he was alarmed at the scarlet brightness of its complexion, and the burning heat of its skin. He carried it to its mother. It was the last time the cherub ever slumbered on his bosom. It never again lifted up its head, but faded away like a flower scorched by a noonday sun.

Day and night Adellan knelt by the couch of the dying infant, and prayed in agony for its life; yet even in the intensity of his anguish, he felt how sublime was the resignation of its parents. They wept, but no murmur escaped their lips. They prayed, but every prayer ended with the submissive ejaculation of their Saviour, "Not our will, O Father! but thine be done." And when the sweet, wistful eyes were at last closed in death, and the waxen limbs grew stiff and cold, when Adellan could not restrain the bitterness of his grief, still the mourners bowed their heads and cried, "The Lord gave, the Lord taketh away—blessed be the name of the Lord."

Adellan had witnessed the stormy sorrow of his country-women, whose custom it is to rend their hair, and lacerate their faces with their nails, and grovel, shrieking, in the dust; but never had his heart been so touched as by the resignation of this Christian mother. But, though she murmured not, she was stricken by the blow, and her fragile frame trembled beneath the shock. Her husband felt that she leaned more heavily on his arm, and though she smiled upon him as wont, the smile was so sad, it often brought tears into his eyes. At length she fell sick, and the missionary saw her laid upon the same bed on which his infant had died. Now, indeed, it might be said that the hand of God was on him. She, the bride of his youth, the wife of his fondest affections, who had given up all the luxuries of wealth, and the tender indulgences of her father's home, for the love of him and her God; who had followed him not only with meekness, but joy, to those benighted regions, that she might share and sweeten his labours, and join to his, her prayers and her efforts for the extension of the Redeemer's kingdom; she, whose presence had been able to transform their present lowly and lonely dwelling into a place lovely as the Garden of Eden—could he see *her* taken from him, and repeat, from his heart, as he had done over the grave of his only child, "Father, thy will be done?"

Bitter was the conflict, but the watchful ear of Adellan again heard the same low, submissive accents, which were so lately breathed over his lost darling. Here, too, Adellan acted a brother's part; but female care was requisite, and this his watchful tenderness supplied. He left them for a while, and returned with a young maiden, whose olive complexion, graceful figure, and long braided locks, declared her of Abyssinian birth. Her voice was gentle, and her step light, when she approached the bed of the sufferer. Ozora, for such was the name of the maiden, was a treasure in the house of sickness. Mary's languid eye followed her movements, and often brightened with pleasure, while receiving her sympathizing attentions. In her hours of delirious agony, she would hold her hand, and call her sister in the most endearing tone, and ask her how she had found her in that land of strangers. Sometimes she would talk of the home of her childhood, and imagine she heard the green leaves of her native bowers rustling in the gale. Then she thought she was wandering through the groves of Paradise, and heard the angel voice of her child singing amid the flowers.

Ozora was familiar with all the medicinal arts and cooling drinks of her country. She possessed not only native gentleness, but skill and experience as a nurse. She was an orphan, and the death-bed of her mother had witnessed her filial tenderness and care. She was an idolater, but she loved Adellan, and for his sake would gladly embrace the faith of the European. Adellan was actuated by a twofold motive in bringing her to the sick-bed of Mary; one was, that she might exercise a healing influence on the invalid, and another, that she might witness the triumphs of Christian faith over disease, sorrow, and death. But Mary was not doomed to make her grave in the stranger's land. The fever left her burning veins, and her mind recovered its wonted clearness. She was able to rise from her couch, and sit in the door of the cabin, and feel the balmy air flowing over her pallid brow.

She sat thus one evening, supported by the arm of her husband, in the soft light of the sinking sunbeams. Adellan and her gentle nurse were seated near. The eyes of all were simultaneously turned to a small green mound, beneath the shade of a spreading cedar, and they thought of the fairy form that had so often sported around them in the twilight hour.

"Oh! not there," cried Mary, raising her glistening eyes from that lonely grave to heaven—"Not there must we seek our child. Even now doth her glorified spirit behold the face of our Father in heaven. She is folded in the arms of Him, who, when on earth, took little children to his bosom and blessed them. And I, my beloved husband—a little while and ye shall see my face no more. Though the Almighty has raised me from that couch of pain, there is something tells me," continued she, laying her hand on her heart, "that my days are numbered; and when my ashes sleep beside that grassy bed, mourn not for me, but think that I have gone to my Father and your Father, to my God and your God." Then, leaning her head on her husband's shoulder, she added, in a low trembling voice—"to my child and your child."

It was long before Mr. M—— spoke; at length he turned to Adellan, and addressed him in the Amharic language: "My brother! it must be that I leave you. The air of her native climes may revive this drooping flower. I will bear her back to her own home, and, if God wills it, I will return and finish the work he has destined me to do."

Mary clasped her hands with irrepressible rapture as he uttered these words; then, as if reproaching herself for the momentary selfishness, she exclaimed, "And leave the poor Abyssinians!"

"I will leave them with Adellan," he answered, "whom I firmly believe God has chosen, to declare his unsearchable riches to this portion of the Gentile world. The seed that has been sown has taken root, and the sacred plant will spring up and increase, till the birds of the air nestle in its branches, and the beasts of the forest lie down beneath its shade. Adellan, does your faith waver?"

"Never," answered the youth, with energy, "but the arm of my brother is weak. Let me go with him on his homeward journey, and help him to support the being he loves. I shall gather wisdom from his lips, and knowledge from the glimpse of a Christian land. Then shall I be more worthy to minister to my brethren the word of life."

A sudden thought flashed into the mind of the missionary. "And would you, Adellan," asked he, "would you indeed wish to visit our land, and gain instruction in our institutions of learning, that you might return to enrich your country with the best treasures of our own? You are very young, and might be spared awhile now, that you may be fitted for more extensive usefulness hereafter."

Adellan's ardent eye told more expressively than words could utter, the joy which filled his soul at this proposition. "Too happy to follow you," cried he; "how can I be sufficiently grateful for an added blessing?"

Ozora, who had listened to the conversation, held in her own language, with intense interest, here turned her eyes upon Adellan, with a look of piercing reproach, and suddenly rising, left the cabin.

"Poor girl!" exclaimed Mary, as Adellan, with a saddened countenance, followed the steps of Ozora; "how tenderly has she nursed me, and what is the recompense she meets? We are about to deprive her of the light that gladdens her existence. She has not yet anchored her hopes on the Rock of Ages, and where else can the human heart find refuge, when the wild surges of passion sweep over it!"

"Adellan is in the hands of an all-wise and all-controlling power," answered the missionary, thoughtfully; "the tears of Ozora may be necessary to prove the strength of his resolution; if so, they will not fall in vain."

A few weeks after, everything being in readiness for the departure of the missionary and his family, he bade farewell to the Abyssinians, who crowded round his door to hear his parting words. He took them with him to the hillside, and, under the shadow of the odoriferous trees, and the covering of the heavens, he addressed them with a solemnity and fervour adapted to the august temple that surrounded him. His deep and sweet-toned voice rolled through the leafy colonnades and verdant aisles, like the rich notes of an organ in some ancient cathedral. The Amharic language, soft and musical in itself, derived new melody from the lips of Mr. M——.

"And now," added he, in conclusion, "I consign you to the guardianship of a gracious and long-suffering God. Forget not the words I have just delivered unto you, for remember they will rise up in judgment against you in that day when we shall meet face to face before the bar of eternal justice. This day has the Gospel been preached in your ears. Every tree that waves its boughs over your heads, every flower that embalms the atmosphere, and every stream that flows down into the valley, will bear witness that the hallowed name of the Redeemer has been breathed in these shades, and promises of mercy so sweet that angels stoop down from heaven to listen to the strains that have been offered, free, free as the very air you inhale. I go, my friends, but should I never return, this place will be for ever precious to my remembrance. It contains the ashes of my child. That child was yielded up in faith to its Maker, and the spot where it sleeps is, therefore, holy ground. Will ye not guard it from the foot of the stranger, and the wild beast of the mountain? Let the flower of the hills bloom ungathered upon it, and the dew of heaven rest untrodden on its turf, till he, who is the resurrection and the life, shall appear, and the grave give back its trust."

He paused, overpowered by the strength of his emotions, and the sobs of many of his auditors attested the sympathy of these untutored children of nature. He came down from the elevated position on which he had been standing, and taking the hand of Adellan, led him to the place he had just occupied. The people welcomed him with shouts, for it was the first time he had presented himself in public, to declare the change in his religious creed, and such was the character he had previously obtained for sanctity and devotion, they looked upon him with reverence, notwithstanding his youth. He spoke at first with diffidence and agitation, but gathering confidence as he proceeded, he boldly and eloquently set forth and defended the faith he had embraced. That young, enthusiastic preacher would have been a novel spectacle to an European audience, as well as that wild, promiscuous assembly. His long, white robes, girded about his waist, according to the custom of his country, his black, floating hair, large, lustrous eyes, and dark but now glowing complexion, formed a striking contrast with the sable garments, pallid hue, and subdued expression of the European minister. They interrupted him with tumultuous shouts, and when he spoke of his intended departure and attempted to bid them farewell, their excitement became so great, he was compelled to pause, for his voice strove in vain to lift itself above the mingled sounds of grief and indignation.

"I leave you, my brethren," cried he, at length, "only to return more worthy to minister unto you. My brother will open my path to the temples of religion and knowledge. He needs my helping arm in bearing his sick through the lonely desert and over the deep sea—what do I not owe him? I was a stranger and he took me in; I was naked and he clothed me; hungry and he fed me, thirsty and he gave me drink; and more than all, he has given me to eat the bread of heaven, and water to drink from the wells of salvation. Oh! next to God, he is my best friend and yours."

The shades of night began to fall, before the excited crowd were all dispersed, and Mr. M——, and Adellan were left in tranquillity. Mary had listened to the multitudinous sounds, with extreme agitation. She reproached herself for allowing her husband to withdraw from the scene of his missionary labours out of tenderness for her. She thought it would be better for her to die and be laid by her infant's grave, than the awakened minds of these half Pagan, half Jewish people, be allowed to relapse into their ancient idolatries. When the clods of the valley were once laid upon her breast, her slumbers would not be

147

less sweet because they were of the dust of a foreign land.

Thus she reasoned with her husband, who, feeling that her life was a sacred trust committed to his care, and that it was his first duty to guard it from danger, was not moved from his purpose by her tearful entreaties. They were to depart on the following morning.

That night Adellan sat with Ozora by the side of a fountain, that shone like a bed of liquid silver in the rising moonbeams. Nature always looks lovely in the moonlight, but it seemed to the imagination of Adellan he had never seen her clothed with such resplendent lustre as at this moment, when every star shone with a farewell ray, and every bough, as it sparkled in the radiance, whispered a melancholy adieu.

Ozora sat with her face bent over the fountain, which lately had often been fed by her tears. Her hair, which she had been accustomed to braid with oriental care, hung dishevelled over her shoulders. Her whole appearance presented the abandonment of despair. Almost every night since his contemplated departure, had Adellan followed her to that spot, and mingled the holiest teachings of religion with the purest vows of love. He had long loved Ozora, but he had struggled with the passion, as opposed to that dedication of himself to heaven, he had contemplated in the gloom of his conventual life. Now enlightened by the example of the missionary, and the evangelical principles he had embraced, he believed Christianity sanctioned and hallowed the natural affections of the heart. He no longer tried to conquer his love, but to make it subservient to higher duties.

Mary, grieved at the sorrow of Ozora, would have gladly taken her with her, but Adellan feared her influence. He knew he would be unable to devote himself so entirely to the eternal truths he was one day to teach to others, if those soft and loving eyes were always looking into the depths of his heart, to discover their own image there. He resisted the proposition, and Mr. M——— applauded the heroic resolution. But now Adellan was no hero; he was a young, impassioned lover, and the bitterness of parting pressed heavily on his soul.

"Promise me, Ozora," repeated he, "that when I am gone, you will never return to the idolatrous worship you have abjured. Promise me, that you will never kneel to any but the one, invisible God, and that this blessed book, which I give you, as a parting pledge, shall be as a lamp to your feet and a light to your path. Oh! should you forget the faith you have vowed to embrace, and should I, when I come back to my country, find you an alien from God, I should mourn, I should weep tears of blood over your fall; but you could never be the wife of Adellan. The friend of his bosom must be a Christian."

"I cannot be a Christian," sobbed the disconsolate girl, "for I love you better than God himself, and I am still an idolater. Oh! Adellan, you are dearer to me than ten thousand worlds, and yet you are going to leave me."

The grief she had struggled to restrain, here burst its bounds. Like the unchastened daughters of those ardent climes, she gave way to the wildest paroxysms of agony. She threw herself on the ground, tore out her long raven locks, and startled the silence of night by her wild, hysterical screams. Adellan in vain endeavoured to soothe and restore her to reason; when, finding his caresses and sympathy worse than unavailing, he knelt down by her side, and lifting his hands above her head, prayed to the Almighty to forgive her for her sacrilegious love. As the stormy waves are said to subside, when the wing of the halcyon passes over them, so were the tempestuous emotions that raged in the bosom of this unhappy maiden, lulled into calmness by the holy breath of prayer. As Adellan continued his deep and fervent aspirations, a sense of the omnipresence, the omnipotence and holiness of God stole over her. She raised her weeping eyes, and as the moonbeams glittered on her tears, they seemed but the glances of his all-seeing eye. As the wind sighed through the branches, she felt as if *His* breath were passing by her, in mercy and in love. Filled with melting and penitential feelings, she lifted herself on her knees, by the side of Adellan, and softly whispered a response to every supplication for pardon.

"Oh! Father, I thank thee for this hour!" exclaimed Adellan, overpowered by so unlooked-for a change, and throwing his arms around her, he wept from alternate ecstasy and sorrow. Let not the feelings of Adellan be deemed too refined and exalted for the region in which he dwelt. From early boyhood he had been kept apart from the companionship of the ruder throng; his adolescence had been passed in the shades of a convent, in study, and deep observation, and more than all he was a Christian; and wherever Christianity sheds its pure and purifying light, it imparts an elevation, a sublimity to the character and the language, which princes, untaught of God, may vainly emulate.

The morning sunbeam lighted the pilgrims on their way. The slight and feeble frame of Mary was borne on a litter by four sturdy Ethiopians. Seven or eight more accompanied to rest them, when weary, and to bear Mr. M—— in the same manner, when overcome by fatigue, for it was a long distance to Massowak. Their journey led them through a desert wilderness, where they might vainly sigh for the shadow of the rock, or the murmur of the stream. Adellan walked in silence by the side of his friend. His thoughts were with the weeping Ozora, and of the parting hour by the banks of the moonlighted fountain. Mary remembered the grave of her infant, and wept, as she caught a last glimpse of the hill where she had dwelt. The spirit of the missionary was lingering with the beings for whose salvation he had laboured, and he made a solemn covenant with his own soul, that he would return with Adellan, if God spared his life, and leave his Mary under the shelter of the paternal roof, if she indeed lived to behold it. On the third day, Mr. M—— was overcome with such excessive languor, he was compelled to be borne constantly by the side of his wife, unable to direct, or to exercise any controlling influence on his followers. Adellan alone, unwearied and energetic, presided over all, encouraged, sustained, and soothed. He assisted the bearers in upholding their burdens, and whenever he put his shoulder to the litter, the invalids immediately felt with what gentleness and steadiness they were supported. When they reached the desert, and camels were provided for the travellers, they were still often obliged to exchange their backs for the litter, unable long to endure the fatigue. Adellan was still unwilling to intrust his friends to any guidance but his own. He travelled day after day through the burning sands, animating by his example the exhausted slaves, and personally administering to the wants of the sufferers. When they paused for rest or refreshment, before he carried the cup to his own parched lips, he brought it to theirs. It was his hand that bathed with water their feverish brows, and drew the curtain around them at night, when slumber shed its dews upon their eyelids. And often, in the stillness of the midnight, when the tired bearers and weary camels rested and slept after their toils, the voice of Adellan rose sweet and solemn in the loneliness of the desert, holding communion with the high and holy One who inhabiteth eternity.

There was a boy among the negro attendants, who was the object of Adellan's peculiar kindness. He seemed feeble and incapable of bearing long fatigue, and at the commencement of the journey Adellan urged him to stay behind, but he expressed so strong a desire to follow the good missionary, he could not refuse his request. He wore his face muffled in a handkerchief, on account of some natural deformity, a circumstance which exposed him to the derision of his fellow slaves, but which only excited the sympathy of the compassionate Adellan. Often, when the boy, panting and exhausted, would throw himself for breath on the hot sand, Adellan placed him on his own camel and compelled him to ride. And when they rested at night, and Adellan thought every one but himself wrapped in slumber, he would steal towards him, and ask him to tell him something out of God's book, that he, Adellan, had been reading. It was a delightful task to Adellan to pour the light of divine truth into the dark mind of this poor negro boy, and every moment he could spare from his friends was devoted to his instruction.

One evening, after a day of unusual toil and exertion, they reached one of those verdant spots, called the Oases of the desert; and sweet to the weary travellers was the fragrance and coolness of this green resting-place. They made their tent under the boughs of the flowering acacia, whose pure white blossoms diffused their odours even over the sandy waste they had passed. The date tree, too, was blooming luxuriantly there, and, more delicious than all, the waters of a fountain, gushing out of the rock, reminded them how God had provided for the wants of his ancient people in the wilderness. The missionary and his wife were able to lift their languid heads, and drink in the freshness of the balmy atmosphere. All seemed invigorated and revived but the negro boy, who lay drooping on the ground, and refused the nourishment which the others eagerly shared.

"What is the matter, my boy?" asked Adellan, kindly, and taking his hand in his, was struck by its burning heat. "You are ill," continued he, "and have not complained." He made a pallet for him under the trees, and they brought him a medicinal draught. Seeing him sink after a while in a deep sleep, Adellan's anxiety abated. But about midnight he was awakened by the moanings of the boy, and bending over him, laid his hand on his forehead. The sufferer opened his eyes, and gasped, "Water, or I die!" Adellan ran to the fountain, and brought the water immediately to his lips. Then kneeling down, he removed the muffling folds of the handkerchief from his face, and unbound the same from his head, that he might bathe his temples in the cooling stream. The moon shone as clearly and resplendently as when it beamed on Ozora's parting tears, and lighted up with an intense radiance the features of the apparently expiring negro. Adellan was astonished that no disfiguring traces appeared on the regular outline of his youthful face; his hair, too, instead of the woolly locks of the Ethiopian, was of shining length and profusion, and as Adellan's hand bathed his brow with water, he discovered beneath the jetty dye of his complexion the olive skin of the Abyssinian.

"Ozora!" exclaimed Adellan, throwing himself in agony by her side; "Ozora, you have followed me, but to die!"

"Forgive me, Adellan," cried she, faintly; "it was death to live without you; but oh! I have found everlasting life, in dying at your feet. Your prayers have been heard in the desert, and I die in the faith and the hope of a Christian."

Adellan's fearful cry had roused the slumberers of the tent. Mr. M——, and Mary, herself, gathering strength from terror, drew near the spot. What was her astonishment to behold her beloved nurse, supported in the arms of Adellan, and seemingly breathing out her last sighs! Every restorative was applied, but in vain. The blood was literally burning up in her veins.

This last fatal proof of her love and constancy wrung the heart of Adellan. He remembered how often he had seen her slender arms bearing the litter, her feet blistering in the sands; and when he knew, too, that it was for the love of him she had done this, he felt as if he would willingly lay down his life for hers. But when he saw her mind, clear and undimmed by the mists of disease, bearing its spontaneous testimony to the truth of that religion which reserves its most glorious triumphs for the dying hour, he was filled with rejoicing emotions.

"My Saviour found me in the wilderness," cried she, "while listening to the prayers of Adellan. His head was filled with dew, and his locks were heavy with the drops of night. Oh, Adellan, there is a love stronger than that which has bound my soul to yours. In the strength of that love I am willing to resign you. I feel there is forgiveness even for me."

She paused, and lifting her eyes to heaven, with a serene expression, folded her hands on her bosom. The missionary saw that her soul was about to take its flight, and kneeling over her, his feeble voice rose in prayer and adoration. While the holy incense was ascending up to heaven, her spirit winged its upward way, so peacefully and silently, that Adellan still clasped her cold hand, unconscious that he was clinging to dust and ashes.

They made her grave beneath the acacia, whose blossoms were strewed over her dying couch. They placed a rude stone at the head, and the hand of Adellan carved upon it this simple, but sublime inscription, "I know that my Redeemer liveth." The name of *Ozora*, on the opposite side, was all the memorial left in the desert, of her whose memory was immortal in the bosom of her friends. But there was a grandeur in that lonely grave which no marble monument could exalt. It was the grave of a Christian:

And angels with their silver wings o'ershade

The ground now sacred by her relics made."

It would be a weary task to follow the travellers through every step of their journey. Adellan still continued his unwearied offices to his grateful and now convalescent friends, but his spirit mourned for his lost Ozora. When, however, he set foot on Christian land, he felt something of the rapture that swelled the breast of Columbus on the discovery of a new world. It was, indeed, a new world to him, and almost realized his dreams of Paradise.

The friends of Mary and her husband welcomed him, as the guardian angel who had watched over their lives in the desert, at the hazard of his own; and Christians pressed forward to open their hearts and their homes to their Abyssinian brother. Mary, once more surrounded by the loved scenes of her youth, and all the appliances of kindred love, and all the medicinal balms the healing art can furnish, slowly recovered her former strength. All that female gratitude and tenderness could do, she exerted to interest and enliven the feelings of Adellan, when, after each day of intense study, he returned to their domestic circle. The rapidity with which he acquired the German language was extraordinary. He found it, however, only a key, opening to him treasures of unknown value. Mr. M—— feared the effects of his excessive application, and endeavoured to draw him from his books and studies. He led him abroad amongst the works of nature, and the wonders of art, and tried to engage him in the athletic exercises the youth of the country delighted in.

Whatever Adellan undertook he performed with an ardour which no obstacles could damp, no difficulties subdue. Knowledge, purified by religion, was now the object of his existence; and, while it was flowing in upon his mind, from such various sources, finding, instead of its capacities being filled, that they were constantly enlarging and multiplying, and the fountains, though overflowing, still undrained: and knowing too, that it was only for a short time that his spirit could drink in these immortal influences, and that through them he was to fertilize and refresh, hereafter, the waste places of his country, he considered every moment devoted to relaxation alone, as something robbed from eternity.

One day, Adellan accompanied a number of young men belonging to the institution in which he was placed, in an excursion for the collection of minerals. Their path led them through the wildest and most luxuriant country, through scenes where nature rioted in all its virgin bloom; yet, where the eye glancing around, could discern the gilding traces of art, the triumphs of man's creating hand. Adellan, who beheld in every object, whether of nature or of art, the manifestation of God's glory, became lost in a trance of ecstasy. He wandered from his companions. He knelt down amid the rocks, upon the green turf, and on the banks of the streams. In every place he found an altar, and consecrated it with the incense of prayer and of praise. The shades of night fell around him, before he was conscious that the sun had declined. The dews fell heavy on his temples, that still throbbed with the heat and the exertions of the day. He returned chilled and exhausted. The smile of rapture yet lingered on his lips, but the damps of death had descended with the dews of night, and from that hour consumption commenced its slow but certain progress. When his friends became aware of his danger, they sought by every possible means to ward off the fatal blow. Mr. M—— induced him to travel, that he might wean him from his too sedentary habits. He carried him with him, through the magnificent valleys of Switzerland, those valleys, embosomed in hills, on whose white and glittering summits Adellan imagined he could see the visible footprints of the Deity. "Up to the hills," he exclaimed, with the sweet singer of Israel, in a kind of holy rapture, "up to the hills do I lift mine eyes, from whence cometh my help." When returning, they lingered on the lovely banks of the Rhine, his devout mind, imbued with sacred lore, recalled "the green fields and still waters," where the Shepherd of Israel gathered his flock.

The languid frame of Adellan seemed to have gathered strength, and his friends rejoiced in their reviving hopes; but "He who seeth not as man seeth," had sent forth his messenger to call him to his heavenly home. Gentle was the summons, but Adellan knew the voice of his divine Master, and prepared to obey. One night, as he reclined in his easy chair, and Mr. M—— was seated near, he stretched out his hand towards him, with a bright and earnest glance: "My brother," said he, "I can now say from my heart, the will of God be done. It was hard to give up my beloved Abyssinians, but I leave them in the hands of One who is strong to deliver, and mighty to save. You, too, will return, when you have laid this wasted frame in its clay-cold bed."

"I made a vow unto my God," answered Mr. M——, "that I would see them again, and that vow shall not be broken. When they ask me the parting words of Adellan, tell me what I shall utter."

"Tell them," exclaimed Adellan, raising himself up, with an energy that was startling, and in a voice surprisingly clear, while the glow of sensibility mingled with the hectic fires that burned upon his cheek; "tell them that the only reflection that planted a thorn in my dying pillow, was the sorrow I felt that I was not permitted to declare to them once more, the eternal truths of the

Gospel. Tell them, with the solemnities of death gathering around me, in the near prospect of judgment and eternity, I declare my triumphant faith in that religion your lips revealed unto me, that religion which was sealed by the blood of Jesus, and attested by the Spirit of Almighty God; and say, too, that had I ten thousand lives, and for every life ten thousand years to live, I should deem them all too short to devote to the glory of God, and the service of my Redeemer."

He sunk back exhausted in his chair, and continued, in a lower voice, "You will travel once more through the desert, but the hand of Adellan will no longer minister to the friend he loves. Remember him when you pass the grave of Ozora, and hallow it once more with the breath of prayer. She died for love of me, but she is gone to him who loved her *as man never loved*. Her spirit awaits my coming."

The last tear that ever dimmed the eye of Adellan here fell to the memory of Ozora. It seemed a parting tribute to the world he was about to leave. His future hours were gilded by anticipations of the happiness of heaven, and by visions of glory too bright, too holy for description. He died in the arms of the missionary, while the hand of Mary wiped from his brow the dews of dissolution. Their united tears embalmed the body of one, who, had he lived, would have been a burning and a shining light, in the midst of the dark places of the earth; one, who combined in his character, notwithstanding his youth and his country, the humility of the Publican, the ardour of Peter, the love of John, and the faith and zeal of the great Apostle of the Gentiles. Perhaps it should rather be said, with the reverence due to these holy evangelists and saints, that a large portion of their divine attributes animated the spirit of the Abyssinian Neophyte.

THE VILLAGE ANTHEM.

"What is that bell ringing for?" asked Villeneuve of the waiter, who was leaving the room.

"For church," was the reply.

"For church! Oh! is it Sunday? I had forgotten it. I did not think there was a church in this little village."

"Yes, indeed," answered the boy, his village pride taking the alarm, "and a very handsome one, too. Just look out at that window, sir. Do you see that tall, white steeple, behind those big trees there? That is the church, and I know there is not a better preacher in the whole world than Parson Blandford. He was never pestered for a word yet, and his voice makes one feel so warm and tender about the heart, it does one good to hear him."

Villeneuve cast a languid glance through the window, from the sofa on which he was reclining, thinking that Parson Blandford was very probably some old hum-drum, puritanical preacher, whose nasal twang was considered melodious by the vulgar ears which were accustomed to listen to him. Dull as his present position was, he was resolved to keep it, rather than inflict upon himself such an intolerable bore. The boy, who had mounted his hobby, continued, regardless of the unpropitious countenance of his auditor.

"Then there is Miss Grace Blandford, his daughter, plays so beautifully on the organ! You never heard such music in your life. When she sits behind the red curtains, and you can't see anything but the edge of her white skirt below, I can't help thinking there's an angel hid there; and when she comes down and takes her father's arm, to walk out of church, she looks like an angel, sure enough."

Villeneuve's countenance brightened. Allowing for all the hyperbole of ignorance, there were two positive things which were agreeable in themselves —music and a young maiden. He rose from the sofa, threw aside his dressing-gown, called for his coat and hat, and commanded the delighted boy to direct him to the church, the nearest way. His guide, proud of ushering in such a handsome and aristocratic-looking stranger, conducted him to one of the most conspicuous seats in the broad aisle, in full view of the pulpit and the orchestra, and Villeneuve's first glance was towards the red curtains, which were drawn so close, not even a glimpse of white was granted to the beholder. He smiled at his own curiosity. Very likely this angel of the village boy was a great red-faced, hard-handed country girl, who had been taught imperfectly to thrum the keys of an instrument, and consequently transformed by rustic simplicity into a being of superior order. No matter, any kind of excitement was better than the ennui from which he had been aroused. A low, sweet, trembling prelude stole on his ear. "Surely," thought he, "no vulgar fingers press those keys—that is the key-note of true harmony." He listened, the sound swelled, deepened, rolled through the arch of the building, and sank again with such a melting cadence, the tears involuntarily sprang into his eyes. Ashamed of his emotions, he leaned his head on his hand, and yielded unseen to an influence, which, coming over him so unexpectedly, had all the force of enchantment. The notes died away, then swelled again in solemn accompaniment with the opening hymn. The hymn closed with the melodious vibrations of the instrument, and for a few moments there was a most profound silence.

"The Lord is in his holy temple; let all the earth keep silence before him:" uttered a deep, solemn voice.

Villeneuve raised his head and gazed upon the speaker. He was a man rather past the meridian of life, but wearing unmarred the noblest attributes of manhood. His brow was unwrinkled, his piercing eye undimmed, and his tall figure majestic and unbowed. The sun inclined from the zenith, but the light, the warmth, the splendour remained in all their power, and the hearts of the hearers radiated that light and warmth, till an intense glow pervaded the assembly, and the opening words of the preacher seemed realized. Villeneuve was an Infidel; he looked upon the rites of Christianity as theatrical machinery, necessary, perhaps, towards carrying on the great drama of life, and when the springs were well adjusted and oiled, and the pulleys worked without confusion, and every appearance of art was kept successfully in the background, he was willing to sit and listen as he would to a fine actor when reciting the impassioned language of the stage. "This man is a very fine actor," was his first thought, "he knows his part well. It is astonishing, however, that he is willing to remain in such a limited sphere—with such an eye and voice—such flowing language and graceful elocution, he might make his fortune in any city. It is incomprehensible that he is content to linger in obscurity." Thus Villeneuve speculated, till his whole attention became absorbed in the sermon, which as a literary production was exactly suited to his fastidiously refined taste. The language was simple, the sentiments sublime. The preacher did not bring himself down to the capacities of his auditors, he lifted them to his, he elevated them, he spiritualized them. He was deeply read in the mysteries of the human heart, and he knew that however ignorant it might be of the truths of science and the laws of metaphysics, it contained many a divine spark which only required an eliciting touch to kindle. He looked down into the eyes upturned to him in breathless interest, and he read in them the same yearnings after immortality, the same reverence for the Infinite Majesty of the Universe, which moved and solemnized his own soul. His manner was in general calm and affectionate, yet there were moments when he swept the chords of human passion with a master's hand, and the hectic flush of his cheek told of the fire burning within.

"He is a scholar, a metaphysician, a philosopher, and a gentleman," said Villeneuve to himself, at the close of his discourse. "If he is an actor, he is the best one I ever saw. He is probably an enthusiast, who, if he had lived in ancient days, would have worn the blazing crown of martyrdom. I should like to see his daughter." The low notes of the organ again rose, as if in response to his heart's desire. This time there was the accompaniment of a new female voice. The congregation rose as the words of the anthem began. It was a kind of doxology, the chorus terminating with the solemn expression—"for ever and ever." The hand of the organist no longer trembled. It swept over the keys, as if the enthusiasm of an exalted spirit were communicated to every pulse and sinew. The undulating strains rolled and reverberated till the whole house was filled with the waves of harmony. But high, and clear, and sweet above those waves of harmony and the mingling voices of the choir, rose that single female voice, uttering the burden of the anthem, "for ever and ever." Villeneuve closed his eyes. He was oppressed by the novelty of his sensations. Where was he? In a simple village church, listening to the minstrelsy of a simple village maiden, and he had frequented the magnificent cathedral of Notre Dame, been familiar there with the splendid ritual of the national religion, and heard its sublime chantings from the finest choirs in the Universe. Why did those few monotonous words so thrill through every nerve of his being? That eternity which he believed was the dream of fanaticism, seemed for a moment an awful reality, as the last notes of the pæan echoed on his ear.

When the benediction was given, and the congregation was leaving the church, he watched impatiently for the foldings of the red curtains to part, and his heart palpitated when he saw a white-robed figure glide through the opening and immediately disappear. The next minute she was seen at the entrance of the church, evidently waiting the approach of her father, who, surrounded by his people, pressing on each other to catch a kindly greeting, always found it difficult to make his egress. As she thus stood against a column which supported the entrance, Villeneuve had a most favourable opportunity of scanning her figure, which he did with a practised and scrutinizing glance. He was accustomed to Parisian and English beauty, and comparing Grace Blandford to the high-born and high-bred beauties of the old world, she certainly lost in the comparison. She was very simply dressed, her eyes were downcast, and her features were in complete repose. Still there was a quiet grace about her that pleased him—a blending of perfect simplicity and perfect refinement that was extraordinary. Mr. Blandford paused as he came down the aisle. He had noticed the young and interesting looking stranger, who listened with such devout attention to all the exercises. He had heard, for in a country village such things are rapidly communicated, that there was a traveller at the inn, a foreigner and an invalid—two strong claims to sympathy and kindness. The pallid complexion of the young man was a sufficient indication of the latter, and the air of high breeding which distinguished him was equal to a letter of recommendation in his behalf. The minister accosted him with great benignity, and invited him to accompany him home.

"You are a stranger," said he, "and I understand an invalid. Perhaps you will find the quiet of our household more congenial this day than the bustle of a public dwelling."

Villeneuve bowed his delighted acceptance of this most unexpected invitation. He grasped the proffered hand of the minister with more warmth than he was aware of, and followed him to the door where Grace yet stood, with downcast eyes.

"My daughter," said Mr. Blandford, drawing her hand through his arm. This simple introduction well befitted the place where it was made, and was acknowledged by her with a gentle bending of the head and a lifting of the eyes, and they walked in silence from the portals of the church. What a change had the mere uplifting of those veiled lids made in her countenance! Two lines of a noble bard flashed across his memory—

The light of love, the purity of grace,

The mind, the music breathing from her face."

Then another line instantaneously succeeded—

And oh! that eye is in itself a soul."

There was one thing which disappointed him. He did not notice a single blush flitting over her fair cheek. He feared she was deficient in sensibility. It was so natural to blush at a stranger's greeting. He did not understand the nature of her feelings. He could not know that one so recently engaged in sublime worship of the Creator, must be lifted above fear or confusion in the presence of the creature. Villeneuve had seen much of the world, and understood the art of adaptedness, in the best sense of the word. He could conform to the circumstances in which he might be placed with grace and ease, and though he was too sincere to express sentiments he did not feel, he felt justified in concealing those he did feel, when he knew their avowal would give pain or displeasure. It was a very singular way for him to pass the Sabbath. The guest of a village pastor, breathing an atmosphere redolent of the sweets of piety, spirituality, and holy love. The language of levity and flattery, so current in society, would be considered profanation here; and a conviction deeply mortifying to his vanity forced itself upon him, that all those accomplishments for which he had been so much admired, would gain him no favour with the minister and his daughter. He could not forbear expressing his surprise at the location Mr. Blandford had chosen.

"I would not insult you by flattery," said Villeneuve, ingenuously, "but I am astonished you do not seek a wider sphere of usefulness. It is impossible that the people here should appreciate your talents, or estimate the sacrifices you make to enlighten and exalt them."

Mr. Blandford smiled as he answered—"You think my sphere too small, while I tremble at the weight of responsibility I have assumed. If I have the talents which you kindly ascribe to me, I find here an ample field for their exercise. There are hundreds of minds around me that mingle their aspirations with mine, and even assist me in the heavenward journey. In a larger, more brilliant circle, I might perhaps gain a more sounding name and exercise a wider influence, but that influence would not be half as deep and heartfelt. I was born and bred in a city, and know the advantages such a life can offer; but I would not exchange the tranquillity of this rural residence, the serenity of my pastoral life, the paternal influence I wield over this secluded village, and the love and reverence of its upright and pure-minded inhabitants, for the splendid sinecure of the Archbishops of our motherland."

Villeneuve was astonished to see a man so nobly endowed, entirely destitute of the principle of ambition. He wanted to ask him how he had thus trampled under his feet the honours and distinctions of the world. "You consider ambition a vice, then?" said he.

"You are mistaken," replied Mr. Blandford, "if you believe me destitute of ambition. I am one of the most ambitious men in the world. But I aspire after honours that can resist the mutations of time, and partake of the imperishability of their Great Bestower."

There was a silence of some moments, during which Mr. Blandford looked upward, and the eyes of Grace followed her father's with kindling ray.

"But, your daughter," continued Villeneuve, "can she find contentment in a situation for which nature and education have so evidently unfitted her?"

"Let Grace answer for herself," said Mr. Blandford, mildly; "I have consulted her happiness as well as my own, in the choice I have made."

Villeneuve was delighted to see a bright blush suffuse the modest cheek of

Grace—but it was the blush of feeling, not of shame.

"I love the country rather than the town," said she, "for I prefer nature to art, meditation to action, and the works of God to the works of man; and in the constant companionship of my father I find more than contentment—I find happiness, joy."

Villeneuve sighed—he felt the isolation of his own destiny. The last of his family, a traveller in a strange land, in pursuit of health; which had been sacrificed in the too eager pursuit of the pleasures of this world, without one hope to link him to another. Affluent and uncontrolled, yet sated and desponding, he envied the uncorrupted taste of the minister's daughter. He would have bartered all his wealth for the enthusiasm that warmed the character of her father. That night he was awakened by a singular dream. He thought he was alone in the horror of thick darkness. It seemed that he was in the midst of infinity, and yet chained to one dark spot, an immovable speck in the boundless ocean of space. "Must I remain here for ever?" he cried in agony, such as is only known in dreams, when the spirit's nerves are all unsheathed. "For ever and ever," answered a sweet, seraphic voice, high above his head, and looking up he beheld Grace, reclining on silver-bosomed clouds, so distant she appeared like a star in the heavens, yet every lineament perfectly defined. "Am I then parted from thee for ever?" exclaimed he, endeavouring to stretch out his arms towards the luminous point. "For ever and ever," responded the same heavenly accents, mournfully echoing till they died away, and the vision fled. He was not superstitious, but he did not like the impression of his dream. He rose feverish and unrefreshed, and felt himself unable to continue his journey. Mr. Blandford came to see him. He was deeply interested in the young stranger, and experienced the pleasure which every sensitive and intellectual being feels in meeting with kindred sensibility and intellect. The intimacy, thus commenced, continued to increase, and week after week passed away, and Villeneuve still lingered near the minister and his daughter. His health was invigorated, his spirits excited by the novel yet powerful influences that surrounded him. It was impossible, in the course of this deepening intimacy, that the real sentiments of Villeneuve should remain concealed, for hypocrisy formed no part of his character. Mr. Blandford, relying on the reverence and affection Villeneuve evidently felt for him, believed it would be an easy task to interest him in the great truths of religion. And it was an easy task to interest him, particularly when the father's arguments were backed by the daughter's persuasive eloquence; but it was a most difficult one to convince. The prejudices of education, the power of habit, the hardening influence of a worldly life, presented an apparently impenetrable shield against the arrows of divine truth.

"I respect, I revere the principles of your religion," Villeneuve was accustomed to say at the close of their long and interesting conversations. "I would willingly endure the pangs of death; yea, the agonies of martyrdom, for the possession of a faith like yours. But it is a gift denied to me. I cannot force my belief, nor give a cold assent with my lips to what my reason and my conscience belie."

Mr. Blandford ceased not his efforts, notwithstanding the unexpected resistance he encountered, but Grace gradually retired from the conflict, and Villeneuve found to his sorrow and mortification that she no longer appeared to rejoice in his society. There was a reserve in her manners which would have excited his resentment, had not the sadness of her countenance touched his heart. Sometimes when he met her eye it had an earnest, reproachful, pitying expression, that thrilled to his soul. One evening he came to the Parsonage at a later hour than usual. He was agitated and pale. "I have received letters of importance," said he; "I must leave you immediately. I did not know that all my happiness was centered in the intercourse I have been holding with your family, till this summons came." Grace, unable to conceal her emotions, rose and left the apartment. Villeneuve's eyes followed her with an expression which made her father tremble. He anticipated the scene which followed. "Mr. Blandford," continued Villeneuve, "I love your daughter. I cannot live without her—I cannot depart without an assurance of her love and your approbation."

Mr. Blandford was too much agitated to reply—the blood rushed to his temples, then retreating as suddenly, left his brow and cheek as colourless as marble. "I should have foreseen this," at length he said. "It would have spared us all much misery."

"Misery!" replied Villeneuve, in a startling tone.

"Yes," replied Mr. Blandford, "I have been greatly to blame—I have suffered my feelings to triumph over my judgment. Villeneuve, I have never met a young man who won upon my affections as you have done. The ingenuousness, ardour, and generosity of your character impelled me to love you. I still love you; but I pity you still more. I can never trust my daughter's happiness in your hands. There is a gulf between you—a wall of separation—high as the heavens and deeper than the foundations of the earth." He paused, and bowed his face upon his hands. The possibility that his daughter's happiness might be no longer in her own keeping, completely overpowered him. Villeneuve listened in astonishment and dismay. He, in all the pride of affluence and rank (for noble blood ran in lineal streams through his veins), to be rejected by an obscure village pastor, from mere religious scruples. It was incredible—one moment his eye flashed haughtily on the bending figure before him; the next it wavered, in the apprehension that Grace might yield to her father's decision, and seal their final separation. "Mr. Blandford," cried he, passionately, "I can take my rejection only from your daughter—I have never sought her love unsanctioned by your approbation—I have scorned the guise of a hypocrite, and I have a right to claim this from you. You may destroy *my* happiness—it is in your power—but tremble lest you sacrifice a daughter's peace."

Mr. Blandford recovered his self-command, as the passions of the young man burst their bounds. He summoned Grace into his presence. "I yield to your impetuous desire," said he, "but I would to Heaven you had spared me a scene like this. Painful as it is, I must remain to be a witness to it." He took his daughter's hand as she entered, and drew her towards him. He watched her countenance while the first vows of love to which she had ever listened were breathed into her ear with an eloquence and a fervour which seemed irresistible, and these were aided by the powerful auxiliary of a most handsome and engaging person, and he trembled as he gazed. Her cheek kindled, her eye lighted up with rapture, her heart panted with excessive emotion. She leaned on her father's arm, unable to speak, but looked up in his face with an expression that spoke volumes.

"You love him, then, Grace," said he mournfully. "Oh, my God! forgive me the folly, the blindness, the madness of which I have been guilty!"

Grace started, as if wakening from a dream. Her father's words recalled her to herself—one brief moment of ecstasy had been hers—to be followed, she knew, by hours of darkness and sorrow. The warm glow faded from her cheek, and throwing her arms round her father's neck, she wept unrestrainedly.

"She loves me," exclaimed Villeneuve; "you yourself witness her emotions—you will not separate us—you will not suffer a cruel fanaticism to destroy us both."

"Grace," said Mr. Blandford, in a firm voice, "look up. Let not the feelings of a moment, but the principles of a life decide. Will you hazard, for the enjoyment of a few fleeting years, the unutterable interests of eternity? Will you forsake the Master *he* abjures for the bosom of a stranger? In one word, my daughter, will you wed an Infidel?"

Grace lifted her head, and clasping her hands together, looked fervently upward.

"Thou art answered," cried Mr. Blandford, with a repelling motion towards Villeneuve. "The God she invokes will give her strength to resist temptation. Go, then, most unhappy yet beloved young man—you have chosen your

163

destiny, and we have chosen ours. *You* live for time. *We*, for eternity. As I said before, there is a deep gulf between us. Seek not to drag her down into the abyss into which you would madly plunge. My soul hath wrestled with yours, and you have resisted, though I fought with weapons drawn from Heaven's own armory. Farewell—our prayers and our tears will follow you."

He extended his hand to grasp Villeneuve's for the last time, but Villeneuve, with every passion excited beyond the power of control, rejected the motion; and, snatching the hand of Grace, which hung powerless over her father's shoulder, drew her impetuously towards him. "She loves me," exclaimed he, "and I will never resign her; I swear it by the inexorable Power you so blindly worship. Perish the religion that would crush the dearest and holiest feelings of the human heart! Perish the faith that exults in the sacrifice of nature and of love!"

With one powerful arm Mr. Blandford separated his daughter from the embrace of her lover, and holding him back with the other, commanded him to depart. He was dreadfully agitated, the veins of his temples started out like cords, and his eyes flashed with imprisoned fires. Villeneuve writhed for a moment in his unrelaxing grasp, then, reeling backward, sunk upon a sofa. He turned deadly pale, and held his handkerchief to his face.

"Oh! father! you have killed him!" shrieked Grace, springing to his side; "he faints! he bleeds, he dies!"

Even while Grace was speaking, the white handkerchief was crimsoned with blood, the eyes of the young man closed, and he fell back insensible.

"Just Heaven! spare me this curse!" cried Mr. Blandford. "Great God! I have killed them both!"

They did indeed look like two murdered victims, for the blood which oozed from the young man's lips not only dyed his own handkerchief and neckcloth, but reddened the white dress of Grace and stiffened on her fair locks, as her head drooped unconsciously on his breast. All was horror and confusion in the household. The physician was immediately summoned, who declared that a blood-vessel was ruptured, and that the life of the young man was in the most imminent danger. Grace was borne to her own apartment and consigned to the care of some kind neighbours, but Mr. Blandford remained the whole night by Villeneuve's side, holding his hand in his, with his eyes fixed on his pallid countenance, trembling lest every fluttering breath should be his last. About daybreak he opened his eyes, and seeing who was watching so tenderly over him, pressed his hand and attempted to speak, but the doctor commanded perfect silence, assuring him that the slightest exertion would be at the hazard of his life. For two or three days he hovered on the brink of the grave, during which time Mr. Blandford scarcely left his side, and Grace lingered near the threshold of the door, pale and sleepless, the image of despair. One night, when he seemed to be in a deep sleep, Mr. Blandford knelt by his couch, and in a low voice breathed out his soul in prayer. His vigil had been one long prayer, but he felt that he must find vent in language for the depth and strength of his emotions. He prayed in agony for the life of the young man; for his soul's life. He pleaded, he supplicated; till, language failing, sigh and tears alone bore witness to the strivings of his spirit. "Yet, not my will, oh! God!" ejaculated he again, "but thine be done."

"Amen!" uttered a faint voice. The minister started as if he had heard a voice from the dead. It was Villeneuve who spoke, and whose eyes fixed upon him had a most intense and thrilling expression. "Your prayer is heard," continued he. "I feel that God is merciful. A ray of divine light illumines my parting hour. Let me see Grace before I die, that our souls may mingle once on earth, in earnest of their union hereafter."

The minister led his daughter to the couch of Villeneuve. He joined her hand in his. "My daughter," cried he, "rejoice. I asked for him life. God giveth unto him long life; yea, life for evermore."

Grace bowed her head on the pale hand that clasped her own, and even in that awful moment, a torrent of joy gushed into her soul. It was the foretaste of an eternal wedlock, and death seemed indeed swallowed up in victory. Mr. Blandford knelt by his kneeling daughter, and many a time during that night they thought they saw the spirit of Villeneuve about to take its upward flight; but he sunk at length into a gentle slumber, and when the doctor again saw him, he perceived a favourable change in his pulse, and told Mr. Blandford there was a faint hope of his recovery. "With perfect quiet and tender nursing," said he, looking meaningly at Grace, "he may yet possibly be saved."

The predictions of the excellent physician were indeed fulfilled, for in less than three weeks Villeneuve, though still weak and languid, was able to take his seat in the family circle. Mr. Blandford saw with joy that the faith which he had embraced in what he believed his dying hour, was not abandoned with returning health. He had always relied on the rectitude of his principles, and now, when religion strengthened and sanctified them, he felt it his duty to sanction his union with his daughter. The business which had summoned him so unexpectedly to his native country still remained unsettled, and as the physician prescribed a milder climate, he resolved to try the genial air of France. It was no light sacrifice for Mr. Blandford to give up his daughter, the sole treasury of his affections, and doom himself to a solitary home; but he did it without murmuring, since he hoped the blessing of heaven would hallow their nuptials. Villeneuve promised to return the ensuing year, and restore Grace again to her beloved parsonage.

The Sunday before their departure, Grace accompanied her father and husband to the village church. Villeneuve saw the boy who had guided him there the first time, standing at the portal. He returned his respectful salutation with a warm grasp of the hand. "He led me to the gate of heaven," thought he; "he shall not go unrewarded."

"She will be too proud to play on the organ any more," said the boy to himself, "now that she has married a great man and a foreigner;" but Grace ascended the steps as usual, and drew the red curtains closely round her. What the feelings of the musician were, within that sacred sanctuary, as she pressed the keys, probably for the last time, could only be judged from a trembling touch; but at the close of the services, when the same sublime anthem, with the burden "for ever and ever," was sung by the choir, Villeneuve recognised the same clear, adoring accents which first fell so thrillingly on his ear. He remembered his dream. It no longer filled him with superstitious horror. It was caused by the workings of his dark and troubled mind. Now every thought flowed in a new channel; he seemed a new being to himself.

"Are we indeed united?" said he, while his soul hung on the echoes of that sweet strain, "and shall we be united for ever?"

"For ever and ever," returned the voice of the worshipper; and the whole choir, joining in, in a full burst of harmony, repeated again and again, "for ever and ever."

THE BOSOM SERPENT.

"I have something to tell you, Rosamond," said Cecil Dormer, taking Rosamond Clifford on his knee and seating himself in a corner of her mother's sofa—"Don't you want to hear a story to-night?"

"Is it a sure enough story?" asked Rosamond, "or a fairy tale, like the Arabian Nights Entertainment?"

"Every word of it truth," answered Cecil—"though some portions of it may 'freeze your young blood.' It is of a little girl, about your own age, and a woman who I verily believe is Lucifer himself, dressed in woman's clothes."

"You have excited my curiosity," said Mrs. Clifford closing her book, and taking a seat on the sofa—"for as every story must have a hero, I suspect you are the hero of your own."

"Please tell it," cried Rosamond, with the impatience of a petted child—"I want to hear about the little girl."

"Well," said Cecil, "you recollect how bright and beautiful the moon shone last night, and how peaceful and lovely everything looked. As I was returning to my lodgings, rather later than usual, I passed through a lane, which shortened the distance, though the walk itself was rough and unpleasant. As I was indulging in my old habit of building castles by the moonlight, I heard the most piercing shrieks issuing from a low building to which I was directly opposite. There must be murder going on, thought I, and like the giant, I imagined I could 'smell the blood of an Englishman.' I rushed to the door, almost shook it from its hinges in opening it, and found myself in the narrow, dark passage—but, guided by the cries, I soon reached another door, which I opened with as little ceremony, and what do you think I saw?"

"Were they killing the poor little girl?" cried Rosamond, drawing a long breath, her eyes growing larger and darker.

"You shall hear. In the centre of the room, there was a large, iron-framed woman, with her right hand extended, brandishing a leathern thong over the head of a pale, shrinking girl, whom she grasped with her left hand, and from whose bare shoulders the blood was oozing through grooves that thong had cut. You may well start and shudder, for a more hideous spectacle never met the eye. She was just in the act of inflicting another lash, when I arrested her arm with a force which must have made it ache to the marrow of the bones, and caused her involuntarily to loosen her hold of her victim, who fell exhausted to the floor. The woman turned on me, with the fury of a wolf

167

interrupted in its bloody banquet."

"Did she look like the picture of the wolf in little *Red Riding Hood*?" asked Rosamond.

"Yes, a most striking resemblance. Her cap was blown back to the crown of her head by the barbarous exercise in which she had been engaged, her tongue actually protruded from her mouth, in the impotence of her rage, and her hard, dull-coloured eyes glowed like red-hot stones in their deep sockets."

"'What do you want?' cried she, in a voice between a growl and a scream—'and who are you, and what is your business? You had better take care, or I'll make your back smart, in spite of your fine coat.'

"I could not help smiling at the idea of being whipped by a woman, but I answered as sternly as possible—'I want humanity, for I am a man. My business is to snatch this child from your clutches, and to give you up to the city authorities for disturbing the public peace.'

"'It is her fault, not mine,' replied she, a little intimidated by my threat—'she always screams and hollows when I whip her, as if I were murdering her, if I but scratch her skin. I gave her a task to do, and told her if she did not do it I would whip her—a good-for-nothing, lazy thing!—mope, mope from morning to night, nothing but mope and fret, while I'm drudging like a slave. I'm not going to support her any longer, if I have to turn her out of doors. She thinks because her mother happened to die here, I must give her a home, forsooth, and she do nothing to pay for it, the ungrateful hussy!'"

"Oh! don't tell any more about that horrid old woman," interrupted Rosamond—"I want to hear about the little girl. What did she do?"

"Why, she wept and sobbed, and said she did all she could, but that she was sick and weak, and she wished she was in the grave, by her poor mother's side, for there was nobody in the world to take care of her, and she knew not what would become of her. I told her impulsively that *I* would see she was taken care of, and if that vile woman but lifted her finger against her once more, she should rue it to her heart's core."

"There, Cecil, you have made a rhyme, so you must wish before you speak again," said Rosamond, laughing.

"Well, I wish that poor, desolate child had a home like this, and a mother like Mrs. Clifford, and a companion like Rosamond—or I wish that I had a kind mother and sister, to whose care I could intrust her, or a sweet gentle wife—and it is the first time in my life I ever breathed that wish—who would be willing to protect and cherish her for my sake."

"Is she a pretty child?" interrogated Mrs. Clifford, feelings best known to herself prompting the question.

"Yes!" repeated Rosamond, eagerly, stealing a look in the glass at her own bright eyes, fair complexion, and curling locks—"is she pretty, and was she dressed nice?"

"No!" answered Cecil, "the only emotion she could excite is that of the deepest pity. She is thin to emaciation, sallow to cadaverousness, and her eyes occupy the greatest portion of her face, they look so large and hollow and wild. She might sit for a miniature representation of famine, disease, or woe. There is something about her, however, that speaks of gentle blood and early gentle breeding. Her name at least is aristocratic, and bespeaks a French extraction—Eugenia St. Clair."

Rosamond was delighted with the name, and wondered how she could help being pretty with such a beautiful name.

"Poor child!" said Mrs. Clifford, "it is a pity she is not handsome, it would add so much to the romance of the adventure."

"She is helpless and oppressed," cried Cecil warmly, "and if she had the beauty of a cherub her claims would not plead more eloquently than they do in my heart. I should think I were guilty of murder, if I left her in the hands of that virago. It is true I put a *douceur* in her hand, terrifying her at the same time with the threatenings of the law, but this will only purchase the child's security for a short time. I made a vow to myself, when she clung to me convulsively, as I attempted to leave her, that I would place her in some situation where she could find kindness and protection, till fitting arrangements can be made for her education."

"You are indeed romantic," said Mrs. Clifford, seriously, "and know not what you may entail upon yourself."

"I am sorry if you think me so," said Cecil, with a look of mortification and disappointment—"I see I have as usual drawn too hasty conclusions. You have been so very kind to me, so kind as to make me forget in your household the absence of domestic ties. I dared to hope you would assist me in my design, and perhaps receive for a little while, under your own roof, this neglected child of orphanage and want. I have no other friend of whom I could ask a similar favour, and if I find I am presuming too much on you, I believe I must try to fall in love and get married, so that I can take my protegée to a home of my own."

Mrs. Clifford had not the most distant idea of permitting him to do so preposterous a thing, for she had long since appropriated him to Rosamond, whom as a child he now petted and caressed, and whom, if he continued as he now was, fancy free, as a woman he must inevitably love. When he first mentioned the girl, and expressed such a strong interest in her behalf, she began to tremble in anticipation, fearing a future rival in her views; but the lean, sallow face, half eyes and half bone, just delineated, tranquillized her fears, and as her fears subsided, her pity strengthened. And Rosamond, though too young to enter into her mother's speculations, felt her sympathy increased tenfold since she had learned that nature had gone hand in hand with fortune, and been equally niggard of her boons. She was unfortunately an only child, and accustomed to be an object of exclusive attention in the household, from her idolizing mother down to the lowest menial. The guests too easily understood the way to Mrs. Clifford's heart, and as Rosamond was pretty and sprightly, they derived amusement from her little airs and graces. But what flattered her vanity and elated her pride more than anything else, Cecil Dormer, so distinguished for wealth and accomplishments, so courted and admired, seemed to prefer her company to the society of grown ladies, who had often declared themselves jealous of her, and threatened, when she was a few years older, to shut her up in some convent or cell. Thus imperceptibly acquiring an exaggerated idea of her own consequence, and believing the love and admiration of all her inalienable right, had Cecil represented the orphan Eugenia as beautiful and charming, it is more than probable she would have regarded her as a dreaded encroacher on boundaries which nature had prescribed and fortune guarded—but for the ugly Eugenia all her sympathies were enlisted, and she pleaded her mother so warmly to bring her there directly, and take her away from that dreadful woman *for good and all*, that Cecil was delighted with her sensibility and benevolence, and rejoiced in such a juvenile coadjutor.

The next morning Mrs. Clifford accompanied Dormer to Mrs. Grundy's, the woman of the leathern thong, of whom she requested the history of Eugenia. Mrs. Grundy was sullen, and but little disposed to be communicative. She declared she knew nothing about her mother, only that she came there as a boarder, with barely sufficient to pay the expenses of her lodgings; that she fell sick soon after, and died, leaving the little girl on her hands, with nothing in the world but a grand name for her support. She expressed no gratitude or pleasure at the prospect of being released from the burthen under which she groaned, but grumbled about her own hard lot, insinuating that idleness and ingratitude were always sure to be rewarded. Eugenia's appearance was a living commentary on the truth of Dormer's story. Her neck and shoulders were streaked with swollen and livid lines, and her large, blood-shot eyes spoke of repressed and unutterable anguish. When told of the new home to which she was to be transferred, that she was to be placed by Dormer under the protection of Mrs. Clifford, and that if she were a good girl, and merited such advantages, she should be sent to school, and be fitted for a respectable station in society—she stood like one bewildered, as if awaking from a dream. Then, after taking in the truth of her position, she turned towards Dormer with wonderful quickness and even grace of motion, and clasping her hands together, attempted to speak, but burst into a passionate fit of weeping.

"There!" cried Mrs. Grundy, "you see what an ungrateful cretur she is. Do what you will for her, she does nothing but cry. Well, all I hope, you'll not be sick of your bargain, and be imposing her on me, before the week comes round again. But I give you warning, when once she gets out of my doors, she never darkens them a second time."

Dormer cast upon her a withering look, but, disdaining to reply to mere vulgarity and insolence, he took the hand of the sobbing child, and motioning to Mrs. Clifford, they left the room, while Mrs. Grundy's voice, keeping up a deep thorough bass, followed them till the door of the carriage was closed and the rumbling of the wheels drowned accents which certainly "by distance were made more sweet."

Eugenia had not been an hour under the roof of Mrs. Clifford, before a complete transformation was effected, by the supervising care of the proud and busy Rosamond. Her waiting-maid was put in active employment, in combing, brushing, and perfuming Eugenia's neglected hair, her wardrobe was ransacked to supply her fitting apparel, her mother's medicine chest was opened to furnish a healing liniment for her lacerated neck, which was afterwards covered by a neat muslin apron.

"Now look at yourself in the glass," said Rosamond, leading her to a large mirror, which reflected the figure at full length; "don't you look nice?"

Eugenia cast one glance, then turned away with a deep sigh. The contrast of her own tawny visage and meagre limbs with the fair, bright, round, joyous face and glowing lineaments of Rosamond, was too painful; but Rosamond loved to linger where a comparison so favourable to herself could be drawn, and her kind feelings to Eugenia rose in proportion to the self-complacency of which she was the cause.

It was a happy little circle which met that evening around Mrs. Clifford's table. Mrs. Clifford was happy in the new claim she had acquired over Cecil Dormer, and the probable influence it might exert on her future plans. Rosamond was happy in enacting the character of Lady Bountiful, and being praised by Cecil Dormer; and Cecil himself was happy in the consciousness of having performed a benevolent action. Eugenia's spirits had been so crushed by sorrow and unkindness, it seemed as if their elastic principle were destroyed. She was gentle, but passive, and appeared oppressed by the strangeness of her situation. Yet, as she expressed no vulgar amazement at the elegancies that surrounded her, and had evidently been taught the courtesies of society, Mrs. Clifford became convinced that Dormer was right in his belief that she was of gentle blood, and the fear that Rosamond's manners might be injured by contact with an unpolished plebeian subsided. When Eugenia was somewhat accustomed to her new situation, Mrs. Clifford questioned her minutely with regard to her parentage and the peculiar circumstances of her mother's death. She gathered from her broken and timid answers, that her father was wealthy, and that the first years of her life were passed in affluence; that as she grew older her mother seemed unhappy and her father stern and gloomy, why she could not tell; that one night, during her father's absence, her mother had left her home, accompanied by herself and one servant girl, and taken passage in a steamboat for that city. They boarded in obscure lodgings, never went abroad, or received visiters at home. Her mother grew paler and sadder. At length the servant girl, who seemed greatly attached to them, died. Then she described her mother as being much distressed for money to pay her board, being obliged to part with her watch and jewels, and when these resources failed, thankful to obtain sewing from her landlady, or, through her, from others. As they became more wretched and helpless, they were compelled to go from house to house, where her mother could find employment, till she was taken sick at Mrs. Grundy's, and never lifted her head again from the pillow so grudgingly supplied. A diamond ring, the most valued and carefully preserved of all her jewels, procured for her the sad privilege of dying there. Over her consequent sufferings Eugenia only wept, and on this subject Mrs. Clifford had no curiosity.

It was about six years after these events, that Cecil Dormer again was seated on the sofa in Mrs. Clifford's drawing-room, but Rosamond no longer sat upon his knee. The rosy-cheeked child, with short curling hair, short frock, and ruffled pantalettes, had disappeared, and, in her stead, a maiden with longer and more closely fitting robes, smoother and darker hair, and cheeks of paler and more mutable roses. Cecil was unchanged in face, but there was that in his air and manner which spoke a higher degree of elegance and fashion, and a deeper acquaintance with the world. He had passed several years at Paris. Rosamond had been in the mean time at a distant boarding-school, where Eugenia still remained.

"What are you going to do with Eugenia," asked Mrs. Clifford, "when she returns? Will you not find a young female protegée rather an embarrassing appendage to a bachelor's establishment?"

"I have just been thinking of the same thing," replied Cecil. "I believe I must still encroach on your kindness as I was wont to do in former days, and request you to receive her under your protection, till some permanent arrangement can be made for her home."

"That permanent arrangement must be your own marriage, I should presume," said Mrs. Clifford; "and indeed, Cecil, I wonder that with your fortune and rare endowments, you do not think seriously of assuming the responsibility of a household."

"What! the sensible Benedict a married man?" cried Cecil, with a theatrical start. "I shall lose all my consequence in society—I shall dwindle down into complete insignificance. No—I am not quite old enough to be married yet. I must act, too, as protector and elder brother to Rosamond, on her entrance into the world, an office which I promised to perform, when I dandled her a child in my arms."

"I am sure Rosamond would not wish to interfere with your personal arrangements," replied Mrs. Clifford, in a tone of pique—she was vexed and astonished at Cecil's coldness and indifference. She could not imagine the stoicism which could resist the influence of Rosamond's blooming beauty. She had looked forward to their meeting, after an absence of years, as the moment which should realize her long-cherished hopes, and nothing could be more provoking than the nonchalance of Cecil, unless it was the warm interest he manifested in everything respecting Eugenia.

"No, indeed," said Rosamond, laughing, "I willingly relinquish every claim on your protection, for Eugenia's sake. Perhaps some one else will take pity on my forlorn condition, and volunteer as my champion." Rosamond laughed, but her voice was unsteady, and a bright blush suffused her cheek.

Cecil noticed the vibration of her voice, and the sudden crimson rushing even to her temples. Her emotion surprised—interested him—was it possible, his marriage was an event capable of awakening such visible agitation? He looked at her more intently. Sensibility had added wonderful charms to her features. His vanity was flattered. He had been much admired in the world, and the language of adulation was familiar to his ear. But here was a young girl, in all the freshness and purity of life's vernal season, incapable of artifice, unpractised in the blandishments of society, one too whom he had known and loved as a beautiful child, and caressed with the familiarity of a brother, who was paying him an involuntary homage, as unexpected as it was fascinating. It was surprising what a long train of images swept over his mind, rapid and dazzling as lightning, called up by that deep maiden blush. How delightful it would be to secure the possession of a heart which had never yet known the pulsations of passion, whose master chords were waiting the magic of his touch to respond the deep music of feeling and love! How happy

Eugenia would be in the constant companionship of her juvenile benefactress, her schoolmate and friend! Mrs. Clifford, too, had always shown him the tenderness of a mother, and was so interested in his future establishment. Strange, what slight circumstances sometimes decide the most solemn, the most important events of life! The opportune blush of Rosamond sealed her own destiny, and that of Cecil Dormer. In less than one month the "sensible Benedict" was indeed a married man, the husband of the young and happy Rosamond. Seldom indeed was there a prouder and happier bride—ambition, pride, vanity, love—all were gratified, and could she have purchased the lease of immortality on earth, she would have asked no other heaven. But, even in the fulness of love's silver honeymoon, a dark cloud rose. The mother, who had lived but for her, and who was basking in the blaze of her daughter's prosperity, without one thought beyond it, was stricken by a sudden and fatal disease, and Rosamond's bridal paraphernalia was changed to the garments of mourning. It was her first felt misfortune, for her father died in her infancy; and the blow was terrible. At any other time it would have been so, but now this sudden and startling proof of mortality, in the morn of her wedded felicity, was chill and awful. Still there was a consolation in the sympathy of Cecil, that disarmed sorrow of its keenest pang, and there were moments, when she felt it even a joy to weep, since her tears were shed on the bosom of a husband so passionately loved. The arrival of Eugenia, a few weeks after this melancholy event, turned her feelings into a new channel. Cecil had often asked of her a description of Eugenia, whose letters, breathing so eloquently of gratitude and affection, and so indicative of enthusiasm and refinement of character, had been a source of pleasure and pride to him. "If her person has improved only half as much as her mind," he would say, "she cannot be ugly." Rosamond, who had been her daily associate, was hardly sensible of the gradual transformation that was going on in her external appearance. The strength of her first impression remained, and whenever she thought of Eugenia, she remembered her as she stood, pale and hollow-eyed, by her side, before the mirror, which gave back the blooming image of her own juvenile beauty. Still, though she felt her immeasurable superiority to this poor, dependent girl, she was agitated at her coming, and regretted the commanding claims she had on her husband's kindness and protection.

"Can this indeed be Eugenia?" exclaimed Cecil, in a tone of delighted surprise, when, unbonneted and unshawled, she stood before him, tearful, smiling, and agitated. "Rosamond, are we not deceived? Tell me, can this indeed be our Eugenia?"

"It is indeed that Eugenia whom your bounty has cherished, the child whom you"—Eugenia paused in unconquerable emotion, and clasped her hands together with characteristic fervour and grace. Cecil was deeply affected. He recollected the little girl whose emaciated features told a tale of such unutterable woe, whose shoulders were furrowed with bleeding streaks, whose cries of agony had pierced the silence of his evening walk. He contrasted the image drawn on his remembrance, with the figure of exquisite symmetry, the face moulded into the softness of feminine loveliness, the eyes of such rare beauty and lustre, that they actually illuminated her whole countenance. His heart swelled with the consciousness of rewarded benevolence, it softened into tenderness towards every human being, and overflowed with a love for Rosamond, such as he had never felt before. So true it is that the exercise of every kind and generous affection increases the soul's capacities for loving, instead of draining and impoverishing them. "You must henceforth be sisters," said he, taking a hand of each, and seating himself between them. "I need not tell you to love each other as such. I am sure that injunction is unnecessary. But there is one task I must impose upon you, Rosamond. You must teach Eugenia to look upon me as a brother, a friend, not as a benefactor, for I feel repaid a thousand times over, for all I have done for her, in the happiness of this moment. Let the idea of obligation be banished for ever, and we can be the happiest trio in the universe, bound together by a threefold and indissoluble cord."

"My mother!" ejaculated Rosamond, and drawing away her hand from her husband, she covered her face and wept. He reproached himself for his transient oblivion of her sorrow, and in endeavouring to soothe it, Eugenia was for a while forgotten. But he little dreamed of the fountain of Rosamond's tears. It would have been difficult for herself to have analyzed the strange feelings struggling within her. The *bosom serpent*, of whose existence she had been previously unconscious, then wound its first cold coil in her heart, and instead of shuddering at its entrance, and closing its portals on the deadly guest, she allowed it to wind itself in its deepest foldings, where its hissings and writhings were no less terrible, because unheard and unseen. Rosamond from earliest childhood had been the object of exclusive devotion from those she loved. She had never known a sharer in her mother's love, for unhappily she was an only child. The undivided fondness of her husband had hitherto been all that her exacting heart required. Now, she must admit an acknowledged sharer of his thoughts and affections, not as an occasional visiter, but as an constant inmate, an inseparable companion. The hallowed privacy of the domestic altar was destroyed, for the foot of the stranger had desecrated it. She could no longer appropriate to herself every look and smile of him, whose glances and smiles she believed her own inalienable right. If she walked abroad, another beside herself, must henceforth lean upon his arm. If she remained at home, another must also be seated at his side. And this invasion of her most precious immunities, was not to be endured for a short season, for weeks or months, but years, perhaps for life. These new and evil anticipations swept darkly across the troubled surface of Rosamond's mind, as she gazed on the varying countenance of Eugenia, and wondered she had never thought her handsome before. The gratitude and sensibility that beamed from her eyes whenever they turned on her benefactor, seemed to her diseased imagination the harbingers of a warmer emotion, and the constitutional ardour and frankness of her expressions were indicative of the most dangerous of characters. It was well for Rosamond that the recent death of her mother was a legitimate excuse for her pensiveness and gloom, as the incipient stage of the malady that was beginning to steal into her soul must otherwise have been perceived. Cecil, frank, confident, and unsuspecting, never dreamed that every attention bestowed on Eugenia was considered as a robbery to herself. Eugenia, warm-hearted, impulsive, and grateful, as little imagined that the overflowings of her gratitude were construed into feelings she would have blushed to have cherished. Cecil was passionately fond of music. Since her mother's death, Rosamond could not be prevailed upon to touch the keys of the instrument, and he was too kind to urge upon her a task repugnant to her feelings. But when Eugenia discovered that she possessed an accomplishment capable of imparting pleasure to him who had given her the means of acquiring it, she was never weary of exercising it. She sang too with rare sweetness and power, and never refused to sing the songs that Cecil loved to hear. Rosamond could not sing. She had never mourned over this deficiency before, but now she could not bear to think that another should impart a pleasure to her husband, she had not the means of bestowing. She forgot that she had selfishly denied to gratify his taste, in the way she had the power of doing, because it would have interrupted the indulgence of her filial grief. Another thing deeply wounded Rosamond's feelings: always accustomed to being waited upon by others, to have all her wishes anticipated, she never thought of showing her love by those active manifestations which most men love to receive. She would have laid down her life for her husband, if the sacrifice were required, but she never thought of offering him a glass of water with her own hand, because it was the office of the servants to supply his recurring wants. Never till she saw these attentions bestowed by another who was not a menial, did she imagine that affection could give an added relish, even to a cup of cold water, when offered to the thirsty lip. One warm, sultry day, Cecil entered after a long walk, and throwing himself on a sofa exclaimed, "Give me some drink, Titania—for I faint—even as a sick girl." Rosamond smiled at his theatrical assumption of Cæsar's dignity, and reaching out her hand, rang the bell. Eugenia flew out of the room, and returned long before a servant could answer the summons, with a glass of water, and bending one knee to the ground, with sportive grace she offered it to his acceptance.

"Eugenia!" cried Rosamond, colouring very high, "we have no lack of servants. I am sure there is no necessity of your assuming such a trouble."

"Oh! but it is such a pleasure!" exclaimed Eugenia, springing up, and placing the empty glass on the sideboard. "It is all I can do. You would not deprive me of the privilege if you knew how dearly I prize it."

Had Cecil observed the heightened colour of Rosamond, he might have conjectured that all was not right in her bosom, but she sat in the shadow of a curtain, and her emotion was unperceived. A few evenings afterwards, they were walking together, when they met a woman bustling through the streets, with her arm a-kimbo, and an air of boldness and defiance, that spoke the determined Amazon. Eugenia clung closely to Cecil's arm as she approached, and turned deadly pale; she recognised in those stony eyes and iron features the dreaded Mrs. Grundy, the tyrant of her desolate childhood, and she felt as if the thong were again descending on her quivering flesh, and the iron again entering into her soul. Such a rush of painful recollections came over her, she was obliged to lean against a railing for support, while Cecil, who saw what was the cause of her agitation, gave a stern glance at the woman, who had stopped, and was gazing in her face with an undaunted stare.

"Heyday!" cried she, "who's this? 'Tisn't Giny, sure enough? I never should have thought of such a thing, if it hadn't been for the gentleman. Well! can't you speak to a body, now you have got to be such a fine lady? This is all the gratitude one gets in the world."

"Gratitude!" repeated Cecil, "how dare you talk of gratitude to her, before me? Pass on and leave her, and be thankful that your sex shields you a second time from my indignation."

"Well you needn't bristle up so, sir," cried she, with a sneer. "I'm not going to kill her. I suppose you've got married to her by this time. But you'd better look sharp, lest she gets into a rambling way, as her mother did before her." With a malignant laugh the virago passed on, delighted to find that she had drawn quite a crowd to the spot where Eugenia still leaned, incapable of motion, and Rosamond stood, pale as a statue, brooding over the words of the woman, as if, like a Delphian priestess, she had uttered the oracles of fate.

"Why should she imagine *her* to be his wife," whispered the bosom serpent, subtle as its arch prototype in the bowers of Eden, "if she had not witnessed in him evidences of tenderness, such as a husband only should bestow? That random sentence spoke volumes, and justifies thy fearful suspicions. Alas for thee, Rosamond! The young blossoms of thy happiness are blighted in the sweet springtime of their bloom. There is no more greenness or fragrance for thee—better that thou hadst died, and been laid by thy mother's side, than live to experience the bitter pangs of deceived confidence and unrequited love."

Cecil, unconscious of the secret enemy that was operating so powerfully against him in the breast of Rosamond, wondered at her coldness to Eugenia; a coldness which became every day more apparent, and was even assuming the character of dislike. It seemed so natural in one so young and affectionate as Rosamond, to wind her affections round a being of corresponding youth and sensibility, so foreign to her gentle nature to treat one entirely dependent on her kindness, with such reserve and distrust—he wondered, regretted, and at length remonstrated. Eugenia had just anticipated a servant's movements in bringing him a book from the library, which he expressed a desire to see, and he had taken it from her hand with a smile of acknowledgment, when the instantaneous change in the countenance of Rosamond arrested his attention. It was so chilling, so inexplicable, he dropped the book to the ground in his confusion, which Eugenia, with her usual graceful readiness, again lifted and laid upon his knee. In raising her face from her bending position, she encountered the glance of Rosamond, which seemed to have upon her the momentary effect of fascination. She stood as if rooted to the spot, gazing steadfastly on her, then with a cheek as hueless as ashes, turned and precipitately left the apartment. Cecil and Rosamond looked at each other without speaking. Never had they exchanged such a look before. "Good heavens!" he exclaimed, rising and walking two or three times across the apartment, with a resounding tread. "Good heavens! what a transformation! I must know the cause of it. Tell me, Rosamond, and tell me truly and unreservedly, what means your mysterious and unkind behaviour to one who never can have offended you? What has Eugenia done to forfeit your affection as a friend, your consideration as a guest, your respect to the claims of your husband's adopted sister?"

"It were far better to subject your own heart and conscience to this stern inquisition, than mine, Cecil," replied Rosamond bitterly. "Had you informed me sooner of the length and breadth of my duties, I might have fulfilled them better. I did not know, when Eugenia was received into our household, how overwhelming were her claims. I did not know that I was expected to exalt *her* happiness on the ruins of my own."

"Rosamond! Rosamond!" interrupted Cecil, vehemently—"Beware what you say—beware lest you strike a deathblow to our wedded love. I can bear anything in the world but suspicion. Every feeling of my heart has been laid bare before you. There is not a thought that is not as open to your scrutiny as the heavens in the blaze of noonday. How unworthy of yourself, how disgraceful to me, how wounding to Eugenia, this unjustifiable conduct!"

Every chord of Rosamond's heart quivered with agony at this burst of indignant feeling from lips which had never before addressed her but in mild and persuasive tones. Had the wealth of worlds been laid at her feet, she would have given it to recall the last words she had uttered. Still, in the midst of her remorse and horror, she felt the overmastering influence of her imagined wrongs, and that influence triumphed over the suggestions of reason and the admonitions of prudence.

"It is ungenerous—it is unmanly," she cried, "to force me into the confession of sentiments which you blame me for declaring—I had said nothing, done nothing—yet you arraign me before the bar of inexorable justice, as the champion of the injured Eugenia. If the sincerity of my countenance offends you, it is my misfortune, not my fault. I cannot smile on the boldness I condemn, or the arts I despise."

"Boldness! arts!" repeated Cecil. "If there was ever an unaffected, impulsive child of nature, it is she whom you so deeply wrong; but you wrong yourself far more. You let yourself down from the high station where I had enthroned you, and paid you a homage scarcely inferior to an angel of light. You make me an alien from your bosom, and nourish there a serpent which will wind you deeper and deeper in its envenomed folds, till your heart-strings are crushed beneath its coils."

"I am indeed most wretched," exclaimed Rosamond; "and if I have made myself so, I deserve pity rather than upbraiding. Cecil, you never could have loved me, or you would not so lightly cast me from you."

Cecil, who had snatched up his hat, and laid his hand on the latch of the door, turned at the altered tone of her voice. Tears, which she vainly endeavoured to hide, gushed from her eyes, and stole down her colourless cheeks.

"Rosamond," said he, in a softened tone, approaching her as he spoke, "if you believe what you last uttered, turn away from me, and let us henceforth be strangers to each other;—but if your heart belies their meaning, if you can restore me the confidence you have withdrawn, and which is my just due, if you are willing to rely unwaveringly on my integrity, my honour, and my love, come to my arms once more, and they shall shelter you through life with unabated tenderness and undivided devotion."

Poor, foolish Rosamond! she had wrought herself up to a state bordering on despair, and the revulsion of her feelings was so great that she almost fainted in the arms that opened to enfold her. Her folly, her madness, her injustice and selfishness stared her so fearfully in the face, she was appalled and self-condemned. Like the base Judean, she had been about to throw away from her "a gem richer than all its tribe," a gem of whose priceless worth she had never till this moment been fully conscious. She made the most solemn resolutions for the future, invoking upon herself the most awful penalties if she ever again yielded to a passion so degrading. But passion once admitted is not so easily dispossessed of its hold. Every self-relying effort is but a flaxen withe bound round the slumbering giant, broken in the first grasp of temptation. Jealousy is that demon, whose name is Legion, which flies from the rebuking voice of Omnipotence alone. Rosamond did not say, "If God give me strength, I will triumph over my indwelling enemy." She said, "The tempter shall seek me in vain—I am strong, and I defy its power." Rosamond was once more happy, but she had planted a thorn in the bosom of another, sharp, deep, and rankling. No after kindness could obliterate the remembrance of that involuntary, piercing glance. It was but the sheathing of a weapon. Eugenia felt that the cold steel was still lurking in the scabbard, ready to flash forth at the bidding of passion. A few evenings after the scene just described, when she had been playing and singing some of Cecil's favourite songs, at the magnanimous request of Rosamond, she turned suddenly to Cecil and said—

"I think I overheard a friend of yours say to you the other day, that I might make my fortune on the stage. Now," added she, blushing, "I do not wish to go upon the stage, but if my musical talents could give me distinction there, they might be made useful in the domestic circle. I have been told of a lady who wishes an instructress for her daughters. Suffer me to offer myself for the situation. If through your bounty I am possessed of accomplishments which may be subservient to myself or others, is it not my duty to exercise them? I should have done this sooner—I have been too long an idler."

"No, no, Eugenia," said Rosamond, warmly, every good and generous feeling of her heart in full and energetic operation—"we can never sanction such a proposition. Is not this your home as well as mine? Are you not our sister? Remember the threefold cord that never was to be broken." She pressed Eugenia's hand in both her own, and continued, in a trembling voice—"If I have ever seemed cold or unkind, forgive me, Eugenia, for I believe I am a strange, fitful being. You found me a sad mourner over the grave of my mother, with weakened nerves and morbid sensibilities. My mind is getting a healthier tone. Remain with us—we shall be happier by and by."

Completely overcome by this unexpected and candid avowal, Eugenia threw her arms round Rosamond's neck, and exclaimed—"I shall be the happiest being in the world, if you indeed love me. I have no one else in the world to love but you and my benefactor."

Cecil felt as if he could have prostrated himself at Rosamond's feet, and thanked her for her noble and generous conduct. He had waited in trembling eagerness for her reply. It was more than he expected. It was all he wished or required.

"Be but true to yourself, my beloved Rosamond," said he, when he was alone with her, "and you can never be unjust to me. Continue in the path you have now marked out, and you shall be repaid not only with my warmest love, but with my respect, my admiration, and my gratitude."

Thus encouraged, Rosamond felt new life flowing in her veins. Though she could not sing according to scientific rules, her buoyant spirit burst forth in warbling notes, as she moved about her household duties, with light, bounding steps, rejoicing in the consciousness of recovered reason. Week after week glided away, without any circumstance arising to remind them of the past. Indeed all seemed to have forgotten that anything had ever disturbed their domestic peace.

"Oh! what beautiful flowers!" exclaimed Rosamond, as, riding with her husband, on a lovely autumnal evening, they passed a public garden, ornamented with the last flowers of the season. "I wish I had some of them. There are the emblems of love, constancy, and devotion. If I had them now, I would bind them on my heart, in remembrance of this enchanting ride."

"You shall have them speedily, dear Rosamond," replied he, "even if, like the gallant knight who named the sweet flower *Forget-me-not*, I sacrifice my life to purchase them."

Rosamond little thought those flowers, sought with such childish earnestness, and promised with such sportive gallantry, were destined to be so fatal to her newly acquired serenity. As soon as they reached home, Cecil returned to seek the flowers which Rosamond desired, and selecting the most beautiful the garden afforded, brought them with as much enthusiasm of feeling as if it were the bridegroom's first gift. When he entered the room Eugenia was alone, Rosamond being still engaged in changing her riding apparel.

"Oh! what an exquisitely beautiful nosegay," cried Eugenia, involuntarily stretching out her hand—"how rich, how fragrant!"

"Yes! I knew you would admire them," he replied—"I brought them expressly for——" Rosamond, he was just going to add, when he was suddenly called out, leaving the flowers in the hand of Eugenia, and the unfinished sentence in her ear. Not knowing anything of their appropriation, Eugenia believed the bouquet a gift to herself, and she stood turning them to the light in every direction, gazing on their rainbow hues with sparkling eyes, when Rosamond entered the apartment, with a cheek glowing like the roses before her.

"See what beautiful flowers your husband has just given me," cried Eugenia —"he must have been endowed with second sight, for I was just yearning after such a bouquet."

Had Rosamond beheld the leaves of the Bohon-Upas, instead of the blossoms she loved, she could not have experienced a more sickening sensation. She had begged for those flowers—she had pointed out their emblematic beauties —had promised to bind them to her heart, and yet they were wantonly bestowed on another, as if in defiance of her former wretchedness. She grew dizzy from the rapidity of the thoughts that whirled through her brain, and leaning against the mantelpiece, pressed her hand upon her head.

"You are ill, dear Rosamond," cried Eugenia, springing towards her—"lean on me—you are pale and faint."

Rosamond recoiled from her touch, as if a viper were crawling over her. She had lost the power of self-control, and the passion that was threatening to suffocate her, found vent in language.

"Leave me," cried she, "if you would not drive me mad. You have destroyed the peace of my whole life. You have stolen like a serpent into my domestic bower, and robbed me of the affections of a once doting husband. Take them openly, if you will, and triumph in the possession of your ill-gotten treasure."

"Rosamond!" uttered a deep, low voice behind her. She started, turned, and beheld her husband standing on the threshold of the door, pale, dark and stern as the judge who pronounces the doom of the transgressor. Eugenia, who had dropped the flowers at the commencement of Rosamond's indignant accusation, with a wild, bewildered countenance, which kindled as she proceeded, now met her scorching glance, with eyes that literally flashed fire. Her temple veins swelled, her lip quivered, every feature was eloquent with scorn.

"Rosamond," said she, "you have banished me for ever. You have cruelly, wantonly, causelessly insulted me." She walked rapidly to the door, where Cecil yet stood, and glided by him before he could intercept her passage. Then suddenly returning, she snatched his hand, and pressed it to her forehead and to her lips.

"My benefactor, brother, friend!" cried she, "may Heaven for ever bless thee, even as thou hast blessed me!"

"Stay, Eugenia, stay!" he exclaimed, endeavouring to detain her—but it was too late. He heard her footsteps on the stairs, and the door of her chamber hastily close, and he knew he could not follow her.

"Rash, infatuated girl!" cried he, turning to Rosamond, "what have you done? At a moment too when my whole heart was overflowing with tenderness and love towards you. Remember, if you banish Eugenia from the shelter of my roof, I am bound by every tie of honour and humanity still to protect and cherish her."

"I know it well," replied Rosamond; "I remember too that it was to give a home to Eugenia you first consented to bind yourself by marriage vows. That home may still be hers. I am calm now, Cecil—you see I can speak calmly. The certainty of a misfortune gives the spirit and the power of endurance. Those flowers are trifles in themselves, but they contain a world of meaning."

"These worthless flowers!" exclaimed Cecil, trampling them under his feet till their bright leaves lay a soiled and undistinguishable mass—"and have these raised the whirlwind of jealous passion? These fading playthings, left for a moment in another's keeping, accidentally left, to be immediately reclaimed!"

"You gave them to her—with her own lips she told me—rapture sparkling in her eyes."

"It was all a misunderstanding—an innocent mistake. Oh, Rosamond! for a trifle like this you could forget all my faith and affection, every feeling which should be sacred in your eyes—forget your woman's gentleness, and utter words which seem branded in my heart and brain in burning and indelible characters. I dare not go on. I shall say what I may bitterly repent. I wish you no punishment greater than your own reflections."

Rosamond listened to his retreating footsteps, she heard the outer door heavily close, and the sound fell on her ear like the first fall of the damp clods on the coffin, the signal of mortal separation. She remained pale as a statue, gazing on the withering flowers, counting the quick beatings of her lonely heart, believing herself doomed to a widowhood more cruel than that the grave creates. Cecil's simple explanation, stamped with the dignity of truth, had roused her from the delirium of passion, and seeing her conduct in its true light, she shuddered at the review. Her head ached to agony—one moment she shivered with cold, the next the blood in her veins seemed changed to molten lead. "I feel very strangely," thought she—"perhaps I am going to die, and when I am dead, he will pity and forgive me." She had barely strength to seek her own chamber, where, throwing herself on the bed, she lay till the shades of night darkened around her, conscious of but one wish, that her bed might prove her grave, and Cecil, melted by her early fate, might shed one tear of forgiveness over the icy lips that never more could open to offend. The bell rang for supper—she heeded not the summons. A servant came to tell her that Mr. Dormer was below. Her heart bounded, but she remained immovable. Again the servant came.

"Shall I make tea for Mr. Dormer?" she asked. "Miss Eugenia is gone out."

Rosamond started up, and leaned on her elbow. "Gone!" repeated she, wildly —"when? where?"

"I don't know, ma'am," replied the girl; "she put on her bonnet and shawl an hour ago and went out through the back gate."

"Does Mr. Dormer know it?" asked Rosamond faintly.

"I don't know, ma'am—he has just come in," was the reply.—"I saw him reading a note he found on the table in the hall, and he seemed mightily flustered."

There was an insolent curiosity in the countenance of the girl, who had hitherto been respectful and submissive. She placed the lamp near the bedside and left the room; and almost simultaneously, Cecil entered, with an open note in his hand, which he threw upon the bed without speaking. She seized it mechanically, and attempted to read it, but the letters seemed to move and emit electric sparks, flashing on her aching eyeballs. It was with difficulty that she deciphered the following lines, written evidently with a trembling hand:—

"Farewell, kindest, noblest, and best of friends! May the happiness which I have unconsciously blighted, revive in my absence. I go, sustained by the strength of a virtuous resolution, not the excitement of indignant passion. The influence of your bounty remains, and will furnish me an adequate support. Seek not, I pray you, to find the place of my abode. The Heaven in which I trust will protect me. Farewell—deluded, but still beloved Rosamond! Your injustice shall be forgotten, your benefits remembered for ever."

Rosamond dropped the letter, cast one glance towards her husband, who stood with folded arms, pale and immovable, at the foot of the bed, then sinking back upon her pillow, a mist came over her eyes, and all was darkness.

When she again recovered the consciousness of her existence, she found herself in a darkened chamber, the curtains of her bed closely drawn, saving a small aperture, through which she could perceive a neat, matronly figure, moving with soft, careful steps, and occasionally glancing anxiously towards the bed. She attempted to raise herself on her elbow, but she had not strength to lift her head from the pillow; she could scarcely carry her feeble hand to her forehead, to put back the moist hair which fell heavily over her brow.

"How weak I am!" said she faintly. "How long have I slept?"

"Be composed," said the stranger, approaching her gently, "and do not speak. You have been very ill. Everything depends on your keeping perfectly quiet."

Rosamond began to tremble violently as she gazed up in the stranger's face. Why was she committed to *her* charge? Was she forsaken by him whom awakening memory brought before her as an injured and perhaps avenging husband?

"Where is he?" cried she, in a voice so low, the woman bent her ear to her lips, to hear.

"The doctor?" replied she. "Oh, he will soon be here. He said if you waked, no one must come near you, and you must not be allowed to speak one word. It might cost you your life."

Rosamond tried to gasp out her husband's name, but her parched lips were incapable of further articulation. Her eyes closed from exhaustion, and the nurse, supposing she slept, drew the curtains closer, and moved on tiptoe to the window. At length the door slowly opened, and the footstep of a man entered the room. Rosamond knew it was not her husband's step, and such a cold feeling fell on her heart, she thought it the precursor of death. She heard a whispered conversation which set every nerve throbbing with agony. Then the curtains were withdrawn, and she felt a stranger's hand counting the pulsations of her chilled veins. "I am forsaken," thought she, "even in my dying hour. Oh God! it is just." Again the chamber was still, and she must have fallen into a deep slumber, for when she again opened her eyes, she saw a lamp glimmering through the curtains, and the shadow of her nurse reflected in them, seated at a table, reading. She was reading aloud, though in a low voice, as if fearful of disturbing the slumbers she was watching. Rosamond caught the sound, "I the Lord thy God am a jealous God." She repeated it to herself, and it gave her an awful sensation. The commanding claims of her Maker upon her affections, for the first time rose before her in all their height, depth, power, and majesty. "A jealous God!" How tremendous, how appalling the idea. If she, a poor worm of the dust, was so severe and uncompromising in her demands upon a fellow being, what terrible exactions might a neglected Deity make from the creature he had formed for his glory? She remembered the command from which that fearful sentence was extracted. She had broken it, trampled it under her feet. She had bowed down in adoration to an earthly idol, and robbed her God, her *jealous God*, of the homage due to his august name. The light that poured in upon her conscience was like the blazing of a torch through a dark mine. She had felt before the madness of her bosom passion, she now felt its sin and its sacrilege. "I am forsaken," again repeated she to herself, "but I had first forsaken thee, O my God! Thou art drawing me home unto thee." Tears gathering thick and fast, fell down her pale cheeks, till the pillow they pressed was wet as with rain-drops. She wept long, and without one effort to restrain the gushing forth of her melting heart, when exhausted nature once more sought relief in sleep. Her first consciousness, on awakening, was of a soft hand laid gently on her brow, a warm breath stealing over her cheek, and a trembling lip gently pressed upon her own. Had she awakened in the abodes of the blest, in the midst of the hierarchy of heaven, she could hardly have experienced a deeper rapture than that which flooded her breast. Slowly, as if fearing to banish by the act the image drawn on her now glowing heart, she lifted her eyes, and met the eyes of her husband looking down upon her, no longer stern and upbraiding, but softened into woman's tenderness. The next moment he was kneeling by the bedside, his face buried in the covering, which shook from the strong emotion it concealed.

When Rosamond learned that Cecil, instead of having left her to her bitter consequences of her rashness, in just and unappeasable resentment, had never left her in her unconsciousness, and since her restoration to reason had hovered near the threshold of her chamber day and night, forbidden to enter, lest his presence should produce an agitation fatal to a frame apparently trembling on the brink of the grave, she again reproached herself for believing he could have been capable of such unrelenting cruelty. When she was assured too that Eugenia was safe under the protection of an early friend, whom she had most unexpectedly encountered, and only waited a passport from the physician, to come to her bedside, her soul swelled with gratitude that found no language but prayer.

"I have sinned against Heaven and thee, my husband!" exclaimed Rosamond, from the depth of a penitent and chastened spirit—"I am no more worthy to be called thy wife."

"We have both erred, my beloved Rosamond; we have lived too much for the world and ourselves, regardless of higher and holier relations. Never, till I feared to lose thee for ever, did I feel the drawings of that mighty chain which links us inseparably to Him who created us. Let us both commence life anew —awakened to our responsibilities as Christians, and, profiting by the sad experience of the past, let us lay the foundations of our happiness too deep and broad for the storms of passion to overthrow. Let us build it on the Rock of Ages."

And who was the friend whom Eugenia had so providentially discovered? When she left the dwelling of Cecil Dormer, to seek the lady who wished for an instructress for her daughters, one of the first persons who crossed her path was the terrific Mrs. Grundy. This woman, whose hatred for her seemed implacable as the injuries she had inflicted were deep, seeing her alone and in evident disorder of mind, began to revile and threaten her. A stranger, observing the terror and loathing with which a young and attractive-looking girl shrunk from a coarse and masculine woman, paused and offered his protection. The remarkable resemblance which Eugenia bore to her ill-fated mother led to a discovery as unexpected as it was interesting. The melancholy stranger was no other than her own father, who believed his wife and child had perished in their flight, having heard of the destruction of the boat in which they fled. Thus mysteriously had Providence transmuted into a blessing, what seemed the greatest misfortune of her life.

The history of Mr. St. Clair and his unfortunate wife, which he subsequently related to Cecil and Rosamond, was fraught with the most intense interest. Like Rosamond, he had cherished a *bosom serpent*, remorseless as death, "cruel as the grave;" but he had not, like her, found, before it was too late, an antidote for its deadly venom.

MY GRANDMOTHER'S BRACELET.

We were all seated in a piazza, one beautiful summer's night. The moonbeams quivered through the interlacing vines that crept fantastically over the latticework that surrounded it. My grandmother sat in an arm-chair in the centre of the group, her arms quietly folded across her lap, her hair white and silvery as the moonbeams that lingered on its parted folds. She was the handsomest old lady I ever saw, my revered grandmother, and in the spring of her years had been a reigning belle. To me she was still beautiful, in the gentle quietude of life's evening shades, the dignity of chastened passions, waiting hopes, and sustaining religious faith. I was her favourite grandchild, and the place near her feet, the arm laid across her lap, the uplifted eye fixed steadfastly on her face, constant as the recurrence of the still night hour, told a story of love and devotion on my part, which defied all competition. As I sat this night, leaning on her lap, I held her hand in mine, and the thought that, a few more years, that hand must be cold in the grave, incapable of answering the glowing pressure of mine, made me draw a deep inspiration, and I almost imagined her complexion assumed an ashen hue, prophetical of death. The weather was warm, and she wore a large loose wrapper, with flowing sleeves, left unconfined at the wrist. As I moved her hand, the folds of the sleeve fell back, and something pure and bright glittered in the moonlight. She made a movement to draw down the sleeve, but the eager curiosity of childhood was not to be eluded. I caught her wrist, and baring it to the gaze of all, exclaimed —

"Only think—grandmother has got on a bracelet—a pearl bracelet! Who would think of her indulging in such finery? Here are two sweet pearl lilies set together in a golden clasp, with golden leaves below them. Why, grandmother, you must be setting up for a bride!"

"It was a bridal gift," replied she, sliding the bracelet on her shrunken arm; "a bridal gift, made long ago. It was a foolish thought, child. I was looking over a casket, where I have deposited the choicest treasures of my youth, and I clasped it on my wrist, to see how my arm had fallen from its fair proportions. My mind became so lost in thinking of the story of this gem, I forgot to restore it to the place where it has so long lain, slumbering with the hoarded memories of other days."

"A story!" we all eagerly exclaimed,—"please tell it—you promised us one to-night."

"Ah! children, it is no fairy tale, about bright genii, and enchanted palaces, and ladies so beautiful that they bewitch every one who comes within the magic reach of their charms. It is a true tale, and has some sad passages in it."

"Grandmother," said I, in a dignified manner, "I hope you don't think me so silly as not to like anything because it is true. I have got over the Arabian Nights long ago, and I would rather hear something to make me feel sorry than glad—I always do feel sad when the moon shines on me, but I can't tell the reason why."

"Hush! Mina, and let grandmother tell her story—you always talk so much," said little Mitty, who sat on the other side of her venerable relative.

The old lady patted with one hand the golden head of the chider, but the arm clasped by the magic bracelet was still imprisoned by my fingers, and as she proceeded in its history, my grasp tightened and tightened from the intenseness of my interest, till she was compelled to beg me to release her.

"Yes," said she, in a musing tone, "there is a story depending on this, which I remember as vividly as if the events were of yesterday. I may forget what happened an hour ago, but the records of my youth are written in lines that grow deeper as time flows over them."

She looked up steadily for a few moments, appearing to my imagination like an inspired sibyl, then began as follows:

"When I was a young girl, I had no brothers or sisters, as you have, but was an only, I might say a lonely child, for my father was dead and my mother an invalid. When I returned from school, I obtained permission to invite a sweet young cousin of mine, whose name was Eglantine, to be my companion. We were affluent, she was poor; and when my mother proposed to make our house her home, she accepted the offer with gratitude and joy. She was an interesting creature, of a peculiar temperament and exquisite sensibility. She was subject to fits of wonderful buoyancy, and equal despondency; sometimes she would warble all day, gay and untiring as the bird perched on yonder spray, then a soft melancholy would sit brooding on her brow, as if she feared some impending misfortune. This was probably owing to the peculiar circumstances of her infancy, for she was born during her mother's widowhood, and nursed by a mother's tears. A poetical friend had given her the name of Eglantine, and well did her beauty, sweetness, delicacy, and fragility justify the name. In our girlhood we grew together, like the friends of the Midsummer's Night, almost inseparable in body, and never divided in heart, by those little jealousies which sometimes interpose their barriers to young maidens' friendships. But I see little Mitty has fallen asleep already. My story is too grave for the light ears of childhood. I shall be obliged, too, to say something about love, and even you, Mina, are entirely too young to know anything of its influence."

"Oh! but I do know something, grandmother," exclaimed I, impulsively; "that is, I have read—I have thought"—I stammered and stopped, unable to express my own vague ideas.

"You may not be too young to sympathize, but certainly too young to feel," said my grandmother, mildly; "but, ardent and sympathizing as your nature is, it will be hard for you to carry back your mind to the time when all the warm passions and hopes of youth were glowing in my bosom. It is enough to say that there was one who came and rivalled Eglantine in my affections, one to whom I was betrothed, and to whom I was to be shortly wedded. It was on such an eve as this, so clear and bright, that he gave me the pledge of our betrothal, this bracelet of pearl, and clasped it on an arm which then filled the golden circlet. Perhaps you wonder that the first token of love should not have been a ring; but Ronald did not like to follow the track of other men, and even in trifles marked out for himself a peculiar and independent course. That night, when I retired to my chamber, I found Eglantine seated at the open window, apparently absorbed in the contemplation of the starry heavens. She sat in a loose undress, her hair of pale gold hung unbound over her shoulders, and her head, being slightly thrown back, allowed the moonlight to flood her whole face with its unearthly radiance.

"'You look very beautiful and romantic, dear Eglantine,' said I, softly approaching her, and throwing my arms round her neck; 'but come down from the stars a little while, my sweet cousin, and share in my earthborn emotions.' My heart was too full of happiness, my spirits too excited, not to overflow in unreserved confidence in her bosom. She wept as I poured into her ears all my hopes, my recent vows, and future schemes of felicity. It was her usual manner of expressing deep sympathy, and I loved her the better for her tears. 'All I wonder at and blame in Ronald is,' and I spoke this in true sincerity, 'that he does not love you better than me. Never, till this evening, was I sure of his preference.'

"Eglantine withdrew herself from my arms, and turned her face to the shadow of the wall. There was something inexplicable in her manner that chilled, and even alarmed me. A thought, too painful to be admitted, darted for a moment to my mind. Could she be jealous of Ronald's love for me? Was my happiness to be built on the ruin of hers? No! it could not be. She probably feared my affections might become alienated from her in consequence of my new attachment. Such a fear was natural, and I hastened to remove it by the warmest professions, mingled with covert reproaches for her doubts and misgivings.

"I had a young waiting-maid, who, next to Eglantine, was the especial object of my regard. She was the daughter of a gentlewoman, who, from a series of misfortunes, was reduced to penury, to which was added the helplessness of disease. To relieve her mother from the pressure of immediate want, the young Alice offered herself as a candidate for a state of servitude, and I eagerly availed myself of the opportunity of securing the personal attendance of one so refined in manner and so winning in appearance. Alice now came forward, as was her custom, to assist me in preparing for my nightly rest. She was about to unclasp the bracelet from my wrist, but I drew back my arm. 'No, no, Alice,' said I, 'this is an amulet. Sweet dreams will come to my pillow, beckoned by its fairy power. I cannot sleep without it. See how beautifully the lilies gleam in the moonlight that gilds my couch.' Alice seemed as if she could never weary in admiring the beauty of the ornament. She turned my arm to shift the rays, and catch the delicate colouring of the pearls, and looped up the sleeve of my night-dress in a fantastic manner, to display it fully to her gaze. Once or twice I thought I saw the eyes of Eglantine fastened upon it with a sad, wistful expression, and the same exquisitely painful thought again darted to my mind. I struggled against its admission, as degrading both to myself and her, and at last fell asleep, with my arm thrown on the outside of the bed, and the bracelet shining out in the pure night-beams. Alice slept in a little bed by the side of mine, for I could not bear that a creature so young and delicate, and so gentle bred, should share the apartments devoted to the servants, and be exposed to their rude companionship. She generally awoke me with her light touch or gentle voice, but when I awoke the next morning, I saw Alice still sleeping, with a flushed cheek and an attitude that betokened excitement and unrest. Eglantine sat at her window, reading, dressed with her usual care by her own graceful fingers. In the school of early poverty she had learned the glorious lesson of independence, a lesson which, in my more luxurious life, I had never acquired. 'Alice must be ill,' said I, rising, and approaching her bedside; 'she looks feverish, and her brows are knit, as if her dreams were fearful.' I bent down over her, and laid my hand upon her shoulder, to rouse her from her uneasy slumbers, when I started—for the precious bracelet was gone. Eglantine laid down her book at my sudden exclamation, and Alice, wakening, looked round her with a bewildered expression. 'My bracelet!' repeated I—'it is gone.' I flew to my couch; it was not there. I looked upon the carpet, in the vain hope that the clasp had unloosed, and that it had fallen during the night. 'Alice,' cried I, 'rise this moment, and help me to find my bracelet. You must know where it is. It never could have vanished without aid.' I fixed my eyes steadfastly on her face, which turned as hueless as marble. She trembled in every limb, and sunk down again on the side of the bed.

"'You do not think *I* have taken it, Miss Laura?" said she, gasping for breath.

"'I do not know what to think,' I answered, in a raised tone; 'but it is very mysterious, and your whole appearance and manner is very strange this morning, Alice. You must have been up in the night, or you would not have slept so unusually late——

"'Do not be hasty, Laura,' said Eglantine, in a sweet, soothing voice; 'it may yet be found. Perhaps it is clinging to your dress, concealed in its folds. Let me assist you in searching.' She unfolded the sheets, turned up the edges of the carpet, examined every corner where it might have been tossed, but all in vain. In the mean while Alice remained like one stupefied, following our movements with a pale, terrified countenance, without offering to participate in the search.

"'There is no use in looking longer, Eglantine,' said I, bitterly. 'I suspect Alice might assist us effectually to discover it, if she would. Nay, I will not say suspect—I believe—I dare to say, I know—for conscious guilt is written in glaring characters on her countenance.'

"'Do not make any rash accusations, Laura,' cried Eglantine; 'I acknowledge appearances are much against her, but I cannot think Alice capable of such ingratitude, duplicity, and meanness.'

"Alice here burst into a passionate fit of weeping, and declared, with wringing hands and choking sobs, that she would sooner die than commit so base and wicked a deed.

"'Oh! Miss Eglantine,' she exclaimed, 'didn't you take it in sport? It seems as if I saw you in a dream going up to Miss Laura, while she was asleep, and take it from her wrist, softly, and then vanish away. Oh! Miss Eglantine, the more I think of it the more I am sure I saw you,—all in sport, I know,—but please return it, or it will be death to me.'

"The blood seemed to boil up in the cheeks of Eglantine, so sudden and intense was the glow that mantled them.

"'I thought you innocent, Alice,' said she, 'but I see, with pain, that you are an unprincipled girl. How dare you attempt to impose on me the burthen of your crime? How dare you think of sheltering yourself under the shadow of my name?'

"The vague suspicions which the assertion of Alice had excited, vanished before the outraged looks and language of the usually gentle Eglantine. Alice must have been the transgressor, and in proportion to the affection and confidence I had reposed in her, and the transcendent value of the gift, was my indignation at the offence, and the strength of my resolution to banish her from me.

"'Restore it,' said I, 'and leave me. Do it quietly and immediately, and I will inflict no other punishment than your own reflections, for having abused so much love and trust.'

"'Search me, if you please, Miss Laura, and all that belongs to me,' replied Alice, in a firmer tone, 'but I cannot give back what I have never taken. I would not, for fifty thousand worlds, take what was not mine, and least of all from you, who have been so kind and good. I am willing to go, for I would rather beg my bread from door to door, than live upon the bounty of one who thinks me capable of such guilt:' with a composure that strangely contrasted with her late violent agitation, she arranged her dress, and was walking towards the door, when Eglantine arrested her—

"'Alice, Alice, you must be mad to persist in this course. Confess the whole, return the bracelet, and Laura may yet forgive you. Think of your sick mother. How can you go to her in shame and disgrace?'

"At the mention of her mother, Alice wept afresh, and putting her hand to her head, exclaimed—

"'I feel very, very sick. Perhaps we shall die together, and then God will take pity on us. The great God knows I am innocent of this crime.'

"Grandmother," interrupted I, unable to keep silence any longer, "tell me if she was not innocent. I know she must have been. Who could have taken it?"

"Do you think Eglantine more likely to have stolen it from her cousin, who was to her, as it were, another soul and being?"

"Oh! no," I replied, "but I shall feel unhappy till I discover the thief. Please, grandmother, go on. Did Alice really go away?"

"Yes, my child," answered my grandmother, in a faltering voice, "she went, though my relenting heart pleaded for her to linger. Her extreme youth and helplessness, her previous simplicity and truthfulness, and her solemn asseverations of innocence, all staggered my belief in her guilt. It was a mystery which grew darker as I attempted to penetrate it. If Alice were innocent, who could be guilty—Eglantine? Such thought was sacrilege to her pure and elevated character, her tried affection for me, her self-respect, dignity, and truth. Alice returned to her mother, in spite of our permission for her to remain till the subject could be more fully investigated.

"When the door closed upon her retreating form, I sat down by the side of Eglantine, and wept. The fear that I had unjustly accused the innocent, the possibility, nay, the probability that she was guilty, the loss of the first pledge of plighted love, indefinite terrors for the future, a dim shade of superstition brooding over the whole, all conspired to make me gloomy and desponding. We were all unhappy. Ronald tried to laugh at my sadness, and promised me 'gems from the mine, and pearls from the ocean,' to indemnify me for my loss, yet I watched every change of his expressive countenance, and knew he thought deeply and painfully on the subject. The strange suspicion which had risen in my mind the preceding night, with regard to Eglantine's feelings towards him, revived when I saw them together, and I wondered I had not observed before the fluctuations of her complexion, and the agitation of her manner whenever he addressed her. He had always treated her with the kindness of a brother—that kindness now made me unhappy. I was becoming suspicious, jealous, and self-distrustful, with a settled conviction that some strange barrier existed to my union with Ronald, a destiny too bright and too beautiful to be realized in this world of dreams and shadows. My mother was firm in her belief of the guilt of Alice, who had never been a favourite of hers. Perhaps I lavished upon her too many indulgences, which displeased my mother's soberer judgment. She forbade all intercourse with her, all mention of her name, but she was ever present to my imagination; sometimes the shameless ingrate and accomplished deceiver, at others the eloquent pleader of her outraged innocence. One day Eglantine came to me, and laid her hand on mine with a look of unspeakable dismay—

"'I have heard,' said she, 'that Alice is dying. Let us go to her, Laura, and save her, if it be not too late.'

"What I felt at hearing these words I never can tell,—they pressed upon me with such a weight of grief—her innocence seemed as clear to me as noonday—my own unkindness as cruel as the grave. Quickly as possible we sought the cottage where her mother dwelt, and a piteous spectacle met our eyes. There lay Alice, on a little bed, pale, emaciated, and almost unconscious; her once bright hair dim and matted; her sweet blue eyes sunk and half closed; her arms laid listlessly by her side, the breath coming faint and flutteringly from her parted lips. On another bed lay her poor, heart-broken mother, unable to relieve the sufferings of her she would gladly have died to save. Frantic with grief, I threw myself by the side of Alice, and disturbed the solemn stillness of the death-hour with my incoherent ravings. I declared her innocence; I called upon her to live, to live for my sake, and throwing my arms wildly round her wasted form, struggled to hold her back from the grave yawning beneath her. It was in vain to cope with Omnipotence. Alice died, even in the midst of my agonies, and it was long before I was able to listen to the story of her illness, as related by her disconsolate mother. She had returned home sick and feverish, and sick and feverish she evidently was on her first awakening, and that wounded spirit, which none can bear, acting on a diseased frame, accelerated the progress of her fever till it settled on her brain, producing delirium, and ultimately death. During all her delirium, she was pleading her cause with an angel's eloquence, declaring her innocence, and blessing me as her benefactress and friend."

Here my grandmother paused, and covered her eyes with her handkerchief. I laid my head on her lap, and the ringlets of little Mitty's hair were wet with my tears. I felt quite broken-hearted, and ready to murmur at Providence for placing me in a world so full of error and woes.

"Did you ever feel happy again, dear grandmother?" asked I, when I ventured to break the silence,—curiosity was completely merged in sympathy.

"Yes, Mina, I have had hours of happiness, such as seldom falls to the lot of woman, but those bright hours were like the shining of the gold that comes forth purified from the furnace of fire. The mother of Alice soon followed her to the grave, and there they sleep, side by side, in the lonely churchyard. Eglantine soothed and comforted me, and endeavoured to stifle the self-upbraidings that ever sounded dolefully to my heart. Alice had been the victim of inexplicable circumstances, and so far from having been cruel, I had been kind and forbearing, considering the weight of evidence against her. Thus reasoned Eglantine, and I tried to believe her, but all my hopes of joy seemed blighted, for how could I mingle the wreath of love with the cypress boughs that now darkened my path? Ronald pressed an immediate union, but I shrunk with superstitious dread from the proposition, and refused the ring, with which he now sought to bind my faith. 'No, no,' I cried, 'the pledges of love are not for me—I will never accept another.'

"My mother grew angry at my fatalism. 'You are nursing phantasies,' said she, 'that are destroying the brightness of your youth. You are actually making yourself old, ere yet in your bloom. See, if there are not actually streaks of gray threading your jetty hair.' I rose and stood before a mirror, and shaking my hair loose from the confining comb, saw that her words were true. Here and there a gleam of silver wandered through those tresses which had always worn that purple depth of hue peculiar to the raven's plumage. The chill that penetrated my heart on the death-bed of Alice, had thus suddenly and prematurely frosted the dark locks of my youth. My mother became alarmed at my excessive paleness, and proposed a journey for the restoration of my spirits and health. Ronald eagerly supported the suggestion, but Eglantine declined accompanying us. She preferred, she said, being alone. With books at home, and Nature, in the glory of its summer garniture, abroad, she could not want sources of enjoyment. I did not regret her determination, for her presence had become strangely oppressive to me, and even Ronald's manners had assumed an embarrassment and constraint towards her very different from their usual familiarity. The night before our departure I felt more melancholy than ever. It was just such a night as the one that witnessed our ill-starred betrothal. The moon came forth from behind a bed of white clouds, silvering every flake as it floated back from her beauteous face, and diffusing on earth the wondrous secret of heavenly communion. I could not sleep; and as I lay gazing on the solemn tranquillity of the night heavens, I thought of the time when 'those heavens should be rolled together as a scroll, and the elements melt with fervent heat,' and I, still thinking, living, feeling, in other, grander, everlasting scenes, the invisible dweller of my bosom's temple assumed such magnitude and majesty in my eyes, the contemplation became overwhelming and awful. The sublime sound of the clock striking the midnight hour—and all who have heard that sound in the dead silence of the night, can attest that it is sublime—broke in on my deep abstraction. Eglantine, who had lain wrapped in peaceful slumbers, here softly drew back the bed-cover, and rising slowly, walked round with stilly steps to the side where I reclined, and stood looking fixedly upon me. 'Eglantine!' I exclaimed, terrified at her attitude and singular appearance. 'Eglantine, what is the matter?' She answered not, moved not, but remained standing, immovable, with her eyes fixed and expressionless as stone. There she stood, in the white moonlight, in her long, loose night-dress, which hung around her, in her stillness, like the folds of the winding-sheet, her hair streaming down her back in long, lifeless tresses, and lighted up on her brow with a kind of supernatural radiance—and then those death-resembling eyes! I trembled, and tried to draw the sheet over my face, to shut out the appalling vision. After a few moments, which seemed interminable to me, she bent over me, and taking my right hand, felt of my wrist again and again. Her fingers were as cold as marble. My very blood seemed to congeal under her touch. 'It is gone,' murmured she, 'but it is safe—I have it safe. It fits my wrist as well as hers.' Terrified as I was at this unexpected apparition, my mind was clear, and never were my perceptions more vivid. The mystery of the bracelet was about to be unravelled. Poor Alice's assertion that she had seen Eglantine standing by my side, and taking the bracelet from my wrist, came back thundering in my ears. 'It is gone,' replied Eglantine, in the same low, deep voice, 'but I know where it is laid; where the bridegroom or the bride can never find it. Perhaps the moon shines too brightly on it, and reveals the spot.' Thus saying, she glided across the floor, with spirit-like tread, and opening the door, disappeared. In the excess of my excitement I forgot my fears, and hastily rising, followed her footsteps, determined to unravel the mystery, if I died in the act. I could catch the glimpses of her white garments through the shadows of the winding staircase, and I pursued them with rapid steps, till I found myself close behind her, by the door which opened into the garden. There she stood, still as a corpse, and again the cold dew of superstitious terror gathered on my brow. I soon saw a fumbling motion about the keyhole, and the door opening, she again glided onward towards the summer-house, my favourite retreat, the place where I had received this mysterious bracelet—the place where Flora had collected all her wealth of bloom. She put aside the drooping vines, sending out such a cloud of fragrance on the dewy air, I almost fainted from their oppression, and stooping down over a white rose-bush, carefully removed the lower branches, while the rose-leaves fell in a snowy shower over her naked feet. 'Where is it?' said she, feeling about in the long grass. 'It isn't in the spot where I hid it. If she has found it, she may yet be a bride, and Ronald still her own.' She stooped down lower over the rose-bush, then rising hastily, I saw, with inexpressible agitation, the lost bracelet shining in the light that quivered with ghostlike lustre on her pallid face. With a most unearthly smile she clasped it on her wrist, and left the arbour, muttering in a low voice, 'I will not leave it here—lest she find out where it lies, and win back her bridal gift. I will keep it next my own heart, and she cannot reach it there.' Once more I followed the gliding steps of Eglantine, through the chill silence of night, till we ascended the stairs, and entered our own chamber. Quietly she laid herself down, as if she had just risen from her knees in prayer, and I perceived by her closed lids and gentle breathing, that a natural sleep was succeeding the inexplicable mysteries of somnambulism."

"She was walking in her sleep, then, grandmother!" I exclaimed, drawing a long breath. "I thought so all the time; and poor Alice was really innocent! And what did Eglantine say the next morning, when she awaked, and found the bracelet on her arm?"

"She was astonished and bewildered, and knew not what to think; but when I told her of all the events of the night, the truth of which the bracelet itself attested, she sunk back like one stricken with death. So many thoughts crowded upon her at once in such force, it is no wonder they almost crushed her with their power. The conviction that her love for Ronald could no longer be concealed, the remembrance of the accusation of Alice, which she had so indignantly repelled, the apparent meanness and turpitude of the art, though performed without any conscious volition on her part, the belief that another had been the victim of her involuntary crime, all united to bow her spirit to the dust. My heart bled at the sight of her distress, and, every feeling wrought up to unnatural strength by the exciting scenes I had witnessed, I promised never to wed Ronald, since the thought of our union had evidently made her so unhappy. Eglantine contended against this resolution with all her eloquence, but, alas! she was not destined long to oppose the claims of friendship to the pleadings of love. Her constitution was naturally frail, a fragility indicated by the extreme delicacy and mutability of her complexion, and the profusion of her pale golden hair. Day by day she faded—night by night she continued her mysterious rambles to the spot where she had first deposited the bracelet, till she had no longer strength to leave her bed, when her soul seemed to commune with the cherubim and seraphim, which, I doubt not, in their invisible glory surrounded her nightly couch. As she drew near the land of shadows, she lost sight of the phantom of earthly love in aspirations after a heavenly union. She mourned over her ill-directed sensibilities, her wasted opportunities, her selfish brooding over forbidden hopes and imaginings. She gave herself up in penitence and faith to her Redeemer, in submission to her Father and her God; and her soul at last passed away as silently and gently as the perfume from the evening flower into the bosom of eternity."

"Oh! grandmother, what a melancholy story you have told," cried I, looking at the bracelet more intently than ever, the vivid feelings of curiosity subdued and chastened by such sad revelings; "but did not you marry Ronald at last?"

"Yes," replied she, looking upward with mournful earnestness; "the beloved grandfather, who has so often dandled you in his arms, in this very spot where we are now seated, whose head, white with the snows of threescore years and ten, now reposes on the pillow all the living must press,—who now awaits me, I trust, in the dwellings of immortality, was that once youthful Ronald, whose beauty and worth captivated the affections of the too sensitive Eglantine. Many, many years of happiness has it been my blessed lot to share with him on earth. The memories of Alice and Eglantine, softened by time, were robbed of their bitterness, and only served to endear us more tenderly to each other. The knowledge we had gained of the frailty and uncertainty of life, led us to lift our views to a more enduring state of existence, and love, hallowed by religion, became a sublime and holy bond, imperishable as the soul, and lofty as its destinies. I have lived to see my children's children gather around me, like the olive branches of scripture, fair and flourishing. I have lived to see the companion of my youth and age consigned to the darkness of the grave, and I have nothing more to do on earth but to fold the mantle of the spirit quietly around me, and wait the coming of the Son of Man."

I looked up with reverence in my grandmother's face as she thus concluded the eventful history of the Pearl Bracelet, and I thought what a solemn and beautiful thing was old age when the rays of the Sun of Righteousness thus illumed its hoary hair, and converted it into an emblematic crown of glory.

THE MYSTERIOUS RETICULE.

"I own," said Fitzroy, "that I have some foolish prejudices, and this may be one. But I cannot bear to see a lady with a soiled pocket-handkerchief. I never wish to see anything less pure and elegant than this in the hand of a beautiful maiden." He lifted, as he spoke, a superb linen handkerchief, decorated with lace, that lay carelessly folded in the lap of Mary Lee.

"Ah, yes," exclaimed her cousin Kate, laughing, "it looks very nice now, for she has just taken it from her drawer. See, the perfume of the lavender has not begun to evaporate. But wait till to-morrow, and then it will look no nicer than mine."

"To-morrow!" cried the elegant Fitzroy, with an expression of disgust; "surely no lady would think of using a handkerchief more than once. If I were in love with a Venus de Medici herself, and detected her in such an unpardonable act, I believe the spell would be broken."

"I would not give much for your love, then," cried Kate, "if it had no deeper foundation—would you, Mary?"

Mary blushed, for she was already more than half in love with the handsome Fitzroy, and was making an internal resolution to be exceedingly particular in future about her pocket-handkerchiefs.

Fitzroy was a young man of fashion and fortune, of fine person, elegant manners, cultivated mind, and fastidiously refined taste. He had, however, two great defects—one was, attaching too much importance to trifles, and making them the criterion of character; the other, a morbid suspicion of the sincerity of his friends, and a distrust of their motives, which might become the wildest jealousy in the passion of love. He had a most intense admiration of female loveliness, and looked upon woman as a kind of super-angelic being, whose food should be the ambrosiæ and nectar of the gods, and whose garments the spotless white of vestal purity. He had never known misfortune, sickness, or sorrow, therefore had never been dependent on those homely, domestic virtues, those tender, household cares, which can alone entitle woman to the poetical appellation of a ministering angel. He was the spoiled child of affluence and indulgence, who looked, as Kate said, "as if he ought to recline on a crimson velvet sofa, and be fanned with peacocks' feathers all the day long." He was now the guest of Mr. Lee, and consequently the daily companion of the beautiful, sensitive Mary and her gay cousin. With his passionate admiration for beauty, it is not strange that he should become more and more attracted towards Mary, who never forgot, in the adornments of her finished toilet, the robe of vestal white and the pure, delicate, perfumed handkerchief, which Fitzroy seemed to consider the *ne plus ultra* of a lady's perfections. The cousins walked, rode, and visited with the elegant stranger, and never did weeks glide more rapidly away. Mary was happy, inexpressibly happy, for life began to be invested with that soft, purple hue, which, like the rich blush of the grape, is so easily brushed away, and can never be restored.

Fitzroy had often noticed and admired, among the decorations of Mary's dress, a beautiful reticule of white embroidered satin. One evening, on returning from a party, Mary's brow became suddenly clouded. "Oh, how could I be so careless?" exclaimed she, in a tone of vexation; "I have left my reticule behind. How unfortunate!"

Fitzroy immediately offered his services, but Mary persisted in refusing them, and dispatched a servant in his stead.

"You must have something very precious in that bag," said Kate. "I have no doubt it is full of billetdoux or love-letters. I intend to go after it myself, and find out all Mary's secrets."

"How foolish!" cried Mary. "You know there is no such thing in it—nothing in the world but——" She stopped, in evident embarrassment, and lowered her eyes, to avoid Fitzroy's searching glance.

The servant came without the bag, and again Fitzroy renewed his offers of search in the morning.

"No, indeed," said Mary; "I am very grateful, but I cannot allow you to take that trouble. It is of no consequence; I insist that you do not think of going. I am very sorry I said anything about it."

Mary's ill-concealed embarrassment and flitting blushes awakened one of Fitzroy's bosom enemies. Why this strange anxiety and confusion about a simple reticule? It must be the receptacle of secrets she would blush to have revealed. Kate's suggestion was probably true. It contained some confessions or tokens of love which she was holding in her heart's treasury, while her eye and her lip beamed and smiled encouragement and hope of him.

The next morning he rose from his bed at an early hour with a feeling of restlessness and anxiety, and resolved to go himself in search of the lost treasure. He found it suspended on the chair in which he remembered to have seen her last seated, leaning against the window, with the moonbeams shining down on her snowy brow. The soft satin yielded to his touch, and the exquisite beauty of the texture seemed to correspond with the grace and loveliness of the owner. He was beginning to be ashamed of his suspicions, when the resistance of a folded paper against his fingers recalled Kate's laughing assertions about love-letters and billetdoux, and jealous thoughts again tingled in his veins. For one moment he was tempted to open it and satisfy his tantalizing curiosity, but pride and honour resisted the promptings of the evil spirit.

Poor Mary! had she known what sweeping conclusions he brought against her during his homeward walk, she would have wished her unfortunate bag in the bottom of the ocean. She was false, coquettish, and vain! He would never bestow another thought upon her, but bid adieu, as soon as possible, to her father's hospitable mansion, and forget his transient fascination. When he entered the room where Mary and Kate were seated, Mary sprang forward with a crimsoned cheek and extended her hand with an eager, involuntary motion. "I thank you," said she, coldly; "but I am very, very sorry you assumed such unnecessary trouble."

She thanked him with her lips, but her ingenuous countenance expressed anything but gratitude and pleasure. Fitzroy gave it to her with a low, silent bow, and threw himself wearily on the sofa.

"I will know what mystery is wrapped up in this little bag!" exclaimed Kate, suddenly snatching it from her hand. "I know it contains some love talisman or fairy token."

"Ah, Kate, I entreat, I pray you to restore it to me," cried Mary. "No—no—

no," answered Kate, laughing, and holding it high above her head.

Mary sprang to catch it, but Kate only swung it higher and higher with triumphant glee. Fitzroy looked on with a scornful glance; Mary's unaffected alarm confirmed all his suspicions, and he felt a selfish gratification in her increasing trepidation.

"Kate, I did not think you could be rude or unkind before," said Mary, looking reproachfully at Fitzroy, for not assisting her in the contest.

"Since Miss Lee evidently endures so much uneasiness lest the mysteries of her bag should be explored," cried Fitzroy, with a sarcastic smile, "I am sure her friends must sympathize in her sufferings."

"Oh, if you are in earnest, Mary," cried Kate, tossing the reticule over her head, "I would not make you unhappy for the world."

There was a beautiful child, about two or three years old, a little sister of Kate's, who was playing on the carpet with the paraphernalia of her dolls. The bag fell directly in her lap, and she caught it with childish eagerness. "I got it —I got it!" cried she, exultingly; and before Mary could regain possession of it, she had undrawn the silken strings, and emptied the contents in her lap—a parcel of faded rose-leaves scattered on the floor, from a white folded paper that opened as it fell. Fitzroy beheld it, and his jealous fears vanished into air; but another object attracted his too fastidious gaze—a soiled, crumpled pocket-handkerchief lay maliciously displayed in the little plunderer's lap, and then was brandished in her victorious hand. Mary stood for a moment covered with burning blushes, then ran out of the room, stung to the soul by the mocking smile that curled the lip of Fitzroy.

"Cousin Mary been eating cake," said the child, exposing the poor handkerchief still more fully to the shrinking, ultra-refined man of taste and fashion.

The spell was broken, the goddess thrown from her pedestal—the charm of those exquisite, transparent, rose-scented handkerchiefs for ever destroyed. Kate laughed immoderately at the whole scene. There was something truly ridiculous to her in the unfathomable mystery, Mary's preposterous agitation, and Fitzroy's unconcealed disgust. There was a very slight dash of malice mingled with the gayety of her character, and when she recollected how much Fitzroy had admired and Mary displayed her immaculate and superb handkerchiefs, pure from all earthly alloy, she could not but enjoy a *little* her present mortification. She ridiculed Fitzroy so unmercifully that he took refuge in flight, and then the merry girl sought the chamber of Mary, whither she had fled to conceal her mortification and tears.

"Surely you are not weeping for such a ridiculous cause?" said Kate, sobered at the sight of Mary's real suffering. "I had no idea you were so foolish."

Mary turned away in silence; she could not forgive her for having exposed her weakness to the eyes of Fitzroy.

"Mary," continued Kate, "I did not mean to distress you; I did not imagine there was anything in the bag you really wished concealed, and I am sure there was not. What induced you to make such a fuss about a simple pocket-handkerchief? It looks as nice as mine does, I dare say."

"But he is so very particular," sobbed Mary, "he will never forget it. I have always carried a handkerchief in my bag for use, so that I could keep the one which I held in my hand clean and nice. I knew his peculiarities, and thought there was no harm in consulting them. He will never think of me now without disgust."

"And if he never will," cried the spirited Kate, with flashing eyes, "I would spurn him from my thoughts as a being unworthy of respect or admiration. I would not marry such a man were he to lay at my feet the diadem of the East. Forgive me for having made myself merry at your expense, but I could not help laughing at your overwrought sensibility. Answer me seriously, Mary, and tell me if you think that if Fitzroy really loved you, and was worthy of your love, he would become alienated by a trifle like this?"

Mary began to be ashamed of her emotions in the presence of her reasonable cousin;—she was ashamed, and endeavoured to conceal them, but they were not subdued. She was conscious she must appear in a ridiculous light in the eyes of the scrupulously elegant Fitzroy, whose morbid tastes she had so unfortunately studied. When they met again, it was with feelings of mutual estrangement. She was cold and constrained—he polite, but reserved. Mary felt with anguish that the soft, purple hue which had thrown such an enchantment over every scene, was vanished away. The realities of existence began to appear.

Fitzroy soon after took his leave, with very different feelings from what he had once anticipated. He blamed himself, but he could not help the chilled state of his heart. Mary was a mortal, after all; she ate cake, drank lemonade, and used her handkerchiefs like other ladies, only she kept them out of sight. Her loveliness, grace, and feminine gentleness of manner no longer entranced him. He departed, and Mary sighed over the dissolving of her first love's dream; but notwithstanding her weakness on this subject, she had a just estimation of herself, and a spirit which, when once roused, guided her to exertions which astonished herself. Her gay cousin, too, departed, and she was thrown upon her own resources. She read much, and reflected more. She blushed for her past weakness, and learned to think with contempt upon the man who had so false an estimate of the true excellence and glory of a woman's character. "Oh," repeated she to herself a hundred times, as, interested in domestic duties, she devoted herself to the comfort of her widowed father, "how miserable I should have been as the wife of a coxcomb, who would desire me to sit all day with folded hands, holding an embroidered handkerchief, with fingers encased in white kid gloves! How could I ever have been so weak and foolish?" Mary generally concluded these reflections with a sigh, for Fitzroy was handsome, graceful, and intellectual, and he was, moreover, the first person who had ever interested her young heart.

The following summer she accompanied her father to a fashionable watering-place. She was admired and caressed, but she turned coldly from the gaze of admiration, and cared not for the gayety that surrounded her. While others hurried to the ball-room, she lingered over her book, or indulged in meditations unfamiliar to the lovely and the young. One evening, when she had been unusually dilatory, she heard her father call, and taking a lamp, began to thread the passage, which led through a long suite of apartments occupied by the visiters of the spring. As she passed by one of the rooms, the door of which was partially opened, she heard a faint, moaning sound, and paused to listen. It returned again and again, and she was sure some stranger was suffering there, probably forgotten in the gay crowd that filled the mansion. Her first impulse was to enter, but she shrunk from the thought of intruding herself, a young maiden, into the apartment of a stranger. "My father will go in and see who the sufferer is," cried she, hastening to meet him on the stairs.

Mr. Lee required no entreaties from his daughter, for his kind and humane feelings were immediately excited by the idea of a lonely and perhaps dying stranger, in the midst of a heartless crowd. Mary gave the lamp into her father's hand, and stood in the passage while he entered. A sudden exclamation, echoed by a faint low voice, made her heart palpitate with vague apprehensions. Who could this lonely stranger be whom her father evidently recognised? She stood holding her breath painfully, fearing to lose the sound of that faint voice which awakened strange emotions within her, when her father suddenly came to the door and beckoned her to him. "I do believe he is dying," said he, in an agitated tone. "It is Fitzroy himself! You must come to him, while I call a physician."

Mary almost mechanically obeyed the summons, and stood the next moment, pale and trembling, by the bedside of the man she had once loved. Could that, indeed, be the elegant Fitzroy?—with disordered hair, half-closed eyes, parched and trembling lips, which now vainly endeavoured to articulate a sound?—the pillows tossed here and there, as if in wrestling with pain; the white counterpane twisted and tumbled—were these the accompaniments of this fastidious exquisite? These thoughts darted through Mary's mind, as the vision of her soiled handkerchief came ghost-like before her. But she was no longer the weak girl who wept tears of bitter agony at the discovery that she was made of mortal mould; she was a woman awakened to the best energies and virtues of her sex. She found herself alone with the sick man, for her father had flown for the assistance he required, and left her to watch till his return. She saturated her handkerchief with cologne, and bathed his burning temples and feverish hands. Her heart softened over the invalid in his prostrate and dependent state. "Ah, proud Fitzroy," thought she, "this handkerchief is now more soiled and defaced than the one which alienated your fancy from me, and yet you shrink not from its contact. No pride or scorn now flashes from those dim eyes, or curls those pallid lips. Alas! he is very, very ill—I fear even unto death." The tears gathered into her eyes at this appalling idea, and even mingled with the odorous waters with which she embalmed his forehead.

Her father soon came in with the physician, and Mary resigned her watch by his bedside. She withdrew to her own apartment, and waited with intense anxiety the tidings which he promised to bring her. She was surprised at her own emotions. She thought Fitzroy perfectly indifferent to her—nay, more, that she disliked him; but now, when she saw him in suffering and danger, she remembered the charm with which her imagination had once invested him, and accused herself of harsh and vindictive feelings.

"Yes," said Mr. Lee, in answer to her earnest inquiries, "he is very ill—

dangerously ill. Imprudent exposure to the burning mid-day sun has brought on a sudden and violent fever, the consequences of which are more to be dreaded, as he has never been sick before. Could he have commanded immediate attention, perhaps the disease might have been arrested. But in this scene of gayety and confusion—though got up for the express accommodation of invalids—Heaven save the sick and the dying."

"Who will take care of him, father? He has no mother or sister near. Oh, surely we must not let him die for want of these!"

"I know what you are thinking of, Mary," said Mr. Lee, shaking his head; "but I cannot consent to it. The fever may be contagious, and you are too young and too delicate for such a task. Besides, there might be remarks made upon it. No; I will remain with him to-night, and to-morrow we will see what can be done for him."

"But to-night may be the crisis of his fate," pleaded Mary; "to-morrow it may be too late. You are very kind, father, but you are not a woman, and you know there are a thousand gentle cares which only a woman's hand can tender. I am a stranger here; I don't care if they do censure me. Let me act a true woman's, a kind sister's part. You know, by your own experience, what a skilful nurse I am."

Mary pleaded earnestly, and wound her arms caressingly around her father's neck, and looked up into his face with such irresistible eyes, that he could not refuse her. The pallid face of Fitzroy seemed to be leaning beside her own, clothed with that authority which sickness and approaching death impart. So Mary twisted up her shining ringlets, and took the rings from her jeweled fingers, and donned a loose, flowing robe. Behold her, one of the loveliest nurses that ever brought the blessings of Hygea to the chamber of disease. There is a great deal said in romances of the interesting appearance of invalids, of a languor more lovely than the bloom of health, of a debility more graceful than the fullness of strength; but this is all romance. It has been said by one of the greatest moralists of the age, that the slow consuming of beauty is one of the greatest judgments of the Almighty against man for sin. Certainly a sick chamber is not the place for romantic beings to *fall in love*, but it is the place where love, once awakened, can exert its holiest influences, and manifest its death-controlling power; it is the place where religion erects its purest altar, and faith brings its divinest offerings. Yea, verily, it is hallowed ground. Thus Mary thought through the vigils of that long night. She had never been dangerously sick herself, but she felt the entire dependence of one human being upon another, and of all upon God. She felt, too, a kind of generous triumph, if such an expression may be used, in the conviction that this proud and over-sensitive being was so completely abandoned to her cares. Fitzroy lay in the deep lethargy of a burning fever, unconscious whose soft footsteps fell "like snow on snow" around his bed. "He never shall know it," said Mary, to herself. "He would probably feel disgust, instead of gratitude. If he saw this handkerchief, all impregnated with camphor, and stained with medicine, he might well think it unfit for a lady's hand. Shame on me, for cherishing so much malice against him—he so sick and pale!"

For more than a week Fitzroy languished in that almost unconscious condition, and during that interval Mary continued to lavish upon him every attention a kind and gentle sister could bestow. At length he was declared out of danger, and she gradually withdrew from her station in the sick chamber. Her mission was fulfilled, and an angelic one it had been. The physician, her father, and a youthful, unimpaired constitution accomplished the rest.

"What do I not owe you?" said Fitzroy, when, liberated from confinement, he was slowly walking with her through one of the green, shady paths of the enclosure. Now he, indeed, looked interesting. The contrast between his dark brown hair and pale cheek was truly romantic. That dark hair once more exhaled the odours of sweet-scented waters, and his black dress and spotless linen were as distinguished for their elegance as in former days. "What do I not owe you?" repeated he, with more fervour.

Mary smiled. "You were sick, and I ministered unto you. I only obeyed a divine command. A simple act of obedience deserves no reward."

"Then it was only from a sense of duty that you watched over me so kindly?" repeated he, in a mortified tone. "You would have done the same for any stranger?"

"Most certainly I would," replied Mary; "for any stranger as helpless and neglected as you appeared to be."

"Pardon me," said he, evidently disconcerted, "but I thought—I dared to think —that——"

Mary laughed, and *her* rosy lip began to curl with a slight expression of scorn. She was a woman, and her feelings had once been chafed, humiliated through him, if not by him. Her eyes sparkled, not vindictively, but triumphantly. "You dared to think that I was in love with you! Oh, no; that is all passed—long, long ago."

"Passed? Then you acknowledge that you *have* loved?"

"Yes," replied she, in the same laughing tone, though she blushed deeply all the while; "I did love you, Fitzroy, and I could have loved you with a life-long passion. To win your affection I tried to pass myself off as an angel, to whose garments the dust of mortality never adhered. You discovered my folly, and turned from me in contempt. It was a bitter lesson at first, but I thank you for it now. I am not the foolish girl that I was when I first knew you, Fitzroy. You must not think that I am——"

"And *I* am not the fool I was then," interrupted he. "I know now what constitutes the perfection of a woman's character. You only captivated my fancy then, now you have won my whole heart."

"Better lost than won," cried Mary, in the same careless accents. "I could not keep the treasure, and I cannot take it. You think you love me now, but I might fall sick, you know, and people do not look so pretty when they are sick, and you might not like the scent of camphor and medicine, and then one's handkerchiefs get so terribly soiled!"

She stopped, and looked archly at Fitzroy's clouded countenance.

"I understand it all," cried he, bitterly; "you pitied me in sickness, and watched over me. But I must have looked shockingly ugly and slovenly, and you became disgusted. I cannot blame you, for I deserve such a punishment."

"No, no—not ugly, Fitzroy, but helpless, weak, and dependent, proud man that you are. But, oh! you ought to know that this very helplessness and dependence endear the sufferer ten thousand times more to a fond woman's heart than all the pride of beauty and the bloom of health. I have had my revenge; but believe me, Fitzroy, the hours passed in your chamber of sickness will be remembered as the happiest of my life."

The tone of playful mockery which she had assumed, subsided into one of deep feeling, and tears gathered in her downcast eyes. Fitzroy—but it is no matter what Fitzroy said—certainly something that pleased Mary, for when they returned, more than an hour afterwards, her cheeks were glowing with the roses of Eden.

It was about six months after this that Cousin Kate visited Mary—but not *Mary Lee*—once more. Fitzroy, who now often complained of a headache, was leaning back in an easy chair, and Mary was bathing his temples, which she occasionally pressed with her linen handkerchief.

"Oh, shocking!" exclaimed Kate; "how can you bear to see Mary touch anything so rumpled and used, about your elegant person?"

"The hand of affection," replied Fitzroy, pressing Mary's gently on his brow, "can shed a beautifying influence over every object. Mary is a true alchemist, and has separated the gold of my heart from the worthless dross that obscured its lustre. She put me in the crucible, and I have been purified by the fires through which I passed."

Lightning Source UK Ltd.
Milton Keynes UK
UKHW041041100820
367987UK00004B/860

The Devel... Modern ...

C000116443

An Introduction to the Study of Current History
(Volume I)

James Harvey Robinson
Charles Austin Beard

Alpha Editions

PREFACE

It has been a common defect of our historical manuals that, however satisfactorily they have dealt with more or less remote periods, they have ordinarily failed to connect the past with the present. And teachers still pay a mysterious respect to the memory of Datis and Artaphernes which they deny to gentlemen in frock coats, like Gladstone and Gambetta. The gloomy incidents of the capture of Numantia are scrupulously impressed upon the minds of children who have little chance of ever hearing of the siege of Metz. The organization of the Achæan League is given preference to that of the present German Empire.

There are some teachers, perhaps, who would seek to justify the current disregard of recent history, but many others would agree with one of the guild who, when criticised for giving more attention in her instruction to Charlemagne than to Bismarck, complained with truth, "But we know so much more about Charlemagne than about Bismarck." The great majority of those interested in history would no doubt gladly readjust their perspective if they had the means of doing so; and, indeed, there has been a marked improvement in this respect in the newer books which are giving more and more space to recent events.

In preparing the volume in hand, the writers have consistently subordinated the past to the present. It has been their ever-conscious aim to enable the reader to catch up with his own times; to read intelligently the foreign news in the morning paper; to know what was the attitude of Leo XIII toward the social democrats even if he has forgotten that of Innocent III toward the Albigenses.

Yet, in permitting the present to dominate the past, they do not feel that they have dealt less fairly with the general outline of European history during the last two centuries than they would have done had they merely narrated the events with no ulterior object. There has been no distortion of the facts in order to bring them into relation to any particular conception of the present or its tendencies. Even if certain occurrences of merely temporary prominence have been omitted as irrelevant to the purpose of the work, this cannot mean any serious loss.

The way in which the narrative emerges into the living present is, then, one of the claims of this new manual to be regarded as an adventurer in the educational world. A second trait of novelty is the happy reunion of the eighteenth and nineteenth centuries, which should never have been put asunder by the date 1789. The nineteenth century was often too arrogant to recognize its dependence upon the eighteenth, from which it derived most of its inspirations as well as its aversions. It was the eighteenth century which set the problems of progress and suggested their solutions, leaving to its successor the comparatively simple task of working them out in detail and making fuller application of them.

Lastly, the writers have ventured to devote much less space to purely political and military events than has commonly been assigned to them in histories of the nineteenth century. On the other hand, the more fundamental economic matters have been generously treated, — the Industrial Revolution, commerce and the colonies, the internal reforms of the European states, even the general advance of science, have all, so far as possible, been given their just due.

The necessarily succinct outline of events which fills these volumes can be considerably amplified and enlivened by the accompanying *Readings in Modern European History* which follows the narrative chapter by chapter and furnishes examples of the stuff of which history is made.

As for their sources, the writers, who have had at their disposal a very extensive library, would find it difficult to enumerate the debts which they owe to a wide range of historical
writers and to collections of materials, large and small. The
bibliographies given in the *Readings* will indicate fairly the
extent of their investigations. In some of the chapters, especially those relating to the French Revolution and Napoleon,
the writers have borrowed here and there from Robinson's
History of Western Europe. They wish to express their obligations to their colleague, Professor James T. Shotwell, for
many suggestions, and their appreciation of the kindness of
Professor Myers and Professor Cheyney in permitting them to
reproduce several of their maps. While the greatest pains has
been taken to establish the strict accuracy of every assertion
and the authenticity of every alleged fact, the writers cannot
flatter themselves that they have escaped all the pitfalls that
must perforce beset the path of those who boldly undertake to
guide others through the most intricate developments in the
whole recorded history of our planet.

J. H. R.
C. A. B.

COLUMBIA UNIVERSITY
NEW YORK

CONTENTS

LIST OF MAPS

FULL-PAGE ILLUSTRATIONS

THE DEVELOPMENT OF
MODERN EUROPE

VOLUME I

THE EIGHTEENTH CENTURY:
THE FRENCH REVOLUTION AND
THE NAPOLEONIC PERIOD

THE DEVELOPMENT OF
MODERN EUROPE

INTRODUCTORY

History deals with the past and is ordinarily studied with no other aim than that of learning about bygone events and famous men long since dead. Yet it requires no large amount of observation to perceive that history casts light upon the customs and institutions which surround us at the present hour. Consequently students of every branch of human knowledge — science, political economy, philosophy, politics, and religion — are turning more seriously than ever before to the past, not for its own sake merely, but with a hope of coming to know the present better through a knowledge of the past. History essential to an understanding of the present

It is indeed a curious and important discovery of modern times that the existing forms of government and social life are not to be understood by simply examining them, but by taking the trouble to find out how they came to be what they are. Every event in our own lives is determined and explained by preceding events, and this is equally true of the history of nations. Every country — England, Germany, France, Italy, Russia — has its own special past, which serves to explain in a large measure why each differs from all the others. The present situation of each would be incomprehensible except for the key furnished by history. It is history alone that makes clear why Germany is a federation like the United States but nevertheless very different in many respects ; why England is a monarchy but far more like a republic than its fellow-kingdom Prussia ; why France is a republic while Spain remains a monarchy.

I

How one's
personal
conduct is
based upon
a knowledge
of his own
individual
history   The inexorable dependence of the present upon the past
may be clearly illustrated by our own personal experience.
The daily thoughts and actions of each of us rest upon his
knowledge of his own history. Any man would be in a sorry
state if he should forget his own past every night and be compelled to start out afresh every morning, discovering anew his
relatives and friends and puzzling out again once familiar streets.

It is, in short, his knowledge of his own past that makes
a person's surroundings intelligible to him and renders the
doings of the day something more than gropings in an ever
strange and unaccountable world. We must perforce build
our to-day upon the memory of yesterday. And just as our
own private history enables us to interpret what would otherwise have no meaning for us, so the history of nations serves
to show why they are what they are and why they do as they
do. For institutions are, after all, only the habits of nations
and can be understood only by discovering their origin and
following their gradual development.

One may look to history to explain almost everything, great
and small, from the constitution of a state to the form of a
written character or the presence of useless buttons upon a
man's coat sleeve.[1] And it is the special purpose of this volume to dwell as fully as is possible within its limits on those
events, conditions, and public persons that have made the
governments, politics, industries, and intellectual interests of
Europe what they are to-day.

Reasons for
beginning
our study by
reviewing the
history of the
eighteenth
century   Obviously no special date can be fixed as the starting point
of our story, for in some instances it will be necessary to go
farther back than in others in seeking light on the present.
For instance, the conditions that produced the war between

[1] Our characters & and + are both derived from *et*, the Latin word for "and,"
as it was hastily written by mediæval scribes. The abbreviation *viz.* was originally the first two letters of the Latin word for "namely," *videlicet*, followed by
a semicolon (then the sign of abbreviation), which came to be written like a *z*.
The buttons which still adorn the back of a man's coat were, we presume, used
in the time of George Washington to fasten up the tails, while those which still
survive on the sleeves were used to button back the cuffs.

Spain and the United States carry us back to the days of Columbus and the old Spanish colonial policy; whereas for the beginnings of the railway system we need not go beyond the generation of George Stephenson. In general, however, Europe of to-day can be quite well understood if the wonderful achievements since the opening of the eighteenth century are properly grasped.

Could Benjamin Franklin, who visited France in 1776, see that country now, how startling would the changes seem to him! The railroads, the steel steamships, the great towns with well-lighted, smoothly paved, and carefully drained streets; the innumerable newspapers and the beautifully illustrated periodicals, the government schools, the popular elections, the deserted palaces of the king, the vast factories full of machinery, working with a precision and rapidity far surpassing those of an army of skilled workmen; most astonishing of all, the mysterious and multiform applications of that lightning which he himself had years before drawn down his kite string, — all these marvels would combine to convince him that he died on the eve of the greatest revolution in industry, government, and science that the world has ever seen.

It seems best, therefore, to begin our account with a review of the territorial changes, national policies, economic conditions, and intellectual interests of western Europe during a few decades before the French Revolution and before that still more vital Industrial Revolution which has served to alter so profoundly the life of the mass of mankind. The nineteenth century, in one sense, only garnered in the rich harvest which the eighteenth century had not only sown but devotedly cultivated. For it was the eighteenth century that gave us the working steam engine (which was destined to metamorphose the world), brought old ideas and customs sternly to the bar of reason, roused men's slumbering discontent with ancient abuses, pointed the way to reform, and opened up that infinite vista of progress which now stretches before us.

CHAPTER I

FRANCE UNDER LOUIS XIV

FRANCE BEFORE LOUIS XIV

Leading rôle of France during the last two centuries

1. The nation which has unmistakably assumed the leading rôle in European affairs during the past two hundred years is France. At the opening of the eighteenth century she already enjoyed a commanding position. In the wars to which the ambition of her king, Louis XIV, gave rise, almost all the countries of western Europe took part; even their colonies in distant regions were involved, and the map of the world was fundamentally altered. A generation after Louis XIV's death France began to be recognized as the great teacher of Europe; her philosophers and economists denounced the abuses which existed everywhere and urged the reform of ancient, outworn institutions. When, in due time, France wrought a revolution in her own government, she speedily forced other nations to follow her example. Indeed, carried away by the genius of her general, Napoleon Bonaparte, she seemed at one time about to bring all Europe under her sway. Even since that arch-disturber of the peace was finally captured and sent to die on the rock of St. Helena, France has twice precipitated serious crises in European affairs, when in 1848 she proclaimed a new revolution, and in 1870 she assumed the responsibility for the last important war that has afflicted western Europe.

Feudal background of modern France

Of the long history of France from the conquest of Gaul by Julius Cæsar to the accession of Louis XIV in 1643 little can be said here. The French kings had, from about the year 1100, begun to get the better of their vassals and had succeeded, with some setbacks, in forming a tolerably

4

satisfactory kingdom when, about a hundred years before Louis XIV's time, the struggle between Protestants and Catholics produced new and terrible disorder which lasted for a whole generation.

After the close of the wars of religion Henry of Navarre (1589–1610), Louis XIV's grandfather, reformed and strengthened the royal power. He had himself been a Protestant in his earlier days and consequently treated the Huguenots with consideration ; he assigned them fortified cities of refuge, and granted them certain privileges in order to protect them from attacks by their Catholic enemies. But Henry was assassinated in 1610 and his great work was left half done, although he has always remained an heroic and popular figure. *Henry IV strengthens the monarchy*

Henry's son, Louis XIII, had little capacity and he prudently delegated the direction of the government to Cardinal Richelieu, probably the greatest minister that France has ever had. Richelieu found that the Huguenots, owing to the exceptional position in which Henry had placed them, were " sharing the monarchy with the king," as he expressed it. He accordingly reduced them to the position of ordinary subjects by depriving them, after a struggle, of the cities of refuge granted them by Henry IV. *How Richelieu reduced the power of the Huguenots and of the nobles*

The strength of the disorderly tendencies of the nobility had much increased during the turmoil of the prolonged wars of religion. Richelieu accordingly ordered the destruction of all the unnecessary castles and fortresses within the realm, on the ground that they served as so many temptations to resist the king's officers. These officers themselves, who too often acted as if they were absolute rulers in their districts, were strictly watched and corrected by the minister, who was ever jealous of his sovereign's rights.

His successor, the wily Italian, Mazarin, who conducted the government during Louis XIV's boyhood, was able to put down the last preposterous rising of the discontented nobles in the so-called War of the Fronde. *Mazarin and the Fronde*

Results of
the work of
Richelieu
and Mazarin

When Mazarin died in 1661 he left to the young monarch a kingdom such as no previous French king had enjoyed. The nobles, who for centuries had disputed the power with Hugh Capet and his successors, were no longer feudal lords but only courtiers. The Huguenots, whose claim to a place in the state beside the Catholics had led to the terrible civil wars of the sixteenth century, were reduced in numbers and no longer held fortified towns from which they could defy the king's agents. Richelieu and Mazarin had successfully taken part in the Thirty Years' War (1618–1648), and France had come out of it with enlarged territory and increased importance in European affairs.

LOUIS XIV (1643–1715)

General
policy of
Louis XIV

2. Louis XIV carried the work of these great ministers still further. He gave that despotic form to the monarchy which it retained until the French Revolution. He made himself the very mirror of kingship. His brilliant court at Versailles became the model and the despair of other less opulent and powerful princes, who accepted his theory of the absolute authority of kings and would gladly have imitated his luxury. By his incessant wars of aggression he kept Europe in turmoil for over half a century. The distinguished generals — Turenne, Condé, and Vauban — who led his newly organized troops, and the unscrupulous diplomats who arranged his alliances and negotiated his treaties, made France feared and respected by even the most formidable of the other European states.

The theory
of the divine
right of kings

Louis had the same idea of kingship which the first Stuart king of England, James I, had fifty years earlier tried in vain to induce the English people to accept. God had given kings to men, and it was God's will that monarchs should be regarded as his lieutenants and that all those subject to them should obey them absolutely, without asking any questions or making any criticisms ; for in yielding to their princes they were really yielding to God himself. The Bible was used to prove that the person of the king was sacred and that to attack in any way the anointed of the Lord was sacrilege. If the king were good and wise, his subjects should thank the Lord ; if he proved foolish, cruel, or perverse, they must accept their evil ruler as a punishment which God had inflicted upon them for their sins. But in no case might they limit his power or rise against him.[1]

Louis had one distinct advantage over the Stuart kings. The English had generally shown themselves more reluctant than the French to place absolute power in the hands of their rulers. By her Parliament, her courts, and her various declarations of the nation's rights, England had built up traditions which made it impossible for the Stuarts to establish their claim to be absolute rulers.

Different attitude of the English and French nations toward absolute monarchy

In France, on the other hand, there was no Great Charter or Petition of Right ; nor had a representative body like the English Parliament developed which could restrain the king and his officers by refusing to grant them money. The French kings, it is true, had from about the year 1300 been accustomed to call together from time to time representatives of the three estates of the realm, — namely, the nobility, the clergy, and the so-called " third estate," or townspeople. But the Estates General, as this body was called, assembled only at rare intervals, and while they often protested against heavy taxes and bad government, they did not hold the purse strings. The French king was consequently permitted to raise money without asking the permission of the Estates or previously redressing the grievances which they chose to point out. The king could therefore cheerfully dispense with these assemblies, especially as he did not relish their criticisms and demands for reform.

The Estates General

---

[1] The distinguished prelate, Bossuet, wrote a treatise on *Politics drawn from the very words of Scripture.* This was to explain to the heir to the French throne his lofty position and responsibilities toward God. See Robinson and Beard, *Readings in Modern European History*, sect. 2, for extracts.

When Louis XIV took personal charge of the government forty-seven years had passed without a meeting of the Estates General, and a century and a quarter was still to elapse before they were again summoned, in 1789.

England did not need so strongly centralized a government as France

The French people placed far more reliance upon a powerful king than the English, because they were not protected by the sea from their neighbors, as England was. On every side France had enemies ready to take advantage of any weakness or hesitation which might arise from dissension between a parliament and the king; so the French had become accustomed to trust matters of government to the monarch's judgment, even if they suffered at times from his tyranny.

Excessive powers of the absolute monarch

In our democratic age the powers which the French king could legally exercise appear shocking. He was permitted to take as much of his people's money as he could get, and to do with it what he would, since he could both impose new and increase old taxes. No distinction was made between his private funds and the state treasury, from which he could help himself freely, spending what his subjects could ill afford to give him in presents to courtiers, reckless extravagance, or needless wars. What was worse, he could, by simply signing an order, imprison any one he wished for any length of time without any legal proceedings. He could call before him any case which was being tried in the courts and decide it as he pleased. But more will be said of the powers of the French kings when we come to see how they lost them in the great Revolution of 1789.

Personal characteristics of Louis XIV

Louis XIV was personally well adapted to assume the rôle of God's representative on earth. He was a handsome man, of elegant and courtly mien and the most exquisite perfection of manner; even when playing billiards he retained an air of world mastery. The first of the Stuarts, on the contrary, had been a very awkward man, whose slouching gait, intolerable manners, and pedantic conversation were utterly at variance with his lofty pretensions. Louis added to his graceful exterior a sound judgment and quick apprehension. He said neither too much nor too little. He was, for a king, a hard worker and spent several hours a day attending to the business of government.

It requires in fact a great deal of energy and application to be a real despot. In order to understand and to solve the problems which constantly face the ruler of a great state, a monarch must, like Frederick the Great or Napoleon, rise early and toil late. Louis was greatly aided by the able ministers who sat in his council, but he always retained for himself the place of first minister. He would never have consented to be dominated by an adviser, as his father had been by Richelieu. "The profession of the king," he declared, "is great, noble, and delightful if one but feels equal to performing the duties which it involves," and he never harbored a doubt that he himself was born for the business.[1]

Louis XIV was careful that his surroundings should suit the grandeur of his office. His court was magnificent beyond anything that had been dreamed of in the Occident. He had an enormous palace constructed at Versailles, just outside of Paris, with interminable halls and apartments and a vast garden stretching away behind it. About this a town was laid out, where all those lived who were privileged to be near his Majesty or supply the wants of the royal court. This palace and its outlying buildings, including two or three less gorgeous residences for the king when he occasionally tired of the ceremony at Versailles, probably cost the nation about a hundred million dollars, in spite of the fact that thousands of peasants and soldiers were forced to aid in the construction of the buildings and parks without remuneration. The furnishings and decorations were as rich and costly as the palace was splendid. For over a century Versailles continued to be the home of the French kings and the seat of their government.

The king's palace at Versailles

---

[1] There is no reason to suppose that Louis himself ever used the famous expression, "I am the State," but it exactly expresses his idea of government.

Life at Louis
XIV's court

This splendor and luxury helped to attract the nobility, who
no longer lived on their estates in well-fortified castles, planning how they might escape the royal control. They now
dwelt in the effulgence of the king's countenance; they saw
him to bed at night, and in stately procession they greeted him
in the morning. It was deemed a high honor to hand him his
shirt as he was being dressed, or, at dinner, to provide him
with a fresh napkin. Only by living close to the king could
the courtiers hope to gain favors, pensions, and lucrative
offices for themselves and their friends, and perhaps occasionally to exercise some little influence upon the policy of
the government. For they were now entirely dependent upon
the good will of their monarch.

Absolutism
gradually
superseded
by constitu-
tional govern-
ment in the
nineteenth
century

The exalted position of the French king, his claims to concentrate in his person, by God's will, all the powers of government without the coöperation or participation of his people,
is a matter of the utmost significance in appreciating the
history of Europe during the past two centuries. Only in the
light of these pretensions can the French Revolution be understood. It must also be remembered that the other European
sovereigns claimed, in general, similar powers and prerogatives.
The various ways in which each was finally forced, or induced,
during the nineteenth century to accept a constitution which
limited his arbitrary control and gave the people a voice in
the government are among the most important subjects which
we shall have to study.

REFORMS OF COLBERT (1661–1683)

3. Louis XIV was not indifferent, however, to the welfare of
the nation over which he believed God had called him to rule.
He permitted his distinguished adviser, the financier Colbert,
trained in the service of Mazarin, to remedy such abuses as he
could, and even to undertake certain important reforms. Colbert, to whom France still looks back with gratitude, early

LOUIS XIV'S BEDCHAMBER AT VERSAILLES

discovered that Louis's officials were stealing and wasting vast sums. The offenders were arrested and forced to disgorge, and a new system of bookkeeping was introduced similar to that employed by business men.

He then turned his attention to increasing the manufactures of France both by establishing new industries and by seeing that the older ones kept to a high standard, which would make French goods sell readily in foreign markets. He argued justly that if foreigners could be induced to buy French products, these sales would bring gold and silver into the country and so enrich it. He made rigid rules as to the width and quality of cloths which the manufacturers might produce and the dyes which they might use. He even reorganized the old, mediæval guilds and encouraged their monopoly; for through them the government could keep an eye on all the manufacturing that was carried on, and this would have been far more difficult if every one had been free to engage in any trade which he might choose. There were serious drawbacks to this kind of government regulation, but France accepted it, nevertheless, for many years.

Colbert subjects manufactures to government oversight

It was, however, as a patron of art and literature that Louis XIV gained much of his celebrity. Molière, who was at once a playwright and an actor, delighted the court with comedies in which he delicately satirized the foibles of his time. Corneille, who had gained renown by the great tragedy of *The Cid* in Richelieu's day, found a worthy successor in Racine, perhaps the most distinguished of French tragic poets. The charming letters of Madame de Sévigné are models of prose style and serve at the same time to give us a glimpse into the more refined side of the court. In the famous memoirs of Saint-Simon, the weaknesses of the king, as well as the numberless intrigues of the courtiers, are freely exposed with inimitable skill and wit.[1]

Art and literature in the reign of Louis XIV

---

[1] For examples of the writings of both Madame de Sévigné and of Saint-Simon, see *Readings*, sect. 3.

Colbert encourages science

Men of letters were generously aided by the king with pensions. Colbert encouraged the French Academy, which had been created by Richelieu. This body gave special attention to making the French tongue more eloquent and expressive by determining what words should be used. It is to this day the greatest honor that a Frenchman can obtain to be made one of the forty members of this celebrated group. Colbert founded in 1666 the French Academy of Sciences which has since done so much to extend knowledge; he had an astronomical observatory built at Paris, and gave his support and protection to a magazine devoted to careful reviews of new books, the *Journal des Savants*, which is still published regularly. The Royal Library, which then possessed only about sixteen thousand volumes, began to grow into that great collection of two and a half million volumes — the largest in existence — which to-day attracts scholars to Paris from all parts of the world. In short, Louis and his ministers believed one of the chief objects of any government to be the promotion of art, literature, and science, and the example they set has been followed by almost every modern state.

Louis XIV's warlike enterprises

Unfortunately for France, the king's ambitions were by no means altogether peaceful. Indeed, he regarded his wars as his chief glory. He employed a carefully reorganized army and skillful generals in a series of inexcusable attacks on his neighbors by which he not only produced all the incalculable misery at home and abroad which war always brings with it, but finally squandered all the resources of France, which Colbert had so anxiously husbanded, and brought the country to the verge of ruin.

Reason for reviewing the wars of Louis XIV

It might properly be asked at this point why, if our purpose be to explain the present, we should stop for even a short consideration of the criminal aggressions of a despotic king, who only succeeded in slightly extending the boundaries of France and whose victims — the tens of thousands who were killed, maimed, robbed, or maltreated in the battles, sieges, and

devastations to which his projects gave rise — are all dead
and buried these two centuries. There is, however, a good
reason for turning back to the wars of Louis XIV, far off
though they may at first sight seem. They serve to introduce
us to the chief actors who were to appear on the European
stage and to explain their several situations, their loves and
hates and rivalries, and the extent of the possessions of each,
— little Holland with its vast colonial empire, its unrivaled
fleet of merchantmen on the sea, its low meadows, its herds
and windmills, its flourishing cities, its painters and audacious
writers who continually irritated the great Louis; England
with its colonial ambitions in India and North America;
Germany, an empire the innumerable parts of which had
almost fallen asunder; enfeebled Spain, no longer able to take
rank among the formidable powers as it had a century before;
scattered Austria, not yet an empire as it is to-day; Italy, the
disruption of which seemed as hopeless as that of Germany.[1]

REFERENCES

The work of Richelieu and Mazarin: WAKEMAN, *European History, 1598-1715*, chap. vii, pp. 133-165; KITCHIN, *History of
France*, Vol. III, pp. 73-83, 138-142; PERKINS, *Richelieu.*

Louis XIV as a man and ruler: WAKEMAN, pp. 185-194; KIT-
CHIN, Vol. III, pp. 143-164.

The court of Louis XIV: PERKINS, *France under the Regency*,
pp. 129-142.

Colbert and his reforms: PERKINS, *France under the Regency*,
chap. iv, pp. 90-128; WAKEMAN, chap. i, pp. 194-205.

[1] It is scarcely necessary to say that the student must come to cherish the
map, instinctively referring to it when a question of towns, rivers, and mountains
or of any territorial change occurs. One who does not know the difference
between Alsace and Sardinia, who is not sure whether the Danube flows into the
North Sea or the Adriatic, or whether Vienna is in Prussia or Bavaria may easily
fail to understand both the present and the past. In no way can we improve our
geographical knowledge so readily, agreeably, and permanently as by associating
it with history, for thus Versailles, Madrid, the Apennines, and the Zuider Zee
become for the first time for most of us real places. So through history we learn
geography and, on the other hand, without geography, history — even that which
does not have to do directly with wars and treaties about land — is too vague to
be worth much, too ill understood to be interesting.

CHAPTER II

EUROPE AND LOUIS XIV

Louis XIV's Attempt to annex the Spanish Netherlands (1667–1668)

Natural boundaries of France

4. Louis XIV's predecessors had, on the whole, had little time to think of conquest. They had first to consolidate their realms and gain the mastery over their feudal dependents who long shared the government with them; then the claims to French territory advanced by the English Edwards and Henries had to be met, and the French provinces were finally freed from their grasp in the long and exhausting Hundred Years' War; lastly, the great religious dispute between the Catholic and Protestant parties was only settled after many years of disintegrating civil strife. But Louis was finally at liberty to look about him and consider how he might best realize the dream of his ancestors and perhaps reëstablish the ancient boundaries which Julius Cæsar reported that the Gauls had occupied. The "natural limits" of France appeared to be the great river Rhine on the north and northeast, the Jura Mountains and the Alps on the east; to the south, the Mediterranean and the mighty chain of the Pyrenees, and to the west and northwest, the Atlantic Ocean.

Extent of France in 1659

Richelieu had believed it an important part of his policy to endeavor to restore all the territory to France which Nature seemed to have assigned to her. Mazarin looked longingly toward the Rhine and sought vainly to win Savoy and Nice, which lie on the French side of the Alps.[1] But he was forced to content himself with inducing Austria, at the end of the Thirty Years' War, to cede to France such rights as she

---

[1] These regions were added permanently to France some two centuries later.

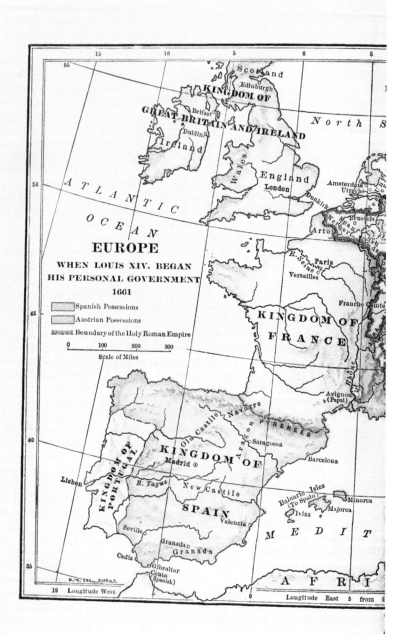

EUROPE

WHEN LOUIS XIV. BEGAN

HIS PERSONAL GOVERNMENT

1661

Spanish Possessions

Austrian Possessions

Boundary of the Holy Roman Empire

0   100   200   300

Scale of Miles

enjoyed in Alsace. A few years later (1659), Mazarin compelled Spain to give up Artois, a few towns on the northern
confines of France, and, to the south, all her trifling possessions
north of the Pyrenees, — that barrier " which," as the treaty
of 1659 recites, "formerly divided the Gauls from Spain."

Louis's efforts to extend the boundaries of France were confined for the most part to the north and east, — to regions
now occupied by France herself, by Belgium, the German
Empire, and the tiny duchy of Luxemburg. But in his time
the map was no such simple matter as it is to-day. France
was still hemmed in by Spain on the south, north, and east,
as she had been since the times of Charles V,[1] for Spain still
held the southern Netherlands and Franche Comté. Then
there was a maze of little duchies, counties, bishoprics, and
more or less independent towns lying between France and
the Rhine, belonging to the weak Holy Roman Empire.[2]
Some of this region France had already added to her possessions, as will be seen on the map, and there was reason to
believe that she might take advantage of the general demoralization of the Empire to add more. Paris, the French capital,
seemed altogether too near the frontier; but, should Louis
succeed in adding territory at the expense of Spain and the
little states toward the Rhine, it might become nearly the
center of an enlarged France.

France hemmed in by Spain in the seventeenth century

Louis had no difficulty in finding an excuse for beginning
his aggressions. He was married to a Spanish princess, Maria
Theresa. When her father died and her younger brother,
Charles II, succeeded to the Spanish throne in 1665, Louis
maintained that his wife, as the firstborn, was legally the

Louis occu- pies the Spanish Netherlands and Franche Comté (1667–1668)

---

[1] It must be remembered that in 1496 the heir of the Austrian and Burgundian
possessions, which included the Netherlands, married the heiress to all the Spanish realms, and that, in consequence, their son, Charles V, became ruler of a very
considerable portion of western Europe. But before his death he divided his
territories between his son, Philip II, to whom Spain and the Netherlands fell,
and his brother, Ferdinand, who received the older Austrian possessions in Germany. See Robinson, *History of Western Europe*, pp. 355 *sq.* and 444 *sq.*

[2] See map, p. 23, below.

heiress to a great part of the Spanish Netherlands, if not to the whole Spanish realm. He had his lawyers write a book to prove this, and then ordered his troops to take possession of the Spanish Netherlands. He insolently announced that he was only about to undertake a "journey" into the region, as if his invasion was merely a visit to an undisputed portion of his territories. He easily took a few towns on the border and then turned southeast and quickly and completely conquered Franche Comté.

Spain unable to resist Louis

Notwithstanding the formidable appearance of the Spanish Empire and the traditions of power and glory handed down from the preceding century, Spain was really in no condition to resist these pretensions of Louis. The new sovereign, Charles II, was a child of only four years when he came to the throne, and a child he remained, in intellect and capacity, until his death in 1700.

Character of Charles II and his government

He is described by contemporaries as being without occupations, pleasures, education, sentiment, or the inclination to do anything serious; he could scarcely read and write; he hated the business of state, and delighted in the game of jackstraws even after reaching the years of maturity. Though king, he did not govern, but was the prey of factious nobles and ecclesiastics who were at once prodigal and without administrative capacity. The offices of state were bestowed on aristocratic favorites or sold to speculators.

State of Spanish finances

The finances of Spain were badly deranged; extravagance was regarded as a virtue, and the systematic accounting for receipts and expenditures was held worthy only of the shopkeeper. A keen observer of the time declared that, so far as the state treasury was concerned, "all was chaos, wrapped in impenetrable obscurity"; and no one wanted to straighten out the tangle. A high functionary vauntingly asserted that Spain did not wish a Colbert to reform finances because " it was beneath so great a prince as his king to live with parsimony." The pension roll was long; the revenues were decreasing and only about one fourth of the taxes remained for the king after the pensions, interest, and charges of the collectors were paid. To meet expenses he was compelled to resort to discreditable methods; the coinage was debased; salaries were only partly paid; and the national debt was cut down by repudiations. The chief reliance was borrowing, although the prudent bankers of Genoa deemed Spain's credit so poor that they exacted an interest of from twenty-five to forty per cent. In spite of all these expedients, the poor king had to pawn his jewels and plate for personal expenses, and even then he was humiliated by finding his servants deserting him and by the refusal of his tradesmen to trust him. This poverty haunted him to the end.

Under such circumstances it was only natural that the military and naval defenses of the Spanish possessions should be neglected. The army and navy had been worn out in the Thirty Years' War. The war footing of the army amounted to less than twenty thousand effective soldiers; the old military spirit was gone, pay was in arrears, and the soldiers were reduced to rags and beggary. Nobles would serve only in high places, and there were more generals than regiments. The ocean-going fleet had less than a dozen ships in good fighting condition, and the coast defenses were so defective that the pirates could not be kept off. *Weakness of military and naval defenses*

The government only reflected the general condition of the country. The gold which flowed in from the colonies, instead of building up Spanish industry and commerce, really checked them, inasmuch as it encouraged idleness and extravagance among the upper classes who disdained mercantile pursuits. The population, which now numbers some eighteen millions, was then but four or five millions; foreigners controlled the manufactures in a large measure; literature had almost perished; and only the Church showed an increase in wealth and in the number of officials. An Italian ambassador declared: "There is no state in Christendom where the ecclesiastics absorb more of the public revenues, or where religious orders are more numerous."

The United
Provinces,
England, and
Sweden com-
bine to check
Louis
The evident inability of Spain to check the operations of the French king threw that burden upon other countries whose interests led them to be alarmed by his high-handed policy of territorial aggrandizement. The encroachments of Louis especially affected the Dutch, for if he succeeded in annexing the Spanish Netherlands, the borders of France would touch those of the Dutch United Provinces; the river Scheldt and the port of Antwerp would be in the hands of the French, and thus Dutch trade would be gravely menaced. Thoroughly aroused to the serious dangers, the Dutch turned to Sweden and England for assistance, and in 1668 the three countries agreed to go to war, if necessary, in order to force Louis to relinquish his pretensions.

Treaty of
Aix-la-
Chapelle,
1668
This formidable combination quickly brought the French monarch to terms, and he consented, in the treaty of Aix-la-Chapelle, to return Franche Comté and the Netherlands to Spain on condition that he might retain about a dozen towns on the north, which gave him a long line of fortresses for frontier defense.

LOUIS XIV'S WAR AGAINST THE DUTCH (1672–1678)

5. The treaty of Aix-la-Chapelle left Louis XIV smarting under the humiliation that he had received through the interference of the Dutch. This little people had forced him to relinquish the Spanish provinces when he had them already in his grasp. He heartily abhorred their Protestantism, their republican tendencies, and their willingness to harbor all the writers and printers who directed attacks against him and against the idea of monarchy by the grace of God. Once their seven provinces had belonged to Spain, and France had helped them to win their independence. Now, instead of favoring their former ally, they raised the duties on French products, and opposed the development of the French navy and the acquisition by France of the Spanish Netherlands.

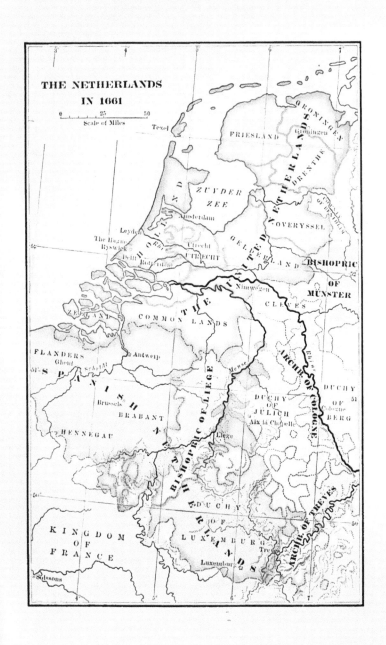

THE NETHERLANDS
IN 1661

0   25   50
Scale of Miles

Texel

FRIESLAND

GRONINGEN

Groningen

U N I T E D   N E T H E R L A N D S

DRENTHE

ZUYDER
ZEE

Amsterdam

OVERYSSEL

Leyden

GELDERLAND

The Hague
Ryswick

Utrecht

Delft
Rotterdam

HOLLAND

UTRECHT

BISHOPRIC

Nimwegen

OF

MÜNSTER

ZEELAND

COMMON   LANDS

CLEVES

FLANDERS

Ghent

Antwerp

Scheldt

THE COMMON LANDS

Meuse

ARCH. OF COLOGNE

Rhine

DUCHY
OF
Cologne
BERG

S P A N I S H

DUCHY
OF
JÜLICH

Brussels

BRABANT

Aix la Chapelle

BISHOPRIC OF LIEGE

Liège

HENNEGAU

NETHERLANDS

KINGDOM
OF
FRANCE

DUCHY
OF
LUXEMBURG

Treves

ARCH. OF TREVES

Luxemburg

Soissons

It seemed consequently both an agreeable and an easy undertaking to crush this confederation of merchants whose whole low, muddy territory did not equal a fifteenth part of the great king's realm.

The United Netherlands was composed of those seven provinces, lying in a circle around the Zuider Zee, which had successfully combined, a century earlier, to free themselves from Spanish oppression.[1] They differed greatly in their laws and in the character and occupations of their inhabitants, and were bound together as loosely as possible, so that each of the members of the union had a right to veto any important measure. The most influential province was Holland with its vast commerce and its celebrated cities of Amsterdam, Rotterdam, Delft, Leyden, and The Hague, which was the seat of government of the united provinces. We commonly refer to the present kingdom of the Netherlands as "Holland," although strictly speaking that is the name of only one province. In the time of Louis XIV the United Netherlands included about the same area as the Dutch kingdom of to-day, which is larger than Massachusetts, but only a quarter the size of the state of New York.[2]

Extent and organization of the United Netherlands

The political troubles in the United Netherlands were due first, to the weakness of the federal congress, the Estates General, in which even the most salutary measures could be defeated by the vote of the representatives of a single province; secondly, to the natural anxiety of Holland to control the affairs of the whole union; thirdly, to the ambition of the descendants of the founder of Dutch liberty, William of Orange, called the Silent, to establish themselves as kings in fact if not in name.

Nature of political troubles in the United Netherlands

[1] See Robinson, *History of Western Europe*, pp. 446 *sq.*

[2] It will be observed on the map that the seven provinces — Holland, Zeeland, Utrecht, Gelderland, Overijssel, Groningen, and Friesland — did not constitute the whole territory of the Confederation, but that there was an eighth, half-dependent, province of Drenthe, besides certain lands to the south, which the union held in common and which were not organized as provinces.

Importance
of the House
of Orange

Each province had a governor or *stadholder*,[1] and as William the Silent owed his power nominally to the fact that he was chosen stadholder by several provinces, so his sons and grandson had the same distinction accorded to them, in grateful recognition of all that the Dutch people owed to the family.

William
of Orange
(b. 1650,
d. 1702)

When Louis XIV began his attack on the provinces, the great grandson of William the Silent, a young man of twenty-two, was the representative of the House of Orange. His enemies, who were in authority at the time, disliked the thought of a strong central power and declared that each province was of right a sovereign republic. But the threatening attitude of Louis XIV and the actual approach of the French troops speedily convinced the Dutch that the provinces must stand together. Every one looked to the descendant of William the Silent for safety in the terrible crisis, and William, Prince of Orange, was chosen commander general of all the troops. He was also appointed hereditary stadholder by some of the more important provinces, beginning with Holland, and while he never became king, he so increased the powers of the stadholder that the Netherlands ceased to be a republic except in name.

The Dutch
stadholder
practically
king

Louis wins
the former
allies of the
Dutch

The ease with which Louis's ambassadors were able to turn against the Dutch all of their former allies casts a sad enough light upon the unscrupulous diplomacy of the time. Charles II of England was induced to join Louis by the promise of money which would enable him to amuse himself in his rather expensive fashion without resorting to Parliament. Sweden, the Emperor, and some of the more important German princes also agreed, in return for money or possible territorial gains, to support Louis. Consequently the Dutch seemed to have no chance of opposing the powerful army which Louis sent around well to the east so as to escape crossing the various

[1] The stadholder, or "stead-holder," as his title may be translated, was originally the lieutenant, or representative, of the King of Spain.

streams which barred the direct way to the provinces. By this route he also kept out of the Spanish Netherlands and so avoided giving Spain any cause for intervening.

In June, 1672, the French were not far east of Amsterdam, and the city expected to have to surrender every moment. The Dutch were ready to conclude peace and offered to cede the southern portions of their territory to France and pay the expenses of the war. Louis, however, asked still more land and money, and demanded, moreover, that the Dutch should reëstablish the Catholic religion on the same footing with the Protestant, and should each year send a solemn embassy to thank him " for having left to the United Provinces the independence which the kings his predecessors had caused them to acquire." These outrageous demands only strengthened the power of William of Orange, who cut the dikes and put a part of the country under water in order to drive out the French ; and after a vain attempt on their part to take Amsterdam on the ice during the winter of 1672–1673, they evacuated Holland.

> The French invade Holland in 1672, but soon evacuate it

William of Orange now became the leader of the European opposition to France. Both as stadholder of the Dutch provinces and later as king of England, he was to be the stanch and unwavering enemy of Louis and the most serious obstacle in his path. Young as he was, William exhibited the capacity for leadership, diplomacy, and dogged perseverance which had shown itself in his ancestors. He induced Louis's recent allies to desert him and organized against the too powerful France a " grand alliance," including Spain, the Emperor, the elector of Brandenburg, and other German princes. England, which had never sympathized with its king's love for Louis, became neutral, leaving only Sweden to support France.

> William of Orange organizes a "grand alliance" against France

When, at the end of six years of intermittent hostilities, a general peace was concluded at Nimwegen, the chief provisions were that France should not only leave the United Netherlands intact but should pledge herself to protect the Dutch

> Peace of Nimwegen, 1678

Franche
Comté goes
to France

merchants and their commerce. France, however, was finally permitted to annex some northern towns and Franche Comté, over which she and Spain had been quarreling for a century and a half.

Louis XIV's Plan of encroaching by "Reunions" upon the Holy Roman Empire

"Reunions"
on the Ger-
man borders

6. Although there was no open war for ten years to follow, Louis found a way to encroach steadily upon the Spanish Netherlands and the German territories which lay between him and the Rhine. Franche Comté and certain towns which had been ceded to him by Spain were, by the terms of the treaty, to include "all their territories, domains, seigneuries, appurtenances, dependencies, and annexes by whatsoever title they might be designated, as well as all the men, vassals, subjects, towns, burgs, villages, hamlets, forests, streams, country districts, salt marshes, and all other things connected with them." These innumerable vestiges of ancient feudal entanglements gave the king of France ample opportunity for extending his claims by reuniting former "dependencies." To carry out these "reunions," as they were called, courts were organized with the special purpose of determining what should of right come to France and, under the king's supervision, they naturally put a liberal construction on the cessions made by the treaty of Nimwegen. Where towns resisted, French troops were sent to bombard them. The Spanish protests received no attention.

Similar uncertainty as to the exact extent of the cessions made to France by the Peace of Westphalia (1648) and by later treaties, led to far more considerable extensions of Louis's power at the expense of the German states on his borders. His courts turned half rights into whole in Alsace, and French troops seized the important city of Strassburg (1681), to which Louis had no claim whatever. In 1684 the diet of the Empire

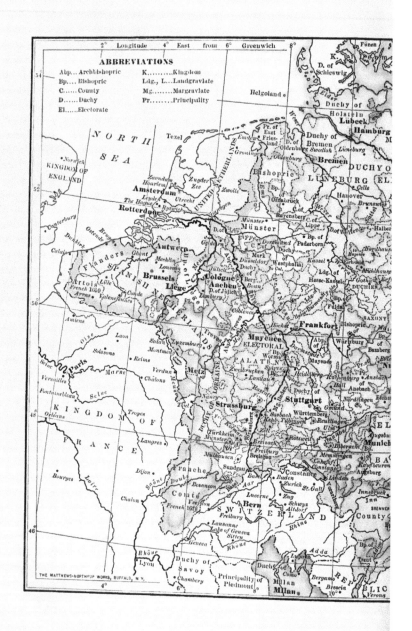

ABBREVIATIONS

Abp... Archbishopric	K.........Kingdom
Bp.... Bishopric	Ldg., L...Landgraviate
C......County	Mg........Margraviate
D......Duchy	Pr.......Principality
El.....Electorate	

THE MATTHEWS-NORTHRUP WORKS, BUFFALO, N. Y.

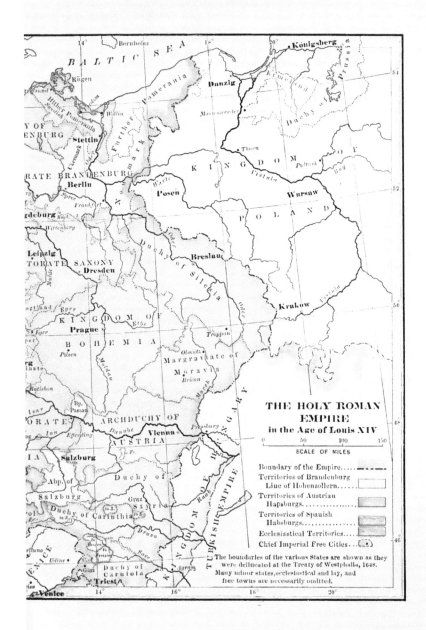

THE HOLY ROMAN
EMPIRE
in the Age of Louis XIV

0   50   100   150
SCALE OF MILES

Boundary of the Empire..... ▬ ▬ ▬
Territories of Brandenburg
  Line of Hohenzollern......
Territories of Austrian
  Hapsburgs................
Territories of Spanish
  Habsburgs................
Ecclesiastical Territories....
Chief Imperial Free Cities...(...)

The boundaries of the various States are shown as they
were delineated at the Treaty of Westphalia, 1648.
Many minor states, ecclesiastical and lay, and
free towns are necessarily omitted.

was induced to ratify the French occupation of Strassburg and of nearly all the territories which had been adjudged to Louis by his courts.

Almost two centuries later Germany was able, as we shall see, to wreak a terrible vengeance upon France and to regain not only Strassburg but the whole of Alsace. But no European state has changed since the time of Louis XIV so completely as Germany, which means to us the German Empire, one of the three or four best organized of the great European powers. It is now a compact federation somewhat like that of the United States, made up of twenty-two monarchies and three city republics. Each member of the union manages its local affairs but leaves all questions of national importance to be settled by the central government at Berlin. Nothing could be more different from this than the " Germanies " — as the French called them — of the seventeenth century. And in order to understand the ease with which Louis appropriated bits of German territory and the alliances which he was constantly making with individual German rulers, we must pause a moment to consider that very anomalous thing known as the Holy Roman Empire.

Contrast between the present German Empire and the " Germanies " of the seventeenth century

In spite of its fine name and long history, it scarcely deserved to be ranked among the states of Europe. The great mediæval emperors, like Henry IV and Frederick Barbarossa, had never succeeded in getting the better of their powerful vassals and binding together their territories into a firm monarchy such as France had become. On the contrary, the central power had grown weaker and weaker, while the various dukes, counts, bishops, abbots, and free towns went their own way, paying less and less attention to the Emperor, coining their own money, raising their own taxes, and, for that matter, fighting their own battles, — for each state was permitted to conclude treaties with other countries as if it were independent.

The Holy Roman Empire

The Emperor, who regarded himself as the successor of the Roman emperors, was selected in a peculiar manner. He did

Selection of the Emperor by eight "electors"

not inherit the crown, but was chosen by a few of the German rulers who had long enjoyed this right and were consequently called "electors." As they often appear in history, it is well worth while to remember their names. There were first, the three ecclesiastical electors, — the archbishops of Mayence, of Treves, and of Cologne, — who were not only prelates but princes, whose possessions lay upon the Rhine and who had consequently much to do with France. Close to them, geographically, was the elector of the Palatinate; then, further east, the elector of Saxony, and, to the north, the elector of Brandenburg, who was soon (1700) to assume the title of King of Prussia. The seventh elector was the king of Bohemia[1]. Lastly there was the duke of Bavaria, who had managed during the troubles of the Thirty Years' War to have himself recognized as a new elector.

The imperial office had long been held by the Austrian ruler

Although the Empire was not hereditary, it had been so in practice for some two hundred and fifty years, since the electors had been accustomed to select as Emperor the ruler of the Austrian dominions. They were free, however, at any time to choose some one else, and Francis I of France, Henry VIII of England, and other foreign candidates had occasionally had some hopes of securing the imperial crown. Even Louis XIV was induced at one time to make an effort to have himself chosen Emperor and spent some money in gaining the good will of the electors.

The imperial diet

The Empire had a general congress, or diet, to which the various members of the union sent representatives and which met at Ratisbon on the Danube. It had little power and was so badly organized and so slow in its proceedings that business dragged along literally for centuries. The Emperor, as emperor, had little or no steady revenue, and the imperial army was made up of contingents from the various states, which came together very reluctantly and tardily. Consequently, although

---

[1] This title had been held for some time by the Emperor himself, since Bohemia formed a part of the Austrian dominions.

one hears of the Empire entering into treaties of alliance, participating in wars and concluding treaties of peace, it must be remembered that no one, not even the diet or the Emperor himself, had any particular interest in the Empire, but that everything really depended upon the individual German princes, among whom the ruler of the Austrian territories was the most important.

The House of Hapsburg, to which the Austrian territories belonged, and which had so long held the office of Emperor, had slowly accumulated its various kingdoms, duchies, counties, etc., by conquest, inheritance, intrigue, and fortunate marriages, running back into the Middle Ages. In the treaty of Nimwegen with France, the Emperor is called " Most serene and mighty Lord Leopold, Emperor elect [1] of the Romans, ever august, King of Germany, Hungary, Bohemia, Dalmatia, Croatia, Slavonia, Archduke of Austria, Duke of Burgundy, Brabant, Styria, Carinthia, Carniola, Margrave of Moravia, Duke of Luxemburg, of Upper and Lower Silesia, Würtemberg and Teck, Prince of Suabia, Count of Hapsburg, Tyrol, Kyburg and Goritz, etc., etc." Some minor possessions are here modestly omitted, but, on the other hand, Leopold's title, King of Germany, was meaningless, and Louis XIV protested against his still calling himself duke of Burgundy since the duchy of Burgundy had belonged to France for over a century.

Possessions of the Austrian ruler

As for Hungary, that was in the hands of the Turks with whom the Hapsburg princes had been warring for two centuries. Just at this period (1683) the Mohammedans were besieging Vienna itself, which was only saved by the timely intervention of the Polish king. After this defeat, however, the power of the Turks rapidly declined, and the Hapsburgs were able in 1699 to force the Sultan to acknowledge their title to

The Turks and other eastern interests of Austria

---

[1] This title "emperor elect" meant that the Emperor had been chosen by the electors but had not as yet been crowned by the pope. It was first assumed by Maximilian in 1580 with the Pope's permission, and after his time no emperor ever went to Rome to be crowned by the Pope, as had been the custom earlier, but they continued to use the title, *imperator electus*.

Hungary. It was but natural that the eyes of the Emperor should be turned rather to the east than to the west, since his realms lay mainly to the east of Germany proper and his capital was Vienna, not Ratisbon where the diet met, nor Frankfurt-on-the-Main where the imperial elections took place.

Importance of elector of Brandenburg
While the Austrian ruler was holding together as best he could his motley aggregation of kingdoms, duchies, counties, and principalities, inhabited by Germans, Bohemians, Slavonians, and Hungarians, the elector of Brandenburg was laying the foundation of a kingdom which was to become Austria's greatest rival and finally the center of the new German Empire from which she has been excluded. Beginning with a strip of territory extending some ninety miles to the east and to the west of the then little town of Berlin, the successive rulers of the House of Hohenzollern have gradually extended their boundaries until the present kingdom of Prussia extends all the way across Germany and embraces nearly two thirds of the present German Empire.

Frederick William, the Great Elector, 1640–1688
The development of Prussia will be described below.[1] Suffice it to say here that it was in the time of Louis XIV that Brandenburg began to play an important part in European affairs. The Great Elector, as he is still honorably designated by Prussians, who reigned from 1640 to 1688, had joined England and Holland in their alliances against Louis, for he was interested in the fate of his territories on the Rhine, Mark and Cleves. He organized an army out of all proportion to his resources and therewith started his country on the way to military glory.

Lesser states of the Holy Roman Empire
As for the rest of the states included in the Holy Roman Empire, two or three hundred in number, they differed widely in size and character. One had a duke, another a count at its head, while others were ruled by prelates, archbishops, bishops, or by the heads of monasteries, — abbots, abbesses, and priors. There were many cities like Nuremberg, Augsburg, Frankfort,

1 See below, sect. 12.

Worms, and Cologne, which were just as independent as Bavaria, Würtemberg, or Saxony. Lastly there were the imperial knights whose whole possessions might consist of a single strong castle with a wretched village lying at its base. The burgravate of Reineck [1] is said to have included one castle and twelve poor subjects; the standing army of Count Leimburg-Styrum-Wilhelmsdorf [1] was composed of one colonel, nine other officers, and two privates.

Now it so happened that it was the southwestern portion of the Empire on both sides of the Rhine and nearest France that were most broken up into weak and helpless little principalities. It is no wonder that Louis was encouraged to add, bit by bit, through war or courts of "reunion," the region between France and the Rhine where he already had so many little "enclaves," or islands of territory. Next to the French boundary lay the duchy of Lorraine, whose duke suffered so much from Louis that he finally took service in the Austrian army. Three bishoprics within his domain — Metz, Verdun, and Toul — had been in the hands of France for a century or more. Alsace, before portions of it were ceded to France in 1648, was divided into some forty independent or dependent little countries, not including the ninety villages of the knights. There were the bishopric of Strassburg, the realms of several abbots and counts, and ten independent towns besides the great free city of Strassburg.

(marginal note: Weakness and minute subdivision of Germany illustrated by Lorraine and Alsace)

To the north of Alsace lay the ragged possessions of the elector of the Palatinate which Louis hoped to add to France; east and west of him were the lands of the ecclesiastical electors of Mayence and Treves, still farther down the Rhine those of the elector of Cologne, and near him the Prussian duchy of Cleves. To the west of Cologne was the duchy of Jülich and then right in the midst of the Spanish Netherlands the bishopric of Liége. Besides these there were other territories,

(marginal note: Louis's other German neighbors)

[1] The reader will search the map in vain for these and other equally insignificant places too small to be indicated.

some too small to appear on even a good map. It will be clear that it is almost impossible to give with any exactness the number of countries which went to make up the singular union known as the Holy Roman Empire. The manner in which Germany finally consolidated itself under the influence of French aggression, which by no means ceased with the death of Louis XIV, will prove one of the most important chapters in this volume.

THE ENGLISH REVOLUTION OF 1688 AND THE WAR OF THE LEAGUE OF AUGSBURG (1688–1697)

7. The "reunions" by which Louis increased the French possessions naturally attracted the attention of his enemies, — the Emperor, William of Orange, the king of Spain, and other rulers whose apprehensions were aroused. A new coalition was therefore preparing against Louis when two startling acts on his part consolidated a great part of Europe against him.

Position of the Huguenots

The first of these was the revocation of the Edict of Nantes which Louis XIV's grandfather, Henry IV, had granted to the Huguenots, as the French Protestants were called. Since they were heretics and as such abhorred by the Catholics, they had no rights except those which the king explicitly accorded them, and to revoke the edict was to make all Protestants outlaws. When the Huguenots were deprived by Richelieu of their former dangerous military independence, they had turned to manufacture, trade, and banking, and "as rich as a Huguenot" had become a proverb in France. There were perhaps a million of them among the fifteen million Frenchmen, and they undoubtedly formed by far the most thrifty and enterprising part of the nation. The Catholic clergy, however, continued to urge the complete suppression of heresy.

Louis XIV had scarcely taken the reins of government into his own hands before the perpetual nagging and injustice to which the Protestants had been subjected at all times took a Louis's policy of suppressing Protestantism more serious form. Upon one pretense or another their churches were demolished. Children were authorized to renounce Protestantism when they reached the age of seven, and might be taken from their parents to be brought up in a Catholic school. In this way Protestant families were pitilessly broken up. Rough and licentious dragoons were quartered upon the Huguenots in the hope that the insulting behavior of the soldiers might drive the heretics to accept the religion of the king.

At last Louis was led by his officials to believe that practi- Revocation of the Edict of Nantes (1685) cally all the Huguenots had been converted by these drastic measures, and in 1685 he accordingly revoked the Edict of Nantes. The Protestants became outlaws, and their ministers subject to the penalty of death if they continued to perform their duties. But even liberal-minded Catholics, like La Fontaine, the kindly writer of fables, and Madame de Sévigné, hailed the reëstablishment of " religious unity " with delight. They honestly believed that only an insignificant and seditious remnant still clung to the beliefs of Calvin. But there could have been no more serious mistake. Thousands of the Huguenots succeeded in eluding the vigilance of the royal officials and fled, — some to the Dutch Netherlands, some to England, some to Brandenburg, some to America, — carrying with them their skill and industry to strengthen the rivals of France.[1]

This revival of ancient fanaticism made a deep impression Louis XIV lays claim to the Palatinate in his sister-in-law's name upon the Protestant powers, especially the Dutch Netherlands, England, and Brandenburg. They had all, at one time or another, been in league with France, but now they all turned against her. Nevertheless, the French king, as if to still further increase the strength and unanimity of his enemies, in the same year that he revoked the Edict of Nantes, laid claim

[1] This was the last great and terrible example of that fierce religious intolerance which had produced the Albigensian Crusade, the Spanish Inquisition, and the Massacre of St. Bartholomew. See Robinson, *History of Western Europe*, pp. 223, 358, and 455.

to the Palatinate in the name of his sister-in-law, Charlotte Elizabeth.[1]

The League of Augsburg

In 1686 the German powers signed an alliance known as the League of Augsburg, which was joined by Spain and the Dutch. Catholics and Protestants alike were ready to fight side by side in order to check the boundless insolence of the French king. Moreover a singular revolution soon greatly increased the strength and resources of Louis's chief adversary, William of Orange, for in 1688 he became king of England.

James II (1685-1688)

Upon the death of Charles II of England, who had been very friendly with Louis, he was succeeded by his brother James, who was an avowed Catholic and had married, as his second wife, Mary of Modena, also a Catholic. He was ready to reëstablish Catholicism in England, regardless of consequences. Mary, James's daughter by his first wife, had married William, prince of Orange, the head of the United Netherlands. The nation, therefore, might have tolerated James so long as they could look forward to the accession of his Protestant daughter Mary. But when a son was born to his Catholic second wife, and James showed unmistakably his purpose of favoring the Catholics, messengers were dispatched by a group of Protestants to William of Orange, asking him to come over with his English wife and be their ruler.[2]

---

1 Louis's younger brother, the duke of Orleans, had married Charlotte Elizabeth, the sister of the elector of the Palatinate, who had died without male heirs in 1685. It was this fact that gave Louis his excuse for intervening to win the Palatinate for her. She is well known on account of the amusing letters which she was accustomed to write to her many German friends about the happenings at the French court.

2 The Revolution of 1688 in England, which called William to the throne, was the culmination of a struggle between the monarchs and the people which had been in progress since the accession of James I in 1603. It originated in the extravagant claim of that king that unlimited authority was vested in him and that he could tax his people without the consent of Parliament. A great number of his subjects, especially the Puritans, who were dissatisfied with the church as established under Elizabeth, resisted the pretensions of the sovereign and, under Charles I, a civil war broke out which was only ended by the execution of the king. A military despotism under Cromwell was then set up; but the very violence of the revolutionists, combined with the innate loyalty of the English people,

William landed in England, November, 1688, and marched upon London, where he received general support from all the English Protestants, regardless of party. James started to oppose William, but his army refused to fight, and his courtiers deserted him. William was glad to forward James's escape to France, as he would hardly have known what to do with him had James insisted on remaining in the country. A new parliament declared the throne vacant, on the ground that King James II, "having violated the fundamental laws and withdrawn himself out of the kingdom, had abdicated the government." The English Revolution of 1688 and the accession of William III

By this peaceful revolution the English rid themselves of the Stuart kings and their claims to rule, like the French kings, by the grace of God. Moreover both Charles II and James II had been Catholics and had threatened to reëstablish their religion against the wishes of the majority of the people. They had both been in constant friendly communication with the French king who favored this plan. Now all was changed. William was unmistakably Protestant and already the head of a Protestant state ; he had come at the bidding of representatives of the people and governed in virtue of an Effects of the English Revolution

brought about a restoration in the person of Charles II, a son of the "martyred ruler," as Charles I was now called. Though a Catholic at heart and opposed therefore to the Protestant church as established by law, and though firmly believing in divine right, Charles II was determined not to risk losing his head, like his father, and succeeded, by dissimulating his views, in keeping his throne until his death in 1685. See Robinson, *History of Western Europe*, chap. xxx.

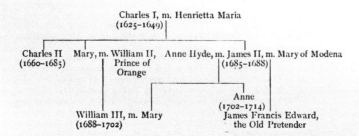

Charles I, m. Henrietta Maria (1625-1649)

Charles II (1660-1685) — Mary, m. William II, Prince of Orange — Anne Hyde, m. James II, m. Mary of Modena (1685-1688)

William III, m. Mary (1688-1702) — Anne (1702-1714) — James Francis Edward, the Old Pretender

act of Parliament,[1] not by the grace of God. Having the people with him, he easily defeated the attempts which James, with Louis's assistance, made to regain his throne.

England joins the League of Augsburg

The effects of the English Revolution were important in their influence upon the course of European affairs, for under William's leadership England immediately joined the League of Augsburg. He was thus able to combine the resources of the Dutch and the English against his arch-enemy, the French king, who made a momentous mistake by occupying the Palatinate in the interests of his sister-in-law, instead of opposing William's designs on England.

The French occupy and then devastate the Palatinate (1688–1689)

France now stood alone against Europe and was really in no condition to begin a new war, for her treasury was empty, her people burdened with taxes, and her best generals dead. Nevertheless Louis seized the Palatinate and the electorate of Cologne where he was trying to establish his own candidate as archbishop. He also sent his fleet to support James II in his attempt to regain his English throne. In 1689 Louis justified the worst apprehensions of his enemies by a frightful devastation of the Palatinate which he had decided to evacuate. He burned whole towns, destroyed the castles, including the beautiful residence of the elector of the Palatinate at Heidelberg, the magnificent ruins of which stand as a reminder of this cruel attempt to destroy permanently the prosperity of one of the most beautiful and flourishing districts of Germany. Mannheim was ruined by fire and gunpowder, Speyer and Worms destroyed, and the country ravaged as Sherman ravaged Georgia on his famous march to the sea. Though this was defended as a war measure, the ancient

---

[1] A " Declaration of Right " was drawn up condemning James's violation of the constitution and appointing William and Mary joint sovereigns. This is a monument in English constitutional history since it once more restated the limitations upon the king which had been imposed by Magna Carta and the Petition of Right drawn up in the time of Charles I. The Declaration bound the king not to levy taxes, or keep a standing army, or suspend the laws without the consent of Parliament, which should enjoy freedom of speech and be assembled frequently. See Robinson, *Readings in European History*, Vol. II, pp. 221 and 261.

grudge of the Germans against France may even to-day be aroused by the sight of the ivy-grown walls which still crown many a hill in the region desolated by Louis's minister of war, the heartless Louvois.

The war dragged on by land and sea for nearly a decade until at last, in 1697, France, England, the United Netherlands, and the Empire signed the treaties of Ryswick. The chief provisions of these will serve to recall the main issues which have been alluded to in this chapter. Louis surrendered practically all the places (except Strassburg) that he had occupied since the treaty of Nimwegen and agreed to recognize William III as king of England, to make no effort to depose him, and to ratify as William's successor his wife's sister, Anne, a stanch Protestant, thus assuring the exclusion of Catholics from the English throne. He restored Lorraine to its rightful ruler, evacuated the right bank of the Rhine, withdrew his candidate for the electorate of Cologne, and accepted a sum of money in lieu of his sister-in-law's claims on the Palatinate.

The treaties of Ryswick, 1697

REFERENCES

Louis XIV's First Attempt on the Spanish Netherlands : WAKEMAN, *European History, 1598–1715*, pp. 207–214 ; KITCHIN, *History of France*, Vol. III, pp. 165–174.

The United Provinces in the Seventeenth Century : WAKEMAN, pp. 216–234.

Louis XIV's First War on Holland : WAKEMAN, pp. 235–248 ; KITCHIN, Vol. III, pp. 175–211 ; TRAILL, *William III*, pp. 1–16.

The Holy Roman Empire : WAKEMAN, pp. 7–11.

The Religious Policy of Louis XIV : WAKEMAN, pp. 248–259 ; KITCHIN, Vol. III, pp. 224–236 ; PERKINS, *France under the Regency*, pp. 164–208.

The Revolution of 1688 in England : CHEYNEY, *Short History of England*, pp. 498–515 ; TRAILL, pp. 17–66 ; GREEN, *Short History of the English People*, chap. ix, pp. 661–683 ; LEE, *Source Book of English History*, pp. 417–442.

Turkey in the Eighteenth Century : WAKEMAN, pp. 266–289.

CHAPTER III

RECONSTRUCTION OF EUROPE AT UTRECHT

THE QUESTION OF THE SPANISH SUCCESSION

8. The willingness of Louis XIV to conclude the Peace of Ryswick, by which he gained so little, is to be explained in part by his anxiety to be ready for a new crisis in European affairs which he and his fellow-monarchs had long foreseen. This was the struggle that was sure to arise when Charles II, the feeble king of Spain, should die. He had neither children nor brothers to whom his vast realms would naturally revert. A successor had therefore to be sought among his more distant kin.

Origin of the French and Austrian claims to the Spanish throne

His father's elder sister had married the French king, Louis XIII, and the younger sister, the Emperor, Ferdinand III, so it had come about that Louis XIV was Charles's cousin, as was also the reigning Emperor (and head of the Austrian house), Leopold I. Matters were further complicated by the circumstance that Charles's own elder sister had married Louis, and his younger, Emperor Leopold, so that it was inevitable that each of these rulers would lay claim to the whole or part of the Spanish possessions either in his own name or in that of his children. Both monarchs, however, were well aware that the other powers of Europe would never permit either of them or the heir to the French or the Austrian crown to become king of Spain and thus found an empire of unprecedented extent. Louis therefore designated his younger grandson, Philip of Anjou, as the rightful successor of Charles II, while Leopold worked in the interests of his younger son, the Archduke Charles.[1]

[1] As the accompanying genealogical table indicates, the situation had originally been complicated by the fact that Charles II's younger sister and Leopold

34

The vital interest of Europe in the settlement of the ques- Extent of the Spanish possessions
tion becomes apparent as we enumerate the more important
of the twenty-two crowns that Charles was so soon to lay down.
Besides the kingdoms of Castile, Aragon, and Navarre with
their dependencies (which embraced all the peninsula except
Portugal), a great part of Italy belonged to the Spanish ruler,
namely, Naples, Sicily, Sardinia, the duchy of Milan and certain coast towns,[1] while to the north of France lay the Spanish
Netherlands, and on the coast of Africa were other Spanish
holdings. But all these territories dwindle into insignificance
when compared with Spain's magnificent colonial empire. This
embraced, far to the east, the Philippine Archipelago and the
Caroline Islands ; to the west — thanks to Columbus — Cuba,
Porto Rico, and Trinidad. In North America, Spain controlled
Florida, Mexico, Texas, and claimed, indeed, all the great

had a daughter who married the elector of Bavaria. Their son, Joseph Ferdinand,
was the candidate favored by poor Charles himself, but the boy's death in 1699
reduced the chief claimants to the two mentioned in the text.

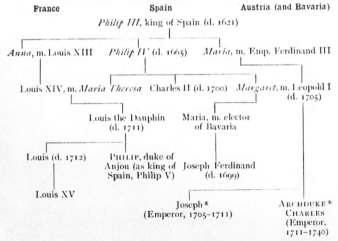

France   **Spain**   **Austria (and Bavaria)**

Philip III, king of Spain (d. 1621)

Anna, m. Louis XIII   *Philip IV* (d. 1665)   *Maria*, m. Emp. Ferdinand III

Louis XIV, m. *Maria Theresa*   Charles II (d. 1700)   *Margaret*, m. Leopold I (d. 1705)

Louis the Dauphin (d. 1711)   Maria, m. elector of Bavaria

Louis (d. 1712)   PHILIP, duke of Anjou (as king of Spain, Philip V)   Joseph Ferdinand (d. 1699)

Louis XV   Joseph* (Emperor, 1705–1711)   ARCHDUKE* CHARLES (Emperor, 1711–1740)

* Joseph and Archduke Charles were sons of Leopold I by his third wife, Eleanor of
Neuburg.

[1] See map, p. 14.

unexplored West. Central America was hers, and all of South America except Brazil, which belonged to the Portuguese.[1]

European history broadens into world history

The Spanish succession was not then a matter of the Spanish kingdom, of a duchy here and there, or a few walled towns which might come into the hands of one European ruler rather than another. The question whether the French king should annex certain fortresses on his northern border, or extend his control over the Alsatian towns, sank into the background. The whole world was now in a sense involved and even the fate of nations yet unborn. The history of Europe was broadening out. The king to whom Madrid, Naples, Milan, and Antwerp should fall was also to be feared — especially by the merchants — as the ruler of Manila, Havana, and Valparaiso.

Both the French and the Austrian claims threaten the European balance of power

Nothing need be said here of the relative strength of the claims made by the French king on the one hand and by the Emperor on the other. Too much was at stake to permit the European powers to leave the matter to be settled by diplomats and lawyers. Should the duke of Anjou succeed to the Spanish throne, on condition that he would give up forever all rights to the French crown, there was no assurance that his promise would be kept. Even if it were, the two branches of the House of Bourbon[2] might combine their strength to the detriment of the rest of Europe. If, on the other hand, Leopold's son should be awarded the prize, there was the risk of a revival of the dangerously extensive empire of Charles V ; for the Archduke Charles might, by the death of his older brother, become heir to the Austrian territories and the most natural candidate for the imperial crown.[3]

Importance of trade with the Spanish colonies

Important as were the issues in the disposal of Spain's European lands and interested as were both England and Holland in maintaining a certain balance of power among

[1] See below, sect. 19.

[2] Henry IV had been the first of the Bourbon family, to which all the succeeding kings of France belonged.

[3] And so it happened, for Charles was elected Emperor in 1711.

the European states, it is probable that they would have hesitated to go to war in support of any particular candidate for the Spanish throne had it not been for the New World and the wealth-bringing trade carried on between the European ports and those of the West Indies, Mexico, and South America.

It is true that Spain had done all she could to keep this trade entirely in her own hands. Columbus had sailed away to the west under the auspices of the queen of Castile, and consequently Castile proposed to retain for herself all the advantages of his discoveries and those of his successors. The idea of the "open door," which would have permitted all shipowners to sail freely back and forth from Dutch, English, or Portuguese ports to Havana, Vera Cruz, or Porto Bello, was unheard of in those days. Castile looked upon her lucky find as a gold prospector would look upon the discovery of a rich claim which he would scarcely expect to share with his less fortunate neighbors. No "open door"

At first Spain forbade all foreign vessels to enter American waters, and Spanish merchants were ordered not to carry on business with traders of other European nations without the express permission of the king. Even in Spain only one port, Seville, was allowed to engage in trade with the colonies. All ships bound for America must leave from that port and must deliver their goods there on their return.[1] For a time Vera Cruz and Porto Bello were the only colonial ports through which trade could be conducted with Spanish America. Moreover all ships were required to sail in fleets with regular convoys which made but very few trips a year. This was doubtless necessary when piracy and buccaneering were rife, but the system was maintained, like other restrictions, with the view of keeping the trade in the hands of the companies in which the government had vested it. How Spain tried to monopolize trade

---

1 Not until 1778 were the special privileges granted to Seville, and later to three or four other towns, abolished and business opened to all Spanish ports.

Why Spain could not maintain her monopoly

Spain was, however, unable to defend her monopoly. In the first place, she could not cover the broad Atlantic with guards and watch every inlet and landing place along the interminable coasts of the Gulf of Mexico and the Caribbean Sea. Moreover her home industries were not so flourishing that she was able to supply her colonies with all that they needed, and so they gladly conducted a secret and illicit trade with the merchants who came to them from England and Holland.

The English and Dutch smuggling trade

These conditions had produced a curious species of trader, — half merchant, half pirate, and necessarily always a smuggler, — who sailed the Spanish main [1] ready, when unduly tempted, to sink a Spanish convoy and capture the unwieldy galleons laden with treasure. The English seamen of Elizabeth's time, — Drake, Hawkins, and others, — had ranged the high seas, first visiting the west coast of Africa to capture a cargo of negroes who could be sold for slaves in the Spanish colonies.[2] When war existed between Spain and her European neighbors her merchants naturally fared worse than usual, for it was considered patriotic as well as profitable to attack her ships. But smuggling flourished at all times, and it is supposed that by the eighteenth century England was carrying on illegally a more considerable trade with the Spanish colonies than did the mother country through her regular channels.

The Bourbon claims a menace to English and Dutch commerce

It was these commercial interests that gave the question of the Spanish succession its chief importance for the English ; for should France obtain the vacant Spanish throne for a member of her reigning house, she would doubtless take pains to assure to herself all possible advantages in the trade with the Spanish colonies, and she would be able to supply the

---

[1] The term " Spanish main " meant perhaps originally the mainland of Central and South America as contrasted with the West Indies, but it is commonly applied to the neighboring waters, especially the Caribbean Sea.

[2] This trade has been the subject of many romances. Some idea of it may be had from the reports of those who actually sailed the Spanish main. See *Readings*, sect. 19.

necessary military and naval forces to aid Spain in keeping out intruders as never before. Nor was it only the western trade that was involved; for should France obtain control, even indirectly, of Spain and southern Italy, she could exclude English merchants from their intercourse with the Levant (as the eastern Mediterranean regions were called), a calamity which England must avoid at any cost.

WILL OF CHARLES II, AND WAR OF THE SPANISH SUCCESSION

9. The vast interests at stake and the danger of a world-wide war had led the European powers to attempt a peaceful partition of the Spanish dominions while Charles was still living. Several plans for a division of the heritage were suggested and given up for one reason or another. But just before Charles died England and Holland had induced Louis XIV to agree that the Archduke Charles should have Spain, the Netherlands, and the colonies, on condition that the Bourbons should receive the Spanish holdings in Italy with the prospect of exchanging Milan for Lorraine. The Emperor, however, stubbornly refused to ratify this partition. Moreover Louis was only temporizing when he acceded to this division, for his clever agents had been busy all along at the Spanish court trying to induce the dying king to maintain the integrity of the Spanish possessions and turn them all over to his French relatives. *Plans for partitioning the Spanish heritage*

In this they succeeded, for when finally the long-expected death of the Spanish king occurred (November, 1700) it was found that he had left a will in which he desired that his twenty-two crowns should fall to the duke of Anjou on condition, however, that the crowns of France and Spain should never rest upon the same head. Should the Bourbons refuse to accept the bequest, the inheritance was to be passed on to the Archduke Charles of Austria, that hereditary enemy of France. *Will of Charles II of Spain*

It was a crucial moment in the history of Europe when the news of Charles's will reached Louis XIV. By the provisions of the Partition Treaty, he had renounced on the part of his family all claims to the Spanish dominions. He clearly fore-saw that war was likely to follow his acceptance and well knew that France was already terribly exhausted by his previ-ous enterprises. Nevertheless the prize was tempting beyond measure. He had been secretly working for it for years, and his refusal meant its transfer to a hated rival. To say "no" meant that, as Torcy, the head of French foreign affairs, urged : " The same courier who has been dispatched to convey the news of the will to France will proceed to Vienna ; and the Spanish nation, without hesitation, will acknowledge the Emperor's second son as their king. The house of Austria will then unite between father and son the power of Charles V, a power hitherto so fatal to France." Such arguments could not but appeal strongly to the king.

For a brief time Louis XIV hesitated, either to save appear-ances or because he realized fully the gravity of the situation ; but at last he decided to accept the privilege for his grandson, and on November 16, 1700, he called the Spanish ambassador to his private chamber and told him to salute the duke of Anjou as the king of Spain. Louis then threw open the fold-ing doors of his cabinet, bade the courtiers enter, and, with the majestic air of which he was the consummate master, he said, " Gentlemen, permit me to present to you the king of Spain. His station called him to that crown ; the late king has called him to it by his will ; and the whole nation has fixed its desire upon him and has eagerly asked me for him. It is the will of Heaven ; I have obeyed it with pleasure." Then turning to his grandson, he said, " Be a good Spaniard ; that is your first duty ; but remember that you are a French-man born, in order that in this way the union between the two nations may be preserved. By this means you will be able to render both peoples happy and preserve the peace of

Europe." The leading French journal of the time boldly proclaimed that the Pyrenees were no more.[1]

Contrary to expectations, Louis's conduct in accepting the throne of Spain for a member of his family failed to arouse general indignation. Both England and the United Provinces concurred in the new arrangement as inevitable, and even acknowledged the duke of Anjou as king of Spain under the title of Philip V. It looked as if Louis were going to have everything his own way; and had he been more discreet he might have secured his prize without war. However, the commercial issue quickly became prominent, for he soon published a series of decrees relating to the Spanish-American trade which clearly indicated that the English and Dutch could expect no favors. He sent French soldiers to reënforce the Spanish troops in the barrier fortresses of the Spanish Netherlands and began to build ships at Cadiz as if Spain were now a part of France. Moveover he had his courts declare solemnly that his grandson, Philip, still retained his rights to the French crown. Finally, in 1701, upon the death of the exiled king, James II, Louis, contrary to the promise he had made in the Treaty of Ryswick, recognized the deposed king's son as sovereign of England.

Louis's indiscreet conduct hastens the outbreak of war

Louis could hardly have discovered more effective methods of irritating and alarming the English and the Dutch. They were now thoroughly aroused, and William easily succeeded in forming a Grand Alliance in which Louis's old enemies, England, Holland, the Emperor, and the king of Prussia, were the important members. The allies reviewed the various examples of Louis's arrogance and his dangerous encroachments upon his neighbors. They proposed to unite in order to wrest his newly acquired advantages from him, restore to the Dutch their barrier towns, win the Italian possessions of Spain for the Emperor, and perhaps the West Indies for England.

William III forms the Grand Alliance

---

[1] For extracts illustrating this matter of the Spanish will, see *Readings*, sect. 9.

Death of
William III,
1702

William himself died (1702) just as hostilities were beginning, and so the Alliance against Louis lost its great leader.
William was succeeded by his sister-in-law, Anne, who was not
distinguished for her capacity as a ruler. The English were,
however, pledged to the Alliance and deeply interested in it.

General
course of the
war

Accordingly the long War of the Spanish Succession was
carried on vigorously by the English general, the duke of
Marlborough, as well as by the Austrian commander, Eugene
of Savoy. Louis, on the contrary, no longer had generals
like Condé and Turenne, who had gained the victories in his
earlier wars. All the important battles, Blenheim, Ramillies, and
Oudenarde, went against him. The conflict was more general
than the Thirty Years' War had been; even in America there
was fighting between the French and English colonists which
passes in American histories under the name of Queen Anne's
War. In the unequal conflict France was rapidly being ruined
by the destruction of her people and her wealth; after some
ten years of war, Louis was willing to consider a compromise
that would bring peace. But as the allies were constantly
quarreling among themselves, charging one another with failure to render the promised help in the war, Louis was able
to save something from the wreck in the treaties which, after
twelve years of fighting in the Netherlands, Germany, Spain,
and Italy, established peace once more.

PEACE OF UTRECHT, 1713

Treaty of
Utrecht

10. The Peace of Utrecht[1] changed the map of Europe
as no previous treaty had done, not even that of Westphalia
which closed the Thirty Years' War in 1648. Each of the

[1] The greater part of the powers which had been involved in the War of the
Spanish Succession concluded peace with one another at Utrecht, April, 1713;
but the Emperor did not sign his treaty with France until the following March at
Rastadt. This was accepted by the representatives of the Holy Roman Empire
a few months later at Baden in Switzerland. So, to be quite accurate, one
should speak of the Peace of Utrecht-Rastadt-Baden, 1713-1714.

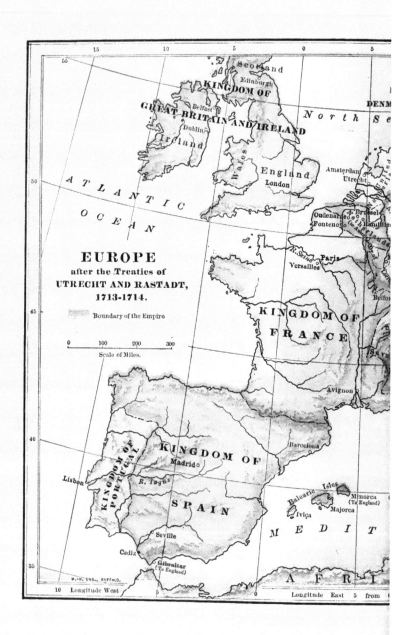

EUROPE
after the Treaties of
UTRECHT AND RASTADT,
1713-1714.

Boundary of the Empire

0   100   200   300
Scale of Miles.

combatants got a share of the Spanish booty over which they had been struggling. The Bourbon Philip was permitted to retain the crown of Spain and all her colonies, but the Spanish and French crowns were never to rest on the same head. Though losing the Spanish Netherlands and the Italian possessions, Spain was really benefited by this arrangement, for, under the new sovereign, attention could be given to those domestic and administrative reforms so long and so sadly needed. *Extent of Philip V's possessions*

The Archduke Charles, now become Emperor after the death of his brother, was of course obliged to surrender his hopes of becoming king of Spain ; but his disappointment was solaced by considerable additions to the Austrian realms. He was awarded the Spanish Netherlands, which were to continue to form a barrier between the Dutch and the French. He also received most of the Spanish possessions in Italy ; namely, Naples, Milan, and the island of Sardinia. In this way it came about that Austria got that hold upon Italy which was not relinquished until 1866. *Austria receives the Spanish Netherlands and portions of Italy*

Of all the countries which participated in the War of the Spanish Succession, England came out with the most considerable and permanent gains. In the first place, the question of the succession to the English crown was set at rest. Louis XIV had always shown himself ready to forward a revolution in England in order to replace a Catholic king upon the throne. But he now agreed to recognize Anne as the legitimate ruler and promised never, either openly or by fomenting sedition, to attack her or her Protestant successors as designated by Parliament. *England's gains*

In America, England acquired from France Nova Scotia, Newfoundland, and the Hudson Bay region, all of which she still holds. In this way the gradual expulsion of the French from North America began. From Spain England received the rock of Gibraltar from which she still commands the narrow entrance to the Mediterranean Sea, now doubly important *England receives the French lands in America* *Gibraltar* since the establishment of the British Empire in India and the opening of the Suez Canal. She also induced Spain to bind herself not to grant to France or any other nation the right to trade freely with her colonies, but secured for herself the highly-prized privilege of supplying the Spanish colonies with African slaves for thirty years. She was also permitted to send each year to Porto Bello, on the isthmus of Panama, a ship of five hundred tons' burden laden with merchandise, — a concession which only served to encourage smuggling on a larger scale than ever before and led finally to a war between the two countries.

Dreary nature of political history after the Peace of Utrecht

The political history during the twenty-five years following the conclusion of the Peace of Utrecht is particularly dreary and unprofitable ; we may therefore neglect it altogether and merely explain here the principal changes, especially those in the map of Italy, which were made during that period.

The Emperor Charles VI and Philip V of Spain reach an agreement in 1720

The Peace of Utrecht had not reconciled the two monarchs chiefly concerned in the War of the Spanish Succession, namely, the new Bourbon king of Spain, Philip V, and the Emperor, Charles VI. The Emperor still refused to recognize Philip as king of Spain, while Philip, on his part, was reluctant to acknowledge the loss of Spain's possessions in Italy, which, according to the treaties, were to fall to Austria. Philip V, moreover, had married an enterprising Italian princess, Elizabeth of Parma, who soon set her heart upon securing some kind of a respectable principality in Italy for their little son, Don Carlos. Under her influence, Spain tried in 1717–1718 to regain Sardinia and Sicily by arms, but was forced by France and England to agree to a peace in 1720 in which Parma and Tuscany were promised to Don Carlos as soon as their rulers, who were without heirs, should die. The Emperor at last

The duke of Savoy becomes king of Sardinia (1720)

acknowledged Philip as king of Spain, but only on condition that he should be given Sicily, which was taken from the duke of Savoy who had to content himself with the island of Sardinia and the title of king.

Austria and Spain, however, were not satisfied to leave Italy alone and before long found an excuse for renewed fighting and another readjustment. Louis XV of France, who succeeded his great-grandfather Louis XIV in 1715, had married the daughter of Stanislas Lesczcynski, a deposed king of Poland, whom he felt it his duty to attempt to restore to his throne. An opportunity offered itself in 1733, and France was forced to go to war in the interest of her king's father-in-law. Spain sided with Stanislas, Austria supported his rival; but it was Italy, not Poland, in which both were really interested. *War of the Polish Succession (1733-1735)*

After two years of hostilities and three years of negotiations, a new agreement was made at Vienna in 1738. The Emperor, who had been badly beaten, agreed to turn over Naples and Sicily to Don Carlos on condition that the latter should give up all claim to Parma and Tuscany. In this way the queen of Spain secured the coveted kingdom of the Two Sicilies [1] for her son and his heirs. This younger branch of the Spanish Bourbons held all southern Italy until the last of them was driven out by Garibaldi in 1860. *The Spanish Bourbons established in southern Italy*

As Louis XV had not succeeded in replacing his father-in-law on the Polish throne, he looked about for a dukedom to solace the ex-king's declining years. Since there was none vacant, the duke of Lorraine was induced to surrender his patrimony to Stanislas Lesczcynski, after whose death (which occurred in 1766) France was to be allowed to annex this long-coveted region. In view of this advantageous arrangement, France gave her consent to a marriage between Francis, the dispossessed duke of Lorraine, and the Emperor's daughter, Maria Theresa, of whom we shall hear more anon. As an indemnity for the loss of his duchy, Francis was given Tuscany with its famous city of Florence. This had long been under the rule of the Medici, but the line died out in 1737 and their lands thus passed to a stranger from across the Alps. *How France got Lorraine (1766) and Tuscany fell to Austria*

The end of the Medici

---

[1] This singular name owes its origin to the fact that during the Middle Ages the kingdom of Naples was commonly called "Sicily" as well as the island of Sicily.

The disruption of Italy in the eighteenth century

Italy's fate was sealed for more than a century. As we glance at the map (in 1750), we find a Spanish ruler once more controlling, as of old, all the southern portions of the peninsula. Another foreign power, Austria, holds Milan and indirectly Tuscany. (Parma she agreed in 1748 to hand over to a younger son of the queen of Spain.) Across the peninsula, between the Austrian and the Spanish lands, lay the Papal States, which for hundreds of years had belonged to the head of the Roman Catholic Church. The two ancient republics, Venice and Genoa, once the glory of Italy, had lost a great part of their former importance, nor were the two little independent duchies of Modena and Lucca in a position to resist foreign interference.

The king of Sardinia and his later importance

As later history showed, the hope of Italy lay in the king of Sardinia, whose capital was Turin. His realms consisted of Piedmont and the mountainous Savoy together with the unimportant island from which he derived the royal title that he was destined one day to exchange for the far more glorious one of King of Italy. We shall later describe the extraordinary series of events in the nineteenth century which enabled Italy to free herself from the control of foreign nations which had so long and so impudently disposed of her possessions and which permitted her, after many vicissitudes, to unite all her scattered members into a firm national union.

Holy Roman Empire unaffected by the Peace of Utrecht

The Peace of Utrecht did not affect the Holy Roman Empire, which remained for almost another century the same loose union of practically independent dukedoms, principalities, bishoprics, and towns that it had long been. The new kingdom of Prussia was, however, preparing to assume an important place in European affairs.

Death of Louis XIV and accession of Louis XV (1715)

When Louis XIV had died in 1715, after a reign of more than seventy years, France experienced a feeling of relief. There was no one to spoil the general satisfaction by foretelling that the new king, then but five years old, was beginning a long and inglorious reign during which he would exhibit a love of

THE ITALIAN STATES
IN 1750

Under Spanish Bourbons
Under the House of Austria
Papal States
Remaining Italian States

SWITZERLAND

AUSTRIAN DOMAINS

REP. OF VENICE

DALMATIA

FRANCE

SAVOY
Turin
Milan
PIEDMONT
KINGDOM
GENOA
PARMA
MODENA
Lucca Florence
TUSCANY
Venice

PAPAL STATES

CORSICA
(To Genoa)

SARDINIA

Rome

Naples

KINGDOM

OF THE

TWO SICILIES

Palermo
SICILY

AFRICA

0   50   100   200
Scale of Miles

low debauchery and a cruel indifference to the public welfare quite alien to his great-grandfather, whose death was mistaken as a harbinger of better times to come. France was greatly exhausted by many wars, and under Louis XV her military power ceased to be a terror to her neighbors.

But even if her king was incompetent, her generals inferior, and her campaigns resulted in shameful defeats; though she lost her colonies and was weighed down by bad taxes and the survivals of feudal dues and privileges, France nevertheless became under Louis XV the leader of European thought and the teacher of the nations. Her scientists, philosophers, and economists, as we shall see, pointed the way toward progress by denouncing the old abuses and errors — sometimes too hotly, it is true, but in such a manner that no one could refuse to listen to them. At last, in the Revolution of 1789, France gave Europe an example of thorough-going reform which was sooner or later followed by all the western powers.

France declines as a military power but becomes the teacher of Europe

England had gained much in the settlement at Utrecht[1] and was able to overshadow France as a naval and colonial power. Indeed at the end of the War of the Spanish Succession her navy was the finest in the world, since both of her chief rivals, the Dutch and the French, had been decidedly weakened in the conflict. For a quarter of a century after the close of the war England managed to keep out of the conflicts on the continent,[2] but later she felt obliged to intervene, as

England lays the foundation of her commercial greatness in the eighteenth century

---

[1] During the War of the Spanish Succession, England had strengthened herself by a final union with Scotland. For centuries the difficulties between the two countries had led to much bloodshed and suffering. In 1603, on the accession to the English throne of the Scotch king, James VI, as James I of England, the two countries had come under the same ruler, but each had maintained its own independent parliament and system of government. Finally, in 1707, both countries agreed to unite in one government. Forty-five members of the British House of Commons were thereafter to be chosen in Scotland, and sixteen Scotch lords were added to the British House of Lords. In this way the whole island of Great Britain was at last placed under a single government, and the occasions for strife and misunderstanding thereby greatly reduced.

[2] Except when, in 1718–1720, England allied herself with France against Spain, and her admiral, Byng, destroyed the Spanish fleet.

we shall see, in order to maintain "the balance of power" among her neighbors across the channel. Her great wars, however, were waged in distant parts of the world and on sea more often than on land. Fifty years after the Peace of Utrecht, England succeeded in driving the French from both India and North America [1] and laid the foundation of that vast colonial empire which gives her the commercial supremacy among European nations to-day.

In order to make the later history clear, it is necessary to notice here a remarkable change in the English line of kings. None of Queen Anne's children survived her, and she was succeeded, according to an arrangement made before her accession, by the nearest Protestant heir. This was George I, son of James I's granddaughter, Sophia.[2] She had married the elector of Hanover [3]; consequently the king who came to the English throne in 1714 was a German, and as elector of Hanover his continental realms belonged to the Holy Roman Empire.

[1] See below, Chapters VI–VII.

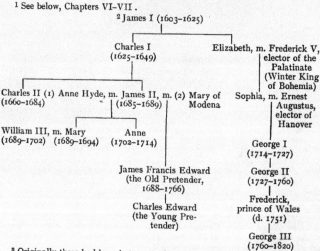

[2] James I (1603–1625)

Charles I (1625–1649)

Elizabeth, m. Frederick V, elector of the Palatinate (Winter King of Bohemia)

Charles II (1) Anne Hyde, m. James II, m. (2) Mary of Modena
(1660–1684)   (1685–1689)

Sophia, m. Ernest Augustus, elector of Hanover

William III, m. Mary   Anne
(1689–1702) (1689–1694)   (1702–1714)

George I (1714–1727)

James Francis Edward (the Old Pretender, 1688–1766)

George II (1727–1760)

Charles Edward (the Young Pretender)

Frederick, prince of Wales (d. 1751)

George III (1760–1820)

[3] Originally there had been but seven electors (see above, p. 24), but the duke of Bavaria had been made an elector during the Thirty Years' War, and in 1692 the father of George I had been permitted to assume the title of Elector of Hanover.

This circumstance did not cause as much trouble as might   Hanover and England were not united
have been expected. There was no question of uniting Han-
over and Great Britain in any way. Indeed, England assumed
no responsibility for her king's German territory. Nevertheless the policy of the Hanoverian kings was from time to time
influenced by attacks made upon their electorate. The inability of George I to speak English led to an important result,
since he was compelled to turn over most of the business of
government to his ministers and, as will be shown later, this
led to the development of the famous English cabinet.

REFERENCES

Attempts to Settle Claims to the Spanish Throne: WAKEMAN,
European History, 1598–1715, pp. 312–330 ; TRAILL, *William III*,
pp. 156–170 ; PERKINS, *France under the Regency*, pp. 239–251 ;
KITCHIN, *History of France*, Vol. III, pp. 277–287.

The Spanish Will and Louis XIV: WAKEMAN, pp. 330–340 ;
TRAILL, pp. 187–195 ; PERKINS, pp. 253–271 ; KITCHIN, Vol. III,
pp. 287–291.

Marlborough and the War of the Spanish Succession: WAKEMAN,
pp. 345–365 ; GREEN, *Short History of the English People*, chap.
ix, pp. 705–720 ; PERKINS, pp. 273–285 ; KITCHIN, Vol. III,
pp. 296–330.

Europe at the Peace of Utrecht: WAKEMAN, pp. 366–373 ; HAS-
SALL, *European History, 1715–1789*, pp. 1–24 ; PERKINS, pp.
285–290 ; KITCHIN, Vol. III, pp. 330–342.

The Union of England and Scotland: GREEN, chap. ix, sect. 9,
pp. 714–715 ; COLBY, *Selections from the Sources of English History*, pp. 227–229 ; LEE, *Source Book of English History*, pp.
443–445.

The Closing Years of Louis XIV's Reign: PERKINS, pp. 293–323 ;
KITCHIN, Vol. III, pp. 343–359.

CHAPTER IV

RUSSIA AND PRUSSIA BECOME EUROPEAN POWERS

Peter the Great plans to make Russia a European Power

11. Hitherto our attention has been fixed upon western and southern Europe. We have reviewed the chief events of Louis XIV's reign, his theory of kingship, his warlike policy, and have briefly introduced the several actors in the successive struggles, — England, Spain, the Netherlands, the Holy Roman Empire, and the Italian states. We must now turn from the Rhine and the Pyrenees to the shores of the Baltic and the vast plains of Russia; for while the War of the Spanish Succession was in progress another conflict was raging in the North, and changes were taking place there comparable in importance to those which were ratified by the Peace of Utrecht. Russia, which had hitherto faced eastward, was turning toward the West, upon which she was destined to exert an ever-increasing influence. The newly founded kingdom of Prussia was gathering its forces for a series of brilliant military exploits under the leadership of Frederick the Great, one of the most celebrated rulers of all times.

The Slavic peoples of Europe and the extent of Russia

There has been no occasion in dealing with the situation in western Europe to speak heretofore of the Slavic peoples to which the Russians, as well as the Poles, Bohemians, Bulgarians, and other nations of eastern Europe belong, although together they constitute the most numerous race in Europe. Not until the opening of the eighteenth century did Russia begin to take an active part in western affairs. Now she is one of the most important factors in the politics of the world. Of the realms of the Tsar, that portion which lies in Europe exceeds in extent the territories of all the other rulers of the continent put together, and yet European Russia comprises scarcely a quarter of the Tsar's whole dominion, which embraces northern and central Asia, extends to the Pacific Ocean, and forms altogether an empire covering about three times the area of the United States.

The beginnings of the Russian state fall in the ninth century ; some of the Northmen invaded the districts to the east of the Baltic, while their relatives were causing grievous trouble in France and England. It is generally supposed that one of their leaders, Rurik, was the first to consolidate the Slavic tribes about Novgorod into a sort of state in 862. Rurik's successor extended the bounds of the new empire so as to include the important town of Kiev on the Dnieper. The word "Russia" is probably derived from *Rous*, the name given by the neighboring Finns to the Norman adventurers. Before the end of the tenth century the Greek form of Christianity was introduced and the Russian ruler was baptized. The frequent intercourse with Constantinople might have led to rapid advance in civilization had it not been for a great disaster which put Russia back for centuries.

Beginnings of Russia

Russia is geographically nothing more than an extension of the vast plain of northern Asia, which the Russians were destined finally to conquer. It was therefore exposed to the great invasion of the Tartars, or Mongols, who swept in from the East in the thirteenth century. The powerful Tartar ruler, Genghis Khan (1162–1227), conquered northern China and central Asia, and the mounted hordes of his successors crossed into Europe and overran Russia, which had fallen apart into numerous principalities. The Russian princes became the dependents of the great Khan, and had frequently to seek his far-distant court, some three thousand miles away, where he freely disposed of both their crowns and their heads. The Tartars exacted tribute of the Russians, but left them undisturbed in their laws and religion.

The Tartar invasion in the thirteenth century

Influence of
the Tartar
occupation on
manners and
customs
Of the Russian princes who went to prostrate themselves at the foot of the Great Khan's throne, none made a more favorable impression upon him than the prince of Moscow, in whose favor the Khan was wont to decide all cases of dispute between the prince and his rivals. When the Mongol power had begun to decline in strength and the princes of Moscow had grown stronger, they ventured, in 1480, to kill the Mongol ambassadors sent to demand tribute, and thus freed themselves from the Mongol yoke. But the Tartar occupation had left its mark, for the princes of Moscow imitated the Khans rather than the western rulers, of whom, in fact, they knew nothing. In 1547

Ivan the Terrible assumes
the title of
Tsar
Ivan the Terrible assumed the Asiatic title of Tsar,[1] which appeared to him more worthy than that of king or emperor. The costumes and etiquette of the court were also Asiatic. The Russian armor suggested that of the Chinese, and their headdress was a turban. It was the task of Peter the Great to Europeanize Russia.

Peter the
Great
(1672-1725)
At the time of Peter's accession, Russia, which had grown greatly under Ivan the Terrible and other enterprising rulers, still had no outlet to the sea. In manners and customs the kingdom was Asiatic, and its government was that of a Tartar prince. Peter had no quarrel with the despotic power which fell to him and which the Russian monarchs still exercise.[2] But he knew that Russia was very much behind the rest of Europe, and that his crudely equipped soldiers could never make head against the well-armed and disciplined troops of the West. He had no seaport and no ships, without which Russia could never hope to take part in the world's affairs. His two great tasks were, therefore, to introduce western habits and to " make a window," as he expressed it, through which Russia might look abroad.

[1] The title Tsar, or Czar, was formerly supposed to be connected with Cæsar (German *Kaiser*), i.e. emperor, but this appears to have been a mistake.

[2] At the time of writing (summer, 1907) it is impossible to foretell how long the latter part of this statement will continue to be true. The Russian revolution now in progress will be described below. See chap. xxviii.

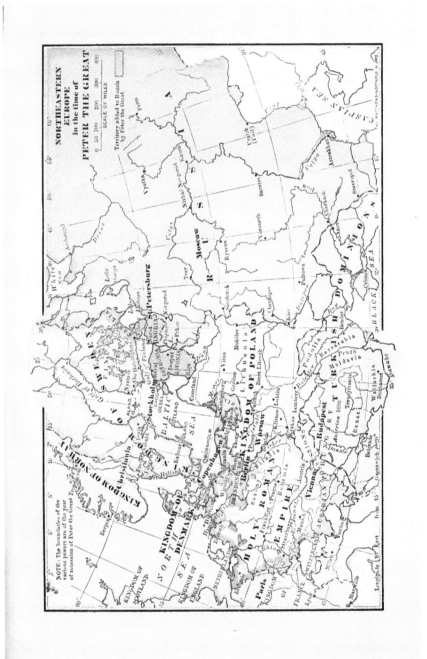

NORTHEASTERN
EUROPE
in the time of
PETER THE GREAT

SCALE OF MILES
0 50 100 200 300 400

Territory added to Russia
by Peter the Great.

NOTE: The boundaries of the
various powers are of the year
of accession of Peter the Great.

In 1697–1698, when the western powers were enjoying the peace concluded at Ryswick, Peter himself visited Germany, Holland, and England, with a view to investigating every art and science of the West, as well as the most approved methods of manufacture, from the making of a man-of-war to the etching of an engraving. Nothing escaped the keen eyes of this rude, half-savage northern giant. For a week he put on the wide breeches of a Dutch laborer and worked in the shipyard at Saardam near Amsterdam. In England, Holland, and Germany he engaged artisans, scientific men, architects, ship captains, and those versed in artillery and the training of troops, all of whom he took back with him to aid in the reform and development of Russia.

Peter's travels in Europe

He was called home by the revolt of the royal guard, who had allied themselves with the very large party of nobles and churchmen who were horrified at Peter's desertion of the habits and customs of his forefathers. They hated what they called "German ideas," such as short coats, tobacco smoking, and beardless faces. The clergy even suggested that Peter was perhaps Antichrist. Peter took a fearful revenge upon the rebels, and is said to have himself cut off the heads of many of them.

Suppression of revolt against foreign ideas

Peter's reforms extended through his whole reign. He made his people give up their cherished oriental beards and long flowing garments. He forced the women of the better class, who had been kept in a sort of oriental harem, to come out and meet the men in social assemblies, such as were common in the West. He invited foreigners to settle in Russia, and insured them protection, privileges, and the free exercise of their religion. He sent young Russians abroad to study. He reorganized the government officials on the model of a western kingdom, and made over his army in the same way.[1]

Peter's reform measures

Finding that the old capital of Moscow clung persistently to its ancient habits, he prepared to found a new capital for

[1] See *Readings*, sect. 11.

his new Russia. He selected for this purpose a bit of territory on the Baltic which he had conquered from Sweden, — very marshy, it is true, but where he might hope to construct Russia's first real port. Here he built St. Petersburg at enormous expense and colonized it with Russians and foreigners.

In his ambition to get to the sea, Peter naturally collided with Sweden, to which the provinces between Russia and the Baltic belonged. Never had Sweden, or any other country, had a more warlike king than the one with whom Peter had to contend, — the youthful prodigy, Charles XII. When Charles came to the throne in 1697 he was only fifteen years old, and it seemed to the natural enemies of Sweden an auspicious time to profit by the supposed weakness of the boy ruler. So a union was formed between Denmark, Poland, and Russia, with the object of increasing their territories at Sweden's expense. But Charles turned out to be a second Alexander the Great in military prowess. He astonished Europe by promptly besieging Copenhagen and forcing the king of Denmark to sign a treaty of peace. He then turned like lightning against Peter, who was industriously besieging Narva, and with eight thousand Swedes wiped out an army of fifty thousand Russians (1700). Lastly he defeated the king of Poland.

Though Charles was a remarkable military leader, he was a foolish ruler. He undertook to wrest Poland from its king, to whom he attributed the formation of the league against him. He had a new king crowned at Warsaw, whom he at last succeeded in getting recognized. He then turned his attention to Peter, who had meanwhile been conquering the Baltic provinces. This time fortune turned against the Swedes. The long march to Moscow proved as fatal to them as to Napoleon a century later, Charles XII being totally defeated in the battle of Pultowa (1709). He fled to Turkey, where he spent some years in vainly urging the Sultan to attack Peter. Returning at last to his own kingdom, which he had utterly neglected for years, he was killed in 1718 while besieging a town.

Soon after Charles's death a treaty was concluded between Sweden and Russia by which Russia gained Livonia, Esthonia, and the other Swedish provinces at the eastern end of the Baltic. Peter had made less successful attempts to get a footing on the Black Sea. He had first taken Azof, which he soon lost during the war with Sweden, and then several towns on the Caspian. It had become evident that if the Turks should be driven out of Europe, Russia would be a mighty rival of the western powers in the division of the spoils.   *Russia acquires the Baltic provinces and attempts to get a footing on the Black Sea*

For a generation after the death of Peter the Great, Russia fell into the hands of incompetent rulers. It appears again as a European state when the great Catharine II came to the throne in 1762. From that time on, the western powers had always to consider the vast Slavic empire in all their great struggles. They had also to consider a new kingdom in northern Germany, Prussia, which was just growing into a great power as Peter began his work.

Rise of Prussia

12. The electorate of Brandenburg had figured on the map of Europe for centuries, and there was no particular reason to suppose that it was one day to become the dominant state in Germany. Early in the fifteenth century the old line of electors had died out, and the impecunious Emperor Sigismund had sold it to a hitherto inconspicuous house, the Hohenzollerns, who are known to us now through such names as those of Frederick the Great, William I, the first German emperor, and his grandson, the present emperor. While it has always been the pride of the Hohenzollern family that practically every one of its reigning members has added something to what his ancestors handed down to him, nothing need be said of the little earlier annexations; no great extension took place until 1614, when the elector of Brandenburg inherited Cleves and Mark, and thus got his first hold on the Rhine district.   *The House of Hohenzollern*

Prussia acquired by the elector of Brandenburg

What was quite as important, he won, four years later, far to the east, the duchy of Prussia, which was separated from Brandenburg by Polish territory. Prussia was originally the name of a region on the Baltic inhabited by heathen Slavs. These had been conquered in the thirteenth century by one of the orders of crusading knights, who, when the conquest of the Holy Land was abandoned, looked about for other occupations. The region filled up with German colonists, but it came under the sovereignty of the neighboring kingdom of Poland, whose ruler annexed the western half of the territory of the Teutonic Order, as the German knights were called. In Luther's day (1525) the knights accepted Protestantism and dissolved their order. They then formed their lands into the duchy of Prussia and made their Grand Master, who was a relative of the elector of Brandenburg, their first duke, under the suzerainty of the king of Poland. About a hundred years later (1618) this branch of the Hohenzollerns died out, and the duchy then fell to the elector of Brandenburg.

The territories of the Great Elector (1640–1688)

Notwithstanding this substantial territorial gain, there was little promise that the hitherto obscure electorate would ever become a formidable power when, in 1640, Frederick William, known as the Great Elector, came to his inheritance. His territories were scattered from the Rhine to the Vistula, his army was of small account, and his authority disputed by powerful nobles and local assemblies. The center of his domain was Brandenburg. Far to the west was Mark, bordering on the Rhine valley, and Cleves lying on both banks of that river. Far to the east, beyond the Vistula, was the duchy of Prussia, outside the borders of the Empire and subject to the overlordship of the king of Poland.

Character of the Great Elector

Frederick William was, however, well fitted for the task of welding these domains into a powerful state. He was coarse by nature, heartless in destroying opponents, treacherous in diplomatic negotiations, and entirely devoid of the culture which distinguished Louis XIV and his court. He set resolutely to work to build up a great army, destroy the local assemblies in his provinces, place all government in the hands of his officials, and add new territories to his patrimony.

In all of these undertakings he was largely successful. By shrewd tactics during the closing days of the Thirty Years' War he managed to secure, by the treaties of Westphalia, the bishoprics of Minden and Halberstadt and the duchy of Farther

The Great Elector makes important gains in territory

Territories of the Great Elector of Brandenburg

Pomerania, which gave him a good shore line on the Baltic. He also forced Poland to surrender her overlordship of the duchy of Prussia and thus made himself a duke independent of the Empire.

Knowing that the interests of his house depended on military strength, he organized, in spite of the protests of the taxpayers, an army out of all proportion to the size and wealth of his dominions. He reformed the system of administration and succeeded in creating an absolute monarchy on the model furnished by his contemporary, Louis XIV. He joined England and Holland in their alliances against Louis, and the army of Brandenburg began to be known and feared.

Reforms of the Great Elector

Though a good Protestant, the Great Elector permitted religious freedom to a remarkable degree. He made Catholics eligible to office and, on the other hand, gave asylum to the

Huguenots received in Brandenburg

persecuted Huguenots of France, even offering them special inducements to settle in his realms. In short, as his illustrious descendant, Frederick the Great, wrote : " He was the restorer and defender of Brandenburg, and an arbiter among his equals. With slight means he did great things; he was his own prime minister and commander-in-chief and rendered flourishing a state which he found buried beneath its own ruins."

Brandenburg becomes the kingdom of Prussia, 1701

It was accordingly a splendid legacy which the Great Elector left in 1688 to his son, Frederick III, and although the career of the latter was by no means as brilliant as that of his father, he was able by a bold stroke to transform his electorate into a kingdom. The opportunity for this achievement was offered by the need of the powers for his assistance against the designs of Louis XIV. When the Emperor called upon Frederick III in 1700 to assist him in securing a division of the Spanish dominions, the elector exacted as the price of his help the recognition of his right to take the title of king.

Frederick III, elector of Brandenburg, becomes King Frederick I of Prussia

The title King of Prussia was deemed preferable to the more natural King of Brandenburg because Prussia lay wholly without the bounds of the Empire and consequently its ruler was not in any sense subject to the Emperor but was entirely independent. Since West Prussia still belonged to Poland in 1701, the new king satisfied himself at first with the title King *in* Prussia.

Government of Frederick William I (1713-1740)

The second ruler of the new kingdom, Frederick William I, the father of Frederick the Great, is known to history as the rough and boorish barrack king who devoted himself entirely to governing his realm, collecting tall soldiers, drilling his battalions, hunting wild game, and smoking strong tobacco. He ruled his family and his country with an iron hand, declaring to those who remonstrated, "Salvation belongs to the Lord; everything else is my business."

Frederick William and his soldiers

Frederick William was passionately fond of military life from his childhood. He took special pride in stalwart soldiers and collected them at great expense from all parts of Europe. He raised the army, which numbered twenty-seven thousand in the days of the Great Elector, to eighty-four thousand, making it almost equal to that maintained by France or Austria. He reserved to himself the right to appoint subordinates as well as high officials in the service and based promotion on excellence in discipline rather than on family connections. He was constantly drilling and reviewing his men, whom he addressed affectionately as "my blue children."

Moreover, by wise management, miserly thrift, and entire indifference to the amenities of life, Frederick William treasured up a large sum of money. He discharged a large number of court servants; sold at auction many of the royal jewels; and had a great portion of the family plate coined into money. Consequently he was able to leave to his son, Frederick II, not only an admirable army but an ample supply of gold. Indeed it was his toil and economy that made possible the achievements of his far more distinguished son.

Miserly economy in finances

REFERENCES

Russia under Peter the Great: WAKEMAN, *European History, 1598-1715*, pp. 298-304; RAMBAUD, *History of Russia*, Vol. II, pp. 76-105.

Peter the Great and Charles XII: WAKEMAN, pp. 304-311; HASSALL, *European History, 1715-1789*, pp. 57-62; RAMBAUD, Vol. II, pp. 51-75; BAIN, *Charles XII and the Collapse of the Swedish Empire* (Heroes of the Nations Series).

Peter the Great's European Journeys: RAMBAUD, Vol. II, pp. 33-39, 112-118.

Brandenburg and the Great Elector: WAKEMAN, pp. 173-181, 292-297; HENDERSON, *Short History of Germany*, Vol. II, pp. 9-29; CARLYLE, *Frederick the Great*, Vol. I, Book III, chap. xviii; TUTTLE, *History of Prussia to the Accession of Frederick the Great*, pp. 208-250.

Frederick William, the Father of Frederick the Great: TUTTLE, pp. 337-487; HENDERSON, Vol. II, pp. 87-111; CARLYLE, Vol. I, Book IV, chaps. iii and iv.

CHAPTER V

THE WARS OF FREDERICK THE GREAT

Frederick the Great and Maria Theresa

Frederick's literary tastes, and troubles with his father

13. It was reserved for Frederick II of Prussia to stir Europe to its depths, to win for his little kingdom a place among the European powers, and to earn for himself the title of "the Great." As a youth he had grieved and disgusted his father by his fondness for books and his passion for writing verses and playing the flute. A French tutor had instilled in him a love for the polished language of France and an enthusiasm for her literature and for her philosophers who were busy attacking the traditional religious ideas to which Frederick's father stoutly clung. When eighteen years old Frederick had tried to run away in order to escape the harsh military discipline to which he was subjected. He was captured and brought before the king, who was in such a rage that he seemed upon the point of killing his renegade son with his sword. He contented himself, however, with imprisoning Frederick in the citadel of Küstrin, with no books except a Bible, and forced him to witness the execution of one of his companions, who had aided his flight.

After this Frederick consented to give some contemptuous attention to public affairs. He inspected the royal domains near Küstrin and began, for the first time, to study the peasants, their farms, and their cattle. He even agreed to marry a princess whom his father had selected for him, and settled down to a scholarly life, studying literature, philosophy, history, and mathematics, and carrying on a correspondence with learned men of all nations, especially with Voltaire,[1] whom he greatly

_____
[1] See below, p. 168.

admired. He was very fond indeed of writing himself and seized every spare moment of a busy life to push forward his works upon history, politics, and military matters. No less than twenty-four volumes of his writings, all in French, were published shortly after his death, and these did not include everything that he had managed to write.

Frederick did not neglect to give some attention to the duties which were to devolve upon him when he should become king. He accompanied the Prussian contingent which took part in the War of the Polish Succession (1733–1735)[1] and noted certain weaknesses in the Austrian army, with which he was soon to engage. He took occasion to maneuver a regiment before his father and showed such skill that Frederick William conceded that literature had not completely demoralized his son after all. *Frederick begins to attend to business*

Frederick had no trouble, when the time came, in showing the world that he was one of the greatest generals of all the ages; but his military prowess and his statesmanship did not prevent his continuing to gratify his literary and scientific tastes. Upon his father's death in 1740 it seemed for a moment as if he proposed to inaugurate an era of peaceful devotion to the arts and sciences. He dismissed the giant guards whom his father had taken such pains to get together, and recalled to Berlin a famous philosopher and mathematician, Wolf, who years before had been sent off by the devout Frederick William on account of his heretical teachings. He reorganized the Academy of Berlin and hastened to confer personally with the great Voltaire in regard to the new responsibilities which he had now to meet. *Accession of Frederick II, 1740*

Frederick came to the throne in the spring of 1740. In the autumn the Emperor, Charles VI, died and left his Austrian domains to his eldest daughter, Maria Theresa, then only twenty-three years old, five years younger than her future rival, the king of Prussia. Her father, it will be remembered, *The Pragmatic Sanction insures the succession to Maria Theresa*

[1] See above, p. 45.

had aspired to the throne of Spain and had most reluctantly acknowledged the Bourbon Philip V, with whom he had continued to fight over their respective claims to Italian territory. Since he had no male relatives to whom the Hapsburg possessions would descend after his death, he labored for years to insure to his daughter, Maria Theresa, the inheritance of all the Austrian lands. In order to do this, he drew up a revised code of laws relating to the rights of succession, which was called the Pragmatic Sanction. This he so arranged as to exclude the daughters of his elder brother and give preference to his own.[1] By promises, concessions of territory, and tedious negotiations, he induced the more important powers of Europe — Russia, Prussia, Holland, Spain, England, and France — to agree to his plan.

Queenly traits of Maria Theresa

For a time it seemed as if no one was going to take advantage of Maria Theresa's inexperience to rob her of any of her outlying possessions. She began immediately to display astonishing energy and aptitude for the business of governing. She patiently attended to all the tiresome matters of state, read long documents and reports, conscientiously consulted her ministers, and conferred with the ambassadors of foreign

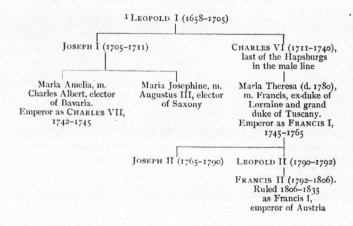

[1] LEOPOLD I (1658-1705)

courts. Her clear judgment, her distinguished bearing, her love of pomp and ceremony, — all helped her to sustain her dignity in the trying circumstances in which she soon found herself. She had none of Frederick's appreciation of culture and, unlike most of her royal contemporaries, she exhibited a contempt for science and philosophy. Nor had she any sympathy with religious toleration ; on the contrary she abhorred the sceptical notions of the Prussian king and his admiration for Voltaire.

The problems which confronted her would have been diffi- Polyglot Austrian dominions
cult enough if her realms had been compact and inhabited by people of a single race. The Austrian possessions were, however, as has already been pointed out, a most miscellaneous and scattered collection of territories, great and small, inhabited by a great variety of widely differing races, — Germans in Austria proper, Czechs mixed with Germans in Bohemia and Moravia, Magyars in Hungary, Croatians and Slovenes to the south, Italians in Milan and Tuscany, French and Walloons in the Netherlands. The chief cities of the young queen included such scattered and varied places as Vienna, Pesth, Prague, Milan, Brussels, and Antwerp.

While the Spanish Bourbons might try to increase their Claimants to the Hapsburg lands
Italian territories at her expense, or France encroach upon the Netherlands, Maria Theresa's more natural enemies were nearer home. One of her cousins (the daughters of her father's elder brother, Emperor Joseph I), had married the elector of Saxony ; the other, the elector of Bavaria. Both of these princes accordingly laid claim to portions of Maria Theresa's lands ; the elector of Saxony wanted Moravia and the elector of Bavaria, Bohemia.

It was however none of Maria Theresa's more or less distant Frederick II seizes Silesia in 1740
relatives that first attacked her, but Frederick of Prussia, whose anxiety to increase the bounds of his kingdom precipitated a series of wars which lasted with scarcely any interruption for nearly a quarter of a century and altered the map of the world

more fundamentally than even the weary War of the Spanish Succession had done. He saw no easier way of forwarding his designs than by robbing the seemingly defenseless Maria Theresa of Silesia, a strip of territory lying to the southeast of Brandenburg.

To save appearances, he offered to join Austria in a firm alliance if she would peacefully cede Silesia to him, but Maria Theresa indignantly replied that she was prepared to defend, not to sell, her subjects. Thereupon, scarcely two months after the death of Charles VI, Frederick marched his army into the coveted district, occupied the important city of Breslau and had soon gained possession of the whole province. He did not take the trouble to declare war, and offered as an excuse for his attack only a vague claim to a part of the land. He remarked, impudently enough, that he was engaged in the finest game in the world and the boldest and most rapidly executed of all the enterprises which princes of his house had ever undertaken.

General alliance directed against Maria Theresa

Maria Theresa got together an army with difficulty, but her troops were hopelessly defeated by the Prussian king at Mollwitz early in April, 1741. Here Frederick's infantry showed the results of all his father's care and discipline, for they withstood like a rock the desperate charges of the Austrian cavalry. This brilliant victory attracted the attention of all the European monarchs, especially those who saw a prospect of following Frederick's example and seizing some part of the defenseless queen's territory. In June France joined Prussia, hoping to weaken her old enemy Austria; to secure the election of her friend, the elector of Bavaria, as Emperor instead of Maria Theresa's husband, Francis; and lastly, to gain the long-coveted Austrian Netherlands. Spain, Sardinia, and Bavaria joined

England supports Austria

France and Prussia. But Maria Theresa's appeal to England had brought a prompt response from George II who, as elector of Hanover,[1] had reason to fear the increasing power of Prussia,

[1] See above, p. 48.

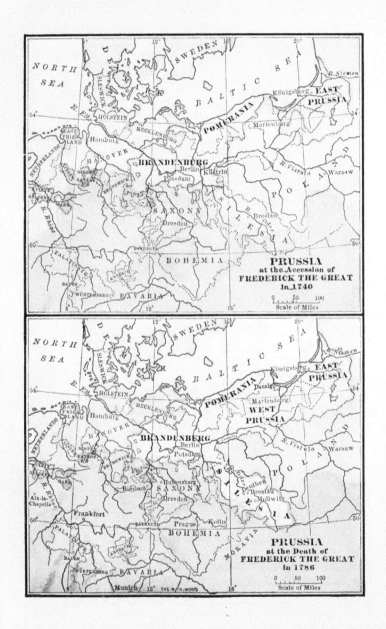

NORTH SEA

SWEDEN

BALTIC SEA

R. Niemen

Königsberg EAST PRUSSIA

DENMARK

SLESWICK

HOLSTEIN

R. Elbe

EAST FRIESLAND

Hamburg

MECKLENBURG

POMERANIA

Marienburg

HANOVER

NETHERLANDS

MINDEN

RAVENS.

BRUNSWICK

BRANDENBURG

Berlin

Küstrin

R. Vistula

Warsaw

CLEVE

GELDERS

MARK

Potsdam

P O L A N D

R. Rhine

SAXONY

Dresden

R. Oder

Breslau

S I L E S I A

PALAT.

BAREUTH

BADEN

WÜRTEMBERG

BAVARIA

BOHEMIA

PRUSSIA
at the Accession of
FREDERICK THE GREAT
in 1740

0   50   100
Scale of Miles

NORTH SEA

SWEDEN

BALTIC SEA

R. Niemen

Königsberg EAST PRUSSIA

DENMARK

SLESWICK

HOLSTEIN

R. Elbe

EAST FRIESLAND

Hamburg

MECKLENBURG

POMERANIA

Danzig

Marienburg

WEST PRUSSIA

HANOVER

NETHERLANDS

MINDEN

RAVENS.

BRUNSWICK

BRANDENBURG

Berlin

Potsdam

R. Vistula

Warsaw

CLEVE

GELDERS

MARK

Aix-la-Chapelle

Frankfort

Rossbach

Hubertusburg

SAXONY

Dresden

R. Oder

Leuthen

Breslau

Mollwitz

P O L A N D

S I L E S I A

PALAT.

BAREUTH

ANSPACH

Prague

Kollin

MORAVIA

BOHEMIA

BADEN

WÜRTEMBERG

BAVARIA

Munich

THE W.-N. WORLD

PRUSSIA
at the Death of
FREDERICK THE GREAT
in 1786

0   50   100
Scale of Miles

and consequently induced Parliament to make a grant to aid the young queen in defending herself.

The French army joined that of the elector of Bavaria and advanced into Austria. They might easily have taken Vienna itself had it not been that France was not anxious to increase unduly the power of her ally, the Bavarian elector. They accordingly turned into Bohemia, took Prague in November, 1741, and forced the representatives of Bohemia to recognize Charles Albert as their king. Early next year he was duly chosen Emperor, as Charles VII, at Frankfort. Success of the French and Bavarian troops

A great part of Maria Theresa's possessions were now in the hands of her numerous enemies; her army was disorganized and she could look for no considerable aid either from England or Russia, her natural allies. Nevertheless, her courage did not fail, even in the darkest hour. She appealed to her Hungarian subjects. It took a good deal of negotiation to induce them to take part in a war that had already proved so disastrous; but at last their queen roused their enthusiasm and they provided her with soldiers so that she was able in a short time to turn the tide of fortune in her favor. Maria Theresa appeals to Hungary

In February, 1742, on the very day on which Charles Albert was crowned Emperor, one of her armies swept into his capital of Munich, while the other was defeating his French allies. In the summer she came to terms with the Prussian king, who perfidiously deserted his French ally on condition that Maria Theresa should give him Silesia. The Austrian troops forced the French across the Rhine and Charles VII, in spite of his august title, became a sort of vagrant who had to rely upon the French commander for pocket money. Austria recovers herself

The war, instead of coming to an end as might have been expected, now broadened out by combining with a war between England and Spain which had begun in 1739, just before the seizure of Silesia by Frederick. The first Bourbon king of Spain, Philip V, became in later life a sad mental and The war broadens out physical wreck; but his energetic wife, Elizabeth of Parma,[1] did what she could, with the aid of a succession of able ministers, to strengthen her adopted country. The marine forces were increased and the heavy old galleons replaced by more modern ships. Efforts were made, too, to check the smuggling which the English continued to carry on.

War of
Jenkins's ear

The English merchants, who had long violated with impunity the Spanish laws which prohibited them from trading with the West Indies and South America, began to bring home stories of the hardships they had suffered in Spanish prisons. Public opinion was inflamed by the exhibition in the streets of London of the filthy food which was alleged to have been furnished to English seamen who had been so unfortunate as to be caught. It was further reported that Englishmen on lawful voyages had been seized and cruelly dealt with by Spanish officials. One of the many stories in circulation alleged that a certain Captain Jenkins, while engaged in legitimate commerce, had been arrested by the ferocious Spaniards, who had cut off his ear. Whether true or not, Captain Jenkins's tale helped to excite the populace to fever heat.

The pacific Sir Robert Walpole, who was then at the head of English affairs, discouraged a resort to arms and urged a careful investigation of the charges; but he was forced to agree to war in 1739. He declared, when he heard the clamor of bells announcing to the people the commencement of hostilities, "They are ringing the bells now; they will be wringing their hands soon."

France joins
Spain against
England

The momentous results in India and America of the war thus begun will form the subject of the following chapters. So far as the continent of Europe was concerned, the conflict between England and Spain merged into the general turmoil; for France, instead of being discouraged by her reverses in 1743, made advances to Spain and concluded a "family compact" by which each branch of the Bourbons agreed to

[1] See above, p. 44.

defend the territories of the other. France promised also to help Spain to regain Gibraltar and Minorca, which she had been forced to cede to England,[1] and to win the English colony of Georgia in North America.[2] France, as an ally of Spain, was now at war with England as well as with Austria and at once threw her troops into the Austrian Netherlands, where they won for a time victories as brilliant as those achieved by Louis XIV upon the same battle ground.[3]

Frederick of Prussia knew full well that Maria Theresa was not reconciled to the loss of Silesia, and, with the hope of assuring to himself the continued possession of his new province and perhaps gaining some of Bohemia in addition, he again entered the war. He withdrew, however, a year or so later when Maria Theresa reaffirmed her cession of Silesia to him. France was thus left in the lurch once more while Frederick remarked with easy philosophy, " Happy are they who, having secured their own advantage, can look tranquilly upon the embarrassments of others." *Frederick again attacks Austria*

For four years the war raged in the Austrian Netherlands, in the Rhine valley, in Silesia, Saxony, Italy, North America, and India without bringing permanent gain or glory to any of the combatants, for all the fearful sacrifices of life and treasure. Finally all parties, weary of the long conflict, laid down their arms and agreed to what is called in diplomacy the *status quo ante bellum*, which meant that everything should be restored in general to the conditions which existed before hostilities began. *The slight changes ratified at Aix-la-Chapelle, 1748*

In the Peace of Aix-la-Chapelle in 1748, France agreed once again to make no further attempt to aid the Stuart pretenders

---

[1] At the close of the War of the Spanish Succession. See above, p. 43.

[2] See below, p. 110.

[3] The French forces ventured to invade the territory of the United Provinces in 1747. The Dutch, frightened as they had been in 1672 (see above, p. 21), proclaimed William IV, Prince of Orange, *hereditary* stadholder of all the provinces, and so transformed the former republic into a monarchy in all but name.

to regain the English throne.[1] The Pragmatic Sanction and the election of Maria Theresa's husband as Emperor Francis I were ratified by the powers. Little Parma was turned over by Austria to a younger son of Elizabeth of Parma, queen of Spain. England had spent some three hundred and twenty millions of dollars and yet had not succeeded in forcing Spain to promise to stop searching English vessels suspected of smuggling or to remedy any of the other abuses which had led to the war.

THE SEVEN YEARS' WAR (1756–1763)

The powers discontented with the settlement of 1748

14. The Peace of Aix-la-Chapelle proved to be only a truce, for none of the parties to the settlement were satisfied with the outcome. The question of French and English predominance on the seas and in India and North America was left undecided. Maria Theresa could not reconcile herself to the loss of Silesia; according to an English envoy she forgot that she was a queen and broke into tears like a woman whenever she saw a Silesian. Therefore, when the Tsarina Elizabeth offered her aid in recovering the lost province, she gladly accepted it. Louis XV harbored bitter feelings against his former ally, Frederick, whom he charged with breach of faith in withdrawing from the conflict when he had gained his own ends. On the other hand, Frederick made fun of the French generals and retorted that Louis likewise had thought only of his own interests.

Seven Years' War opens in America

The renewed conflict, which was to involve the Indian rajahs of Hindustan and the colonists of Virginia and New England, began, singularly enough, near the site now occupied by smoky Pittsburg, where General Braddock was defeated

---

[1] During the war Charles Edward, grandson of James II, had landed in Scotland, gathered the Highland clans about him, and marched southward into England with the hope of wresting the English scepter from George II. France having failed to send the expected aid, he was utterly defeated at Culloden in 1746 and regained the continent only after the most romantic adventures. This episode forever put an end to the attempts of the Stuarts to win back the English throne.

(1755) by the French and their Indian allies in his attempt to take Fort Duquesne. The English captured two French frigates off the coast of Newfoundland and war commenced on the high seas before it was declared in 1756. Frederick the Great was well aware that Maria Theresa was forming a coalition against him and accordingly prudently entered into an alliance with England, who was thereby ranged among the enemies of Austria instead of among her friends as formerly.

The news of Frederick's alliance with England had a powerful effect upon the court of Louis XV. Kaunitz, the able ambassador of Maria Theresa, had been busy trying to bring France over to his side, and he now succeeded; in spite of two hundred years of hostility to the House of Hapsburg, France bound herself to her inveterate enemy in an alliance of friendship and defense. After this astonishing diplomatic revolution the new friends proceeded to plan a partition of Prussia. Maria Theresa was to reduce Frederick's territories to the confined boundaries of a hundred years before, deprive him of his rank of king, and thus thoroughly humiliate him. Russia, Saxony, and Sweden also agreed to join in the concerted attack upon Prussia, and armies gathering from all points of the compass threatened the complete annihilation of Austria's rival. Diplomatic revolution brings Austria and France together

However, it was in this very war that Frederick earned his title of "the Great" and showed himself the equal of the ablest generals that the world has seen, from Alexander of Macedon to Napoleon. Learning the object of the allies, he did not wait for them to declare war upon him; with entire disregard of international law, he invaded Saxony, expelled the elector, assumed the administration of the province, and defeated the Austrians sent against him (1756). The next year, however, he found himself thickly beset with difficulties. Sweden, having joined the coalition against him, occupied East Pomerania; France began to pour an enormous army into his Rhenish provinces; Russian troops invaded Prussia Critical position of Frederick in 1756 and overwhelmed the general whom Frederick dispatched against them; and Frederick himself was badly beaten at Kolin by the imperial army.

Frederick wins the battle of Rossbach (November 5, 1757)
Undaunted, nevertheless, Frederick recruited fresh levies, turned to the western part of Saxony to meet the oncoming French troops, and gained one of his most famous victories at the battle of Rossbach against the French and imperial forces. Then swinging back to the east, he worsted the Austrians and Russians a month later at Leuthen in Silesia in a memorable battle which Napoleon afterwards declared would alone have placed the Prussian king among the great generals of all time. For five years more Frederick continued the unequal struggle in Saxony, Silesia, Brandenburg, and Bohemia, sometimes in victory and sometimes in bitter defeat, but subjected to a constant strain on his resources which eventually shattered his splendid army and embittered its intrepid commander.

Frederick's English subsidy is withdrawn
During these trying years one of Frederick's principal sources of support was the annual subsidy of six hundred and seventy thousand pounds, furnished him by William Pitt, then the chief minister in England and director of English operations on land and sea. Unfortunately for Frederick, in the autumn of 1761 Pitt was forced to resign his office owing to the fact that the new sovereign, George III (1760–1820), longed for peace and was especially opposed to the minister's plan for increasing the war burden by fighting the king of Spain, who had just renewed the family compact with France. The subsidies that had so materially helped Frederick in his struggle were now withdrawn and he was advised to make terms with his enemies. Naturally this reversal of the English policy greatly incensed Frederick and inspired him with a stanch hatred for England which he cherished until his death.

Frederick comes to terms with Maria Theresa
The outlook would now have been gloomy indeed for Frederick had it not been for the death of his bitter enemy, the Tsarina Elizabeth of Russia, in 1762. Her successor, Peter III, was a great admirer of Frederick, and promptly concluded peace

with him. Freed thus from further danger on the Russian side, Frederick turned upon the Austrians, drove them out of Silesia, and in November agreed to a truce with Maria Theresa, as a preliminary to a final settlement which was reached at Hubertsburg in Saxony in February, 1763. The Seven Years' War brought to Frederick only a renewed confirmation of his claim to the Silesian province; to Austria an enormous war debt and the promise of the Prussian king to assist Maria Theresa's son, Joseph II, in securing the succession to his father as Emperor.

Meanwhile France and England brought their maritime and colonial struggle to a close in a treaty of peace signed at Paris in February, 1763. This settlement was most disastrous for Louis XV who, instead of the glory and dominion he had sought, found only defeat and ruin. The great empire which the French colonists had been building up in the valley of the St. Lawrence and east of the Mississippi for more than a century had to be surrendered to England. Though France retained five trading posts in India, they were not to be fortified, and thus the hopes of conquering Hindustan which she had cherished during recent years came to naught. England, on the other hand, emerged from the conflict incontestably mistress of the seas and the world's greatest colonial power.

Treaty of Paris, 1763; France forced to cede Canada to England

In addition to the discredit resulting from these grave territorial losses, Louis XV had become burdened by a connection with the House of Austria, which was thoroughly unpopular with his subjects, and he had incurred a great war debt which helped materially to bring on in later years the financial disaster which precipitated the French Revolution.

Disastrous results of France's alliance with Austria

THREE PARTITIONS OF POLAND, 1772, 1793, AND 1795

15. Frederick's success in seizing and holding one of Austria's finest provinces did not satisfy him. The central portions of his kingdom — Brandenburg, Silesia, and Pomerania

— were completely cut off from East Prussia by a considerable tract known as West Prussia, which belonged to the kingdom of Poland. The map will show how great must have been Frederick's temptation to fill this gap, especially as Poland was in no condition to defend its possessions.

Origin of the kingdom of Poland

The Poles, a Slavic people, begin to be heard of in the history of the tenth century. Their first great ruler, Boleslav I (992–1025), built up a considerable kingdom between the Oder and the Vistula, and his people were converted to the Roman Catholic faith. After a long period of weakness, the kingdom was revived and strengthened in the fourteenth century.

Lithuania added to Poland

In 1386 a Polish princess married Jagello, grand duke of Lithuania, a region twice as large as Poland, which lay to the east of it and was inhabited chiefly by Russians. As time went on Poland and Lithuania were gradually welded together and came to be considered a single country. To the north of Poland lay the region conquered by the Teutonic Knights [1] and

Poland gains West Prussia

colonized by Germans. After long conflicts, one of Jagello's successors wrested from the knights the province of West Prussia, with its strong fortress of Marienburg and the flourishing German towns of Danzig and Thorn. A single diet, or national assembly, was established in 1468 for the whole motley realm of the king of Poland.

Mixed population and discordant religions in Poland

With the exception of Russia, Poland was the largest kingdom in Europe. It covered an immense plain with no natural boundaries, and the population, which was very thinly scattered, belonged to several races. Besides the Poles themselves there were Germans in the cities of West Prussia, and the Lithuanians and Russians in Lithuania. The Jews were very numerous everywhere, forming half of the population in some of the towns. The Poles were usually Catholics, while the Germans were Protestants, and the Russians adhered to the Greek Church. These differences in religion, added to those of race, created endless difficulties and dissensions. There were many

[1] See above, p. 56.

Jesuits in Poland and the intolerance of the Roman Catholics led to the expulsion from the diet of all "dissenters," as the members of the Protestant and the Greek churches were called. In 1733 the dissenters were deprived of all political rights.

The government of Poland was the worst imaginable. Instead of having developed a strong monarchy, as her neighbors — Prussia, Russia, and Austria — had done, she remained in a state of feudal anarchy which the nobles had taken the greatest pains to perpetuate by binding their kings in such a way that they had no power either to maintain order or to defend the country from attack. The king could not declare war, make peace, impose taxes, or pass any law without the consent of the diet. As the diet was composed of representatives of the nobility, any one of whom could freely veto any measure, — for no measure could pass that had even one vote against it, — most of the diets broke up without accomplishing anything. *The defective system of government*

The liberum veto

The kingship was not hereditary in Poland, but each time the ruler died the nobles assembled and chose a new one, commonly a foreigner. These elections were tumultuous and the various European powers regularly interfered, by force or bribery, to secure the election of a candidate whom they believed would favor their interests. *The elective kingship*

The nobles in Poland were very numerous. There were perhaps a million and a half of them, mostly very poor, owning only a trifling bit of land. There was a saying that the poor noble's dog, even if he sat in the middle of the estate, was sure to have his tail upon a neighbor's land. It was the few rich and powerful families that really controlled such government as might be said to have existed in Poland. There was no middle class except in the few German towns. In the Polish and Lithuanian towns such industry and commerce as existed were in the hands of the Jews, who were not recognized as citizens and who both oppressed and were oppressed. The peasants were miserable indeed. They had sunk from serfs to slaves *The Polish nobles and peasants* over whom their lords had the right of life and death. They owed all the fruits of their labor to their lords and were mere chattels, living in incredible and hopeless filth and misery. There was for them no king, no law but the will of their masters, no country but the manor on which they were born and to which they belonged like the cattle in the fields.

Rousseau's view of Poland

The French philosopher Rousseau thus describes the conditions : " As one reads the history of Poland, he wonders how a government so fantastically arranged could have lasted so long : a huge body made up of a great number of dead members and a few live ones which are so disunited as to be independent of one another ; a body which acts violently but accomplishes nothing ; which cannot resist any one who chooses to attack it ; which breaks up altogether five or six times in a century, and which has a stroke of paralysis when any effort is necessary ; and yet in spite of all this still survives and exhibits no little vigor." [1]

Catharine II and Frederick II agree on Polish matters, 1764

It required no great insight to foresee that Poland was in danger of falling a prey to its greedy and powerful neighbors, Russia, Prussia, and Austria, who clamped in the unfortunate kingdom on all sides. They had long shamelessly interfered in its affairs and had actually taken active measures to oppose all reforms of the constitution in order that they might profit by the existing anarchy. As we have seen, a general war had broken out in 1733 when Louis XV, backed up by Spain, endeavored to place his father-in-law, Stanislas Lesczinski, upon the throne in opposition to a Saxon prince, Augustus III, who was supported by Austria and Russia. Augustus III died in 1763, just as the Seven Years' War had been brought to a close, and Frederick immediately arranged with the new Russian ruler, the famous Catharine II, to put upon the vacant throne her favorite, Poniatowski, who took the title of Stanislas II.

[1] Rousseau's *Considerations upon the Government of Poland*, written in 1771, just before the first partition.

Since Catharine was to play a conspicuous rôle in all the affairs of Europe for thirty-five years, a word must be said of the manner in which this German woman became the ruler of all the Russias. She was the daughter of one of Frederick the Great's officers and had been selected by him in 1743, at the request of the Tsarina Elizabeth, as a suitable wife for Peter, the heir to the throne. At the age of fourteen this inexperienced girl found herself in the midst of the intrigues of the court at St. Petersburg; she joined the Greek Church, exchanged her name of Sophia for that of Catharine, and, by zealous study of both books and men, prepared to make her new name famous.

Catharine II, empress of Russia (1762–1796)

Her husband proved to be a worthless fellow who early began to neglect and maltreat her. When he came to the throne in 1762, he frightened the clergy by threatening to confiscate their lands, alienated the soldiers by his admiration for the Prussian uniforms and discipline, and lost the respect of every one by his drunken and dissolute life. Catharine won over the imperial guard and had herself proclaimed empress. Peter was forced to abdicate and was carried off by some of Catharine's supporters, who put him to death, probably with her tacit consent.

Murder of Tsar Peter, 1762

In the spirit of Peter the Great, Catharine determined to carry on the Europeanizing of Russia and extend her empire. She was unquestionably a bad woman morally, thoroughly unscrupulous and hypocritical, but she was shrewd in the choice and management of her ministers and was herself a hard worker. She rose at six o'clock in the morning, hurried through her toilet, prepared her own light breakfast, and turned to the exacting and dull business of government, carefully considering the reports laid before her relating to the army, the navy, finances, and foreign affairs. She read and admired the writings of Voltaire and the various other French philosophers and reformers, whom she welcomed at her court whenever she could induce them to visit her. She was, in short, a sort of

Catharine's character

Frederick the Great, sharing his energy and patience, his anxiety to better his country, his love of learning and of power, and his cynical unscrupulousness.

Russia and Prussia agree to prevent reforms in Poland

To return to Poland, Catharine was disappointed in Stanislas Poniatowski, who showed himself favorable to reform. He even proposed to do away with the *liberum veto*, — the sacred right of any member of the diet to block a measure no matter how salutary. Russia, however, supported by Prussia, intervened to demand that the *liberum veto*, which insured continued anarchy, should be maintained and that the adherents of the Protestant and Greek churches should be granted reasonable rights. The diet most unwisely determined to maintain the *liberum veto*, but refused to exhibit the least tolerance toward the dissenters. Then came several years of civil war between the several factions, a war in which the Russians freely intervened.

Catharine involved in war with Turkey

Meanwhile France, in order to direct Catharine's attention to another quarter, encouraged the Turks to attack her; but Catharine's armies gained victory after victory. She sent a fleet around through the North Sea into the Mediterranean (1770) which destroyed the Turkish squadron in the Ægean Sea. Her forces occupied the coast of the Black Sea and seemed ready to cross the Balkan Mountains and perhaps put an end to the Turkish power in Europe.

Austria agrees to the partition of Poland

Austria was thoroughly alarmed by the prospect of having Russia for a neighbor on the southeast instead of the ever-weakening Turks. She consequently approached her old enemy, Frederick, and between them, they decided that Russia should be allowed to take a portion of Poland if she would consent to give up most of her Turkish conquests; then Austria, in order to maintain the balance of power, should be given a slice of Poland and Frederick should take the longed-for West Prussia.

Accordingly in 1772 Poland's three neighbors arranged to take each a portion of the distracted kingdom. Austria was

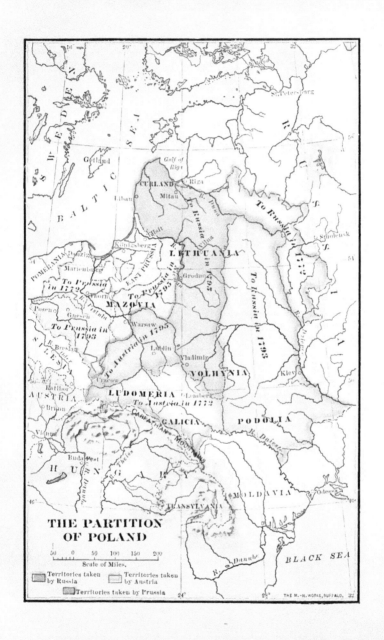

THE M.-N. WORKS, BUFFALO.

THE PARTITION
OF POLAND

Scale of Miles.

Territories taken
by Russia

Territories taken
by Austria

Territories taken by Prussia

assigned a strip inhabited by almost three million Poles and Russians and thus added two new kinds of people and two new languages to her already varied collection of races and tongues. Prussia was given a smaller piece, but it was the coveted West Prussia which she needed to fill out her boundaries, and its inhabitants were to a considerable extent Germans and Protestants. Russia's strip on the east was inhabited entirely by Russians. The Polish diet was forced, by the advance of Russian troops to Warsaw, to approve the partition. First partition of Poland, 1772

This outrageous mutilation of an ancient kingdom, which had once been one of the most important in Europe, awakened general indignation and touched the seared consciences of men who had become accustomed to see thousands of soldiers killed and hundreds of towns sacked in order to secure a trifling addition of territory to France or a throne for the queen of Spain's son. Even those who had shared the booty showed signs of shame, especially Maria Theresa, who wept while she reached out her hand for her share. But this first dismemberment of Poland was only the prelude to its complete extinction and to other equally scandalous and violent depredations during the French Revolution and Napoleonic periods, as will appear in good time. Europe shocked by the partition of Poland

Poland seemed at first, however, to have learned a great lesson from the disaster. During the twenty years following its first dismemberment there was an extraordinary revival in education, art, and literature; the old universities at Vilna and Cracow were reorganized and many new schools established. King Stanislas Poniatowski summoned French and Italian artists and entered into correspondence with the French philosophers and reformers. Historians and poets sprang up to give distinction to the last days of Polish independence. The old intolerance and bigotry decreased and, above all, the constitution which had made Poland the laughingstock and the victim of its neighbors was abolished and an entirely new one worked out. Revival of Poland, 1772–1791

The new Polish constitution, approved on May 3, 1791, did away with the *liberum veto*, made the crown hereditary, established a parliament something like that of England — in short, gave to the king power enough to conduct the government efficiently and yet made him and his ministers dependent upon the representatives of the nation.

There was a party, however, which regretted the changes and feared that they might result in time in doing away with the absolute control of the nobles over the peasants. These opponents of reform appealed to Catharine for aid. She, mindful as always of her own interests, denounced all changes in a government " under which the Polish republic had flourished for so many centuries," and declared that the reformers were no better than the abhorred French Jacobins who were busy destroying the power of their king.[1] She sent her soldiers and her wild Cossacks into Poland, and the enemies of the new constitution were able with her help to undo all that had been done and to reëstablish the *liberum veto*.

Not satisfied with plunging Poland into its former anarchy, Russia and Prussia determined to rob her of still more territory. Frederick the Great's successor, Frederick William II, ordered his forces across his eastern boundary on the ground that Danzig was sending grain to the French Revolutionists, that Poland was infested with Jacobins, and that, in general, she threatened the tranquillity of her neighbors. Prussia cut deep into Poland, added a million and a half of Poles to her subjects and acquired the towns of Thorn, Danzig, and Posen. Russia's gains were three millions of people, who at least belonged to her own race. On this occasion Austria was put off with the promises of her confederates, Russia and Prussia, that they would use their good offices to secure Bavaria for her in exchange for the Austrian Netherlands.

At this juncture the Poles found a national leader in the brave Kosciusco, who had fought under Washington for American

The new Polish constitution of 1791

Catharine frustrates the reform

Second partition of Poland, 1793

[1] See below, sect. 37.

liberty. With the utmost care and secrecy, he organized an in-surrection in the spring of 1794 and summoned the Polish people to join his standard of national independence. The Poles who had been incorporated into the Prussian monarchy thereupon rose and forced Frederick William to withdraw his forces.

Revolt of Poles under Kosciusco, 1794

Catharine was ready, however, to crush the patriots. Kos-ciusco was wounded and captured in battle, and by the end of the year Russia was in control of Warsaw. The Polish king was compelled to abdicate, and the remnants of the dismembered kingdom were divided, after much bitter contention, among Austria, Russia, and Prussia. In the three partitions which blotted out the kingdom of Poland from the map of Europe, Russia received nearly all of the old grand duchy of Lithuania, or nearly twice the combined shares of Austria and Prussia.

Third and final partition, 1795

REFERENCES

The Youth of Frederick the Great: HENDERSON, *Short History of Germany*, Vol. II, pp. 111–122.

Maria Theresa and the First Silesian War: HENDERSON, Vol. II, pp. 123–148; KITCHIN, *History of France*, Vol. III, pp. 409–425; PERKINS, *France under Louis XV*, Vol. I, pp. 164–205, 346–378; BRIGHT, *Maria Theresa*, pp. 1–63.

Walpole and the Spanish War: GREEN, *Short History of the English People*, chap. ix, pp. 732–734; MORLEY, *Walpole*.

Frederick the Great and the Seven Years' War: HASSALL, *European History, 1715–1789*, pp. 241–279; KITCHIN, Vol. III, pp. 445–468; PERKINS, Vol. II, pp. 85–177; HENDERSON, Vol. II, pp. 149–181; BRIGHT, pp. 135–187.

Pitt and the Seven Years' War: GREEN, chap. x, pp. 735–757.

Poland in the Eighteenth Century: RAMBAUD, *History of Russia*, Vol. II, pp. 184–192; MORFILL, *Poland*.

The Partition of Poland: HASSALL, pp. 312–318; RAMBAUD, Vol. II, pp. 192–197, 232–245; PERKINS, Vol. II, pp. 285–309.

Final Destruction of Poland: *Cambridge Modern History*, Vol. VIII, chap. xvii; STEPHENS, *European History, 1789–1815*, pp. 103–105, 151–153.

Catharine II: RAMBAUD, Vol. II, pp. 183–247; BURY, *Catherine II* (Foreign Statesmen Series).

CHAPTER VI

THE STRUGGLE BETWEEN FRANCE AND ENGLAND FOR INDIA

How Europe began to extend its Commerce over the Whole World

16. The long and disastrous wars of the eighteenth century which we have been reviewing seem, from the standpoint of the changes they produced in Europe, to have been scarcely worth our attention. It was not a vital question in the world's history whether a member of the House of Bourbon or of the House of Hapsburg sat on the throne of Spain, whether Silesia belonged to Frederick or Maria Theresa, or even whether Poland continued to exist or not. But alongside of these contentions among the various dynasties and these shiftings of territory were other interests far beyond the confines of Europe, and to these we must now turn.

The history of Europe only to be explained by the history of Europe's colonies

Constant wars have been waged during the past two centuries by the European nations in their efforts to extend and defend their distant possessions. The War of the Spanish Succession concerned the trade as well as the throne of Spain. The internal affairs of each country have been constantly influenced by the demands of its merchants and the achievements of its sailors and soldiers, fighting rival nations or alien peoples thousands of miles from London, Paris, or Vienna. The great manufacturing towns of England — Leeds, Manchester, and Birmingham — owe their prosperity to India, China, and Australia. Liverpool, Amsterdam, and Hamburg, with their long lines of docks and warehouses and their fleets of merchant vessels, would dwindle away if their trade were confined to the demands of their European neighbors. It was in the eighteenth century that European history became linked for the first time with world history.

Europe includes scarcely a twelfth of the land upon the globe and yet over three fifths of the world is to-day either occupied by peoples of European origin or ruled by European states. The possessions of France in Asia and Africa exceed the entire area of Europe ; even the little kingdom of the Netherlands administers a colonial dominion three times the size of the German Empire. The British Empire, of which the island of Great Britain constitutes but a hundredth part, includes one fifth of the world's dry land. Moreover European peoples have populated the United States, which is nearly as large as all of Europe, and rule all of Mexico and South America. Vast extent of the European colonial dominion

In the present chapter the origin of European coloniza- tion will be briefly explained, as well as the manner in which England succeeded in extending her sway over the teeming millions of India. In the next chapter we shall review Eng- land's victory over France in the western hemisphere. In this way the real meaning of the Seven Years' War will become clear.

The widening of the field of European history is one of the most striking features of modern times. Though the Greeks and Romans carried on a large trade in silks, spices, and pre- cious stones with India and China, they really knew little of the world beyond southern Europe, northern Africa, and western Asia, and much that they knew was forgotten during the Middle Ages. Slowly, however, the interest in the East revived and travelers began to add to the scanty knowledge handed down from antiquity. Narrow limits of the ancient and mediæval world

The Crusades took many Europeans as far east as Egypt and Syria. In the latter part of the thirteenth century two Venetian merchants, the Polo brothers, visited China and were kindly received at Pekin by the emperor of the Mongols. On a second journey they were accompanied by Marco Polo, the son of one of the brothers. When he got safely back to Venice Travels of Marco Polo in the thirteenth century in 1295, after a journey of twenty years, Marco gave an account of his experiences which filled his readers with wonder. Nothing stimulated the interest of the West in the East more than his fabulous description of the golden island of Zipango (Japan) and of the spice markets of the Moluccas and Ceylon.

About the same year Venice and Genoa opened up direct communication by sea with the towns of the Netherlands and with England. Their fleets touched at the ports of Lisbon and aroused the commercial enterprise of the Portuguese, who soon began to undertake extended maritime expeditions. By the middle of the fourteenth century they had discovered the Canary Islands, Madeira, and the Azores. Before this time no one had ventured along the coast of Africa beyond the arid region of the Sahara. The country was forbidding, there were no ports, and mariners, moreover, were discouraged in their progress by the general belief that the torrid region was uninhabitable. In 1445, however, some adventurous sailors came in sight of a headland beyond the desert and, struck by its luxuriant growth of tropical trees, they called it Cape Verde (the green cape). Its discovery put an end once for all to the idea that there were only parched deserts to the south.

For a generation longer the Portuguese continued to venture farther and farther along the coast in the hope of finding it coming to an end so that they might make their way by sea to India. At last, in 1486, Diaz rounded the Cape of Good Hope. Twelve years later (1498) Vasco da Gama, spurred on by Columbus's great discovery, after sailing around the Cape of Good Hope and northward beyond Zanzibar, steered straight across the Indian Ocean and reached Calicut in India by sea, thus opening up a new trade route of which Portuguese sailors, under the direction of the government, were not slow to take advantage.

As fleet after fleet of Portuguese merchantmen appeared in Eastern waters, they excited the natural suspicion of the Mohammedan merchants who had long enjoyed a monopoly

The Voyages of Discovery

of the trade between the East Indies and the eastern ports of the Mediterranean, where the products were handed over to Italian merchants to distribute to Western nations. They were unable, however, to drive the newcomers away. So for a long time the Portuguese held a preëminent place as a maritime power and had the satisfaction of seeing the Italian towns decay as Lisbon grew in wealth and importance. They occupied Muscat in Arabia, Ormuz at the entrance of the Persian Gulf, Goa, Calicut, and other points on the Indian peninsula and the shores of the neighboring island of Ceylon.

The Portuguese were, however, by no means content with supplanting the Mohammedan merchants in the Indian Ocean. Albuquerque got control of Malacca in 1511 and sent on three ships through the narrow straits into the mysterious Malay Archipelago whence came the specially rare spices, nutmeg and cloves. The adventurous mariners crossed the equator, skirted along Sumatra and Java, and, passing the great island of Borneo, finally reached their goal, the Moluccas or Spice Islands *par excellence*, which lie two thousand miles beyond the straits of Malacca.[1]

In order to give a just idea of the vast extent of the Malay Archipelago a little map on the following page shows the outlines of the United States superimposed upon the region which lies between the Andaman Islands and the Spice Islands. It will be observed that it is about as far from the western point of Sumatra to the western point of New Guinea as from Portland, Maine, to San Francisco, that is, some three thousand

---

[1] There is no doubt that the desire to obtain spices was the main reason for the exploration of the globe. This motive led European navigators to try in succession every possible way to reach the East — by going around Africa, by sailing west in the hope of reaching the Indies, before they knew of the existence of America; then, after America was discovered, by sailing around it to the north or south, and even sailing around Europe to the north. It is hard for us to understand this enthusiasm for spices, for which we care much less nowadays. One former use of spices was to preserve food, which could not then, as now, be carried rapidly, while still fresh, from place to place; nor did our conveniences then exist for keeping it by the use of ice. Moreover, spice served to make even spoiled food more palatable than it would otherwise have been.

miles. The island of Sumatra is a good deal larger than Great Britain and Ireland, and Borneo considerably exceeds in size the whole of France or of the present German Empire. Java, which is but a little smaller than England and Wales, has a population now of nearly thirty millions. The other islands are, however, much less densely populated, and much of Borneo is still unexplored to the present day. Australia scarcely attracted

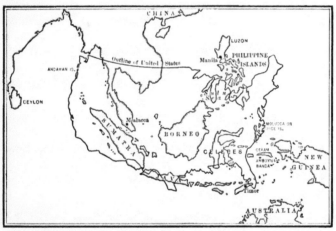

The Malay Archipelago as compared with the Area of
the United States

the attention of the early navigators, and it was left for England to occupy that continent in the nineteenth century and establish flourishing colonies there.[1]

In accordance with the spirit of the time the Portuguese sought to monopolize their new trade and exclude all other nations. They succeeded in this only for a short time. The Dutch, who had learned something of the profits of the spice trade by distributing among the northern ports of Europe the products which the Portuguese ships landed at Lisbon, decided to engage in the Eastern trade on their own account. Portugal

The Dutch supplant the Portuguese in the seventeenth century

[1] See below, sect. 90.

found itself at a serious disadvantage in the contest with the Dutch, for she had come under the Spanish crown in 1580 and the Spanish were much more interested in the gold and silver mines of America than in the trade with the East. They did not have ships enough to police the seas of two hemispheres, especially after the English had destroyed their mighty Armada in 1588. The Dutch had therefore little to fear from the Portuguese when, in 1595, they sent out their first expedition to India. They rapidly established trading houses and seized one by one the most favorable stations which the Portuguese had selected and occupied, until by the close of the seventeenth century only Goa and a few minor trading posts remained from the vast commercial empire which the Portuguese had built up.[1]

Origin of the English East India Company

Meanwhile the energetic Dutch discovered redoubtable competitors in the English, who were not inclined to sit idly by and have their neighbors reap an enormous profit from the products which they brought to England to sell. As early as 1591 some English traders had sent out an expedition of their own from Plymouth and, although it was not successful, other merchants, in London, were not daunted, for in 1600 they organized the English East India Company and secured a charter from Queen Elizabeth. This company was given a monopoly of the Indian trade, authorized to make rules for its own government, to secure trading posts, and to defend its own interests.

Nature of the early rivalry among the trading companies

The organization of companies by the English, Dutch, and French was rendered necessary by reason of the considerable capital required in fitting out ships and maintaining numerous trading stations; and also on account of the jealousy which existed among the traders of the various European nations. The doors of a great treasure-house had been thrown open, and the share which each was to get depended on his prowess and

---

[1] These points the Portuguese managed to hold through the wars and revolutions of the eighteenth and nineteenth centuries and they retain in the East to-day Goa and Diu in India, Timor in the Malay Archipelago, Macao near Hongkong, and two or three minor stations.

fighting strength. Whatever the terms of their charters, the great companies were practically licensed to wage war against one another, and they equipped their vessels with guns and men to carry on naval and land operations.[1]

Private warfare for trade

ENGLAND GAINS A FOOTHOLD IN INDIA

17. It was therefore really a war for trade into which the English company entered when it sent out its first fleet in 1601 under the command of James Lancaster. The expedition reached Sumatra in June of the following year, and, after the ships were loaded with spices from the Moluccas, it was decided to establish an English station at Bantam in Java. Other voyages followed at intervals of from two to three years, and in 1612 the English, after defeating the Portuguese at sea near Surat, on the west coast of Hindustan, were permitted to establish a trading center there. Four years later Jehangir, the Great Mogul of India, was induced by Sir Thomas Roe, the ambassador of King James I, to permit the English merchants to live and trade in his kingdoms. He gives a general command that " what goods soever they desire to sell or buy they may have free liberty without any restraint ; and at what port soever they shall arrive, that neither Portugal nor any other shall dare to molest their quiet ; and in what city soever they shall have residence, I have commanded all my governors and captains to give them freedom answerable to their own desires, to sell, buy, and to transport into their country at their pleasure." [2]

The Great Mogul permits the English merchants to trade freely in India, 1616

---

[1] So general was the recognition of this private warfare among the merchants of the different nations that Spain and France, in a treaty in 1598, frankly stipulated that everything west of the Canary Islands should be left to the test of force. In 1622, when England and Portugal were at peace, the agents of the English company at Surat fitted out a small fleet, sailed to Ormuz, bombarded the town, took the Portuguese on board their ships, and transferred them to Goa. This wanton act, which apparently caused no trouble at home, would to-day be regarded as a just cause of war.

[2] See whole of this letter from Jehangir to James I in *Readings*, sect. 17.

Originally the English had no idea of conquering any part
of Hindustan. They did no more than establish agencies, or
" factories," [1] as they were called. These were trading settlements where one would find a great warehouse in which were
stored the goods brought from England for sale in India, and
the Indian commodities which the native merchants, or the
Englishmen who penetrated into the interior, collected to be
shipped to England. Around the warehouse were the houses
of the agents of the East India Company built in a fashion
more suited to European needs than were the native dwellings.
Sometimes the entire settlement was surrounded by fortifications, especially after it was found that the richly stocked warehouses might be sacked by native marauders. About 1640 the
English established a factory at Hugli, near the mouths of the
Ganges in Bengal, one of the richest of the Indian provinces.[2]
About the same time they built Fort St. George at Madras,
nearly a thousand miles down the coast, on the first land
actually acquired by them.

As has been said, it was the Dutch, not the Portuguese, who
were the most serious rivals of the English merchants, especially when the latter sent their ships three thousand miles to
the eastward of India to the Spice Islands, where they proposed
to get their share of the nutmeg, mace, and cloves. The Dutch
claimed exclusive rights to the particularly precious islands of
Banda and Amboyna, where the rarest spices grew; and for a
time they seemed to have the advantage. They owned more
than half of the merchant ships of Europe, and consequently
Rotterdam and Amsterdam enjoyed a great part of the profits
which resulted from carrying goods to the East and then
returning to supply England and the ports of the continent
with the spices, precious stones, ivory, and rich fabrics of
the Orient.

[1] Derived from "factor," which means "agent," especially a commission
merchant.

[2] This station was later transferred to Calcutta, a few miles away.

Oliver Cromwell, during his brief period of power, tried to reduce the Dutch trade and encourage English shipping by the Navigation Act which Parliament passed in 1651. This provided that only English vessels should be permitted to bring to England commodities produced in Asia, Africa, or America. The result was a short, brisk commercial war between the Dutch and the English, fought at sea, in which sometimes one fleet, sometimes the other, gained the upper hand. This conflict is notable as the first example of a distinctly commercial struggle. Nations were beginning to go to war over trade instead of over religion. The Navigation Act of 1651

On the restoration of Charles II in 1660, the English, after almost twenty years of civil war and disorder, were ready to devote themselves more seriously to the defending and extending of their trade and their colonies in the East and the West. The king granted a new charter to the East India Company which gave it a monopoly of the trade with the right to coin money, administer justice, punish independent English merchants who sailed ships into eastern waters on their own account, and finally to wage war and make peace with non-Christian states. Cromwell's Navigation Act was reënforced by additional provisions to the effect that not only must the ships be owned and manned by Englishmen but they must be English-built as well; and English agents were ordered to prevent the Dutch from getting any of the English trade. Charles II also dispatched troops to the company's settlements to help defend them against attacks from Europeans and natives. He also turned over to the company the town of Bombay, which his Portuguese wife had brought him as her dowry. This soon (1685) became the headquarters of the company (instead of Surat) and is now the second greatest emporium of Indian trade. The English government favors the East India Company

The old war with Holland, begun under Cromwell, was renewed under Charles II. The two nations were very evenly matched on the sea, but in 1664 the English succeeded in seizing some of the West Indian Islands from the Dutch as Second commercial war with Holland well as their colony upon Manhattan Island, which was renamed New York in honor of the king's brother, the duke of York. On the other hand, the Dutch expelled the English from their last foothold in the Spice Islands (1667). Five years later Charles II was induced by his friend Louis XIV to attack the Dutch once more, — those "eternal enemies" of England, who were to be utterly destroyed as Carthage had been blotted out by the Romans.

Dutch and English ally themselves against France

But the war, as we have already seen, resulted in a victory for the Dutch,[1] who soon joined the English against the menacing power of Louis XIV and in 1688 sent their stadholder over to occupy the vacant English throne. Their strength had, however, been exhausted in the long wars with Louis XIV and they gave up the attempt to oppose England in India. Yet, although they no longer dominated the seas as they had earlier done, the Dutch still held important possessions and enjoyed a flourishing trade at the opening of the eighteenth century.

The Dutch during the eighteenth century

The business of their East India Company was so profitable and the dividends so large that the stock continued to be rated at two or three times its original value. The Dutch held the Cape of Good Hope, which they had taken as a half-way post on the way to India, the island of Ceylon, some important centers on the mainland of India, actual dominion or predominance in the Spice Islands, Java, Sumatra, Borneo, Celebes, the Malaccan peninsula, and Siam. They monopolized the European trade with Japan and the greater portion of the spice business. Nevertheless their advance was checked, and it was not they but the French who were now to fight with England for the control of India and North America.[2]

---

[1] See above, p. 21.

[2] In spite of the severe losses growing out of the wars at the close of the eighteenth and beginning of the nineteenth centuries, the Dutch now hold Java, Sumatra, Celebes, the Molucca Islands, portions of Borneo, and other islands in the East, comprising an area of over 700,000 square miles with a population of some 36,000,000.

The ambitions of Louis XIV had not been confined to punishing the Dutch, making "reunions" at the expense of his neighbors, and assuring the Spanish throne to his grandson. In 1664, under the influence of Colbert, the king chartered the French East India Company, granting it a monopoly of trade for fifty years, the right to cast cannons, raise troops, and garrison posts, and to declare war and make peace in the name of their sovereign. The king also assisted the company with large grants from the royal treasury in overcoming the difficulties which the enterprise necessarily involved.[1] *How France established herself in India*

In 1669 the first French expedition under the new company arrived at Surat where they established a factory beside those of the English and Portuguese, from which they sent out their agents in every direction. Three years later the French became the rivals of the English in Bengal by fortifying themselves at Chandarnagar just north of Calcutta. They also purchased from the ruler of the Carnatic, on the eastern shores of the Deccan, a plot of ground of about one hundred and thirteen acres, upon which was the village of Pondicherry, destined to be the capital of the French dominions in India.[2] *Extent of French holdings in India*

In order to follow the approaching struggle between the English and French companies for the control of India, we must pause a moment to consider this extraordinary country and the conditions which existed at the opening of the eighteenth century.

INDIA AND THE STRUGGLE BETWEEN ENGLAND AND FRANCE FOR ITS POSSESSION

18. India was neither a group of half-savage islands nor, like North America, a sparsely inhabited region awaiting development; it was a vast empire, swarming with millions of people,

[1] For fifty or sixty years French merchants had been going to India; and Richelieu had reorganized a company which had been established as early as 1604. It is unnecessary to say more of these beginnings.

[2] They had also a factory at Masulipatam and minor stations at Calicut, Golconda, and a few other points.

the seat of an ancient and highly elaborate civilization. It had given birth to philosophies and religions which had dominated the lives of myriads of men not only in India itself but in China and Japan. Geographically, India occupies the triangular peninsula which juts southward from the continent of Asia and is shut in by lofty mountain ranges from the countries to the north and west. One may gain an idea of its extent by laying the map of Hindustan upon that of the United States. If the southernmost point, Cape Comorin, be placed over New Orleans, Calcutta will lie nearly over New York City, and Bombay in the neighborhood of Des Moines, Iowa.

Geographical divisions of Hindustan

The Indian peninsula is separated into three great divisions. In the extreme north are the regions of the Himalaya Mountains and their foothills. South of these are plains and the valleys of a network of rivers draining into the mighty Ganges, which flows southeastward for fifteen hundred miles into the Bay of Bengal, refreshing and fertilizing one of the most thickly populated districts of the world. The third region is the table-land of southern India, broken in many places, especially near the seacoast, by minor mountain ranges and principally drained by rivers running eastward into the Bay of Bengal.

Climate and products of India

While all variations of climate may be found in India, from the extreme heat of the tropical regions near the equator to the temperate climate of the north and the eternal winter of the Himalayas, generally speaking the heat and humidity of the atmosphere make the country rather unsuited to men accustomed to the colder and drier climes of the North. India yields almost all the mineral and vegetable products which are the objects of modern commerce. The northern valleys of the Ganges and its tributaries furnish cotton, tobacco, indigo, spices, dyes, opium, silk, rice, and grain; while the southern table-lands, in addition to grain and cotton, afford a variety of minerals and precious stones, among which are the famous diamonds of Golconda.

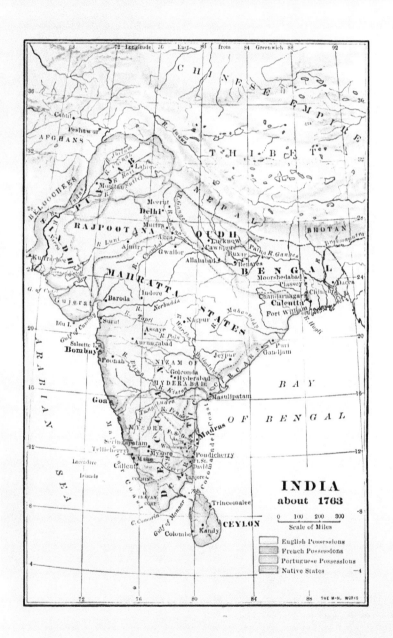

INDIA
about 1763

0   100   200   300
Scale of Miles

English Possessions
French Possessions
Portuguese Possessions
Native States

India has long been and still is the home of many peoples, The various peoples of India differing greatly in race, language, religion, and civilization, from the dog-faced man-eaters of the Bay of Bengal to the highly cultivated and spiritual Brahmins. At the bottom of the scale are the miserable inhabitants of the Andaman Islands, living almost without clothes and shelter, and exhibiting few signs of intelligence.

The Hindus form the most important portion of the popu- The Hindus lation. They speak various dialects derived from the ancient Sanskrit, a language related to Greek and Latin. They penetrated into India in the remote past and drove the original inhabitants into the mountains or reduced them to servitude. The Hindus developed a noble literature, which is studied in the universities of western Europe, and their religious teachings find adherents to-day in England and America. It was they who appear to have invented the nine arithmetical figures and the cipher, which are now used throughout the civilized world.

The Hindus are separated into rigid social classes or The castes "castes," the highest being that of the Brahmins, or priests, a class which furnishes the poets, lawgivers, and scholars ; the Rajputs or warriors come next ; then the Vaisyas or husbandmen and merchants. Lowest of all are the Pariahs, who are not supposed to belong to any *caste* but are regarded as mere *outcasts* from society. Familiar association between those of different castes is regarded as sinful, and one can never escape from the group into which one is born. Besides the Hindus there are many Mohammedans who have swept into India from the north in wave after wave, adding to the general confusion of races and religions.

A generation after Vasco da Gama landed in Calicut, a Mongolian conqueror, Baber,[1] had established his empire in

[1] Baber claimed to be descended from an earlier invader, the famous Timur (or Tamerlane), who died in 1405. The so-called Mongol (or Mogul) emperors were really Turkish rather than Mongolian in origin. A very interesting account of them and their enlightenment may be found in Holden, *The Mogul Emperors of Hindustan.*

The Mongolian emperors of Hindustan
India. The dynasty of Mongolian rulers which he founded had been able to keep the whole country under its control for nearly two centuries; but in 1707 Aurangzeb, the last Mongolian emperor of importance, died. In his old age he saw that anarchy would come after he was gone and he wrote a sad letter to a friend in which he bemoaned a wasted life.[1]

Subahdars, nawabs, and rajahs
He was right in his forebodings, for his empire fell apart in much the same way as that of Charlemagne had done. Like the counts and dukes of the Carolingian period, the emperor's officials, the subahdars and nawabs (nabobs), and the rajahs— i.e. the Hindu princes temporarily subjugated by the Mongols — gradually got the power in their respective districts into their own hands. Although the emperor, or Great Mogul, as the English called him, continued to maintain himself in his capital of Delhi, he could no longer be said to rule the country at the opening of the eighteenth century when the French and English were seriously beginning to turn their attention to his coasts.

Dupleix plans to conquer India for France
The real situation in India had long been apparent to the French governors, and in 1741 when Dupleix, the most remarkable of them, received his appointment, he openly adopted the policy of establishing French power by allying himself with the native rulers and playing them off one against another. He strongly fortified the French capital, Pondicherry. He assumed princely titles granted him by the Great Mogul and introduced Oriental pomp into his processions and ceremonies. As he had but few soldiers, he enlisted great numbers of natives —a custom which was also quickly adopted on a large scale by the English. These native soldiers, whom the English called
The sepoys
"sepoys," were taught to fight in the manner of the Europeans and, under the sterner discipline of western military rules, soon developed into capable soldiers, especially when supported by some European officers and privates.

[1] See *Readings*, sect. 18.

During the wars which raged in Europe over the realms of Maria Theresa, the French and English East India companies were also fighting to extend their power. One question at issue was whether the French or the English candidate should become nawab of the Carnatic. Dupleix appeared at first to have the advantage over the English, but his magnificent plan of creating a vast French colonial empire in India was frustrated by an English commander of even greater genius than his. This was Robert Clive, who had become a clerk in the service of the English company at Madras in 1744. He had discovered that the sword was more to his taste than the quill of the bookkeeper and had taken service in the army when hostilities with the French broke out. His skill in organizing the native troops was such that Dupleix was unable to maintain his reputation and was recalled to France in disgrace in 1754.

The final crisis in India came in 1756 when France, casting in her fortunes with Austria, was forced to wage war at one and the same time with Prussia on land and England on the sea. The French government dispatched Count Lally to India with a large force for the purpose of destroying the English settlements along the Madras coast. Though for a time successful, he was finally beaten and his fleet disorganized and driven away, so that the French land forces were not supported from the sea as were the English. Count Lally was hopelessly defeated at the decisive battle of Wandewash in 1760 and fell back to Pondicherry where, blockaded by land and sea, he was compelled the next year to surrender the French capital in India. The dream cherished by Dupleix was now dispelled and never again were the French seriously to menace the rising power of England in India.

The treaty of Paris of 1763, which brought the Seven Years' War to a close, returned Pondicherry to France, as well as the other posts which she had held prior to Dupleix's territorial gains, but these posts were not to be fortified and French troops could not be stationed in Bengal, the seat of the growing

Marginal notes:

Dupleix fights the English

Robert Clive

The Seven Years' War in India

Battle of Wandewash, 1760

End of French political power in India

power of England. France ceased to be a rival in the contest for the possession of the peninsula and the English were left free scope in the work of conquering and ruling India.[1]

Clive and Surajah Dowlah

While the troops of the English East India Company under their able commander, Clive, were successfully fighting the French under Lally, they were also beginning the conquest of Bengal. This important province on the Ganges was under one of the Great Mogul's nawabs, or viceroys, whose seat of government was at Moorshedabad, about a hundred miles north of Calcutta. With the decline of the Mogul's power, the nawab had become practically independent. Now the English, in their anxiety to get the better of their French enemies, had taken the liberty of fortifying their posts in the nawab's possessions without obtaining his consent. This gave offense to the new nawab, Surajah Dowlah, a headstrong young fellow who had just come into power. The English further irritated him by giving shelter to his relatives, who were fleeing from his wrath.

The "Black Hole of Calcutta"

Surajah Dowlah thereupon marched upon Calcutta, seized some of the property of the company, and shut up one hundred and forty-five Englishmen in a little room about eighteen feet square, with only two small windows. Whether the nawab had really intended to destroy the unfortunate prisoners or not, only twenty-three of them staggered out of the dungeon when the door was opened the following morning. This tragedy of the "Black Hole of Calcutta," as it was called, raised a cry for revenge on the part of the English and a call for help was immediately sent to Madras, where Clive was stationed with some troops.[2]

Clive wins the battle of Plassey, 1757

In response to this call, Clive hastened at once to Bengal by sea and, by show of force, compelled Surajah Dowlah to restore the English prisoners and make compensation for the

[1] The French still have ten posts in India aggregating about two hundred square miles, with the old town of Pondicherry as their capital. The colony has a governor and is represented in the French Parliament by a senator and one deputy.
[2] See *Readings*, sect. 18.

injuries he had inflicted. Not content with this achievement, Clive seized the French settlement at Chandarnagar in the nawab's dominions, whereupon Surajah Dowlah allied himself with the French against the English. The quarrel was finally decided at the battle of Plassey where Clive, with about nine hundred English soldiers and two thousand sepoys, defeated the nawab's force of nearly fifty thousand natives aided by a few French.

After the great victory of Plassey, Surajah Dowlah was deposed and murdered and Clive's nominee was proclaimed nawab on condition of rewarding his English friends with enormous gifts from Surajah Dowlah's treasury. The new nawab proved unsatisfactory however, despite his liberality, and he was deposed in favor of another nominee of the English who, to their surprise, showed such independence when he got into power that they were forced to make war upon him in order to reduce him to submission. Like the war with Surajah Dowlah, this new conflict turned out in favor of the English in spite of the fact that the Great Mogul came to the aid of his nominal vassal. At the battle of Buxar, the Mogul himself was captured and compelled to grant to the company the right to administer his imperial revenues in Bengal. This meant that, for all practical purposes, the victors became governors of this vast region, though a nominal nawab was retained in office. **English control established in Bengal**

Thus by a series of unexpected events, a trading company was transformed into a great governing body supporting thousands of soldiers, waging war, making treaties, acquiring territory, administering a portion of the Great Mogul's finances, and enjoying immense revenues from taxes and trading monopolies. Exceptional advantages for enriching themselves were now offered to the agents of the company in India because the directors, ten thousand miles away, could exercise very little control over officials, traders, and agents in a strange land with no strong government to keep the foreigners in order. **Corruption among the agents of the East India Company**

The English
government
begins to con-
trol the East
India Com-
pany
Huge fortunes were consequently accumulated rapidly
through corruption and by exploiting the defenseless natives;
penniless young men who had gone out in the service of the
company returned to England in ten or twelve years in the
possession of such wealth as to excite the astonishment of
the English people at home.[1] Clive himself was poor when he
first entered the employ of the company, but at the age of
thirty-four he enjoyed an income of forty thousand pounds a
year and yet regarded himself as moderate in his accumula-
tions. He frankly declared that the evil of corruption was
contagious in India and that it had spread among the civil
and military employees down to the lowest rank.

Strange as it may seem, in spite of its remarkable achievements and the trading advantages it had won, the East India
Company was sadly in debt and was confronted by the most
difficult problems in managing its unwieldy undertakings.
This state of affairs, coupled with the conduct of the company's agents in India and the news of a terrible famine in
Bengal in 1770, which destroyed nearly one half of the population, called the attention of the British government to the
necessity of exercising a stricter supervision over the English
enterprises in India. Parliament thereupon vested the control of Bombay and Madras in the hands of a governor and
four councilors in Bengal, to be appointed by Parliament in
the first instance, and by the directors of the East India Company thereafter, but always subject to the approval of the
crown. The measure also provided that all reports sent to
London by the company's agents should be open to inspection
by the British government.

The English possessions were surrounded by the domains
of native rulers, great and small, who had ordinarily risen to
power through military prowess and were liable to sudden and
violent overthrow. The peninsula was thus kept in a constant

[1] Those who returned from India to spend their ill-gotten gains in London
were popularly known as "nabobs." They often figure in Thackeray's novels.

state of turmoil and there could be no hope of peace until some one power suppressed the petty rulers. Warren Hastings became governor general of India in 1774. For various reasons, for which he was not always responsible, his administration was filled with military conflicts with the natives, although the company was not intent on extending its possessions. Serious accusations of cruelty and misgovernment were brought against him, and on his return to England in 1788 he was impeached by the House of Commons, the charges being presented in a long and impassioned speech by the celebrated orator, Burke.[1] This famous trial dragged on for seven years and finally ended in the acquittal of Hastings.

Impeachment of Hastings

The extensive wars in which the company was engaged during Hastings's administration led Parliament in 1784 to assume a more direct management of Indian affairs. A board appointed by the king was to reside in England, supervise the civil, military, and financial transactions of the company and examine their accounts and reports. In matters pertaining to the expenditure of revenue, to diplomacy, peace and war, power was vested in the governor general and three advisers appointed by the company with the king's approval and liable to be dismissed by him at will. This meant that the highest authority in India was thereafter to be in the hands of officials whose choice was practically determined by Parliament.[2]

Parliament controls the British government in India after 1784

Although, in assuming control of the political affairs of the company, Parliament distinctly repudiated any intention of making further conquests in India, the governor generals who

Increase of British possessions in India

[1] Later writers defend Hastings against the charges advanced by Burke, and seem to agree that only his heroic measures could have saved India for the English. See Lyall, *Warren Hastings*, in English Men of Action Series.

[2] The first of the governors under the new arrangement was Lord Cornwallis, who retrieved in war and government in India the reputation he had lost in the unhappy conflict with the American colonies. The third governor general, Lord Wellesley, with the assistance of his more famous brother, later Duke of Wellington, carried forward the policy which Cornwallis and his predecessors had found unavoidable, and steadily annexed new territories whose rulers had disturbed the English rule. See below, chap. xxvii.

were sent out found themselves irresistibly drawn into wars by the restlessness of native rulers whose domains bordered on the English possessions. By 1805 the British dominion had been extended far up the Ganges valley, southward along the eastern coast, and over a great portion of the southern end of the peninsula.

REFERENCES

The Mohammedan Empire in India : HUNTER, *A Brief History of the Indian Peoples*, pp. 132–155 ; LYALL, *Rise of British Dominion in India*, pp. 32–37, 50–53.

Early Rivalry for the Indian Trade : LYALL, pp. 1–23 ; HUNTER, pp. 164–175.

Dupleix and French Dominion in India : LYALL, pp. 59–84 ; PERKINS, *France under Louis XV*, Vol. I, pp. 379–430.

The Seven Years' War in India : LYALL, pp. 85–97 ; PERKINS, Vol. I, pp. 431–453.

Clive and English Conquests in Bengal : LYALL, pp. 98–111, 130–136 ; HUNTER, pp. 176–186 ; COLBY, *Selections from the Sources of English History*, pp. 245–247 ; WILSON, *Clive* (English Men of Action Series).

Warren Hastings as Governor General : LYALL, pp. 157–178 ; HUNTER, pp. 186–190 ; LYALL, *Warren Hastings* (English Men of Action Series).

CHAPTER VII

THE RIVALRY OF FRANCE AND ENGLAND IN NORTH AMERICA

How the European Nations established themselves in the New World

19. While the Portuguese, Dutch, English, and French merchants and trading companies were busy in India and the Spice Islands establishing trading posts, fighting one another, and gradually conquering territory, a new world on the other side of the globe was being opened up which was to exercise a great influence upon European affairs. We must now turn to the discovery and settlement of the western hemisphere.

All through the Middle Ages scholars had known that the earth was a globe although, like the ancient geographers, they somewhat underrated its size, and supposed it to be about one sixth smaller than it is. It was inevitable therefore that, just when the Portuguese navigators were creeping gradually down the African coast with the expectation of getting around it and reaching the Orient by sea, it should have occurred to other adventurous mariners to try to reach Asia and the Spice Islands by sailing westward. This plan seemed the more promising since Marco Polo and other travelers had given an exaggerated idea of the distance which they had traveled eastward, and it was supposed that it could not be a very long journey from Europe across the Atlantic to Japan. *The earth known during the Middle Ages to be a globe*

In the year 1492, as we all know, a Genoese navigator, Columbus, who had had much experience on the sea, got together three little ships and undertook the journey westward to Zipango, or Japan, which he hoped to reach in five *Columbus discovers America, 1492* weeks. Thirty-six days from the time he left the Canary Islands he came upon land, the island of San Salvador, and believed himself to be in the East Indies. Going on from there he discovered the island of Cuba, which he believed to be the mainland of Asia, and then Haiti, which he mistook for the longed-for Zipango. Although he made three later expeditions and sailed down the coast of South America as far as the Orinoco, he died without realizing that he had not been exploring the coast of Asia. Columbus had been supplied by the Spanish queen, Isabella, with the money necessary to carry out his undertaking and consequently the new-found islands and the adjacent mainland were claimed by Spain.

Cabral happens upon Brazil in 1500

While Columbus and others were exploring the Caribbean Sea in the interests of Spain, Cabral, a Portuguese commander on his way around Africa to India, sailed so far west that he came upon Brazil. Thereupon the coast southward was rapidly investigated by the Portuguese, who in this way came into possession of a vast region in the New World.

The Spanish hope to reach the Pacific

Strange as it may seem, the brilliant exploits of Columbus were at first disappointing to the Spaniards, for the islands of the West Indies yielded a poor return for the outlay necessitated by the various expeditions. The Portuguese, on the other hand, were deriving fabulous sums from the Eastern trade, and the Spaniards therefore determined to find a western route to India. They at once began an energetic search for a passage which would open into the waters of the Pacific, and it was this motive, together with their natural taste for exploration and adventure, that led to the foundation of their power on the mainland.

The Spanish cross the Isthmus of Panama

In 1508 Pinzon set out on a voyage to discover what lay beyond the islands which Columbus had found, and, sailing across the Gulf of Mexico, he skirted along the coast of Central and South America. Five years later the spirited Balboa with a small troop pushed his way through the jungles and swamps of the Isthmus of Panama, and, on the morning of

September 25, 1513, saw from the mountain heights the waters of the Pacific. After prostrating himself upon the earth, he raised himself to his knees and "poured forth his boundless gratitude to God and all the heavenly hosts who had reserved the prize of so great a thing unto him, a man of small wit and knowledge, of little experience, and lowly parentage."

It remained for Magellan, a Portuguese who had deserted to Spain, to find his way down the barren and seemingly interminable coast of Patagonia, reach the straits which bear his name, and thus penetrate into the Pacific. This he crossed and reached the Philippine Islands after accomplishing the greatest feat of continuous seamanship that the world has ever known. Here he was killed by a native, but his vessel, the Victoria, reached home in 1522. This first voyage ever made around the globe required very nearly three years.

The earth is first circumnavigated, 1519–1522

From Cuba the Spaniards found their way into Mexico, which was inhabited by a people that had made some beginnings in civilization. They lived in *pueblos*, or towns, cultivated the soil, and exhibited great skill in working up gold and silver into utensils and ornaments of which they had stored up vast quantities. But they had a rule that they must fight their neighbors at least once every twenty days in order to obtain victims for sacrifice and for their cannibal feasts. Human sacrifice they believed essential in order to support the sun, which would otherwise perish.

The ancient inhabitants of Mexico

In 1521 Cortes captured the city of Mexico and began the conquest of New Spain, as he called the region, — a tract eight hundred miles in length and extending from the Gulf of Mexico to the Pacific Ocean. The chief object in conquering this territory was the great supply of gold and silver articles which the natives had been accumulating for centuries, and which were sent to Spain to be recast into coin. Before long, rumors reached the Spaniards of untold wealth among the Incas of Peru, and ten years after Cortes had won Mexico, Pizarro, with a company of one hundred and eighty-three

Cortes conquers Mexico in 1521, and Pizarro conquers Peru in 1532

soldiers, invaded and cruelly subjugated the land. He and his
followers gratified their thirst for gold by plundering the burial
places where the gold and silver articles which had belonged
to the dead were deposited with them.[1]

After the conquest of Peru, Spain's stream of treasure from
the New World was trebled; the silver mines of Europe were
abandoned, and soon all the gold supply also was derived from
America. It is no wonder that English, French, and other
mariners found excuses for capturing Spanish galleons, and by
piracy and smuggling strove to share in the advantages which
Spain enjoyed in the West Indies.

The Spaniards lose interest in North America after the failure of De Soto's expedition, 1542

The Spaniards naturally sent expeditions to explore what
are now the southernmost of the United States. After Pizarro
had conquered Peru, one of his lieutenants, De Soto, traversed
this region in search of gold and silver such as had been found
in Mexico and Peru. He struggled through forests and swamps
for four years, finding only an Indian village here and there,
and at last reached the Mississippi, where he died, leaving
his disheartened followers to make their way back to Mexico.
After this, Spain lost interest in North America and left it, with
the exception of Mexico and Florida, to be fought over by
other European powers, especially France and England.[2]

Spain occupies the Philippine Archipelago, 1565

Spain, however, pressed on westward where Magellan had
shown the way. Forty-four years after he had laid claim in
her name to the archipelago which he had discovered far to

---

[1] The Spanish built churches and made every effort to convert the natives to
Christianity. "The aboriginal population, freed from the grinding tyranny of
their old masters, increased and throve; new mines, especially of silver, were discovered and wrought. Both Peru and Mexico assumed gradually the semblance
of civilized life; and their prosperity testified to the benefits conferred on them
by conquests which, however unjustifiable upon abstract grounds, in both cases
redeemed the populations affected by them from cruel and oppressive [native]
governments, and bloody and senseless religions." — E. J. Payne in *Cambridge
Modern History*, Vol. I, chaps. i–ii. This rosy view of the Spanish conquest
deserves respectful consideration, since it is that of an eminent scholar; but it
should be said that earlier historians reached entirely opposite conclusions and
accuse the Spaniards of practically exterminating the natives by their cruelty.

[2] Spain, however, founded, to the north of her main possessions, St. Augustine
in 1565, and Santa Fe (New Mexico) in 1598.

the south of Japan, an expedition of soldiers and friars was sent out from New Spain (Mexico) to occupy the islands. These they discovered to be " large and rich, well provided with inhabitants, food, and gold." The group had earlier been named the Philippine Islands after Philip II, who was then heir to the Spanish throne. In 1571 a well-sheltered bay was discovered upon the west shore of the island of Luzon, and there the town of Manila was established and made the seat of the Spanish government in the islands.

The archipelago consists of seventeen or eighteen hundred islands, large and small, inhabited by three distinct races which are divided into many tribes differing from one another both in language and civilization. The Spaniards were early defeated by the Sultan of Sulu and never gained complete control over the more savage tribes, especially the Moros, who still cling to Mohammedanism. The friars and Jesuits, however, Christianized a great part of the islands, and the natural products, such as hemp, tobacco, coffee, sugar, and rice, were developed. Development by Spain of the Philippines

It was the policy of Spain to keep a firm hold on her possessions in the New World, and for three centuries she ruled the subjugated natives by means of viceroys. As the conversion of the heathen was always regarded as important by the Spaniards, friars followed the explorers, establishing missions from Chile to California,[1] and in 1600 there were four hundred monasteries in New Spain alone. The Spaniards did not emigrate in great numbers but, by the close of the eighteenth century, there were in all the colonies probably some three or four millions of them whose blood was unmixed with that of the native races, beside many half-breeds. How Spain ruled and converted the natives

England, although she was later to be so great an influence in the New World, allowed a hundred years or more to elapse

---

[1] The mission monasteries in California (especially that which may still be seen at Santa Barbara) have exercised a very happy influence upon the architecture of the region.

after its discovery before her mariners did much more than hunt in vain for a western passage to India and plunder such Spanish ships as they might encounter. In 1497 John Cabot, an Italian by birth, sailed from Bristol westward with the hope of reaching " the island of Zipango and the lands from which Oriental caravans brought their goods to Alexandria." But he found only the barren coast of Labrador, which he believed to be a part of Asia. For at least a century and a half thereafter so little was known of North America that mariners continued to search for a convenient passage westward to the Pacific and the Spice Islands.

Under Elizabeth there was an outburst of maritime enthusiasm. The adventures of Sir Francis Drake afford an example of the way in which the English raided the Spanish posts. Setting sail from Plymouth in November, 1577, with five vessels and one hundred and sixty-four men, he passed the Straits of Magellan, in August, and then turned northward, following the west coast to Santiago in Chile, where he rifled the chapel, carrying off a " silver chalice, two cruets, and one altar cloth " ; and, from a Spanish vessel which they seized near there, his men got upwards of thirty-seven thousand ducats of pure gold. Later they plundered three barks, taking from them fifty-seven wedges of silver, each weighing twenty pounds. Near Panama they captured a Spanish vessel from which they took " great riches, such as precious stones, thirteen chests full of reals of plate, fourscore pound weight of gold, and six and twenty tons of silver." Drake then sailed northward along the coast of North America and, turning westward across the Pacific, reached Borneo on February 8, 1580, and England, by way of the Cape of Good Hope, in November of the same year. Drake was only one of the many English seamen engaged in capturing the treasure ships of the hated Philip II, but the first two or three attempts of the English to establish colonies in North America failed ; nor were the efforts of the French before 1600 more successful.

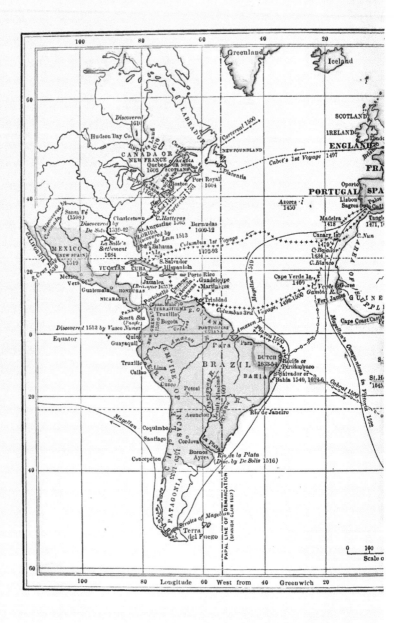

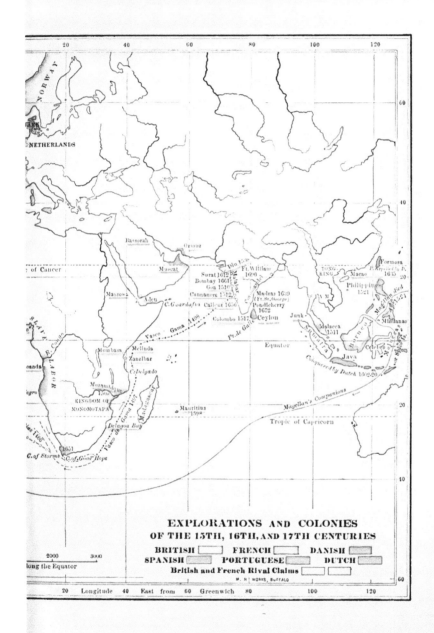

EXPLORATIONS AND COLONIES
OF THE 15TH, 16TH, AND 17TH CENTURIES

BRITISH ☐   FRENCH ☐   DANISH ☐
SPANISH ☐   PORTUGUESE ☐   DUTCH ☐
British and French Rival Claims ☐ ☐

M. N. WORKS, BUFFALO

Verrazano, an Italian commander in the French service, had captured two of the treasure ships dispatched by Cortes to Spain in 1522 and turned them over to the French king, Francis I, who was so impressed by the riches which were flowing into Spain that he commissioned Verrazano to explore the shore from Florida to Newfoundland and to search for a northwest passage to the East Indies. Upon this exploration, France based her claim to North America, which she named New France. Ten years later another Frenchman, Jacques Cartier, made his way up the St. Lawrence River and took possession of the land in the name of his sovereign. He even made an unsuccessful attempt to found a colony on the present site of Montreal. Verrazano (1524) and Cartier (1534) claim North America for France

A company having been formed in France for colonizing Acadia (as Nova Scotia was then called) and Canada, a group of Frenchmen succeeded in 1604 in establishing a permanent settlement in Acadia at Port Royal and four years later the famous Champlain, " the father of New France," as he has been fittingly called, founded a settlement at Quebec. With this as a basis the French explorers, traders, and missionaries worked their way westward and southward, the long reaches of navigable waters and the rich fur trade luring them farther and farther inland. Champlain, like Livingstone, was at once a missionary and an ardent explorer. He discovered (1609) the beautiful lake which bears his name and wrote a number of books which served to make the great virgin forests and their savage inhabitants known to his countrymen. The French establish themselves at Port Royal and Quebec, 1604–1608 Champlain

Montreal was permanently founded in 1642, a generation later than Quebec, and the French companies offered every inducement to settlers who would agree to go to Canada; but the severe climate and the hard life deterred all except the more adventurous, and when Louis XIV came to the throne there were not more than three thousand of his subjects dwelling in the valley of the St. Lawrence. The French explorers and missionaries pressed westward in the hope of finding the The French in Canada

Pacific. They discovered the Great Lakes, raised a cross at Sault Ste. Marie and, in the name of Louis XIV, laid claim to all the lands about the lakes, discovered or undiscovered, "bounded on the one side by the seas of the north and of the west, and on the other by the South Sea."

How Marquette explored the Mississippi, 1673

Rumors began to reach the French explorers of a mighty river flowing across the continent which might enable them at last to reach the Pacific. In 1673, under the guidance of friendly Indians, Marquette, a Jesuit missionary, and Joliet, a veteran explorer and trader, reached the upper Mississippi. Father Marquette gives a fascinating account of their experiences. Undeterred by the warnings of the Indians, who declared that the river was full of monsters which would devour them and their canoes, and lined with savage peoples who would kill them without mercy, Marquette and his companions committed themselves to the stream and for days floated down with its current, stopping to smoke a pipe with the Illinois Indians, observing the buffaloes on the banks and noting the muddy Missouri River as they passed the site of St. Louis. They finally satisfied themselves, as they approached the Gulf of Mexico, that "the Mississippi discharged itself into it and not to the eastward of the Cape of Florida or westward into the California Sea." Fearful lest they should meet the Spanish they turned back.[1]

La Salle claims Louisiana for France, 1682

Their work was completed by La Salle, a determined and experienced explorer, who had already discovered the Ohio River. Encouraged by Louis XIV, he set out from Lake Michigan in January, 1682, with a band of twenty-three Frenchmen and eighteen Indians, all inured to hardship. After passing down the Illinois River and the Mississippi, whose mouth they reached in April, La Salle solemnly took possession of all the region watered by the great river and its tributaries and named it Louisiana after his king. His later attempt to colonize the country was, however, a failure.

[1] See *Readings*, sect. 19, for Marquette's story.

While the French were roaming about the Great Lakes and the Mississippi Valley, the English were slowly occupying the Atlantic coast from New England to Florida. A year before Champlain founded Quebec, Englishmen had established their first successful colony, which they had named Jamestown after their king, James I. After a period of deprivation and suffering, the colonists began to find their way inland and take possession of the fertile valleys of Virginia. Under Charles II North and South Carolina were colonized. *The English found Jamestown, 1607*

The New England colonists differed essentially from those of Virginia. In 1620 the *Mayflower* had landed at Plymouth bringing stern, religious Englishmen, who could not endure the ceremonies of the English church as it had been organized under Elizabeth[1] and had fled to the New World to found permanent homes where they might worship as they pleased. Nine years later the Massachusetts Bay Company began to attract thousands of well-to-do Puritans, whose worldly prosperity contributed not a little to the success of the colony. Off-shoots of this colony established themselves in Connecticut and Rhode Island. The climate and the soil of New England did not encourage the use of slave labor, which became the bane of the southern colonies. The northern colonists, instead of scattering upon great plantations, kept together and formed compact settlements, which tended to develop a spirit of independence and well-organized governments. *The New England colonies*

Henry Hudson, an English mariner sailing under the Dutch flag, had discovered (1609) the river which bears his name and the island of Manhattan at its mouth. On this island the Dutch West India Company established its colony of New Amsterdam and the Dutch occupied the valley of the Hudson and what is now New Jersey under the name of the New Netherlands. But the short history of the Dutch in North America came to an end in 1664, when their possessions were conquered by the English. *Brief rôle of the Dutch in North America*

[1] See below, p. 150.

Pennsylvania and Maryland

Maryland became the refuge for persecuted Roman Catholics. Pennsylvania, granted to William Penn by Charles II in 1681, developed into a thriving colony of Quakers, whose simple habits and opposition to war had made them hated in England.

England gains Nova Scotia, Newfoundland, and the Hudson Bay region

Many changes took place in the various companies which received grants and established colonies in the New World; there was much fighting with the Indians and constant uncertainty and disputes in regard to boundaries. The wars in Europe, moreover, were usually accompanied by little wars among the colonists of the various nations involved. Into these matters we need not go. During the War of the Spanish Succession (called Queen Anne's War by the colonists), the New England settlers had captured the French stronghold of Port Royal [1] in Nova Scotia (then Acadia). This was important for them on account of the cod which their fishermen caught every year on the neighboring Newfoundland banks. By the Peace of Utrecht at the end of the war, France ceded Nova Scotia to England and acknowledged her right to Newfoundland and the region about Hudson Bay which had been in dispute between the two countries.[2]

Georgia, and its troubles with the neighboring Spaniards

In the South a new English colony called Georgia had been established by Oglethorpe, and the town of Savannah founded in 1733 very near the Spanish boundary of Florida. When England went to war with Spain in 1739, Oglethorpe organized a little army of the colonists in Georgia and South Carolina and laid siege to the Spanish fortress of St. Augustine, but sickness in his army forced him to give up his attempt to take the town.

The map of the New World in 1750 indicates that it was divided up as follows among the various European countries which had participated in its exploration and colonization

---

[1] Now Annapolis.

[2] The English had organized a Hudson Bay Company in 1670, and laid claim to the vast region north of New France.

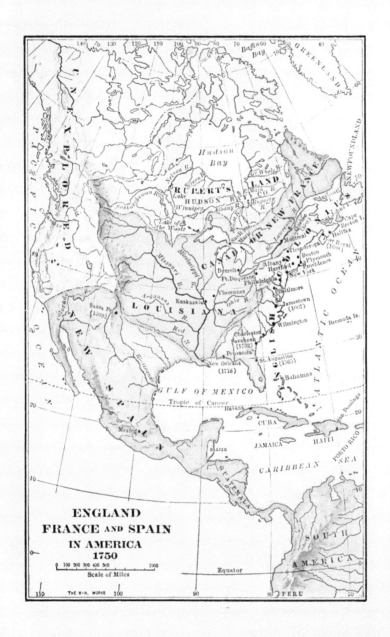

ENGLAND
FRANCE AND SPAIN
IN AMERICA
1750

0 100 200 300 400 500   1000
Scale of Miles

THE M-N. WORKS

during the two centuries and a half that they had known of
its existence. Besides New France (Canada), the French held
Louisiana, extending from the Alleghenies to the Rocky Mountains and from the Great Lakes to the Gulf of Mexico. This
was defended by scattered forts, extending from New Orleans
(founded by the French Mississippi Company in 1718) to Montreal. France also held a portion of the island of Haiti and of
Guiana (Cayenne) on the northeastern coast of South America.
The English Hudson Bay Company claimed the great ill-explored
region, frequented by adventurous trappers, which lay to the
north of New France. English colonies occupied all the Atlantic coast from Newfoundland to a point south of Savannah.
England had settlements besides in the Bahamas, Jamaica,
and Belize (British Honduras). She had also, like France,
colonized a portion of Guiana on the coast of South America,
but this she ceded to the Dutch in 1667 in exchange for New
Amsterdam and their other North American possessions. In
general, however, all the region to the south of Santa Fe and
St. Augustine, including Mexico, Florida, Central America, the
West Indies, and all of South America, except Brazil (which
was Portuguese) and Guiana, belonged to the Spanish crown.
All the outlying regions, such as the northwestern parts of
North America, the interior of Brazil, and the southern part
of South America, were little known or entirely unexplored.

marginal note: How the New World was apportioned in 1750 among the European powers — England, France, Spain, Hol-land, and Portugal

STRUGGLE BETWEEN FRANCE AND ENGLAND FOR NORTH AMERICA

20. In the final struggle which was approaching between
France and England for the possession of North America, the
French found themselves at a great disadvantage. Their
claims included an immense territory upon which, in the
nature of things, they could have only a very precarious hold.
The exhausting wars of Louis XIV affected the colonies by
checking immigration and preventing their proper financial

marginal note: Weakness of the French colonies

support by the home government. The Huguenots, after the revocation of the Edict of Nantes, would gladly have found homes in the New World and built up the French power as the Puritans had the English. But New France and Louisiana had been explored by the Jesuits, and both the home government and the priests scattered about North America stoutly opposed the coming of the heretical Huguenots, who were therefore forced to flee to Protestant countries in search of freedom.

Scarcely a hundred thousand French colonists in 1754

The French who came to America were, in general, too engrossed in the fur trade, in exploring, in converting the Indians to Christianity, or in fighting the English colonists, to form strong settled communities. They were not permitted to govern themselves when they did collect in settlements, but were carefully watched by the officials of a king who forbade them to trade with any one except Frenchmen and Indians. As a result of these conditions the scattered French population of North America was less than a hundred thousand souls when the war broke out with England in 1754.

Strength of the English colonies

The situation of the English colonies from Massachusetts to Georgia was quite different. They varied greatly, it is true, in population, religion, trade, and industry, but they had much in common and could combine far more easily than the French. Four fifths of the English lived within a short distance of the seacoast and were consequently in ready communication with the mother country compared with a Frenchman in Kaskaskia or Detroit, or even in New Orleans. Each of the colonies had its own government and its representative assembly which voted taxes and passed laws subject to the approval of the king.

Character and number of the English colonists

Moreover the English settlers were, for the most part, seeking permanent homes for themselves and their families; there were few mere traders, trappers, missionaries, or wandering adventurers. In spite of the rule made by Parliament that they must trade only with England, industry and commerce increased, for it was always possible to evade the navigation laws, which were not strictly enforced. The population of the English colonies increased very rapidly. By the close of the War of the Spanish Succession there must have been toward half a million, and by 1750 this number had almost trebled. A great part of the colonists at this latter date had been born in America, but they were still loyal to their English king, and were now able to vote money, men, and ships to aid him in his wars.

As the English colonies grew they gradually pressed inland and so inevitably came into conflict with the French, who claimed all the region south of the Great Lakes. The New England population expanded toward the St. Lawrence, that of New York and Virginia westward toward Lake Erie and into what is now Ohio. In 1749 the Ohio Company was formed by London merchants and leading Virginians with a view of forwarding colonization beyond the Alleghenies. The French were alarmed, established a fort at Erie, and prepared to defend, as the boundary between them and the English, a line which would to-day lie within the limits of western Pennsylvania. *The English colonists press westward and meet the French*

Virginia now raised a little army of four hundred men which set out under George Washington to protect a fort that the Ohio Company was building where Pittsburg now stands. The French, with their allies the Indians, reached the spot first, captured the fort, which they named Fort Duquesne, and compelled Washington to surrender on condition that he and his men should be permitted to return to Virginia. In this way the French and Indian War originated, quite independently of any trouble between England and France, which were then at peace. *Opening of the French and Indian War, 1754*

It was clear that a struggle was not to be avoided, and both France and England began to send forces to America. The English colonies even considered a plan of federation (which for the moment came to nothing) and collected troops to fight side by side with the forces sent from England. Of the English troops, which amounted in 1758 to about fifty thousand, more than half were supplied by the colonies. An expedition was sent to Nova Scotia from Boston with a view of completing the conquest of a region which had been already in part ceded to England. The English commander, General Braddock, tried to recapture Fort Duquesne but, failing to heed the warnings of Washington, he was defeated by the French and Indians and killed (1755).

The English successes

In 1756 the Seven Years' War opened and England, as the ally of Frederick the Great, went to war against France and Austria.[1] In America the French troops were under the able command of Montcalm, who was supported by all the Indians in the disputed region. For a time the English were kept out of the mooted territory, but when William Pitt was put at the head of the English government in 1757 all was changed. He not only aided the hard-pressed Frederick with men and money in the European war but sent out reënforcements to the American colonists which enabled them to take Louisburg on Cape Breton Island, capture Fort Duquesne (which they renamed after Pitt), and drive the French out of western New York.

The French lose Canada, 1759–1760

The following year the English were able to begin the conquest of Canada. They took Ticonderoga and Crown Point on Lake Champlain, and Fort Niagara. Then, from the recently captured Louisburg, the English under General Wolfe made their way up the St. Lawrence to attack Quebec, the key to the French power in Canada, which was defended by Montcalm. After an unsuccessful siege of three months, Wolfe's troops one night scaled the heights upon which the town stands and next day defeated the French who had come out to meet him. Both Montcalm and Wolfe were killed in this memorable engagement. From this time on the conquest of Canada progressed rapidly. The French forts surrendered

[1] See above, p. 69.

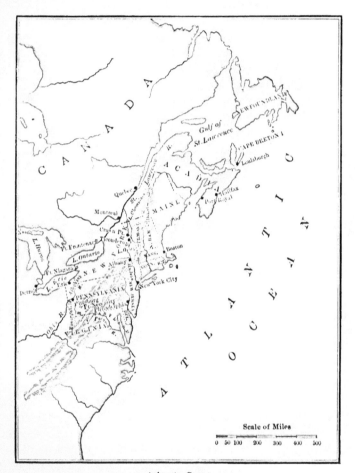

Atlantic Coast

in quick succession and when Montreal was captured (1760), the French gave up the unequal conquest and recalled their troops.

Strength of the English colonies at the end of the war

Just before the close of the Seven Years' War Spain entered the conflict in America as an ally of France, and this gave the English an excuse for organizing an expedition which succeeded in taking Havana. The colonists, who eagerly attacked the Spanish merchantmen on the seas, were now able to outnumber in vessels, guns, and men the whole navy that England had possessed when the English colonies had first been established a century and a half earlier.

By the Peace of Paris (1763) the French possessions in North America were ceded to England and Spain

In the Peace of Paris (1763), which brought the Seven Years' War to a close, France gave up all her territory in North America. That to the east of the Mississippi she ceded to England; that to the west of the river, including the city of New Orleans, she gave to her ally Spain. Spain, on her part, ceded Florida to England on condition that England would restore to her Havana and Manila, both of which the English had captured. In this way England got possession of practically all that part of North America which had as yet been explored and developed, with the exception, of course, of Mexico. While Spain's territory was greatly augmented by Louisiana she was not in a position to colonize the region which, so to speak, lay fallow until, forty years later, it was purchased by the United States.

Traces of the French occupation

The only remnants of the French occupation of North America to-day are the French-speaking Creoles of New Orleans and the French Canadians in and about Quebec and Montreal. We still retain the name "prairie" which the French explorers gave to the grassy plains of Illinois. Names like Detroit, Vincennes, Terre Haute, Des Moines, and Baton Rouge still remind us of the nationality of the first explorers and missionaries, and it is pleasant to think that Joliet, La Salle, and Marquette each has a town dedicated to his memory although no word of his language be spoken there.

REVOLT OF THE AMERICAN COLONIES FROM ENGLAND

21. England had, however, no sooner added Canada to her possessions and driven the French from the broad region which lay between her colonies and the Mississippi than she lost the better part of her American empire by the revolt of the irritated colonists, who refused to submit to her interference in their government and commerce.

The English settlers had been left alone, for the most part, by the home government and had enjoyed far greater freedom in the management of their affairs than the French and Spanish colonies. Virginia established its own assembly in 1619 and Massachusetts became almost an independent commonwealth. Regular constitutions developed which were later used as the basis for those of the several states when the colonies gained their independence. England had been busied during the seventeenth century with a great struggle at home and with the wars stirred up by Louis XIV. After the Peace of Utrecht Walpole for twenty years prudently refused to interfere with the colonies. The result was that by the end of the Seven Years' War the colonists numbered over two millions. Their rapidly increasing wealth and strength, their free life in a new land, and the confidence they had gained in their successful conflict with the French, — all combined to render the renewed interference of the home government intolerable to them.

For a long period England left her colonies very free

During the war with the French England began to realize for the first time that the colonies had money, and so Parliament decided that they should be required to pay part of the expenses of the recent conflict and support a small standing army of English soldiers. The Stamp Act was therefore passed, which taxed the colonists by requiring them to pay the English government for stamps which had to be used upon leases, deeds, and other legal documents in order to make them binding. But the indignant colonists declared that they had already

England taxes the colonies

Stamp Act of 1765

borne the brunt of the war and that in any case Parliament, in which they were not represented, had no right to tax them. Representatives of the colonies met in New York and denounced the Stamp Act as indicating "a manifest tendency to subvert the rights and liberties of the colonists."

Navigation laws

More irritating than the attempts of Great Britain to tax the colonists were the vexatious navigation and trade laws by which she tried to keep all the benefits of colonial trade and industry to herself. The early navigation laws passed under Cromwell and Charles II were specially directed against the Dutch and have already been mentioned in connection with the rivalry of England and Holland.[1] They provided that all products grown or manufactured in Asia, Africa, or America should be imported into England or her colonies only in English ships. Thus if a Dutch merchant vessel laden with cloves, cinnamon, teas, and silks from the Far East anchored in the harbor of New York, the inhabitants could not lawfully buy of the ship's master, no matter how much lower his prices were than those offered by English shippers. Furthermore, another act provided that no commodity of European production or manufacture should be imported into any of the colonies without being shipped through England and carried in ships built in England or the colonies. So if a colonial merchant wished to buy French wines or Dutch watches, he would have to order through English merchants. Again, if a colonist desired to sell to a European merchant such products as the law permitted him to sell to foreigners, he had to export them in English ships and even send them by way of England.

Trade laws

What was still worse for the colonists, certain articles in which they were most interested, such as sugar, tobacco, cotton, and indigo, could be sold only in England. Other things they were forbidden to export at all, or even to produce. For instance, though they possessed the finest furs in abundance, they could not export any caps or hats to England or to any

[1] See above, p. 86.

foreign country. They had iron ore in inexhaustible quantities at their disposal, but by a law of 1750 they were forbidden to erect any rolling mill or furnace for making steel, in order that English steel manufacturers might enjoy a monopoly of that trade. The colonists had built up a lucrative lumber and provision trade with the French West Indies, from which they imported large quantities of rum, sugar, and molasses, but in order to keep this trade within British dominions the importation of these commodities was forbidden.

The colonists naturally evaded these laws as far as possible; they carried on a flourishing smuggling trade and built up industries in spite of them. Tobacco, sugar, hemp, flax, and cotton were grown and cloth was manufactured. Furnaces, foundries, nail and wire mills supplied pig and bar iron, chains, anchors, and other hardware. It is clear that where so many people were interested in both manufacturing and commerce a loud protest was sure to be raised against the continued attempts of England to restrict the business of the colonists in the interests of her own merchants. *The colonists evade the English restrictions*

Parliament withdrew the unpopular stamp tax, but declared that it had a perfect right to tax the colonies as well as to make laws for them. Soon new duties on glass, paper, and tea were imposed, and a board was established to secure a strict observance of the navigation laws and other restrictions. But the protests of the colonists finally moved Parliament to remove all the duties except that on tea, which was retained to prove England's right to tax the colonists. *Taxes withdrawn except that on tea*

This effort to make the Americans pay a very moderate import duty on tea produced further trouble in 1773. The young men of Boston seditiously boarded a tea ship in the harbor and threw the cargo into the water. Burke, perhaps the most able member of the House of Commons, urged the ministry to leave the Americans to tax themselves, but George III, and Parliament as a whole, could not forgive the colonists for their opposition. They believed that the trouble was largely *Opposition to " taxation without representation "* confined to New England and could easily be overcome. In 1774 acts were passed prohibiting the landing and shipping of goods at Boston ; and the colony of Massachusetts was deprived of its former right to choose its judges and the members of the upper house of its legislature, who were thereafter to be selected by the king.

The Conti- nental Con- gress

These measures, instead of bringing Massachusetts to terms, so roused the apprehension of the rest of the colonists that a congress of all the colonies was summoned which met at Phila- delphia. This decided that all trade with Great Britain should cease until the grievances of the colonies had been redressed. The following year the Americans attacked the British troops at Lexington and made a brave stand against them in the battle of Bunker Hill. The new congress decided to prepare for war and raised an army which was put under the command of George Washington, a Virginia planter who had gained

Declaration of Independ- ence, July 4, 1776

some distinction in the late French and Indian War. Up to this time the colonies had not intended to secede from the mother country, but the proposed compromises came to noth- ing, and in July, 1776, Congress declared that " these United States are, and of right ought to be, free and independent."

The United States seeks and receives aid from France

This occurrence naturally excited great interest in France. The outcome of the Seven Years' War had been most lamen- table for that country, and any trouble which came to her old enemy, England, could not but be a source of congratulation to the French. The United States therefore regarded France as their natural ally and immediately sent Benjamin Franklin to Versailles in the hope of obtaining the aid of the new French king, Louis XVI. The king's ministers were uncertain whether the colonies could long maintain their resistance against the overwhelming strength of the mother country. It was only after the Americans had defeated Burgoyne at Saratoga that France, in 1778, concluded a treaty with the United States in which the independence of the new republic was recog- nized. This was tantamount to declaring war upon England.

The enthusiasm for the Americans was so great in France that a number of the younger nobles, the most conspicuous of whom was the Marquis of Lafayette, crossed the Atlantic to fight in the American army.

In spite of the skill and heroic self-sacrifice of Washington, the Americans lost more battles than they gained. It is extremely doubtful whether they would have succeeded in bringing the war to a favorable close, by forcing the English general, Cornwallis, to capitulate at Yorktown (1781), had it not been for the aid of the French fleet. The chief result of the war was the recognition by England of the independence of the United States, whose territory was to extend to the Mississippi River. To the west of the Mississippi, the vast territory of Louisiana still remained in the hands of Spain, as well as Florida, which England had held since 1763 but now gave back.

Spain and Portugal were able to hold their American possessions a generation longer than the English, but in the end practically all of the western hemisphere, with the exception of Canada, completely freed itself from the domination of the European powers. Cuba, one of the very last vestiges of Spanish rule in the West, gained its independence with the aid of the United States in 1899.

Close of the war, 1783

England acknowledges the independence of the United State

Revolt of the English colonies the beginning of the emancipation of the western hemisphere

REFERENCES

Early English Explorations in America: TYLER, *England in America* (American Nation Series), pp. 1–33; THWAITES, *The Colonies* (Epochs of American History Series), chap. ii, pp. 21–44.

The French in Canada: THWAITES, *The Colonies*, chap. xii, pp. 246–257; *France in America* (American Nation Series), pp. 124–142.

Struggle between England and France: HART, *Formation of the Union* (Epochs of American History Series), pp. 22–41; THWAITES, *France in America*, pp. 157–280.

British Colonial Policy: HART, pp. 44–63; HOWARD, *Preliminaries of the Revolution* (American Nation Series), pp. 22–67, 174–192; LEE, *Source Book of English History*, pp. 474–483.

A Sketch of the American Revolution: HART, pp. 70–101.

CHAPTER VIII

THE OLD RÉGIME IN EUROPE

CONDITION OF THE COUNTRY PEOPLE: SERFDOM

22. If a peasant who lived on a manor in the times of the Crusades had been permitted to return to earth and travel about Europe at the close of the Seven Years' War, he would have found much to remind him of the conditions under which, seven centuries earlier, he had extracted a scanty living from the soil. On the other hand, an American farmer of to-day would find great difficulty in understanding the situation of a Prussian peasant even a century ago. We must therefore glance at the ancient manorial system of the Middle Ages which, in the eighteenth century, still existed in most of the countries of Europe.

Those who till the soil have usually not owned the land The modern farmer who either owns his land or leases it from the owner for a certain sum annually and then cultivates it in any way he pleases, with the aid of such men as he may hire to help him, is, in fact, a rather novel thing in the world's history. In the past, those who have tilled the soil have commonly been slaves, or half slaves, who worked upon large estates belonging to others. They neither owned nor rented the land in the modern sense of the terms, and yet they often had a certain claim upon it and, so long as they fulfilled their obligations, were not deprived of it.

Slaves replaced by serfs in the Roman Empire The system of great estates prevailed under the Roman Empire, and the land had originally been cultivated by armies of slaves. Later, however, the slaves disappeared, or merged into a curious intermediate class neither free nor slave, the so-called serfs, which included practically all those who tilled the soil in the Middle Ages. Indeed, a free farmer who had

122

no means of protecting himself would have stood but a poor chance amidst the violence and disorder which prevailed during the barbarian invasions and the feudal period. Consequently all through the Middle Ages the great estates still continued to exist, peopled by serfs who were protected to a certain degree by the lord of the manor.

The lord, who lived in a castle or solidly built house, reserved for himself a goodly number of fields. The rest of the estate was divided up among the serfs, who were not ordinarily deprived of their holdings so long as they served their lord and paid him the customary dues. These holdings passed down from father to son; and in case the manor changed hands, the peasants went with it, just as did the wretched hovels in which they lived and the trees and brooks. For the serf was not at liberty to leave the manor, and in case of flight he might be pursued like a fugitive slave. He was, in short, bound to the land.

The serf bound to the soil

The serfs were required to till those fields which the lord reserved for himself and to gather his crops. They might not marry without the lord's permission, and their wives and children must render such assistance as was required in the manor house. We have many exact statements of what the serfs owed the lord upon whose estate they were fixed. To take a single instance from an English village in 1279: William Modi, a serf, holds from Sir Baldwin a cottage and twelve acres of land. For this he must, among other things, work for the lord two days a week for the greater part of the year and, during August and September, must see that at least two acres of Sir Baldwin's grain are harvested each day. He must put his cart at the lord's disposal on certain occasions and mow in his field the whole of one day. "And he owes at Christmas four hens and a cock and forty eggs, and on St. Peter's day he shall give five ducks. And about Christmas time he shall thresh in the barn of his lord sixteen bushels of barley and make malt of this at his house and dry it, and then carry it to the mill to be ground, and then from the mill to the kitchen of his lord."

Services required from the serf by the lord of the manor

All the men were, moreover, expected to be present at the "court" of the lord where the business of the manor was transacted under the supervision of his representative. Here disputes were settled and fines were imposed for disorder or for violating the customs of the manor. These fines were a somewhat important source of income to the lord, who found this privilege of administering justice a valuable one. While the services and dues varied on different manors those enumerated above give a very just idea of the general conditions which prevailed for centuries throughout western Europe.

The serf an
inferior
farmer who
could only
exist when
there was
plenty of
land
The serf was ordinarily a bad farmer and workman. He cultivated the soil in a very crude manner, and his crops were accordingly scanty and inferior. Obviously serfdom could exist only as long as land was plentiful. Serfdom would, therefore, naturally tend to disappear when the population so increased that the carelessly cultivated fields no longer supplied the food necessary for the growing numbers.

Disappear-
ance of serf-
dom begins in
France and
England
Serfdom began to die out first in France and England. As time went on, neither the lord nor the serf was satisfied with the ancient primitive arrangements which had answered well enough in the time of Charlemagne. The serfs, on the one hand, began to obtain money by the sale of their products in the markets of neighboring towns. They soon found it more profitable to pay the lord a certain sum instead of working for him, for they could then turn their whole attention to their own holdings. The land owners, on the other hand, found it to their advantage to accept money in place of the services of their tenants. With this money they could hire laborers to cultivate their own fields and buy the luxuries which were brought to their notice as commerce increased. So it came about that the lords gradually renounced their control over the peasants, and the serf was no longer easily distinguishable from the freeman who paid a regular rent for his land.[1]

[1] A serf might gain his liberty by fleeing to a town. In England, if he remained undiscovered by his lord for a year and a day, he became a freeman.

The gradual extinction of serfdom in western Europe appears to have begun as early as the twelfth century, but proceeded at very different rates in the various countries. In France the old type of serf had largely disappeared by the fourteenth century and in England a hundred years later. In Prussia, Austria, Poland, Russia, Italy, and Spain, on the contrary, the great mass of the country people were still bound to the soil in the eighteenth century.

Serfdom still existed in the eighteenth century

Even in France there were still many aggravating traces of the old system. The peasant was, it is true, no longer bound to a particular manor; he could buy or sell his land at will, could marry without consulting the lord, and could go and come as he pleased. Many bought their land outright, while others disposed of their holdings and settled in town. But the lord might still require all those on his manor to grind their grain at his mill, bake their bread in his oven, and press their grapes in his winepress. The peasant might have to pay a toll to cross a bridge or ferry which was under the lord's control, or a certain sum for driving his flock past the lord's mansion. Many of the old arrangements still forced the peasant occupying a particular plot of land to turn over to the lord a certain portion of his crops and, if he sold his land, to pay the lord a part of the money he received for it.

Survivals of manorial system in France in the eighteenth century

In England in the eighteenth century the prominent features of serfdom had disappeared more completely than in France. The services in labor due to the lord had long been commuted into money payments and the peasant was thus transformed into a renter or owner of his holding. He still took off his hat to the squire of his village and was liable to be severely punished by his lord, who was usually a justice of the peace, if he was caught shooting a hare on the game preserves. Moreover, many traces of feudal dues and restrictions remained in their old form until the nineteenth century and the subserviency of the agricultural laborers to the landed proprietors is still strongly marked. As late as 1809 the town

Survivals in England of the manorial system

of Manchester had to get the consent of the lord of the manor before it could incorporate a waterworks company; and in 1839 the town of Leeds had to pay thirteen thousand pounds to its former lord in order to extinguish the old obligation of grinding corn at his mill.

Condition of the serfs in a great part of Europe in the eighteenth century

In central, southern, and eastern Europe the mediæval system still prevailed; the peasant lived and died upon the same manor and worked for his lord in the same way that his ancestors had worked a thousand years before. Everywhere the same crude agricultural instruments were still used and most of the implements and tools were roughly made in the village itself. The wooden plows commonly found even on English farms were constructed on the model of the old Roman plow; wheat was cut with a sickle, grass with an unwieldy scythe, and the wretched cart wheels were supplied only with wooden rims.

Wretched houses of the peasants

The houses occupied by the country people differed greatly from Sicily to Pomerania, and from Ireland to Poland; but, in general, they were small, with little light or ventilation, and often they were nothing but wretched hovels with dirt floors and neglected thatch roofs. The pigs and the cows were frequently better housed than the people, with whom they associated upon very familiar terms since the barn and the house were commonly in the same building. The drinking water was bad and there was no attempt to secure proper drainage. Fortunately every one was out of doors a great deal of the time, for the women as well as the men usually worked in the fields cultivating the soil and helping to gather in the crops.

Unattractive character of country life

Country life in the eighteenth century was obviously very arduous and unattractive for the most part. The peasant had no newspapers to tell him of the world outside his manor, nor could he have read them had he had them. Even in England not one farmer in five thousand, it is said, could read at all; and in France the local tax collectors were too uneducated to make out their own reports. Farther east conditions must have been still more cheerless, for a Hungarian peasant complains that he owed four days of his labor to his lord, spent the fifth and sixth hunting and fishing for him, while the seventh belonged to God.

THE TOWNS AND THE GUILDS

23. Even in the towns there was much to remind one of the Middle Ages. The narrow, crooked streets, darkened by the overhanging buildings and scarcely lighted at all by night, the rough cobblestones, the disgusting odors even in the best quarters, — all offered a marked contrast to the European cities of to-day, which have grown tremendously in the last hundred years in size, beauty, and comfort. *(margin: Towns still mediæval in the eighteenth century)*

In 1760 London had half a million inhabitants, or about a tenth of its present population. There were of course no street cars or omnibuses, to say nothing of the thousands of hansom cabs which now thread their way in and out through the press of traffic. A few hundred hackney coaches and sedan chairs served to carry those who had not private conveyances and could not, or would not, walk. The ill-lighted streets were guarded at night by watchmen who went about with lanterns but afforded so little protection against the roughs and robbers that gentlemen were compelled to carry arms when passing through the streets after nightfall. *(margin: London)*

Paris was somewhat larger than London and had outgrown its mediæval walls. The police were more efficient there, and the highway robberies which disgraced London and its suburbs were almost unknown. The great park, the "Elysian fields," and the boulevards which now form so distinguished a feature of Paris, were already laid out ; but, in general, the streets were still narrow, and there were none of the fine broad avenues which now radiate from a hundred centers. There were few sewers to carry off the water which, when it rained, flowed through the middle of the streets. The filth and the bad *(margin: Paris)* smells of former times still remained and the people relied upon easily polluted wells or the dirty river Seine for their water supply.

German towns

In Germany very few of the towns had spread beyond their mediæval walls. They had, for the most part, lost their former prosperity, which was still attested by the fine houses of the merchants and of the once flourishing guilds. Berlin had a population of about two hundred thousand, and Vienna slightly more. The latter city, now one of the most beautiful in the world, then employed from thirty to a hundred street cleaners and boasted that the street lamps were lighted every night, while many towns contented themselves with dirty streets and with light during the winter months, and then only when the moon was not scheduled to shine.

Italian cities

Even the famous cities of Italy, — Milan, Genoa, Florence, Rome, — notwithstanding their beautiful palaces and public buildings, were, with the exception of water-bound Venice, crowded into the narrow compass of the town wall and their streets were narrow and crooked.

Trade and industry conducted upon a small scale

Another contrast between the towns of the eighteenth century and those of to-day lay in the absence of the great wholesale warehouses, the vast factories with their tall chimneys, and the attractive department stores which may now be found in every city from Dublin to Budapest. Commerce and industry were in general conducted upon a very small scale, except at the great ports like London, Antwerp, or Hamburg, where goods coming from and going to the colonies were brought together.

The growth of industry under the influence of the various machines which were being invented during the latter part of the eighteenth century will form the subject of a later chapter. It is clear, however, that before the introduction of railroads, steamships, and machine-equipped factories, all business operations must have been carried on in what would seem to us a slow and primitive fashion.

A great part of the manufacturing still took place in little shops where the articles when completed were offered for sale. Generally all those who owned the several shops carrying on a particular trade, such as tailoring, shoemaking, baking, tanning, bookbinding, hair cutting, or the making of candles, knives, hats, artificial flowers, swords, or wigs, were organized into a guild—a union — the main object of which was to prevent all other citizens from making or selling the articles in which the members of the guild dealt. The number of master workmen who might open a shop of their own was often limited by the guild as well as the number of apprentices each master could train. The period of apprenticeship was long, sometimes seven or even nine years, on the ground that it took years to learn the trade properly, but really because the guild wished to maintain its monopoly by keeping down the number who could become masters. When the apprenticeship was over, the workman became a " journeyman " and might never perhaps become a master workman and open a shop of his own.

The trades organized into guilds

This guild system had originated in the Middle Ages and was consequently hundreds of years old. In England the term of seven years was required for apprenticeship in all the staple trades, although the rule was by no means universally enforced. In Sheffield no master cutler could have more than one apprentice at a time ; the master weavers of Norfolk and Norwich were limited to two apprentices each, and no master hatter in England could have more than two.

Guilds in England

In France the guilds were more powerful than in England since they had been supported and encouraged by Colbert, who believed that they kept up the standard of French products. In Germany the organization was much stricter and more widespread than either in England or in France. Old regulations concerning apprenticeship and the conduct of the various trades were still enforced. No master could have more than one apprentice, manage more than one workshop, or sell goods that he had not himself produced.

Guilds in France and Germany

Strife among
the guilds

Everywhere a workman had to stick to his trade ; if a cobbler should venture to make a pair of new boots, or a baker should roast a piece of meat in his oven, he might be expelled from the guild unless he made amends. In Paris a hatter, who had greatly increased his trade by making hats of wool mixed with silk, had his stock destroyed by the guild authorities on the ground that the rules only permitted hats to be made of wool and said nothing of silk. The trimming makers had an edict passed forbidding any one to make buttons that were cast, or turned, or made of horn.

The guilds not only protected themselves against workmen who opened a shop without their permission but each particular trade was in more or less constant disagreement with the other trades as to what each might make. The goldsmiths were the natural enemies of all who used gold in their respective operations, such as the clock and watch makers, the money changers, and those who set precious stones. Those who dealt in natural flowers were not allowed to encroach upon those who made artificial ones. One who baked bread must not make pies or cakes. The tailor who mended clothes must not permit himself to make new garments.

Three
important
differences
between the
guilds and
the modern
trade unions

The guilds differed from the modern trade unions in several important respects. In the first place, it was only the master workmen, who owned the shops, tools, or machines, who belonged to them. The apprentices and journeymen, i.e. the ordinary workmen, were excluded and had no influence whatever upon the policy of the organization. In the second place, the government enforced the decisions of the guilds. For example, in Paris, if it were learned that a journeyman goldbeater was working for himself, a representative of the guild betook himself to the offender's house, accompanied by a town officer, and seized his tools and materials, after which the unfortunate man might be sent to the galleys for three years or perhaps get off with a heavy fine, imprisonment, and the loss of every chance of ever becoming a master. Lastly, the guilds were confined to the old-established industries which were still carried on, as they had been during the Middle Ages, on a small scale in the master's house.

In spite, however, of the seeming strength of the guilds, they were really giving way before the entirely new conditions which had arisen. Thoughtful persons disapproved of them on the ground that they hampered industry and prevented progress by their outworn restrictions. In many towns the regulations were evaded or had broken down altogether, so that enterprising workmen and dealers carried on their business as they pleased. Then, as we have said, it was only the old industries that were included in the guild system. The newer manufactures, of silk and cotton goods, porcelain, fine glassware, etc., which had been introduced into Europe, were under the control of individuals or companies who were independent of the old guilds and relied upon monopolies and privileges granted by the rulers, who, in France at least, were glad to foster new industries. *Decline of the guilds*

THE NOBILITY

24. Not only had the mediæval manor and the mediæval guilds maintained themselves down into the eighteenth century but the successors of the feudal lords continued to exist as a conspicuous and powerful class which enjoyed various privileges and distinctions denied to the ordinary citizen, although they were, of course, shorn of the great power that the more important dukes and counts had enjoyed in the Middle Ages, when they ruled over vast tracts, could summon their vassals to assist them in their constant wars with their neighbors, and dared defy even the authority of the king himself.

It is impossible to recount here how the English, French, and Spanish kings gradually subjugated the turbulent barons and brought the great fiefs directly under royal control. Suffice it to say that the monarchs met with such success that in the eighteenth century the nobles no. longer held aloof but *The former independence of the feudal nobles lost by the eighteenth century* eagerly sought the king's court. Those whose predecessors had once been veritable sovereigns within their own domains, had declared war even against the king, coined money, made laws for their subjects, and meted out justice in their castle halls, had, by the eighteenth century, deserted their war horses and laid aside their long swords; in their velvet coats and high-heeled shoes they were contented with the privilege of helping the king to dress in the morning and attending him at dinner. The battlemented castle, once the stronghold of independent chieftains, was transformed into a tasteful country residence where, if the king honored the owner with a visit, the host was no longer tempted, as his ancestors had been, to shower arrows and stones upon the royal intruder.

The French nobility

The French noble, unlike the English, was not fond of the country but lived with the court at Versailles whenever he could afford to do so, and often when he could not. He liked the excitement of the court, and it was there that he could best advance his own and his friends' interests by obtaining lucrative offices in the army or Church or in the king's palace. By their prolonged absence from their estates the nobles lost the esteem of their tenants, while their stewards roused the hatred of the peasants by strictly collecting all the ancient manorial dues in order that the lord might enjoy the gayeties at Versailles.

The French nobility a privileged class

The unpopularity of the French nobility was further increased by their exemptions from some of the heavy taxes, on the ground that they were still supposed to shed their blood in fighting for their king instead of paying him money like the unsoldierly burghers and peasants. They enjoyed, moreover, the preference when the king had desirable positions to grant. They also claimed a certain social superiority, since they were excluded by their traditions of birth from engaging in any ordinary trade or industry, although they might enter some professions, such as medicine, law, the Church, or the army, or even participate in maritime trade without derogating from their rank. In short, the French nobility, including some one hundred and thirty thousand or one hundred and forty thousand persons, constituted a privileged class, although they no longer performed any of the high functions which had been exercised by their predecessors.

To make matters worse, very few of the nobles really belonged to old feudal families. For the most part they had been ennobled by the king for some supposed service, or had bought an office, or a judgeship in the higher courts, to which noble rank was attached. Naturally this circumstance served to rob them of much of the respect that their hereditary dignity and titles might otherwise have gained for them. *The ennobled*

In England the feudal castles had disappeared earlier even than in France, and the English law did not grant to any one, however long and distinguished his lineage, special rights or privileges not enjoyed by every freeman. Nevertheless there was a distinct noble class in England. The monarch had formerly been accustomed to summon his counts and some of his barons to take council with him and in this way the peerage developed; this included those whose title permitted them to sit in the House of Lords and to transmit this honorable prerogative to their eldest sons. But the peers paid the same taxes as did every other subject and were punished in the same manner if they were convicted of an offense. Moreover only the eldest surviving son of a noble father inherited his rank, while on the Continent all the children became nobles. In this way the number of the English nobility was greatly restricted and their social distinction roused little antagonism. *Peculiar position of the English peerage*

In Germany, however, the nobles continued to occupy very much the same position which their ancestors held in the Middle Ages. There had been no king to do for all Germany what the French kings had done for France; no mighty man had risen strong enough to batter down castle walls and bend all barons, great and small, to his will. The result was that there were in Germany in the eighteenth century hundreds *The German knights still resembled mediæval lords* of nobles dwelling in strong old castles and ruling with a high hand domains which were sometimes no larger than an American township. They levied taxes, held courts, coined money, and maintained standing armies of perhaps only a handful of soldiers.

The chief noble was the king

In all the countries of Europe the chief noble was of course the monarch himself,[1] to whose favor almost all the lesser nobles owed their titles and rank. He was, except in England, always despotic, permitting the people no share in the man-

His arbitrary powers

agement of the government and often rendering them miserable by needless wars and ill-advised and oppressive taxes. He commonly maintained a very expensive court and gave away to unworthy courtiers much of the money which he had wrung from his people. He was permitted to imprison his subjects upon the slightest grounds and in the most unjust manner. Nevertheless, he usually enjoyed the loyalty and respect of all classes of his subjects, who were generally ready to attribute his bad acts to evil councilors.

The services performed by even despotic kings

On the whole the king merited the respect paid him. He it was who had destroyed the power of innumerable lesser despots and created something like a nation. He had put a stop to the private warfare and feudal brigandage which had disgraced the Middle Ages. His officers maintained order throughout the country so that merchants and travelers could go to and fro with little danger. He opened highroads for them and established a general system of coinage which greatly facilitated business operations. He interested himself more and more in commerce and industry and often encouraged learning. Finally, by consolidating his realms and establishing a regular system of government, he prepared the way for the European State of to-day in which the people are either accorded an effective control of the lawmaking and the disposition of the

[1] All the European countries were monarchies in the eighteenth century except the half-monarchical United Netherlands, Switzerland, and the tiny republics of San Marino in Italy and of Andorra in the Pyrenees. The monarchs of the eighteenth century are discussed in chap. x.

public revenue or, as in the case of France, the monarch has been discarded altogether as no longer needful.

THE CATHOLIC CHURCH

25. The eighteenth century had inherited from the Middle Ages not only the nobility but the clergy, who, except in England, were set off by their peculiar powers and privileges from the nation at large. They were far more powerful and better organized than the nobility and exercised a potent influence in the State. The clergy owed their authority to the Church, which for many centuries had been the great central institution of Europe. The mediæval Church serves to explain more of the problems which have faced reformers in modern times than even the feudal and manorial systems. We must therefore look back for a moment to a time — let us say five hundred years before the period with which we are dealing — when all western Europe was still loyal to its head, the Pope, when the Church was still the soul of almost every great enterprise, and the State had not yet gained the necessary strength to wrest from it gradually many of its prerogatives and a part of its wealth.

In the first place, every one, in the Middle Ages, was required to belong to the Church, somewhat in the same way that we to-day all belong as a matter of course to the State. It is true that one was not born into the Church as we are into the State, but he was ordinarily baptized into it before he had any opinion in the matter. All western Europe formed a single religious association, from which it was a crime to revolt. To refuse allegiance to the Church, or to question its authority or teachings, was reputed treason against God, the most terrible of all crimes. When the clergy declared a person guilty of heresy (as a rejection of the Church's doctrines was called), the king's officials were by law required to execute him, since doubt and disbelief were regarded not merely as sinful, but as

Importance of the mediæval Church in explaining modern problems

Every one required to belong to the Church in the Middle Ages

a criminal revolt against an institution which practically every one esteemed more essential to the existence of order and civilization than was even the king's authority.

The income of the Church from its land and the tithe

·The Church did not rely for its support, as churches usually must to-day, upon the voluntary contributions of its members, but enjoyed the revenue from vast domains which kings, nobles, and other landholders had from time to time given to the churches and monasteries. Practically none of this land was ever sold or given up, and consequently the Church's income continued to increase from generation to generation as new gifts were made. This accumulation of property in the hands of those who could not part with it has been a source of much trouble between the clergy and the various European governments. In addition to the income from its lands and from a considerable variety of fees and contributions, the Church had the right, like the State, to impose a regular tax called the *tithe*. All who were subject to this were forced to pay it whether they cared anything about religion or not, just as we are all compelled to pay taxes imposed by the government under which we live, even if we should prefer an entirely different constitution.

Many cases decided by Church courts

Like the State the Church had, moreover, an elaborate system of law and its own courts in which its officials tried many cases which are now settled in the civil tribunals. One may get some idea of the business of the ecclesiastical courts from the fact that the Church claimed the right to try all cases in which a clergyman was involved, or any one connected with the Church or under its special protection, such as monks, students, crusaders, widows, orphans, and the helpless in general. Then all cases where matters of religion were involved, such as the sacraments of the Church, or its prohibitions, came ordinarily before its courts, as for example, those concerning marriage, wills, sworn contracts, usury, blasphemy, sorcery, heresy, and so forth. The Church had its prisons, too, to which it might sentence offenders to lifelong detention.

The Church not only performed the functions of a state, making laws for its members, taxing them, and trying and punishing them if they broke its laws ; it had also the organization of a state. Unlike the Protestant ministers of to-day, all churchmen and all religious associations of mediæval Europe were under one supreme head, the Roman pontiff, who made laws for all and controlled every Church officer, bishop, or priest, wherever he might be, whether in Italy, Spain, Germany, or Ireland. The Pope's control was facilitated by the circumstance that the Church had one official language — Latin — in which all communications were written and its services everywhere conducted.

The mediæval Church may, therefore, properly be called a great international monarchy embracing all the peoples of western Europe regardless of their race or the character of their civil government. The Pope was its all-powerful and absolute ruler in the same sense that Louis XIV was legally the absolute ruler of the French state. The Pope concentrated in his person, according to the laws of the Church, its entire spiritual and temporal authority. He was the supreme lawgiver. No council of the Church, no matter how large and representative, could make laws against his will; for its decrees, to be valid, required his sanction. He could set aside or abrogate any law of the Church, however ancient, so long as it was not ordained by the Bible or by nature. He might, for good reasons, make exceptions to all merely human law. He was not only the supreme lawgiver but the supreme judge as well. Any one in any part of Europe could appeal to him at any stage in almost any case.

As supreme head of the Church the Pope naturally claimed the right under certain circumstances to annul the decrees of all other earthly powers. Ordinarily the Church left the kings and princes to make laws and rule their peoples, so far as the interests of this world were concerned, as they pleased, but the Pope felt in duty bound — since he was answerable for the eternal welfare of every Christian — to restrain a sinful and perverse prince and to declare unrighteous laws null and void. Should all else fail, he claimed the right to free a nation which was being led to disaster in this world and to perdition in the next from its allegiance to a wicked monarch.

Great service of the Church in supplying the deficiencies of feudalism

The influence which the Church and its head exercised over the civil government in the Middle Ages was due largely to the absence of any orderly states in the modern sense of the term. There were only weak kings and refractory feudal lords to whom disorder was the very breath of life. There were few, if any, strong, efficient rulers who could count upon the support of a large body of prosperous and loyal subjects. So long as this feudal anarchy continued, the Church endeavored to supply the deficiencies of the turbulent and ignorant princes by striving to maintain order, administer justice, protect the weak, and encourage learning.

The problem of the relation of Church and State

So soon, however, as the modern State began to develop, difficulties arose. The clergy naturally clung to the powers and privileges which they had long enjoyed, and which they believed to be rightly theirs. On the other hand, the State, so soon as it felt itself able to manage its own affairs, protect its subjects, and provide for their worldly interests, was less and less inclined to tolerate the interference of the clergy and of their head, the Pope.

Laymen replace the clergy in the king's government

Educated laymen were becoming more and more common — above all, lawyers trained in the Roman law — and the king was no longer obliged to rely mainly upon the assistance of the clergy in conducting his government. It was natural that he should look with disfavor upon their privileges, which put them upon a different footing from the great mass of his subjects, and upon their wealth, which he would deem excessive and dangerous to his power. This situation raised the fundamental problem of the proper relation of Church and State, upon which Europe has been working ever since the fourteenth century and has not yet completely solved.

Among the many difficulties and contentions which were constantly arising between the clergy and the various European governments were the following: Four chief subjects of contention between the Church and the State

1. Should the king or the Pope enjoy the privilege of selecting the important Church officials, — the archbishops and bishops and the abbots of the great and rich monasteries? Naturally both king and Pope were anxious to place their own friends and supporters in these influential positions. Moreover the Pope came to claim a considerable contribution from those he appointed and the king grudged him the money. 1. Who should choose the Church officials?

2. How far might the king venture to tax the lands and other property of the clergy which he, or his predecessors, and the feudal lords had donated for the support of the churches and monasteries? Was this vast amount of property to be permitted to increase indefinitely and yet contribute nothing to the maintenance of the government? The clergy commonly maintained that their possessions were dedicated to God's service and that they needed all their revenue in order to support themselves with proper dignity, conduct the religious services, keep up the churches and monasteries, aid the poor and afflicted, and carry on the schools, since the State left them to bear all these burdens. The law of the Church permitted the clergy to make voluntary contributions to the king when there was urgent necessity and the resources of the laity proved inadequate, but the Pope maintained that except in the most critical cases his consent must be obtained for such grants upon the part of the clergy. 2. How far could the king tax the clergy?

3. There was inevitable jealousy on the part of the king and his judges in respect to the cases which the clergy had drawn into their own courts and the exemption from trial before the regular courts which they claimed. Still graver disadvantages were to be ascribed to the misuse of the right of appeal to the Pope's great central court at Rome, whither cases were carried upon every pretense. The head of the Church maintained that no one might prevent cases being freely brought before him, 3. Question of Church courts and appeals to the Pope

and he did not hesitate to reverse the decisions of the royal courts. The result was that matters which should have been adjusted in London or Paris, where the facts were known and the witnesses were readily assembled, were frequently carried to a distant city where the best intentioned Pope could hardly expect to see justice done.

4. How far might the Pope interfere in the affairs of a state?

4. Lastly, there was the most fundamental problem of all; namely, the extent to which the Pope, as the universally recognized religious head of the Church, was justified in interfering with the temporal or worldly concerns of a particular state. Unfortunately almost every matter could be viewed from a religious as well as from a worldly standpoint. A contract might relate to purely secular affairs but, if it was solemnized by an oath, it received a religious sanction which seemed to bring the question of its violation within the scope of the ecclesiastical courts. Marriage was held to be a sacrament, a holy act, and was not legitimate unless performed by the priest, but dowries and rights of inheritance seemed to be matters for adjustment by the state officials. Every crime or misdemeanor was, in the last analysis, a *sin*, so there seemed no limit to the questions which the Pope and clergy might claim the right to consider. The Pope's powers were consequently very great and very vague, and there has always been a wide range of difference even among devout Catholics in regard to their extent.

The Pope never surrenders any powers once conceded to him

It may be said in general that the Pope has always laid claim to all the authority which any of his predecessors, or the theologians, have at any time attributed to the Roman see. He does not, however, exercise it in its plenitude, sometimes because he is unable to enforce his will, sometimes because he judges it best, in the interest of the Church, to make exceptions and concessions in special agreements with various Catholic rulers. He does not thereby surrender, however, any of the imposing prerogatives which he believes that God has vested in him as the successor of Saint Peter, the chief of the apostles, to whom the right of loosing and binding upon earth and in heaven was granted by Christ himself.

The Popes have, through the centuries, been forced to accept many insults and some personal violence from princes who, although they believed the Pope to be the divinely appointed head of the Church, nevertheless protested against his interference in secular matters. The German emperors fought with him over the question of patronage, which was a vital matter to them; Philip the Fair of France, about the year 1300, engaged in a bitter controversy with Boniface VIII over the king's right to tax the property of the clergy. Fifty years later the English Parliament forbade any representative of the Pope bearing a papal appointment to an English benefice to enter the kingdom. No one was to appeal to the Pope in such matters; and to act under the Pope's authority, except with the king's special permission, was declared a crime punishable with death. Struggles between the Popes and the German, French, and English rulers

Yet the gradual reduction of the powers of the clergy was due not so much to violent altercations with the papacy as to peaceful arrangements; for example, those by which the clergy undertook to make " free gifts " to the king of France, or the Pope agreed to share his patronage with the Emperor, allowing him to fill the benefices which fell vacant every other month beginning with January. In 1516 the Pope agreed to permit the French kings to nominate archbishops, bishops, and abbots, and pledged himself to appoint the king's candidates, if suitable men, on the understanding that he should receive a contribution, called the *Annates*, from each benefice which was so filled. Peaceful arrangements made between the Pope and the rulers Concordat of 1516

As to the important controversy over lawsuits, the king had always stoutly maintained his right to try all cases involving land, since that was certainly a purely worldly matter. Then the king's lawyers claimed many other cases on the ground that their religious aspects were merely accidental and thus brought a great part of the matrimonial cases and those concerning Ways in which the kings got cases into their own courts contracts and wills into the king's tribunals. The "benefit of clergy," as their right to be tried by their own courts was called, was also steadily reduced in one way or another. In England many new laws were passed whose violation was made felony "without benefit of clergy." In France the same end was reached rather more indirectly. Moreover the French and English kings only regarded as law such of the papal decrees as they had ratified, and they permitted no lands to be given to the Church without their permission.

The Protestant revolt from the Pope

After several great Church congresses, known as general councils, had vainly attempted in the fifteenth century to remedy the abuses that had grown up in the Church and limit the general powers of the Pope, a considerable portion of northern Europe finally revolted from the papacy altogether, namely, northern Germany, Norway and Sweden, England, Scotland, the Dutch Netherlands, and parts of Switzerland. The Protestant rulers of these countries refused longer to recognize the Pope except as an Italian prince. They took matters boldly into their own hands, adopted new doctrines (which they usually imposed upon their subjects), confiscated the property of the monasteries, and scattered the monks and nuns. They brought all the property of the Church under their control and used such part of it as they saw fit to support the particular form of Christianity which they professed. Nevertheless, even in Protestant lands many vestiges of the old system still remained in the eighteenth century, especially in England.

The importance of the Council of Trent (1545–1563)

After the Protestant revolt, representatives of the clergy from the countries which still remained Catholic — France, Italy, Spain, Austria, and southern Germany — assembled at Trent, where prolonged sessions were held from 1545 to 1563 to consider once more the reform of the Church. This Council of Trent is memorable in the history of Europe. Its decrees, far more numerous and detailed than those of any previous council, provided a new and solid basis for the doctrines and law of the Roman Catholic Church. The old doctrines were ratified and the Protestant innovations declared accursed. Certain abuses were corrected but all attempts to limit the power of the Pope failed, since his delegates really guided the deliberation of the council. Some of the Catholic princes were disappointed in the results, and the French courts refused to sanction the council's decrees.

THE JESUITS AND ULTRAMONTANISM

26. Among those who, during the final sessions of the Council of Trent, sturdily opposed every attempt to reduce in any way the exalted powers of the Pope, was the head of a new religious society which was becoming the most powerful organization in Europe, — the Society of Jesus, or Jesuits, as they are commonly called. This most faithful of all the Pope's allies was founded by a Spaniard named Ignatius Loyola. He conceived of a new association which, unlike the older monastic orders, should aim not so much at the salvation of its own members through fasts and chants and spiritual meditation as to promote the glory of God by serving the Church and its head, the Roman pontiff.

In 1538 Loyola summoned his followers to Rome, and there they worked out the principles of their order. The Pope then incorporated these in a bull in which he gave his sanction to the new organization. The society was to be under the absolute control of a *general*, who was to be chosen for life by the great assembly of the order. Loyola had been a soldier, and he laid great and constant stress upon the source of all efficient military discipline, namely, absolute and unquestioning obedience. This he declared to be the mother of all virtue and happiness. Not only were the members to obey the Pope as Christ's representative on earth, and undertake without hesitation any journey, no matter how distant or perilous, which he might command, but each was to obey his superiors in the order as if he were receiving directions from Christ in person.

Rigid organization and discipline of the Jesuits

He must have no will or preference of his own, but must be as the staff which supports and aids its bearer in any way in which he sees fit to use it. This admirable organization and incomparable discipline were the great secret of the later influence of the Jesuits.

Objects and methods of the new order

The object of the society was to cultivate piety and the love of God, especially through example. The members were to pledge themselves to lead a pure life of poverty and devotion. Their humility was to show itself in face and attitude, so that their very appearance should attract to the service of God those with whom they came in contact. The methods adopted by the society for reaching its ends are of the utmost importance. A great number of its members were priests, who went about preaching, hearing confession, and encouraging devotional exercises. But the Jesuits were teachers as well as preachers and confessors. They clearly perceived the advantage of bringing young people under their influence, and they became the schoolmasters of Catholic Europe. So successful were their methods of instruction that even Protestants sometimes sent their children to them.

Rapid increase of the Jesuits in numbers

It was originally proposed that the number of persons admitted to the order should not exceed sixty; but this limit was speedily removed, and before the death of Loyola over a thousand persons had joined the society. Under his successor the number was trebled and it went on increasing for two centuries.

Their missions and explorations

The founder of the order had been attracted to missionary work from the first, and the Jesuits rapidly spread not only throughout Europe but over the whole world. Francis Xavier, one of Loyola's original little band, went to Hindustan, the Moluccas, and Japan. Brazil, Florida, Mexico, and Peru were soon fields of active missionary work at a time when Protestants did not dream as yet of carrying Christianity to the heathen. We owe to the reports of Jesuits like Marquette much of our knowledge of the condition of America when white men first began to explore Canada and the Mississippi Valley; for the followers of Loyola boldly penetrated into regions unknown to Europeans, and settled among the natives with the purpose of bringing the Gospel to them.

Dedicated as they were to the service of the Pope, the Jesuits early directed their energies against Protestantism. They sent their members into Germany and the Netherlands, and even made strenuous efforts to reclaim England. Their success was most apparent in southern Germany and Austria, where they became the confessors and confidential advisers of the rulers. They not only succeeded in checking the progress of Protestantism but were able to reconquer for the Pope some districts in which the old faith had been abandoned. *Their fight against the Protestants*

The Jesuits were naturally abhorred in Protestant countries, where they were popularly believed to be absolutely unscrupulous in working for their ends.[1] Even in Catholic countries there were many thoughtful persons who disapproved of their tendency to exalt the papal prerogatives at the cost of the rights of the bishops and of the king. Thus the Jesuits came to be regarded as the chief defenders of what is now known in France, Germany, and Austria as *ultramontanism*. *Sources of unpopularity of the Jesuits*

The ultramontane, or "beyond-the-mountain," party was so called by its enemies because it looked across the Alps *Ultramontanism*

[1] Protestants realized that the new order was their most powerful and dangerous enemy. Their apprehensions produced a bitter hatred which blinded them to the high purposes of the founders of the order and led them to attribute an evil motive to every act of the Jesuits. The Jesuits' air of humility the Protestants declared to be a mere cloak of hypocrisy under which they carried on their intrigues. The Jesuits' readiness to adjust themselves to circumstances, and the variety of the tasks that they undertook, seemed to their enemies a willingness to resort to any means in order to reach their ends. They were supposed to justify the most deceitful and immoral measures on the ground that the result would be "for the greater glory of God." The very obedience on which the Jesuits laid so much stress was viewed by the hostile Protestant as one of their worst offenses, for he believed that the members of the order were the blind tools of their superiors, and that they would not hesitate even to commit a crime if so ordered.

Doubtless there have been many Jesuits who have not lived up to the principles of their society, and as time went on the order fell away from its standards, as earlier ones had done. It was, as we shall see, abolished by the Pope in 1773, but was restored in 1814, and now has some fifteen thousand members and is growing steadily.

into Italy for the source of authority, and attributed to the bishop of Rome all the powers over churches and governments throughout Christendom which he had asserted during the Middle Ages. The doctrines of the Jesuits were opposed in France by the so-called Gallican, or patriotic, national party which maintained that the authority of the Pope was supreme only in religious matters, and that even in those it was subordinate to that of a general council of Christendom.

The Declaration of Gallican Liberties of 1682   In 1682 the old trouble between the French king and the Pope in regard to filling certain benefices had once more arisen and Louis XIV summoned an assembly of the French clergy. They approved a statement drawn up by the famous Bossuet and known as the Declaration of Gallican Liberties of 1682. This aimed to define in a general way the limits of the spiritual and temporal powers as they were interpreted in France. The first article declared that "Saint Peter and his successors, vicars of Jesus Christ, and even the Church as a whole, has been granted authority from God only in spiritual matters and those which have to do with salvation, and not in temporal or civil affairs; that accordingly the kings and princes are, by God's command, subject (as princes) to no ecclesiastical authority in temporal matters; they may not be deposed directly or indirectly by the Church, and their subjects may not be released from their obedience to them or freed from their oath of fidelity." [1]

Febronius and his book on the Pope and the Church   The Declaration of Gallican Liberties helped later to spread and consolidate the opposition to the extreme papal claims and the doctrines of the Jesuits. A German scholar, Hontheim, associated with the archbishop of Treves, after a careful investigation of the development of the papal power, wrote an elaborate Latin treatise *On the Present State of the Church and the Legitimate Powers of the Roman Pontiff*.

[1] Other articles added that a general council was superior to the Pope and that only such decrees of the Pope should be observed as had been accepted everywhere or had been sanctioned by the French government and by the French national church.

This he published in 1763, under the assumed name of Justinus Febronius, with the lively hope that the Pope would accept his views. He brought forward evidence to show that the Church was not properly a monarchy, and that all the bishops had originally enjoyed the same powers as the bishop of Rome who, he declared, owed his exaltation mainly to certain forged documents — namely, the pseudo-Isidorian decretals — which some unknown person had invented in the ninth century. The Church had, it is true, made the Pope its head in spiritual matters, but he remained subordinate to a general council. In short, Febronius defended the Gallican liberties and advocated the general adoption in Catholic countries of the policy pursued by France.

His book was immediately condemned by the Pope, who declared that to undermine the papacy, which was the very foundation of the Church, was to destroy the Church itself. Nevertheless the work was translated into German, Italian, Spanish, and Portuguese, and became a sort of handbook for the princes who were aiming to limit the activities of the clergy and their head.[1] It served to emphasize once more the contrast between the ultramontane theory and that of those Catholics who wished to have the various national churches retain a certain independence of the central papal government.

In spite of the changes which had overtaken the Church since the Middle Ages, it still retained its ancient external appearance in the eighteenth century, — its gorgeous ceremonial, its wealth, its influence over the lives of men, its intolerance of those who ventured to differ from the conceptions of Christianity which it believed to be its duty to impose upon every one. The ecclesiastical courts still tried many cases, in spite of the widening jurisdiction of the royal judges. The Church could fine and imprison those whom it convicted of blasphemy, contempt of religion, or heresy. The clergy

The Pope condemns the work of Febronius

Great powers still retained by the Catholic Church in the eighteenth century

[1] See below, chap. xi.

managed the schools and saw to it that the children were
brought up in the orthodox faith. Hospitals and other charitable institutions were under their control. They registered
all births and deaths, and only the marriages which they sanctified were regarded by the State as legal. The monasteries
still existed in great numbers and owned vast tracts of land.
A map of Paris made in 1789 shows no less than sixty-eight
monasteries and seventy-three nunneries within the walls. The
clergy still forced the laity to pay the tithe as in the Middle
Ages and still enjoyed exemption from the direct taxes.

Intolerance of
both Catho-
lics and
Protestants

Both the Catholic and the Protestant churches were very
intolerant, and in this were usually supported by the government, which was ready to punish or persecute those who refused
to conform to the State religion, whatever it might be, or ventured to speak or write against its doctrines. There was none
of that freedom which is so general now and which permits a
man to worship or not as he pleases, and even to denounce
religion in any or all its forms without danger of imprisonment,
loss of citizenship, or death.

Position of
the Protes-
tants in
France

In France, after the revocation of the Edict of Nantes in
1685, Protestants had lost all civil rights. According to a
decree of 1724, those who assembled for any form of worship
other than the Roman Catholic were condemned to lose their
property; the men were to be sent to the galleys and the
women imprisoned for life. The preachers who convoked such
assemblies or performed Protestant ceremonies were punishable with death; yet but few executions took place, for happily
the old enthusiasm for persecution was abating. None the less
all who did not accept the Catholic teachings were practically
outlawed, for the priests would neither recognize the marriages
nor register the births and deaths over which they were not
called to preside. This made it impossible for Protestants to
marry legally and have legitimate children, or to inherit or
devise property. A royal proclamation in 1712 forbade physicians to visit such sick people as refused to call in a Catholic

confessor, and the kings still pledged themselves in their coronation oaths to extirpate heretics.

Books and pamphlets were carefully examined in order to see if they contained any attacks upon the orthodox Catholic beliefs or might in any way serve to undermine the authority of the Church or of the king. The Pope had long maintained a commission (which still exists) to examine new books, and to publish from time to time a list, called the "Index," of all those which the Church condemned and forbade the faithful to read. The king of France, as late as 1757, issued a declaration establishing the death penalty for those who wrote, printed, or distributed any work which appeared to be an attack upon religion. The teachings of the professors in the university were watched. A clergyman who ventured to compare the healing of the sick by Christ to the cures ascribed to Æsculapius was arrested (about 1750) by order of the king's judges at Paris and forced to leave the country. A considerable number of the most enlightened books issued in France in the eighteenth century were condemned either by the clergy or the king's courts, and were burned by the common hangman or suppressed. Not infrequently the authors, if they could be discovered, were imprisoned. *Censorship of the press*

This did not check speculation, however, and books attacking the old ideas and suggesting reforms in Church and State constantly appeared and were freely circulated.[1] The writers took care not to place their names, or that of the publisher, upon the title-page, and many such books were printed at Geneva or in Holland, where great freedom prevailed. *Censorship ineffective*

In Spain, Austria, and Italy, however, and especially in the Papal States, the clergy, particularly the Jesuits, were more powerful and enjoyed more privileges than in France. In Spain the censorship of the press and the Inquisition constituted a double bulwark against change until the latter half of the eighteenth century. *Strength of the Church in Spain, Austria, and Italy*

[1] See following chapter.

Peculiar situation of the great German prelates

In Germany the position of the Church varied greatly. The southern states were Catholic, while Prussia and the northern rulers had embraced Protestantism. Many of the archbishops, bishops, and abbots ruled as princes over their own lands and made the best arrangements they could with the Pope.

THE ENGLISH ESTABLISHED CHURCH AND THE PROTESTANT SECTS

The Anglican Church as established under Queen Elizabeth (1558–1603)

27. In England Henry VIII had thrown off his allegiance to the Pope and declared himself the head of the English Church. Under his daughter, Queen Elizabeth (1558–1603), Parliament had established the Church of England. It abolished the mass and sanctioned the Book of Common Prayer which has since remained the official guide to the services in the Anglican Church. The beliefs of the Church were brought together in the Thirty-Nine Articles, from which no one was to vary or depart in the least degree. The system of government of the Roman Catholic Church, with its archbishops, bishops, and priests, was retained but the general charge of religious matters and the appointment of bishops were put in the hands of the monarch or his ministers. All clergymen and government officers were required to subscribe solemnly to the Thirty-Nine Articles. All public religious services were to be conducted according to the Prayer Book, and those who failed to attend services on Sunday and holy days were to be fined.

Persecution of the Catholics in England

Those who persisted in adhering to the Roman Catholic faith fared badly, although happily there were no such general massacres as overwhelmed the Protestants in France. Under the influence of the Jesuits some of the English Catholics became involved in plots against the heretical queen, Elizabeth, who had been deposed by the Pope. These alleged "traitors" were in some instances executed for treason.

Indeed, any one who brought a papal bull to England, who embraced Catholicism, or converted a Protestant was declared a traitor. Fines and imprisonment were inflicted upon those who dared to say or to hear mass.

But there were many Protestants who did not approve of the Anglican Church as established by law. Those who came under the influence of Calvin, the reformer at Geneva, or of his treatise on *The Institutes of the Christian Religion*, felt that Parliament had not gone far enough but should have abolished the bishops and priests and all suggestions of the older Roman Catholic service, such as the surplice worn by the priest, kneeling during the communion, and using the sign of the cross at baptism. They made themselves very unpopular by denouncing pastimes, especially on Sunday, and advocating an austere life, and were contemptuously called Puritans. They finally began to defy the government and hold meetings of their own outside the churches. Elizabeth then took measures to break up the custom and imprisoned those who attended these unlawful religious meetings. {The Puritans}

From these Puritans, or Dissenters, several parties or sects with differing views developed. There was a " Low Church " party ready to support the Established Church if all " superstitious usages " which suggested the Catholic Church were done away with. Then there were the Presbyterians, followers of Calvin, who held that the Church should rightly be governed by ministers and elders instead of by bishops. Lastly there was an ever-increasing number of Separatists, or Independents. These rejected both the organization of the Church of England and that advocated by the Presbyterians and desired that each religious community should organize itself independently. {Classes of Puritans. The " Low Church " party} {The Presbyterians} {The Separatists, or Independents}

Since the government had forbidden the meetings of the Separatists, some of them fled to Holland about the year 1600 and a community of them, under Reverend John Robinson, established themselves at Leyden. In 1620 they determined {The Plymouth colony} to send out a band of colonists to the New World. After many difficulties their ship, the *Mayflower*, reached land in Plymouth Bay, Massachusetts, and there they founded a colony which practiced their form of worship.

Eight years later a new band of English Puritans landed to the north of Plymouth and founded Salem and the Massachusetts Bay colony. They agreed in the main in their theological· beliefs with the people who had come in the *Mayflower* and soon gave up all connection with the English Church. Their

descendants became merged with those of the Plymouth colonists and in this way the Congregational Church was formed, which now has a membership in the United States of about seven hundred thousand.

Meanwhile the opposition to the Established Church was growing in England. The Presbyterians began their attempt to do away with the bishops and replace them, according to Calvin's system, by elders (presbyters).[1] They succeeded in controlling the Long Parliament which assembled in 1640. This body accordingly summoned a great conclave of Presbyterian divines, who held their sessions in Westminster Abbey for several years (1643–1652) and formulated a new system of doctrines, known as the Westminster Confession, which was

to replace the Book of Common Prayer. But with the death of Cromwell and the restoration of Charles II, who was a Catholic at heart, all chance of making Presbyterianism the state religion in England disappeared. Many Dutch, Huguenot, and Scotch-Irish Presbyterians settled, however, in America and there are to-day nearly twice as many Presbyterians in the United States as there are Congregationalists.

---

[1] Calvin established his church in Geneva about 1540. The name Presbyterian is of course derived from the emphasis which he laid upon the rôle of the *presbyters*, or elders, in the government of the Church. His doctrines spread to southern Germany and Holland. They were espoused by the French Huguenots and introduced into Scotland by John Knox. The Westminster Confession of Faith, while it claims to be based directly upon the Bible, accepts Calvin's interpretations and is really a statement of his teachings. See Robinson, *Readings in European History*, Vol. II, pp. 122 *sqq.*

By far the most numerous of the sects which developed in England was that of the Baptists. They held that infants should not be baptized into the Church but that baptism should be postponed until the believer had reached the age of discretion. Most of them also held that it should be performed by immersion instead of by sprinkling. Not until 1640 did they begin forming churches of their own in England after sending Richard Blount to the Baptist community at Rynsburg, in Holland, where he was duly immersed and then returned to England to immerse his fellow-believers. Like other dissenters they suffered persecution under Charles II. John Bunyan was one of those who were cast into prison, and while there he wrote his *Pilgrim's Progress*.

Their first prominent representative in America was Roger Williams, who founded a Baptist community in Rhode Island. Since then they have flourished mightily and now have in the United States over forty-six thousand churches and nearly five million members. They were the first Protestant sect to undertake foreign missions on a large scale, having founded a society for that purpose as early as 1792.[1]

Another English sect which was destined also to be conspic- uous in America was the Society of Friends, or Quakers, as they are commonly called. This group owes its origin to George Fox, who began his preaching in 1647. The Friends were distinguished by their simplicity of life and dress, their abhorrence of war, and their rejection of all ceremonial, including even the Lord's Supper. While there have been fanatics among them whose practices brought discredit upon them both in Old England and New, no branch of the Christian Church

---

[1] It may be noted here that the Catholics found a refuge in America from their Protestant persecutors as did the Huguenots who fled from the oppression of the Catholic government in France. The colony of Maryland was founded by Lord Baltimore in 1634 and named after the French wife of Charles I. In the nineteenth century the number of Catholics in the United States was vastly increased by immigration from Ireland, Italy, and other countries, so that there are over thirteen millions to-day who have been baptized into the Roman Catholic Church.

has ever shown their religion more consistently or beautifully
in their lives than the Friends. Their chief stronghold in
America has always been Pennsylvania, more particularly Phil-
adelphia and its neighborhood, where they settled under the
leadership of William Penn.

John Wesley
and the
Methodists

The last of the great Protestant sects to appear was that of
the Methodists. Their founder, John Wesley, when at Oxford
had founded a religious society among his fellow-students.
Their piety and the regularity of their habits gained for them
the nickname of " Methodists." After leaving Oxford, Wesley
spent some time in the colony of Georgia. On his return to
England in 1738 he came to believe in the sudden and complete forgiveness of sins known as " conversion," which he later
made the basis of his teaching. He thus describes his own
experience : As he entered a meeting in London in 1738 he
found the preacher reading Luther's preface to " The Epistle to

John Wes-
ley's conver-
sion, 1738

the Romans." " About a quarter before nine," Wesley reports,
" while he was describing the change which God works in the
heart through faith in Christ I felt my heart strangely warmed.
I felt I did trust in Christ and in Christ alone for salvation,
and an assurance was given me that he had taken away my
sins, even mine, and saved me from the law of sin and death."

This memorable evening marked a turning point in the life
of Wesley. He soon began a series of great revival meetings
in London and other large towns. He journeyed up and down
the land, aided in his preaching by his brother Charles and by
the impassioned Whitefield. Only gradually did the Methodists separate themselves from the Church of England, of which
they at first considered themselves members. In 1784 the
numerous American Methodists were formally organized into
the Methodist Episcopal Church, and early in the nineteenth
century they became an independent organization in England.
At the time of Wesley's death his followers numbered over
fifty thousand and there are now in the United States over
three millions, including the various branches of the Church.

Parliament under Charles II showed itself very intolerant towards all Dissenters alike, — Presbyterians, Independents, Baptists, Quakers, Unitarians. Any clergyman who refused to accept everything in the Book of Common Prayer was to lose his benefice, and two thousand clergymen resigned for conscience' sake. In 1664 the Conventicle Act declared that any one attending any religious meeting not held in accordance with the practices of the English Church was liable, for repeated offenses, to be transported to some distant colony, and some of the more obstinate Dissenters were actually exiled. Finally, by the Test Act, every one was excluded from office who did not adhere to the Thirty-Nine Articles.

Persecution of the Dissenters under Charles II

Test Act

Upon the accession of William and Mary an Act of Toleration was passed in 1689 which permitted Dissenters to hold meetings; but " Papists and such as deny the Trinity " were explicitly excluded, so England still continued to maintain an intolerant system in the eighteenth century. It had a State Church with a particular form of belief and of services which was established by the government in Elizabeth's time. Even if the Dissenters were permitted to hold services in their own way, they were excluded from government offices unless they accepted the Thirty-Nine Articles; nor could they obtain a degree at the universities. Only the members of the Anglican Church could hold a benefice. Its bishops had seats in the House of Lords and its priests enjoyed a social preëminence denied to the dissenting ministers.

Legal intolerance in England

The privileges of the Anglican clergy

Those who clung to the Roman Catholic faith, to the Pope and the mass, were forbidden to enter England. The celebration of the mass was strictly prohibited. All public offices were closed to Catholics and of course they could not sit in Parliament. Indeed, legally, they had no right whatever to be in England at all. In the middle of the eighteenth century an English court decided that the law did not recognize the existence of Roman Catholics within the realm and that their presence was only made possible by the lax enforcement of the law.

Existence of Catholics not recognized in England

The Church courts still existed in England and could punish
laymen for not attending church, for heresy, and for certain
immoral acts. As late as 1812 a young woman was imprisoned
for two years by a Church court because she failed to perform
the penance it had imposed and had no money to pay the fees
involved in the trial. The ecclesiastical tribunals still tried
matrimonial cases and those concerned with wills. But one
who published a book or pamphlet did not have to obtain the
permission of the government as in France, and nowhere was
there such unrestrained discussion of scientific and religious
matters at this period as in England. As we shall see in the
following chapter, England, in the early eighteenth century,
was the center of progressive thought from which the French
philosophers and reformers drew their inspiration.

REFERENCES

Germany in the Eighteenth Century: FYFFE, *History of Modern
Europe*, pp. 23–27; HENDERSON, *A Short History of Germany*,
Vol. II, pp. 219–226.

The French Nobility: LOWELL, *The Eve of the French Revolution*, pp. 70–82.

The English Peerage: MAY, *Constitutional History of England*,
chap. v.

Town Life in France: LOWELL, pp. 154–185.

Town Life in England: LECKY, *History of England in the
Eighteenth Century*, Vol. II, chap. iv, pp. 97–115; chap. v,
pp. 211–228.

Country Life in France: LOWELL, pp. 186–206.

Country Life in England: LECKY, Vol. II, chap. v, pp. 203–211;
Vol. VII, chap. xxi, pp. 241–265.

The Clergy in France: LOWELL, pp. 25–39.

Religious Sects in England: LECKY, Vol. III, chap. viii,
pp. 1–154; Vol. VI, chap. xvii, pp. 1–47; MAY, chap. xii.

CHAPTER IX

THE SPIRIT OF REFORM

THE DEVELOPMENT OF MODERN SCIENCE

28. A thoughtful observer in the eighteenth century would, as we have seen, have discovered many mediæval institutions which had persisted in spite of the considerable changes which had taken place in conditions and ideas during the previous five hundred years. Serfdom, the guilds, the feudal dues, the nobility and clergy with their peculiar privileges, the declining monastic orders, the confused and cruel laws, — these were a part of the heritage which Europe had received from what was coming to be regarded as a dark and barbarous period. People began to be keenly alive to the deficiencies of the past, and to look to the future for better things, even to dream of progress beyond the happiest times of which they had any record. They came to feel that the chief obstacles to progress were the outworn institutions, the ignorance and prejudices of their forefathers, and that if they could only be freed from this incubus, they would find it easy to create new and enlightened laws and institutions to suit their needs.

This attitude of mind seems natural enough in our progress- ive age, but two centuries ago it was distinctly new. Mankind has in general shown an unreasoning respect and veneration for the past. Until the opening of the eighteenth century the former times were commonly held to have been better than the present, for the evils of the past were little known while those of the present were, as always, only too apparent. Men looked backward rather than forward. They aspired to fight as well, or be as saintly, or write as good books, or paint as beautiful pictures, as the great men of old. That they might excel the

157

achievements of their predecessors did not occur to them. Knowledge was sought not by studying the world about them but in some ancient authority. In Aristotle's vast range of works on various branches of science, the Middle Ages felt that they had a mass of authentic information which it should be the main business of the universities to explain and impart rather than to increase or correct it by new investigations. Men's ideals centered in the past, and improvement seemed to them to consist in reviving, so far as possible, the "good old days."[1]

How the scientists have created the spirit of progress and reform

It was mainly to the patient men of science that the western world owed its first hopes of future improvement. It is they who have shown that the ancient writers were mistaken about many serious matters and that they had at best a very crude and imperfect notion of the world. They have gradually robbed men of their old blind respect for the past and, by their discoveries, have pointed the way to indefinite advance, so that now we expect constant change and improvement and are scarcely astonished at the most marvelous inventions.

Roger Bacon advocates experimental science in the thirteenth century

In the Middle Ages the scholars and learned men had been but little interested in the world about them. They devoted far more attention to philosophy and theology than to what we should call the natural sciences. They were satisfied in the main to get their knowledge of nature from reading the works of the ancients, — above all, those of Aristotle. But, as early as the thirteenth century, a very extraordinary Franciscan friar, Roger Bacon, showed his insight by protesting against the exaggerated veneration for books. He foresaw that a careful examination of the things about us — such as water, air, light,

[1] It may be noted that the men of the Renaissance, in renewing the interest in the literature of Greece, carried men's minds back to the writers and heroes of a distant past and so obscured the importance of the world about them. The Protestants did not claim to create a new theology but to return once more to the old ways and teachings which had prevailed in the early Church. Both of these movements, therefore, illustrate the conservative tendency of mankind and the natural respect for the past.

animals, and plants — would lead to important and useful discoveries which would greatly benefit mankind.[1]

He advocated three methods of reaching truth which are now followed by all scientific men. In the first place, he proposed that natural objects and changes should be examined with great care, in order that the observer might determine exactly what happened in any given case. This has led in modern times to incredibly refined measurement and analysis. The chemist, for example, can now determine the exact nature and amount of every substance in a cup of impure water which may appear perfectly limpid to the casual observer. Then, secondly, Roger Bacon advocated experimentation. He was not contented with mere observation of what actually happened but tried new and artificial combinations and processes. Nowadays experimentation is, of course, constantly used by scientific investigators, and by means of it they ascertain many things which the most careful observation would never reveal. Thirdly, in order to carry on investigation and make careful measurements and experiments, apparatus designed for this special purpose was found to be necessary. As early as the thirteenth century it was discovered, for example, that a convex crystal or bit of glass would magnify objects, although several centuries elapsed before the microscope and telescope were devised.

The progress of scientific discovery was hastened, strangely enough, by two grave misapprehensions, — the belief in alchemy and the confidence in astrology, both of which had been handed down from the Greeks and Romans to the scholars and investigators of the Middle Ages. Modern chemistry developed from alchemy and modern astronomy from astrology.

---

[1] He believed that huge vessels could be made to move at great speed without rowers, "that carriages can be constructed to move without animals to draw them, and with incredible velocity," that flying machines could be devised and suspension bridges be built. See Robinson, *Readings in European History*, Vol. I, p. 461.

The alchemist carried on his experiments with the hope of finding a so-called "elixir," or philosopher's stone, which, if added to baser metals, like lead, mercury, or even silver, should transmute them into gold. It was also believed that the same marvelous elixir would, if taken in small quantities, restore youth to the aged and prolong life indefinitely. Mysterious directions were passed on from the Greeks and Arabs which roused hope in western Europe that some of the strange substances produced in retort, crucible, and mortar would at last prove to be the potent and long-sought combination. Although no one discovered the philosopher's stone, the patient search for it brought to light curious and useful compounds which could be used in medicine and in the industries. To these picturesque names were given, such as spirits of wine and of hartshorn, cream of tartar, oil of vitriol.

The progress of chemistry was much impeded by the respect for the old idea, which even Aristotle had maintained, that there were four "elements" — earth, air, fire, and water — and that heat and cold, dryness and dampness were the fundamental qualities of matter. Even in the eighteenth century the arguments of a German chemist to prove that flame was an element which was latent in bodies until they were subjected to heat, were accepted by the greatest minds of the time. The old hopes of finding the philosopher's stone had, however, been dissipated, chiefly by the English chemist, Boyle (1626–1691).[1] New substances were discovered and the various gases, or "airs" as they were first called, were isolated : first, "inflammable air," or hydrogen, by Boyle ; later carbonic acid gas, or "fixed air," and "nitrous air," or nitrogen.

[1] The impossibility of transmuting other metals into gold was first scientifically proved when it was discovered that gold was an element, or simple substance, which could not therefore be formed by any combination of other elements. Very recently, however, the strange action of the newly discovered radium and similar substances have aroused the suspicion that even the elements may some day be decomposed and perhaps transformed.

Modern chemistry was not, however, really established until the latter part of the eighteenth century, when the celebrated French chemist, Lavoisier (born in 1743 and beheaded by the guillotine in 1794), during some fifteen years of experimentation, succeeded in decomposing air and in showing that combustion was really the violent combination of the oxygen in the air with any material capable of rapid oxidization. By careful weighing he showed that the products of combustion were always exactly equal to the burned substance plus the oxygen used up in the burning. It was he also who first decomposed water into oxygen and hydrogen and then recombined these gases into water. He coöperated in drawing up a new system for renaming chemical substances which was presented to the French Academy of Sciences in 1787. The names adopted — sulphates, nitrates, oxides, etc. — are still employed in our text-books of chemistry. Lavoisier's use of the balance, his successful analyses and recombinations, his correct conception of combustion and of the more important gases, enabled the chemists rapidly to multiply their discoveries and apply their knowledge to all manner of practical processes which have given us such diverse and important results as photography, the new and powerful explosives, aniline dyes, celluloid, anæsthetics, and many other potent drugs.

Lavoisier (1743–1794), the father of modern chemistry

Just as the false hopes of alchemy promoted the development of chemistry, so the vain hopes of forecasting the future from the stars forwarded astronomy. Until recent times, even the most intelligent persons have believed that the heavenly bodies influenced the fate of mankind; consequently, that a careful observation of the position of the planets at the time of a child's birth would make it possible to forecast his life. In the same way important enterprises were only to be undertaken when the influence of the stars was auspicious. Physicians believed that the efficacy of their medicines depended upon the position of the planets. This whole subject of the influence of the stars upon human affairs was called astrology,

Astrology

and was, in some cases, taught in the mediæval universities. Those who studied the heavens gradually came, however, to the conclusion that the movements of the planets had no effect upon humanity; but the facts which the astrologers had discovered through careful observation became the basis of modern astronomy.

Idea that the earth was the center of the universe   All through the Middle Ages, even in the darkest period, learned men had known that the earth was a globe, and had not greatly underrated its size. They also knew that the planets and stars were very large and millions of miles away from the earth. But they nevertheless had a very inadequate notion of the tremendous extent of the universe. They mistakenly believed that the earth was its center and that the sun and all the heavenly host revolved about it every day. Some of the Greek thinkers had suspected that this was not true, but a Polish astronomer, Kopernick (commonly known by his Latinized name of Copernicus), was the first modern writer to maintain boldly that the earth and the other planets revolved about the sun. His great work, *Upon the Revolutions of the Heavenly Bodies*, was published in 1543 just after his death. But he was unable to prove his theory, which was declared to be foolish and wicked by Catholics and Protestants alike, since it appeared to contradict the teachings of the Bible. Nevertheless, Copernicus opened the way for an entirely new conception of the heavenly bodies and their motions, which continued to be studied with the help of new mathematical knowledge.

Copernicus (1473-1543)

Galileo and his telescope   The truths which had been only suspected by earlier astronomers were demonstrated to the eye by Galileo (1564-1642). By means of a little telescope, which was not so powerful as the best modern opera glasses, he discovered (in 1610) the spots on the sun. These made it plain that the sun was turning on its axis in the same way that astronomers were already convinced that the earth turned. His little telescope showed, too, that the moons of Jupiter were revolving about their planet in the same way that the planets revolve about the sun.

The year that Galileo died, the famous English mathematician, Isaac Newton, was born (1642–1727). He carried on the work of earlier astronomers by the application of mathematics, and proved that the force of attraction which we call gravitation was a universal one, and that the sun, the moon, the earth, and all the heavenly bodies are attracted to one another inversely as the square of the distance. Sir Isaac Newton and his discovery of universal gravitation

While the telescope aided the astronomer, the microscope contributed far more to the extension of practical knowledge. Rude and simple microscopes were used with advantage as early as the seventeenth century. Leuwenhoek, a Dutch linen merchant, so far improved his lenses that he discovered (1665) the blood corpuscles and the "animalculæ," or minute organisms of various kinds found in pond water and elsewhere. The microscope has been rapidly perfected since the introduction of better kinds of lenses early in the nineteenth century, so that it is now possible to magnify minute objects to more than four thousand times their diameters. Development of the microscope

It is very clear to us now that all the natural sciences are in some sort dependent upon one another. The physiologist, the physicist, the geologist, and the botanist must all know something of chemistry because they must all reckon with chemical processes at some stage of their investigations. The astronomer must know physics and mathematics and some chemistry. The psychologist must base his work upon physiology and biology. Dependence of the various sciences upon one another

The first scholar to draw up a great scheme of all the known sciences and work out a method of research which, if conscientiously followed, promised wonderful discoveries, was Francis Bacon, a versatile English statesman and author who wrote in the time of James I. It seemed to him (as it had seemed to his namesake, Roger Bacon, three centuries earlier) that the discoveries which had hitherto been made were as nothing Francis Bacon (1561 1626) compared with what could be done if men would but study and experiment with things themselves, abandon their confidence in vague words, like "moist" and "dry," "matter" and "form," and repudiate altogether "the thorny philosophy" of Aristotle which was taught in the universities. "No one," he declares, "has yet been found so firm of mind and purpose as resolutely to compel himself to sweep away all theories and common notions, and to apply the understanding, thus made fair and even, to a fresh examination of details. Thus it comes about that human knowledge is as yet a mere medley and ill-digested mass, made up of much credulity and much accident, and also of childish notions which we early have imbibed."

Founding of royal scientific academies in England, France, and Prussia

Not many years after Bacon's death, the government in England and France began to take an interest in promoting general scientific progress. The Royal Society was incorporated in London in 1662 under the king's patronage and soon began to issue its *Proceedings*, which still appear regularly. Four years later Colbert definitely organized the French Academy of Sciences. These academies — together with that founded by the Prussian king in 1700 in Berlin — by their discussions, by the publication of their proceedings, and by their encouragement and support of special investigations, have served greatly to hasten scientific progress. Colbert established the

Astronomical observatories

famous observatory of Paris in 1667 ; a few years later, 1676, the still more famous observatory at Greenwich, near London, was completed. Periodicals devoted to scientific matters began to appear. One of the very earliest and most important was the *Journal des Savants*, encouraged by Colbert, which, except for a few years during the French Revolution, has been issued regularly for well-nigh two centuries and a half.

Scientific expeditions in the eighteenth century

Scientific expeditions to distant parts of the earth were also subsidized by the European governments, especially by France, to determine by simultaneous observations at widely distant points the exact size and shape of the globe and the distance

SIR ISAAC NEWTON

of the moon from the earth. In 1769, when Venus crossed
the face of the sun, an event that would not occur again for
over a hundred years, astronomers were anxious to avail themselves of this unusual opportunity with a view of calculating
more exactly than ever before the distance of the sun from the
earth. Accordingly various governments arranged to dispatch
observers to suitable places, — the English to Hudson Bay,
Tahiti, and Madras; the French to California and India; the
Danes to North Cape; the Russians to Siberia. This was an
early instance of what has now become an established practice
in the case of any unusual astronomical event.

The observation and experimentation of which we have Discovery of
been speaking deeply influenced men's conceptions of the natural laws
earth and of the universe at large. Of the many scientific discoveries, by far the most fundamental was the conviction that
all things about us follow certain natural and immutable laws;
and it is the determination of these laws and the seeking out
of their applications to which the modern scientific investigator devotes his efforts, whether he be calculating the distance of a nebula or noting the effect of a drop of acid upon
a frog's foot. He has given up all hope of reading man's fate
in the stars, or of producing any results by magical processes.
He is convinced that the natural laws have been found to
work regularly in every instance where they have been carefully observed. Unlike the mediæval scholars, therefore, he
hesitates to accept as true the reports which reach him of
alleged miracles, that is, of exceptions to the general laws in
which he has come to have such confidence. Moreover his
study of the regular processes of nature has enabled him, as
Roger Bacon foresaw,[1] to work wonders far more marvelous
than any attributed to the mediæval magician.

The path of the scientific investigator has not always been Opposition to
without its thorns. Mankind has changed its notions with reluc- scientific
tance. The churchmen and the professors in the universities discoveries

[1] See note, p. 159, above.

were wedded to the conceptions of the world which the mediæval theologians and philosophers had worked out, mainly from the Bible and Aristotle. They clung to the old books that they and their predecessors had long used in teaching, and had no desire to begin a long and painful examination of the innumerable substances and organisms from a study of which the newer scientists were gathering information that refuted the venerated theories of the past.

Hostile atti-
tude of the
theologians

The theologians were especially prone to denounce scientific discoveries on the ground that they did not harmonize with the teachings of the Bible as commonly accepted. It was naturally a great shock to them, and also to the public at large, to have it suggested that man's dwelling place, instead of being God's greatest work, to which he had subordinated everything and around which the whole starry firmament revolved, was after all but a tiny speck in comparison with the whole universe, and its sun but one of an innumerable host of similar glowing bodies of stupendous size, each of which might have its particular family of planets revolving about it.

Galileo pun-
ished for
advocating
new ideas

The bolder thinkers were consequently sometimes made to suffer for their ideas, and their books prohibited or burned. Galileo was forced to say that he did not really believe that the sun revolved about the earth; and he was kept in partial confinement for a time and ordered to recite certain psalms every day for three years for having ventured to question the received views in a book which he wrote in Italian, instead of Latin, so that the public at large might read it.[1]

[1] But even the scientists themselves did not always readily accept new discoveries. Francis Bacon, who lived some seventy years after Copernicus, still clung to the old idea of the revolution of the sun about the earth and still believed in many quite preposterous illusions, as for example, that "it hath been observed by the ancients that where a rainbow seemeth to hang over or to touch, there breatheth forth a sweet smell"; and that "since the ape is a merry and a bold beast, its heart worn near the heart of a man comforteth the heart and increaseth audacity." In the latter half of the eighteenth century Lavoisier was burned in effigy in Berlin because his discovery of oxygen threatened the accepted explanation of combustion.

How the Scientific Discoveries produced a Spirit of Reform

29. Those who accepted the traditional views of the world and of religion, and opposed change, were quite justified in suspecting that scientific investigation would sooner or later make them trouble. It taught men to distrust, and even to scorn, the past which furnished so many instances of ignorance and gross superstition. Instead of accepting the teachings of the theologians, both Catholic and Protestant, that mankind through Adam's fall was rendered utterly vile, and incapable, (except through God's special grace) of good thoughts or deeds, certain thinkers began to urge that man was by nature good ; that he should freely use his own God-given reason ; that he was capable of becoming increasingly wise by a study of nature's laws, and that he could indefinitely better his own condition and that of his fellows if he would but free himself from the shackles of error and superstition. Those who had broadened their views of mankind and of the universe refused longer to believe that God had revealed himself only to the Jewish people, but maintained that he must be equally solicitous for all his creatures in all ages and in all parts of a boundless universe where everything was controlled by his immutable laws. This tendency to "enlarge God" is illustrated in the famous "Universal Prayer" of Alexander Pope, written about 1737 :

Effects of scientific discoveries on religious belief

> Father of all! in ev'ry age,
>   In ev'ry clime adored,
> By saint, by savage, and by sage,
>   Jehova, Jove, or Lord!
>
> .   .   .   .
>
> Yet not to earth's contracted span
>   Thy goodness let me bound,
> Or think Thee Lord alone of man,
>   When thousand worlds are 'round.

The deists Pope was suspected of " infidelity " to the Christian religion and of rejecting the Bible as God's revelation to man, although nowadays the most devout Christian could read without offense his long poem called " An Essay on Man." But there were in his day a considerable number of " freethinkers " in England who attacked the Christian religion in no doubtful terms, and whose books were eagerly read and discussed. These " deists " maintained that their conception of God was far worthier than that of the Christian believer who, they declared, accused the deity of violating his own laws by miracles and of condemning a great part of his children to eternal torment.

How Voltaire came to England, 1726 In the year 1726 there landed in England a young and gifted Frenchman who was to become the great prophet of deism in all lands. Voltaire, who was then thirty-two years old, had already deserted the older religious beliefs and was consequently ready to follow enthusiastically the more radical of the English thinkers, who discussed matters with an openness which filled him with astonishment. He became an ardent admirer of the teachings of Newton, whose stately funeral he attended shortly after his arrival. He regarded the discoverer of universal gravitation as greater than an Alexander or a Cæsar, and did all he could to popularize Newton's work in France. " It is to him who masters our minds by the force of truth, not to those who enslave men by violence; it is to him who understands the universe, not to those who disfigure it, that we owe our reverence."

Voltaire charmed by the English freedom of speech Voltaire was deeply impressed by the Quakers,—their simple life and their hatred of war. He was delighted with the English philosophers, especially with John Locke[1] (died in 1704);

---

[1] Locke rejected the notion that man was born with certain divinely implanted ideas, and maintained that we owe all that we know to the sensations and impressions which come to us from without. Locke was a man of extraordinary modesty, good sense, and caution, and he and his gifted successor, Bishop Berkeley, did much to found modern psychology by helping to rid the world of certain meaningless abstractions and encouraging the careful study of our own mental processes to which so much attention is now being given. Berkeley's *New Theory of Vision* is a clear account of the gradual way in which we learn to

he thought Pope's "Essay on Man" the finest moral poem ever composed; he admired the English liberty of speech and writing; he respected the general esteem for the merchant class. In France, he said, "the merchant so constantly hears his business spoken of with disdain that he is fool enough to blush for it; yet I am not sure that the merchant who enriches his country, gives orders from his countinghouse at Surat or Cairo, and contributes to the happiness of the globe is not more useful to a state than the thickly-bepowdered lord who knows exactly what time the king rises and what time he goes to bed, and gives himself mighty airs of greatness while he plays the part of a slave in the minister's ante-room."

Voltaire proceeded to enlighten his countrymen by a volume of essays in which he set forth his impressions of England; but the high court of justice (the *parlement*) of Paris condemned these *Letters on the English* to be publicly burned, as scandalous and contrary alike to good manners and to the respect due to the principalities and powers. In this way they furnished one more illustration of the need of such men as Voltaire, who was to become, during the remainder of a long life, the chief advocate throughout Europe of unremitting reliance upon reason and of confidence in enlightenment and progress. And since a great part of the institutions of his day were not based upon reason but upon mere tradition, and were often quite opposed to common sense, "the touch of reason was fatal to the whole structure, which instantly began to crumble." His keen eye was continually discovering some new absurdity in the existing order, which, with incomparable wit and literary skill, he would expose to his eager readers. He was interested in almost everything; he wrote histories, dramas, philosophic treatises, romances, epics, and

Voltaire's Letters on the English

Voltaire's wide influence and popularity

see. He shows that a blind man, if suddenly restored to sight, would make little or nothing of the confused colors and shapes which would first strike his eye. He would learn only from prolonged experience that one set of colors and contours meant a man and another a horse or a table, no matter how readily he might recognize the several objects by touch.

innumerable letters to his innumerable admirers. The vast range of his writings enabled him to bring his bold questionings to the attention of all sorts and conditions of men, — not only to the general reader, but even to the careless playgoer.

While Voltaire was successfully inculcating free criticism in general, he led a relentless attack upon the most venerable, probably the most powerful, institution in Europe, the Roman Catholic Church. The absolute power of the king did not trouble him, but the Church, with what appeared to him to be its deep-seated opposition to a free exercise of reason and its hostility to reform, seemed fatally to block all human progress. He was wont to close his letters with the exhortation, "Crush the infamous thing." The Church, as it fully realized, had never encountered a more deadly enemy. Not only was Voltaire supremely skillful in his varied methods of attack, but there were thousands of both the thoughtful and the thoughtless ready to applaud him; for not only was he always brilliant and entertaining in his diatribes, but many of his readers had reached the same conclusions, although they might not be able to express their thoughts so persuasively as he.[1]

Voltaire
maintains
that the
Church
should not
encroach
upon the
functions of
the State

Voltaire was scandalized not only by what he regarded as the gloomy superstition of the Church, its cruel intolerance, and the hateful conflicts over seemingly unimportant matters of belief; but he held that it exercised a pernicious control over the government. In his famous *Handy Philosophic Dictionary*, a little volume of witty essays on a variety of themes which he published anonymously in 1764, he maintains that no law of the Church should have the least force unless expressly sanctioned by the government; that all ecclesiastics should be subject to the government, should pay taxes like

---

[1] Voltaire repudiated the beliefs of the Protestant churches as well as of the Roman Church. He was, however, no atheist, as his enemies — and they have been many and bitter — have so often asserted. He believed in God, and at his country home near Geneva he dedicated a temple to him. Like many of his contemporaries, he was a deist, and held that God had revealed himself in nature and in our own hearts, not in Bible or Church.

VOLTAIRE

every one else, and should have no power to deprive a citizen
of the least of his rights on the ground that he is a sinner,
"since the priest — himself a sinner — should pray for other
sinners, not judge them." Marriage should be entirely under
the control of the civil government, and the shameful custom, as he calls it, of paying a part of the clergy's revenue to
a "foreign priest," namely the Pope, should no longer be
maintained. But the *parlement* of Paris condemned the book
to be burned, on the ground that it defended license and
incredulity; that it attacked all that was sacred in religious
teachings, mysteries, and authority; and that the writer glo-
ried in sinking to the level of the brutes and dragging others
down into his own degradation.

Were there space at command, a great many good things,
as well as plenty of bad ones, might be told of this extraordinary man. He was often superficial in his judgments, and
sometimes jumped to unwarranted conclusions. He saw only
the evil in the Church and seemed incapable of understanding all that it had done for mankind during the bygone ages.
He maliciously attributed to evil motives teachings which
were accepted by the best and loftiest of men. He bitterly
ridiculed even the holiest and purest aspirations, along with
the alleged deceptions of the Jesuits and the quarrels of the
theologians. *(Weaknesses of Voltaire)*

He could, and did, however, fight bravely against wrong
and oppression. The abuses which he attacked were in large
part abolished by the Revolution. It is unfair to notice only
Voltaire's mistakes and exaggerations, as many writers, both
Catholic and Protestant, have done, for he certainly did more
than any one else to prepare the way for the great and permanent reform of the Church, as a political and social institution,
in 1789–1790. "When the right sense of historical proportion is more fully developed in men's minds," John Morley
writes, "the name of Voltaire will stand out like the names of
the great decisive movements in the European advance, like *(Real greatness of Voltaire)*

the Revival of Learning or the Reformation. The existence, character, and career of this extraordinary person constituted in themselves a new and prodigious era."

Diderot's *En-cyclopædia*

Voltaire had many admirers and powerful allies. Among these none were more important than Denis Diderot and the scholars whom Diderot induced to coöperate with him in preparing articles for a new *Encyclopædia* which should serve to spread among a wide range of intelligent readers a knowledge of scientific advance and rouse enthusiasm for reform and progress. An encyclopædia was by no means a new thing. Diderot's plan had been suggested by a proposal to publish a French translation of Chambers *Cyclopædia*.[1] Before his first volume appeared, a vast *Universal Dictionary* had been completed in Germany in sixty-four volumes. But few people outside of that country could read German in those days, whereas the well-written and popular articles of Diderot and his helpers, ranging from " abacus," " abbey," and "abdication " to " Zoroaster," " Zurich," and " zymology," were in a language that many people all over Europe could understand.

Diderot
(1713–1784)

Diderot was one of the broadest, most alert and genial of the French philosophers. Like Voltaire, he had learned English and had become acquainted with the writings of Bacon, Locke, and some of the more sceptical later writers. Under their influence he prepared a little volume of *Philosophic Thoughts*, in which he urges people to dare to think for themselves, since no one should believe that he is honoring God by refusing to use his reason. He asserted that what has never been questioned has never been proved ; we must doubt before we have a right to believe. Consequently scepticism, which is only legitimate doubt, leads us on to truth. "It is as hazardous to believe too much as to believe too little." The *parlement* of Paris ordered this book burned,

[1] This was first published by an English Quaker in 1727, and new editions of it still continue to appear from time to time.

and Diderot was later imprisoned for a time on account of his *Letter on the Blind for the Use of Those Who See*, in which he questioned some of the proofs usually assigned for the existence of God.

Diderot chose for his main collaborator in preparing the *Encyclopædia*, D'Alembert, perhaps the most distinguished mathematician of his age, who was well qualified by his exactness and his special knowledge of the various fields of mathematical investigation to supplement Diderot's efforts. He lived in poverty and independence and refused invitations which came to him from Frederick the Great and later from Catharine of Russia to leave his humble surroundings for a life at court. D'Alembert aids Diderot

The editors endeavored to rouse as little opposition as possible. They respected current prejudices and gave space to ideas and opinions with which they were not personally in sympathy. They furnished material, however, for refuting what they believed to be mistaken notions, and Diderot declared that " time will enable people to distinguish what we have thought from what we have said." But no sooner did the first two volumes appear in 1752 than the king's ministers, to please the Church, suppressed them, as containing principles hostile to royal authority and religion, although they did not forbid the continuation of the work. The attitude of the clergy led Diderot to exclaim angrily: " I know nothing so indecent as these vague declamations of the theologians against reason. To hear them, one would suppose that men could only enter into the bosom of Christianity as a herd of cattle enters a stable ; and that we must renounce our common sense if we are either to embrace our religion or to remain in it." The *Encyclopædia* rouses the hostility of the theologians

As volume after volume appeared the subscribers increased ; but so did the opposition. The Encyclopædists were declared to be a band bent upon the destruction of religion and the undermining of society; the government again interfered, D'Alembert, discouraged, leaves Diderot to complete the *Encyclopædia*

withdrew the license to publish the work, and prohibited the sale of the seven volumes that were already out. D'Alembert was disheartened, and resolved to give up any attempt to carry the work further, although they had only just reached the letter "H." He wrote to Voltaire : " I am worn out with the affronts and vexations of every kind that this work draws down upon us. The hateful and even infamous satires which they print against us and which are not only tolerated but protected, authorized, applauded, nay, actually commanded, by those in power; the sermons, or rather the alarm bells, that are rung out against us at Versailles in the king's presence . . . all these reasons and some others drive me to give up this accursed work once for all." Voltaire naturally encouraged the editors to persevere. " We are on the eve of a great revolution in the human mind," he argued, "and it is you to whom we are most of all indebted." He urged Diderot to leave France and seek a country where he could complete his work in peace; but this he refused to do, for he knew that was just what his enemies desired.

Completion of the *Encyclopædia* and accompanying volumes of plates

Seven years later he was able to deliver the remaining ten volumes to the subscribers in spite of the government's prohibition. Still later eleven volumes of beautiful plates illustrating the various arts — such as weaving, printing, engraving, mining, dyeing, cabinet making, surgery — were added. In spite of the denunciation by the clergy of the completed enterprise the government refused to interfere any further.

Scope of the *Encyclopædia*

As one looks through these fine volumes, which may now and then be found in our larger libraries, he is struck with the light which they must have shed upon thousands of matters, great and small, from a lady's headdress to the constitution of the universe. The peaceful arts received especial attention. Great care was exercised in order to secure those to write for the *Encyclopædia* who really knew the details of the various trades; an inspector of glass works dealt with his particular subject, and the article on brewing was assigned to an intelligent brewer.

The *Encyclopædia* attacked temperately, but effectively, religious intolerance, the bad taxes, the slave trade, and the atrocities of the criminal law; it encouraged men to turn their minds to natural science with all its beneficent possibilities, and this helped to discourage the old interest in theology and barren metaphysics. The article, " Legislator," written by Diderot, says: " All the men of all lands have become necessary to one another for the exchange of the fruits of industry and the products of the soil. Commerce is a new bond among men. Every nation has an interest in these days in the preservation by every other nation of its wealth, its industry, its banks, its luxury, its agriculture. The ruin of Leipzig, of Lisbon, of Lima has led to bankruptcies on all the exchanges of Europe and has affected the fortunes of many millions of persons." The English statesman, John Morley, is doubtless right when he says, in his enthusiastic account of Diderot and his companions, that "it was this band of writers, organized by a harassed man of letters, and not the nobles swarming around Louis XV, nor the churchmen singing masses, who first grasped the great principle of modern society, the honour that is owed to productive industry. They were vehement for the glories of peace and passionate against the brazen glories of war." *Value of the Encyclopædia*

Neither Voltaire nor Diderot had attacked the kings and their despotic system of government. Montesquieu, however, while expressing great loyalty to French institutions, opened the eyes of his fellow-citizens to the disadvantages and abuses of their government by his enthusiastic eulogy of the limited monarchy of England. In his celebrated work, *The Spirit of Laws, or the Relation which Laws should bear to the Constitution of each Country, its Customs, Climate, Religion, Commerce, etc.*, he proves from history that governments are not arbitrary arrangements, but that they are the natural products of special conditions and should meet the needs of a particular people at a particular period. England, he thought, had developed an especially happy system. *Montesquieu (1689–1755) and his Spirit of Laws*

Montesquieu's doctrine of the separation of powers

Montesquieu maintained that the freedom which Englishmen enjoyed was due to the fact that the three powers of government — legislative, executive, and judicial — were not, as in France, in the same hands. Parliament made the laws, the king executed them, and the courts, independent of both, saw that they were observed. He believed that the English would lose their liberties as soon as these powers fell under the control of one person or body of persons. This principle of " the separation of powers " is now recognized in many modern governments, notably in that of the United States.

Montesquieu familiarizes Frenchmen with the advantages of the English constitution

Through Montesquieu's very readable book many thoughtful people became familiar for the first time with the English Parliament, its division into the House of Commons and the House of Lords, its annual budget which prevented the king from arbitrarily taxing his people, and the *habeas corpus* proceedings which stood in the way of his unjustly imprisoning his subjects, as the king of France could do. And there can be no doubt that English methods of government have exercised the most profound influence in bringing about the gradual reduction of the absolute powers of the monarchs upon the Continent.

Rousseau (1712–1778) attacks civilization

Next to Voltaire, the writer who did most to cultivate discontent with existing conditions was Jean Jacques Rousseau (1712–1778). Unlike Voltaire, Diderot, and D'Alembert, he believed that people thought too much, not too little; that we should trust to our hearts rather than to our heads, and may safely rely upon our natural feelings and sentiments to guide us. He declared that Europe was over-civilized, and summoned men to return to nature and simplicity. His first work was a prize essay written in 1750, in which he sought to prove that the development of the arts and sciences had demoralized mankind, inasmuch as they had produced luxury, insincerity, and arrogance. He extolled the rude vigor of Sparta and denounced the refined and degenerate life of the Athenians.

Later Rousseau wrote a book on education, called *Émile*, which is still famous. In this he protests against the efforts made by teachers to improve upon nature for, he maintains, "All things are good as their Author made them, but everything degenerates in the hands of man.... To form this rare creature, man, what have we to do? Much doubtless, but chiefly to prevent anything from being done.... All our wisdom consists in servile prejudices; all our customs are but anxiety and restraint. Civilized man is born, lives, dies in a state of slavery. At his birth he is sewed in swaddling clothes; at his death he is nailed in a coffin; as long as he preserves the human form he is fettered by our institutions." Rousseau's *Émile* deals with education

Rousseau's plea for the simple life went to the heart of many a person who was weary of complications and artificiality. Others were attracted by his firm belief in the natural equality of mankind and the right of every man to have a voice in the government. In his celebrated little treatise, *The Social Contract*, he takes up the question, By what right does one man rule over others? The book opens with the words: "Man is born free and yet is now everywhere in chains. One man believes himself the master of others and yet is after all more of a slave than they. How did this change come about? I do not know. What can render it legitimate? I believe that I can answer that question." It is, Rousseau declares, the will of the people that renders government legitimate. The real sovereign is the people. Although they may appoint a single person, such as a king, to manage the government for them, they should make the laws, since it is they who must obey them. We shall find that the first French constitution accepted Rousseau's doctrine and defined law as "the expression of the general will," — not the will of a king reigning by the grace of God. *The Social Contract* Popular sovereignty

Among all the books advocating urgent reforms which appeared in the eighteenth century none accomplished more than a little volume by the Italian economist and jurist, Beccaria (1738–1794) and his book on *Crimes and Punishments*

Beccaria, which exposed with great clearness and vigor the atrocities of the criminal law. The trials (even in England) were scandalously unfair and the punishments incredibly cruel. The accused was not ordinarily allowed any counsel and was

Unfairness of criminal trials

required to give evidence against himself. Indeed, it was common enough to use torture to force a confession from him. Witnesses were examined secretly and separately and their evidence recorded before they faced the accused. Informers were rewarded, and the flimsiest evidence was considered sufficient in the case of atrocious crimes. After a criminal had been convicted he might be tortured by the rack, thumb screws, applying fire to different parts of his body, or in other ways, to induce him to reveal the names of his accomplices.

Cruelty of the punishments

The death penalty was established for a great variety of offenses besides murder, — for example, heresy, counterfeiting, highway robbery, even sacrilege. In England there were, according to the great jurist, Blackstone, a hundred and sixty offenses punishable with death, including cutting down trees in an orchard, and stealing a sum over five shillings in a shop, or of more than twelve pence from a person's pocket. Yet in spite of the long list of capital offenses the trials in England were far more reasonable than on the Continent, for they were public and conducted before a jury, and there was no torture used.

Beccaria advocates public trials and milder but certain punishments

Beccaria advocated public trials in which the accused should be confronted by those who gave evidence against him. Secret accusations should no longer be considered. Like Voltaire, Montesquieu, and many others, he denounced the practice of torturing a suspected person with a view of compelling him by bodily anguish to confess himself guilty of crimes of which he might be quite innocent. As for punishments, he advocated the entire abolition of the death penalty, on the ground that it did not deter the evil doer as life imprisonment at hard labor would, and that in its various hideous forms — beheading, hanging, mutilation, breaking on the wheel — it was a source of demoralization to the spectators. Punishments should be less harsh but more certain and more carefully proportioned to the danger of the offense to society. Nobles and magistrates convicted of crime should be treated exactly like offenders of the lowest class. Confiscation of property should be abolished, since it brought suffering to the innocent members of the criminal's family. It was better, he urged, to prevent crimes than to punish them, and this could be done by making the laws very clear and the punishments for their violation very certain, but above all by spreading enlightenment through better education.

About the middle of the eighteenth century a new social science was born, namely, political economy. Scholars began to investigate the sources of a nation's wealth, the manner in which commodities were produced and distributed, the laws determining demand and supply, the function of money and credit, and their influence upon industry and commerce. Previous to the eighteenth century these matters had seemed unworthy of scientific discussion. Few suspected that there were any great laws underlying the varying amount of wheat that could be bought for a shilling, or the rate of interest that a bank could charge. The ancient philosophers of Greece and Rome had despised the tiller of the soil, the shopkeeper, and the artisan, for these indispensable members of society at that period were commonly slaves. The contempt for manual labor had decreased in the Middle Ages, but the learned men who studied theology, or pondered over Aristotle's teachings in regard to "form" and "essence," never thought of considering the effect of the growth of population upon serfdom, or of an export duty upon commerce, any more than they tried to determine why the housewife's milk soured more readily in warm weather than in cold, or why a field left fallow regained its fertility.[1]

> The science of political economy develops in the eighteenth century

---

[1] The mediæval philosophers and theologians discussed, it is true, the question whether it was right or not to charge interest for money loaned, and what might be a "just price." But both matters were considered as ethical or theological problems rather than in their economic aspects. See Ashley, *English Economic History*, Vol. I, chap. iii; Vol. II, chap. vi.

Tendency of
the govern-
ments to
regulate
commerce
and industry

Although ignorant of economic laws, the governments had come gradually to regulate more and more both commerce and industry. We have seen how each country tried to keep all the trade for its own merchants by issuing elaborate regulations and restrictions, and how the king's officers enforced the monopoly of the guilds. Indeed the French government, under Colbert's influence, fell into the habit of regulating well-nigh everything. In order that the goods which were produced in France might find a ready sale abroad, the government fixed the quality and width of the cloth which might be manufactured and the character of the dyes which should be used. The king's ministers kept a constant eye upon the dealers in grain and breadstuffs, forbidding the storing up of these products or their sale outside a market. In this way they had hoped to prevent speculators from accumulating grain in order to sell it at a high rate in times of scarcity.

Doctrines of
the " mercan-
tilists "

In short, at the opening of the eighteenth century statesmen, merchants, and such scholars as gave any attention to the subject believed that the wealth of a country could be greatly increased by government regulation and encouragement, just ·as in the United States to-day it is held by the majority of citizens that the government can increase prosperity and improve the conditions of the wage-earners by imposing high· duties upon imported articles. It was also commonly believed that a country, to be really prosperous, must export more than it imported, so that foreign nations would each year owe it a cash balance which would have to be paid in gold or silver and in this way increase its stock of precious metals. Those who advocated using the powers of government to encourage and protect shipping, to develop colonies, and to regulate manufactures are known as "mercantilists."

Origin of
the "free
trade"
school of
economists

About the year 1700, however, certain writers in France and England reached the conclusion that the government did no good by interfering with natural economic laws which it did not understand and whose workings it did not reckon with.

They argued that the government restrictions often produced the worst possible results ; that industry would advance far more rapidly if manufacturers were free to adopt new inventions instead of being confined by the government's restrictions to old and discredited methods ; that, in France, the government's frantic efforts to prevent famines by making all sorts of rules in regard to selling grain only increased the distress, since even the most powerful king could not violate with impunity an economic law. So the new economists rejected the formerly popular mercantile policy. They accused the mercantilists of identifying gold and silver with wealth, and maintained that a country might be prosperous without a favorable cash balance. In short, the new school advocated "free trade." A French economist urged his king to adopt the motto, *Laissez faire* (Let things alone), if he would see his realms prosper.

The leading economist of France in the eighteenth century was Turgot who, as head of the government for a brief period, made, as we shall see, an unsuccessful effort to remedy the existing abuses.[1] He argued that it would be quite sufficient if "the government should always protect the natural liberty of the buyer to buy and of the seller to sell. For the buyer being always the master to buy or not to buy, it is certain that he will select among the sellers the man who will give him at the best bargain the goods that suit him best. It is not less certain that every seller, it being his chief interest to merit preference over his competitors, will sell in general the best goods and at the lowest price at which he can make a profit in order to attract customers. The merchant or manufacturer who cheats will be quickly discredited and lose his custom without the interference of government."

Doctrines of Turgot

The first great systematic work upon political economy was published by a Scotch philosopher, Adam Smith, in 1776. His *Inquiry into the Nature and Causes of the Wealth of*

Adam Smith's *Wealth of Nations* (1776)

[1] See below, p. 219.

Nations became the basis of all further progress in the science. He attacked the doctrines of the mercantilists and the various expedients which they had favored, — import duties, bounties, restrictions upon exporting grain, etc., — all of which he believed "retard instead of accelerating the progress of society toward real wealth and greatness; and diminish instead of increasing the real value of the annual produce of its labor and land." In general he agreed with Turgot that the State should content itself with protecting traders and business men and seeing that justice was done; but he sympathized with the English navigation laws, although they obviously hampered commerce, and was not as thoroughgoing a free trader as many of the later English economists.

The economists attack existing abuses

While the economists in France and England by no means agreed in details, they were at one in believing that it was useless and harmful to interfere with what they held to be the economic laws. They brought the light of reason to bear, for example, upon the various bungling and iniquitous old methods of taxation then in vogue, and many of them advocated a single tax which should fall directly upon the landowner. They wrote treatises on practical questions, scattered pamphlets broadcast, and even conducted a magazine or two in the hope of bringing home to the people at large the existing economic evils.

The eighteenth century a period of rapidly increasing enlightenment

It is clear from what has been said that the eighteenth century was a period of unexampled advance in general enlightenment. New knowledge spread abroad by the Encyclopædists, the economists, and writers on government — Turgot, Adam Smith, Montesquieu, Rousseau, Beccaria, and many others of lesser fame — led people to see the vices of the existing system and gave them at the same time new hope of bettering themselves by abandoning the mistaken beliefs and imperfect methods of their predecessors. The spirit of reform penetrated even into kings' palaces, and we must now turn to the actual attempts to better affairs made by the more enlightened rulers of Europe.

REFERENCES

Voltaire: LOWELL, *The Eve of the French Revolution*, pp. 51–69; MORLEY, *Voltaire*.

Montesquieu: LOWELL, pp. 126–153; SOREL, *Montesquieu* (in the Great French Writers Series).

Rousseau: LOWELL, pp. 274–321; MORLEY, *Rousseau*.

The Encyclopædia: PERKINS, *France under Louis XV*, Vol. II, pp. 437–446; LOWELL, pp. 243–260; MORLEY, *Diderot and the Encyclopædists*, Vol. I.

Criminal Law in France: LOWELL, pp. 107–118.

Criminal Law in England: LECKY, *History of England in the Eighteenth Century*, Vol. II, chap. iv, pp. 126–138; Vol. II, chap. xxi, pp. 315–347.

The French Economists: PERKINS, Vol. II, pp. 424–437; SAY, *Turgot* (in the Great French Writers Series).

Adam Smith: HIRST, *Adam Smith* (English Men of Letters Series).

CHAPTER X

THE ENLIGHTENED DESPOTS OF THE EIGHTEENTH CENTURY

REFORMS OF FREDERICK II, CATHARINE II, JOSEPH II AND CHARLES III

30. We have now described the general conditions which prevailed in western Europe in the eighteenth century, and discovered that many mediæval institutions still existed, such, for example, as the serfs, the guilds, and the privileged classes of the nobles and clergy. We have also seen how, under the influence of increasing knowledge, thoughtful men began to lose their confidence in the old customs and institutions and to demand thoroughgoing reforms. It remains to see how such reforms were attempted, and at last carried out, so that there are now few vestiges of the old system left.

The "enlightened despots"

It happened in the eighteenth century that there were several remarkably intelligent monarchs, — Frederick II of Prussia, Catharine the Great of Russia, Emperor Joseph II and his brother Leopold (grand duke of Tuscany), and Charles III of Spain. These rulers read the works of the reformers, and planned all sorts of ways in which they might better the conditions in their realms by removing old restrictions which hampered the farmer and merchant, by making new and clearer laws, by depriving the clergy of wealth and power which seemed to them excessive, and by encouraging manufactures and promoting commerce.

These monarchs are commonly known as the "enlightened" or "benevolent" despots. They were no doubt more "enlightened" than the older kings; at least they all read books and associated with learned men. But they were not more

184

" benevolent " than Charlemagne, or Canute, or St. Louis, or Henry IV, all of whom, as well as many other European monarchs of earlier centuries, had believed it their duty to do all they could for the welfare of their people. On the other hand, the monarchs of the eighteenth century were certainly despots in the full sense of the word. They held that all the powers of the State were vested in them, and had no idea of permitting their subjects any share in the government.

One of the most striking and practical of the reforming rulers was Frederick the Great, who maintained that the king was merely the first servant of the State. He believed that the ruler owed the State an account of the uses to which he put the taxes raised for its support and defense. He allowed the people no part in the government, it is true, but he worked very hard himself. He rose early and was busy all day. He was his own prime minister and the real head of all branches of the government, watching over the army and leading it in battle, attending to foreign affairs, guarding the finances, overseeing the courts, journeying up and down the land investigating the conduct of his officials and examining into the condition of his people.

Frederick the Great, a very hard-working king

After the exhausting wars by which he had succeeded in rounding out his realms, Frederick bent his energies toward recruiting his wasted country. He did not approve of serfdom, and even declared that " the fact that the peasant belongs to the land and is the serf of the lord is revolting to mankind." Nevertheless he did not attempt to abolish the system. Indeed he sanctioned the old division of his subjects into three classes, — nobles, burghers, and peasants. Not only was every one bound to remain in the class in which he happened to be born but no noble was permitted to acquire burgher or peasant land ; no burgher, noble or peasant land ; and no peasant, noble or burgher land.

How Frederick clung to the old system of serfdom

While retaining these old restrictions the king endeavored to improve the methods of farming and increased the amount of agricultural land by draining the swamps. From two great marshes he recovered four hundred thousand acres upon which he had several hundred villages built. These he peopled with foreigners, for he was intent upon increasing the population by immigration. Manufactures were also fostered and Prussia began to develop some important industries.

In religious matters Frederick was extremely tolerant; he held that his subjects should be allowed to worship God freely in any way they pleased. His kingdom had long been Protestant, but there were many Catholics in parts of his scattered dominions. He welcomed Huguenots and Jesuits with equal cordiality and admitted Catholics as well as Protestants to his service. "I stand neutral between Rome and Geneva," he once said; "he who wrongs his brother of a different faith shall be punished; were I to declare for one or the other creed I should excite party spirit and persecution; my aim, on the contrary, is to show the adherents of the different churches that they are all fellow-citizens." [1]

Frederick found the laws of his kingdom (like those of the other European countries) in a very confused condition, — cumbersome, contradictory, and the cause of innumerable delays and constant injustice. He determined to have a new code drawn up which should establish one clear system of law for all his territories. He died before it was completed, but it was issued by his successor. It declared that the object of all government is the welfare of the people; proclaimed the right of every man to pursue his own interests so long as he did not injure any one else, and even maintained that it is the duty of the State to care for the poor and those out of work. On the other hand, it vested all the power in the king, gave to the people no part in the government, sanctioned serfdom

Agriculture and manufactures fostered

Religious toleration in Prussia

Frederick's code furnishes a good example of benevolent despotism

[1] Frederick agreed with Voltaire in his contempt for theological disputes. A clergyman of Valangin was expelled from his pulpit by his congregation because he questioned eternal punishment; when he petitioned Frederick to reinstate him, the king replied, "If my loving subjects of Valangin choose to be eternally damned it is not for me to interfere."

and the old division of the people into classes, and empowered the king to check at any moment freedom of speech and the publication of books and periodicals which were distasteful to him. Frederick's code is, in short, a picture of the benevolent despot who proclaims his anxiety to reform all things and help everybody, but who really clings to the old institutions and refuses to permit his subjects to express any opinion in regard to what should be done.

In spite of his long wars and his constant attention to the duties of government, Frederick found time, as we have seen, for reading and writing books, for music and art. He built a palace near Berlin which he called *Sans Souci* where, "free from care" (as the name may be translated), he could collect his library, dine with the learned and witty men whom he chose for his companions, and play the flute. Voltaire lived with him for a time, and after his departure the king and the philosopher kept up an intimate correspondence until Voltaire's death.

Catharine II of Russia showed herself almost as interested in the philosophers and reformers as did Frederick. She invited Diderot to spend a month with her and was disappointed that d'Alembert would not consent to become the tutor of the grand duke Paul, the heir to the throne. She subscribed for the *Encyclopædia*, and bought Diderot's library when he got into trouble, permitting him to continue to use the books as long as he wished. In her frequent letters to Voltaire she explained to him her various plans for reform.

She read Montesquieu's *Spirit of Laws*, and Beccaria's *Crimes and Punishments*. Under their influence she summoned a great assembly to Moscow in 1766 which represented all the various peoples under her scepter — Russians, Tartars, Kalmucks, Cossacks, Laplanders — as well as the different classes, namely, nobles, townspeople, and peasants. She submitted to this assembly a draft of a new code of laws for Russia which she had based upon the western writers, especially

Frederick's interest in literature

Catharine II's interest in the French philosophers

Catharine calls together a great assembly to revise the laws of Russia (1766)

Montesquieu and Beccaria. In this she declared that "the nation is not made for the ruler but the ruler for the nation"; "liberty is the right to do anything that is not forbidden by law"; "better that ten guilty should escape than that one innocent should suffer unjust punishment." Intolerance, religious persecution, and the use of torture were condemned. When war broke out with Turkey the assembly was dismissed without finishing a task which it was, in any case, ill qualified to accomplish on account of its size and its mixed character.

Catharine maintains serfdom but secularizes the Church lands

There was some talk of abolishing serfdom in Russia, but Catharine rather increased than decreased the number of serfs and she made their lot harder than it had been before by forbidding them to complain of the treatment they received at the hands of their masters. She appropriated the vast property of the churches and monasteries, using the revenue to support the clergy and monks, and such surplus as remained she devoted to schools and hospitals.

Rash reforms of Joseph II of Austria (Emperor, 1765-1790)

It is clear that while Frederick and Catharine expressed great admiration for the reformers, they did not attempt to make any sweeping changes in the laws or the social order. Emperor Joseph II, who, after the death of his mother, Maria Theresa, in 1780, became ruler of the Austrian dominions, had

Attempt to convert the Austrian dominions into a well-organized state

however the courage of his convictions. He proposed to transform the scattered and heterogeneous territories over which he ruled into a well-organized state in which disorder, confusion, prejudice, fanaticism, and intellectual bondage should disappear and all his subjects be put in possession of their natural rights. Germans, Hungarians, Italians, Poles, Bohemians, and Belgians were all to use the German language in official communications. The old irregular territorial divisions were abolished and his realms divided up into thirteen new provinces. All the ancient privileges enjoyed by the towns and the local assemblies were done away with and replaced by a uniform system of government in which his own officials enjoyed the control.

JOSEPH II

Joseph visited France and was personally acquainted with d'Alembert, Rousseau, and Turgot. He also read with approval the work of Febronius[1] attacking the power of the Pope. So it is no wonder that, while he still claimed to be a good Catholic, he undertook a radical reform of the Church. He was heartily opposed to the monks. "The principles of monasticism," he declared, "are in flat contradiction to human reason; monks are the most useless and dangerous subjects that a country can possess." He particularly objected to those orders whose members devoted themselves to religious contemplation, which he regarded as worse than a waste of time; he consequently abolished some six hundred of their monasteries and used their property for charitable purposes and to establish schools. He appointed the bishops without consulting the Pope and forbade money to be sent to Rome. Marriage was declared to be merely a civil contract and so was taken out of the control of the priests. Lutherans, Calvinists, and other heretics were allowed to worship in their own way. Only "enlightened" professors, that is, those who sympathized with Joseph's views, were to teach in the theological schools. The Emperor's object was, in short, to free the Austrian Church from the papal control and bring it under his own. Pope Pius VI became so anxious in regard to the situation that in 1782 he actually traveled to Vienna in order to expostulate with Joseph personally. But the Emperor was firm; he forbade any one to confer with the Pope without his permission and even walled up all but one door of the palace where he was entertained and had it carefully guarded lest his Holiness should gain the ear of the people.

Joseph II reforms the Church

Joseph II sought to complete his work by attacking the surviving features of feudalism and encouraging the development of manufactures. He freed the serfs in Bohemia, Moravia, Galicia, and Hungary, transforming the peasants into tenants; elsewhere he reduced the services due from them

Joseph attacks the survivals of feudalism and encourages manufactures

[1] See above, p. 146.

to the lord. He taxed nobles and clergy without regard to their claims to exemption and supplanted the confused and uncertain laws by a uniform system which is the basis of Austrian law to-day. He introduced a protective tariff and caused a large number of factories to be built. He illustrated his preference for home industries by giving away to the hospitals all the foreign wines in his cellars, and his spirit of economy, by forbidding the use of gold and silver for candlesticks, and prohibiting the burial of the dead in coffins for the reason that this was a waste of wood which might be better employed.

Opposition to Joseph's reforms

Naturally Joseph met opposition on every hand. The clergy abhorred him as an oppressor, and all who were forced to sacrifice their old privileges did what they could to frustrate his reforms, however salutary they might be. The Nether-

Revolt of the Austrian Netherlands (1790)

lands, which he proposed to transform into an Austrian province, finally followed the example of the American colonies and declared themselves independent in 1790. The same year Joseph died, a sadly disappointed man, having been forced to undo almost all that he had hoped to accomplish.

Accession of Leopold II (1790-1792)

Joseph was followed by his brother Leopold who, although he had introduced important reforms in the grand duchy of Tuscany over which he had ruled, deemed it wise to restore the Austrian dominions, so far as possible, to the condition in which they were when Joseph had begun his reckless improvements. In this way he brought back the Netherlands to the Austrian fold and reassured those who had been terrified by the prospect of change.

Charles III's reforms in Spain (1759-1788)

In Italy Don Carlos, the first Bourbon king of the Two Sicilies,[1] had, like Leopold, striven to improve his very backward kingdom, and when in 1759 he became king of Spain as Charles III, he adopted the career of a reformer in earnest. He began, however, like his fellow-monarchs, by excluding the nation from all share in the government. He ignored the

---

[1] See above, p. 45.

national assembly, or *Cortes*, and placed the control of all branches of government in the hands of his own ministers and officials.

Like the other benevolent despots Charles III endeavored to increase the wealth of his kingdom by encouraging industry. Domestic manufactures were protected against foreign competition by a tariff. An agricultural college and trade schools were established, and highways, bridges, and canals were constructed. Formerly all ships coming from the American colonies had been required to land their goods either at Seville or one or two other ports. Now all the Spanish ports were thrown open to colonial commerce. Manufactures and commerce

Scientific and economic questions began to be discussed in the newspapers and periodicals. The schools were taken out of the hands of the clergy. Modern science and philosophy were introduced into the universities of Alcala and Valencia; but that at Salamanca refused to make any change, on the ground that Aristotle was still satisfactory to all. Reform of education

In no respect were Charles's reforms more striking than in his method of dealing with the Church. There were within his realm sixty-six thousand priests and three thousand monasteries with eighty-five thousand monks. The lands of the monasteries and churches amounted to about one fifth of the entire area of Spain. The king strictly limited the right of the Church to acquire more property and subjected its lands to taxation. Although Charles III, like Joseph, regarded himself as a devout Catholic, he adhered to the principles advocated by Febronius, whose book had been translated into Spanish. He forbade any papal bull or decree to be executed before it had received his approbation, and when the Pope expostulated with him he replied that he was responsible to God alone for his acts as king. Charles III and the Spanish Church

Spain had long been proud of its vigilance in defending the purity of its religion. The Inquisition, which was an ancient Church court originally established by the Pope in the middle The Inquisition of the thirteenth century for the discovery and punishment of heretics, had been revived by the Spanish monarchs, Ferdinand and Isabella, in 1483, with a view of purging their kingdoms of the religious errors of the numerous Jews and Moors, and it had developed into a great national institution. Thousands and thousands were convicted by this tribunal of holding false beliefs, uttering blasphemies, or practicing forbidden arts like sorcery or magic, and were condemned to be burned, whipped, imprisoned, or sent to the galleys.[1] While the Inquisition was no longer so active in the eighteenth century as it had once been, no less than fourteen thousand persons are said to have been convicted by it of more or less grave offenses during the reign of the Bourbon king, Philip V, and nearly eight hundred of these were burned alive. Charles III thought that the Inquisition contributed materially to the maintenance of public morals by condemning wrong teachings and books which were indecent or which attacked the government or religion. He did not, therefore, abolish it, but there were only four persons sent to the stake during his reign.

The expulsion of the Jesuits begun by Portugal (1759)

On one matter most of the Catholic monarchs were in hearty agreement; they were all opposed to the Jesuits, who had become increasingly unpopular during the eighteenth century. They had aroused the hostility of the kings by exalting the power of the Pope and they had excited the enmity of the merchant class by their success in carrying on trade with India and the New World. The first country to expel the Jesuits was Portugal, where they were accused of stirring up disorder

[1] In order to impress the people with the horror of heresy and the majesty of the Inquisition, the sentencing of those guilty of heresy was made a gorgeous public ceremony held in a great square "for the glory of God and the exaltation of our holy Catholic faith." Everything was arranged to terrify and humiliate the victims. For example, those who were to be burned wore miters and yellow cloaks adorned with flames. These *autos-da-fé*, or "acts of faith," were regarded as a pious and fitting form of celebrating the advent of a new monarch. The last great public *auto-da-fé* was held in Madrid in 1680 to celebrate the marriage of Charles II. The first French king, Philip V, refused to be present at a similar performance proposed for him and it was given up. Thereafter the *autos-da-fé* were held in churches and became less and less important.

and plotting the death of the king. In 1759 large numbers of them were loaded on to ships and sent to the papal dominions, while others were imprisoned. The property of the order was confiscated.

In France the quarrel between the Jesuits and the Jansenists — a party which clung to the Gallican liberties [1] — had been long and bitter. About the middle of the eighteenth century an association was formed by the enemies of the Jesuits for the express purpose of publishing pamphlets denouncing them and their teachings and rousing public opinion against them. Matters were brought to a crisis by the failure of a great Jesuit commercial house in Martinique. Its creditors declared the whole order responsible for the losses involved and the case reached the *parlement* of Paris, the chief French court. When the lawyer representing the Jesuits argued that their property should be protected on the ground that it was used to train youths in piety and learning, he was greeted with jeers from the crowd in the court room. The *parlement* decided against

Dissolution of the order of Jesuits in France

---

[1] See above, p. 146. The Jansenists derived their name from a theologian, Cornelius Jansen, who wrote a long Latin treatise upon the teachings of St. Augustine. This contained certain doctrines resembling those of Calvin, although Jansen believed himself a devout Catholic and submitted all that he said to the judgment of the Pope. The Jesuits attacked the work when it appeared in 1640 and the Pope forbade the reading of the *Augustinus*. Nevertheless a party adhered to the teachings of Jansen, and one of their number, the famous Pascal, attacked the Jesuits in his *Provincial Letters*, which is regarded as a French classic. After interminable discussions, the Pope, urged by the Jesuits, issued the important bull "Unigenitus" in 1713 in which he condemned one hundred and one propositions of a Jansenist work, — *Moral Reflections* by Quesnel, a prominent Jansenist. This led to forty years of disturbance, for the Pope ordered those to be cast out of the Church who refused to accept the "Unigenitus." A part of the clergy accepted the bull but others refused to do so and were supported in their opposition by the king's courts; for many of the judges were Jansenists, or, at any rate, hated the Jesuits on account of their ultramontane views. Finally, in 1752, a priest refused to perform the last sacraments in the case of a man accused of Jansenism. Other priests who had accepted the bull declined to perform the funeral services for those who rejected it and bodies remained unburied, to the scandal and disgust of the community. This long struggle within the French Church, which did not come to an end until 1756, prepared the way for the abolition in France of the Jesuits, and helped to discredit religion in the minds of those who read the writings of Voltaire, Diderot, and the other philosophers.

the Jesuits, ordered an investigation of their alleged pernicious teachings, and in 1762 dissolved the order on account of the perversity of their conduct and doctrines. Louis XV reluctantly ratified this measure two years later and the Jesuits, to the number of four thousand, ceased to form an order in France, although they were permitted to remain in the country as individuals.

The Spanish and Italian Bourbons suppress the order and induce the Pope to abolish it (1773)

Three years later Charles III of Spain followed the example set by Portugal and France and abolished the order in Spain without giving any reasons. He ordered the Jesuits to be taken to the seacoast and shipped to the papal dominions. After the king of the Two Sicilies and the duke of Parma had also suppressed the order in their realms, all the various Bourbon rulers combined to induce the Pope to complete their work by putting an end to the Society of Jesus throughout Christendom. This he most reluctantly consented to do. In 1773 Clement XIV issued the bull "Dominus ac redemptor," in which he confessed that the order no longer performed the services for which it had been founded, that it roused innumerable complaints by mixing in politics, and that its continued existence was an obstacle in the way of a good understanding between the Pope and the House of Bourbon. He accordingly abolished the society, permitting its members to enter other orders or to become ordinary priests.[1] At the time when the attack on the Jesuits began the society numbered 22,589 members and maintained nearly 800 colleges and seminaries and 270 mission stations.

Summary of the activities of the benevolent despots

It has become clear, as we have reviewed the activities of the various benevolent despots, that all of them were chiefly intent upon increasing their own power; they were more despotic than they were benevolent. They opposed the interference of the Pope and brought the clergy under their own control. In some cases they took a portion of the property of the churches and monasteries. They tried to improve the laws

---

[1] For the bull itself, see *Readings*, sect. 30.

and do away with the existing contradictions and obscurities. They endeavored to "centralize" the administration and to place all the power in the hands of their own officials instead of leaving it with the nobles or the old local assemblies. They encouraged agriculture, commerce, and industries in various ways. All of these measures were undertaken primarily with a view to strengthening the autocratic power of the ruler and augmenting the revenue and the military strength of his government, for none of these energetic monarchs showed any willingness to admit the people to a share in the government, and only Joseph II ventured to attempt to free the serfs.

Peculiarities of the English Government in the Eighteenth Century

31. The government of England in the eighteenth century differed in many respects from that which prevailed across the Channel. Frederick the Great and Louis XV could fix the amount of the taxes and decide who should pay them without asking the consent, or even the advice, of any of their subjects. They could borrow all the money that the bankers would lend them and spend it as they pleased, without giving any account of it. The English king, on the contrary, could impose no taxes and borrow no money on the national credit without the sanction of Parliament; and a definite sum was assigned to him as an allowance with which to keep up his royal establishment, defray his personal expenses, and pay the salaries of important government officials.

Parliament holds the purse strings

The benevolent despots, as we have seen, made any change they wished in the laws by a simple edict. In England the king could neither issue a new law nor suspend an old one without the consent of Parliament. Even the right which he had formerly enjoyed to veto the bills passed by Parliament fell into disuse and was exercised for the last time by Queen Anne in 1707.

Parliament controls lawmaking

The king of
England did
not control
the courts
of law

On the Continent the monarch could remove judges who made decisions which did not please him. In England, since 1701, the judges have held their positions during good behavior, unless removed on request of both houses of Parliament. The English king could not arbitrarily arrest his subjects or call before his own council, to be decided by himself personally, cases which were being tried in the regular courts. The Habeas Corpus Act of 1679 provided that any one who was arrested should be informed of the reason and should be speedily tried by a regular tribunal and dealt with according to the law of the land. In France there were none of these restrictions placed upon the king, who could arrest his subjects on *lettres de cachet*, imprison them indefinitely without assigning a reason, and could interfere in any suit and decide it as he chose.

Contrast between the
English Parliament and
similar bodies
on the Continent

The English Parliament, which had originated in the thirteenth century, was by no means unique in the Middle Ages. For example, we find the king of Aragon summoning an assembly of nobles, clergy, and "rich men" as early as 1162. In 1255 the representatives of the cities appeared in the diet of the Holy Roman Empire along with the various princes and prelates. In France, about 1300, the Estates General had come to be made up of representatives of the three classes of the realm, — nobles, clergy, and the "third estate," or townspeople.

The two
houses of
Parliament

But all these bodies, and others of the same kind, gradually lost all their importance with the sole exception of the English Parliament. This had from the middle of the fourteenth century consisted of two houses. The higher nobility — dukes, marquises, earls, viscounts, and barons — sat, together with the prelates, — archbishops, bishops, and abbots [1] — in the House of Lords. Accordingly the representatives of the nobles and the clergy were not separated as they often were on the Continent. In the second chamber, the House of Commons, there were not only representatives of the towns but those chosen by

---

[1] The abbots disappeared when Henry VIII dissolved the monasteries.

the landed proprietors of the counties, — thus giving the lesser landholders a voice in the nation's councils.[1]

Remarkable as was the English Parliament in the eighteenth century, in its organization and its power to control the king, it nevertheless represented only a small part of the nation. In the Middle Ages, when the towns were small and the country population tolerably evenly scattered, the House of Commons fairly represented the property owners throughout England. But as time went on no effort was made to read-just the apportionment to meet the changes which gradually took place. Many towns dwindled away, some disappeared altogether, and the lords upon whose lands they had been situated came to control the choice of those members of the House of Commons who represented these so-called "rotten boroughs." On the other hand, great towns like Manchester, Birmingham, and Leeds grew up, which had no representa-tives. As a result the great majority of the English people had no more share in the government than the subjects of Louis XV. In 1768 there were only one hundred and sixty thousand voters, although the whole population of Great Britain amounted to some eight millions ; that is to say, about one in every ten adult males had a voice in the government. More-over, no poor man could sit in Parliament, since all members were required to hold considerable land.[2]

The House of Commons represented only a small part of the nation

Despite the small number who could actually participate in the choice of representatives, political questions were hotly discussed among the upper classes, who were divided into two well-defined parties, Tories and Whigs. These owed their origin to the excitement of the Civil War, when those who supported Charles I were called Cavaliers and those who op-posed him, Roundheads. During the latter years of Charles II,

Origin of the Tories and Whigs

[1] The lower clergy was not represented in Parliament as it was in the Estates General. For a time its representatives met and voted the taxes that they were to pay, but after 1664 the assembly confined itself exclusively to religious matters.
[2] For a fuller description of the parliamentary system and its reform, see below, chap. xxv.

the former party, which upheld the divine right of kings and the supremacy of the Anglican Church, received the name of " Tory." Their opponents, who advocated the supremacy of Parliament and championed toleration for the Dissenters, came to be called Whigs.[1]

Whig suprem-
acy in the
early eight-
eenth
century

After the death of Anne, many of the Tories favored calling to the throne the son of James II (popularly called " the old Pretender "), whereupon the Whigs succeeded in discrediting their rivals by denouncing them as Jacobites[2] and traitors. They made the new Hanoverian king, George I,[3] believe that he owed everything to the Whigs, and for a period of nearly fifty years, under George I and George II, they were able to control Parliament. George I himself spoke no English, was ignorant of English politics, and was much more interested in Hanover than in his new kingdom. He did not attend the meetings of his ministers, as his predecessors had done, and turned over the management of affairs to the Whig

Robert
Walpole,
prime minis-
ter (1721–
1742)

leaders. They found a skillful " boss " and a judicious statesman in Sir Robert Walpole, who maintained his own power and that of his party by avoiding war and preventing religious dissensions at home. He used the king's funds to buy the votes necessary to maintain the Whig majority in the House of Commons and for getting his measures through that body. He was England's first " prime minister."

Origin of the
cabinet

The existence of two well-defined political parties standing for widely different policies forced the king to choose all his ministers from either one or the other. The more prominent among his advisers came gradually to form a little group which resigned together if Parliament refused to accept the measures they advocated. So the English rulers from the time of William III were generally compelled to select their ministers

---

[1] Not until after the reform of 1832 did the Tories become " Conservatives " and the Whigs assume the name of " Liberals."

[2] This name applied to the supporters of James is derived from the Latin form of his name, *Jacobus.*

[3] See above, p. 48.

from the party which had a majority in Parliament; otherwise their plans would be pretty sure to be frustrated. In this way "cabinet government" originated, that is, government by a small group of the heads of departments (like the Chancellor of the Exchequer, the First Commissioner of the Admiralty, etc.) who belong to the party which has a majority in Parliament, or at least in the House of Commons, and who resign together when the House votes down any measure which they propose.

Walpole secured a cabinet which he could control and declared that it, not the king, was really responsible for the whole conduct of the government while its members remained in office. Moreover, he frankly confessed that he owed his power not to the king but to the House of Commons. In a debate there he said : " I have lived long enough to know that the safety of a minister lies in having the approbation of this house. Formerly, ministers neglected this and fell; I have always made it my first study to obtain it and therefore I hope to stand." On another occasion he said, "When I speak here as a minister I speak as possessing my powers from his Majesty, but as being answerable to this house for the exercise of those powers." And so it came about that Parliament acquired the right not only to grant taxes and make laws but actually to force the king to turn over the conduct of the government to ministers who enjoyed its approval.

Walpole acknowledges his dependence upon the House of Commons

Nevertheless after Walpole's fall in 1742 cabinet government did not flourish for a generation or so, especially under George III, who came to the throne in 1760, for he proposed to follow his mother's advice, "George, be king." Indeed many thoughtful men felt that Walpole had been what we should call nowadays a corrupt boss, and accordingly they encouraged the king to keep the government in his own hands. During the war with the American colonies George III was practically his own prime minister and freely resorted to what he called

King George III bribes the Commons when necessary

"golden pills" to cure those who opposed him and to gain a majority in the House of Commons.

General
interest in
politics
aroused

George III, in spite of his exalted notion of his royal prerogatives, could not revive any general enthusiasm for absolute monarchy. Indeed, during the latter half of the eighteenth century the people at large began to pay especial attention to political questions, to draw up petitions,[1] and hold monster meetings in which they demanded that all adult males, rich and poor alike, should be permitted to vote for members of the House of Commons.

John Wilkes
and his
North Briton

The newspapers, which had become common in England as the eighteenth century advanced, freely discussed politics in a way absolutely unknown on the Continent. John Wilkes, the editor of the *North Briton*, who held that the members of Parliament were merely delegates of the people and were, like the ministers, accountable to them, ventured in 1763 to describe George III's speech at the opening of Parliament as "the most abandoned instance of political effrontery." This enraged the king and his ministers who, while they could not shut up the obnoxious journalist as Louis XV would have done, had him prosecuted for libel in a regular court. Though Wilkes was found guilty of the charge, his cause was so popular that riots broke out in his favor. He stood for Parliament and was elected twice by a large majority but was expelled both times and not allowed to take his seat until the excitement had died away.

Growing
demand for
reform

The real victory was therefore with Wilkes, and except in times of danger the government did not seriously interfere with political criticism. There was accordingly an increasing number of writers to point out to the people the defects in the

[1] Dr. Johnson declared that every politician who lost his office got signatures to a petition attacking the policy of the ministers who dismissed him. "One man signs because he hates the papists, another because he had vowed destruction to the turnpikes; one because it will vex the parson, another because he owes his landlord nothing; one because he is rich, another because he is poor; one to show that he is not afraid, and another to show that he can write."

English system. They urged that every man should have the right to participate in the government by casting his vote, and that the constitution should be written and so made clear and unmistakable. Political clubs were founded which entered into correspondence with political societies in France ; newspapers and pamphlets poured from the press in enormous quantities, and political reform found champions in the House of Commons. Even so influential a politician as the younger Pitt, who was prime minister from 1783 to 1801, introduced bills into the House of Commons for remedying some inequalities in representation. But the violence and disorder which accompanied the French Revolution involved England in a long and tedious war and discredited reform with Englishmen who had formerly favored change, to say nothing of the Tories, who regarded with horror any proposal to modify the venerated English constitution. The younger Pitt

It is clear that England possessed the elements of a modern free government, for her king was master neither of the persons nor the purses of his subjects, nor could he issue arbitrary laws. Political affairs were discussed in newspapers and petitions so that weighty matters of government could not be decided secretly in the king's closet without the knowledge of his subjects. Nevertheless it would be far from correct to regard the English system as democratic. The mass of the people had no political rights whatever ; an hereditary House of Lords could block any measure introduced in the House of Commons ; and the House of Commons itself represented not the nation but a small minority of landowners and traders. Government offices were monopolized by members of the Established Church and the poor were oppressed by cruel criminal laws administered by officials chosen by the king. Workingmen were prohibited from forming associations to promote their interests. It was more than a century after the accession of George III before the English peasant could go to the ballot box and vote for members of Parliament. England had already the elements of a modern free government, but the political system was not democratic

REFERENCES

Frederick the Great: HENDERSON, *A Short History of Germany*, Vol. II, chap. v, pp. 182–218.

Reforms of Catharine the Great: RAMBAUD, *History of Russia*, Vol. II, chap. x, pp. 203–220.

Joseph II and Austria: FYFFE, *History of Modern Europe*, pp. 15–20; HASSALL, *Balance of Power* (European History, 1715–1789), pp. 357–366.

Charles III of Spain: HASSALL, pp. 287–289.

Enlightened Despotism in Portugal and Italy: HASSALL, pp. 291–294.

Dissolution of the Jesuit Order: HASSALL, pp. 294–301; PERKINS, *France under Louis XV*, Vol. II, pp. 206–225.

Walpole and the Cabinet System: MORLEY, *Walpole* (English Statesmen Series), pp. 139–165; LECKY, *History of England in the Eighteenth Century*, Vol. I, chap. iii, pp. 364–437.

The English Parliament: LECKY, Vol. II, chap. iv, pp. 45–63; MAY, *Constitutional History of England*, chaps. v and vi.

Political Parties in England: LECKY, Vol. I, chap. ii, pp. 212–270; MAY, chap. viii.

CHAPTER XI

THE EVE OF THE FRENCH REVOLUTION

THE *ANCIEN RÉGIME* IN FRANCE

32. The benevolent despots had not succeeded in ridding Europe of the old institutions and confusion which had come down from the Middle Ages, — indeed, there were many things which they had no desire to change. Even in England little was done in the eighteenth century to meet the most reasonable demands of the reformers. But in 1789 the king of France asked his people to submit their grievances to him and to send representatives to Versailles to confer with him upon the state of the realm and the ways in which the government might be improved so as to increase the general happiness and the prosperity of the kingdom. And then the miracle happened! The French National Assembly swept away the old abuses with an ease and thoroughness which put the petty reforms of the benevolent despots to shame. It accomplished more in a few months than the reforming kings had done in a century; for the kings had never dreamed of calling in their people to aid them. Instead of availing themselves of the great forces of the nation, they had tried to do everything alone by royal decrees, and so had failed.

How the French people accomplished reforms which had foiled the benevolent despots

The unique greatness of the reformation accomplished by the French Assembly is, however, often obscured by the disorder which accompanied it. When one meets the words " French Revolution," he is pretty sure to call up before his mind's eye the storming of the Bastille, the guillotine and its hundreds of victims, and the Paris mob shouting the hymn of the Marseillaise as they parade the streets with the heads of unfortunate " aristocrats " on their pikes. Every one has heard of this

The real French Revolution not to be confused with the Reign of Terror

terrible episode in French history, even if he knows practically nothing of the permanent good which was accomplished at the time. Indeed, it has made so deep an impression on posterity that the Reign of Terror is often mistaken for the real Revolution. It was, however, only a sequel to it, an unhappy accident which will seem less and less important as the years go on, while the achievements of the Revolution itself will loom larger and larger. The Reign of Terror will be explained and described in good time, but it is a matter of far greater importance to understand clearly how the fundamental and permanent reforms were wrought out, and how France won the proud distinction of being the first nation to do away with the absurd and vexatious institutions which weighed upon Europe in the eighteenth century.

Meaning of the term *Ancien Régime*

We have already examined these institutions which were common to most of the European countries, — despotic kings, arbitrary imprisonment, unfair taxation, censorship of the press, serfdom, feudal dues, friction between Church and State, — all of which the reformers had been busy denouncing as contrary to reason and humanity, and some of which the benevolent despots and their ministers had, in a half-hearted way, attempted to remedy. The various relics of bygone times and of outlived conditions which the Revolution abolished forever are commonly called in France the *Ancien Régime* (the old system). In order to see why France took the lead of other European countries in modernizing itself, it is necessary to examine somewhat carefully the particular causes of discontent there. We shall then see how almost every one, from the king to the peasant, came to realize that the old system was bad and consequently resolved to do away with it and substitute a more rational plan of government for the long-standing disorder.

France not a well-organized state in the eighteenth century

Of the evils which the Revolution abolished, none was more important than the confusion due to the fact that France was not in the eighteenth century a well-organized, homogeneous state whose citizens all enjoyed the same rights and privileges. A long line of kings had patched it together, adding bit by bit as they could. By conquest and bargain, by marrying heiresses, and through the extinction of the feudal dynasties, the original restricted domains of Hugh Capet about Paris and Orleans had been gradually increased by his descendants. We have seen how Louis XIV gained Alsace and Strassburg and some towns on the borders of the Spanish Netherlands, how Louis XV added Lorraine on the death of his father-in-law in 1766. Two years later the island of Corsica was ceded to France by Genoa. So when Louis XVI came to the throne in 1774 he found himself ruler of practically the whole territory which makes up France to-day.

Some of the districts which the kings of France brought under their sway, like Languedoc, Provence, Brittany, and Dauphiny, were considerable states in themselves, each with its own laws, customs, and system of government. When these provinces had come, at different times, into the possession of the king of France, he had not changed their laws so as to make them correspond with those of his other domains. He was satisfied if a new province paid its due share of the taxes and treated his officials with respect. In some cases the provinces retained their local assemblies, and controlled, to a certain extent, their own affairs. The provinces into which France was divided before the Revolution were not, therefore, merely artificial divisions created for the purposes of administrative convenience, like the modern French departments,[1] but represented real historical differences. *The old provinces of France*

While in a considerable portion of southern France the Roman law still prevailed, in the central parts and in the west and north there were no less than two hundred and eighty-five different local codes of law in force; so that one who moved from his own to a neighboring town might find a wholly unfamiliar legal system. *Various systems of law*

[1] See below, p. 238.

Neither was France commercially a single state. The chief customs duties were not collected upon goods as they entered French territory from a foreign country ; for the customs lines lay within France itself, so that the central provinces about Paris were cut off from the outlying ones as from a foreign

The Provinces of France in the Eighteenth Century, showing Interior Customs Lines

land. A merchant of Bordeaux sending goods to Paris would have to see that the duties were paid on them as they passed the customs line, and, conversely, a merchant of Paris would have to pay a like duty on commodities sent to places without the line.

The monstrous inequalities in levying one of the oldest and heaviest of the taxes, i.e. the salt tax, still better illustrate

the strange disorder that existed in France in the eighteenth
century. The government collected this form of revenue by
monopolizing the sale of salt and then charging a high price
for it. There would have been nothing remarkable in this had
the same price been charged everywhere, but as it was, the

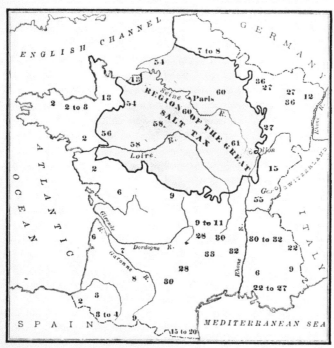

Map showing the Amount paid in the Eighteenth Century for Salt
in Various Parts of France [1]

people in one town might be forced to pay thirty times as
much as their neighbors in an adjacent district. The accompanying map shows how arbitrarily France was divided. To
take a single example : in the city of Dijon a certain amount
of salt cost seven francs ; a few miles to the east, on entering

[1] The figures indicate the various prices of a given amount of salt.

Franche-Comté, one had to pay for the same amount twenty-five francs; a little to the north, fifty-eight francs; to the south, in the region of the little salt tax, twenty-eight francs; while still farther off, in Gex, there was no tax whatever. The government had to go to great expense to guard the boundary lines between the various districts, for there was every inducement to smugglers to carry salt from those parts of the country where it was cheap into the land of the great salt tax.

The privileged classes   Besides these unfortunate local differences, there were class differences which caused great discontent. All Frenchmen did not enjoy the same rights as citizens. Two small but very important classes, the nobility and the clergy, were treated differently by the State from the rest of the people. They did not have to pay one of the heaviest of the taxes, the notorious *taille;* and on one ground or another they escaped other burdens which the rest of the citizens bore. For instance, they were not required to serve in the militia or help build the roads.

The Church   We have seen how great and powerful the mediæval Church was. In France, as in other Catholic countries of Europe, it still retained in the eighteenth century a considerable part of the power that it had possessed in the thirteenth, and it still performed important public functions. It took charge of education and of the relief of the sick and the poor. It was very wealthy and is supposed to have owned one fifth of all the land in France. The clergy claimed that their property, being dedicated to God, was not subject to taxation. They consented, however, to help the king from time to time by a "free gift," as they called it. The Church still collected the tithes from the people, and its vast possessions made it very independent. It will be remembered that those who did not call themselves Roman Catholics were excluded from some of the most important rights of citizenship. Since the revocation of the Edict of Nantes no Protestant could be legally married, or have the births of his children registered, or make a legal will.

A great part of the enormous income of the Church went The clergy
to the higher clergy, — the bishops, archbishops, and abbots.
Since these were appointed by the king,[1] often from among
his courtiers, they paid but little attention to their duties as
officers of the Church and were generally nothing more than
"great lords with a hundred thousand francs income." While
they amused themselves at Versailles the real work was performed — and well performed — by the lower clergy, who
often received scarcely enough to keep soul and body together.
This explains why, when the Revolution began, the parish
priests sided with the people instead of with their ecclesiastical
superiors.

The privileges of the nobles, like those of the clergy, had The privi-
originated in the mediæval conditions described in an earlier leges of the nobility
chapter.[2] A detailed study of their rights would reveal many
survivals of the institutions which prevailed in the eleventh
and twelfth centuries, when the great majority of the people
were serfs living upon the manors. While serfdom had largely
disappeared in France long before the eighteenth century, and
the peasants were generally free men who owned or rented
their land, it was still the theory of the French law that there
was "no land without its lord." Consequently the lords still
enjoyed the right to collect a variety of time-honored dues
from the inhabitants living within the limits of the former
manors.

The privileges and dues enjoyed by the nobles varied greatly The feudal
in different parts of France. It was quite common for the noble dues
landowner to have a right to a certain portion of the peasant's crops; occasionally he could still collect a toll on sheep
and cattle driven past his house. In some cases the lord maintained, as he had done in the Middle Ages, the only mill, wine
press, or oven within a certain district, and could require every

---

[1] According to the agreement made by Francis I with the Pope in 1516. See
above, p. 141.
[2] See above, sects. 24 and 25.

one to make use of these and pay him a share of the product. Even when a peasant owned his land, the neighboring lord usually had the right to exact one fifth of its value every time it was sold.

The hunting rights

The nobles, too, enjoyed the exclusive privilege of hunting, which was deemed an aristocratic pastime. The game which they preserved for their amusement often did great damage to the crops of the peasants, who were forbidden to interfere with hares and deer. Many of the manors had great pigeon houses, built in the form of a tower, in which there were one or two thousand nests. No wonder the peasants detested these, for they were not permitted to protect themselves against the innumerable pigeons and their progeny, which spread over the fields devouring newly sown seed. These dovecotes constituted, in fact, one of the chief grievances of the peasants.

Offices at court and in the Church and army reserved for nobles

The higher offices in the army were reserved for the nobles, as well as the easiest and most lucrative places in the Church and about the king's person. All these privileges were vestiges of the powers which the nobles had enjoyed when they ruled their estates as feudal lords. Louis XIV had, as we know, induced them to leave their domains and gather round him at Versailles, where all who could afford it lived for at least a part of the year.

Only a small part of the nobles belonged to old families

Only a small part of the nobility in the eighteenth century were, however, descendants of the ancient and illustrious feudal families of France. The greater part of them had been ennobled in recent times by the king, or had purchased or inherited a government office or judgeship which carried the privileges of nobility with it. This fact rendered the rights and exemptions claimed by the nobility even more odious to the people at large than they would otherwise have been.

The third estate

Everybody who did not belong to either the clergy or nobility was regarded as being of the third estate. The third estate was therefore nothing more than the nation at large, which was made up in 1789 of about twenty-five million souls. The privileged classes can scarcely have counted altogether more than two hundred or two hundred and fifty thousand individuals. A great part of the third estate lived in the country and tilled the soil. Most historians have been inclined to make out their condition as very wretched. They were certainly oppressed by an abominable system of taxation and were irritated by the dues which they had to pay to the lords. They also suffered frequently from local famines. Yet there is no doubt that the evils of their situation have been greatly exaggerated. When Thomas Jefferson traveled through France in 1787 he reports that the country people appeared to be comfortable and that they had plenty to eat. Arthur Young, a famous English traveler who has left us an admirable account of his journeys in France during the years 1787 and 1789, found much prosperity and contentment, although he gives, too, some forlorn pictures of destitution.

The latter have often been unduly emphasized by historical writers; for it has commonly been thought that the Revolution was to be explained by the misery and despair of the people, who could bear their burdens no longer. If, however, instead of comparing the situation of the French peasant under the old régime with that of an English or American farmer to-day, we contrast his position with that of his fellow-peasant in Prussia, Russia, Austria, Italy, or Spain, in the eighteenth century, it will be clear that in France the agricultural classes were really much better off than elsewhere on the Continent. In almost all the other European countries, except England, the peasants were still serfs : they had to work certain days in each week for their lord ; they could not marry or dispose of their land without his permission. Moreover the fact that the population of France had steadily increased from seventeen millions after the close of the wars of Louis XIV to about twenty-five millions at the opening of the Revolution, indicates that the general condition of the people was improving rather than growing worse.

Favorable situation of the peasant in France compared with other countries

Rapid increase of population in the eighteenth century

The real reason why France was the first among the European countries to carry out a great reform and do away with the irritating survivals of feudalism was not that the nation was miserable and oppressed above all others, but that it was sufficiently free and enlightened to realize the evils and absurdities of the old régime. Mere oppression and misery does not account for a revolution; there must also be active *discontent;* and of that there was a great abundance in France, as we shall see. The French peasant no longer looked up to his lord as his ruler and protector, but viewed him as a sort of legalized robber who demanded a share of his precious harvest, whose officers awaited the farmer at the crossing of the river to claim a toll, who would not let him sell his produce when he wished, or permit him to protect his fields from the ravages of the pigeons which it pleased his lord to keep.

In the eighteenth century France was still the despotism that Louis XIV had made it. Louis XVI once described it very well in the following words: "The sovereign authority resides exclusively in my person. To me solely belongs the power of making the laws, and without dependence or coöperation. The entire public order emanates from me, and I am its supreme protector. My people are one with me. The rights and interests of the nation are necessarily identical with mine and rest solely in my hands." In short, the king still ruled "by the grace of God," as Louis XIV had done. He needed to render account to no man for his governmental acts; he was responsible to God alone. The following illustrations will make clear the dangerous extent of the king's power.

In the first place, it was he who levied each year the heaviest of the taxes, the hated *taille,* from which the privileged classes were exempted. This tax brought in about one sixth of the whole revenue of the State. The amount collected was kept secret, and no report was made to the nation of what was done with it or, for that matter, with any other part of the king's income. Indeed no distinction was made between the king's private funds and the State treasury, whereas in England the monarch was given a stated allowance. The king of France could issue as many drafts payable to bearer as he wished; the royal officials must pay all such orders and ask no questions. Louis XV is said to have spent no less than seventy million dollars in this irresponsible fashion in a single year.

But the king not only controlled his subjects' purses; he had a terrible authority over their persons as well. He could issue orders for the arrest and arbitrary imprisonment of any one he pleased. Without trial or formality of any sort a person might be cast into a dungeon for an indefinite period, until the king happened to remember him again or was reminded of him by the poor man's friends. These notorious orders of arrest were called *lettres de cachet*, i.e. sealed letters. They were not difficult to obtain for any one who had influence with the king or his favorites, and they furnished a particularly easy and efficacious way of disposing of an enemy. These arbitrary orders lead one to appreciate the importance of the provision of Magna Carta which runs: " No freeman shall be taken or imprisoned except by the lawful judgment of his peers and in accordance with the law of the land." Some of the most eminent men of the time were shut up by the king's order, often on account of books or pamphlets written by them which displeased the king or those about him. The distinguished statesman, Mirabeau, when a young man, was imprisoned several times through *lettres de cachet* obtained by his father as a means of checking his reckless dissipation.

Lettres de cachet

Yet, notwithstanding the seemingly unlimited powers of the French king, and in spite of the fact that France had no written constitution and no legislative body to which the nation sent representatives, the monarch was by no means absolutely free to do just as he pleased. He had not the time nor inclination to carry on personally the government of twenty-five million subjects, and he necessarily, and willingly, left much of the

Limitations on the power of the French king

work to his ministers and the numerous public officials, who were bound to obey the laws and regulations established for their control and guidance.

The *parle-
ments* and
their
protests
Next to the king's council the most important governmental bodies were the higher courts of law, the *parlements*. These resembled the English Parliament in almost nothing but name. The French *parlements* — of which the most important one was at Paris and a dozen more were scattered about the provinces — did not, however, confine themselves solely to the business of trying lawsuits. They claimed, and quite properly, that when the king decided to make a new law he must send it to them to be registered, for how, otherwise, could they adjust their decisions to it? Now although they acknowledged that the right to make the laws belonged to the monarch, they nevertheless often sent a "protest" to the king instead of registering an edict which they disapproved. They would urge that the ministers had abused his Majesty's confidence. They would also take pains to have their protest printed and sold on the streets at a penny or two a copy, so that people should get the idea that the *parlement* was defending the nation against the oppressive measures of the king's ministers.

When the king received one of these protests two alternatives were open to him. He might recall the distasteful decree altogether, or modify it so as to suit the court; or he could summon the *parlement* before him and in a solemn session (called a *lit de justice*) command it with his own mouth to register the law in its records. The *parlement* would then reluctantly obey; but as the Revolution approached it began to claim that a decree registered against its will was not valid.

The *parle-
ments* help
to prepare
the way for
the Revo-
lution
Struggles between the *parlements* and the king's ministers were very frequent in the eighteenth century. They prepared the way for the Revolution, first, by bringing important questions to the attention of the people; for there were no newspapers, and no parliamentary or congressional debates, to enable the

public to understand the policy of the government. Secondly, the *parlements* not only frankly criticised the proposed measures of the king and his ministers, but they familiarized the nation with the idea that the king was not really at liberty to alter what they called " the fundamental laws " of the State. By this they meant that there was an unwritten constitution, which limited the king's power and of which they were the guardians. In this way they promoted the growing discontent with a government which was carried on in secret, and which left the nation at the mercy of the men in whom the king might for the moment repose confidence.

It is a great mistake to suppose that public opinion did not exercise a powerful check upon the king, even under the autocratic old régime. It was, as one of Louis XVI's ministers declared, " an invisible power which, without treasury, guards, or an army, ruled Paris and the court, — yes, the very palace of the king." The latter half of the eighteenth century was a period of outspoken and acrid criticism of the whole existing social and governmental system. Reformers, among whom many of the king's ministers were counted, loudly and eloquently discussed the numerous abuses and the vicious character of the government, which gradually came to seem just as bad to the people of that day as it does to us now. *Public opinion*

Although there were no daily newspapers to discuss public questions, large numbers of pamphlets were written and circulated by individuals whenever there was an important crisis, and they answered much the same purpose as the editorials in a modern newspaper. We have already seen how French philosophers and reformers, like Voltaire, Diderot, and Montesquieu, had been encouraged by the freedom of speech which prevailed in England, and how industriously they had sown the seeds of discontent in their own country. We have seen how in popular works, in poems and stories and plays, and above all in the *Encyclopædia*, they explained the new scientific discoveries, attacked the old beliefs and misapprehensions, and *Attempts to check the discussion of public questions* encouraged progress. Only the most ignorant could escape their influence altogether.

The censorship of the press serves to advertise the reformers

Sometimes the pamphlets and books treated the government, the clergy, or the Catholic religion with such open contempt that either the king, or the clergy, or the courts felt it necessary to prevent their circulation. The *parlement* of Paris now and then ordered some offensive writing, such as Diderot's *Philosophic Thoughts*, Voltaire's *Handy Philosophic Dictionary*, certain of Rousseau's works, pamphlets defending the Jesuits, etc., to be burned by the common hangman. The authors, if they could be discovered, were in some cases imprisoned, and the printers and publishers fined or banished, but in general the courts satisfied themselves with suppressing the books and pamphlets of which they disapproved. But the attempted suppression only advertised the attacks upon existing abuses, which followed one another in rapid succession. The efforts of the government and the clergy to check free discussion seemed an outrage to the more thoughtful among the citizens, and so rather promoted than prevented the consideration of the weaknesses of the Church and of the king's government.

Economists argue against government restrictions on trade and manufacture

The economists exposed and brought home to the people the many evils of which their new science took note. The unjust system of taxation, which tended to exempt the richer classes from their fair share of the public burdens ; the wasteful and irritating methods of collecting the taxes ; the interior customs lines, preventing the easy passage of goods from one part of France to another ; the extravagance of the king's household ; the pensions granted to undeserving persons ; every evil of the bungling, iniquitous old régime was brought under the scrutiny of the new thinkers, who tested the existing system by the light of reason and the welfare of the great mass of the people.

The French government, as has already been explained, had been in the habit of regulating manufactures with the hope of maintaining a standard which would insure large and regular

sales in foreign lands and in this way bring money into France.
Governmental officials watched those who handled grain, forbade them to accumulate wheat, barley, rye, or bread stuffs, or
to make any sales except in the public markets, and required
them to report all their transactions to the government. The
economists were flatly opposed to this system of regulation.
They pointed out that these government restrictions produced
some very bad results. They failed to prevent famine, and, in
the case of industry, they discouraged new inventions and the
adoption of better methods. The economists claimed that it
would be far better to leave the manufacturer to carry on his
business in his own way.[1]

How Louis XVI Tried to Play the Benevolent Despot

33. In 1774 Louis XV died, after a disgraceful reign of
which it has not seemed necessary to say much. His unsuccessful wars, which had ended with the loss of all his American
possessions and the victory of his enemies in India, had brought
France to the verge of bankruptcy; indeed in his last years
his ministers repudiated a portion of the government's obligations. The taxes were already so oppressive as to arouse universal discontent and yet the government was running behind
seventy millions of dollars a year. The king's personal conduct
was scandalous, and he allowed his mistresses and courtiers to
meddle in public affairs and plunder the royal treasury for
themselves and their favorites. When at last he was carried off
by smallpox every one hailed, with hopes of better times, the
accession of his grandson and successor, Louis XVI.

Death of Louis XV and the accession of Louis XVI (1774)

The new king was but twenty years old, ill educated, indo-
lent, unsociable, and very fond of hunting and of pottering
about in a workshop where he spent his happiest hours. He
was a well-meaning young man, with none of his grandfather's

Character of Louis XVI

[1] See above, pp. 180 *sqq.*

vices, who tried now and then to attend to the disagreeable business of government, and would gladly have made his people happy if that had not required more energy than he possessed. He had none of the restless interest in public affairs that we found in Frederick the Great, Catharine II, or his brother-in-law, Joseph II; he was never tempted to rise at five o'clock in the morning in order to read State papers.

Marie Antoinette

His wife was the beautiful Marie Antoinette, daughter of Maria Theresa. The marriage had been arranged in 1770 with a view of maintaining the alliance which had been concluded between France and Austria in 1756. The queen was only nineteen years old when she came to the throne, light-hearted and on pleasure bent. She disliked the formal etiquette of the court at Versailles and shocked people by her thoughtless pranks. She rather despised her heavy husband, who did not care to share in the amusements which pleased her best. She did not hesitate to interfere in the government when she wished to help one of her favorites or to make trouble for some one she disliked.

Turgot, controller general (1774–1776)

At first Louis XVI took his duties very seriously. It seemed for a time that he might find a place among the benevolent despots who were then ruling in Europe. He almost immediately placed the ablest of all the French economists, Turgot, in the most important of the government offices, that of controller general. Turgot was an experienced government official as well as a scholar. For thirteen years he had been the king's representative in Limoges, one of the least prosperous portions of France. There he had had ample opportunity to see the vices of the prevailing system of taxation. He had made every effort to induce the government to better its methods, and had tried to familiarize the people with the principles of political economy. Consequently, when he was put in charge of the nation's finances, it seemed as if he and the conscientious young king might find some remedy for the recognized abuses.

The first and most natural measure was economy, for only in that way could the government be saved from bankruptcy and the burden of taxation be lightened. Turgot felt that the vast amount spent in maintaining the luxury of the royal court at Versailles should be reduced. The establishments of the king, the queen, and the princes of the blood royal cost the State annually toward twelve million dollars. Then the French king had long been accustomed to grant " pensions " in a reckless manner to his favorites, and this required nearly twelve million dollars more.

Turgot advocates economy

Any attempt, however, to reduce this amount would arouse the immediate opposition of the courtiers, and it was the courtiers who really governed France. They had every opportunity to influence the king's mind against a man whose economies they disliked. They were constantly about the monarch from the moment when he awoke in the morning until he went to bed at night ; therefore they had an obvious advantage over the controller general, who only saw him in business hours.[1]

How the courtiers governed France

Immediately upon coming into power Turgot removed a great part of the restrictions on the grain trade. He prefaced the edict with a very frank denunciation of the government's traditional policy of preventing persons from buying and selling their grain when and where they wished. He showed that this did not obviate famines, as the government hoped that it might, and that it caused great loss and hardship. If the government would only let matters alone the grain would always go to those provinces where it was most needed, for there it would bring the best price. Turgot seized this and every similar opportunity to impress important economic truths upon the minds of the people.

Turgot frees the grain trade and endeavors to teach political economy to the people

Early in 1776 Turgot brought forward two edicts which could not fail to rouse much opposition. The first of these abolished the guilds, which he declared exercised " a vast tyranny

Turgot abolishes the guilds

[1] See Turgot's letter to the king, August, 1774, in *Readings*, sect. 33.

over trade and industry." In almost all the towns the various trades of the baker, tailor, barber, swordmaker, hatter, cooper, and all the rest, were each in the hands of a small number of masters who formed a union to keep every one else out, and who made such rules as they pleased about the way in which the trade should be conducted. Sometimes only the sons of masters or those who married masters' widows would be permitted to carry on a trade. Employers could not select the workmen they wished. " Often," Turgot declared, " one cannot get the simplest job done without having it go through the hands of several workmen of different guilds and without suffering the delays, tricks, and exactions which the prétensions of the various guilds encourage." The king, therefore, ordered that " it shall be free to all persons of whatever quality or condition they may be, even to all foreigners, to exercise in all our kingdom, and particularly in our good city of Paris, whatever profession or industry may seem good to them." All the guilds were abolished, in spite of those who declared that industry would be ruined as soon as everybody was free to open a shop and offer his goods to the public.

Turgot abolishes the *corvée* and so attacks the privileges of the clergy and the nobility

At the same time Turgot proposed an even more important reform. The government had been accustomed to build and repair the public roads, forcing the peasants to bring out their horses and carts and work for a certain time every year without remuneration. This was of course a form of taxation and was known as the *corvée*. Turgot held that the peasants should not be required to bear this burden and proposed to substitute for it a tax to be paid by the landholders. Both the clergy and nobility hotly opposed this reform on the ground that their privileges exempted them from the *corvée*, which was an ignoble exaction which could fall only upon a peasant. Turgot confessed that his main aim was to begin a great reform of the vicious system of taxation which exempted the privileged classes from the *corvée*, the *taille*, and other contributions which should be borne by everybody according to his capacity.

Turgot forced the *parlement* of Paris to register these edicts; but he had become very unpopular, for each one of his reforms injured a particular class who thereafter became his enemies. The nobles disliked him for substituting the land tax, which fell upon them, for the *corvée*, which only the peasants had borne. The clergy believed him a wicked philosopher, for it was known that he had urged the pious Louis XVI, when he took his coronation oath, to omit the pledge to extirpate heresy from his realms. The tradespeople hated him for doing away with the guilds.

An Italian economist, when he heard of Turgot's appointment, wrote to a friend in France: "So Turgot is controller general! He will not remain in office long enough to carry out his plans. He will punish some scoundrels; he will bluster about and lose his temper; he will be anxious to do good, but will run against obstacles and rogues at every turn. Public credit will fall; he will be detested; it will be said that he is not fitted for his task. Enthusiasm will cool; he will retire or be sent off, and we shall have a new proof of the mistake of filling a position like his in a monarchy like yours with an upright man and a philosopher."

The Italian could not have made a more accurate statement of the case had he waited until after the dismissal of Turgot, which took place in May, 1776, much to the satisfaction of the court. The king, although upright and well-intentioned, was not fond of the governmental duties to which Turgot was always calling his attention. It was much easier to let things go along in the old way; for reforms not only required much extra work, but they also forced him to refuse the customary favors to those around him. It was not perhaps unnatural that the discontent of his young queen or of an intimate companion should outweigh the woes of the distant peasant.

Although the privileged classes, especially the courtiers who had the king's ear and the conservative lawyers in the *parlements*, prevented Turgot from carrying out the extensive

[marginal notes:] Turgot's enemies

Turgot's position

Turgot dismissed, May, 1776

Turgot's plan for local assemblies

reforms that he had in mind, and even induced the king to restore the guilds and to continue the *corvée*, Turgot's administration nevertheless forwarded the French Revolution. In the preambles to his edicts he carefully explained the nature of the abuses which the king was trying to remedy and so strove to enlist the sympathy of the public. He proposed that the king should form local assemblies to help him in the government, as otherwise too much power was left in the hands of the king's officials. In short, while Turgot was quite satisfied to have a benevolent despot in France so long as the king allowed himself to be led along the path of reform by a wise philosopher and economist, he was anxious to encourage public interest in the policy of the government, and believed it essential to have the people's representatives help in assessing the taxes and in managing local affairs.

Necker succeeds Turgot

Necker, who, after a brief interval, succeeded Turgot, also contributed to the progress of the coming Revolution in two ways. He borrowed vast sums of money in order to carry on the war which France, as the ally of the United States, had undertaken against England. This greatly embarrassed the treasury later and helped to produce the financial crisis which was the immediate cause of the Revolution. Secondly, he gave the nation its first opportunity of learning what was done with the public funds by presenting to the king (February, 1781) a *report* on the financial condition of the kingdom which was publicly printed and eagerly read. There the people could see for the first time how much the *taille* and the salt tax actually took from them, and how much the king spent on himself and his favorites.

Necker's financial report

Calonne, controller general (1783-1787)

Necker was soon followed by Calonne, who may be said to have precipitated the momentous reform which constitutes the French Revolution. He was very popular at first with king and courtiers, for he spent the public funds far more recklessly than his predecessors. But naturally he soon found himself in a position where he could obtain no more money. The *parlements* would consent to no more loans in a period of peace, and the taxes were as high as it was deemed possible to make them. At last Calonne, finding himself desperately put to it, informed the astonished king that the State was on the verge of bankruptcy, and that in order to save it a radical reformation of "the whole public order" was necessary. This report of Calonne's may be taken as the beginning of the French Revolution, for it was the first of the series of events that led to the calling of a representative assembly which abolished the old régime and gave France a written constitution.

Calonne informs the king that France is on the verge of bankruptcy, August, 1786

REFERENCES

The Government of Louis XVI: LOWELL, *The Eve of the French Revolution*, pp. 4–24; *Cambridge Modern History*, Vol. VIII, chap. ii, pp. 36–65; MATHEWS, *The French Revolution*, pp. 1–11.

Taxation and Finance: LOWELL, pp. 207–242; *Cambridge Modern History*, Vol. VIII, chap. iii, pp. 66–78.

Agitation by Pamphlets: LOWELL, pp. 322–341.

Lettres de Cachet: PERKINS, *France under Louis XV*, Vol. II, pp. 352–358.

Turgot and Necker: MATHEWS, pp. 92–101; *Cambridge Modern History*, Vol. VIII, chap. iii, pp. 66–78; HASSALL, *Balance of Power*, pp. 405–412; SAY, *Turgot* (Great French Writers Series).

Early Years of Louis XVI's Reign: HASSALL, pp. 401–424; *Cambridge Modern History*, Vol. VIII, chap. iv, pp. 79–98.

CHAPTER XII

THE FRENCH REVOLUTION

How the Estates General were summoned in 1789

Reforms proposed by Calonne

34. Calonne claimed that it was necessary, in order to avoid ruin, " to reform everything vicious in the State." He proposed, therefore, to reduce the *taille*, reform the salt tax, do away with the interior customs lines, correct the abuses of the guilds, etc. But the chief reform, and by far the most difficult one, was to force the privileged classes to surrender their important exemptions from taxation. He hoped that if certain concessions were made to them they might be brought to consent to a land tax which should be levied on the nobility and clergy as well as on the third estate. So he proposed to the king that he should summon an assembly of persons prominent in Church and State, called " Notables," to ratify certain changes which would increase the prosperity of the country and bring money enough into the treasury to meet the necessary expenses.

Summoning of the Notables, 1786

The summoning of the Notables late in 1786 was really a revolution in itself. It was a confession on the part of the king that he found himself in a predicament from which he could not escape without the aid of his people. The Notables whom he selected — bishops, archbishops, dukes, judges, high government officials — were practically all members of the privileged classes ; but they still represented the nation, after a fashion, as distinguished from the king's immediate circle of courtiers.

In his opening address Calonne gave the Notables an idea of the sad financial condition of the country. The government

was running behind some forty million dollars a year. He
could not continue to borrow, and economy, however strict,
would not suffice to cover the deficit. " What, then," he
asked, " remains to fill this frightful void and enable us to
raise the revenue to the desired level? *The Abuses !* Yes,
gentlemen, the abuses offer a source of wealth which the
State should appropriate, and which should serve to reëstablish order in the finances. . . . Those abuses which must now
be destroyed for the welfare of the people are the most
important and the best guarded of all, the very ones which
have the deepest roots and the most spreading branches. For
example, those which weigh on the laboring classes, the
pecuniary privileges, exceptions to the law which should be
common to all, and many an unjust exemption which can
only relieve certain taxpayers by embittering the conditions
of others ; the general want of uniformity in the assessment
of the taxes and the enormous difference which exists between
the contributions of different provinces and of the subjects of
the same sovereign ; the severity and arbitrariness in the collection of the *taille ;* the apprehension, embarrassment, almost
dishonor, associated with the trade in breadstuffs ; the interior
customhouses and barriers which make the various parts of
the kingdom like foreign countries to one another . . . ," —
all these evils, which public-spirited citizens had long depre-
cated, Calonne proposed to do away with forthwith.

The Notables, however, had no confidence in Calonne ;
most of them were determined not to give up their privileges,
and they refused to ratify his program of reform. The king
then dismissed Calonne and soon sent the Notables home, too
(May, 1787). He then attempted to carry through some of
the more pressing financial reforms in the usual way by drawing up edicts and sending them to the *parlements* to be
registered.

The *parlement* of Paris resolved, as usual, to make the
king's ministry trouble and gain popularity for itself. This

time it resorted to a truly extraordinary measure. It not only refused to register two new taxes which the king desired, but asserted that " *Only the nation assembled in the Estates General can give the consent necessary to the establishment of a permanent tax.*" " Only the nation," the *parlement* continued, "after it has learned the true state of the finances, can destroy the great abuses and open up important resources." This declaration was followed in a few days by the respectful request that the king assemble the Estates General of his kingdom.

The refusal of the *parlement* to register the new taxes led to one of the old struggles between it and the king's ministers. A compromise was arranged in the autumn of 1787 ; the *parlement* agreed to register a great loan, and the king pledged himself to assemble the Estates General within five years. During the early months of 1788 a flood of pamphlets appeared, criticising the system of taxation and the unjust privileges and exemptions enjoyed by a few citizens to the detriment of the great mass of the nation.

Suddenly the *parlement* of Paris learned that the king's ministers were planning to put an end to its troublesome habit of opposing their measures. They proposed to remodel the whole judicial system and take from the *parlement* the right to register new decrees and consequently the right to protest. This the *parlement* loudly proclaimed was in reality a blow at the nation itself. The ministers were attacking it simply because it had acknowledged its lack of power to grant new taxes and had requested the king to assemble the representatives of the nation. The ministers, it claimed, were bent upon establishing an out-and-out despotism in which there should no longer be any check whatever on the arbitrary power of the king.

The *parlement* had long been wont to refer to certain "fundamental laws " which formed a sort of unwritten constitution limiting the powers of the king. It now ventured to formulate some of these : (1) the right of the nation to grant all taxes voluntarily through their representatives in the Estates General ; (2) the right of the provinces which had been annexed to France to retain all the liberties which the king had guaranteed to them when they came under his rule ; and the right of the local *parlement* in each of these provinces to examine every edict of the king and refuse to register it if it did not conform to the constitutional laws of the province, or violated its rights ; (3) the right of the judges to retain their offices no matter how anxious the king might be to dismiss them ; (4) the right of every citizen, if arrested, to be brought immediately before a competent court and only to be tried by the regular judges.

The *parlement* of Paris draws up a Declaration of Rights (May, 1788)

This was a very poor and inadequate sketch of a constitution, but it was a definite protest against allowing the king to become an absolute and uncontrolled despot. According to the new edicts against which the *parlement* of Paris protested, tyrannical ministers might freely make new laws for the whole realm and completely ignore the special privileges which the king had pledged himself to maintain when Languedoc, Provence, Dauphiny, Brittany, Béarn, Navarre, and other important provinces had originally been added to his kingdom. The cause of the *parlements* seemed the cause of the nation, and their protest contributed to the excitement and indignation which spread throughout France and which was to continue until the whole system of government was completely reformed.

The provinces of France support the *parlements*

When the king's commissioners tried to proclaim the edicts which robbed the *parlements* of their right to register new laws, mobs collected and insulted them. At Rennes, in Brittany, they were besieged by the townspeople and had to be protected by soldiers. At Toulouse the mob tore up the pavement to build barricades and prepared to resist the entry of the commissioners. At Bordeaux the new laws were proclaimed under the protection of bayonets. Everywhere there were protests, usually accompanied by disorder.

Opposition
roused in
Dauphiny

The most interesting events took place at Grenoble, where
the *parlement* of Dauphiny was accustomed to meet. It
declared that, if the king persisted in his plan, he would
break all the bonds which bound that province to France and
that Dauphiny would consider itself entirely freed from the
oath of fidelity to him. When the king's officers arrived to
punish the *parlement* for its audacious utterances, they found
the city ready to defend it. An assembly was convened at

Meeting at
Vizille

the neighboring Vizille where representatives of the nobility,
clergy, and third estate came together. They denounced the
policy of the king's ministers, demanded the speedy convocation of the Estates General, and reiterated the right of the
nation to grant all taxes and to be protected from arbitrary punishment. They claimed that they were vindicating the rights
of the nation at large, and that they were ready, if necessary,
to sacrifice any of their special privileges in the interest of the
whole kingdom.

The Estates
General sum-
moned for
1789

This demonstration on the part of Dauphiny and similar
ones in the other provinces forced the king to dismiss the
unpopular ministry and to recall Necker, who had followed
Turgot as controller general and in whom everybody had great
confidence. Necker restored the *parlements* to their old power
and, as the treasury was absolutely empty, there seemed nothing to do but to call together the representatives of the people.
Necker therefore announced that the Estates General would
convene early the next year.[1]

General igno-
rance in
regard to the
Estates
General

It was now discovered that no one knew much about this
body of which every one was talking, for it had not met since
1614. The king accordingly issued a general invitation to
scholars to find out all they could about the customs observed

---

[1] The *parlements* immediately lost all their importance. They had helped to
precipitate the reform but they did not sympathize with any change which would
deprive the privileged classes, to which their members belonged, of their ancient
exemptions. They therefore forfeited their popularity when in September, 1788,
they declared that the Estates General should meet in its old way, which would
have enabled the privileged classes to stop any distasteful reforms.

in the former meetings of the Estates. The public naturally became very much interested in a matter which touched them so closely, and there were plenty of readers for the pamphlets which now began to appear in greater numbers than ever before.

The old Estates General had been organized in a way appropriate enough to the feudal conditions under which it originated. Each of the three estates of the realm — clergy, nobility, and third estate — sent an equal number of representatives, who were expected to consider not the interests of the nation but the special interests of the particular social class to which they respectively belonged. Accordingly the deputies of the three estates did not sit together or vote as a single body. The members of each group first came to an agreement among themselves and then cast a single vote for the whole order. The Estates General thus had three houses instead of two, like the English Parliament and the Congress of the United States, which had just been established.

The old system of voting by classes in the Estates General

It was natural that this system should seem preposterous to the average Frenchman in 1788. If the Estates should be convoked according to the ancient forms, the two privileged classes would together be entitled to twice the number of representatives allotted to the other twenty-five million inhabitants of France. What was much worse, it seemed impossible that any important reforms could be adopted in an assembly where those who had every selfish reason for opposing the most necessary changes were given two votes out of three. Necker, whom the king had recalled in the hope that he might succeed in adjusting the finances, agreed that the third estate might have as many deputies as both the other orders put together, namely six hundred, but he would not consent to having the three orders sit and vote together, as the nation at large desired.

Objections to the system

Of the innumerable pamphlets which now appeared, the most famous was that written by Sieyès, called *What is the*

Sieyès's pamphlet, *What is the Third Estate?* (*Qu'est-ce que le tiers état?*)

Third Estate? He claimed that the "aristocrats," or privileged classes, should be simply neglected, since the deputies of the third estate would represent practically the whole nation, namely, some twenty-five million or more individuals of whom less than two hundred thousand, as he estimated, were nobles and priests. "It is impossible," he says, "to answer the question, What place should the privileged orders be assigned in the social body, for it is like asking Where, in the human body, does the malign ulcer belong which torments and weakens the unhappy victim?"

The *cahiers*

Besides the great question as to whether the deputies should vote by head or by order, the pamphlets discussed what reforms the Estates should undertake. We have, however, a still more interesting and important expression of public opinion in France at this time, in the *cahiers*,[1] or lists of grievances and suggestions for reform, which, in pursuance of an old custom, the king asked the nation to prepare. Each village and town throughout France had an opportunity to tell quite frankly exactly what it suffered from the existing system, and what reforms it desired that the Estates General should bring about. These *cahiers*[2] were the "last will and testament" of the old régime, and they constitute a unique historical document of unparalleled completeness and authenticity. No one can read the *cahiers* without seeing that the nation was ready for the great transformation which, within a year, was to destroy a great part of the social and political system under which the French had lived for centuries.

Desire of the nation for a constitutional, instead of an absolute, monarchy

Almost all the *cahiers* agreed that the prevailing disorder and the vast and ill-defined powers of the king and his ministers were perhaps the fundamental evils. One of them says: "Since arbitrary power has been the source of all the evils which afflict the State, our first desire is the establishment of a really national constitution, which shall define the rights of all and provide the

[1] Pronounced kä-yä'.
[2] An example of the *cahiers* may be found in the *Readings*, sect. 34.

laws to maintain them." No one dreamed at this time of displacing the king or of taking the government out of his hands.
The people only wished to change an absolute monarchy into
a limited, or constitutional, one. All that was necessary was
that the things which the government might *not* do should be
solemnly and irrevocably determined and put upon record, and
that the Estates General should meet periodically to grant the
taxes, give the king advice in national crises, and expostulate,
if necessary, against any violations of the proposed charter of
liberties.

The king expressed the wish that he might reach all his
subjects, no matter how remote or humble they might be. He
consequently permitted every one whose name appeared upon
the list of taxpayers to vote, either directly or indirectly, for
deputies. As he and his predecessors had always been careful
to have every one pay taxes that had anything whatever to
pay, this was practically equivalent to modern universal manhood suffrage.

Practically universal manhood suffrage

The village priests were all allowed to vote directly for
deputies of their order. Since they hated the rich prelates
who spent their time at the court of Versailles, they naturally
elected as many as they could of their own rank. The result
was that two thirds of the representatives of the clergy in the
Estates General were simple parish priests who were in sympathy with the people and more commonly sided with the
third estate than with the bishops and abbots, who were bent
upon defending the old privileges and blocking reform.

Many parish priests elected

With these ideas expressed in the *cahiers* in mind, the
Estates assembled in Versailles and held their first session on
May 5, 1789. The king had ordered the deputies to wear the
same costumes that had been worn at the last meeting of the
Estates in 1614 ; but no royal edict could call back the spirit
of earlier centuries. The representatives of the third estate
refused to organize themselves in the old way as a separate
order. They sent invitation after invitation to the deputies of

The Estates General meets, May 5, 1789

the clergy and nobility, requesting them to join the people's representatives and deliberate in common on the great interests of the nation. Some of the more liberal of the nobles — Lafayette, for example — and a large minority of the clergy wished to meet with the deputies of the third estate.[1] But they were outvoted, and finally the deputies of the third estate (under the influence of Sieyès), losing patience, declared themselves on June 17 a " National Assembly." They argued that, since they represented at least ninety-six per cent of the nation, the deputies of the privileged orders might be neglected altogether. This usurpation of power on the part of the third estate transformed the old feudal Estates, voting by orders, into the first modern national representative assembly on the continent of Europe.

The representatives of the third estate declare themselves a " National Assembly "

Under the influence of his courtiers the king tried to restore the old system by arranging a solemn joint session of the three orders, at which he presided in person. He presented a long program of excellent reforms, and then bade the Estates sit apart, according to the former custom. But it was like bidding water to run up hill. Three days before, when the commons had found themselves excluded from their regular place of meeting on account of the preparations for the royal session, they had betaken themselves to a neighboring building called the " Tennis Court." Here, on June 20, they took the famous " Tennis-Court " oath, never to separate " until the constitution of the kingdom should be established and placed upon a firm foundation." They were emboldened in their purpose to resist all schemes to frustrate a general reform by the support of over half of the deputies of the clergy, who joined them the day before the royal session.

The " Tennis-Court " oath

Consequently, when the king finished his address and commanded the three orders to disperse immediately in order to

[1] The nobles, of whom a few sympathized with the third estate, rejected the proposed union by a vote of 188 to 47. The vote of the clergy, made up largely of parish priests, stood 133 to 114, so ten more noes, in their case, would have turned the scale.

resume their separate sessions, most of the bishops, some of the parish priests, and a great part of the nobility obeyed ; the rest sat still, uncertain what they should do. When the master of ceremonies ordered them to comply with the king's commands, Count Mirabeau, who was to prove himself the most distinguished statesman among the deputies, told him bluntly that they would not leave their places except at the point of the bayonet. The weak king almost immediately gave in, and a few days later ordered all the deputies of the privileged orders, who had not already done so, to join the commons. The nobility and clergy forced to join the third estate

This was a momentous victory for the nation. The representatives of the privileged classes had been forced to unite with the third estate, to deliberate with them, and to vote " by head." Moreover the National Assembly had pledged itself never to separate until it had regenerated the kingdom and given France a constitution. It was no longer simply to vote taxes and help the king's treasury out of its perennial difficulties. First momentous victory of the nation

FIRST REFORMS OF THE NATIONAL ASSEMBLY, JULY–OCTOBER, 1789

35. The National Assembly now began in earnest the great task of preparing a constitution for France. It was, however, soon interrupted. The little group of noblemen and prelates who spent much of their time in the king's palace formed what was known as the court party. They were not numerous but could influence the king as no other group in the nation could do. They naturally opposed reform ; they neither wished to give up their own privileges nor to have the king come under the control of the National Assembly, for that would mean that he would no longer be able to give them the pensions and lucrative positions which they now readily obtained. This court " ring " enjoyed the hearty support of the queen, Marie Antoinette, and of the king's younger brother, the count of Artois, both of whom regarded the deputies of the third estate as The court party determines to disperse the National Assembly

insolent and dangerous agitators who proposed to rob the
monarch of the powers which had been conferred upon him
by God himself. The queen and her friends had got rid of
Turgot and Calonne, who had endeavored to change the old
order ; why should they not disperse the Estates General, which
was escaping from the control of the clergy and nobility?

Troops sent
to Paris;
Necker's dis-
missal, July,
1789

The king agreed to the court party's plans. He summoned
the Swiss and German troops in the employ of France and
sent a company of them into Paris in order that they might
suppress any violence on the part of the townspeople, should
he decide to send the arrogant deputies home. He was also
induced to dismiss Necker, who enjoyed a popularity that he
had, in reality, done little to merit. When the people of Paris
saw the troops gathering and heard of the dismissal of Necker

Camille
Desmoulins
excites the
Parisians,
July 12, 1789

they became excited. Camille Desmoulins, a brilliant young
journalist, rushed into the garden of the Palais Royal, where
crowds of people were discussing the situation, and, leaping
upon a table, announced that the Swiss and German soldiers
would soon be slaughtering all the "patriots." He urged the
people to arm and defend both themselves and the National
Assembly from the attacks of the court party, which wished to
betray the nation. All night the mob surged about the streets,
seeking arms in the shops of the gunsmiths and breaking into
bakeries and taverns to satisfy their hunger and thirst.

Attack on
the Bastille,
July 14, 1789

This was but the prelude to the great day of July 14, when
crowds of people assembled to renew the search for arms, and
to perform, mayhap, some deed of patriotism. One of the law-
less bands made its way to the ancient fortress of the Bastille, which stood in the poorer quarter of the city. Here the
mob expected to find arms, but the governor of the fortress,
de Launay, naturally refused to supply the crowd with weapons.
He had, moreover, mounted cannons on the parapets, which
made the inhabitants of the region very nervous. The people
hated the castle, which they imagined to be full of dark dun-
geons and instruments of torture. It appeared to them a symbol

of tyranny, for it had long been used as a place of confinement for those whom the king imprisoned by his arbitrary orders, the *lettres de cachet.* While there seemed no hope of taking the fortress, whose walls, ten feet thick, towered high above them, the attempt was made. Negotiations with the governor were opened and, during these, a part of the crowd pressed across a drawbridge into the court. Here, for some reason that has never been explained, the troops in the castle fired upon the people and killed nearly a hundred of them. Meanwhile the mob on the outside continued an ineffectual but desperate attack until de Launay was forced by the garrison to surrender on condition that they should be allowed to retire unmolested. The drawbridge was then let down and the crowd rushed into the gloomy pile. They found only seven prisoners, whom they freed with great enthusiasm. But the better element in the crowd was unable to restrain the violent and cruel class, represented in every mob, who proposed to avenge the slaughter of their companions in the courtyard of the Bastille. Consequently the Swiss soldiers, who formed the garrison, were killed, and their heads, with that of de Launay, were paraded about the streets on pikes.

The fall of the Bastille is one of the most impressive, striking, and dramatic events in modern history, and its anniversary is still celebrated in France as the chief national holiday. On that day the people of Paris rose to protect themselves against the plots of the courtiers, who wished to maintain the old despotic system. They attacked an ancient monument of despotism, forced the king's officer in charge of it to capitulate, and then destroyed the walls of the fortress so that nothing now remains except a line of white stones to mark its former site. The events of the 14th of July, 1789, have been "disfigured and transfigured by legends," but none the less they opened a new era of freedom inasmuch as they put an end to the danger of a return to the *Ancien Régime.* It is true that the court party continued to make trouble, but its

Significance of the fall of the Bastille

Beginning of the emigration of the nobles

opposition served to hasten rather than to impede reform. Some of the leaders of the group, among them the king's younger brother, the count of Artois (who was destined to become king as Charles X), left France immediately after the fall of the Bastille and began actively urging foreign monarchs to intervene to protect Louis XVI from the reformers.

The national guard

It had become clear that the king could not maintain order in Paris. The shopkeepers and other respectable citizens were compelled to protect themselves against the wild crowds made up of the criminal and disorderly class of the capital and reënforced by half-starving men who had drifted to Paris on account of the famine which prevailed in the provinces. In order to prevent attacks on individuals and the sacking of shops, a " national guard " was organized, made up of volunteers from the well-to-do citizens. General Lafayette, one of the most liberal-minded of the nobles, was put in command. This deprived the king of every excuse for calling in his regular troops to insure order in Paris, and put the military power into the hands of the *bourgeoisie*, as the French call the class made up of the more prosperous business men.

Establishment of *communes* in Paris and other cities

The government of Paris was reorganized, and a mayor, chosen from among the members of the National Assembly, was put at the head of the new *commune*, as the municipal government was called. The other cities of France also began with one accord, after the dismissal of Necker and the fall of the Bastille, to promote the Revolution by displacing or supplementing their former governments by committees of their citizens. These improvised communes, or city governments, established national guards, as Paris had done, and thus maintained order. The news that the king had approved the changes at Paris confirmed the citizens of other cities in the conviction that they had done right in taking the control into their own hands. We shall hear a good deal of the commune, or municipal government, of Paris later, as it played a very important rôle in the Reign of Terror.

By the end of the month of July the commotion reached the country districts. A curious panic swept over the land, which the peasants long remembered as " the great fear." A mysterious rumor arose that the " brigands " were coming! The terrified people did what they could to prepare for the danger, although they had no clear idea of what it was ; neighboring communities combined with one another for mutual protection. When the panic was over and people saw that there were no brigands after all, they turned their attention to an enemy by no means imaginary, i.e. the old régime. The peasants assembled on the village common, or in the parish church, and voted to pay the feudal dues no longer. The next step was to burn the *châteaux*, or castles of the nobles, in order to destroy the records of the peasants' obligations to their feudal lords.

About the 1st of August news reached the National Assem- bly of the burning of *châteaux* in various parts of the kingdom, and of the obstinate refusal of the country people to pay the tithes, taxes, rents, and feudal dues. It seemed absolutely necessary to pacify and encourage the people by announcing sweeping reforms. Consequently during the celebrated night session of August 4–5, amid great excitement, the members of the privileged orders, led by the viscount of Noailles, a relative of Lafayette who had fought with him in America, vied with one another in surrendering their ancient privileges.[1]

The exclusive right of the nobility to hunt and to maintain their huge pigeon houses was abolished, and the peasant was

[1] Of course the nobles and clergy had very little prospect of retaining their privileges even if they did not give them up voluntarily. This was bitterly emphasized by Marat in his newspaper, *The Friend of the People.* " Let us not be duped! If these sacrifices of privileges were due to benevolence, it must be confessed that the voice of benevolence has been raised rather late in the day. When the lurid flames of their burning *châteaux* have illuminated France, these people have been good enough to give up the privilege of keeping in fetters men who had already gained their liberty by force of arms. When they see the punishment that awaits robbers, extortioners, and tyrants like themselves they generously abandon the feudal dues and agree to stop bleeding the wretched people who can barely keep body and soul together."

Decree abolishing the feudal dues, hunting rights, and other privileges

permitted to kill game which he found on his land. The tithes of the Church were done away with. Exemptions from the payment of taxes were abolished forever. It was decreed that "taxes shall be collected from all citizens and from all property in the same manner and in the same form," and that "all citizens, without distinction of birth, are eligible to any office or dignity." Moreover, inasmuch as a national constitution would be of more advantage to the provinces than the privileges which some of these enjoyed, and — so the decree continues — "inasmuch as the surrender of such privileges is essential to the intimate union of all parts of the realm, it is decreed that all the peculiar privileges, pecuniary or otherwise, of the provinces, principalities, districts, cantons, cities, and communes, are once for all abolished and are absorbed into the law common to all Frenchmen." [1]

Unification of France through the abolition of the ancient provinces and the creation of the present departments

This decree thus proclaimed the equality and uniformity for which the French people had so long sighed. The injustice of the former system of taxation could never be reintroduced. All France was to have the same laws, and its citizens were henceforth to be treated in the same way by the State, whether they lived in Brittany or Dauphiny, in the Pyrenees or on the Rhine. A few months later the Assembly went a step farther in consolidating and unifying France. It wiped out the old provinces altogether by dividing the whole country into districts of convenient size, called *départements*. These were much more numerous than the ancient divisions, and were named after rivers and mountains. This obliterated from the map all reminiscences of the feudal disunion.

The Declaration of the Rights of Man

Many of the *cahiers* had suggested that the Estates should draw up a clear statement of the rights of the individual citizen. It was urged that the recurrence of abuses and the insidious encroachments of despotism might in this way be forever prevented. The National Assembly consequently determined

---

[1] This edict is given in the *Readings*, sect. 35. The nobles were to be indemnified for some of the important but less offensive of the feudal dues.

to prepare such a declaration in order to gratify and reassure the people and to form a basis for the new constitution.

This Declaration of the Rights of Man (completed August 26) is one of the most notable documents in the history of Europe. It not only aroused general enthusiasm when it was first published, but it appeared over and over again, in a modified form, in the succeeding French constitutions down to 1848, and has been the model for similar declarations in many of the other continental states. It was a dignified repudiation of the abuses described in the preceding chapter. Behind each article there was some crying evil of long standing against which the people wished to be forever protected, — *lettres de cachet*, religious persecution, censorship of the press, and despotism in general.

The Declaration sets forth that " Men are born and remain equal in rights. Social distinctions can only be founded upon the general good." "Law is the expression of the general will. Every citizen has a right to participate, personally or through his representative, in its formation. It must be the same for all." "No person shall be accused, arrested, or imprisoned except in the cases and according to the forms prescribed by law." "No one shall be disquieted on account of his opinions, including his religious views, provided that their manifestation does not disturb the public order established by law." "The free communication of ideas and opinions is one of the most precious of the rights of man. Every citizen may, accordingly, speak, write, and print with freedom, being responsible, however, for such abuses of this freedom as shall be defined by law." " All citizens have a right to decide, either personally or by their representative, as to the necessity of the contribution to the public treasury, to grant this freely, to know to what uses it is put, and to fix the proportion, the mode of assessment and of collection, and the duration of the taxes." "Society has the right to require of every public agent an account of his administration." Well might the Assembly claim,

Contents of the Declaration

in its address to the people, that " the rights of man had been misconceived and insulted for centuries," and boast that they were " reëstablished for all humanity in this declaration, which shall serve as an everlasting war cry against oppressors."

THE NATIONAL ASSEMBLY IN PARIS, OCTOBER, 1789 TO SEPTEMBER, 1791

The court party once more plans a counter-revolution

36. The king hesitated to ratify the Declaration of the Rights of Man, and about the first of October rumors became current that, under the influence of the courtiers, he was calling together troops and preparing for another attempt to put an end to the Revolution, similar to that which the attack on the Bastille had frustrated. A regiment arrived from Flanders and was entertained at a banquet given by the king's guard at Versailles. The queen was present, and it was reported in Paris that the officers, in their enthusiasm for her, had trampled under foot the new national colors, — the red, white, and blue, — which had been adopted after the fall of the Bastille. These things, along with the scarcity of food due to the poor crops of the year, aroused the excitable Paris populace to fever heat.

A Paris mob invades the king's palace and carries him off to Paris

On October 5 several thousand women and a number of armed men marched out to Versailles to ask bread of the king, in whom they had great confidence personally, however suspicious they might be of his friends and advisers. Lafayette marched after the crowd with the national guard, but did not prevent some of the people from invading the king's palace the next morning and nearly murdering the queen, who had become very unpopular. She was believed to be still an Austrian at heart and to be in league with the counter-revolutionary party.

The people declared that the king must accompany them to Paris, and he was obliged to consent. Far from being disloyal, they assumed that the presence of the royal family would insure plenty and prosperity. So they gayly escorted the " baker and the baker's wife and the baker's boy," as they jocularly termed

the king and queen and the little dauphin, to the Palace of
the Tuileries, where the king took up his residence, practically a prisoner, as it proved. The National Assembly soon
followed him and resumed its sittings in a riding school near
the Tuileries.

This transfer of the king and the Assembly to the capital
was the first great misfortune of the Revolution. The work of
reform was by no means completed, and now the disorderly
element of Paris could at any time invade the galleries and interrupt those deputies who proposed measures that did not
meet with their approval. Marat's newspaper, *The Friend of
the People*, assured the poor of the city that they were the
real " patriots." Before long they came to hate the well-to-do
middle class (the *bourgeoisie*) almost as heartily as they hated
the nobles, and were ready to follow any leader who talked to
them about " liberty " and vaguely denounced " traitors."
Under these circumstances the populace might at any time get
control of Paris, and Paris of the National Assembly. And so
it fell out, as we shall see.

No one was more impressed by the danger than Mirabeau,
whose keen insight cannot fail to fill every student of the
French Revolution with admiration. After the transfer of the
royal family to Paris, Mirabeau became a sort of official adviser to the king, who, however, never acted upon the advice,
for both he and the queen abhorred the great orator and statesman on account of his views and his immorality. So it did no
good when Mirabeau pointed out to Louis that both he and
the Assembly were really prisoners in Paris, which was constantly subject to the most serious disturbances. " Its inhabitants when excited are irresistible. Winter is approaching and
food may be wanting. Bankruptcy may be declared. What
will Paris be three months hence? — assuredly a poorhouse,
perhaps a theater of horrors. Is it to such a place that the
head of the nation should intrust his existence and our only
hope? " The king, he urged, should openly retire to Rouen

Disastrous results of transferring the king and the Assembly to Paris

Mirabeau advises the king to leave Paris and call the Assembly to him and summon the Assembly to him there, where reforms could be completed without interruption or coercion. Above all things, the king must not go eastward, else he would be suspected of joining the runaway nobles who were hanging about the boundaries. Yet, as we shall see, when the king finally decided to escape from Paris eighteen months later this was precisely what he did.

The new constitution

But for some time there was no considerable disorder. The deputies worked away on the constitution, and on February 4, 1790, the king visited the National Assembly and solemnly pledged himself and the queen to accept the new form of government. This provided that the sovereign should rule both by the grace of God and by the constitutional law of the State, but the nation was to be superior to the law and the law to the king. The king was to be the chief executive and to be permitted to veto bills passed by the Assembly, unless they were passed by three successive Assemblies, in which case they would become law without his ratification. This was called the suspensive veto and was supposed to be modeled upon that granted to the President of the United States.

The Legislative Assembly established by the new constitution

The constitution naturally provided that the laws should be made and the taxes granted by a representative body that should meet regularly. This was to consist, like the National Assembly, of one house, instead of two like the English Parliament. Many had favored the system of two houses, but the nobility and clergy, who would have composed the upper house on the English analogy, were still viewed with suspicion as likely to wish to restore the privileges of which they had just been deprived. Only those citizens who paid a tax equal to three days' labor were permitted to vote for deputies to the Legislative Assembly. The poorer people had, consequently, no voice in the government in spite of the Declaration of the Rights of Man, which assured equal rights to all. This and other restrictions tended to keep the power in the hands of the middle class.

Of the other reforms of the National Assembly, the most important related to the Church, which, as has been explained, continued up to the time of the Revolution to be very rich and powerful, and to retain many of its mediæval prerogatives and privileges. Its higher officials, the bishops and abbots, received very large revenues and often one prelate held a number of rich benefices, the duties of which he utterly neglected while he amused himself at Versailles. The parish priests, on the other hand, who really performed the manifold and important functions of the Church, were scarcely able to live on their incomes. This unjust apportionment of the vast revenue of the Church naturally suggested the idea that, if the State confiscated the ecclesiastical possessions, it could see that those who did the work were properly paid for it, and might, at the same time, secure a handsome sum which would help the government out of its financial troubles. Those who sympathized with Voltaire's views were naturally delighted to see their old enemy deprived of its independence and made subservient to the State, and even many good Catholics hoped that the new system would be an improvement upon the old.

The tithes had been abolished in August along with the feudal dues. This deprived the Church of perhaps thirty million dollars a year. On November 2, 1789, a decree was passed providing that " All the ecclesiastical possessions are at the disposal of the nation on condition that it provides properly for the expenses of maintaining religious services, for the support of those who conduct them, and for the succor of the poor." This decree deprived the bishops and priests of their benefices and made them dependent on salaries paid by the State. The monasteries and convents were also, when called upon, to give up their property to meet the needs of the State.[1]

The Assembly reforms the Church

Unjust division of the revenue of the Church

The National Assembly declares the property of the Church to be at the disposal of the nation

---

[1] The mediæval monastic orders, feeble and often degenerate, still continued to exist in France at the opening of the Revolution, — Benedictines, Carthusians, Cistercians, Franciscans, Dominicans. The State still recognized the solemn vows of poverty taken by the monks and viewed them as incapable of holding any property or receiving any bequests. It also regarded it as its duty to arrest

The *assignats*, or paper currency

The National Assembly a little later ordered inventories to be made of the lands and buildings and various sources of revenue which the bishops, priests, and monks had so long enjoyed, and then the Church property was offered for sale. Meanwhile, in order to supply an empty treasury, the Assembly determined to issue a paper currency for which the newly acquired lands would serve as security. Of these *assignats*, as this paper money was called, we hear a great deal during the revolutionary period. They soon began to depreciate, and ultimately a great part of the forty billions of francs issued during the next seven years was repudiated.

The Civil Constitution of the Clergy, completed July, 1790

After depriving the Church of its property, the Assembly deemed it necessary to completely reorganize it, and drew up the so-called Civil Constitution of the Clergy. The one hundred and thirty-four ancient bishoprics, some of which dated back to the Roman Empire, were reduced to eighty-three, so as to correspond with the new "departments" into which France had just been divided. Each of these became the diocese of a bishop, who was no longer to be appointed by the king and confirmed by the Pope [1] but was looked upon as a government

a runaway monk and restore him to his monastery. The National Assembly, shortly after declaring the property of the monasteries at the disposal of the nation, refused (February 13, 1790) longer legally to recognize perpetual monastic vows, and abolished all the orders which required them. The monks and nuns were to be free to leave their monasteries and were, in that case, to receive a pension from the government of from seven hundred to twelve hundred francs. Those, however, who preferred to remain were to be grouped in such houses as the government assigned them. In a year or so a good many of the monks appear to have deserted their old life, but very few of the nuns. Those who remained were naturally the most conservative of all; they opposed the Revolution and sided with the nonjuring clergy. This made them very unpopular with the Legislative Assembly, which in August, 1792, ordered all the monasteries to be vacated and turned over to the government for its use. At the same time it abolished all the other religious communities and associations, like the Oratorians and the Sisters of Charity, which, without requiring any solemn vows, had devoted themselves to teaching or charitable works. Many of these religious *congregations*, as the French call them, were revived in the nineteenth century and have been the cause of a good deal of agitation. See below, sect. 77.

[1] See above, p. 141. The decrees abolishing the feudal system (August 11, 1789) had already prohibited all remittances to the Pope in the shape of *annates* or other payments. The bishoprics were grouped into ten districts, each presided over by a " metropolitan " who corresponded to the former archbishop.

official, to be elected, like other government officials, by the people, and paid a regular salary. The priests, too, were to be chosen by the people instead, as formerly, by the bishop or lord of the manor ; and their salaries were to be substantially increased. In Paris they were to have six thousand francs, in smaller places less, but never an amount below twelve hundred francs ; even in the smallest villages they received over twice the minimum paid under the old régime. Lastly, it was provided that clergymen, upon accepting office, must all take an oath, like other government officials, to be faithful to the nation, the law, and the king, and to "maintain with all their might the constitution decreed by the Assembly." [1]

The Civil Constitution of the Clergy proved a serious mistake. While the half-feudalized Church had sadly needed reform, the worst abuses might have been remedied without overturning the whole system, which was hallowed in the minds of most of the French people by age and religious veneration. The arbitrary suppression of fifty-one bishoprics, the election of the bishops by the ordinary voters, who included Protestants, Jews, and unbelievers, the neglect of the Pope's rights, — all shocked and alienated thousands of those who had hitherto enthusiastically applauded the reforms which the Assembly had effected. The king gave his assent to the Civil Constitution, but with the fearful apprehension that he might be losing his soul by so doing. From that time on he became an enemy of the Revolution on religious grounds.

Opposition aroused by the Civil Constitution

The bishops, with very few exceptions, opposed the changes and did all they could to prevent the reforms from being carried out. Accordingly (November 27, 1790) the irritated Assembly ordered all the bishops and priests to take the oath to the Constitution (which, of course, included the new laws in regard to the Church) within a week. Those who refused were to be regarded as having resigned ; and if any of them

Oath to the Constitution required of the clergy

[1] For the text of the Civil Constitution of the Clergy, see the *Readings*, sect. 36.

still continued to perform their functions they were to be treated as "disturbers of the peace."

Only four of the bishops consented to take the required oath and but a third of the lower clergy, although they were much better off under the new system. Forty-six thousand parish priests refused to sacrifice their religious scruples. Before long the Pope condemned the Civil Constitution and forbade the clergy to take the oath. As time went on the "nonjuring" clergy were dealt with more and more harshly by the government, and the way was prepared for the horrors of the Reign of Terror. The Revolution ceased to stand for liberty, order, and the abolition of ancient abuses, and came to mean — in the minds of many besides those who had lost their former privileges — irreligion, violence, and a new kind of oppression more cruel than the old.

A year after the fall of the Bastille a great festival was held in Paris to celebrate the glorious anniversary which has been commemorated on the 14th of July ever since. Delegates were sent to Paris from all parts of France to express the sympathy of the country at large. This occasion made a deep impression upon all, as well it might. It was more than a year later, however, before the National Assembly at last finished its work and dissolved, to give place to the Legislative Assembly for which the constitution provided.

It was little more than two years that the National Assembly had been engaged upon its tremendous task of modernizing France. No body of men has ever accomplished so much in so short a period. The English Parliament, during an existence of five hundred years, had done far less to reform England; and no monarch, with the possible exception of the unhappy Joseph II, has ever even attempted to make such deep and far-reaching changes as were permanently accomplished by the first French Assembly.

Despite the marvelous success of the Assembly, as measured by the multiplicity and the decisiveness of its reforms, it had made many and dangerous enemies. The king and queen and the courtiers were in correspondence with the king of Prussia and the Emperor, with a hope of inducing them to intervene to check the Revolution. The runaway nobles were ready to call in foreign forces to restore the old system, and many of the clergy now regarded the Revolution as hostile to religion. Moreover the populace in Paris and in other large towns had been aroused against the Assembly by their radical leaders, their newspapers, and the political clubs. They felt that the deputies had worked only for the prosperous classes and had done little for the poor people, who should have been supplied with bread and allowed to vote. They were irritated also by the national guard commanded by that ex-noble, the marquis of Lafayette, who looked altogether too fine on his white horse. The members of the guard, too, were well dressed and only too ready to fire on the "patriots" if they dared to make a demonstration. Altogether it is easy to see that there was trouble ahead. The Revolution had gone much too far for some and not far enough for others.

The hostility aroused by the policy of the Assembly

REFERENCES

The Cahiers : LOWELL, *Eve of the French Revolution*, chaps. xxi–xxii, pp. 342–376 ; *Cambridge Modern History*, Vol. VIII, pp. 134–144.

The Pamphlets : LOWELL, chap. xx, pp. 322–341.

Convocation of the Estates General : MATHEWS, *The French Revolution*, chap. viii, pp. 102–110 ; STEPHENS, *History of the French Revolution*, Vol. I, Prologue, and chap. i, pp. 1–54 ; *Cambridge Modern History*, Vol. VIII, pp. 96–118.

Opening of the National Assembly : MATHEWS, chap. ix, pp. 111–124 ; STEPHENS, Vol. I, chap. ii, pp. 55–74 ; *Cambridge Modern History*, Vol. VIII, pp. 145–158.

Fall of the Bastille : MATHEWS, chap. x, pp. 125–137 ; STEPHENS, Vol. I, pp. 128–145 ; *Cambridge Modern History*, Vol. VIII, pp. 159–169.

The Country at Large in the Summer of 1789 : STEPHENS, Vol. I, chap. vi, pp. 169–197.

Abolition of the Old Régime : MATHEWS, chaps. xi–xii, pp. 138–165.

The Civil Constitution of the Clergy : STEPHENS, Vol. I, chap. x, pp. 291–309.

English Attitude toward the Revolution : LECKY, *History of England in the Eighteenth Century*, Vol. VI, chap. xix, pp. 365–487 ; *Cambridge Modern History*, Vol. VIII, chap. xxv, pp. 754–771.

CHAPTER XIII

THE FIRST FRENCH REPUBLIC

THE ABOLITION OF THE MONARCHY, 1791-1792

37. We have now studied the progress and nature of the revolution which destroyed the old régime and created modern France. Through it the unjust privileges, the perplexing irregularities, and the local differences were abolished, and the people admitted to a share in the government. This vast reform had been accomplished without serious disturbance and, with the exception of some of the changes in the Church, it had been welcomed with enthusiasm by the French nation.

This permanent, peaceful revolution, or reformation, was followed by a second, violent revolution, which for a time destroyed the French monarchy. It also introduced a series of further changes, many of which were fantastic and unnecessary and could not endure, since they were approved by only a few fanatical leaders. France, moreover, became involved in a war with most of the powers of western Europe. The weakness of her government, which permitted the forces of disorder and fanaticism to prevail, combined with the imminent danger of an invasion by the united powers of Europe, produced the Reign of Terror. After a period of national excitement and partial anarchy, France gladly accepted the rule of one of her military commanders, who was to prove himself far more despotic than her former kings had been. This general, Napoleon Bonaparte, did not, however, undo the great work of 1789; his colossal ambition was, on the contrary, the means of extending, directly or indirectly, many of the benefits of the Revolution to other parts of western Europe. When, after Napoleon's fall, the elder

The second revolution

249

brother of Louis XVI came to the throne, the first thing that he did was solemnly to assure the people that all the great gains of the first revolution should be maintained.

The emigration of the nobles

While practically the whole of the nation heartily rejoiced in the earlier reforms introduced by the National Assembly, and celebrated the general satisfaction and harmony by that great national festival held in Paris on the first anniversary of the fall of the Bastille, of which mention has been made,[1] some of the higher nobility refused to remain in France. The count of Artois (the king's younger brother), Calonne, the prince of Condé, and others, set the example by leaving the country just after the events of July 14, 1789. They were followed by others who were terrified or disgusted by the burning of the *châteaux*, the loss of their privileges, and the injudicious abolition of hereditary nobility by the National Assembly in June, 1790. Before long these emigrant nobles (*émigrés*), among whom were many military officers like Condé, organized a little army across the Rhine, and the count of Artois began to plan an invasion of France. He was ready to ally himself with Austria, Prussia, or any other foreign government which he could induce to help undo the Revolution and give back to the French king his former absolute power, and to the nobles their old privileges.

The conduct of the emigrant nobles discredits the king and queen

The threats and insolence of the emigrant nobles and their shameful negotiations with foreign powers discredited the members of their class who still remained in France. The people suspected that the plans of the runaways met with the secret approval of the king, and more especially of the queen, whose brother, Leopold II, was now Emperor, and ruler of the Austrian dominions. This, added to the opposition of the nonjuring clergy, produced a bitter hostility between the so-called "patriots" and those who, on the other hand, were supposed to be secretly hoping for a counter-revolution which would reëstablish the old régime.

[1] See above, p. 246.

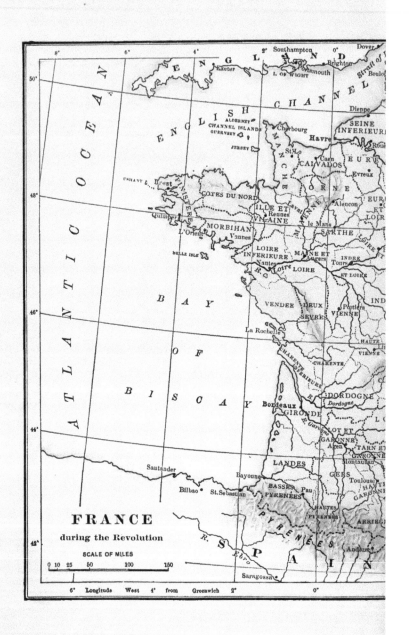

FRANCE
during the Revolution

SCALE OF MILES

0 10 25   50   100   150

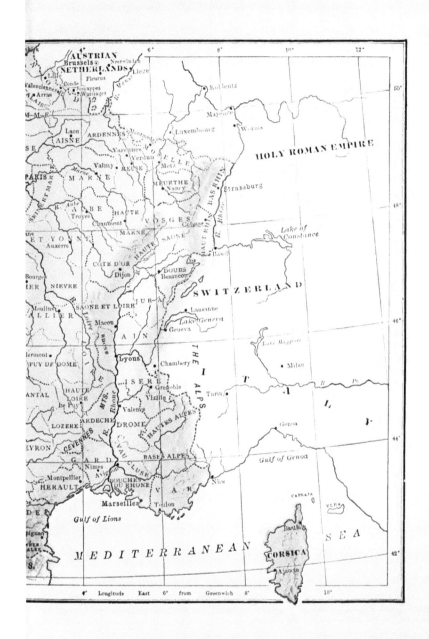

Had the king been willing to follow the advice of Mirabeau, the tragedy of the approaching Reign of Terror might probably have been avoided. France needed a strong king who would adjust himself to the new constitution, guide the Assembly, maintain order in Paris and the other great cities, and, above all, avoid any suspicion of wishing for a restoration of the old régime. Mirabeau saw clearly that the welfare of France at this juncture depended upon strengthening the monarchy. His efforts to forward this end were, however, unavailing. The fact that he accepted money from the king for advice roused the natural suspicions of the radical members of the Assembly and he was denounced as a traitor. On the other hand, he never really enjoyed the confidence of Louis XVI, who, like the queen, heartily detested him. He died April 2, 1791, at the age of forty-three, worn out by a life of dissipation, and the king was thus left with no one to hold him back from destruction.

Mirabeau fails to strengthen the monarchy and dies, April, 1791

The worst fears of the people seemed to be justified by the secret flight of the royal family from Paris, in June, 1791. Ever since the king had reluctantly signed the Civil Constitution of the Clergy, flight had seemed to him his only resource. A body of regular troops was collected on the northeastern boundary ready to receive and protect him. If he could escape and join them at Montmédy, which was just on the frontier, about a hundred and seventy miles from Paris, he hoped that, aided by a demonstration on the part of the queen's brother, Leopold, he might march back and check the further progress of the revolutionary movement. He had, it is true, no liking for the emigrants and disapproved of their policy, nor did he believe that the old régime could ever be restored. But, unfortunately, his plans led him to attempt to reach the boundary just at the point where the emigrants were collected, viz. at Coblenz and Worms. He and the queen were, however, arrested at Varennes, when within twenty-five miles of their destination, and speedily brought back to Paris.

The flight to Varennes (June 21, 1791)

Effect of the king's flight

The desertion of the king appears to have terrified rather than angered the nation. The consternation of the people at the thought of losing, and their relief at regaining, a poor weak ruler like Louis XVI clearly shows that France was still profoundly royalist in its sympathies. The National Assembly pretended that the king had not fled but had been carried off. This gratified France at large; in Paris, however, there were some who advocated the deposition of the king, on the ground that he was clearly a traitor. Indeed, for the first time a *republican* party, small as yet, made its appearance, which urged the complete abolition of the monarchical form of government and the substitution of a democracy.

The leaders of the new republican party

Of those who had lost confidence in the king and in the monarchy, the most prominent was Dr. Marat, a physician and scholar, who before the Revolution had published several scientific works, but was now conducting the very violent newspaper already quoted, *The Friend of the People*. In this he denounced in the most extravagant language both the "aristocrats" and the "bourgeoisie," — for by "the people" he meant the great mass of workingmen in the towns and the peasants in the fields. Then there was the gentle and witty Camille Desmoulins, who had made the famous address in the Palais Royal on the 12th of July, 1789, which roused the populace to defend themselves against the plots of the courtiers. He too edited a newspaper and was a leader in the radical club called the *Cordeliers*.[1] Lastly Desmoulins's good friend Danton, with his coarse, strong face, his big voice, and his fiery eloquence, was becoming a sort of Mirabeau of the masses. He had much good sense and was not so virulent in his language as Marat, but his superabundant vitality led him to condone violence and cruelty in carrying on the Revolution and destroying its enemies.

[1] So named after the monastery where the club held its meetings. The monks had belonged to the order of St. Francis and were called *Cordeliers* on account of the heavy "cord," a rope with three knots, which they wore instead of a girdle.

DANTON

Under the influence of these men a petition was drawn up demanding that the Assembly should regard the king as having abdicated by his flight, and that a new convention should be called to draw up a better constitution. On July 17 this petition was taken to the Champ de Mars (a great open space used for military maneuvers, where the festival had been held during the previous July), and here the people of Paris were called together to sign it. The mayor of Paris disapproved of the affair and decided to disperse the people. He marched out with Lafayette and the national guard and ordered the petitioners to go home. Unhappily the crowd did not take the warnings of the mayor seriously; some stones were thrown at the troops, who were thereupon ordered to fire, and a number of men, women, and children were killed. This unfortunate and quite needless " Massacre of the Champ de Mars " served to weaken the monarchy still farther. It was not forgotten, although the king remained on the throne for a year longer, and Marat, Danton, and Desmoulins were intimidated and thought it prudent to remain in hiding for a time.

Massacre of the Champ de Mars (July 17, 1791)

It was in the following September that the National Assembly at last put the finishing touches on the constitution which had occupied them for more than two years. The king swore to obey it faithfully, and a general amnesty was proclaimed so that all the discord and suspicion of the past few months might be forgotten. The Assembly then broke up and gave way to the regular congress provided for by the new constitution, — the Legislative Assembly, — which held its first meeting October 1, 1791.

The National Assembly gives way to the Legislative Assembly (September, 1791)

In spite of the great achievements of the National Assembly it left France in a critical situation. Besides the emigrant nobles abroad there were the nonjuring clergy at home, and a king who was treacherously corresponding with foreign powers in the hope of securing their aid. When the news of the capture of the king and queen at Varennes reached the ears of Marie Antoinette's brother, Leopold II, he declared that the

Sources of danger at the opening of the Legislative Assembly, October, 1791

violent arrest of the king sealed with unlawfulness all that had been done in France and "compromised directly the honor of all the sovereigns and the security of every government." He therefore proposed to the rulers of Russia, England, Prussia, Spain, Naples, and Sardinia that they should come to some understanding between themselves as to how they might " reëstablish the liberty and honor of the most Christian king and his family, and place a check upon the dangerous excesses of the French Revolution, the fatal example of which it behooves every government to repress."

The Declaration of Pillnitz, August 27, 1791

On August 27 Leopold, in conjunction with the king of Prussia, had issued the famous Declaration of Pillnitz. In this the two sovereigns state that, in accordance with the wishes of the king's brothers (the leaders of the emigrant nobles), they are ready to join the other European rulers in an attempt to place the king of France in a position to establish a form of government "that shall be once more in harmony with the rights of sovereigns and shall promote the welfare of the French nation." They agreed in the meantime to prepare their troops for active service.

Effect of the Declaration

The Declaration was little more than an empty threat; but it seemed to the French people a sufficient proof that the monarchs were ready to help the seditious French nobles to reëstablish the old régime against the wishes of the nation and at the cost of infinite bloodshed. The idea of foreign rulers intermeddling with their internal affairs would in itself have been intolerable to a proud people like the French, even if the new reforms had not been endangered. Had it been the object of the allied monarchs to hasten instead of to prevent the deposition of Louis XVI, they could hardly have chosen a more efficient means than the Declaration of Pillnitz.

The newspapers

Political excitement and enthusiasm for the Revolution were kept up by the newspapers which had been established, especially in Paris, since the convening of the Estates General. Except in England there had been no daily newspapers before the French Revolution, and those journals that were issued weekly or at longer intervals had little to say of politics, — commonly a dangerous subject on the Continent. But after 1789 the public did not need longer to rely upon an occasional pamphlet, as was the case earlier. Many journals of the most divergent kinds and representing the most various opinions were published. Some, like the notorious *Friend of the People*, were no more than a periodical editorial written by one man. Others, like the famous *Moniteur*, were much like our papers of to-day and contained news, both foreign and domestic, reports of the debates in the assembly and the text of its decrees, announcements of theaters, etc. The royalists had their organ called *The Acts of the Apostles*, witty and irreverent as the court party itself. Some of the papers were illustrated, and the representations of contemporaneous events, especially the numerous caricatures, are highly diverting.[1]

Of the numerous political clubs, by far the most famous was that of the *Jacobins*. When the Assembly moved into Paris some of the provincial representatives of the third estate rented a large room in the monastery of the Jacobin monks, not far from the building where the National Assembly itself met. A hundred deputies perhaps were present at the first meeting. The next day the number had doubled. The aim of this society was to discuss questions which were about to come before the National Assembly. The club decided at its meetings what should be the policy of its members and how they should vote ; and in this way they successfully combined to counteract the schemes of the aristocratic party in the Assembly. The club rapidly grew, and soon admitted to its sessions some who were not deputies. In October, 1791, it decided to permit the public to attend its discussions.

The Jacobi

[1] For example, in one of the caricatures, the formerly despotic king is represented as safely confined by the National Assembly in a huge parrot cage. When asked by his brother-in-law, Leopold II, what he is about, Louis XVI replies, "I am signing my name," — that is, he had nothing to do except meekly to ratify the measures which the Assembly chose to pass.

Gradually similar societies were formed in the provinces.[1] These affiliated themselves with the "mother" society at Paris and kept in constant communication with it. In this way the Jacobins of Paris stimulated and controlled public opinion throughout France and kept the opponents of the old régime alert. When the Legislative Assembly met, the Jacobins had not as yet become republicans but they believed that the king should have hardly more power than the president of a republic. They were even ready to promote his deposition if he failed to stand by the Revolution.

Parties in the Legislative Assembly

The new Legislative Assembly was not well qualified to cope with the many difficulties which faced it. It was made up almost entirely of young and inexperienced men, for the National Assembly, on motion of the virtuous Robespierre, had passed a self-denying ordinance excluding all its members from election to the new body. The Jacobin clubs in the provinces had succeeded in securing the election of a good many of their candidates, sometimes by resorting to violence in order to defeat the more conservative candidates. Consequently the most active and powerful party in the Legislative Assembly was, on the whole, hostile to the king.

The Girondists

Many young and ardent lawyers had been elected, among whom the most prominent were from the department of the Gironde, in which the important city of Bordeaux was situated. They and their followers were called Girondists. They had much to say in their brilliant speeches of the glories of Sparta and of the Roman Republic; they too longed for a republic and inveighed against "tyrants." They applauded the eloquence of their chief orator, Vergniaud, and frequently assembled at the house of the ardent and fascinating Madame Roland to consider the regeneration of their beloved country. But in spite of their enthusiasm they were not statesmen and showed no skill in meeting the troublesome problems that kept arising.

[1] By June, 1791, there were 406 of these affiliated Jacobin clubs. See *Readings*, sect. 37.

The Assembly, not unnaturally, promptly turned its atten- The emigrant nobles declared traitors
tion to the emigrant nobles. These had been joined by the
king's elder brother, the count of Provence, who had managed
to escape at the time that the royal family had been arrested
at Varennes. Having succeeded in inducing the Emperor and
the king of Prussia to issue the Declaration of Pillnitz, they
continued to collect troops on the Rhine. The Assembly declared that "the Frenchmen assembled on the frontier" were
under suspicion of conspiring against their country. The count
of Provence was ordered to return within two months or forfeit
any possible claim to the throne.[1] Should the other *émigrés*
fail to return to France by January 1, 1792, they were to be
regarded as convicted traitors, and punished, if caught, with
death ; their property was to be confiscated.

The harsh treatment of the emigrant nobles was perhaps Harsh measures of the Assembly toward nonjuring clergy
justified by their desertion and treasonable intrigues; but the
conduct of the Assembly toward the clergy was impolitic as
well as cruel. Those who had refused to pledge themselves to
support a system which was in conflict with their religious convictions and which had been condemned by the Pope were
commanded to take the prescribed oath within a week, on
penalty of losing their income from the State and being put
under surveillance as "suspects." As this failed to bring the
clergy to terms, the Assembly later (May, 1792) ordered the
deportation from the country of those who steadily persisted
in their refusal to accept the Civil Constitution of the Clergy.
In this way the Assembly aroused the active hostility of a great
part of the most conscientious among the lower clergy, who
had loyally supported the commons in their fight against the
privileged orders. It also lost the confidence of the great mass
of faithful Catholics, — merchants, artisans, and peasants, —
who had gladly accepted the abolition of the old abuses, but
who would not consent to desert their priests at the bidding of
the Assembly.

[1] See *Readings*, sect. 37, for the count of Provence's saucy reply.

The Legislative Assembly precipitates a war with Europe

By far the most important act of the Legislative Assembly during the one year of its existence was its precipitation of a war between France and Austria.[1] To many in the Assembly, including the Girondists, it seemed that the existing conditions were intolerable. The emigrant nobles were forming little armies on the boundaries of France and had induced Austria and Prussia to consider interfering in French affairs. The Assembly suspected — what was quite true [2] — that Louis was negotiating with foreign rulers and would be glad to have them intervene and reëstablish him in his old despotic power. The Girondist deputies argued, therefore, that a war against the hated Austria would unite the sympathies of the nation and force the king to show his true character; for he would be obliged either to become the nation's leader or to show himself the traitor they believed him to be.

France declares war on Austria (April 20, 1792)

It was with a heavy heart that Louis XVI, urged on by the clamors of the Girondists, declared war upon Austria on April 20, 1792. Little did the ardent young lawyers of the Assembly surmise that this was the beginning of the most terrific and momentous series of wars that ever swept over Europe, involving, during twenty-three years of almost continuous conflict, every country and people from Ireland to Turkey, and from Norway to Naples. Although the Girondist leaders, Vergniaud, Brissot, Guadet, and their friend Madame Roland, were the first to be destroyed by the storm they had conjured up, could they have looked forward they would have been consoled to see that the tyrants they hated never permanently regained their old power; that the long wars served to bring the principles of the French Revolution home to all the European peoples, everywhere slowly but surely destroyed the old régime, and gave to the people the liberty and the control of the government which the Girondists had so hotly defended.

[1] See *Readings*, sect. 37, for reasons assigned by the French for going to war.
[2] Ibid., for letter of Louis XVI, December 3, 1791, to the king of Prussia, suggesting the intervention of the foreign powers in French affairs.

The French army was in no condition for war. The officers, who, according to the law, were all nobles, had many of them deserted and joined the *émigrés*. The regular troops were consequently demoralized, and the new national guard had not yet been employed except to maintain order in the towns. Naturally Dumouriez, the Girondist minister of war, first turned his attention to the Austrian Netherlands, which promised to be an easy conquest. The reforms of Joseph II and his attempt to make the Netherlands an integral part of the Austrian state had roused a revolt in 1789. It is true that when Leopold II came to the throne and undid his brother's rash changes, all resistance had subsided. Still there was a strong party in the Netherlands which greeted the French Revolution with enthusiasm, and Dumouriez had good reason to think that the attempts made a century before by Louis XIV to add that region to France might at last be successful. But the raw troops that he collected for the invasion of Belgium ran away as soon as they caught sight of Austrian cavalry. The emigrant nobles rejoiced, and Europe concluded that the "patriots" were made of poor stuff.

Meanwhile matters were going badly for the king of France. The Assembly had passed two bills, one ordering those priests who refused to take the oath to the constitution to leave the country within a month; the other directing the formation, just without the walls of Paris, of a camp of twenty thousand volunteers from various parts of France as a protection to the capital. The king resolved, for very good reasons, to veto both of these measures and to dismiss his Girondist ministry, with the exception of Dumouriez, his really able minister of war, who immediately resigned.

All this served to make the king far more unpopular than ever. The "Austrian woman" or "Madame Veto," as the queen was called, was rightly believed to be actively betraying France, and it is now known that she did send to Austria the plan of campaign which had been adopted before the war began.

On June 20 some of the lesser leaders of the Paris populace resolved to celebrate the anniversary of the Tennis-Court oath. They arranged a procession which was permitted to march through the Riding School where the Assembly sat.

The *sans-culottes*

The ensigns of the mob were a calf's heart on the point of a pike, labeled " the heart of an aristocrat," and a pair of knee breeches representing the older costume of a gentleman, which was now going out of fashion since the Girondists, in order to exhibit their democratic sentiments, had adopted the long trousers which had hitherto been worn only by workingmen. To give up knee breeches and become a " sans-culotte," or breeches-less patriot, had come to be considered an unmistakable indication of love for the Revolution.

Invasion of the Tuileries

After visiting the Assembly, the crowd found their way into the neighboring palace of the Tuileries. They wandered through the beautiful apartments shouting, " Down with Monsieur Veto ! " The king might have been killed by some ruffian had he not consented to drink to the health of the " nation " — whose representatives were roughly crowding him into the recess of a window — and put on a red " liberty cap," the badge of the " citizen patriots."

Approach of the Prussian army

This invasion of the Tuileries seemed to the European rulers a new and conclusive proof that the Revolution meant anarchy. Had not the populace of Paris treated the king of France as they might have disported themselves with a poor drunken fellow in the street? Prussia had immediately joined Austria when France declared war against the latter in April, and now the army which Frederick the Great had led to victory was moving, under his old general, the duke of Brunswick, toward the French boundary with a view of restoring Louis XVI to his former independent position.

The country declared in danger (July 11, 1792)

The Assembly now declared the country in danger. Every citizen, whether in town or country, was to report, under penalty of imprisonment, what arms or munitions he possessed. The national guards were to select from their ranks those who could best join the active army. Every citizen was ordered to wear the tricolored cockade, — the red, white, and blue of the Revolution. In this way the peasants, who had been accustomed to regard war as a matter of purely personal interest to kings, were given to understand that they were not now called upon to risk their lives, as formerly, because the Polish king had lost his throne, or because Maria Theresa had a grudge against Frederick the Great. Now, if they shed their blood, it would be to keep out of France two " tyrants " who proposed to force them to surrender the precious reforms of the past three years and restore to the hated runaway nobles their former privileges.

As the allies approached the French frontier it became clearer and clearer that the king was utterly incapable of defending the country, even if he were willing to oppose the armies which claimed to be coming to his rescue and with which he was believed to be in league. France seemed almost compelled under the circumstances to rid herself of her traitorous and utterly incompetent ruler. The duke of Brunswick, who was in command of the Prussian army, sealed the king's fate by issuing a manifesto in the name of both the Emperor and the king of Prussia, in which he declared that the allies proposed to put an end to anarchy in France and restore the king to his rightful powers ; that the inhabitants of France who dared to oppose the Austrian and Prussian troops " shall be punished immediately according to the most stringent laws of war, and their houses shall be burned." If Paris offered the least violence to king or queen, or again permitted the Tuileries to be invaded, the allies promised to " inflict an ever-to-be-remembered vengeance by delivering over the city of Paris to military execution and complete destruction."

The proclamation of the duke of Brunswick (July 25, 1792)

The leaders in Paris now determined to force the Assembly to depose the king. Five hundred members of the national guard of Marseilles were summoned to their aid. This little troop of "patriots" came marching up through France singing

The volunteers of Marseilles and their war song

that most stirring of all national hymns, the " Marseillaise,"
which has ever since borne their name.[1]

The Tuileries again attacked (August 10, 1792)   Danton and other leaders of the insurrection had set their
hearts on doing away with the king altogether and establish-
ing a republic. After careful preparations, which were scarcely
concealed, the various sections into which Paris was divided
arranged to attack the Tuileries on August 10. The men
from Marseilles led in this attack. The king, who had been
warned, retired from the palace with the queen and the dauphin
to the neighboring Riding School where they were respectfully
received by the Assembly and assigned a safe place in the
newspaper reporters' gallery. The king's Swiss guards fired
upon the insurgents, but were overpowered and almost all of
them slain. Then the ruffianly element in the mob ransacked
the palace and killed the servants. Napoleon Bonaparte, an
unknown lieutenant who was watching affairs from across the
river, declared that the palace could easily have been defended

---

[1] This famous song was not meant originally as a republican chant. It had
been composed a few months before by Rouget de Lisle at Strassburg. War had
just been declared, and it was designed to give heart to the French army on the
Rhine. The "tyrants" it refers to were the foreign kings Frederick William II
of Prussia and the Emperor, who were attacking France, not Louis XVI. The
"Marseillaise" begins as follows :

> Allons, enfants de la patrie,
> Le jour de gloire est arrivé ;
> Contre nous de la tyrannie
> L'étendard sanglant est levé. (repeat)
> Entendez-vous, dans ces campagnes,
> Mugir ces féroces soldats?
> Ils viennent jusque dans vos bras
> Égorger vos fils, vos compagnes !
> Aux armes, citoyens ! formez vos bataillons !
> Marchons, qu'un sang impure abreuve nos sillons.
>
> Que veut cette horde d'esclaves,
> De traîtres, de rois conjurés?
> Pour qui ces ignobles entraves,
> Ces fers dès longtemps préparés? (repeat)
> Français, pour nous, ah ! quel outrage !
> Quels transports il doit exciter !
> C'est nous qu'on ose méditer
> De rendre à l'antique esclavage !
> Aux armes, citoyens ! formez vos bataillons !
> Marchons, qu'un sang impure abreuve nos sillons.

had not the commander of the guards been brutally murdered before hostilities opened.[1]

Meanwhile the representatives of the various quarters of Paris had taken possession of the City Hall. They pushed the members of the municipal council off their seats and took their places. In this way a new revolutionary commune was formed, which seized the government of the capital and then sent messengers to demand that the Assembly dethrone the king.

The revolutionary commune of Paris

The Assembly refused to abolish kingship, but " suspended " the monarch and put him under guard. They regarded the attack on the Tuileries merely as a reply to the threats of the allies, and endeavored to reassure Europe by proclaiming that France had no idea of making any conquests, but desired to secure the brotherhood of mankind. To illustrate this universal brotherhood, the privileges of French citizenship were conferred upon a number of distinguished foreigners, — Priestley, Wilberforce, Schiller, Washington, and Kosciusko among others. The suffrage in France, which had been limited by the previous Assembly to the citizens who could pay taxes equal to three days' labor, was extended to all, rich and poor alike. Lastly, a new ministry was formed in which Danton, the most conspicuous leader in the insurrection, was made minister of justice.

Attitude of the Legislative Assembly

Three days later a decree which had been proposed by Vergniaud was passed, summoning a national convention to

[1] Of the many patriotic songs which express the spirit of the people during the Revolution, the famous " Carmagnole," which deals with the events of August 10, may be cited. It begins :

> Madame Veto avait promis,
> Madame Veto avait promis,
> De faire égorger tout Paris,
> De faire égorger tout Paris.
> Mais le coup a manqué
> Grâce à nos cannoniers !
> Dansons la Carmagnole !
> Vive le son, vive le son,
> Dansons la Carmagnole,
> Vive le son du canon !

Why monarchy was doomed in France

draft a new constitution. Although a great part of France was still loyal to the monarchy, it was evident that under the circumstances this convention would be forced to establish a republic. What else could it do? The king and queen were in league with the foreign enemy whom the king's two brothers had induced to invade France. The natural heir to the throne was a boy of seven to whose weak hands it was impossible to intrust the public welfare. These were strong arguments for the republican leaders and newspaper editors, especially as they had behind them the resolute insurrectionary commune of Paris. France must find a substitute for her ancient kings, who had come to seem little better than the feudal lords of whom they had been, after all, the chief. In short, the monarchial constitution which had not yet been in force a year had already become an anachronism.

Appalling task of the Convention

So the Legislative Assembly gave way to the Convention, whose task was truly appalling since it had not only to draft a new constitution to suit both monarchists and republicans, but to conduct the government, repel invading armies, keep down the Paris mob, — in a word, see France through the Reign of Terror.

THE REIGN OF TERROR

France proclaimed a republic (September 22, 1792)

38. The Convention met on the 21st of September, and its first act was to abolish the ancient monarchy and proclaim France a republic. It seemed to the enthusiasts of the time that a new era of liberty had dawned, now that the long oppression by "despots" was ended forever. The twenty-second day of September, 1792, was reckoned as the first day of the Year One of French Liberty.[1]

[1] A committee of the Convention was appointed to draw up a new republican calendar. The year was divided into twelve months of thirty days each. The five days preceding September 22, at the end of the year, were holidays. Each month was divided into three *décades*, and each "tenth day" (*décadi*) was a holiday. The days were no longer dedicated to saints, but to agricultural implements, vegetables, domestic animals, etc.

Meanwhile the usurping Paris commune had taken matters into its own hands and had brought discredit upon the cause of liberty by one of the most atrocious acts in history. On the pretext that Paris was full of traitors who sympathized with the Austrians and the emigrant nobles, they had filled the prisons with three thousand citizens, including many of the priests who had refused to take the oath required by the Constitution. On September 2 and 3, hundreds of these were executed with scarcely a pretense of a trial. The excuse offered was: "How can we go away to the war and leave behind us three thousand prisoners who may break out and destroy our wives and our children!" The members of the commune who perpetrated this deed probably hoped to terrify those who might still dream of returning to the old system of government. *The September massacres (1792)*

Late in August the Prussians crossed the French boundary and on September 2 took the fortress of Verdun. It now seemed as if there was nothing to prevent their marching upon Paris. The French general, Dumouriez, blocked the advance of the Prussian army, however, at Valmy, scarcely a hundred miles from the capital, and forced the enemy to retreat without fighting a pitched battle. Notwithstanding the fear of the French, King Frederick William II of Prussia (who had succeeded his uncle, Frederick the Great, six years before) had but little interest in the war. As for the Austrian troops, they were lagging far behind, for both powers were far more absorbed in a second partition of Poland, which was approaching, than in the fate of the French king. *The Prussian army checked at Valmy*

The French were able, therefore, in spite of their disorganization, not only to expel the Prussians but to carry the Revolution beyond the bounds of France. They invaded Germany and took several important towns on the Rhine, including Mayence, which gladly opened its gates to them. They also occupied Savoy on the southeast. Then Dumouriez led his barefooted, ill-equipped volunteers into the Austrian Netherlands. *The French occupy Savoy, the Rhine valley, and the Netherlands*

This time they did not run away, but, shouting the "Marseillaise," they defeated the Austrians at Jemappes (November 6) and were soon in possession of the whole country.

How the Convention proposed to spread the Revolution abroad (December 15, 1792)

The Convention now proposed to use its armies to revolutionize Europe. It issued a proclamation addressed to the peoples of the countries that France was occupying: "We have driven out your tyrants. Show yourselves freemen and we will protect you from their vengeance." Feudal dues, unjust taxes, and all the burdens which had been devised by the "tyrants" were forthwith abolished, and the French nation declared that it would treat as enemies every people who, "refusing liberty and equality, or renouncing them, may wish to maintain or recall its prince or the privileged classes."[1]

Trial and execution of the king (January, 1793)

Meanwhile the Convention was puzzled to determine what would best be done with the king. A considerable party felt that he was guilty of treason in secretly encouraging the foreign powers to come to his aid. He was therefore brought to trial, and when it came to a final vote he was, by a small majority, condemned to death. He mounted the scaffold on January 21, 1793, with the fortitude of a martyr. Nevertheless it cannot be denied that, through his earlier weakness and indecision, he brought untold misery upon his own kingdom and upon Europe at large. The French people had not dreamed of a republic until his absolute incompetence forced them, in self-defense, to abolish the monarchy in the hope of securing a more efficient government.

The execution of Louis XVI solidifies the alliance against France

The execution of Louis XVI had immediate and unhappy effects. The Convention had thrown down the head of their king as a challenge to the "despots" of Europe; the monarchs accepted the challenge and the French republic soon found all the powers of Europe ranged against it. Nowhere did the tragic event of January 21 produce more momentous results than in England. George III went into mourning and ordered the French envoy to be expelled from the kingdom;

---

[1] This decree may be found in the *Readings*, sect. 38.

even Pitt, forgetting the work of Cromwell and the Puritan revolutionists, declared the killing of the French king to be the most awful and atrocious crime in all recorded history. All England's old fears of French aggression were aroused. It was clear that the Republic was bent upon carrying out the plans of Louis XIV for annexing the Austrian Netherlands and Holland and thereby extending her frontiers to the Rhine. Indeed there was no telling where the excited nation, in its fanatical hatred of kings, would stop.

On February 1 Pitt made a speech in the House of Commons in which he accused the French of having broken their promises not to conquer their neighbors or mix in their affairs. They had seized the Netherlands and had declared the river Scheldt open to commerce although it had been closed by the Treaty of Westphalia (1648) in the interests of the Dutch ports. They had already occupied Savoy and now threatened Holland. They loudly proclaimed their intention to free all peoples from the dominion of their rulers. Consequently the Revolution was, Pitt urged, incompatible with the peace of Europe, and England must in honor join the allies and save Europe from falling under the yoke of France.[1]

Pitt declares that England must oppose the Revolution

On the same day that Pitt made his speech, the French Convention boldly declared war upon England and Holland on the ground that "the king of England has not ceased, especially since the Revolution of August 10, 1792, to give the French nation proofs of his ill-will and his attachment to the coalition of crowned heads." He had expelled the French envoy, flooded France with forged *assignats*, prevented grain from reaching French ports, and drawn the "servile" Dutch Stadholder into an alliance against France. No one could have foreseen that England, the last of the European powers to join the coalition against France, was to prove her most

France declares war on England (February 1, 1793) and gives her reasons

[1] Many Englishmen sympathized with the Revolution. Against Pitt's arguments some of the Whigs, especially Fox, urged in vain the bloody manifesto of the duke of Brunswick which had maddened the French, and the atrocious conduct of the allies in the partition of Poland upon which they were just then engaged.

persistent enemy. For over twenty years the struggle was to continue, until an English ship carried Napoleon Bonaparte to his island prison.

Second partition of Poland (1793)
Catharine the Great abhorred the revolutionists, but she had contented herself with encouraging Austria and Prussia to fight for Louis XVI and the rights of monarchs in general, while she prepared to seize more than her share of Poland. Frederick William and the Emperor were well aware of her plans, and consequently felt that they must keep their eyes on her rather than move on Paris. This accounts, in a measure, for the ease with which the French had repulsed the allies and taken possession of the Austrian Netherlands in the autumn of 1792. It was in the following January that Prussia and Russia arranged the second partition of Poland. Austria, as has been explained,[1] was treated very shabbily and forced to go without her share on the flimsy pretense that Frederick William and Catharine would use their good offices to induce the elector of Bavaria to exchange his possessions for the Austrian Netherlands, — which were at that moment in the hands of Dumouriez's republican troops.

French driven from the Netherlands; desertion of Dumouriez
This adjustment of the differences between the allies gave a wholly new aspect to the war with France. When, in March, 1793, Spain and the Holy Roman Empire joined the coalition, France was at war with all her neighbors. The Austrians defeated Dumouriez at Neerwinden, March 18, and drove the French out of the Netherlands. Thereupon Dumouriez, disgusted by the failure of the Convention to support him and by their execution of the king, and angered by the outrageous manner in which their commissioners levied contributions from the people to whom they had brought "liberty," deserted to the enemy with a few hundred soldiers who consented to follow him.

Encouraged by this success, the allies began to consider partitioning France as they had Poland. Austria might take

---

[1] See above, p. 78.

the northern regions for herself and then assign Alsace and Lorraine to Bavaria in exchange for the Bavarian territory on her boundaries, which Austria had long wished to annex. England could have Dunkirk and what remained of the French colonies. A Russian diplomat suggested that Spain and the king of Sardinia should also help themselves. "This done, let us all work in concert to give what remains of France a stable and permanent monarchical government. She will in this way become a second-rate power which will harm no one, and we shall get rid of this democratic firebrand which threatens to set Europe aflame." The allies consider a possible partition of France

The loss of the Netherlands and the treason of their best general made a deep impression upon the members of the Convention. If the new French republic was to defend itself against the "tyrants" without and its many enemies within, it could not wait for the Convention to draw up an elaborate, permanent constitution. An efficient government must be devised immediately to maintain the loyalty of the nation to the republic, and to raise and equip armies and direct their commanders. The Convention accordingly put the government into the hands of a small committee, consisting originally of nine, later of twelve, of its members. This famous Committee of Public Safety was given practically unlimited powers. "We must," one of the leaders exclaimed, "establish the despotism of liberty in order to crush the despotism of kings." The French government put in the hands of the Committee of Public Safety, April, 1793

Within the Convention itself there was dissension, especially between two groups of active men who came into bitter conflict over the policy to be pursued. There was, first, the party of the Girondists, led by Vergniaud, Brissot, and others. They were enthusiastic republicans and counted among their numbers some speakers of remarkable eloquence. The Girondists had enjoyed the control of the Legislative Assembly in 1792 and had been active in bringing on the war with Austria and Prussia. They hoped in that way to complete the Revolution by exposing the bad faith of the king and his sympathy with the The Girondists emigrant nobles. They were not, however, men of sufficient decision to direct affairs in the terrible difficulties in which France found herself after the execution of the king. They consequently lost their influence, and a new party, called the "Mountain" from the high seats that they occupied in the Convention, gained the ascendency.

The extreme republicans, called the "Mountain"

This was composed of the most vigorous and uncompromising republicans, like Danton, Robespierre, and Saint-Just, who had obtained control of the Jacobin clubs and were supported by the commune of Paris. They believed that the French people had been depraved by the slavery to which their kings had subjected them. Everything, they argued, which suggested the former rule of kings must be wiped out. A new France should be created, in which liberty, equality, and fraternity should take the place of the tyranny of princes, the insolence of nobles, and the impostures of the priests. The leaders of the Mountain held that the mass of the people were by nature good and upright, but that there were a number of adherents of the old system who would, if they could, undo the great work of the Revolution and lead the people back to slavery under king and Church. All who were suspected by the Mountain of having the least sympathy with the nobles or the persecuted priests were branded as "counter-revolutionary." The Mountain was willing to resort to any measures, however shocking, to rid the nation of those suspected of counter-revolutionary tendencies, and its leaders relied upon the populace of Paris to aid them in carrying out their designs.

Girondist leaders expelled from the Convention, June 2, 1793

The Girondists, on the other hand, abhorred the restless populace of Paris and the fanatics who composed the commune of the capital. They argued that Paris was not France, and that it had no right to assume a despotic rule over the nation. They proposed that the commune should be dissolved and that the Convention should remove to another town where they would not be subject to the intimidation of the Paris mob. The Mountain thereupon accused the Girondists of an attempt to break up the republic, " one and indivisible," by questioning the supremacy of Paris and the duty of the provinces to follow the lead of the capital. The mob, thus encouraged, rose against the Girondists. On June 2 it surrounded the meeting place of the Convention, and deputies of the commune demanded the expulsion from the Convention of the Girondist leaders, who were placed under arrest.

The conduct of the Mountain and its ally, the Paris commune, now began to arouse opposition in various parts of France, and the country was threatened with civil war at a time when it was absolutely necessary that all Frenchmen should combine in the loyal defense of their country against the invaders who were again approaching its boundaries.

France threatened with civil war

The first and most serious opposition came from the peasants of Brittany, especially in the department of La Vendée. There the people still loved the monarchy and their priests, and even the nobles; they refused to send their sons to fight for a republic which had killed their king and was persecuting those clergymen who declined to take an oath which their conscience forbade.

The revolt of the peasants of Brittany against the Convention

The cities of Marseilles and Bordeaux were indignant at the treatment to which the Girondist deputies were subjected in Paris, and they also organized a revolt against the Convention. In the manufacturing city of Lyons the merchants hated the Jacobins and their republic, since the demand for silk and other luxuries produced at Lyons had come from the nobility and clergy, who were now no longer in a position to buy. The prosperous classes were therefore exasperated when the commissioners of the Convention demanded money and troops. The citizens gathered an army of ten thousand men, placed it under a royalist leader, and prepared to bid defiance to the Jacobins who controlled the Convention.

Revolt of the cities against the Convention

Meanwhile France's enemies were again advancing against her. The Austrians laid siege to the border fortress of Condé, which they captured on July 10, 1793, and two weeks later

French fortresses fall into the hands of Austria and England (July, 1793)

the English took Valenciennes. In this way the allies gained a foothold in France itself. Once more they were hardly more than a hundred miles away from the capital, and there appeared to be no reason why they should not immediately march upon Paris and wreak the vengeance which the duke of Brunswick had threatened in his proclamation of the previous year. The Prussians had driven the French garrison out of Mayence and were ready to advance into Alsace. Toulon, the great naval station of southern France, now revolted against the Convention. It proclaimed the little dauphin as king, under the title of Louis XVII, and welcomed the English fleet as an ally.

Carnot organizes the French armies

The French Republic seemed to be lost; but never did a body of men exhibit such marvelous energy as the Committee of Public Safety. Carnot, who was to earn the title of Organizer of Victory, became a member of the committee in August. He immediately called for a general levy of troops and soon had no less than seven hundred and fifty thousand men. These he divided into thirteen armies which he dispatched against the allies. Each general was accompanied by two " deputies on mission " who were always on the watch lest the commanders desert, as Lafayette had done after August 10, 1792, and Dumouriez a few months later. These Jacobin deputies not only roused the patriotism of the raw recruits, but they let it be known that for a general to lose a battle meant death.

The French easily repulse the allies

Fortunately for the Convention the allies did not march on Paris, but Austria began occupying the border towns and the English moved westward to seize the coveted Dunkirk. The French were able to drive off the English and Hanoverians who were besieging Dunkirk, and in October General Jourdan defeated the Austrians at Wattignies. Since Frederick William continued to give his attention mainly to Poland, there was little danger from the duke of Brunswick and his army, so that by the close of 1793 all danger from foreign invasion was over for the time being.

As for the revolt of the cities and of the Vendean peasants, the Committee of Public Safety showed itself able to cope with that danger too. It first turned its attention to Lyons. Some of the troops from the armies on the frontiers were recalled and the city was bombarded and captured. Then Collot d'Herbois, one of the stanchest believers in terrorism, was sent down to demonstrate to the conquered city what a fearful thing it was to rise against the Mountain. Nearly two thousand persons were executed, or rather massacred, as traitors, within five months. Indeed the Convention declared its intention to annihilate the great and flourishing city and rename its site Freedville (*Commune affranchie*). Happily a close friend of Robespierre, who was sent to execute this decree, contented himself with destroying forty houses.

The revolt of the cities suppressed by the Committee of Public Safety

Frightened by the awful fate of Lyons, the cities of Bordeaux and Marseilles judged it useless to oppose the Convention and admitted its representatives, who executed three or four hundred "traitors" in each place. Toulon held out until an artillery officer hitherto entirely unknown, a young Corsican by the name of Napoleon Bonaparte, suggested occupying a certain promontory in the harbor, from which he was able to train his cannon on the British fleet which was supporting the city. It sailed away with some refugees, leaving the town to the vengeance of the Convention, December 19, 1793.

Bonaparte at Toulon

Although the Vendean peasants fought bravely and defeated several corps of the national guard sent against them, their insurrection was also put down in the autumn — at least for a time — with atrocious cruelty. A representative of the Convention at Nantes had perhaps two thousand Vendean insurgents shot or drowned in the Loire. This was probably the most horrible episode of the Revolution, and was not approved by the Convention, which recalled its bloodthirsty agent, who was finally sent to the scaffold for his crimes.

Defeat of the peasants of the Vendée

In spite of the extraordinary success with which the Committee of Public Safety had crushed its opponents at home and

The Reign of Terror

repelled the armies of the monarchs who proposed to dismember France, it was clear that the task of rendering the Revolution complete and permanent was by no means accomplished. The revolt of the Vendée and of the cities had shown that there were thousands of Frenchmen who hated the Jacobins. All such were viewed by the Convention as guilty of holding counter-revolutionary sentiments and therefore "suspect." It was argued that any one who was not an ardent and demonstrative *sans-culotte* might at any time become a traitor. In order to prevent this and force people to be faithful to the republic, the Convention decided that they must be terrorized by observing the fearful vengeance which the republic wrought upon traitors. The Reign of Terror was only a systematic attempt to secure the success of the Revolution by summarily punishing or intimidating its enemies. While it had no definite beginning or end, it lasted, in its more acute stages, for about ten months, — from September, 1793 to July, 1794.

The Revolutionary Tribunal

Even before the fall of the Girondists a special court had been established in Paris, known as the Revolutionary Tribunal. Its function was to try all those who were suspected of treasonable acts. At first the cases were very carefully considered and few persons were condemned. In September, after the revolt of the cities, two new men who had been implicated in the September massacres were added to the Committee of Public Safety. They were selected with the particular purpose of intimidating the counter-revolutionary party by bringing all the disaffected to the guillotine.[1] A terrible law was passed, declaring all those to be suspects who by their conduct or remarks had shown themselves enemies of liberty. The former nobles, including the wives, fathers, mothers, and children of the "emigrants,"

[1] In former times it had been customary to inflict capital punishment by decapitating the victim with a sword. At the opening of the Revolution a certain Dr. Guillotin recommended a new device, which consisted of a heavy knife sliding downward between two uprights. This instrument, called after him the guillotine, which has until very recently been used in France, was more speedy and certain in its action than the sword in the hands of the executioner.

unless they had constantly manifested their attachment to the Revolution, were ordered to be imprisoned.

In October Marie Antoinette, after a trial in which false and atrocious charges were urged against her in addition to the treasonable acts of which she had been guilty, was executed in Paris. A number of high-minded and distinguished persons, including Madame Roland and a group of Girondists, suffered a like fate. But the most horrible acts of the Reign of Terror were, as has been noted, perpetrated in the provinces, especially at Lyons and Nantes. Execution of Marie Antoinette (October, 1793)

It was not long before the members of the radical party who were conducting the government began to disagree among themselves. Danton, a man of fiery zeal for the republic, who had hitherto enjoyed great popularity with the Jacobins, became tired of bloodshed and convinced that the system of terror was no longer necessary. Camille Desmoulins, another ardent republican, began to attack the harsher Jacobins as he had earlier attacked the unpractical Girondists. He started a witty but very serious little newspaper, called *The Old Cordelier*, in the interests of moderation. Schism in the party of the Mountain

Desmoulins began by showing that the severities of the Reign of Terror were, after all, as nothing compared with the atrocities of the earlier Roman emperors which one read about in Tacitus. "Vice, pillage, and crime are diseases in republics, whereas rogues are absolutely necessary to the maintenance of a monarchy." In his next issue he ceased to extenuate the work of the guillotine and pleaded for clemency. " You would exterminate all your enemies by the guillotine ! What madness ! Can you possibly destroy one enemy on the scaffold without making ten others among his family and friends? " The strong and courageous, as Desmoulins urged, had emigrated or perished at Lyons or in the Vendée. The cowardly or sick who remained were no source of danger. So Terror should no longer be the order of the day, and a committee of clemency should take the place of the revolutionary army that The *Vieux Cordelier* of Desmoulins

was traveling about the country with a movable guillotine. "This committee of clemency," he said, "will complete the Revolution, for clemency itself is a revolutionary measure, the most efficient of all, when it is wisely dealt out."[1]

Hébert and the ultra-radicals

On the other hand, the radical leader of the Paris commune, Hébert, had also his newspaper, an indecent sheet which called on the people to complete the Revolution. He proposed that the worship of Reason should be substituted for that of God and arranged a service in the cathedral of Notre Dame where Reason, in the person of a handsome actress, took her place on the altar.

Robespierre and Saint-Just

Robespierre, who was a member of the Committee of Public Safety, sympathized neither with the moderates nor with Hébert and his Goddess of Reason. He himself enjoyed a great reputation for high ideals, republican virtue, and incorruptibility. He and Saint-Just had read their Rousseau with prayerful attention and dreamed of a glorious republic in which there should be neither rich nor poor; in which men and women should live in independence and rear robust and healthy children. These should be turned over to the republic at five years of age to be educated in Spartan fashion by the nation; they were to eat together and to live on roots, fruit, vegetables, milk, cheese, bread, and water. The Eternal was to be worshiped in temples, and in these temples at certain times every man should be required publicly to state who were his friends. Any man who said he had no friends, or was convicted of ingratitude, was to be banished.[2]

Robespierre has the leaders of both the moderates and extremists executed (March and April, 1794)

Robespierre was, however, insignificant and unattractive in person and a tiresome speaker. He had none of the magnetism of Danton and none of the wit and charm of Desmoulins. He coldly advocated the execution of these two former associates for attempting to betray the republic and frustrate the

[1] See extracts from *The Old Cordelier* in *Readings*, sect. 38.

[2] See *Readings*, sect. 38, for extracts from Saint-Just's book on *Republican Institutions*.

Revolution by their ill-timed moderation. On the other hand, as a deist, he believed that Hébert and his followers were discrediting the Revolution by their atheism. Accordingly, through his influence, the leaders of both the moderate and the extreme parties were arrested and sent to the guillotine (March and April, 1794).

Robespierre now enjoyed a brief dictatorship. He read in the Convention a report on a system of festivals which were to help regenerate the land by celebrating such abstractions as liberty, equality, glory, immortality, frugality, stoicism, and old age. He had a decree passed proclaiming that the French nation believed in God and the immortality of the soul, and organized a ceremony in honor of the Supreme Being in which he himself assumed a very conspicuous rôle as a sort of high priest of deism. The Convention was so far in sympathy with the aspirations of Robespierre and Saint-Just as to assert that " it is necessary to refashion a people completely if it is to be made free. Its prejudices must be destroyed, its habits changed, its needs limited, its vices eradicated, and its desires purified. Strong forces must be invoked to develop social virtues and repress the passions of men." Robespierre's brief period of influence

In order the more effectively to destroy his enemies and those who opposed his designs for the regeneration of society, Robespierre had the Revolutionary Tribunal divided into four sections (June 10, 1794), so that it could work far more rapidly than hitherto. It could condemn any suspected "enemy of the people " on almost any evidence. The accused were in many cases deprived of counsel and no witnesses were examined. The result was that in seven weeks thirteen hundred and seventy-six persons were sent to the guillotine in Paris, whereas only eleven hundred and sixty-five had been executed from December 1 of the previous year to the passage of Robespierre's terrible new law in June. Law of 22d Prairial heightens the Reign of Terror

It was of course impossible for Robespierre to maintain his power long. Many of his colleagues in the Convention began

Fall of
Robespierre
on the 9th
Thermidor
(July 27,
1794)
to fear that they might at any moment follow Danton and Hébert to the guillotine. They did not sympathize very deeply with Robespierre's ideas ; as one of the most ardent terrorists said, " Robespierre begins to bore me with his Supreme Being." A conspiracy was formed against him and the Convention was induced to order his arrest. When, on July 27, — the 9th Thermidor of the new republican calendar,— he appeared in the Convention and attempted to speak he was silenced by cries of "Down with the tyrant ! " In his consternation he could not at first recover his voice, whereupon one of the deputies shouted, "The blood of Danton chokes him ! " Finally he called upon the commune of Paris to defend him, but the Convention was able to maintain its authority and to send Robespierre and Saint-Just, his fellow-idealist, to the guillotine. It is sad enough that two of the most sincere and upright of all the revolutionists should, in their misguided and over-earnest efforts to better the condition of their fellow-men, have become objects of execration to posterity.

Reaction
after the
overthrow of
Robespierre
In successfully overthrowing Robespierre the Convention and Committee of Public Safety had rid the country of the only man who, owing to his popularity and his reputation for uprightness, could have prolonged the Reign of Terror. There was almost an immediate reaction after his death, for the country was weary of executions. The Revolutionary Tribunal henceforth convicted very few indeed of those who were brought before it. It made an exception, however, of those who had themselves been the leaders in the worst atrocities, as, for example, the public prosecutor, who had brought hundreds of victims to the guillotine in Paris, and the terrorists who had ordered the massacres at Nantes and Lyons. Within a few months the Jacobin Club at Paris was closed by the Convention and the commune of Paris abolished.

Review of
the Reign
of Terror
The importance and nature of the Reign of Terror are so commonly misunderstood that it is worth our while to stop a moment to reconsider it as a whole. When the Estates

General met, the people of France were loyal to their king First stage but wished to establish a more orderly government; they wanted to vote the taxes, have some share in making the laws, and abolish the old feudal abuses, including the unreasonable privileges of the nobility and the clergy. The nobility were frightened and began to run away. The king and queen urged foreign powers to intervene and even tried to escape to join the traitorous emigrant nobles. Austrian and Prussian troops reached the frontier and the Prussian commander threatened to destroy Paris unless the royal family were given complete liberty. Paris, aided by the men of Marseilles, retaliated by deposing the king, and the Convention decided by a narrow majority to execute Louis XVI for treason, of which he was manifestly guilty. In the summer, just as Austria and England were taking the French border fortresses of Condé and Valenciennes, the cities of Lyons, Marseilles, and Toulon and the peasants of the Vendée revolted. The necessity of making head against invasion and putting down the insurrection at home led to harsh measures on the part of the Convention and its Committee of Public Safety.

When the immediate danger was dispelled Robespierre, Second stage Saint-Just, and others sought to exterminate the enemies of that utopian republic of which they dreamed and in which every man was to have a fair chance in life. This led to the second, and perhaps less excusable, phase of the Reign of Terror. To the executions sanctioned by the government must be added the massacres and lynchings perpetrated by mobs or by irresponsible agents of the Convention. Yet Camille Desmoulins was right when he claimed that the blood that had flowed "for the eternal emancipation of a nation of twenty-five millions" was as nothing to that shed by the Roman emperors (and it may be added, by bishops and kings), often in less worthy causes.

Then it should be remembered that a great part of the French people were nearly or quite unaffected by the Reign

A great part of the French people unaffected by the Reign of Terror

of Terror. In Paris very few of the citizens stood in any fear of the guillotine. The city was not the gloomy place that it has been pictured by Dickens and other story-tellers. Never did the inhabitants appear happier than when the country was being purged of the supposed traitors; never were the theaters and restaurants more crowded. The guillotine was making way with the enemies of liberty, so the women wore tiny guillotines as ornaments, and the children were given toy guillotines and amused themselves decapitating the figures of "aristocrats."

Sound reforms introduced by the Convention

Moreover the Convention had by no means confined its attention during the months of the Reign of Terror to hunting down "suspects" and executing traitors. Its committees had raised a million troops, organized and equipped them with arms, and sent them forth to victory. The reforms sketched out by the National Assembly had been developed and carried on. The Convention had worked out a great system of elementary education which should form the basis of the new republic. It had drafted a new code of laws which should replace the confusion of the *ancien régime*, although it was left for Napoleon to order its revision and gain the credit of the enterprise. The republican calendar was not destined to sur-

The metric system

vive, but the rational system of weights and measures known as the metric system, which the Convention introduced, has been adopted by most of the nations of Continental Europe and is used by men of science in England and America.

Anxiety of the Convention to blot out all suggestions of the past

In its anxiety to obliterate every suggestion of the old order of things, the Convention went to excess. The old terms of address, Monsieur and Madame, seemed to smack of the *ancien régime* and so were replaced by " citizen " and " citizeness." The days were no longer dedicated to St. Peter, St. James, St. Bridget, or St. Catharine, but to the cow, the horse, celery, the turnip, the harrow, the pitchfork, or other useful creature or utensil. The Place Louis XV became Place de la Revolution. Throne Square was rechristened Place of the Overturned

Throne. The Convention endeavored to better the condition of the poor man and deprive the rich of their superfluity. The land which had been taken from the Church and the runaway nobles was sold in small parcels and the number of small land-holders was thus greatly increased. In May, 1793, the Convention tried to keep down the price of grain by passing the Law of the Maximum, which forbade the selling of grain and flour at a higher price than that fixed by each commune. This was later extended to other forms of food and worked quite as badly as the grain laws which Turgot had abolished.

The Convention's efforts to improve the condition of the poorer classes

The reckless increase of the paper currency, or *assignats*, and the efforts to prevent their depreciation by a law which made it a capital offense to refuse to accept them at par caused infinite confusion. There were about forty billions of francs of these *assignats* in circulation at the opening of the year 1796. At that time it required nearly three hundred francs in paper to procure one in specie.

Trouble with depreciated paper money

At last the Convention turned its attention once more to the special work for which it had been summoned in September, 1792, and drew up a constitution for the republic. This was preceded by a " Declaration of the Rights and Duties of Man and the Citizen," which summed up, as the first Declaration of Rights had done, the great principles of the Revolution.[1] The lawmaking power is vested by the Constitution of the Year III in a Legislative Body to be composed of two chambers, the Council of Five Hundred and the Council of the Elders (consisting of two hundred and fifty members). Members of the latter were to be at least forty years old and either married or widowers. Practically all men over twenty-one years of age were permitted to vote for the members of the electoral colleges, which in turn chose the members of the

Constitution of the Year III

---

[1] All the duties of man and the citizen are derived, according to this constitution, from two principles which are graven by nature in the hearts of all: Ne faites pas à autrui ce que vous ne voudriez pas qu'on vous fît. Faites constamment aux autres le bien que vous voudriez en recevoir. This is after all only an amplification of the Golden Rule.

Legislative Body. To take the place of a king, a Directory composed of five members chosen by the Legislative Body was invested with the executive power. One director was to retire each year, as well as one third of the members of the Legislative Body (a system suggesting that of the United States Senate).

Before the Convention completed the constitution its enemies had become very strong. The richer classes had once more got the upper hand ; they abhorred the Convention which had killed their king and oppressed them, and they favored the reëstablishment of the monarchy without the abuses of the *ancien régime*. The Convention, fearing for itself and the republic, decreed that in the approaching election, at least two thirds of the new Legislative Body were to be chosen from the existing members of the Convention. Believing that it could rely upon the armies, it ordered that the constitution should be submitted to the soldiers for ratification and that bodies of troops should be collected near Paris to maintain order during the elections. These decrees roused the anger of the wealthier districts of Paris which did not hesitate to organize a revolt and prepare to attack the Convention.

The latter, however, chose for its defender that same Napoleon Bonaparte who, after helping to take Toulon, had resigned his commission rather than leave the artillery and join the infantry as he had been ordered to do, and was earning a bare subsistence as a clerk in a government office. Bonaparte stationed the regulars around the building in which the Convention sat and then loaded his cannon with grapeshot. When the bourgeois national guard attacked him, he gave the order to fire and easily swept them from the streets.[1] The royalists were defeated. The day had been saved for the Convention by the army and by a military genius who was destined soon not only to make himself master of France but to build up an empire comprising a great part of western Europe.

[1] More people were killed on the 13th Vendémiaire than on August 10, 1792, when the monarchy was overthrown.

REFERENCES

End of the National Assembly: MATHEWS, *French Revolution*, chap. xiii, pp. 166–181; STEPHENS, *History of the French Revolution*, Vol. I, chap. xv, pp. 434–470; *Cambridge Modern History*, Vol. VIII, pp. 199–210.

Opening of the War with Europe: MATHEWS, pp. 182–195; STEPHENS, Vol. II, pp. 27–44; FYFFE, *History of Modern Europe*, pp. 28–40.

Conditions in Europe in 1792: FYFFE, chap. i, pp. 1–27.

Tenth of August and the September Massacres: STEPHENS, Vol. II, chap. iv, pp. 107–150; MATHEWS, pp. 195–206; *Cambridge Modern History*, Vol. VIII, pp. 228–244.

Establishment of the Republic: MATHEWS, chap. xv, pp. 207–224; STEPHENS, Vol. II, chap. v, pp. 151–180.

Reign of Terror in Paris: STEPHENS, Vol. II, chap. x, pp. 321–361; MATHEWS, chap. xvi, pp. 224–233; *Cambridge Modern History*, Vol. VIII, chap. xii, pp. 338–371.

Reign of Terror in the Provinces: MATHEWS, chap. xvii, pp. 234–251; STEPHENS, Vol. II, chap. xi, pp. 362–414.

Robespierre: MATHEWS, chap. xviii, pp. 252–265.

Reaction after Thermidor: MATHEWS, chap. xix, pp. 266–285; *Cambridge Modern History*, Vol. VIII, chap. xiii, pp. 372–397.

Course of the War to 1795: FYFFE, chap. ii, pp. 28–73; *Cambridge Modern History*, chap. xiv, pp. 398–446.

CHAPTER XIV

NAPOLEON BONAPARTE

BONAPARTE'S FIRST ITALIAN CAMPAIGN

How the
Revolution
transformed
and democ-
ratized the
army

39. The French army had undergone a complete transformation during the Revolution. The rules of the *ancien régime*
had required all officers to be nobles, and many of these had
left France after the fall of the Bastille. Others, like Lafayette
and Dumouriez, who had at first favored the Revolution, deserted soon after the opening of the war. Still others, like
Custine and Beauharnais (the Empress Josephine's first husband), were executed because the "deputies on mission"
believed that they were responsible for the defeats that the
armies of the French republic had suffered.

The former rigid discipline disappeared, and the hundreds
of thousands of volunteers who pressed forward to defend and
extend the boundaries of the Republic found new leaders, who
rose from the ranks, and who hit upon novel and quite uncon-
ventional ways of beating the enemy. Any one might now become a general if he could prove his ability to lead troops to
victory. Moreau was a lawyer from Brittany, Murat had been
a waiter, Jourdan before the Revolution had been selling
cloth in Limoges. In short, the army, like the State, had
become democratic.

The Napo-
leonic Period

Among the commanders who by means of their talents
rose to take the places of the "aristocrats" was one who was
to dominate the history of Europe as no man before him had
ever done. For fifteen years his biography and the political
history of Europe are so nearly synonymous that the period
we are now entering upon may properly be called after him,
the Napoleonic Period.

Napoleon Bonaparte was hardly a Frenchman by birth. It is true that the island of Corsica where he was born, August 15, 1769, had at that time belonged to France for a year,[1] but Napoleon's native language was Italian, and he was descended from Italian ancestors who had come to the island in the sixteenth century. His father, Carlo Buonaparte, although he claimed to be of noble extraction, busied himself with the profession of the law in the town of Ajaccio where Napoleon was probably born. He was poor and found it hard to support his eight boys and girls, all of whom were one day to become kings and queens, or at worst, princes and princesses. Accordingly he took his two elder sons, Joseph and Napoleon, to France, where Joseph was to be educated for the priesthood and Napoleon, who was but ten years old, after learning a little French was to prepare for the army in the military academy at Brienne.

Napoleon Bonaparte (b. 1769), a Corsican by birth, an Italian by descent

Here the boy led an unhappy life for five or six years. He soon came to hate the young French nobles with whom he was associated. He wrote to his father, "I am tired of exposing my poverty and seeing these shameless boys laughing over it, for they are superior to me only in wealth and infinitely beneath me in noble sentiments." Gradually the ambition to free his little island country from French control developed in him.

Bonaparte at the military school (1779–1784)

On completing his course in the military school he was made second lieutenant. Poor and without influence, he had little hope of any considerable advance in the French army, and he was drawn to his own country both by a desire to play a political rôle there and to help his family, which had been left in straitened circumstances by his father's death. He therefore absented himself from his command as often and as long as he could, and engaged in a series of intrigues in Corsica in the hope of getting control of the forces of the island. He

His political intrigues in Corsica

The Bonapartes banished from Corsica (1793)

[1] It is possible that Bonaparte was born in the previous year, when Corsica still belonged to the republic of Genoa.

fell into disfavor, however, with the authorities, and he and his family were banished in 1793, and fled to France.

How Bonaparte won the confidence of Barras and the Directory

The following three years were for Bonaparte a period of great uncertainty. He had lost his love for Corsica and as yet had found no foothold in France. Soon after his return his knowledge of artillery enabled him, as we have seen, to suggest a successful method of capturing Toulon; and two years later his friend Barras selected him to defend the Convention against its enemies on the 13th Vendémiaire. This was the beginning of his career, for Barras, who had been chosen a member of the Directory, introduced him into the gay and reckless social circle to which he belonged. Here he met and fell in love

Napoleon marries Josephine Beauharnais

with the charming widow of poor General Beauharnais, who had lost his head just before Thermidor. Madame Beauharnais accepted the pale, nervous little republican officer in spite of his awkward manners and ill-fitting uniform. Nine years later he was able to place an imperial crown upon her brow.

Bonaparte made commander in chief of the army of Italy (1796)

In the spring of 1796 Bonaparte was selected by the Directory to command one of the three armies which it was sending against Austria. This important appointment at the age of twenty-seven forms the opening of an astonishing military career which can be compared only with that of Alexander the Great.

How Prussia and Austria neglected the war with France in 1794

France, as has been pointed out, found herself in 1793 at war with Austria, Prussia, England, Holland, Spain, the Holy Roman Empire, Sardinia, the Kingdom of Naples (i.e. of the Two Sicilies), and Tuscany. This formidable alliance, however, only succeeded in taking a few border fortresses which the French easily regained. Prussia and Austria were far more interested in Poland, where a third and last partition was pending, than in fighting the Revolution and keeping the French out of the Austrian Netherlands. The Polish patriot, Kosciusko, had led a revolt of the Poles against their oppressors, and the Russian garrison which Catharine had placed in Warsaw was cut down by the Polish rebels in April, 1794. Catharine then appealed to Frederick William for assistance. He therefore turned his whole attention to Poland,[1] and Pitt had to pay him handsomely to induce him to leave sixty thousand Prussian troops to protect the Netherlands from the French invaders. But England's money was wasted, for the Prussians refused to take active measures, and even Austria, after one or two reverses, decided to evacuate the Netherlands, in the summer of 1794, in order to center all her energies upon Polish affairs and prevent Russia and Prussia from excluding her, as they had done the last time, when it came to a division of the booty.

England was naturally disgusted. She had joined the war in order to aid Austria and Prussia to maintain the balance of power and defend the Netherlands, which formed a protective barrier between Holland and France. Lord Malmesbury, one of the English diplomats, declared that in his dealings with the allies he encountered only "shabby art and cunning, ill will, jealousy and every sort of dirty passion." By October, 1794, the Austrians had disappeared beyond the Rhine; the English were forced to give up Holland and to retreat forlornly into Hanover before the French under General Pichegru, who captured the Dutch fleet imprisoned in the ice near Texel. The Dutch towns contained some enthusiastic republicans who received the French cordially. The office of hereditary stadholder,[2] which was really that of a king except in name, was abolished, and the United Netherlands became the Batavian Republic under French control. *England unable to check the French, who occupy Holland and the Rhine region*

Instead of being crushed by the overwhelming forces of the allies, the armies of the French republic had, in the three years since the opening of the war, conquered the Spanish Netherlands, Savoy, and Nice; they had metamorphosed Holland into a friendly sister republic, and had occupied western Germany as far as the Rhine. The Convention was now ready to conclude its first treaties of peace. Prussia signed the Treaty of Basel with the new republic (April, 1795), in which she secretly *The French republic concludes the Treaties of Basel with Prussia and Spain (April and July, 1795)*

[1] See above, pp. 79–80.   [2] See above, p. 67.

agreed not to oppose the permanent acquisition by France of the left bank of the Rhine provided Prussia were indemnified for the territory which she would in that case lose. Three months later Spain also made peace with France. Early in 1796 the Directory decided, in accordance with General Bonaparte's advice, to undertake a triple movement upon Vienna, the capital of its chief remaining enemy. Jourdan was to take a northerly route along the river Main; Moreau was to lead an army through the Black Forest and down the Danube, while Bonaparte invaded Lombardy, which was, since the French had occupied the Netherlands, the nearest of the Austrian possessions.

Divisions of Italy

Italy was still in the same condition in which it had been left some fifty years before at the Peace of Aix-la-Chapelle, when the Austrian Hapsburgs and the Spanish Bourbons had come to a final agreement as to what each was to have for the younger members of the two families.[1] In the kingdom of Naples [2] the feeble Ferdinand IV [3] reigned with Caroline his wife, the sister of Marie Antoinette. To the north, stretching across the peninsula, lay the Papal States. Tuscany enjoyed the mild and enlightened rule of the successors of Joseph of Lorraine. Parma's duke was related to the Spanish house and Modena's to the Austrian, but the only part of Italy actually under foreign rule was Lombardy and its capital, Milan, which had fallen to Austria after the War of the Spanish Succession. The once flourishing republics of Venice and Genoa still existed, but had long since ceased to play a rôle in European affairs. The only vigorous and promising state in Italy that was not more or less under the influence of either Austria or Spain was the kingdom of Sardinia, composed of Piedmont, Savoy, Nice, and the island of Sardinia.

[1] See above, pp. 45–46.

[2] We shall use this name hereafter instead of the more cumbersome title, Kingdom of the Two Sicilies.

[3] The successor of Don Carlos, who had become Charles III of Spain (see above, pp. 45 and 190).

General Bonaparte had to face the combined forces of Austria and Sardinia, which had joined the enemies of France in 1793. By marching north from Savona he skillfully separated his two enemies. He forced the Sardinian troops back toward Turin and compelled the king to conclude a treaty by which Savoy and Nice were ceded to France. Bonaparte was now free to advance into Lombardy. He marched down the Po, and the Austrians, fearing that he might cut them off, hastened eastward, leaving Milan to be occupied by the French. Here Bonaparte made a triumphal entry on May 15, 1796, scarcely more than a month after the campaign opened.

Bonaparte forces Sardinia to conclude peace and enters Milan (May, 1796)

As he descended the mountains into the plains of Lombardy, Bonaparte had announced that the French army came to break the chains of the tyrants, for the French people was the friend of all peoples. Nevertheless the Directory expected him to force those that he "freed" to support the French armies. Their directions to Bonaparte were sufficiently explicit: "Leave nothing in Italy which will be useful to us and which the political situation will permit you to remove." Accordingly Milan was not only required to pay its deliverers twenty million francs but also to give up some of the finest old masterpieces in its churches and galleries. The dukes of Parma and Modena made similar "contributions" on condition that Bonaparte would grant them an armistice.

The French begin to plunder Italy

Bonaparte soon moved east and defeated the Austrian army, a part of which took refuge in the impregnable fortress of Mantua to which the French promptly laid siege. There is no more fascinating chapter in the history of warfare than the story of the audacious maneuvers by which Bonaparte successfully repulsed the Austrian armies sent to relieve Mantua. Toward the end of July an Austrian army nearly twice the size of Bonaparte's descended in three divisions from Tyrol. The situation of the French was critical, but Bonaparte managed to defeat each of the three divisions before they had an opportunity to join forces. In five days the Austrians retired, leaving

The campaign about Mantua (May, 1796–February, 1797)

fifteen thousand prisoners in the hands of the French. Bonaparte now determined to advance up the river Adige into
Germany. He again routed the Austrians and took possession
of Trent. Wurmser, the Austrian commander, tried to cut him

Central Europe to illustrate Napoleon's Campaigns, 1796–1801

off from Italy but was himself shut up in Mantua with the
remains of his army.

Bonaparte
defeats the
Austrians at
Arcole (No-
vember 15–17,
1796) and at
Rivoli (Janua-
ry 14–15, 1797)
In November two more armies were sent down to relieve
Mantua, one approaching by the Adige and the other descending the Piave. Bonaparte met and defeated the Piave army
in a three days' battle at Arcole, after which the other Austrian
division retreated. The last effort to relieve the fortress was

frustrated by Bonaparte at Rivoli (January 14–15, 1797) and resulted in the surrender of Mantua, which gave the French complete control of northern Italy.

Fall of Mantua

All danger of an attack in the rear was now removed, and the victorious French general could lead his army through the mountains to Vienna. He forced back the Austrians, who attempted to block the road, and when, on April 7, he was within eighty miles of the capital, the Austrian commander requested a truce, which Bonaparte was not unwilling to grant, since he was now far from home, and both the other armies which the Directory had sent out, under Moreau and Jourdan, had been routed and forced back over the Rhine. A preliminary peace was accordingly arranged, which was followed by the definitive Treaty of Campo Formio (October, 1797).

Truce at Leoben (April, 1797)

The provisions of the Treaty of Campo Formio illustrate the unscrupulous manner in which Bonaparte and Austria disposed of the helpless lesser states. It inaugurated the bewilderingly rapid territorial redistribution of Europe which was so characteristic of the Napoleonic period. Austria ceded to France the Austrian Netherlands and secretly agreed to use its good offices to secure for France a great part of the left bank of the Rhine. Austria also recognized the Cisalpine Republic, which Bonaparte had created out of the smaller states of northern Italy, and which was under the " protection " of France. This new state included Lombardy, which Bonaparte had conquered, the duchy of Modena, some of the papal dominions, and, lastly, a part of the possessions of the venerable and renowned but now defenseless republic of Venice, which Napoleon had ruthlessly destroyed. Austria received as an indemnity for the Netherlands and Lombardy the rest of the possessions of the Venetian republic, including Venice itself.

Provisions of the Treaty of Campo Formio (October, 1797)

Creation of the Cisalpine Republic

While the negotiations were going on, the young general had established a brilliant court at a villa near Milan. "His salons," an observer informs us, " were filled with a throng of generals, officials, and purveyors, as well as the highest nobility and the

General Bonaparte establishes a court

most distinguished men of Italy, who came to solicit the favor of a glance or a moment's conversation." It would appear, from the report of a most extraordinary conversation which occurred at this time, that he had already conceived the rôle that he was to play later.

"What I have done so far," he declared, "is nothing. I am but at the opening of the career that I am to run. Do you suppose that I have gained my victories in Italy in order to advance the lawyers of the Directory, — the Carnots and the Barras'? Do you think either that my object is to establish a republic? What a notion! . . . What the French want is Glory and the satisfaction of their vanity; as for Liberty, of that they have no conception. Look at the army! The victories that we have just gained have given the French soldier his true character. I am everything to him. Let the Directory attempt to deprive me of my command and they will see who is the master. The nation must have a head, a head who is rendered illustrious by glory and not by theories of government, fine phrases, or the talk of idealists, of which the French understand not a whit."

There is no doubt whom General Bonaparte had in mind when he spoke of the needed head of the French nation who should be "rendered illustrious by glory." This son of a poor Corsican lawyer, but yesterday a mere unlucky adventurer, had arranged his program; two years and a half later he was the master of the French republic.

We naturally ask what manner of person this was who could frame such audacious schemes at twenty-eight and realize them at thirty years of age. He was a little man, less than five feet two inches in height. At this time he was extremely thin, but his striking features, quick, searching eye, abrupt, animated gestures, and rapid speech, incorrect as it was, made a deep impression upon those who came in contact with him. He possessed in a supreme degree two qualities that are ordinarily considered incompatible. He was a dreamer and, at the same time, a man whose practical skill and mastery of detail amounted to genius. He once told a friend that he was wont, when a poor lieutenant, to allow his imagination full play and fancy things just as he would have them. Then he would coolly consider the exact steps to be taken if he were to try to make his dream come true.

In order to explain Bonaparte's success it must be remembered that he was not hampered or held back by the fear of doing wrong. He was utterly unscrupulous, whether dealing with an individual or a nation, and appears to have been absolutely without any sense of moral responsibility. Neither did affection for his friends and relatives ever stand in the way of his personal aggrandizement. To these traits must be added unrivaled military genius and the power of intense and almost uninterrupted work. *Sources of power in Napoleon's character*

But even Bonaparte, unexampled as were his abilities, could never have extended his power over all of western Europe, had it not been for the peculiar political weakness of most of the states with which he had to deal. There was no strong German Empire in his day, no united Italy, no Belgium whose neutrality was guaranteed — as it now is — by the other powers of Europe. The French republic was surrounded by petty, independent, or practically independent, principalities, which were defenseless against an unscrupulous invader. Prussia, much smaller than it now is, offered, as we shall see, no efficient opposition to the extension of French control, while Austria had been forced to capitulate, after a short campaign, by an enemy far from its source of supplies and led by a young and inexperienced general. *The political conditions which rendered Napoleon's wonderful successes possible*

How Bonaparte made Himself Master of France

40. After arranging the Peace of Campo Formio, General Bonaparte returned to Paris. He at once perceived that

Bonaparte
conceives the
plan of an
expedition
to Egypt

France, in spite of her enthusiasm over his victories, was not yet ready to accept him as her ruler. The pear was not yet ripe, as he observed. He saw, too, that he would soon sacrifice his prestige if he lived quietly in Paris like an ordinary person. His active mind promptly conceived a plan which would forward his interests. France was still at war with England, its most persevering enemy during this period. Bonaparte convinced the Directory that England could best be ruined in the long run by occupying Egypt and so threatening her commerce in the Mediterranean, and perhaps ultimately her dominion in the East. Fascinated by the career of Alexander the Great, Bonaparte pictured himself riding to India on the back of an elephant and dispossessing England of her most precious colonial dependencies. He had, however, still another and a characteristic reason for undertaking the expedition. France was on the eve of a new war with the European powers. Bonaparte foresaw that, if he could withdraw with him some of France's best officers, the Directory might soon find itself so embarrassed that he could return as a national savior. And even so it fell out.

Accordingly General Bonaparte, under authority of the Directory, collected forty thousand of the best troops and fitted out a strong fleet, which should serve to give France the control of the Mediterranean. He did not forget to add to the expedition a hundred and twenty scientists and engineers, who were to study the country and prepare the way for French colonists to be sent out later.[1]

The campaign in Egypt (1798–1799)

The French fleet left Toulon, May 19, 1798. It was so fortunate as to escape the English squadron under Nelson, which sailed by it in the night. Bonaparte arrived at Alexandria, July 1, and easily defeated the Turkish troops in the famous

---

[1] One of the most noteworthy scientific results of Bonaparte's expedition to Egypt was the discovery of the Rosetta Stone, which the soldiers dug up at the mouth of the Nile. This has inscribed upon it a passage in Egyptian hieroglyphics accompanied by a Greek translation which furnished the modern world with the key to ancient hieroglyphic inscriptions. The stone is now in the British Museum.

battle of the Pyramids. Meanwhile Nelson, who did not know the destination of the enemy's fleet, had returned from the Syrian coast, where he had looked for the French in vain. He discovered Bonaparte's ships in the harbor of Alexandria and completely annihilated them in the first battle of the Nile

Nelson destroys the French fleet

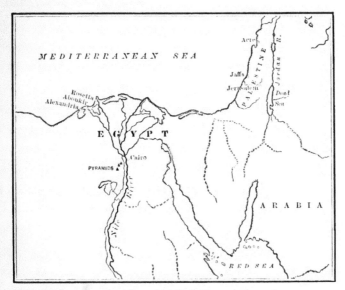

Egyptian Campaign

(August 1, 1798). The French troops were now completely cut off from Europe.

The Porte (i.e. the Turkish government) having declared war against France, Bonaparte resolved to attack Turkey by land. He accordingly marched into Syria in the spring of 1799, but was repulsed at Acre, where the Turkish forces were aided by the English fleet. Pursued by pestilence, the army regained Cairo in June, after terrible suffering and loss. It was still strong enough to annihilate a Turkish army that landed at Alexandria ; but news now reached Bonaparte from Europe

Syrian campaign

Bonaparte deserts the army in Egypt and returns to Paris

which convinced him that the time had come for him to hasten back. The powers had formed a new coalition against France. Northern Italy, which he had won, was lost; the allies were about to invade France itself, and the Directory was hopelessly demoralized. Bonaparte accordingly secretly deserted his army and managed, by a series of happy accidents, to reach France by October 9, 1799.

The *coup d'état* of the 18th Brumaire, November 9, 1799

The Directory, one of the most corrupt and inefficient governmental bodies that the world has ever seen, had completely disgraced itself and Bonaparte readily found others to join with him in a conspiracy to overthrow it. A plan was formed for abruptly destroying the old government and replacing it by a new one without observing any constitutional forms. This is a procedure so familiar in France during the past century that it is known even in English as a *coup d'état* (literally translated, a "stroke of state"). The conspirators had a good many friends in the two assemblies, especially among the " Elders." Nevertheless Bonaparte had to order his soldiers to invade the hall in which the Assembly of the Five Hundred was in session and scatter his opponents before he could accomplish his purpose. A chosen few were then reassembled under the presidency of Lucien Bonaparte, one of Napoleon's brothers, who was a member of the Assembly. They voted to put the government in the hands of three men, — General Bonaparte and two others, — to be called "Consuls." These were to proceed, with the aid of a commission and of the Elders, to draw up a new constitution.

Bonaparte made First Consul

The consti- tution of the Year VIII

The new constitution was a very cumbrous and elaborate one. It provided for no less than four assemblies, one to propose the laws, one to consider them, one to vote upon them, and one to decide on their constitutionality. But Bonaparte saw to it that as First Consul he himself had practically all the power in his own hands. The Council of State, to which he called talented men from all parties and over which he presided, was the most important of the governmental bodies.

The Council of State

Bonaparte's chief aim was to *centralize* the government. The centralized administrative system established by Bonaparte Nothing was left to local assemblies, for he proposed to control everything from Paris. Accordingly, in each department he put an officer called a *prefect;* in each subdivision of the department a *subprefect.* These, together with the mayors and police commissioners of the towns, were all appointed by the First Consul. The prefects — "little First Consuls," as Bonaparte called them — resembled the former intendants, the king's officers under the old régime. Indeed, the new government suggested in several important respects that of Louis XIV. This administrative system which Bonaparte perfected has endured, with a few changes, down to the present day. It has rendered the French government very stable in spite of the startling changes in the constitution which have occurred. There is no surer proof of Napoleon's genius than that, with no previous experience, he could conceive a plan of government that should serve a great state like France through all its vicissitudes for a century.

The new ruler objected as decidedly as Louis XIV had done The new government accepted by a plebiscite to the idea of being controlled by the people, who, he believed, knew nothing of public affairs. It was enough, he thought, if they were allowed to say whether they wished a certain form of government or not. He therefore introduced what he called a *plebiscite.*[1] The new constitution when completed was submitted to the nation at large, and all were allowed to vote " yes " or " no " on the expediency of its adoption. Over three million voted in favor of it and only fifteen hundred and sixty-two against it. This did not necessarily mean, however, that practically the whole nation wished to have General Bonaparte as its ruler. A great many may have preferred what seemed to them an objectionable form of government to the risk of rejecting it. Herein lies the injustice of the plebiscite; there are many questions that cannot be answered by a simple "yes" or "no."

[1] The *plebiscitum* of the Romans, from which the French derived their term *plébiscite*, was originally a law voted in the Assembly of the *plebs*, or people.

Bonaparte
generally
acceptable to
France as
First Consul Yet the accession to power of the popular young general was undoubtedly grateful to the majority of citizens, who longed above all for a stable government. The Swedish envoy wrote, just after the *coup d'état:* "A legitimate monarch has perhaps never found a people more ready to do his bidding than Bonaparte, and it would be inexcusable if this talented general did not take advantage of this to introduce a better form of government upon a firmer basis. It is literally true that France will perform impossibilities in order to aid him in this. The people (with the exception of a despicable horde of anarchists) are so sick and weary of revolutionary horrors and folly that they believe that any change cannot fail to be for the better. . . . Even the royalists, whatever their views may be, are sincerely devoted to Bonaparte, for they attribute to him the intention of gradually restoring the old order of things. The indifferent element cling to him as the one most likely to give France peace. The enlightened republicans, although they tremble for their form of government, prefer to see a single man of talent possess himself of the power than a club of intriguers."

THE SECOND COALITION AGAINST FRANCE

The Directory strikes at English commerce **41.** Upon becoming First Consul, General Bonaparte found France at war with England, Russia, Austria, Turkey, and Naples, — a somewhat strange coalition which must be explained. After the treaties of Basel and Campo Formio, England had been left to fight the Revolution single-handed. The Directory issued a decree excluding her products from all lands under French control, especially cotton and woolen goods, hardware, pottery, and refined sugar, which were not to be imported on pain of confiscation. Although this was exactly the kind of law that England had been trying to enforce in her own interest for a century or so,[1] the English merchants were

[1] See above, pp. 117–118.

exasperated at the unprincipled French, and Pitt was encouraged to continue the struggle.

He found an unexpected ally in the Tsar Paul.[1] Like his mother, Catharine II, whom he succeeded in 1796, he hated the Revolution ; but, unlike her, he consented to send troops to fight against France, for which Pitt agreed (December, 1798) to help pay. Austria was willing to take up the war again since she saw no prospect of getting all the territory that Bonaparte had half promised her in the Treaty of Campo Formio. As for the Sultan, Bonaparte's Egyptian expedition brought the French to his very doors and led him to join his ancient enemy, Russia, in a common cause. *Russia enters the war as England's ally* *The Sultan*

It certainly appeared to be high time to check the restless new republic which was busily engaged in spreading " liberty " in her own interest. Holland had first been *republicanized ;* then Bonaparte had established the Cisalpine Republic in northern Italy ; and the French had stirred up a revolution in Genoa, which led to the abolition of the old aristocratic government and the founding of a new Ligurian Republic which was to be the friend and ally of France. *France republicanizes her neighbors*

Next, with the encouragement of Joseph Bonaparte, Napoleon's brother, who was the French ambassador in Rome, the few republicans in the Pope's capital proclaimed a republic. In the disturbance which ensued a French general was killed, a fact which gave the Directory an excuse for declaring war and occupying Rome. On February 15, 1798, the republicans assembled in the ancient forum and declared that the Roman Republic was once more restored. The brutal French commissioner insulted the Pope, snatched his staff and ring from his hand, and ordered him out of town. The French *The Roman Republic proclaimed (February, 1798)*

1 Paul was an ill-balanced person whose chief grievance against the French was that Bonaparte had captured the island of Malta on the way to Egypt. Malta had for centuries been held by the Order of the Knights of Malta, which had originated during the Crusades. Now the knights had chosen Paul as their " Protector," an honor which enchanted his simple soul and led him to dream of annexing Malta to his empire. Bonaparte's seizure of the island interfered with his plans and served to rouse a desire for vengeance.

seized the pictures and statues in the Vatican and sent them to Paris and managed to rob the new republic of some sixty million francs besides.

More scandalous still was the conduct of the Directory and its commissioners in dealing with Switzerland. In that little country, certain of the *cantons*, or provinces, had long been subject to others which possessed superior rights. A few persons in the canton of Vaud were readily induced by the French agitators to petition the Directory to free their canton from the overlordship of Berne. In January, 1798, a French army entered Switzerland and easily overpowered the troops of Berne and occupied the city (in March), where they seized the treasure — some four millions of dollars — which had been gradually brought together through a long period by the thrifty

government of the confederation. A new Helvetic Republic, "one and indivisible," was proclaimed, in which all the cantons should be equal and all the old feudal customs and inequalities should be abolished. The mountaineers of the conservative cantons about the lake of Lucerne rose in vain against the intruders, who mercilessly massacred those who dared to oppose the changes which their "deliverers" chose to introduce. The money and supplies which the French appropriated were sent to Toulon to be used in the Egyptian expedition.

The new outbreak of war against France was due to Naples, where Marie Antoinette's sister, Caroline, watched with horror the occupation of Rome by the French troops. Nelson, after destroying Bonaparte's fleet in the battle of the Nile, had returned to Naples and there arranged a plan for driving the French from the Papal States. But everything went badly ;

the French easily defeated the Bourbon armies and the members of the royal family of Naples were glad to embark on the British ships and make their way to Palermo. Thereupon the French republicanized Naples, seized millions of francs as usual, and carried off to Paris the best works of art.

At the same time Piedmont was occupied by the French, and the king was forced to abdicate. He retired to Sardinia, where he remained until Napoleon's downfall fifteen years later.

Early in the year 1799 the French republic seemed everywhere victorious. It had at last reached its "natural boundaries" by adding to the Austrian Netherlands those portions of the Holy Roman Empire which lay on the left bank[1] of the Rhine, and, to the south, the duchy of Savoy. It had reorganized its neighbors, the Batavian Republic, the Helvetic Republic, the Ligurian Republic, the Cisalpine Republic, the Roman Republic, and the Parthenopean Republic, — all of which were to accept its counsel and aid it with money, troops, and supplies. Bonaparte had occupied Egypt and was on his way to Syria with gorgeous visions of subjugating the whole Orient.

Within a few months, however, the situation was completely changed. The Austrians defeated Jourdan at Stockach in southern Germany, and the French retreated to the Rhine. In Italy the brave Russian general, Suvaroff, with the small but valiant army which the Tsar had sent to the west, forced the French out of northern Italy and, with the aid of the Austrians, repeatedly defeated their armies and shut up the remains of their forces in Genoa, to which the Austrians laid siege. Suvaroff, after expelling the French from Piedmont, burned to push on into France. But the Austrian minister, Thugut, opposed the restoration of the king of Sardinia to his throne, and urged that Austria should be permitted to annex Piedmont since she alone would be powerful enough to keep the French out of Italy. Thereupon, utterly disgusted with his Austrian ally, Suvaroff turned northward through the Swiss mountains, across which he forced his way in spite of incredible difficulties, only to find that a second Russian army, which he had expected would join him, had been defeated by the French. Thereupon the Tsar, attributing the reverses of his armies to the

[1] That is to say, the bank which would lie to the left of one traveling down the river, in this case the west bank.

intrigues of the land-greedy Austria, broke off all relations with her and recalled his generals (October, 1799).[1]

The First Consul writes to George III and Francis II in the interests of peace

In November, 1799, the corrupt and inefficient Directory was, as we have seen, thrust aside by a victorious general to whom France now looked for peace and order. The First Consul sought to make a happy impression upon France by writing personal letters on Christmas Day to both George III and Emperor Francis II, in which he deplored a continuation of war among the most enlightened nations of Europe. Why should they "sacrifice to ideas of empty greatness the blessings of commerce, internal prosperity, and domestic happiness? Should they not recognize that peace was at once their first need and their chief glory?"

His advances not well received

The English returned a gruff reply in which Pitt declared that France had been entirely at fault and had precipitated war by her aggressions in Holland, Switzerland, and Egypt. England must continue the struggle until France offered pledges of peace, and the best security would be the recall of the Bourbon dynasty.[2] The Austrians also refused, though somewhat more graciously, to come to terms, and Bonaparte began secretly collecting troops which he could direct against the Austrian army that was besieging the French in Genoa.

Bonaparte crosses the St. Bernard Pass (May, 1800)

Bonaparte now proceeded to devise one of the boldest and most brilliant of campaigns. Instead of following one of the usual roads into Italy, either along the coast to Genoa or across the Alps of Savoy, he resolved to take the enemy in the rear. In order to do this he concentrated his forces in Switzerland and, emulating Hannibal, he led them over the difficult Alpine pass of the Great St. Bernard. There was no carriage road then as there is now, and the cannons had to be dragged over

---

[1] Naturally the republics which had been formed in Italy under French influence collapsed. Ferdinand returned to Naples and instituted a royalist reign of terror in which Nelson took part. His conduct met with hearty disapproval in England.

[2] This suggestion irritated the French and convinced them that England was their implacable enemy.

in trunks of trees which had been hollowed out for the purpose.
Bonaparte arrived safely in Milan on June 2, 1800, to the
utter astonishment of the Austrians, who had received no
definite news of his line of approach. He immediately restored
the Cisalpine Republic, wrote to Paris that he had delivered
the Lombards from the "Austrian rod," and then moved westward to find and crush the enemy.

In his uncertainty as to the exact whereabouts of the Austrians, Bonaparte divided his forces when near the village of
Marengo (June 14) and sent a contingent under Desaix southward to head off the enemy in that direction. In the meantime the whole Austrian army approached from Alessandria
and the engagement began. The Austrians at first repulsed
the French, and Bonaparte saw all his great plans in jeopardy
as he vainly besought his soldiers to make another stand. The
defeat was soon turned, however, into one of his most brilliant
victories, for Desaix had heard the firing and returned with
his division. Meanwhile the aged and infirm Austrian commander had returned to Alessandria, supposing that the battle
was won. The result was that the French troops, reënforced,
returned to the attack and carried all before them. The brave
Desaix, who had really saved the day, was killed; Bonaparte simply said nothing of his own temporary defeat, and
added one more to the list of his great military triumphs.
A truce was signed next day, and the Austrians retreated behind
the Mincio River, leaving Bonaparte to restore French influence in Lombardy. The districts that he had "freed" were
obliged to support his army, and the reëstablished Cisalpine
Republic was forced to pay a monthly tax of two million francs.

The battle of Marengo (June 14, 1800)

While Bonaparte had been making his last preparations to
cross the St. Bernard, a French army under Moreau, a very
able commander, had invaded southern Germany and prevented
the Austrian forces there from taking the road to Italy. Some
months later, in the early winter, when the truce concluded
after Marengo had expired, he was ordered to march on Vienna.

Moreau defeats the Austrian army in the forest of Hohenlinden (December, 1800)

On December 3 he met the Austrian army in the snowy roads of the forest of Hohenlinden and overwhelmingly defeated it. This brought Austria to terms and she agreed to a treaty of peace at Lunéville, February, 1801.

Provisions of the Treaty of Lunéville (February, 1801)

In this, the arrangements made at Campo Formio were in general reaffirmed. France was to retain possession of the Austrian Netherlands and the left bank of the Rhine. The Batavian, Helvetic, Ligurian, and Cisalpine republics were to be recognized and included in the peace. Austria was to keep Venice.[1]

General peace of 1801

Austria's retirement from the war was the signal for a general peace. Even England, who had not laid down her arms since hostilities first opened in 1793, saw no advantage in continuing a struggle in which the continental powers refused longer to participate. After defeating the French army which Bonaparte had left in Egypt, she suspended hostilities and opened negotiations with France in the autumn of 1801, although the definite peace was not signed until the following March, at Amiens.

Two most important results of the treaties of 1801

Among many merely transitory results of these treaties, there were two provisions of momentous import. The first of these, Spain's cession of Louisiana to France in exchange for certain advantages in Italy, does not concern us here directly. But

(*a*) Bonaparte sells Louisiana to the United States (1803)

when war again broke out Bonaparte sold the district to the United States, and among the many transfers of territory that he made during his reign, none was more important than this. We must, however, treat with some detail the second of the great changes, which led to the complete reorganization of Germany and ultimately rendered possible the establishment of the present powerful German Empire.

(*b*) Effects of the cession of the left bank of the Rhine to France

In the Treaty of Lunéville, the Emperor had agreed on his own part, as the ruler of Austria, and on the part of the Holy Roman Empire, that the French republic should thereafter possess in full sovereignty the territories of the Empire which lay on the left bank of the Rhine, and that thereafter the Rhine

[1] The text of this treaty may be found in the *Readings*, sect. 42.

should form the boundary of France from the point where it left the Helvetic Republic to the point where it entered the Batavian Republic. As an inevitable consequence of this cession, numerous rulers and towns — nearly a hundred in number — found themselves dispossessed wholly or in part of their lands. The territories involved included the Palatinate and the duchy of Jülich (both of which then belonged to Bavaria), the possessions of the archbishops of Treves and Cologne and of the bishop of Liége, the ancient free cities of Worms, Speyer, and Cologne, Prussia's duchy of Cleves, besides the tiny realms of dozens of counts and abbots.

The Empire bound itself by the treaty to furnish the *heredi-* *tary* princes who had been forced to give up their territories to France "an indemnity within the Empire." Those who did not belong to the class of hereditary rulers were of course the bishops and abbots and the free cities. The ecclesiastical princes were forbidden as clergymen to marry, and consequently could have no lawful heirs. Hence if they were deprived of their realms they might be adequately indemnified by a pension for life, with no fear of injustice to their heirs, since they could have none. As for the towns, once so prosperous and important, they now seemed scarcely worth considering to the more powerful rulers of Germany. Indeed it seemed absurd at the opening of the nineteenth century that a single town should be permitted to constitute an independent state with its own system of coinage and its particular customs lines. *Only the hereditary princes to be indemnified*

There was, however, no unoccupied land within the Empire with which to indemnify even the hereditary princes, like the elector of Bavaria, the margrave of Baden, the king of Prussia, or the Emperor himself, who had seen their possessions on the left bank of the Rhine divided up into French departments. It was understood by France, and by the princes concerned, that the ecclesiastical rulers and the free towns should pay the costs of this cession by sacrificing their territories on the right bank as well as on the left. The *secularization* of *The ecclesiastical states and the free towns to be used to indemnify the hereditary rulers* the church lands, — as the process of transferring them to lay rulers was called, — and the annexation of the free towns implied a veritable revolution in the old Holy Roman Empire, as one may readily see who will turn back to the map given above (p. 22) and note the purple areas which represent the vast possessions of the ecclesiastical rulers.

The work of the imperial commission in reconstructing Germany

A commission of German princes was appointed to undertake the reconstruction of the map; and the final distribution was preceded by an undignified scramble among the hereditary rulers for bits of territory. All turned to Paris for favors, since it was really the First Consul and his minister, Talleyrand, who determined the distribution. Needy princelings are said to have caressed Talleyrand's poodle and played "drop the handkerchief" with his niece in the hope of adding a monastery or a shabby village to their share. At last the Imperial Commission, with France's help, finished its intricate task and the *Reichsdeputationshauptschluss*, as the outcome of their labors was officially called, was ratified by the diet in 1803.

Destruction of the ecclesiastical states and free towns

All the ecclesiastical states except Mayence were turned over to lay rulers, while of the forty-eight imperial cities only six were left. Three of these — Hamburg, Bremen, and Lübeck — still exist as members of the new German Empire. No map could make clear all the shiftings of territory which the Imperial Commission sanctioned. A few examples will serve to illustrate the complexity of their procedure and the strange microscopic divisions of the Empire.[1]

Examples of indemnification

Prussia received in return for Cleves and other small territories the bishoprics of Hildesheim and Paderborn, a part of the bishopric of Münster and of the lands of the elector of Mayence, the territories of the abbots, or abbesses, of Herford, Quedlinburg, Elten, Essen, Werden, and Kappenberg, and the free towns of Mühlhausen, Nordhausen, and Goslar, — over

[1] It has not been deemed feasible to give a map here to illustrate the innumerable changes effected by the *Reichsdeputationshauptschluss*. See map in Droysen, *Historischer Handatlas*, and the extraordinary maps at the end of Putzger's *Historischer Schul-Atlas*.

four times the area that she had lost. The elector of Bavaria, for more considerable sacrifices on the left bank, was rewarded with the bishoprics of Würzburg, Bamberg, Freising, Augsburg, and Passau, besides the lands of twelve abbots and of seventeen free towns; which materially extended his boundaries. Austria got the bishoprics of Brixen and Trent; the duke of Würtemberg and the margrave of Baden also rounded out and consolidated their dominions. A host of princes and counts received their little allotments of land or were assigned an income of a few thousand gulden to solace their woes,[1] but the more important rulers carried off the lion's share of the spoils. Bonaparte wished to add Parma as well as Piedmont to France, so the duke of Parma was given Tuscany, and the grand duke of Tuscany was indemnified with the archbishopric of Salzburg.[2]

These bewildering details are only given here to make clear the hopelessly minute subdivision of the old Holy Roman Empire and the importance of the partial amalgamation which took place in 1803. One hundred and twelve sovereign and independent states lying to the east of the Rhine were wiped out by being annexed to larger states, such as Prussia, Austria, Bavaria, Würtemberg, Baden, Hesse, etc., while nearly a hundred more had disappeared when the left bank of the Rhine was converted into departments by the French.

Over two hundred independent states extinguished

Although Germany never sank to a lower degree of national degradation than at this period, this consolidation was nevertheless the beginning of her political regeneration. Bonaparte, it is true, hoped to weaken rather than to strengthen the Empire, for by increasing the territory and power of the

Bonaparte's purpose to gain allies in southern Germany

---

[1] For example, the prince of Bretzenheim, for the loss of the villages of Bretzenheim and Winzenheim, was given a "princely" nunnery on the lake of Constance; the poor princess of Isenburg, countess of Parkstein, who lost a part of the tiny Reipoltskirchen, received an annuity of twenty-three thousand gulden and a share in the tolls paid by boats on the Rhine, and so on.

[2] As for the knights, who were the least among the German rulers, those who had lost their few acres on the left bank were not indemnified, and those on the right bank were quietly deprived of their political rights within the next two or three years by the princes within whose territories they happened to lie.

southern states — Bavaria, Würtemberg, Hesse, and Baden —
he expected to gain the permanent friendship of their rulers
and so create a "third Germany" which he could play off
against Austria and Prussia. He succeeded for a time in this
design, but the consolidation of 1803 paved the way, as we
shall see, for the creation sixty-seven years later of the present
German Empire.

REFERENCES

Youth of Bonaparte: FOURNIER, *Napoleon*, chaps. i and ii,
pp. 1–37; JOHNSTON, *Napoleon*, chap. i, pp. 1–13; ROSE, *The
Life of Napoleon I*, Vol. I, chap. i, pp. 1–21.

The Beginning of Bonaparte's Military Career: JOHNSTON, chap.
ii, pp. 14–26; *Cambridge Modern History*, Vol. VIII, chap. xviii,
pp. 560 *sqq.*; ROSE, Vol. I, chaps. ii and iii, pp. 22–69.

The First Italian Campaign: FOURNIER, chap. v, pp. 72–110;
FYFFE, *History of Modern Europe*, chap. iii, pp. 74–103; *Cambridge Modern History*, Vol. VIII, chap. xviii, pp. 553–593;
JOHNSTON, pp. 27–44; ROSE, Vol. I, chaps. iv–vii, pp. 70–158.

The Egyptian Expedition: FOURNIER, chap. vi, pp. 111–153;
JOHNSTON, pp. 44–58; *Cambridge Modern History*, Vol. VIII,
chap. xix, pp. 594–619; ROSE, Vol. I, chaps. viii and ix,
pp. 159–197.

Overthrow of the Directory and Establishment of the Consulate:
FOURNIER, chap. vii, pp. 154–187; FYFFE, chap. iv, pp. 104–144; JOHNSTON, pp. 59–78; *Cambridge Modern History*, Vol. IX,
chap. i, pp. 1–33; ROSE, Vol. I, chap. x, pp. 198–220.

CHAPTER XV

EUROPE AND NAPOLEON

BONAPARTE RESTORES ORDER AND PROSPERITY
IN FRANCE

42. Bonaparte was by no means merely a military genius; he was a distinguished statesman as well. He found France in a sad plight after ten years of rapid and radical change, incompetent government, and general disorder. The turmoil of the Reign of Terror had been followed by the mismanagement and corruption of the Directory. There had been no opportunity to perfect the elaborate and thoroughgoing reforms introduced by the first National Assembly, and the work of the Revolution remained but half done. Bonaparte's officials reported to him that the highways were infested with murderous bands of robbers, that the roads and bridges were dilapidated and the harbors filled with sand. The manufacturers and business men were discouraged and industry was demoralized. *General disorder in France under the Directory*

The financial situation was intolerable. The disorder had reached such a pitch that scarcely any taxes were paid in the year 1800. The *assignats* had so depreciated in March, 1796, that three hundred francs in paper were required to procure one in gold. Thereupon the Directory had withdrawn them at one thirtieth of their value and substituted another kind of paper money which rapidly declined in value in the same way that the *assignats* had done. The hard-beset government had issued all sorts of government securities which were at a hopeless discount, and had repudiated a considerable part of the public debt. *The paper money*

The First Consul and his able ministers began at once to devise measures to remedy the difficulties, and his officials, scattered throughout France, saw to it that the new laws were enforced. The police was everywhere reorganized and the robbers brought to summary justice. The tax rate was fixed and the taxes regularly collected. A sinking fund was established designed gradually to extinguish the public debt; this served to raise the credit of the State. New government securities replaced the old ones, and a Bank of France was founded to stimulate business. The Directory had so grossly mismanaged the disposal of the lands of the clergy and emigrant nobles that they had brought in very little to the government. Bonaparte carefully cherished what remained unsold and made the most of it.

In no respect had the revolutionary governments been less successful than in dealing with the Church. We have seen how those priests who refused to swear to support the Civil Constitution of the Clergy had been persecuted. After Hébert's attempt to replace Christianity by the worship of Reason, and that of Robespierre to establish a new deistic worship of the Supreme Being, the Catholic churches began early in 1795 to be opened once more, and the Convention declared (February 21, 1795) that the government would no longer concern itself with religion; it would not in the future pay salaries to any clergyman, and every one should be free to worship in any way he pleased.[1] Thereupon both the "constitutional" and the non-juring clergy began actively to reorganize their churches. But while thousands of priests managed to perform their duties, the Convention, and later the Directory, continued

---

[1] This first law separating Church and State is interesting in view of the efforts which are now being made in France to effect the same result (see below, sect. 77). The Convention's decree read as follows : " No form of worship shall be interfered with. The Republic will subsidize none of them. It will furnish no buildings for religious exercises nor any dwellings for clergymen. The ceremonies of all religions are forbidden outside of the confines of the place chosen for their performance. The law recognizes no minister of religion and no one is to appear in public with costumes or ornaments used in religious ceremonies." The Convention gruffly added other limitations on religious freedom. It required, for example, that all services be conducted in a semi-private manner, with none of the old gorgeous display or public ceremonials and processions.

to persecute those who did not take a new oath to submit
to the laws of the republic, and many suspected of hostility to
the government were exiled or imprisoned.

General Bonaparte, although himself a deist, nevertheless
fully appreciated the importance of gaining the support of the
Church and the Pope, and consequently, immediately upon becoming First Consul, he set to work to settle the religious difficulties. He freed the imprisoned priests upon their promising
not to oppose the constitution, while those who had been
exiled began to return in considerable numbers after the 18th
Brumaire. Sunday, which had been abolished by the republican calendar, was once more generally observed, and all
the revolutionary holidays, except July 14, the anniversary
of the fall of the Bastille, and September 22, the first day of
the republican year, were done away with.

Bonaparte hopes to gain the support of the Church

A formal treaty with the Pope, known as the *Concordat*, was
concluded in September, 1801, which was destined to remain
in force for over a hundred years. It declared that the Roman
Catholic religion was that of the great majority of the French
citizens and that its rites might be freely observed; that the
Pope and the French government should arrange a new division of the country into bishoprics; that the bishops should be
appointed by the First Consul and confirmed by the Pope, and
the priests should be chosen by the bishops. Both bishops and
priests were to receive a suitable remuneration from the government, but were to be required to swear to support the Constitution of the republic. The churches which had not been sold
should be put at the disposition of the bishops, but the Pope
agreed never to disturb in any way those who had acquired
the former property of the clergy.

The Concordat of 1801

It is to be observed that Bonaparte showed no inclination to
separate Church and State, but carefully brought the Church
under the control of the State by vesting the appointment of
the bishops in the head of the government, — the First Consul.
The Pope's confirmation was likely to be a mere form. The

Bonaparte brings the Church under the control of the State

bishops were to choose no priests who were not agreeable to the government, nor was any papal bull or decree to be published in France without its permission.[1]

How the Revolution had changed the Church

In some ways the arrangements of the Concordat of 1801 resembled those which prevailed under the *ancien régime*, but the Revolution had swept away the whole mediæval substructure of the Church, its lands and feudal rights, the tithes, the monks and nuns with their irrevocable vows enforced by law, the Church courts, the monopoly of religion, and the right to persecute heretics, — all of these had disappeared and General Bonaparte saw no reason for restoring any of them.

The emigrant nobles permitted to return

As for the emigrant nobles, Bonaparte decreed that no more names should be added to the lists. The striking of names from the list, and the return of confiscated lands that had not already been sold, he made favors to be granted by himself. Parents and relatives of emigrants were no longer to be regarded as incapable of holding public offices. In April, 1802, a general amnesty was issued, and no less than forty thousand families returned to France.

Old habits resumed

There was a gradual reaction from some of the innovations of the Reign of Terror. The old titles of address, Monsieur and Madame, again came into use instead of the revolutionary "Citizen." Streets which had been rebaptized with republican names resumed their former ones. Old titles of nobility were revived, and something very like a royal court began to develop at the Palace of the Tuileries; for Bonaparte, in all but his title, was already a king, and his wife, Josephine, a queen.

The grateful reliance of the nation on Bonaparte

It had been clear for some years that the nation was weary of political agitation. How great a blessing, after the anarchy of the past, to put all responsibility upon one who showed himself capable of concluding a long war with unprecedented glory for France and of reëstablishing order and the security of

---

[1] In the "Organic articles" which, at the instigation of the First Consul, were passed by the Legislative Body, all the old Gallican liberties were reaffirmed and all the teachers in the theological seminaries were to subscribe to, and agree to inculcate, the Declaration of 1682 (see above, p. 146).

person and property, the necessary conditions for renewed prosperity! How natural that the French should welcome a despotism to which they had been accustomed for centuries, after suffering as they had under nominally republican institutions!

One of the greatest and most permanent of Bonaparte's achievements still remains to be noted. The heterogeneous laws of the old régime had been much modified by the legislation of the successive assemblies. All this needed a final revision and Bonaparte appointed a commission to undertake this task. Their draft of the new code was discussed in the Council of State, and the First Consul had many suggestions to make. The resulting codification of the civil law — the *Code Napoléon* — is still used to-day, not only in France but also, with some modifications, in Rhenish Prussia, Bavaria, Baden, Holland, Belgium, Italy, and even in the state of Louisiana. The criminal and commercial law was also codified. These codes carried with them into foreign lands the principles of equality upon which they were based, and thus diffused the benefits of the Revolution beyond the borders of France.

The *Code Napoléon*

Bonaparte had always shown the instincts of a despotic ruler, and France really ceased to be a republic except in name after the 18th Brumaire. The First Consul was able to bring about changes, one by one, in the constitution, which rendered his own power more and more absolute. In 1802 he was appointed Consul for life with the right to choose his successor. But this did not satisfy his insatiable ambition. He longed to be a monarch in name as well as in fact. He believed heartily in kingship and was not averse to its traditional splendor, its palaces, ermine robes, and gay courtiers. A royalist plot gave him an excuse for secretly urging that he be made emperor. France might, he argued, be replunged into civil war as long as there was any chance of overthrowing the government. The only safety for a great nation lay in hereditary power " which can alone assure a continuous political life which may endure

General Bonaparte becomes Napoleon I, emperor of the French (1804)

for generations, even for centuries." [1] The Senate was induced to ask him (May, 1804) to accept the title of Emperor of the French, which he was to hand down to his children or adopted heirs. [2]

A new royal court established in the Tuileries

December 2, 1804, General Bonaparte was crowned, in the Cathedral of Notre Dame, as Napoleon I, emperor of the French. The Pope consented to grace the occasion, but the new monarch seized the golden laurel chaplet before the Pope could take it up, and placed it on his own head, since he wished the world to understand that he owed the crown not to the head of the Church but to his own sagacity and military genius. A royal court was reëstablished in the Tuileries, and Ségur, an emigrant noble, and Madame de Campan — one of Marie Antoinette's ladies-in-waiting, who had been earning an honest livelihood by conducting a girls' school — were called in to show the new courtiers how to deport themselves according to the rules of etiquette which had prevailed before the red cap of liberty had come into fashion. A new nobility was established to take the place of that abolished by the first National Assembly in 1790: Bonaparte's uncle was made Grand Almoner; Talleyrand, Lord High Chamberlain; General Duroc, High Constable; and fourteen of the most important generals were exalted to the rank of Marshals of France. The stanch republicans, who had believed that the court pageantry of the *old régime* had gone to stay, were either disgusted or amused by these proceedings, according to their temperaments. But Emperor Napoleon would brook no strictures or sarcastic comment.

Napoleon's censorship of the press

From this time on he became increasingly tyrannical and hostile to criticism. At the very beginning of his administration he had suppressed a great part of the numerous political newspapers and forbidden the establishment of new ones. As

---

[1] See *Readings*, sect. 42, for Napoleon's report of recent events submitted at the close of the year 1804.

[2] Josephine had borne him no children.

emperor he showed himself still more exacting. His police furnished the news to the papers, and carefully omitted all that might offend their suspicious master. He ordered the journals to "put in quarantine all news that might be disadvantageous or disagreeable to France."[1] He would have liked to suppress all newspapers but one, which should be used for official purposes.

NAPOLEON DESTROYS THE HOLY ROMAN EMPIRE AND REORGANIZES GERMANY

43. A great majority of the French undoubtedly longed for peace, but Napoleon's position made war a personal necessity for him. No one saw this more clearly than he. "If," he said to his Council of State in the summer of 1802, "the European states intend ever to renew the war, the sooner it comes the better. Every day the remembrance of their defeats grows dimmer and at the same time the prestige of our victories pales. . . . France needs glorious deeds, and hence war. She must be the first among the states or she is lost. I shall put up with peace as long as our neighbors can maintain it, but I shall regard it as an advantage if they force me to take up my arms again before they rust. . . . In our position I shall look on each conclusion of peace as simply a short armistice, and I regard myself as destined during my term of office to fight almost without intermission."

Napoleon on the necessity of war for France

On another occasion, in 1804, Napoleon said, "There will be no rest in Europe until it is under a single chief — an emperor who shall have kings for officers, who shall distribute kingdoms to his lieutenants, and shall make this one king of Italy, that one of Bavaria; this one ruler of Switzerland, that one governor of Holland, each having an office of honor in the imperial household." This was the ideal that he now found himself in a position to carry out with marvelous exactness.

Napoleon dreams of becoming emperor of Europe

[1] When the French fleet was annihilated by Nelson at Trafalgar in 1805, the event was not mentioned in the *Moniteur*, the official newspaper.

316 The Development of Modern Europe

Reasons for England's persistent opposition to Napoleon

There were many reasons why the peace with England (concluded at Amiens in March, 1802) should be speedily broken, especially as the First Consul was not averse to a renewal of the war. The obvious intention of Napoleon to bring as much of Europe under his control as he could, and the imposition of high duties on English goods in those territories that he already controlled, filled commercial and industrial England with apprehension. The English people longed for peace, but peace appeared only to offer an opportunity to Napoleon to develop French commerce at their expense. This was the secret of England's pertinacity. All the other European powers concluded treaties with Napoleon at some time during his reign. England alone did not lay down her arms a second time until the emperor of the French was a prisoner.

War between France and England renewed in 1803. Napoleon institutes a coast blockade

War was renewed between England and France, May, 1803. Bonaparte promptly occupied Hanover, of which it will be remembered that the English king was elector, and declared the coast blockaded from Hanover to Otranto. Holland, Spain, and the Ligurian Republic — formerly the republic of Genoa — were, by hook or by crook, induced to agree to furnish each their contingent of men or money to the French army and to exclude English ships from their ports.

Napoleon threatens to invade England

To cap the climax, England was alarmed by the appearance of a French army at Boulogne, just across the Channel. A great number of flatboats were collected and troops trained to embark and disembark. Apparently Napoleon harbored the firm purpose of invading the British Isles. Yet the transportation of a large body of troops across the English Channel, trifling as is the distance, would have been very hazardous, and by many it was deemed downright impossible.[1] No one knows whether Napoleon really intended to make the trial. It is quite possible that his main purpose in collecting an army

---

[1] The waves and currents caused by winds and tides make the Channel very uncertain for all except steam navigation. Robert Fulton offered to put his newly invented steamboat at Napoleon's disposal, but his offer was declined.

at Boulogne was to have it in readiness for the continental war which he saw immediately ahead of him. He succeeded, at any rate, in terrifying England, who prepared to defend her coasts against the French invaders.

The new Tsar, Alexander I,[1] had submitted a plan for the reconciliation of France and England in August, 1803; the rejection of this, the continued aggressions of Napoleon, and above all, his shocking execution of the duke of Enghien, a Bourbon prince whom he had arrested on the ground that he was plotting against the First Consul, roused the Tsar's indignation and led him to conclude an alliance with England, the objects of which were the expulsion of the French from Holland, Switzerland, Italy, and Hanover, and the settlement of European affairs upon a sound and permanent basis by a great international congress.

Alexander I joins England, April, 1805

Russia and England were immediately joined by Austria, who found Napoleon intent upon developing in northern Italy a strong power which would threaten her borders. He had been crowned king of Italy in May, 1805, and had annexed the Ligurian Republic to France. There were rumors, too, that he was planning to seize the Venetian territories which had been assigned to Austria at Campo Formio. The timid king of Prussia, Frederick William III, could not be induced to join the alliance, nor would he ally himself with Napoleon, although he was offered the electorate of Hanover, a very substantial inducement. He persisted in maintaining a neutrality which was to cost him dear.

Austria joins the coalition of 1805, but Prussia remains neutral

Napoleon had been endeavoring to get the advantage of the English on the sea, for there was no possibility of ferrying his armies across to England so long as English men-of-war were blockading the French squadrons and guarding the Channel. His efforts to free the French ships and concentrate them in the Channel proved vain, for Lord Cornwallis continued to

Napoleon fails to get control of the sea and turns his attention to Austria

1 Alexander had succeeded his father, Paul, when the latter was assassinated in a palace plot, March, 1801.

blockade one fleet in Brest while the other was forced to take refuge in the harbor of Cadiz where Lord Nelson watched it. These circumstances and the approach of the Austrian army through southern Germany led Napoleon to give up all thought of invading England and to turn his whole attention toward the east.

Napoleon
captures
Mack's army
at Ulm (Oc-
tober 20,
1805) and
then occupies
Vienna

He misled Austria by massing troops about Strassburg and pretending that he was going to march through the Black Forest. Consequently, the Austrian general, Mack, concentrated his forces about Ulm in order to be ready for the French when they should appear. Napoleon was, however, really taking his armies around to the north through Mayence and Coblenz, so that he occupied Munich, October 14, and cut off the Austrians from Vienna in somewhat the same way that he had done when he crossed the St. Bernard Pass in 1800. He then moved westward, and six days later General Mack, finding himself surrounded and shut up in Ulm, was forced to capitulate, and Napoleon made prisoners of a whole Austrian army, sixty thousand strong, without losing more than a few hundred of his own men. The French could now safely march down the Danube to Vienna, which they reached, October 31.

Battle of
Austerlitz
(December 2,
1805)

Emperor Francis II had retired before the approaching enemy and was concentrating his troops north of Vienna in Moravia. Here he had been joined by the Russian army. The allies determined to risk a battle with the French and occupied a favorable position on a hill near the village of Austerlitz, which was to be made forever famous by the terrible winter battle which occurred there, December 2. The Russians having descended the hill to attack the weaker wing of Napoleon's army, the French occupied the heights which the Russians had deserted, and poured a deadly fire upon the enemy's rear. The allies were routed and thousands of their troops were drowned as they sought to escape across the thin ice of a little lake which lay at the foot of the hill. The Tsar withdrew the remnants of his forces, while the Emperor in despair agreed to submit to a humiliating peace, the Treaty of Pressburg.

By this treaty Austria recognized all Napoleon's changes in Italy, and ceded to his kingdom of Italy that portion of the Venetian territory which she had received at Campo Formio. Moreover, she ceded Tyrol to Bavaria, which was friendly to Napoleon, and other of her possessions to Würtemberg and Baden, also friends of the French emperor. As head of the Holy Roman Empire, Francis II also agreed that the rulers of Bavaria and Würtemberg should be raised to the rank of kings, and that they and the grand duke of Baden should enjoy "the plenitude of sovereignty" and all rights derived therefrom, precisely as did the rulers of Austria and Prussia.

The Treaty of Pressburg (December 26, 1805)

These provisions of the Treaty of Pressburg are of vital importance in the history of Germany. By explicitly declaring several of the larger of the German states altogether independent of the Emperor, Napoleon prepared the way for the formation in Germany of another dependency which, like Holland and the kingdom of Italy, should support France in future wars. In the summer of 1806 Bavaria, Würtemberg, Baden, and thirteen lesser German states united into a league known as the Confederation of the Rhine. This union was to be under the "protection" of the French emperor and to furnish him with sixty-three thousand soldiers, who were to be organized by French officers and to be at his disposal when he needed them.

Napoleon forms a new dependency, — the Confederation of the Rhine (1806)

On August 1 Napoleon announced to the diet of the Holy Roman Empire at Ratisbon that he had, "in the dearest interests of his people and of his neighbors," accepted the title of Protector of the Confederation of the Rhine, and that he could therefore no longer recognize the existence of the Holy Roman Empire, which had long been merely a shadow of its former self. A considerable number of its members had become sovereign powers and its continuation could only be a source of dissension and confusion.

Napoleon refuses longer to recognize the existence of the Holy Roman Empire

Francis II assumes the title of Emperor of Austria (1804)

The Emperor, Francis II, like his predecessors for several hundred years, was the ruler of the various Austrian dominions. He was officially known as King of Hungary, Bohemia, Dalmatia, Croatia, Galicia, and Laodomeria, Duke of Lorraine, Venice, Salzburg, etc., etc. When, however, the First Consul received as ruler of France the title of Emperor of the French, Francis determined to substitute for his long array of individual titles the brief and dignified formula, Hereditary Emperor of Austria and King of Hungary.

Francis abdicates as Emperor (August 6, 1806) and the Holy Roman Empire is dissolved

After the Treaty of Pressburg and the formation of the Confederation of the Rhine, he became convinced of the utter impossibility of longer fulfilling the duties of his office as head of the Holy Roman Empire and accordingly abdicated on August 6, 1806. In this way he formally put an end to a line of rulers who had, for well-nigh eighteen centuries, proudly maintained that they were the successors of Augustus Cæsar, the first Roman emperor. The slight bond that had held the practically independent German states together was now dissolved, and the way was left clear for a series of reconstructions which have resulted in the formation of a new and powerful German Empire with the king of Prussia at its head. But the story of this must be deferred.

Napoleon assigns Naples to Joseph Bonaparte and Holland to Louis

Napoleon went on steadily developing what he called "the real French Empire," namely, the dependent states under his control which lay outside the bounds of France itself. Immediately after the battle of Austerlitz, he had proclaimed that Ferdinand IV, the Bourbon king of Naples, had ceased to reign. He ordered one of his generals to proceed to southern Italy and "hurl from the throne that guilty woman," Queen Caroline, who had favored the English and entertained Lord Nelson. In March he appointed his elder brother, Joseph, king of Naples and Sicily, and a younger brother, Louis, king of Holland.

One of the most important of the continental states, it will have been noticed, had taken no part as yet in the opposition to the extension of Napoleon's influence. Prussia, the first power to conclude peace with the new French republic in 1795, had since that time maintained a strict neutrality. Had it yielded to Tsar Alexander's persuasions and joined the coalition in 1805, it might have turned the tide at Austerlitz, or at any rate have encouraged further resistance to the conqueror. The hesitation of Frederick William III at that juncture proved a grave mistake, for Napoleon now forced him into war at a time when he could look for no efficient assistance from Russia or the other powers. Prussia forced into war with France

The immediate cause of the declaration of war was the disposal of Hanover. This electorate Frederick William had consented to hold provisionally, pending its possible transfer to him should the English king give his assent. Prussia was anxious to get possession of Hanover because it lay just between her older possessions and the territory which she had gained in the redistribution of 1803. Question of Hanover

Napoleon, as usual, did not fail either to see or to use his advantage. His conduct toward Prussia was most insolent. After setting her at enmity with England and promising that she should have Hanover, he unblushingly offered to restore the electorate to George III. His insults now began to arouse the national spirit in Prussia, and the reluctant Frederick William was forced by the party in favor of war, which included his beautiful queen, Louise, and the great statesman Stein, to break with Napoleon. Napoleon's insolent behavior toward Prussia

The Prussian army was, however, as has been well said, "only that of Frederick the Great grown twenty years older"; one of Frederick's generals, the aged duke of Brunswick, who had issued the famous manifesto in 1792, was its leader. A double defeat near Jena (October 14, 1806) put Prussia entirely in the hands of her enemy. This one disaster produced complete demoralization throughout the country. Fortresses were surrendered without resistance and the king fled to the uttermost parts of his realm on the Russian boundary. Decisive defeat of the Prussian army at Jena, 1806

The campaign in Poland (November–June, 1806–1807)

After crushing Prussia, Napoleon led his army into what had once been the kingdom of Poland. Here he spent a winter of great hardships and dangers in operations against the Russians and their feeble allies, the Prussians. He closed a difficult campaign far from France by the signal victory of Friedland (not far from Königsberg), and then arranged for an interview with the Tsar. The two rulers met on a raft in the river Niemen (June 25, 1807), and there privately arranged the provisions of the Treaty of Tilsit between France, Russia, and Prussia. The Tsar, Alexander I, was completely won over by Napoleon's skillful diplomacy. He shamefully deserted his helpless ally, Frederick William III of Prussia, and turned against England, whose subsidies he had been accepting.

Napoleon dismembers Prussia in order to create the grand duchy of Warsaw and the kingdom of Westphalia

Napoleon had no mercy upon Prussia, which he ruthlessly dismembered by depriving it of all its possessions west of the Elbe River, and all that it had gained in the second and third partitions of Poland. From the lands which he forced Frederick William to cede to him at Tilsit, Napoleon established two new French dependencies by forming the Polish territories into the grand duchy of Warsaw, of which his friend, the king of Saxony, was made ruler; and creating from the western territory (to which he later added Hanover) the kingdom of Westphalia for his brother Jerome.

Terms of the secret alliance of Tilsit between Napoleon and the Tsar

Russia, on the other hand, he treated with marked consideration, and proposed that he and the Tsar should form an alliance which would enable him to have his way in western Europe and Alexander in the east. The Tsar consented to the dismemberment of Prussia and agreed to recognize all the sweeping changes which Napoleon had made during previous years. He secretly promised, if George III refused to conclude peace, to join France against England, and to force Denmark and Portugal to exclude English ships from their ports. In this way England would be cut off from all of western Europe, since Napoleon would have the whole coast practically under his control. In return for these promises, Napoleon engaged to aid the Tsar in seizing Finland from Sweden and annexing the so-called Danubian provinces, — Moldavia and Wallachia, — which belonged to the Sultan of Turkey.[1]

THE CONTINENTAL BLOCKADE

44. In arranging the Treaty of Tilsit, it is evident that Napoleon had constantly in mind his most persistent and inaccessible enemy, England. However marvelous his successes by land might be, he had no luck on the sea. He had beheld his Egyptian fleet sink under Nelson's attack in 1798. When he was making preparations to transport his army across the Channel in 1805, he was humiliated to discover that the English were keeping his main squadron penned up in the harbors of Brest and Cadiz. The day after he captured General Mack's whole army with such ease at Ulm, Nelson had annihilated off Cape Trafalgar the French squadron which had ventured out from Cadiz. After Tilsit, Napoleon set himself more earnestly than ever to bring England to terms by ruining her commerce and industry, since he had no hope of subduing her by arms. He proposed to make " that race of shopkeepers " cry for peace by absolutely cutting them off from trade with the continent of Europe and so drying up their sources of prosperity. *Napoleon's plan of bringing England to terms by ruining her commerce*

In May, 1806, England had declared the coast from the mouth of the Elbe to Brest to be " blockaded," that is to say, she gave warning that her war vessels and privateers would capture any vessel that attempted to enter or leave any of the ports between these two points. After he had won the battle of Jena, Napoleon replied to this by his Berlin Decree (November, 1806) in which he proclaimed that England had " disregarded all ideas of justice and every high sentiment which civilization should bring to mankind "; that it was a monstrous abuse on her part to declare great stretches of coast in a state of blockade which her whole fleet would be *Napoleon's Berlin Decree (November 21, 1806)*

[1] They now form the kingdom of Roumania.

unable to enforce. Nevertheless he believed it a natural right to use the same measures against her that she employed against him. He therefore retaliated by declaring the British Isles in a state of blockade and forbidding all commerce with them. Letters or packages addressed to England or to an Englishman, or even written in the English language, were not to be permitted to pass through the mails in the countries he controlled. All trade in English goods was prohibited. Any British subject discovered in the countries occupied by French troops, or in the territories of Napoleon's allies, was to be regarded as a prisoner of war and his property as a lawful prize. This was, of course, only a "paper" blockade, since France and her allies could do little more than capture, now and then, some unfortunate vessel which was supposed to be coming from, or bound to, an English port.

England prepared to grant licenses to neutral ships. Napoleon's Milan Decree (December 7, 1807)

A year later England established a similar paper blockade of the ports of the French Empire and its allies, but hit upon the happy idea of permitting the ships of neutral powers to proceed, provided that they touched at an English port, secured a license from the English government, and paid a heavy export duty. Napoleon was ready with a still more outrageous measure. In a decree issued from "our royal palace at Milan" (December, 1807), he ordered that all vessels, of whatever nationality, which submitted to the humiliating regulations of England, should be regarded as lawful prizes by the French privateers.

Sad plight of the vessels of the United States

The ships of the United States were at this time the most numerous and important of the neutral vessels carrying on the world's trade, and a very hard time they had between the Scylla of the English orders and the Charybdis of Napoleon's Berlin and Milan decrees.[1] The Baltimore *Evening Post* in September, 1808, calculated that if an American ship bound for Holland with four hundred hogsheads of tobacco should decide to meet England's requirements and touch at London

[1] For the text of the Berlin and Milan decrees, see *Readings*, sect. 44.

on the way, its owners would pay one and a half pence per pound on the tobacco, and twelve shillings for each ton of the ship. With a hundred dollars for England's license to proceed on her way, and sundry other dues, the total would come to about thirteen thousand dollars. On the way home, if the neutral vessel wished to avoid the chance of capture by an English cruiser, she might pay, perhaps, sixteen thousand five hundred dollars more to England for the privilege of returning to Baltimore with a cargo of Holland gin. This would make the total contributions paid to Great Britain for a single voyage about thirty thousand dollars.

Alarmed and exasperated at the conduct of England and France, the Congress of the United States, at the suggestion of President Jefferson, passed an embargo act (December, 1807), which forbade all vessels to leave port. It was hoped that this would prevent the further loss of American ships and at the same time so interfere with the trade of England and France that they would make some concessions. But the only obvious result was the destruction of the previously flourishing commerce of the Atlantic coast towns, especially in New England. Early in 1809 Congress was induced to permit trade once more with the European nations, excepting France and England, whose vessels were still to be strictly excluded from all the ports of the United States.

Napoleon expressed the utmost confidence in his plan of ruining England by cutting her off from the Continent. He was cheered to observe that a pound sterling was no longer worth twenty-five francs but only seventeen, and that the discouraged English merchants were beginning to urge Parliament to conclude peace. In order to cripple England permanently, he proposed to wean Europe from the use of those colonial products with which it had been supplied by English ships. He therefore encouraged the substitution of chicory for coffee, the cultivation of the sugar beet, and the discovery of new dyes to replace those — such as indigo and cochineal —

which came from the tropics. This "Continental System" caused a great deal of distress and discontent and contributed to his downfall, inasmuch as he had to resort to despotic measures to break up the old system of trade. Then he was led to make continual additions to his already unwieldy empire in order to get control of the whole coast line of western Europe, from the boundaries of Prussia around to those of the Turkish Empire.

NAPOLEON AT THE ZENITH OF HIS POWER (1808–1812)

Napoleon's policy in France

45. France owed much to Napoleon, for he had restored order and guaranteed many of the beneficent achievements of the Revolution of 1789. His boundless ambition was, it is true, sapping her strength by forcing younger and younger men into his armies in order to build up the vast international federation which he planned. But his victories and the commanding position to which he had raised France could not but fill the nation with pride.

Public works

He sought to gain popular approval by great public improvements. He built magnificent roads along the Rhine and the Mediterranean and across the Alps, which still fill the traveler with admiration. He beautified Paris by opening up wide streets and quays and constructing bridges and triumphal arches that kept fresh in the people's minds the recollection of his victories. By these means he gradually converted a mediæval town into the most beautiful of modern capitals.

The "university" established by Napoleon in 1806

In order to be sure that the young people were brought up to venerate his name and support his government, Napoleon completely reorganized the schools and colleges of France. These he consolidated into a single "university"[1] which

[1] Only the theological seminaries and the polytechnic schools were excluded from the university. Napoleon's plan resembled the Board of Regents which constitutes the University of the State of New York.

comprised all the instruction from the most elementary to the
most advanced. A "grand master" was put at its head, and
a university council of thirty members drew up regulations for
all the schools, prepared the text-books, and controlled the
teachers, high and low, throughout France. The university
had its own large endowment, and its instructors were to be suit-
ably prepared in a normal school established for the purpose.

The government could at any time interfere if it disapproved
of the teaching; the prefect was to visit the schools in his department and report on their condition to the minister of the
interior. The first schoolbook to be drawn up was the *Imperial Catechism;* in this the children were taught to say:
"Christians owe to the princes who govern them, and we in
particular owe to Napoleon I, our emperor, love, respect,
obedience, fidelity, military service, and the taxes levied for
the preservation and defense of the empire and of his throne.
We also owe him fervent prayers for his safety and for the
spiritual and temporal prosperity of the State." [1]

The *Imperial Catechism*

Napoleon not only created a new nobility but he endeavored to assure the support of distinguished individuals by
making them members of the Legion of Honor which he
founded. The "princes," whom he nominated, received an
annual income of two hundred thousand francs. The ministers
of state, senators, members of his Council of State, and the
archbishops received the title of Count and a revenue of thirty
thousand francs, and so on. The army was not forgotten, for
Napoleon felt that to be his chief support. The incomes of
his marshals were enormous, and brave actions among the
soldiers were rewarded with the decoration of the Legion
of Honor.

The new nobility and the Legion of Honor

Napoleon was, however, never content with his achievements
or his glory. On the day of his coronation he complained to
his minister, Decrès, that he had been born too late, that there
was nothing great to be done any more. On his minister's

Napoleon's discontent with his achievements

[1] See *Readings*, sect. 43, for further extracts from this extraordinary document.

remonstrating, he added : " I admit that my career has been brilliant and that I have made a good record. But what a difference is there if we compare ours with ancient times. Take Alexander the Great, for example. When he announced himself the son of Jupiter, the whole East, except his mother, Aristotle, and a few Athenian pedants, believed this to be true. But now, should I nowadays declare myself the son of the Eternal Father, there is n't a fishwife who would n't hiss me. No, the nations are too sophisticated, nothing great is any longer possible."

Napoleon's despotism in France

As time went on Napoleon's despotism grew more and more oppressive. No less than thirty-five hundred prisoners of state were arrested at his command, one because he hated Napoleon, another because in his letters he expressed sentiments adverse to the government. No grievance was too petty to attract the attention of the emperor's jealous eye. He ordered the title of *A History of Bonaparte* to be changed to *The History of the Campaigns of Napoleon the Great*. He forbade the performance of certain of Schiller's and Goethe's plays in German towns, as tending to arouse the patriotic discontent of the people with his rule.

Napoleon's European power threatened by the growth of national opposition to him

Up to this time Napoleon had had only the opposition of the several European courts to overcome in the extension of his power. The people of the various states which he had conquered showed an extraordinary indifference toward the political changes. It was clear, however, that as soon as the national spirit was once awakened, the highly artificial system created by the French emperor would collapse. His first serious reverse came from the people, and from an unexpected quarter.

A French army occupies Portugal (November, 1807)

After concluding the Treaty of Tilsit, Napoleon turned his attention to the Spanish peninsula. He was on friendly terms with the court of Spain, but little Portugal continued to admit English ships to her harbors. In October he ordered the Portuguese government to declare war on England and to confiscate

EMPEROR NAPOLEON I

all English property. Upon its refusal to obey the second part
of the order, he commanded General Junot to invade Portugal and take charge of the government. Thereupon the royal
family resolved to take refuge in their vast Brazilian empire,
and when Junot reached Lisbon they were receiving the
salutes of the English squadron as they moved down the Tagus
on the way to their new home across the Atlantic. Easy and
simple as was the subsequent occupation of Portugal, it proved
one of Napoleon's serious mistakes.

Owing to quarrels and dissensions in the Spanish royal
family, Spain also seemed to Napoleon an easy prey and he
determined to add it to his subject kingdoms. In the spring
of 1808 he induced both Charles IV of Spain and the crown
prince Ferdinand to meet him at Bayonne. Here he was able
to persuade or force both of them to surrender their rights to
the throne,[1] and on June 6 he appointed his brother Joseph
king of Spain. Murat, one of Napoleon's ablest generals, who
had married his sister, succeeded Joseph on the throne of
Naples.

Napoleon makes his brother Joseph king of Spain (1808)

Joseph entered Madrid in July, armed with excellent intentions and a new constitution. The general rebellion in favor
of the Crown Prince Ferdinand, which immediately broke out,
had an element of religious enthusiasm in it; for the monks
stirred up the people against Napoleon, on the ground that he
was an enemy of the Pope and an oppressor of the Church.
One French army was captured at Bailén, and another capitu-
lated to the English forces which had landed in Portugal.
Before the end of July Joseph and the French troops had
been compelled to retreat behind the Ebro River.

Revolt in Spain against the foreign ruler (1808)

---

[1] Charles IV resigned all his rights to the crown of Spain and the Indies "to
the emperor of the French as the only person who, in the existing state of
affairs, can reëstablish order." He and his disreputable queen retired to Rome,
while Napoleon kept Ferdinand under guard in Talleyrand's country estate.
Here this despicable prince lived for six years, occasionally writing a cringing
letter to Napoleon. In 1814 he was restored to the Spanish throne as Ferdinand VII, and, as we shall see later, showed himself the consistent enemy of
reform. See below, sect. 52.

Spain sub-
dued by arms
(December,
1808)

In November the French emperor himself led into Spain a magnificent army, two hundred thousand strong, in the best of condition and commanded by his ablest marshals. The Spanish troops, perhaps one hundred thousand in number, were ill clad and inadequately equipped; what was worse, they were over-confident in view of their late victory. They were, of course, defeated, and Madrid surrendered on December 4. Napoleon thereupon issued a proclamation to the Spanish people in which he said, "It depends upon you alone whether this moderate constitution that I offer you shall henceforth be your law. Should all my efforts prove vain, and should you refuse to justify my confidence, then nothing will remain for me but to treat you as a conquered province and find a new throne for my brother. In that case I shall myself assume the crown of Spain and teach the ill-disposed to respect that crown, for God has given me the power and the will to overcome all obstacles."

Napoleon
begins radi-
cal reform
in Spain

Decrees were immediately issued in which Napoleon abol-ished all vestiges of the feudal system, and declared that it should be free to every one who conformed to the laws to carry on any industry that he pleased. The tribunal of the Inquisition, for which Spain had been noted for hundreds of years,[1] was abolished and its property seized. The monasteries and convents were to be reduced to one third of their number, and no one, for the time being, was to be permitted to take any monastic vows. The customs lines which separated the Spanish provinces and hampered trade were obliterated and the customhouses transferred to the frontiers of the kingdom. These measures illustrate the way in which Napoleon spread the principles of the French Revolution by arms in those states which, in spite of their benevolent despots, still clung to their half-mediæval institutions.

The next month Napoleon was back in Paris, as he saw that he had another war with Austria on his hands. He left Joseph

---

[1] See above, p. 192.

on a very insecure throne, and, in spite of the arrogant confidence of his proclamation to the Spaniards, he was soon to discover that they could maintain a guerilla warfare against which his best troops and most distinguished generals were powerless. His ultimate downfall was in no small measure due to the persistent hostility of the Spanish people. Spain continues to require the presence of French troops

Austria was fearful, since Napoleon had gained Russia's friendship, that he might be tempted, should he succeed in putting down the stubborn resistance of the Spaniards, still further to increase his empire at her expense. She had been reorganizing and increasing her army, and decided that it was best to strike while some two hundred thousand of Napoleon's troops were busy in Spain. So the Austrian emperor's brother, the Archduke Charles, led his forces westward in April, 1809, and issued an appeal to the German nation in which he urged them to imitate the heroic Spaniards and rise against their oppressors. Although there was an ever-growing party in Prussia and southern Germany which longed to throw off Napoleon's yoke, the king of Prussia refused to join Austria unless Russia would lend her aid. The monarchs who composed the Confederation of the Rhine also clung to their " Protector," so Austria was left to meet " the enemy of Europe " single-handed. Austria takes the field against Napoleon (April, 1809)

After defeating the Archduke Charles in Bavaria, Napoleon marched on to Vienna, but he did not succeed in crushing the Austrian forces as easily and promptly as he had done at Austerlitz in 1805. Indeed he was actually defeated at the battle of Aspern (May 21-22), but finally gained a rather doubtful victory in the fearful battle of Wagram, near Vienna (July 5-6). Austria was disheartened and again consented to conclude a peace quite as humiliating as that of Pressburg. Battles of Aspern and Wagram (May and July, 1808)

She had announced that her object in going to war once more was the destruction of Napoleon's system of dependent states and had proposed " to restore to their rightful possessors all those lands belonging to them respectively before the Napoleonic usurpation." The battle of Wagram put an The Treaty of Vienna (October, 1809) end to these dreams and the emperor of Austria was forced to surrender to the victor and his friends extensive territories, together with four million Austrian subjects. A strip of land, including Salzburg, was given to the king of Bavaria; on the north, Galicia (which Austria had received in the first partition of Poland) was ceded to Napoleon's ally, the grand duke of Warsaw; and finally, along the Adriatic, Napoleon exacted a district which he added to his own empire under the name of the Illyrian Provinces. This last cession served to cut Austria entirely off from the sea.

Napoleon marries the Archduchess Maria Louisa (April, 1810)

The new Austrian minister, Metternich, was anxious to establish a permanent alliance with the seemingly invincible emperor of the French and did all he could to heal the breach between Austria and France by a royal marriage. Napoleon ardently desired an heir to whom he could transmit his vast dominions. As Josephine had borne him no children, he decided to divorce her, and, after considering and rejecting a Russian princess, he married (April, 1810) the Archduchess Maria Louisa, the daughter of the Austrian emperor and a grand-niece of Marie Antoinette. In this way the former Corsican adventurer gained admission to one of the oldest and proudest of reigning families, the Hapsburgs. His second wife soon bore him a son, who was styled "King of Rome."

Napoleon "reunites" the Papal States to France (1809)

While Napoleon was in the midst of the war with Austria, he had issued a proclamation "reuniting" the Papal States to the French Empire. He argued that it was Charlemagne, emperor of the French, his august predecessor, who had given the lands to the Popes and that now, since the tranquillity and welfare of his people required that the territory be reunited to France, it was his obvious duty to deprive the Pope of his dominions.

Annexation of Holland and the Hanseatic towns (1810)

Holland, it will be remembered, had been formed into a kingdom under the rule of Napoleon's brother Louis. The brothers had never agreed,[1] and in 1810 Holland was annexed

---

[1] Louis Bonaparte, the father of Napoleon III, and the most conscientious of the Bonaparte family, had been so harassed by Napoleon that he had abdicated.

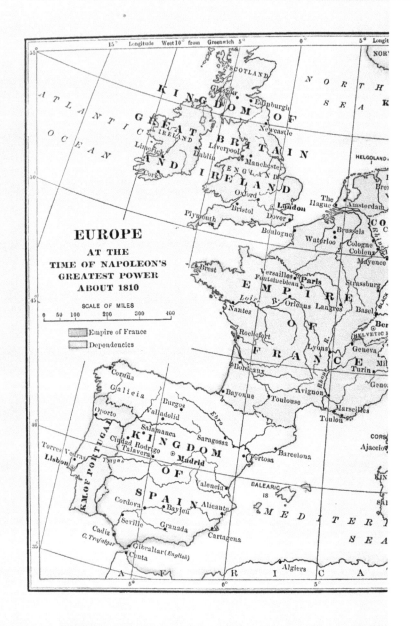

EUROPE

AT THE
TIME OF NAPOLEON'S
GREATEST POWER
ABOUT 1810

SCALE OF MILES
0   50   100   200   300   400

Empire of France
Dependencies

KINGDOM OF SWEDEN

Moscow

Borodino

Copenhagen

Riga

Vitebsk

Smolensk

EMPIRE

Königsberg

Korno

Tilsit

Friedland

Vilna

Rep.of Danzig

Swedish Pomerania

Stettin

K.M. OF PRUSSIA

Berlin

Posen

Thorn

G.R. DUCHY

Podubin

OF WARSAW

RUSSIA

Kiev

Pultowa

WARSAW

Dnieper R.

Breslau

Krakow

Galicia

Prague

Bohemia

INE

Brunn

Austerlitz

EMPIRE

Aspern

Wagram

Pressburg

Munich

Vienna

OF

Innsbruck

AUSTRIA

HUNGARY

Jassy

Moldavia

Tyrol

Trent

Trieste

Temesvar

Venice

Wallachia

Bucharest

Silistria

BLACK

Belgrade

Danube R.

Varna

SEA

ITALY

Ragusa

Cattaro

Sophia

TURKISH

Adrianople

Constantinople

Scutari

K.M. OF NAPLES

ADRIATIC SEA

Rome

Naples

Brindisi

Saloniki

EMPIRE

Otranto

Janina

Smyrna

Cosenza

IONIAN ISLANDS

NEAN

Palermo

KINGDOM OF SICILY

Messina

Syracuse

to France, as well as the German territory to the north, including the great ports of Bremen, Hamburg, and Lübeck.

Napoleon had now reached the zenith of his power. All of western Europe, except England, was apparently under his control. France itself reached from the Baltic nearly to the Bay of Naples and included a considerable district beyond the Adriatic. The emperor of the French was also king of Italy and "protector" of the Confederation of the Rhine, which now included all of the German states except Austria and the remains of the kingdom of Prussia. Napoleon's brother Joseph was king of Spain, and his brother-in-law, Murat, king of Naples. Poland once more appeared on the map as the grand duchy of Warsaw, a faithful ally of its "restorer." The possessions of the emperor of Austria had so shrunk on the west that Hungary was now by far the most important part of Francis I's realms,[1] but he had the satisfaction of beholding in his grandson, the king of Rome, the heir to unprecedented power. Surely in the history of the world there is nothing comparable to the career of Napoleon Bonaparte! He was, as a sage Frenchman has said, "as great as a man can be without virtue."

Maximum extent of Napoleon's power

THE FALL OF NAPOLEON

46. But all Napoleon's military genius, his statesmanship, his tireless vigilance, and his absolute unscrupulousness could not invent means by which an empire such as he had built up could be held together permanently. Even if he could, by force or persuasion, have induced the monarchs to remain his vassals, he could not cope with the growing spirit of nationality among their subjects which made subordination to a French ruler seem a more and more shameful thing to Spaniards, Germans, and Italians alike. Moreover there were two governments that he had not succeeded in conquering, — England and Russia.

Insecurity of Napoleon's achievements

[1] Emperor Francis II of the Holy Roman Empire had become Francis I, emperor of Austria.

Wellington
and the Eng-
lish in Spain
(1808-1812)
The English, far from begging for peace on account of the continental blockade, had annihilated the French sea power and now began to attack Napoleon on land. Sir Arthur Wellesley (a commander who had made a reputation in India, and who is better known by his later title of the Duke of Wellington) had landed English troops in Portugal (August, 1808) and forced Junot and the French army to evacuate the country. While Napoleon was busy about Vienna in 1809 Wellesley had invaded Spain and gained a victory over the French there. He then retired again to Portugal where he The lines of
Torres
Vedras spent the winter constructing a system of fortifications — the lines of Torres Vedras — on a rocky promontory near Lisbon. From here he could carry on his operations against the French with security and success. He and his Spanish allies continued to occupy the attention of about three hundred thousand of Napoleon's troops and some of his very best generals. So Napoleon never really conquered Spain, which proved a constant drain on his resources, a source of humiliation to him and of exultation and encouragement to his enemies.

Relations
between
Napoleon
and Alexan-
der I of
Russia
Among the continental states Russia alone was entirely out of Napoleon's control. Up to this time the agreement of Tilsit had been maintained. There were, however, plenty of causes for misunderstanding between the ardent young Tsar, Alexander I, and Napoleon. Napoleon was secretly opposing, instead of aiding, Alexander's plans for adding the Danubian provinces to his possessions. Then the possibility of Napoleon's reëstablishing Poland as a national kingdom, which might threaten Russia's interests, was a constant source of apprehension to Alexander.

Russia could
not afford to
enforce the
continental
blockade
The chief difficulty lay, however, in Russia's unwillingness to enforce the continental blockade. The Tsar was willing, in accordance with the Treaty of Tilsit, to continue to close his harbors to English ships, but he refused to accede to Napoleon's demand that he shut out vessels sailing under a neutral flag. Russia had to dispose of her own products in some way

and to obtain English manufactures, as well as coffee, sugar, spices, and other tropical and semi-tropical products which she had no hope of producing herself. Her comfort and prosperity depended, therefore, upon the neutral vessels which visited her Baltic ports.

Napoleon viewed the open Russian ports as a fatal flaw in his continental system and began to make preparations for an attack upon his doubtful friend, who was already beginning to look like an enemy. In 1812 he believed that he was ready to subdue even distant Russia. His more far-sighted counselors vainly attempted to dissuade him by pointing out the fearful risks that he was taking. Deaf to their warnings, he collected on the Russian frontier a vast army of half a million men, composed to a great extent of young French recruits and the contingents furnished by his allies.

Napoleon determines to attack Russia (1812)

The story of the fearful Russian campaign which followed cannot be told here in detail. Napoleon had planned to take three years to conquer Russia, but he was forced on by the necessity of gaining at least one signal victory before he closed the first season's campaign. The Russians simply retreated and led him far within a hostile and devastated country before they offered battle at Borodino (September 7). Napoleon won the battle, but his army was reduced to something over one hundred thousand men when he entered Moscow a week later. The town had been set on fire by the Russians before his arrival; he found his position untenable, and had to retreat as winter came on. The cold, the lack of food, and the harassing attacks of the people along the route made that retreat the most signal military tragedy on record. Napoleon regained Poland early in December, accompanied by scarcely twenty thousand men of the five hundred thousand with whom he had opened the campaign less than six months before.[1]

Napoleon's campaign in Russia (1812)

[1] This does not mean that all but twenty thousand had been killed. Some of the contingents, that of Prussia for example, did not take an active part in the war. Some idea of the horrors of the Russian campaign may be obtained from the descriptions given in the *Readings*, sect. 46.

He hastened back to Paris, where he freely misrepresented
the true state of affairs, even declaring that the army was in
good condition up to the time when he had turned it over to
Murat in December. While the loss of men in the Russian
campaign was enormous, just those few had naturally survived
who would be most essential in the formation of a new army,
namely the officers. With their help Napoleon soon had a force
of no less than six hundred thousand men with which to return
to the attack. This contained one hundred and fifty thousand
conscripts who should not have been called into service until
1814, besides older men who had been hitherto exempted.

The first of his allies to desert Napoleon was Prussia, — and
no wonder. She had felt his tyranny as no other country had.
He had not only taken her lands; he had cajoled and insulted her; he had forced her to send her ablest minister,
Stein, into exile because he had aroused the French emperor's
dislike; he had opposed every measure of reform which might
have served to strengthen the diminished kingdom which he
had left to Frederick William III.

Prussia, notwithstanding the reforms of Frederick the Great,
had retained its half-feudal institutions down to the decisive
defeat of Jena. The agricultural classes were serfs bound to
the soil and compelled to work a certain part of each week for
their lords without remuneration. The population was still divided into three distinct castes, nobles, burghers, and peasants,
who could not acquire one another's land. The disaster of Jena
and the losses at Tilsit convinced the statesmen of Prussia —
among whom Baron von Stein and Prince Hardenberg were
conspicuous — that the country's only hope of recovery was a
complete social and political revolution not unlike that which
had taken place in France. They saw that the old system must
be abolished, the peasants freed, and the restrictions which
hedged about the different classes done away with, before it
would be possible to arouse public spirit to a point where a
great popular uprising might expel the intruder forever.

The first step toward this general reform was the royal decree of October 9, 1807,[1] intended to "remove every obstacle that has hitherto prevented the individual from attaining such a degree of prosperity as he is capable of reaching." Serfdom was abolished and the restrictions on landholding removed, so that any one, regardless of class, was at liberty to purchase and hold landed property of every kind.

Abolition of serfdom in Prussia (October, 1807)

Every thoughtful Prussian had been deeply shocked by the cowardly way in which the enemy had been permitted to occupy the whole country after a single defeat. Men like William von Humboldt and the philosopher, Fichte forwarded a moral and educational reform. The University of Berlin, now one of the foremost institutions of learning in the world, was founded, and four hundred and fifty-eight students matriculated during the first year (1810–1811). The *Gymnasien*, or high schools, were also greatly improved. A League of Virtue (*Tugendbund*), which was formed for the encouragement of morality and public spirit, did much to foster the growing love for the fatherland and the ever-increasing hatred of French domination.

Founding of the University of Berlin

The *Tugend-bund*

The old army of Frederick the Great had been completely discredited, and a few days after the signature of the Treaty of Tilsit, a commission for military reorganization was appointed with a military genius, Scharnhorst, at its head. The main aim of Scharnhorst was to give every man a share in the work of defending his country. Napoleon permitted Prussia to maintain an army of no more than forty-two thousand men, but Scharnhorst arranged that this should constantly be recruited by new men, while those who had had some training in the ranks should retire and form a reserve. In this way, in spite of the small size of the regular army, there were as many as one hundred and fifty thousand men ready to fight when the opportunity should come. (This system was later adopted by

The nationalizing of the Prussian army by Scharnhorst

[1] This decree may be found in the *Readings*, sect. 46.

the other European states and is the basis of all the great armies of to-day.) Moreover the custom of permitting only nobles to be officers was abandoned, and foreign mercenaries were no longer to be employed.

Yorck deserts Napoleon

The Prussian contingent which Napoleon had ordered to support him in his campaign against Alexander was under the command of Yorck. It had held back and so was not involved in the destruction of the main army. On learning of Napoleon's retreat from Moscow, Yorck joined the Russians.

Prussia joins Russia against Napoleon (February, 1813)

This action of Yorck and the influence of public opinion finally induced the faint-hearted king, who was still apprehensive of Napoleon's vengeance, to sign a treaty with the Tsar (February 27, 1813), in which Russia agreed not to lay down arms until Prussia should be restored to a total area equal to that she had possessed before the fatal battle of Jena. It was understood that she should give up to the Tsar all that she had received in the second and third partitions of Poland and be indemnified by annexations in northern Germany. This proved a very important stipulation. On March 17 Frederick William issued a proclamation "To my People," in which he summoned his subjects — Brandenburgers, Prussians, Silesians, Pomeranians, and Lithuanians — to follow the example of the Spaniards and free their country from the rule of a faithless and insolent tyrant.

Napoleon's campaign in Saxony (1813)

Napoleon's situation was, however, by no means desperate so long as Italy, Austria, and the Confederation of the Rhine stood by him. With the new army which he had collected after his disastrous campaign in Russia the previous year, he marched to Leipzig, where he found the Russians and the Prussians under Blücher awaiting him. He once more defeated the allies at Lützen (May 2, 1813), and then moved on to Dresden, the capital of his faithful friend, the king of Saxony. During the summer he inflicted several defeats upon the allies, and on August 26–27 he won his last great victory, the battle of Dresden.

Metternich's friendship had grown cold as Napoleon's position became more and more uncertain. He was willing to maintain the alliance between Austria and France if Napoleon would abandon a considerable portion of his conquests since 1806. As Napoleon refused to do this, Austria joined the allies in August. Meanwhile Sweden, which a year or two before had chosen one of Napoleon's marshals, Bernadotte, as its crown prince,[1] also joined the allies and sent an army into northern Germany. Austria and Sweden turn against Napoleon

Finding that the allied armies of Russia, Prussia, Austria, and Sweden, under excellent generals like Blücher and Bernadotte, had at last learned that it was necessary to coöperate if they hoped to crush their ever-alert enemy, and that they were preparing to cut him off from France, Napoleon retreated early in October to Leipzig. Here the tremendous "Battle of the Nations," as the Germans love to call it, raged for four days. No less than one hundred and twenty thousand men were killed or wounded and Napoleon was totally defeated (October 16–19). Napoleon defeated in the battle of Leipzig (October, 1813).

As the emperor of the French escaped across the Rhine with the remnants of his army, the whole fabric of his vast political edifice crumbled. The members of the Confederation of the Rhine renounced their protector and joined the allies. Jerome fled from his kingdom of Westphalia, and the Dutch drove the French officials out of Holland. Wellington had been steadily and successfully engaged in aiding the Spanish against their common enemy and by the end of 1813 Spain was practically cleared of the French intruders so that Wellington could press on across the Pyrenees into France.[2] The dissolution of Napoleon's empire

---

[1] See below, p. 350.

[2] The United States exasperated by England's interference with her commerce and her impressment of American seamen declared war against Great Britain in June, 1812. This exercised no appreciable effect upon the course of affairs in Europe. The Americans succeeded in capturing a surprising number of English ships and preventing the enemy from invading New England or taking New Orleans. On the other hand, the English succeeded in defending the Canadian boundary and took and destroyed Washington (August, 1814) just before the opening of the Congress of Vienna. Peace was concluded at Ghent before the end of the year, after about a year and a half of hostilities.

Occupation
of Paris by
the allies
(March 31,
1814)

In spite of these disasters, Napoleon refused the propositions of peace made on condition that he would content himself henceforth with his dominion over France. The allies
consequently marched into France, and the almost superhuman
activity of the hard-pressed emperor could not prevent their
occupation of Paris (March 31, 1814). Napoleon was forced
to abdicate, and the allies, in seeming derision, granted him
full sovereignty over the tiny island of Elba, off the coast of
Tuscany, and permitted him to retain his imperial title. In
reality he was a prisoner on his island kingdom, and the
Bourbons reigned again in France.

Napoleon ab-
dicates and
is banished
to the island
of Elba

Return of
Napoleon

Within a year, encouraged by the dissensions of the allies
and the unpopularity of the Bourbons, he made his escape,
landed in France (March 1, 1815), and was received with
enthusiasm by a portion of the army. Yet France as a whole
was indifferent, if not hostile, to his attempt to reëstablish his
power. Certainly no one could place confidence in his talk of
peace and liberty. Moreover, whatever disagreement there
might be among the allies on other matters, there was perfect
unanimity in their attitude toward "the enemy and destroyer
of the world's peace." They solemnly proclaimed him an
outlaw, and devoted him to public vengeance.

Battle of
Waterloo,
June, 1815

Upon learning that English troops under Wellington and a
Prussian army under Blücher had arrived in the Netherlands,
Napoleon decided to attack them with such troops as he
could collect. In the first engagements he defeated and drove
back the Prussians. Wellington then took his station south
of Brussels, at Waterloo. Napoleon advanced against him
(June 18, 1815) and might have defeated the English had
they not been opportunely reënforced by Blücher's Prussians,
who had recovered themselves. As it was, Napoleon lost the
most memorable of modern battles. Yet even if he had not
been defeated at Waterloo, he could not long have opposed
the vast armies which were being concentrated to overthrow
him.

The fugitive emperor hastened to the coast, but found it so carefully guarded by English ships that he decided to throw himself upon the generosity of the English nation. The British government treated him, however, as a dangerous prisoner of war rather than as a retired foreign general and statesman of distinction who desired, as he claimed, to finish his days in peaceful seclusion. He was banished with a few companions and guards to the remote island of Saint Helena.[1] Here he spent the six years until his death on May 5, 1821, brooding over his past glories and dictating his memoirs, in which he strove to justify his career and explain his motives.

(margin: Napoleon banished to St. Helena)

" For the general history of Europe the captivity at St. Helena possesses a double interest. Not only did it invest the career of the fallen hero with an atmosphere of martyrdom and pathos, which gave it a new and distinct appeal, but it enabled him to arrange a pose before the mirror of history, to soften away all that had been ungracious and hard and violent, and to draw in firm and authoritative outline a picture of his splendid achievements and liberal designs. . . . The great captain, hero of adventures wondrous as the *Arabian Nights*, passes over the mysterious ocean to his lonely island and emerges transfigured as in some ennobling mirage." [2]

(margin: The Napoleonic legend)

REFERENCES

Napoleon's Reforms in France: FOURNIER, *Napoleon*, chap. ix, pp. 221–241; JOHNSTON, *Napoleon*, chap. vii, pp. 88–102; ROSE, *Life of Napoleon I*, Vol. I, chap. xii, pp. 245–278; *Cambridge Modern History*, Vol. IX, chaps. v–vii, pp. 107–207.

[1] An isolated rocky island lying south of the equator between Brazil and the African coast, from which it is separated by some thirteen hundred miles of water.

[2] H. A. L. Fisher in the *Cambridge Modern History*, Vol. IX, p. 757. Some historians have accepted Napoleon at his own valuation, among them J. S. C. Abbott, whose popular but misleading life of Napoleon has given thousands of readers a wholly false notion of his character and aims.

Campaign of Austerlitz: FOURNIER, chap. xi, pp. 283–324; FYFFE, *History of Modern Europe*, chap. vi, pp. 179–207; JOHNSTON, chap. ix, pp. 119–129; ROSE, Vol. II, chap. xxii, pp. 1–46.

Napoleon's Creation of New States: FOURNIER, chap. xii, pp. 325–355.

The Continental System: *Cambridge Modern History*, Vol. IX, chap. xiii, pp. 361–389.

Jena and Tilsit: FOURNIER, chap. xiii, pp. 356–390; FYFFE, chap. vii, pp. 208–246; JOHNSTON, pp. 130–147; ROSE, Vol. II, chaps. xxiv–xxvii, pp. 47–145.

Napoleon's Empire at its Height: FOURNIER, chap. xvi, pp. 493–535; FYFFE, chap. ix, pp. 271–306; ROSE, Vol. II, chap. xxxi, pp. 192–212.

Russian Campaign: FOURNIER, chap. xvii, pp. 536–579; FYFFE, chap. x, pp. 307–329; JOHNSTON, pp. 174–188; ROSE, Vol. II, chap. xxxii, pp. 213–245; *Cambridge Modern History*, Vol. IX, chap. xvi, pp. 483–505.

German War of Liberation: FOURNIER, chap. xviii, pp. 580–642; FYFFE, chap. xi, pp. 330–367; JOHNSTON, chap. xiv, pp. 189–209; ROSE, Vol. II, chap. xxxv, pp. 303–366; *Cambridge Modern History*, Vol. IX, chap. xvii, pp. 506–554.

Waterloo: FOURNIER, chap. xx, pp. 694–720; JOHNSTON, chap. xviii, pp. 223–238; ROSE, Vol. II, chap. xxxix, pp. 417–471; *Cambridge Modern History*, Vol. IX, chap. xx, pp. 616–645.

CHAPTER XVI

THE RECONSTRUCTION OF EUROPE AT THE CONGRESS OF VIENNA

The Congress of Vienna and its Work

47. The readjustment of the map of Europe after Napoleon's downfall was an extremely perplexing and delicate operation. Geographical lines centuries old had been swept away by the storms of war and the ambition of the conqueror. Many ancient states had disappeared altogether, — Venice, Genoa, Piedmont, the Papal States, Holland, and scores of little German principalities. These had been either merged into France or the realms of their more fortunate neighbors, or formed into new countries, — the kingdom of Italy, the kingdom of Westphalia, the Confederation of the Rhine, the grand duchy of Warsaw. Those which had survived had, with the exception of England and Russia, received new bounds, new rulers, or new institutions. When Napoleon was forced to abdicate, the princes whose former patrimonies had vanished from the map, or who had been thrust aside, clamored to be restored to their thrones. The great powers, England, Austria, Russia, and Prussia, whose rulers had been able with more or less success to resist the despoiler and had finally combined to bring about his overthrow, naturally assumed the rôle of arbiters in the settlement. But they were far from impartial judges, since each proposed to gain for itself the greatest possible advantages in the reapportionment of territory.

The least troublesome points were settled by the allies in the first Treaty of Paris, which had been concluded in May, 1814, immediately after Napoleon had been sent to Elba. They readily agreed, for instance, that the Bourbon dynasty

Extreme difficulty of adjusting the map of Europe after the great changes of the Napoleonic Period

Some matters settled at the first Peace of Paris, May 30, 1814

343

should be restored to the throne of France in the person of Louis XVI's younger brother, the count of Provence, who took the title of Louis XVIII.[1] They at first permitted France to retain the boundaries she had had on November 1, 1792, but later deprived her of Savoy as a penalty for yielding to Napoleon after his return from Elba.[2] The powers also agreed, at Paris, upon a kingdom of the Netherlands with increased territories to be established under the House of Orange ; the union of Germany into a confederation of sovereign states ; the independence of Switzerland; and the restoration of the monarchical states of Italy. The graver issues and the details of the settlement were left to the consideration of the great congress which was to convene at Vienna in the autumn.

Chief rulers and diplomats present at Vienna
It was an imposing assembly that met in the Austrian capital in September, 1814. The kings of Prussia, Denmark, Bavaria, and Würtemberg, the Tsar, and the emperor of Austria were there in person, besides many minor princes, most of whom had come to reclaim their lost territories. Among the celebrated diplomats were Lord Castlereagh and, later, the duke of Wellington, representing England and her decrepit sovereign, George III, who had now almost lost his mind ; the Prussian minister Stein, who had been driven from his country by Napoleon and was now chosen by Alexander I to advise him upon all matters in which Germany was concerned ; William von Humboldt, the founder of the University of Berlin, and Hardenberg, the Prussian reformer and diplomat, stood by the side of Frederick William III ; Prince Metternich, who for years was to be the chief adversary of further reform in Europe, was in charge of the interests of Austria.

---

[1] The young son of Louis XVI had been imprisoned by the Convention and, according to reports, maltreated by the jailers set to guard him. His fate has been a fruitful theme of historical discussion, but it is probable that he died in 1795. Though he never exercised power in any form, he takes his place in the line of French kings as Louis XVII.

[2] The second Peace of Paris (November, 1815), also provided for the return of the works of art and manuscripts which Napoleon had carried off from Venice, Milan, Rome, Naples, and elsewhere.

Of all the plenipotentiaries none had a more delicate task than the representative of France, Talleyrand, whose strange career mirrored all the extraordinary changes of the previous quarter of a century. A bishop under the old régime, he had been elected to the Estates General and had advocated the fundamental reform of the Church. It was he who moved that its property be placed at the disposal of the State. He was chosen to perform mass at an altar on the Champ de Mars when France sent delegates to Paris to celebrate the first anniversary of the fall of the Bastille. He ordained bishops under the Civil Constitution of the Clergy in spite of the Pope's prohibitions, and when he was finally excommunicated he determined to devote himself frankly to political life. Attaching himself to the fortunes of the rising General Bonaparte, he became minister of foreign affairs during the Consulate, and under the empire was made grand chamberlain and prince of Benevento. He was active in the negotiations which led to the treaties of Lunéville, Amiens, Pressburg, and Tilsit. Alive to the recklessness of Napoleon's later policy, he made overtures during the Russian campaign to the count of Provence and was influential in placing him upon the throne of France. When Louis XVIII selected him to represent France at Vienna, Talleyrand, in spite of his years of experience in difficult negotiations, left Paris with the most gloomy misgivings.[1] He was able, however, to take advantage of the dissensions of the allies, and soon restored his country to an influential place in the councils of the powers.

Although the brilliant assembly at Vienna, which was lav- ishly entertained by the half-bankrupt emperor, is called a "congress," it was in reality merely a meeting of rulers and diplomats who came together, like the brokers on the stock exchange, each to make the best bargain he could with his fellows. The congress was never regularly opened, nor did it assemble as a deliberative body in which motions were

[1] See *Readings*, sect. 47.

submitted to be acted upon by the plenipotentiaries present. On the contrary, the disputes in regard to territory were settled by treaties concluded by the parties chiefly concerned. Indeed the four allied powers, England, Austria, Russia, and Prussia, had come to some sort of an agreement before the congress opened and now proposed to submit their conclusions to the lesser powers for their assent.[1]

Impossibility of restoring the map of Europe to its condition before Napoleon's changes

The restoration of the map to its condition before Napoleon refashioned it was impossible, for Austria, Prussia, and Russia all had schemes for their own advantage which precluded so simple an arrangement. The congress was, in short, a scramble for territory on the part of the powers, who exhibited no more regard for ancient privileges and rights than Napoleon himself had shown. They tried to disguise their selfish schemes, but, as the secretary of the congress, Frederick von Gentz, said, "The grand phrases of 'reconstruction of social order,' 'regeneration of the political system of Europe,' 'a lasting peace founded on a just division of power,' and the like, were uttered to tranquillize the people and give an air of dignity and grandeur to this solemn assembly ; — but the real purpose of the congress was to divide among the conquerors the spoils taken from the vanquished."

Holland made a kingdom, and given the former Austrian Netherlands

Some questions, however, the allies easily settled. They confirmed their former decision that Holland should become an hereditary kingdom under the House of Orange, which had so long played a conspicuous rôle in the nominal republic. In order that Holland might be better able to check any encroachments on the part of France, the Austrian Netherlands (which had been seized by the French Convention early in the revolutionary wars) were joined to the new Dutch kingdom. Metternich was entirely satisfied with this arrangement, for he

1 The chief organ of the congress was a self-appointed "Committee of the Eight," composed of the representatives of Austria, Great Britain, Russia, and Prussia, who permitted the plenipotentiaries of the four other powers who had signed the Peace of Paris — viz. France, Spain, Sweden, and Portugal — to participate in their deliberations.

was relieved to have Austria removed from contact with the troublesome French. Moreover it fitted into the general plan of the congress to consolidate and strengthen, along the borders of France, the petty states whose weakness had for centuries invited French aggressions. The fact that most of the inhabitants of the Austrian Netherlands were not closely connected by language,[1] traditions, or religion with the Dutch had no weight in the councils of the powers, just as no such consideration had arisen in former times when the provinces had passed to Spain by inheritance and, later, to Austria by conquest. The Vienna Congress simply continued the old policy of carving out and distributing states among princes without regard to the wishes of the people concerned.

The territorial settlement of Germany did not prove to be so difficult as might have been expected. No one except the petty princes and the ecclesiastics desired to undo the work of 1803 and restore the old minute subdivisions which had been done away with by the *Reichsdeputationshauptschluss*. The restoration of the Holy Roman Empire could not be seriously considered by any one, but some sort of union between the surviving thirty-eight German states seemed to be expedient. They were accordingly united by a very loose bond, which permitted the former members of the Confederation of the Rhine to continue to enjoy that precious " sovereignty " which Napoleon had granted them. Formerly that portion of Germany which lies on the Rhine had been so broken up into little states that France was constantly tempted to take advantage of this disintegration to encroach upon German territory. After 1815 this source of weakness was partially remedied, for Prussia was assigned a large tract on the Rhine, while Bavaria, Baden, and Würtemberg stood by her side to discourage new aggressions from their dangerous enemy on the west.

The consolidation of Germany leaves only thirty-eight surviving states

Strengthening of Germany's western boundary

---

[1] About half the people of Belgium to-day speak French, while the remainder use Flemish, a dialect akin to Dutch, and a few speak German.

In the read-
justment of
Italy, Austria
assigned a
predominat-
ing influence Italy was not so fortunate as Germany in securing greater
unity than she had enjoyed before the French Revolution.
Napoleon had reduced and consolidated her various divisions
into the kingdom of Italy, of which he was the head, and the
kingdom of Naples, which he had finally bestowed on Murat,
while Piedmont, Genoa, Tuscany, and the Papal States he
had annexed to France.[1] Naturally the powers had no reason
for maintaining this arrangement and determined to restore all
the former monarchical states. Tuscany, Modena, the Papal
States, and Naples [2] were given back to their former princes,
and little Parma was assigned to Napoleon's second wife, the
Austrian princess, Maria Louisa. The king of Sardinia returned from his island and reëstablished himself in Turin.
There were few at the congress to plead for a revival of the
ancient republics of Genoa and Venice. The lands of the
former were therefore added to those of the king of Sardinia,
in order to make as firm a bulwark as possible against France.
Austria deemed the territories of Venice a fair compensation
for the loss of the Netherlands, and was accordingly permitted
to add Venetia to her old duchy of Milan and thus form a new
province in northern Italy, the so-called Lombardo-Venetian
kingdom.

[1] Nothing need be said of a half dozen petty Italian territories, — Lucca, San
Marino, Benevento, etc.

[2] Modena, as well as Tuscany, became a so-called secundo-geniture of Austria,
for an Austrian archduke had married the daughter of the duke of Modena,
who had been dethroned by Bonaparte in 1796. As for southern Italy, it will
be remembered that in 1808, when Napoleon shifted his brother Joseph to the
throne of Spain, he had made Murat king of Naples. Murat remained a faithful
ally of Napoleon until the end of his rule; he distinguished himself in the Moscow campaign, and fought with valor at the battle of Leipzig. At last, however,
to save himself and his throne, he entered into negotiations with England and
Austria, and signed treaties with them in January, 1814. Louis XVIII and Talleyrand were bent on dethroning him and pressed the matter at Vienna. On
Napoleon's return, in 1815, Murat, fearing that he could not maintain himself
with the help of his new allies, and believing that the returning emperor would
carry all before him, hastened northward with troops to aid him, only to be defeated by the Austrians and driven from Italy. Naturally the conquerors then
restored Ferdinand to his ancient kingdom, and when Murat, in the autumn of
1815, made a last attempt to regain it, he was captured and shot.

Switzerland gave the allies but little trouble. Napoleon in 1803 had assumed the rôle of "mediator," and had given the Swiss a new form of government; he had readjusted the old boundaries of the cantons and instituted a federal diet in which each canton, or state, had its representatives. The Congress of Vienna recognized the cantons as all free and equal, and established their "neutrality" by agreeing never to invade Switzerland or send troops through her territory. The cantons (which had been joined by the former free city of Geneva) then drew up a new constitution, which bound them together into a federation consisting of twenty-two little states. Switzerland

Even the Scandinavian countries, Denmark, Norway, and Sweden, were involved in the general settlement of 1815. At first Denmark and Norway, which for several centuries had constituted a single state, had kept out of the war, but when, in 1807, rumors reached England of Napoleon's secret treaty of Tilsit, in which he and the Tsar agreed to force Denmark into the continental system, the English squadron had bombarded Copenhagen, seized the Danish fleet, and carried it off to Portsmouth. This so angered Denmark that she concluded an alliance with Napoleon and remained his faithful ally down to his abdication. Denmark

Sweden had also for a time maintained neutrality, but Gustavus IV, who came to the throne in 1797, was a bitter opponent of revolution, and in 1805 he was so imprudent as to join England, Austria, and Russia in their coalition against Napoleon. It will be remembered that in the Treaty of Tilsit Napoleon had encouraged the Tsar to extend his territories by seizing Sweden's province of Finland. This Alexander had done in 1809, and at the same time the French occupied Swedish Pomerania [1] and added it to the Confederation of the Rhine. The impolitic conduct of Gustavus in joining in the war and the loss of the provinces led to his deposition. Since his uncle Sweden and Bernadotte

---

[1] A German district on the Baltic which had been awarded to Sweden at the close of the Thirty Years' War.

who succeeded him had no sons, the Swedes hit upon the singular notion of conciliating Napoleon by selecting one of his marshals, Bernadotte, as their crown prince and successor to the throne. After the Russian campaign Bernadotte joined the allies against Napoleon and signed a treaty with the Tsar confirming him in his occupation of Finland on condition that Sweden should be permitted to annex Norway if the war against Napoleon proved successful. He then turned his arms against Denmark and forced her to cede Norway to him.

Personal union of Sweden and Norway under the rule of the House of Bernadotte

The Congress of Vienna ratified these arrangements; Finland went to Russia, Norway to Sweden, and Swedish Pomerania was given to Prussia. The Norwegians protested, drew up a constitution of their own, and elected a king, but Bernadotte induced them to accept him as their ruler on condition that Norway should have its own separate constitution and government. This was the origin of the "personal union"[1] of Sweden and Norway under Bernadotte and his successors, which lasted until October, 1905.[2]

In these adjustments all was fairly harmonious, but when it came to the rewards claimed by Russia and Prussia there developed at the congress serious differences of opinion which

[1] This is the term applied in international law to describe the union of two or more independent states under a single ruler.

[2] This personal union worked very well so long as the joint king was tolerably free from control by the Swedish parliament, for the Norwegians had their own constitution and parliament, or Storthing, as it is called, and they could regard themselves as practically independent under a sovereign who also happened to be king of Sweden. However, especially during the past twenty years, the interests of the two countries diverged more and more widely. With the development of parliamentary government the diets of both countries desired to control the king's choice of ministers and the foreign policy of the two kingdoms. So, after a long period of friction, the two states mutually agreed to separate on October 26, 1905. Sweden retained her old king, Oscar II (1872–1907), while Norway elected as king Prince Carl, second son of Frederick, king of Denmark, and gave him the title of Haakon VII. The Norwegians still retain the constitution which was drawn up in 1814, but it has been several times modified by democratic measures. The parliament is chosen by all adult males twenty-five years of age, and when it meets it divides itself into an upper and lower house. Lutheranism is the state religion of Norway and Sweden. See Seignobos, *Political History of Europe since 1814*, pp. 554–566, and the *Statesman's Year-Book* (1907), pp. 1270–1288, 1483–1501.

nearly brought on war between the allies themselves, and which encouraged Napoleon's return from Elba. Russia desired the grand duchy of Warsaw, which Napoleon had formed principally out of the territory seized by Austria and Prussia in the partitions of the previous century. The Tsar proposed to increase this duchy by the addition of a portion of Russian Poland and so form a kingdom to be united in a personal union with his other dominions. The king of Prussia agreed to this plan on condition that he should be indemnified for the loss of a large portion of his former Polish territories by the annexation of the lands of the king of Saxony, who, it was argued, merited this retribution for remaining faithful to Napoleon after the other members of the Confederation of the Rhine had deserted him.

Russia and Prussia agree upon the fate of the grand duchy of Warsaw and of the kingdom of Saxony

Austria and England, on the other hand, were opposed to this arrangement. They did not approve of dispossessing the king of Saxony or of extending the Tsar's influence westward by giving him Poland; and Austria had special grounds for objection because a large portion of the duchy of Warsaw which the Tsar proposed to take had formerly belonged to her.

England, Austria, and France prepare to oppose the plans of Russia and Prussia

The great diplomatist, Talleyrand, now saw his chance to disturb the good will existing between England, Prussia, Austria, and Russia. The allies had resolved to treat France as a black sheep and arrange everything to suit themselves. But now that they were hopelessly at odds Austria and England found the hitherto discredited France a welcome ally. Acting with the consent of Louis XVIII, Talleyrand offered to Austria the aid of French arms in resisting the proposal of Russia and Prussia, and on January 3, 1815, France, England, and Austria joined in a secret treaty against Russia and Prussia, and even went so far as to draw up a plan of campaign. So France, the disturber of the peace of Europe for the last quarter of a century, was received back into the family of nations, and the French ambassador joyfully announced to his king that the coalition against France was dissolved forever.

Skillful diplomacy of Talleyrand

The Tsar
gets Poland,
and Prussia
becomes
powerful on
the Rhine
A compromise was, however, at length arranged without resorting to arms. The Tsar gave up a small portion of the duchy of Warsaw, but was allowed to create the kingdom of Poland on which he had set his heart. Only about one half of the possessions of the king of Saxony were ceded to Prussia, but as a further indemnity Prussia received certain districts on the left bank of the Rhine, which had belonged to petty lay and ecclesiastical princes before the Peace of Lunéville. This proved an important gain for Prussia, although it was not considered so at the time. It gave her a large number of German subjects in exchange for the Poles she lost, and so prepared the way for her to become the dominant power in Germany.

Map of
Europe in
1815 as com-
pared with
the condi-
tions estab-
lished by the
Treaty of
Utrecht
If one compares the map of Europe as it was reconstructed by the plenipotentiaries of the great powers at Vienna with the situation after the Treaty of Utrecht a hundred years before, several very important changes are apparent. A general consolidation had been effected. Holland and the Austrian Netherlands were united under one king. The Holy Roman Empire, with its hundreds of petty principalities, had disappeared and a union of thirty-eight states and free towns had taken its place. Prussia had greatly increased the extent of its German territories, although these remained rather scattered. The kingdom of Poland still appeared on the map, but had lost its independence and been reduced in extent. Portions of it had fallen to Prussia and Austria, but the great mass of Polish territory was now brought under the control of the Tsar, who was no longer regarded by the western nations as an eastern potentate but was regularly admitted to their councils. Austria had lost her outlying provinces of the Netherlands, which had proved so troublesome, but had been indemnified by the lands of the extinct Venetian republic, while her future rival in Italy, the king of Sardinia, had been strengthened by receiving the important city of Genoa and the adjacent territory. Otherwise, Italy remained in her former state of disruption and more completely than ever under the control of Austria.

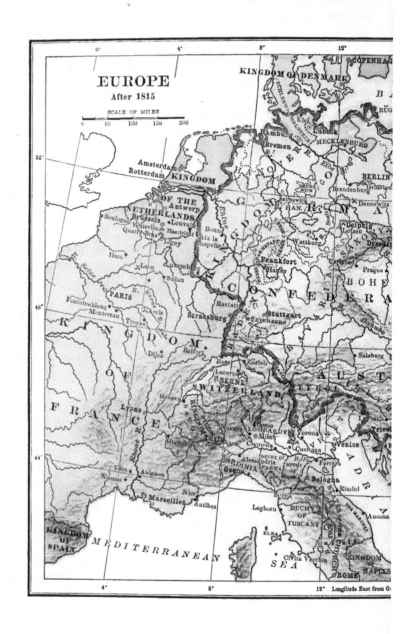

EUROPE

After 1815

SCALE OF MILES

0   50   100   150   200

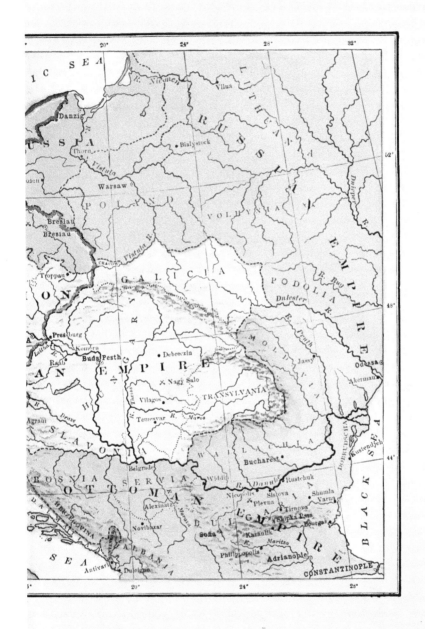

The gains of England resulting from the Napoleonic conflict, like all her other acquisitions since the War of the Spanish Succession, were colonial. The most important of these were Ceylon, off the southeastern coast of the Indian peninsula, and the Cape of Good Hope, which had been wrested from the Dutch (1806) while they were under Napoleon's influence. The latter territory, which had been settled by the Dutch as a halfway post for their ships bound to India and the Spice Islands, had a population of about sixty thousand, two thirds of whom were slaves, and the rest Dutch " Boers," or farmers, with a few French Huguenots, who, fleeing from the wrath of Louis XIV, had found homes in these wilds. Only a small area was then occupied and all the country northward now comprised in the Orange River Colony, Transvaal, and Natal regions was an unexplored wilderness. This seemingly insignificant conquest proved, however, to be the basis of the British expansion which has secured the most valuable portions of southern Africa.[1]

England gains Ceylon and the Cape of Good Hope

In spite of the loss of the American colonies on the eve of the French Revolution, England possessed in 1815 the foundations of the greatest commercial and colonial power which has ever existed. She still held Canada and all the vast northwest of the North American continent, except Alaska. Important islands in the West Indies furnished stations from which a lucrative trade with South America could be carried on. In Gibraltar she had a sentinel at the gateway of the Mediterranean, and the possession of the Cape of Good Hope not only afforded a basis for pressing into the heart of the most habitable part of Africa, but also a halfway port for

Vast extent of England's colonial possessions in 1815

[1] England also received from France the island of Mauritius in the Indian Ocean, east of Madagascar; Tobago, a small island north of the mouth of the Orinoco river, and Saint Lucia, one of the Windward Islands. From Spain England got the island of Trinidad near Tobago, and from Denmark the island of Heligoland, commanding the mouth of the Elbe (recently ceded to Germany). In the Mediterranean England held Malta and, as a protectorate, the Ionian Islands off the coast of Greece, thus securing a basis for operations in the eastern Mediterranean.

vessels bound to distant India. In India the beginnings of empire had already been made in the Bengal region and along the east and west coasts. Finally, in Australia, far away in the southern Pacific, penal settlements had been made which were in time to be supplanted by rich, populous, and prosperous commonwealths. In addition to her colonial strength England possessed the most formidable navy and the largest mercantile marine afloat.

The Congress of Vienna, under the influence of England, condemns the slave trade

The Congress of Vienna marks the disappearance of one of the most atrocious practices which Europe had inherited from an indefinite past, namely, the slave trade.[1] The congress itself did no more than declare the traffic contrary to the principles of civilization and human right but, under the leadership of England, the various states, with the exception of Spain and Portugal, were busy in doing away with the trade in human beings. The horrors of the business had roused the conscience of the more enlightened and humane Englishmen and Frenchmen in the eighteenth century. The English Quakers had been specially urgent in their protests, and in France Montesquieu, Necker, Lafayette, Brissot, and Mirabeau had helped to rouse popular opinion against it. Wilberforce and Clarkson carried on a systematic campaign in England, with a view of forcing Parliament to prohibit the trade in which England had been particularly prominent. Finally, in March, 1807, three weeks after the Congress of the United States had forbidden the importation of slaves,[2] Parliament prohibited Englishmen from engaging in the traffic. Sweden

---

[1] The slave trade, which had prevailed among the Greeks, Romans, and other ancient peoples, had been greatly stimulated by the discovery that African slaves could be profitably used to cultivate the vast plantations of the New World. The English navigator, Hawkins, had carried a cargo of three hundred negroes from Sierra Leone to Hispania in 1562, and so introduced English seamen to a business in which Portugal, Spain, and Holland were already engaged. It is estimated that previous to 1776 at least three million slaves had been imported into French, Spanish, and English colonies, while at least a quarter of a million more had perished during the voyage.

[2] England abolished slavery throughout all her colonies in 1833.

followed England's example in 1813, and Holland a year later. Napoleon, on his return from Elba, in order to gain if possible the confidence of England, abolished the French slave trade.

Napoleon had done more than alter the map of Europe and introduce such reforms in the countries under his control as suited his purposes; he had aroused the modern spirit of nationality, which is one of the forces that helped to make the nineteenth century different from the eighteenth. Before the French Revolution kings went to war without consulting their subjects, and made arrangements with other monarchs in regard to the distribution, division, and annexation of territory without asking the consent of those who lived in the regions involved. Practically no attention was paid to differences in race, for kings gladly added to their realms any lands they could gain by conquest, negotiation, marriage, or inheritance regardless of the particular kind of subjects that they might bring under their scepters. Louis XIV tried to annex the Austrian Netherlands to France, although a great part of the people spoke Flemish; and he claimed the Palatinate where German was spoken. Frederick the Great was willing to have Poles among his subjects as well as Silesians, and Austria added Italian Lombardy on the south and Polish Galicia on the north. There was indeed no reason why the people should be consulted, for the government was vested in the kings, who were responsible not to them but to God alone. When the people of Tuscany woke up to find themselves under a duke of Lorraine instead of the House of Medici, they had no more right to complain than a herd of cattle which is sold to a new owner.

Bishop Bossuet's notions of the divine right of kings, which he based on the Bible's account of the Hebrew rulers, were still in 1815 good enough for Prince Metternich and for many among the nobility and clergy, but the French Declaration of the Rights of Man in 1789 had proclaimed, "under the auspices of the Supreme Being," that the law was the expression

Marginal notes:

Disregard of nationality before the nineteenth century

The French National Assembly declares the monarch responsible to the nation, and so awakens political life among the people

of the general will and that every citizen had a right, personally or through his representatives, to participate in its formation. The king and his officials were made responsible for their public acts not to God but to the people. This idea that the nation had a right to control the making of the laws and the granting of the taxes, and to choose or depose its ruler, who was responsible to it, served to rouse a general interest in political questions, which could not possibly have developed so long as people were content to believe that God had excluded them from all participation in affairs of State. Political leaders appeared, the newspapers began to discuss public questions, and political societies were formed.

The French revolutionists did not emphasize national differences

The leaders of the French Revolution had not, however, been much interested in nationality. They believed that they had discovered a system of government, based upon the eternal rights of man, which was suited by nature to all peoples. The French Convention had promised to aid any nation which wished to free itself from the tyranny of a despot. They showed no inclination, however, to distinguish very carefully between Frenchmen, Dutchmen, Germans, Swiss, or Italians.

How Napoleon's conduct aroused the national spirit

Napoleon was also indifferent to nationality and his arbitrary policy in setting up and pulling down monarchies, and in remodeling the states of Europe to suit his fancy, was only a new, bewildering illustration of the arrogant habits of Louis XIV, Frederick the Great, and Catharine; but the opposition that it called forth, first in Spain and then in Prussia, indicated that the rulers in the nineteenth century would be compelled to consider the sentiments of the people they ruled as well as their own individual interests. The various nations became more and more keenly conscious that each had its own language and traditions which made it different from other peoples. Patriotic orators in Germany, Italy, and Greece recalled the glorious past of the ancient Germans, Romans, and Hellenes, with a view of stimulating this enthusiasm. National feeling may be defined as a general recognition that a people should have a government suited to its particular traditions and needs, and should be ruled by its own native officials, and that (if nations were entitled to political rights, as the French Revolution had taught) it was wrong that one people should be dominated by another, or that monarchs should divide up, redistribute, and transfer territories with no regard to the wishes of the inhabitants, merely to provide some landless prince with a patrimony.

We shall have to reckon hereafter with this national spirit which continued to spread and to increase in strength during the nineteenth century. It has played a great part in the unification of Italy and Germany, in the emancipation of Greece and the Balkan states from Turkish dominion, and in the problems which have faced Austria, with its heterogeneous population. Its demands, however, can scarcely ever be completely realized, since the mixture of people is so considerable that each can hardly expect to have its own territory all to itself and its own independent government. There are still Italians outside of Italy, Germans outside of Germany, Bulgarians outside of Bulgaria; and the laws of Switzerland have to be drawn up in no less than three languages to make them intelligible to the different races which inhabit that limited territory.

The mixture of races precludes the complete realization of the demands of the national spirit

The Holy Alliance: Metternich becomes the Chief Opponent of Revolution

48. In June, 1815, the Congress of Vienna brought together the results of all the treaties and arrangements which its various members had agreed upon among themselves, and issued its " Final Act," in which its work was summed up for convenient reference. A few days later the battle of Waterloo and the subsequent exile of Napoleon freed the powers from their chief cause of solicitude during the past fifteen years. No wonder that the restored monarchs, as they composed themselves

Horror of revolution and suspicion of reform after 1815

upon their thrones and reviewed the wars and turmoil which had begun with the French Revolution and lasted more than a quarter of a century, longed for peace at any cost, and viewed with the utmost suspicion any individual or party who ventured to suggest further changes. The word "revolution" had acquired a hideous sound, not only to the rulers and their immediate advisers, but to all the aristocratic class and the clergy, who thought that they had reason enough to abhor the modern tendencies as they had seen them at work.

Dangers threatening the permanence of the settlement at ViennaThere were plenty of grounds for suspecting that the Congress of Vienna had only checked the revolution in France to awaken it in other countries. The Belgians chafed under their forced union with Holland; the inhabitants of the Rhine districts which had been taken from France disliked the traditions of Frederick the Great's kingdom, of which the Congress of Vienna had made them a part; many Germans were disgusted that no firm national union had been established; while the Italians resented the intrusion of Austria in their affairs, and the Poles rebelled against being driven under the yoke of the hated Russia.

The Holy Alliance devised by Alexander I (September, 1815)It was clear that the powers which had combined to reëstablish order must continue their alliance if they hoped to maintain the arrangements they had made and stifle the fires of revolution which were sure to break out at some unexpected point unless the most constant vigilance were exercised. Alexander I proposed a plan for preserving European tranquillity by the formation of a religious brotherhood of monarchs, which was given the name of "The Holy Alliance." This was accepted by the emperor of Austria and the king of Prussia, and published in September, 1815. In this singular instrument their majesties, "in view of the great events which have taken place in Europe during the past three years, and especially in view of the benefits which it has pleased Divine Providence to shed upon those states whose governments have placed their confidence and sole hope in him, have reached the profound conviction that it is essential to base the policy of the powers, in their mutual relations with one another, upon the sublime truths which are taught by the eternal religion of God our Savior." They solemnly declare " that the present act has for its only aim to manifest to the whole world their firm purpose to have no other rule in the administration of their states and their relations with other governments than the precepts of this holy religion." They agree accordingly to view one another as brothers and compatriots, as "delegates of Providence to govern three branches of the same family." All the other European powers who should recognize the sacred principles of the act were to be welcomed cordially and affectionately into " this holy alliance."

The Tsar and Frederick William took the alliance seriously, but to most of the diplomats who had participated in the scramble for the spoils at Vienna, and who looked back upon the habits of monarchs in dealing with one another, it was an amusing vagary of the devout Tsar. Metternich declared it " verbiage " and Castlereagh, " a piece of sublime mysticism and nonsense." Alexander's well-meant league amounted, in fact, to nothing. It was not, as has often been supposed, a conspiracy of despotic monarchs to repress all liberal movements. It contained no definite allusions to the dangers of revolution or to the necessity of maintaining the settlement of Vienna. The name " Holy Alliance " came nevertheless to be applied by the more liberal newspapers and reformers to a real and effective organization of the powers opposed to change. In this case the monarchs did not unite in " the name of the Most· High " to promote Christian charity, but frankly combined to fight reform under the worldly guidance of Clement Wencelaus Nepomuk Lothaire, Prince of Metternich-Winneburg-Ochsenhausen.

The Holy Alliance not a union to prevent revolution

Metternich, who was destined to succeed Napoleon as the most conspicuous statesman in Europe, was born in 1773 and had followed the course of the French Revolution from the

Metternich's political creed

beginning. He had observed its excesses and the devastating wars which had grown out of it, and he saw only evil in the great changes which were taking place. As a member of a noble family he was opposed to liberal ideas and boasted that the reasoning of the French philosophers had left his stanch old beliefs untouched. The views of kingship entertained by James I and Louis XIV seemed to him perfectly sound. Men had no natural right to govern themselves or to decide upon their religious beliefs. All talk about constitutions and national unity was to him revolutionary, and therefore highly dangerous.

Any development of the spirit of nationality dangerous to Austria

He was doubtless much strengthened in his hostility to reform by the situation of Austria, whose affairs he had been guiding since 1809. No country, except Prussia, had suffered more from the Revolution, which it had been the first to oppose in 1792. Should the idea of nationality gain ground, the various peoples included in the Austrian Empire — Germans, Czechs, Poles, Hungarians, Italians, and the rest — would surely revolt and each demand its own constitution. Liberal ideas, whether in Austria, Italy, or Germany, foreboded the destruction of the highly artificial Austrian realms, which had been accumulated through the centuries by conquest, marriage, and inheritance without regard to the great differences between the races which were gathered together under the scepter of Francis I. Consequently to Metternich the preservation of Austria, the suppression of reformers and of agitators for constitutional government, and "the tranquillity of Europe," all meant one and the same thing.

Secret alliance of November 20, 1815

Accordingly, shortly after the signing of the Holy Alliance, a secret agreement was entered into by Austria, Prussia, England, and Russia, which frankly declared that the tranquillity of Europe depended upon the maintenance in France of the royal authority which the allies had restored, and furthermore, that it was their purpose to prevent renewed disturbance of the peace of Europe. In order to effect their ends the powers agreed to hold periodical meetings with a view to considering their common interests and taking such measures as should be expedient for the preservation of general order. Thus a sort of international congress was established for the purpose of upholding the settlement of Vienna.

The first formal meeting of the powers under this agreement took place at Aix-la-Chapelle in 1818 to arrange for the evacuation of France by the troops of the allies, which had been stationed there since 1814 to suppress any possible disorder. France, once more admitted to the brotherhood of nations, joined Metternich's conservative league, and that judicious statesman could report with complacency that the whole conference was a brilliant triumph for those principles which he held dearest. He was indeed the soul of the alliance and later used it, as we shall see, to crush dangerous reform movements in Italy and Spain; but he did not enjoy the permanent support of England, or even of France, and in spite of his efforts the world continued to move.

Congress of Aix-la-Chapelle, 1818

A glance at the map of Europe to-day will make plain that the Congress of Vienna failed to fix forever the metes and bounds, and the system of government, of the European states. Metternich's flimsy union of German states has given way to the German Empire. Prussia, Austria's old rival, has evidently grown at the expense of its neighbors, as several of the lesser German states of 1815 — Hanover, Nassau, and Hesse-Cassel — no longer appear on the map, and Schleswig-Holstein, which then belonged to Denmark, is now Prussian. It will be noted that the present German Empire does not include any part of the Austrian countries, as did the Confederation of 1815, and that, on the other hand, Prussia is its dominant member. The kingdom of Poland has become an integral part of the Russian dominions. Austria, excluded from the German union, has entered into a dual union with Hungary, in which the two countries are placed upon a footing of equality.

Main changes in the map of Europe since the Congress of Vienna

There was no kingdom of Italy in 1815. Now Austria has lost all hold on Lombardy and Venetia, and all the little Italian states reëstablished by the Congress of Vienna, including the Papal States, have disappeared. A new kingdom, Belgium, has been created out of the old Austrian Netherlands which the Congress gave to the king of Holland. France, now a republic again, has recovered Savoy but has lost all her possessions on the Rhine by the cession of Alsace and Lorraine to the German Empire. Lastly, Turkey in Europe has nearly disappeared, and several new states, Greece, Servia, Roumania, and Bulgaria, have appeared in southeastern Europe. It is the purpose of the following volume to show how the great changes indicated on the map took place and explain the accompanying internal changes, in so far as they represent the general trend of modern development, or have an importance for Europe at large.

REFERENCES

The Character of the Congress of Vienna: *Cambridge Modern History*, Vol. IX, chap. xix, pp. 576–588 ; FYFFE, *History of Modern Europe*, pp. 380–382 ; SEIGNOBOS, *Political History of Europe since 1814*, pp. 2–3 ; ANDREWS, *Historical Development of Modern Europe*, Vol. I, pp. 90–93.

The Polish-Saxon Controversy: *Cambridge Modern History*, Vol. IX, chap. xix, pp. 593–599 ; ANDREWS, Vol. I, pp. 93–97 ; FYFFE, pp. 381–387.

The Territorial Settlement in Italy: *Cambridge Modern History*, Vol. IX, chap. xix, pp. 601–604.

The Final Act of the Vienna Congress : *Cambridge Modern History*, Vol. IX, chap. xxi, pp. 646–663.

Union among the Powers to maintain the Vienna Settlement: *Cambridge Modern History*, Vol. IX, chap. xxi, pp. 663–671 ; FYFFE, pp. 408–411.

ANNOUNCEMENTS

THE DEVELOPMENT OF MODERN EUROPE

An Introduction to the Study of Current History

By JAMES HARVEY ROBINSON, Professor of History in Columbia University,
and Charles A. Beard, Adjunct Professor of Politics in Columbia University

VOLUME I.   The Eighteenth Century: The French Revolution
and the Napoleonic Period.   12mo. Cloth.   362 pages. With illustrations and maps.   List price, $1.50; mailing price, $1.60

VOLUME II.   Europe since the Congress of Vienna.   12mo. Cloth.
448 pages. With illustrations and maps. List price, $1.60; mailing price, $1.75

THESE volumes will meet the demand for a history of recent
times which shall explain the social and economic as well as
the political development of our own age, and shall also prepare
the student to understand the great problems of the world in
which he finds himself.

Their aim is to correct the general disregard of recent history,
— to enable the student to catch up with his own times so that
he may peruse with intelligence the news given in the morning
paper.

Much less space is devoted to purely political and military
events than has been commonly assigned to them in histories of
the nineteenth century.   On the other hand, the more fundamental economic matters — the Industrial Revolution, commerce
and the colonies, the internal reforms of the European states, etc.
— have been generously treated.

The necessarily succinct outline of events which fills the books
can be considerably amplified and enlivened by " Readings in
Modern European History " from the same authors, which follows
the narrative chapter by chapter, and furnishes examples of the
stuff of which history is made.

110½

GINN & COMPANY Publishers

READINGS IN MODERN EURO-PEAN HISTORY

*A collection of extracts from sources chosen with the purpose of illustrating
some of the chief phases of the development of Europe
during the last two hundred years*

By JAMES HARVEY ROBINSON, Professor of History, and CHARLES A. BEARD,
Adjunct Professor of Politics, in Columbia University

Volume I. The Eighteenth Century : The French Revolution and
the Napoleonic Period. 12mo. Cloth. Illustrated. 410 pages. List
price, $1.40 ; mailing price, $1.50

Volume II. Europe since the Congress of Vienna. 12mo. Cloth.
Illustrated. 541 pages. List price, $1.50 ; mailing price, $1.65

"READINGS IN MODERN EUROPEAN HISTORY"
aims to stimulate the student to real thought and interest in
his work by bringing him right to the sources of historical knowledge and enabling him to see the very words of those who, writing when the past was present, can carry him back to themselves
and make their times his own. In this way the book offers the
proper background and atmosphere for "The Development of
Modern Europe," by the same authors, which it accompanies
chapter by chapter and section by section.

Bibliographies provided in the Appendix start the student on
the path to a really thorough study of the field.

A goodly number of the readings in this volume are of the constitutional kind which merit and richly reward careful study. A still larger
number are of the interesting and lively kind which charm and entertain, and which are valuable because they give the flavor of the olden
times. The bibliography is no mere list of unappreciated titles, but an
excellent critical classification which guides the student quickly on to
the fundamental works. — SIDNEY B. FAY, *Assistant Professor of History, Dartmouth College*, in *The American Historical Review*.

GINN AND COMPANY PUBLISHERS

AN INTRODUCTION TO THE
HISTORY OF WESTERN EUROPE

By JAMES HARVEY ROBINSON
Professor of History in Columbia University

IN ONE VOLUME

12mo. Cloth. 714 pages. With maps and illustrations. List price, $1.60; mailing price, $1.80.

IN TWO VOLUMES

VOLUME I. 12mo. Cloth. 368 pages. With maps and illustrations. List price, $1.00; mailing price, $1.10.

VOLUME II. 12mo. Cloth. 364 pages. With maps and illustrations. List price, $1.00; mailing price, $1.10.

THE excellence of Robinson's "History of Western Europe" has been attested by the immediate and widespread adoption of the book in many of the best schools and colleges of the country. It is an epoch-making text-book on the subject, in that it solves in an entirely satisfactory manner the problem of proportion.

The book differs from its predecessors in omitting all isolated, uncorrelated facts, which only obscure the great issues upon which the pupil's attention should be fixed. In this way the writer has gained the space necessary to give a clear and interesting account of the all-important movements, customs, institutions, and achievements of western Europe since the German barbarians conquered the Roman Empire. Such matters of first-rate importance as feudalism, the mediæval Church, the French Revolution, and the development of the modern European states have received much fuller treatment than has been customary in histories of this compass.

The work is thoroughly scholarly and trustworthy, since the writer has relied either upon the most recent treatises of the best European authorities of the day or upon a personal study of the primary sources themselves. Carefully selected illustrations and an abundance of maps accompany the text.

GINN & COMPANY PUBLISHERS

READINGS IN EUROPEAN HISTORY

By JAMES HARVEY ROBINSON, Professor of History in Columbia
University. Designed to supplement his "Introduction
to the History of Western Europe"

VOLUME I. 12mo. Cloth. 551 pages. List price, $1.50; mailing price, $1.65

VOLUME II. 12mo. Cloth. 629 pages. List price, $1.50; mailing price,
$1.65

ABRIDGED EDITION. 12mo. Cloth. 573 pages. List price, $1.50; mailing
price, $1.65

IT is now generally recognized among teachers of history that
the text-book should be supplemented by collateral reading.
Professor Robinson's "Readings" will supply a need that
has long been felt by those dealing with the general history of
Europe. For each chapter of his text he furnishes from twenty
to thirty pages of extracts, mainly from vivid, first-hand accounts
of the persons, events, and institutions discussed in his manual.
In this way the statements in the text-book may be amplified and
given added interest and vividness. He has drawn upon the
greatest variety of material, much of which has never before
found its way into English.

The extensive and carefully classified bibliographies which
accompany each chapter embody the results of careful criticism
and selection. They are carefully arranged to meet the needs of
students of all grades, from the high-school pupil to one engaged
in advanced graduate work.

Volume I corresponds to Chapters I–XXII of the author's
"History of Western Europe," and closes with an account of the
Italian cities during the Renaissance. Volume II begins with
Europe at the opening of the sixteenth century. The Abridged
Edition is intended especially for high schools.

GINN & COMPANY Publishers

9 789354 217333